The Politics of Rape

The Politics of Rape

Sexual Atrocity, Propaganda Wars, and the Restoration Stage

Jennifer L. Airey

UNIVERSITY OF DELAWARE PRESS
Newark

Published by University of Delaware Press
Co-published with The Rowman & Littlefield Publishing Group, Inc.
4501 Forbes Boulevard, Suite 200, Lanham, Maryland 20706
www.rowman.com

10 Thornbury Road, Plymouth PL6 7PP, United Kingdom

British Library Cataloguing in Publication Information Available

Library of Congress Cataloging-in-Publication Data

Airey, Jennifer L., 1980-
The politics of rape : sexual atrocity, propaganda wars, and the Restoration stage / Jennifer L. Airey.
p. cm.
Includes bibliographical references and index.
ISBN 978-1-61149-404-4 (cloth : alk. paper) -- ISBN 978-1-61149-405-1(electronic)
1. English drama--Restoration, 1660-1700--History and criticism. 2. Rape in literature. 3. Rape victims in literature. 4. Violence in literature. 5. Politics and literature--England--History--17th century. 6. Theater--Political aspects--England--History--17th century. 7. Propaganda, British--History--17th century. I. Title.
PR698.R345A37 2012
822'.4093552--dc23
2012021813

™ The paper used in this publication meets the minimum requirements of American National Standard for Information Sciences Permanence of Paper for Printed Library Materials, ANSI/NISO Z39.48-1992.

Printed in the United States of America

Contents

Acknowledgments

I want to begin by expressing my deep gratitude to Boston University's James A. Winn, who has supported this project every step of the way from inception to completion. I am extremely thankful for his mentorship, his wisdom, and his unfailingly correct advice over the years. I could not have completed this book without the support of Erin Murphy, whose unwavering enthusiasm and shrewd commentary guided me through the writing process. I am also very thankful to have had the opportunity to work with Anna Battigelli, whose insightful remarks guided the complete transformation of this project from doctoral dissertation to its present form. I would like to express my gratitude to Bill Carroll, who has supported me at each stage of my career. And I would like to thank John-Paul Riquelme, who first suggested I write about sexual violence in a graduate seminar on Yeats, planting the intellectual seeds for this project.

I have been fortunate to complete this book at the University of Tulsa, where I enjoy a wonderfully caring and brilliant group of colleagues. Lars Engle and Laura Stevens have provided me with unstinting encouragement and advice, and I am extremely grateful for their mentorship. I am especially grateful to Holly Laird for her intellectual generosity; she went above and beyond the call of duty reading drafts of every chapter, and her incisive commentary greatly improved the manuscript. Thanks also to Mark Rideout, my graduate assistant, for his time and careful attention to this manuscript.

This project has been supported by several grants that enabled me to complete my research. I would like to thank the Boston University Humanities Foundation for funding a research trip to London. I am also grateful to the University of Tulsa's Office of Research and Sponsored Programs, which awarded me two Faculty Development Summer Fellowships, enabling me to spend my summers writing. I am also grateful to the staff at Harvard University's Widener and Houghton Libraries, Yale University's Beinecke Library, and the University of Tulsa's McFarlin Library, as well as to the staff at the British National Archives for enabling my research.

I would like to offer my thanks to the insightful readers of the University of Delaware Press, whose feedback has led to a stronger work. I would also like to thank Donald Mell and Julia Oestreich for guiding my book to publication.

Finally, I would like to thank my parents, Barbara and Ron Airey, for their love and support, and my uncle, Stuart Millner, who has read more drafts of each chapter than I could begin to count.

Introduction

A Bloody Tragedie, Or Romish Maske. Acted by five Iesuites and sixteene young Germaine Maides, a 1607 anti-Catholic propaganda tract, claims to offer its reader proof of the dangers posed by Roman Catholicism and Roman Catholic priests. Supposedly a true story, the tract details the actions of five Jesuit priests who took up residence in the town of Miniken, Germany, ostensibly to serve the spiritual needs of the townspeople. Cruel and lascivious by nature, they quickly became enamored of sixteen innocent young women with whose spiritual welfare they had been entrusted: The "five Iesuites became five lascivious Lovers; & no fewer than Sixteen Virgins must sacrifice their chast bodies, to satisfie their lust."[1] Initially, the women refuse to sacrifice their virtue, but the priests assuage their fears, promising to use the powers of their office to absolve the women of sin and shelter them from secular shame. One priest explains, "If you feare to commit the sinne, I can absolve you; if you feare your parents anger, I have strength (by vertue of my Order) to defend you from them; if you feare the scandall of the world, I can plucke out the stings of envie, that they shall not hurt you, and stop up the mouth of slander, that she shall not dare to name you."[2] The priests also insist that no one will know if the women succumb; the sanctity of the confessional is such that "the Infant in the mothers bosome is not more safe, than you are in my chamber," underscoring the anti-Catholic belief that the privacy of the confessional concealed a multitude of sexual sins.[3] Finally, the virgins succumb, some to seduction, others to rape. "[N]ow no more maidens, but holy-mens harlots," they are imprisoned in the church, leaving their families distraught and the women pregnant and miserable: "All of them were great with childe, and more great with calamite."[4]

After several months of imprisonment, the women begin to beg for their freedom. One woman pleads, "if she might not be suffered to behold the face of her parents any more, nor to breathe that ayre in which she was borne, that then [the priests] would commit her to the handes of any hard hearted man, who (as they might not kill her) should bee inioyned to let her upon any foreigne shoare, were it never so farre from her . . . native Countrie."[5] Unfortunately, the Jesuits cannot risk discovery, and with the women becoming more of a liability than a pleasure, they devise a plan of their own. They write and eventually perform a masque: In a parody of the Holy Mass, each woman, big with child, is led to the altar of the church where, instead of being offered the sacrament, she is forced to plead for her life. Then the Jesuits come forward as a group and "with a great Iron Bullet; beate out her braines."[6] None of the women survives the massacre, and the priests are eventually exposed and punished harshly for their crimes: "All the five Iesuites being placed in a Wagon, and drawne through the Citie, had their flesh at nine severall times pinched with hot burning pincers from them; and in three severall parts of their bodies, great peeces sliced along with knyves; then were their arms and legges broken on the Wheele, and were they left languishing till they expired."[7] Thus the town of Minikin—and via the pamphlet, all of England—learns of the dangers posed by the treacherous and violent Jesuit order.

Written in the wake of the successfully disrupted 1605 Gunpowder Plot, *A Bloody Tragedie* represents an example of the most virulent anti-Catholic propaganda. The pamphlet begins by leveling a series of charges at Jesuit priests:

> They say the Iesuites are bloody, and stirrers up [sic] sedition in Christian kingdomes, that they are lyars, that they are proude, that they delight in rich apparell, that they are wherried up and down by Coaches, that they have traines of followers at their heels, as if they were great Earles . . . that they are Epicures, and make their belly their god, that they are lascivious, and love women, having Gentlewomen for their chamber-maides and young wenches for their bedfellowes.[8]

The Jesuits are unspiritually obsessed with secular powers and pleasures; that they are also sexually violent and dangerous links rape imagery with the rhetoric of anti-Catholicism. By constructing the scene of murder as a form of theatrical production in which the priests serve as principal actors, the text also links the combined rhetorics of rape and anti-Catholicism with the discourse of antitheatricalism. The theater in *A Bloody Tragedie's* construction becomes a place of perverted religion, idolatry, sexual immorality, and ultimately hellish murder.

The story of *A Bloody Tragedie*, while horrifying, is not unique in the political culture of the seventeenth century, and it encompasses many of the accusations that would be made against Catholics and Catholic clergy throughout the century. The events that provoked the spread of propaganda—the Gunpowder Plot, the so-called Spanish match,[9] the Irish Rebellion and English Civil Wars, and after the Restoration, the Popish Plot, Exclusion Crisis, and Glorious Revolution—varied throughout the century; the litany of charges remained remarkably static. Perhaps most central to the construction of rape as political discourse, however, was the reaction to the Irish Rebellion of 1641, an event that elicited a powerful contemporary response and whose emotional resonance persisted for over a hundred years. The rhetoric of the Irish Rebellion tracts would be repeatedly resurrected from 1641 onward, providing a consistent set of rhetorical tropes for subsequent generations of propagandists; to reference the Irish Rebellion was to encode via shorthand the worst instances of Catholic barbarity. Historically, the rebellion began on October 23, 1641, feast day of Jesuit founder Ignatius Loyola, when Ireland's Catholic population rose up against the English Protestants. The English were taken by surprise, and before the rebellion could be quashed, anywhere from two thousand to three hundred thousand English Protestants had been killed in extremely brutal and sometimes sexually violent ways.[10] According to the deposition of survivor Occar Butts, the rebels "threatned to Murther him this deponent and his wife, And also some of that Companye offered divers tymes, to violate and ravishe some of his Chilldren."[11] While Butts and his family escaped, others were not so lucky. George Burne described how "the barbarous rebells first ravished" the Protestant "Mr Allens Wiffe as before her husbands face as the rest were murthering him: and instantly after they murthered heir alsoe."[12] Similarly, Samson Moore of Cork County described the death of Robert Scott, along with his wife and children: The Irish confiscated

> most of the said Scotts Goods. And the night following they murdered the said Scott & his ffamily [sic] . . . the Rogues Ravished 2 of the said Scotts Daughters before they murdered them, and that Scotts wife being a lusty woman & passionatley [sic] moued, with these outrages towards her husband & daughters, Stroue & fought with them . . . but therein shee was wounded by them, & therewith falling downe, before shee was dead, they threw her & the rest, into a saw pitt, and Scotts wife yet aliue they threw earth vpon her, & buried her.[13]

Within the year, accounts of the uprising had spread throughout England through a series of tracts that described the inconceivably barbarous acts of violence committed against innocent English citizens. According to the eighteenth-century account included in John Foxe's highly influential *Acts and Monuments,* Irish ruffians attacked the elderly, the young, and the infirm alike, without compassion or surcease. Hundreds were mutilated and left to die painful, lingering deaths:

> Many women, of all ages, were put to deaths of the most cruel nature. Some, in Particular, were fastened with their backs to strong posts, and being stripped to their waists, the inhuman monsters cut off their right breasts with shears, which, of course, put them to the most excruciating torments; and in this position they were left, till, from the loss of blood, they expired.[14]

Nor were pregnant women safe from the carnage. *Acts and Monuments* continues: "Many unhappy mothers were hung naked in the branches of trees, and their bodies being cut open, the innocent offsprings were taken from them, and thrown to dogs and swine. And to increase the horrid scene, they would oblige the husband to be a spectator before suffering himself."[15]

Texts such as Foxe's *Acts and Monuments* constructed a discourse of English Protestant martyrdom in which the events of the Spanish Armada, the Gunpowder Plot, the Irish Rebellion, and later the Popish Plot revealed the continuing dangers posed by the Catholic presence in England. But the *Book of Martyrs* was not alone in describing such atrocities. The violent Irish Catholic savage—what I am terming the figure of the demonic Irishman who vented his spleen on innocent English Protestant martyrs—is omnipresent in the political tracts of the period. *A Bloody Battell: Or the Rebels Overthrow, and Protestants Victorie* (1641), for instance, describes the deaths of one Mr. Atkins and his wife, who were attacked by the Irish. After beating the husband to death, the rebels "layd hold on his wife being big with child, & ravisht her, then ript open her wombe, and like so many *Neroes* undantedly viewing natures bed of Conception, afterward tooke her and her Infant and sacrifiz'd in fire their wounded bodies."[16] James Salmon, author of *Bloudy Newes from Ireland* (1641), likewise relates how the rebels attacked a town of rich merchants, "first deflowering many of the women, then cruelly murdering them, and pulling them about the street by the haire of the head, and dashing their childrens brains out against the posts and stones in the street, and tossing their children upon their pikes."[17] The anonymous author of *The Bloudy Persecution of the Protestants in Ireland* (1641) describes how the Irish rebels raped Sir Patricke Dunson's wife before his eyes and then "cut out his tongue, and afterward to put him out of his paine, they ran a red hot Iron into his bowels and so he died."[18] The encounter between Sir Patricke and the rebels begins with the rape of the wife and concludes with an act of sodomitical rape that implicitly recalls both the death of King Edward II and the accusations of sodomy that frequently followed Catholic clergy.[19]

Similarly violent representations of the demonic Irishman were resurrected after the Restoration, becoming particularly prevalent between the years of the Popish Plot (1678–1681) and the Glorious Revolution (1688–1689), when authors sought either to defend or delegitimize James II's right to the English throne. *A Full and True Account Of The Inhumane and Bloudy Cruelties Of The Papists To The Poor Protestants In Ireland, In the Year. 1641* (1689) reprints the stories of Mr. Atkins and his wife from the 1641 tract *A Bloody Battell*, while *The Manner of the Burning the Pope in Effigies in London On the 5th of November, 1678* (1678) describes how three hundred thousand people were killed or dismembered in Ireland, "some of their Tongues, others of their Hands and Privities."[20] Catholics are, such tracts claim, trained to foment "cruel Massacres, / To murder Kings, and burn their Palaces; / Lay Cities low in Dust, no Treason spare, / Embroil the Nations in a Civil War."[21] They "breathe after the blood of the King, and of all Protestants," and hunt "the blood of Innocents" as they await another opportunity to rebel. [22] Thus *A Scheme Of Popish Cruelties or A Prospect of what wee must Expect under a Popish Successor* (1681) offers a vision of England under Catholic rule: "Ruffians and Hectors, Popish Priests, Jesuites, Monks, and the rest of the Black Guard to the Prince of Darkness, endeavou[r] to Ravish your Wives, your Daughters, your Sisters, and your Mothers."[23] The Catholics beat "out the Brains of Infants, and snatc[h] them out of their tender Mothers Arms; which being done, they likewise put the Mothers also to the Sword."[24] Such threats persisted throughout the century; as late as 1700, *An Abstract of the Bloody Massacre in Ireland* described how the rebels attacked Protestant ministers and violated their wives:

> their manner was first to strip them, and after bind them to a Tree or Post, where they pleased, and then to ravish their Wives and Daughters before their faces (in sight of their merciless rable) with the basest Villain they could pick out, after they hanged up the Husbands and Parents before their faces, then cut them down before they were half dead then quarter'd them, after dismember'd them and stopped their mouths therewith. [25]

William III's rule is all that stands between England and the violence of a Catholic Stuart monarch.

Taken together, all of these tracts reveal how deeply images of rape and sexualized violence saturated the discourse of seventeenth-century English political culture. Sexual violence pervades the pamphlet debates, appearing regularly in works of political propaganda and religious controversy and suggesting that authors relied on the language of rape both to reinforce the righteousness of their positions and to spur the populace to swift and often violent action. Authors of pamphlet tracts also counted on the use of sexual assault to garner popular interest and ensure commercial success. Propaganda sheets openly advertised their sexually violent contents on their cover pages; popular descriptions include a *true relation of all those cruell rapes and murders which have lately beene committed by the Papists in Ireland,*[26] *The Rebels Turkish Tyranny . . . shewing how they . . . ravished religious women,*[27] and *Bloudy News from Ireland, Or The barbarous Crueltie by the Papists used in that Kingdome. By putting men to the sword, deflowring Women; and dragging them up and downe the Streets, and cruelly murdering them, and thrusting their Speeres through their little Infants before their eyes.*[28] The promise of sexually violent atrocities could sell copies to a scandal-obsessed consumer audience.

If rape imagery was particularly popular with audiences of newssheets and propaganda tracts, it was also popular among London's seventeenth-century theater audiences. The Restoration stage, like the propaganda sheets, was suffused with depictions of onstage sexual violence, leading John Dennis to complain in 1721 that "Rape is the peculiar Barbarity of our English stage."[29] Dennis wondered why female spectators would "sit . . . quietly and passively at the Relation of a Rape in a Tragedy, as if they thought that Ravishing gave them a Pleasure."[30] Recently, modern critics have attempted to account for the popularity of such material. Elizabeth Howe and Jean Marsden, for example, have linked the prevalence of onstage rape with the arrival of the first English actresses. Rape, they argue, allowed playwrights to showcase the salacious spectacle of the female body in all its violated and seminude glory. According to Marsden, "the audience, like the rapist, 'enjoys' the actress, deriving its pleasure from the physical presence of the female body."[31] Elizabeth Howe concurs: "Rape became a way of giving the purest, most virginal heroine a sexual quality. It allowed dramatists to create women of such 'greatness' and 'perfect honour' as was felt to be appropriate to tragedy and heroic drama, but at the same time to exploit sexually the new female presence in the theatre."[32] More recently, however, Derek Hughes has disputed such claims, pointing out that very few rape plots accompanied the actual advent of the English actress: "Although the portrayal of rape has been associated with the advent of the actresses, the first scene of accomplished rape in Restoration drama is in fact not until 1672."[33] Although scenes of rape were undeniably titillating, it wasn't until the late 1670s and 1680s that rape became a regular dramatic occurrence, suggesting that a desire to display female flesh did not immediately spark an interest in sexually violent drama.

Perhaps more satisfyingly, then, Susan J. Owen has linked an increase in dramatic sexual violence to the political unrest of the Popish Plot and Exclusion Crisis. The image of the rapist, she argues, merges with the image of the monarchical tyrant, and thus rape features frequently in both Whig and Tory propaganda: "Both Whigs and Tories used rape as a trope of the monstrous, associated by Tories with rebellion, and by Whigs with popery and arbitrary government."[34] Owen's argument is certainly convincing, but it does not account for the growth and change in representations of rape during the wider period, nor does it consider the relationship between the drama and the broader culture of contemporary political writings. To understand fully the treatment of dramatic rape, we need to examine the continuities between depictions of rape onstage and the culture of sexually violent propaganda offstage. This monograph therefore takes as its starting point the assertion that English Civil War propagandists constructed a triad of stock figures or tropes—the aforementioned demonic Irishman, along with what I have named the debauched Cavalier and the poisonous Catholic bride—that were co-opted by the English stage. The demonic Irishman, as we have already seen, was a rapist, a thief, and an infanticide. Closely associated with the demonic Irishman was his political ally, the debauched Cavalier, the royalist supporter who wandered the country like a roving demon in the night, spreading violence, mayhem, and destruction in his wake. The debauched Cavalier, Roundhead polemicists argued, was a thief, a blasphemer, a murderer and a rapist, a drunkard, a cannibal, and most damningly, a secret Catholic, seeking to extend the dominion of the pope's tyranny in England. Frequently, he was married to a poisonous Catholic bride who, as parliamentarian propagandists famously wrote of Queen Henrietta Maria, used her sexual desirability and nighttime access to her husband to poison him against natural English Protestant interests. The poisonous Catholic bride was not herself a rapist, but she suborned, incited, and celebrated sexual assault, encouraging the debauchery of her Cavalier and Catholic allies in an effort to martyr and destroy innocent Protestant women. In all of these instances, authors link the discourse of royalism with descriptions of rape and Catholicism.

Similar rhetoric would be resurrected throughout the latter half of the century, images of rape coming to the political forefront in each new instance of social and governmental turmoil. After the Restoration, the demonic Irishman, debauched Cavalier, and poisonous Catholic bride were joined by a new group of stock political figures also intimately associated with acts of sexual violence: The demonic Dutchman, the ravished monarch, and the cannibal father. The demonic Dutchman, villain of the Anglo-Dutch wars and of early Jacobite writings, was the Protestant counterpart of the demonic Irishman. A rapist, a liar, a murderer, and a thief, the demonic Dutchman was obsessed with the destruction of English trade, seeking to commit "rapes" upon English liberties and to undermine English economic stability by any means possible. Jacobite propaganda, as we shall see, frequently linked such imagery with the trope of the ravished monarch, using the image of a male rape victim to describe and condemn the nation's treatment of James II. James had been "ravished" of his throne by his ungrateful daughter and her corrupt Dutch husband, leaving England at the mercy of the hypocritical and treacherous United Provinces. In contrast, Whig propagandists foregrounded the dangerous figure of the cannibal father, the evil patriarch who rapes his sons' wives before finally and horrifyingly ingesting his own offspring. Through the figure of the cannibal father, Whig authors responded to and dismissed the tenets of patriarchal political theory: If the monarch is allowed absolute and unfettered power, such tracts insisted, even rape and cannibalism are permissible under his regime. Together with the English Civil War stock figures, then, these new characters pervaded late seventeenth-century propaganda and theater, reflecting the centrality of rape imagery to political culture both onstage and off.

The Politics of Rape is a book about sexual violence as a pivotal attribute of the late seventeenth century's literature of atrocity. This literature amasses a shifting and overlapping matrix of tropes used throughout the period to evince feelings of political impotence, hatred, or fear. Integral to all representations of political atrocity, whether Roundhead or Cavalier, Whig or Tory, Williamite or Jacobite, are descriptions of constant, perverse, and explicit sexual violence; to examine the rhetoric of seventeenth-century political tracts is to uncover a deep morass of violent imagery, united above all by the trope of the raped body. From the poisonous Catholic bride of English Civil War pamphlets to the cannibal father of the Exclusion Crisis and the ravished monarch of the Jacobite tracts, the stock characters of propaganda culture are defined by their relationship to sexual assault. While such violence may be unpalatable to the modern reader, it is crucial to understanding contemporary responses to political movements both onstage and off in the later seventeenth century. That authors on either side of each political conflict drew on a single pool of atrocity imagery also helps to explain the difficulty royalists, Tories, and later Jacobites faced in deflecting accusations of violence and developing their own effective counterpropaganda apart from the language of their enemies.

The prevalence of rape imagery in seventeenth-century political discourse begs the question of why such acts feature prominently throughout the period. First and foremost, images of rape could elicit a swift and powerful response from the reader, even as they provided an efficient shorthand for encoding multiple forms of social, political, and economic violation. Legally, rape was treated as a form of property crime until well into the eighteenth century, and thus it provided an emotionally charged vocabulary for property loss. As a woman belonged to her husband or father in accordance with the rules of coverture, her violation represented an encroachment on male property rights. The original financial conception of the crime is evident in the Latin word *rapere*, "to seize," from which the English word "rape" is derived. To commit a rape is to take without permission the female chattel of the man—father, brother, husband—to whom she rightfully belongs. Emily Detmer-Goebel comments, "Early statutory law dating from the late thirteenth-century conflated sexual assault with abduction, blurring the distinction between the two. Long understood as a property crime, 'rape' either by physical abduction (which would often include a forced marriage and sexual consummation) or by 'defilement against her will' fell into the same category of wrong."[35] The First Statute of Westminster (1275)—one of the earliest instances of antirape legislation—emphasized the conflation of abduction with sexual assault when it decreed that "none do ravish, nor take away by Force, any Maiden within Age (neither by her own Consent, nor without) nor any Wife or Maiden of full Age, nor any other Woman against her Will."[36] Ten years later, the Second Statute of Westminster increased the penalty for rape from a fine and two years' imprisonment to death and enacted a provision making rape a capital crime, even in cases where the victim "consent[ed] afterward."[37] Since, in J. B. Post's words, "it is arguable that some couples used [rape accusations] to offset family objections to socially disparaging matches,"[38] through Westminster II, a woman could no longer consent to sex after the fact by agreeing to marry her attacker; this provision limited abductions to circumvent parental matrimonial disapproval. Westminster II thus decreased the law's reliance upon the victim's testimony in the prosecution of rape cases: by "discounting a woman's consent, the wishes of others—technically the Crown, but, by extension, family—were allowed to override her own, despite her nominal status as victim."[39] Rape in this construction is an assault on a family and, more specifically, on a patriarchal estate, not a crime against an individual's will.

Later laws diminished even further the importance of female sexual consent. *6 Richard 2* (1382) established that proof of a woman's permission could no longer free an accused rapist, emphasizing the irrelevance of female subjectivity to the prosecution of rape. According to T. E., author of *The Lawes Resolutions of Womens Rights: Or, the Lawes Provision for Women* (1632), *6 Richard 2* "was made to punish women, which consented to their ravishers."[40] If a woman agreed to marry her attacker, she forfeited her dowry and family inheritance, once again ensuring the economic stability of noble families. Later, *3 Henry 7* (1487) and *4 & 5 Phi. & Mary* also emphasized the economic dangers of rape, declaring that ravishment would be considered a felony only in the case of "takers for lucre, of maids, widdowes, or wives, having substance of lands or goods, or being heires apparent."[41]

The treatment of rape in Shakespeare's *Titus Andronicus* exemplifies the fiscal understanding of sexual violence, while also moving beyond it to reflect new laws established in consideration of consent. Initially, the men of *Titus Andronicus* overwhelmingly view any assault on Lavinia in the older tradition of property crime. When Bassianus seizes Lavinia from Saturninus, the Emperor labels that action a rape: "Traitor," he calls his brother. "[I]f Rome shall have law or we have power, / Thou and thy faction shall repent this rape."[42] Given that Bassianus has not yet consummated his relationship with Lavinia, Saturninus's accusation of rape here refers to Bassianus's unlawful capture of a woman who belongs to another, in this case, Saturninus himself. In response, Bassianus retorts, "'Rape' you call it, my lord, to seize my own, / My true betrothed love, and now my wife? / But let the laws of Rome determine all; / Meanwhile am I possessed of that is mine" (1.1.410–13). Bassianus cannot, he insists, rape a woman who legally and morally belongs to him. His actions are not theft, but rather the redemption of his own property, a legal reclamation of something that had been stolen from him. Importantly, the status of Lavinia's consent to the abduction is irrelevant for the accusation of rape to be leveled; Saturninus subscribes to the older understanding of rape, which made a woman's consent irrelevant before her family's matrimonial wishes.

Lavinia's rape and mutilation at the hands of Chiron and Demetrius, however, subsequently reveal the difference between rape/abduction as a form of property crime and rape as an act against an individual. Bassianus injures his brother and Titus, Lavinia's father; Chiron and Demetrius injure Lavinia herself. A cultural acknowledgment of this distinction was increasingly being enshrined in the laws of the period. From the time of Elizabeth I onward, "statutes begin to redefine rape as a violent crime against a woman rather than as a property crime against her guardians."[43] Modifications to the law under *18 Eliz. 1* (1576) not only reclassified sexual assault as a felony punishable by death without benefit of clergy, but also established that a child under the age of ten could not consent to sex—"the Law adjudgeth her unable to consent, at so tender age"[44] —confirming in the process that a woman over the statutory age did have the ability and the right to exercise the power of sexual choice. *18 Eliz. 1* "redirects the statutory law's attention back to the crime where it is enforced copulation that has nothing to do with a 'taking' for 'lucre.'"[45] While sexual violence was still most easily prosecuted when linked to a form of property crime (i.e., theft), the modern understanding of rape as a crime against an individual's will had begun to emerge.[46]

Anti-Catholic and anti-Cavalier propaganda throughout the Civil War era also reinforced the law's association between loss of property and sexual violation. According to *A barbarous and inhumane Speech Spoken by the Lord Wentworth, Sonne to the late Earle of Straford* (1642), Wentworth reportedly ordered his armies to "Pillage and plunder, ransacke all their Chests," and "Being laden with Wealth, . . . ravish their Virgins, force the timorous maides to clip with you in dalliance, and wreake your utmost spleen upon the roundheads."[47] The Cavaliers will punish their Roundhead enemies first by stealing their goods, then by ruining their women. Later, in the years between the Popish Plot and the Glorious Revolution, Restoration anti-Catholic polemicists resurrected stories of the Irish rebellion to remind English Protestants that neither their lives nor their livelihoods would be safe under

Catholic rule. *An Appeal From the Country To the City, For the Preservation of His Majesties Person, Liberty, Property, and the Protestant Religion* (1679), for instance, asks its reader to

> Imagine you see the whole Town in a flame, occasioned this second time, by the same Popish malice which set it on fire before. At the same instant fancy, that amongst the distracted Crowd, you behold Troops of Papists, ravishing your Wives and your Daughters, dashing your little Childrens brains out against the walls, plundering your Houses, and cutting your own throats, by the Name of Heretick Dogs.[48]

The tract's author recalls the horrifying devastation of the 1666 Great Fire (supposedly ignited by Catholic treachery[49]) and treats Catholic plundering as a form of atrocity on a par with Catholic ravishments and infanticides. Likewise, *An Abstract Of The Unnatural Rebellion And Barbarous Massacre Of The Protestants In the Kingdom of Ireland, In the Year 1641* (1689) explains that the Irish Catholics sought to establish the supremacy of their faith "by destroying the Lives and Properties of different perswasions."[50] The tract proceeds to enumerate crimes committed against both persons and property, "Murthers, Rapes, and the most notorious Robberies."[51] The author lists violation of person alongside violence to possessions, reflecting the correlation of the two in the cultural imagination.

The use of sexually violent imagery to decry the loss of property was not unique to anti-Catholic writings. Throughout the Second and Third Anglo-Dutch wars (1665–1667, 1672–1674), pro-Stuart propagandists adopted a similar rhetoric to foment popular outrage against the United Provinces, describing Dutch attacks on innocent English women and accusing them of "Treachery, and deceit, Cruelty and contempt."[52] In the aftermath of the Glorious Revolution, Jacobite tracts likewise adopted the rhetoric of rape to decry the Dutch effect on English trade; as Robert Ferguson complains, they have committed "Rapines . . . upon our Trade."[53] Such tracts also described the theft of James II's rightful crown as a form of ravishment. According to Charles Blount, for instance, the king's "Crown, as well as his Life" were "most unjustly ravished from him."[54] Meanwhile, Whig proponents of contractual monarchy used the language of rape to condemn kingly overreaching. To rape a man's wife was to attack his property and take something over which fathers or even kings have no claim. According to James Tyrrell, "if a Father . . . should go about to violate his Sons Wife in his presence, or to kill her, or his Grandchildren, I suppose [the son] may as lawfully use the same means for their preservation."[55]

Here we see a point of divergence between the Restoration understanding of rape and our own. For modern critics, the act of rape is an expression of masculine power—in Susan Brownmiller's words, "the vehicle of [the rapist's] victorious conquest over [his victim's] being, the ultimate test of his superior strength, the triumph of his manhood."[56] In contrast, Restoration propaganda most often highlights the *failure* of sexual violence to reaffirm patriarchal prerogative. While the threat of sexual assault momentarily empowers each rapist, the actual moment of physical penetration becomes, paradoxically, the moment of ultimate *dis*empowerment and the justification for political overthrow. Acts of rape prove each of the stock figures of seventeenth-century propaganda unfit to rule. The debauched Cavalier, the demonic Dutchman, the cannibal father, and through her acts of incitement, the poisonous Catholic bride, all seek in their own ways to destroy the English nation, a malicious intent that is revealed in their willingness to violate innocent English women. Throughout the propaganda, rape exposes the degeneracy (and hence illegitimacy) of the governmental regime and authorizes political rebellion. Rape in this construction does not equate phallic power with social and political success. Rather, acts of sexual violence encourage political reactions and undermine patriarchal power structures. They also allegorize wider disturbances to the political realm and emphasize the need for more general civic change.

Acts of rape in political tracts and stage plays therefore transform the female body into a symbol of the suffering nation, a physical representation of the horrific consequences of Catholic, Cavalier, Whig, Tory, Dutch, or Stuart rule. The political resonance of the rape narrative becomes particularly apparent in the dramatic popularity of the story of Lucrece, both a tale of personal violation and a myth of imperial upheaval. Karen Bamford points out that Jacobean plays were constantly rehearsing variants of the stories of Lucrece and Philomel. While the "Lucretia story idealizes the self-destructive rape victim, the Philomela story . . . demonizes the vengeful rape victim."[57] Restoration plays, however, feature primarily variations of Lucrece. Early in the Earl of Rochester's *The Tragedy of Valentinian*, for instance, Lucina expresses her intent to recreate Lucrece's story and kill herself should she find herself similarly victimized. One of the Emperor's bawds reports,

> I askt her
> After my many offers, walking with her,
> And her many downe denyalls, How
> If the Emperour growne mad with love should force her:
> She pointed to a Lucrece that hung by,
> And with an angry looke that from her Eyes
> Shot Vestall Fire against mee, she departed.[58]

Lucina will become Lucrece, reenacting the myth through her own suicide, exposing Valentinian's tyranny, and ensuring the destruction of his regime. Her actions also expose the political power of rape imagery. The Lucrece narrative is the story of the tyrant overthrown; in Bamford's words, the "death of a sexually threatened/violated female becomes instrumental in liberating her community. . . . As an innocent victim she absorbs the evils of political repression—expressed sexually—and pays for them with her death."[59] She also forces the tyrant to pay for his crimes with his demise, her body becoming a rallying symbol for the men of the nation. The spectacle of the violated female body, the Lucrece narrative suggests, can spur real-world political change when effectively harnessed by authors and orators, further accounting for the trope's prevalence in the propaganda of the period.

An analysis of Dryden's 1685 opera, *Albion and Albanius*, also reveals the extent to which female bodies and the sexuality of those female bodies could function as symbolic embodiments of political situations. Dryden's opera opens with a vision of the wretched Augusta, symbol of London. Augusta has been abandoned by her husband, Albion (England/Charles II), in the wake of her infidelity:

> Mercury: Not unknowing came I down,
> Disloyal Town!
> Speak! did'st not Thou
> Forsake thy Faith, and break thy Nuptial Vow?
> Augusta: Ah 'tis too true! too true!
> For what cou'd I, unthinking City, do?
> Faction sway'd me,
> Zeal allur'd me,
> Both assur'd me,
> Both betray'd me.[60]

In depicting Augusta as an unfaithful and abandoned lover, Dryden sexualizes the relationship between monarch and city/subjects and reimagines the English Civil War as an act of marital infidelity.[61] Mercury draws on the language of sexual pollution when he orders Augusta to redeem herself: "Then by some loyal Deed regain / Thy long lost Reputation, / To wash away this stain / That blots a Noble Nation!" (1.1.67–70). Augusta has been soiled by her sexual behavior, and even when she returns to fidelity, her chastity is not safe from assault. Instead, the forces of Democracy and Zealotry cooperate in her attempted rape:

> Democracy: Pull down her Gates Expose her bare;
> I must enjoy the proud disdainful fair.
> Haste, Archon, Haste
> To lay her Waste!
> Zeal: I'll hold her fast
> To be embrac'd. (1.1.117–22)

Dryden represents political strife in the nation as a form of sexual assault; in James Winn's words, Dryden "describes the City, which had been a center of parliamentary opposition to Charles I and remained a hotbed of resistance to Charles II, as the passive victim of a series of violent rapists."[62] Augusta's punishment for her infidelity is her attempted rape at the hands of Democracy; sexual assault is used to regulate and police female rebellion. At the same time, Augusta's experience demonstrates the extent to which sexual violence could serve as an eroticized metaphor for the body politic's inappropriate political choices.

When Dryden's Mercury condemns Augusta's sexual infidelity, he does so using the language of soiling and stains, a rhetoric frequently applied to victims of sexual violence. Rochester's Lucina similarly adopts the language of diseases and blots, warning Valentinian that rape will make her "leprous," a "Blott to Cesars fame" (4.2.150, 1.1.203). In each case, the stain of extramarital sexual contact represents both a personal tragedy and a political act: Augusta has betrayed her rightful monarch, while Lucina has fallen victim to an unscrupulous tyrant. And in each case, the broken body of the rape victim offers a physical manifestation of the spiritual, moral, and political contaminants threatening the nation. Representations of rape both in propaganda and onstage frequently couple images of sexual violence with representations of illness and disease, depicting noncorporeal societal illnesses as real physical woes. This combination of rape and contagion is most apparent at the end of Shakespeare's *The Rape of Lucrece*. In a curious twist on disease imagery, when Shakespeare's Lucrece stabs herself, her blood flows out in two separate streams, her own pure, healthy blood separating from the black, poisonous evidence of Tarquin's assault. In death, the "black" blood "that false Tarquin stained" divides from "some of her blood still pure and red," her black blood evidence both of her tragic personal corruption and of the nation's political contamination.[63] Shakespeare literalizes the metaphoric taint of rape, physicalizing Lucrece's mental and emotional suffering and making horribly apparent the dangers of aristocratic and monarchical tyranny. The foul crime of rape bridges the gap between actual political events and their terrible but hypothetical consequences.

Like Shakespeare, seventeenth-century propagandists trafficked in images of diseased raped bodies to provide concrete evidence of metaphorical contamination. Pamphlet authors treated Roman Catholicism in particular as an insidious form of poison, a disease that infects the individual moral consciousness, destroys the Protestant family, and threatens the body politic with chaos or tyranny. The author of *A Catholick Pill To Purge Popery* (1677) describes the "Poyson and Infection of that Soul and Body destroying Religion,"[64] while Luke Beaulieu, author of *Take heed of Both Extremes* (1675), urges his reader to use truth as "an Antidote against the Infection of some sugared Poisons, which many venture to drink of, not knowing their deadly Qualities."[65] The Roman Catholic Church has caused God's truth to grow "more, and more polluted,"[66] as Jesuit priests seek to "infuse their Mortal Poison of *Adders*, which is under their Lips, into the Souls of *Credulous* Men, through their Ears and Eyes."[67] Papists fill "the Air with Poison in their Word," and traffic in "Poysons, Rapes," and "Massacres."[68] The "Pernicious Swarms of Popish Men / Are such a Plague, we can't enough condemn,"[69] and they cause literal illness in the realm; according to Benjamin Keach's 1679 poem, *Sion in Distress: Or, The Groans Of The Protestant Church*, the "sweeping Plague" of 1666 was the "Messenger of [God's] Wrath" at continued Catholic sacrilege.[70]

The myriad diseases caused by Roman Catholicism come to bear on the rape victim, whose suffering symbolizes the effects of unwelcome penetration and infection. Keach's *Sion in Distress* features one such example of this allegorical use of rape imagery. According to Keach, the English realm has grown sick from a combination of Catholic treachery and Protestant schism, until nature itself has begun to manifest the illness. Keach asks, "What dismal Vapour (in so black a form) is this, that seems to *Harbinger* a Storm? . . . / What interposing *Fog* obscures our *Sun*? / What dire *Eclipse* benights our *Horizon*?"[71] Keach's Sion, allegorical representative of the Protestant Church, then appears in the guise of a rape victim. Although she does not explicitly state she has been sexually assaulted, her cries and disheveled appearance—she comes before the reader with "Arms expanded" to "implore the Skies," with "Streaming Rivulets, flow[ing] from thine Eyes," and she expresses her grief with "deep and piercing sobs" and a "Heart-relenting Moan"—suggest the theater of sexual violation.[72] Sion's suffering form personifies the outrages heaped on the Anglican Church, a physical manifestation of church and state infected, blotted, and insidiously destroyed by the infiltration of Catholic (and for Keach, Nonconformist) evils. If Shakespeare's Lucrece symbolizes the deadly repercussions of kingly overreaching, Sion offers a visible example of the pernicious effects of Catholic poison left to fester in the realm. Rape imagery is here again useful to authors insofar as it transforms esoteric political or religious concerns into literal and wrenching images of physical suffering.

Sion's anguish, horrifying in itself, becomes a bleak foil for the pleasure the "Babylonish Whore," embodiment of the Catholic Church, takes in Sion's distress.[73] While Sion deplores her harsh treatment, begging for the reader's sympathy, the Catholic Church celebrates and compounds her misery: "[M]y pleasure must be done," the Catholic Church insists.[74] The Catholic Church and Sion function as ideological inversions of each other, vividly instancing of the propagandistic tendency to juxtapose a martyred Protestant rape victim and a poisonous Catholic bride who revels in Protestant annihilation. Protestant Sion suffers at the hands of England's enemies; the Catholic Whore revels in her destruction. Protestant Sion represents all that is good and virtuous in English society; the Catholic Whore imports foreign customs, foreign religion, and foreign malice. Protestant Sion is a rape victim; the Catholic Whore commissions rapes and celebrates their accomplishment. Frequently, Catholic female savagery leads to demonic Catholic births. Children raised by Keach's Catholic Church are described as "meer lump[s] of Sin,"[75] while the monstrous women of *A Nest of Nunnes Egges* (1680) "sit on

Egges, with Diligence and Care,"[76] until a priest and a nun finally hatch. Deformed harpies celebrate the birth of the new clergy: "Two Harpies, o're their heads strange Gesture makes, / With heads like Men, and bodies like to Snakes."[77] Catholic women are grotesque fiends whose physical deformities bespeak their inner corruption and who give birth to equally deformed children. Such binaries also play out on the Restoration stage in the contrast between virtuous and evil female characters, Edward Ravenscroft's Lavinia and Tamora, Nathaniel Lee's Teraminta and Tullia, and Elkanah Settle's Aphelia and Fredigond, among others.[78] As we shall see, these plays, like the political tracts, emphasize the contrast between the purity of female English Protestant martyrs and the wickedness of poisonous Catholic brides.

Despite this propensity to demonize Catholic women with images of grotesque physical degeneracy and satanic fertility, female agents of the Catholic Church are almost universally described as seductive, sexualizing the relationship between credulous Protestant and Catholic proselytizer. The Whore of Babylon, in Allison Shell's words "the most powerful anti-Catholic icon of all," represented both the Church's seductive power and the "perennial threat" it posed "to one's spiritual chastity."[79] In the Whore of Babylon, the figure of the dangerous female seducer merges with that of the monstrous mother. The author of *Battering Rams Against Rome's Gates* (1641), for example, describes the Church as the "Whore of Rome and Mother of all our Sorrows," and names her "the Cause of all . . . your Pain, Sorrow and Misery."[80] The Church is both a promiscuous, seductive witch and an unnatural mother who brings harm to her own offspring. She is able to retain her foothold in the kingdom, spreading her poison and destroying her female Protestant rivals because (as we shall see of Ravenscroft's Tamora) her exotic customs and foreign beauty are so dangerously and poisonously enticing.

Catholic women are not, however, the only females capable of producing monstrous progeny. Central to the language of blots and stains so common to rape propaganda is the very real fear that Protestant women could conceive monstrous children, their wombs poisoned by the act of rape. By violating a woman, the rapist creates the possibility that the mother will give birth to an illegitimate child, one that will undermine the sanctity of Protestant lineage and be viewed in the eyes of its society as a monster. In Dolan's words, when a woman is assaulted, "the rapist father puts his stamp on the fetus, erasing the impress of the virtuous English mother."[81] The demonic Irishman and debauched Cavaliers of English Civil War and Exclusion Crisis propaganda, along with the demonic Dutchman of Stuart tracts, thus seek to humiliate Protestant men, first by murdering their legitimate heirs and then by replacing them with monstrous children of their own nonconsensual creation.

Beyond the theft of reproductive rights and heritage, throughout much of the most horrifying anti-Catholic polemic, violence against women is accompanied by violence to children, as England's enemies attempt to destroy future generations of Protestants. Pregnant women in particular become the focus of brutal attacks. The rebels of Foxe's *Acts and Monuments* mutilate women's breasts, attacking their capacity to nurse, and by extension, their capacity to function as mothers. Other tracts describe even more graphic assaults on pregnant women. According to *An Abstract of the Bloody Massacre in Ireland* (1700), "A *Scotish* man they stript, and hewed to pieces, ript up his wifes belly so that her Child dropt out; many other Women they hung up with Child, ript their bellies, and let their infants fall out; some of the Children they gave to the Dogs."[82] Likewise, *An Abstract of Some few of those Barbarous, Cruell Massacres and Murthers, of the Protestants* (1662) describes "one woman great with childe, through whose belly the Rebels thrust their Pikes as shee was hanging, because the childe should not live."[83] Other accounts describe "the most barbarous and execrable Murthers, Villainies, sparing neither Man, Woman, or Child, ripping up Women with Child, ravishing chast Matrons, drowning, putting to the Sword, &c. many thousands of innocent Protestants."[84] Even when the children are not murdered, they are left behind to starve. As *A Collection of Certain Horrid Murthers in Several Counties of Ireland* (1679) describes, "In *Kilbeggan* a boy, and a woman hanged, one of them having a sucking child, desiring it might be buried with her, knowing it would suffer afterwards, but it was cast out, and starved to death."[85] In these various tracts, Catholics seek to destroy future generations of Protestants by whatever violent means possible.

Underscoring seventeenth-century atrocity narratives, then, is anxiety over not only political instability and legitimacy or legal and financial security, but also Protestant lineage and Protestant maternity. Where the suffering of the martyred Protestant rape victim emphasizes the monstrosity of the poisonous Catholic bride, this figuration also reflects the unsettling fear that a raped Protestant virgin may one day become a monstrous Catholic mother. Here fears over lost property—in this case, female chattel and potential heirs—combine with anxieties over societal contagion and poisoned lineage to create an urgent case for the expulsion of the Catholic political threat. A glance at John Milton's *Comus* provides a literary example of such motifs. The Lady's encounter with Comus has most frequently been interpreted as a conflict between Cavalier and Puritan ideologies, or between the demands of desire and the importance of chastity.[86] Comus speaks the language of Cavalier carpe diem rhetoric, asking the Lady, "Why should you be so cruel to your self, / And to those dainty limms which nature lent / For gentle usage, and soft delicacy?"[87] while the Lady responds with the language of Puritan restraint. Comus's status as the son of Circe, however, also invokes the rhetoric of anti-Catholicism, insofar as anti-Catholic propagandists occasionally treated Circe as interchangeable with the Whore of Babylon. In a 1572 tract, Henry Bullinger referred to the people who have "been bewitched by the sorceries of the Roman Circe and her Idolatrous hypocrites,"[88] while in

1603, Samuel Harsnett warned against a Catholic religion "composed of palpable fiction, and diabolicall fascination, whose enchaunted chalice of heathenish drugs . . . hath the power of Circes, and Medaeas cup, to metamorphose men into asses, bayards, & swine."[89] *The English Pope* (1643) also uses Circe to describe the Church's pernicious and seductive influence on European monarchs:

> That cup of fornication which the Circe of Rome, (as the Scripture describes it) mingles and prepares for the K[ing]s of the earth, must needs be very delicious to the sense, as well as it is pernicious to the understanding, it must needs please, as well as intoxicate, or else why should the great Potentates of the world be more apt to yeeld to the infatuation of it than common persons? . . . [T]hat there is a purpose of mischiefe in that strumpet, whose intoxications are so strong to captivate and delude, cannot be doubted.[90]

As Circe is linked with the Catholic Church, Comus is linked with his mother; he is "Deep skill'd in all his mothers witcheries" (l.523). When Comus urges the Lady to drink from his cup, he is therefore symbolically offering her the "false" religion of Catholicism.

The sexually violent overtones of the text thus transform the encounter between Comus and the Lady into a conflict between the monstrous mother, Circe, embodiment of the Catholic Church, and the innocent Protestant virgin who would be victimized by it. The danger for the Lady is twofold. Comus may rape her, leading to the conception of an illegitimate (and hence monstrous) child, or she may succumb to Comus's attractive rhetoric and, like the women of *A Bloody Tragedie* who "are now no more maidens, but holy-mens harlots,"[91] become monstrous herself (and indeed the "gumms of glutenous heat" [l.917] fastening her to Comus's chair may suggest that perhaps the Lady's resolve had begun to waver). In *Comus*, then, Milton merges sexual violence with royalism, Catholicism, and maternal monstrosity. That the text links the figure of Circe with Comus's use of Cavalier rhetoric and carpe diem ideology underscores the propagandistic tendency to link Cavaliers with Catholicism and female poison.

Problems with fertility caused by rape or maternal monstrosity pervade both the drama and the political tracts. The individual Englishwoman martyred by the sexually violent Catholics is contrasted with the monstrous Catholic mother who would infect the individual conscience, commission the rape of the innocent, and destroy the nation to satisfy her Popish masters. As we shall see in detail in chapter 1, Queen Henrietta Maria, wife of Charles I, in particular attracted public hatred, both for her supposed control over her husband and for her insistent Catholicism. Henrietta Maria emerges from the English Civil War tracts as the archetypal poisonous Catholic bride, the Circe inside the kingdom, working from within to poison and destroy. Even after her death, Henrietta Maria's memory would be invoked on the Restoration stage to remind the realm of the dangers posed by Catholic wives. Since, as Frances Dolan points out, Henrietta Maria's fertility was nearly constantly on display in her numerous pregnancies, she became England's own monstrous mother, the inverse mirror of the martyred rape victim.[92] Such parallelisms were adopted again later in the century, when motherhood had a direct impact on history. It was Queen Catherine of Braganza's infertility that necessitated the Exclusion Bill (1679–1681), while Mary of Modena's fertility and successful birthing of a Catholic male heir directly precipitated the Glorious Revolution. Thus rape both in propaganda and onstage offered a way of discussing the place of the maternal in society and in government.

As part of their campaign to humiliate and disenfranchise Protestant men, the monstrous males of propaganda culture frequently attack pregnant women. Such acts are horrifying in themselves, yet Catholic and Cavalier behavior frequently degenerates even further from there. As propaganda authors sought as far as possible to transform their enemies into a distant and fearful monolithic Other, Catholics in these tracts transition from acts of rape and murder to acts of cannibalism and vampirism. Catholics are "barbarous Blood-suckers,"[93] while their mother church is a female vampire who has "drunk of your Blood, until she is made to vomit it up."[94] Demonic Irishmen and debauched Cavaliers are all-too-quick to follow their Church's example, engaging in disgustingly literal acts of blood drinking and flesh eating. In *The Rebels Turkish Tyranny,* for instance, one child is forced to roast his own brother on a spit, possibly as a meal for the rebels, before being himself burned to death. Meanwhile, the author of *The Kings Maiesties speech On the 2. day of December, 1641* describes a young woman gang raped by four Irish rebels. When she stabs one of her attackers, they punish her as follows: they "drew their swords & cut off, first, her right arme, then her left, then both her legs, then they tied a rope about her middle, and drag'd it about, which having done they ript ope her belly, and saved as much of her blood as they could, saying that her puritane sisters should be glad of that to drinke."[95] The tract clearly links the evils of the demonic Irishmen with the horrifying behavior of the royalist faction; allied, these groups commit unimaginable atrocities against Protestant parliamentarians and their families. Thus the author of *Battering Rams* urges his reader to "scale" the Church's "Walls, throw down her Bullworks and Fortresses, and cause to fall to the ground all her Towers of Defence."[96] Given that the language of imperial conquest is often used as a euphemism for rape—women's bodies are towns to be conquered by force—what the author of *Battering Rams* is urging is a rape of the Church to prevent the "Murthers, Rapes, Villaines," and vampiristic acts that this "Whore of Rome, or bad Woman" will perform when left unchecked.[97]

The association of Catholicism with vampirism and cannibalism is primarily designed both to mock and render monstrous the concept of transubstantiation. As Maggie Kilgour explains, "By cleverly pushing the sacrament to a grotesque extreme unimagined by most Catholics and misrepresentative of the official interpretation of the rite, the reformers made the other extreme, their own position, appear as the only alternative for those who did not wish to be cannibals."[98] If Catholics believe in eating the flesh and blood of Christ, anti-Catholic polemicists argue, it is only natural that they would enjoy eating the flesh and blood of their Protestant enemies. At the same time, such accounts deliberately linked the Catholics with other types of distrusted religious and cultural Others. Anthony Horneck likens Catholic rituals of penance to those of the "*Brahmanes* in the Indies, and the religious *Pagans* dispersed through all the Eastern parts."[99] The Irish come to be regarded as more savage than even the Turks—note that Whetcombe's pamphlet *The Rebels Turkish Tyranny* is actually about *Irish* acts of violence—lending credibility to the most outlandish stories of Catholic atrocity. Such stories "were credible not only because Protestant contemporaries believed that Catholics were capable of, if not eager to perform, such acts of barbarity, but also because such acts were committed by the native Irish, commonly regarded by the English as wild and savage heathens who were capable of greater barbarities than the fearsome Turk."[100] Thus the author of *The Manner of the Burning the Pope in Effigies in London On the 5th of November, 1678* says of the Gunpowder Plot, "All the Treacheries of *Europe* compounded would not come near it; nor all the Inhumanity of the *Turks* and *Pagans* give it but a faint resemblance."[101] Such imagery participates in the process of racialization designed to foment hatred of the Irish. According to Dolan, the "difference and inferiority of the Irish, often associated with their Catholicism, was already sometimes understood as racial; that is, as a matter of blood. This racialization would gain momentum in the following centuries."[102] The Irish Catholics, with their blood-drinking and sexually violent ways, are more violent than the Turks and more dangerous than the pagans. They are Other from the English, a different and inferior race of people whose treachery is innate, yet they are allowed to live among virtuous English Protestants.

In the latter half of the century, Catholic and Tory polemicists attempted to redirect accusations of rape, cannibalism, and vampirism against their own enemies, with mixed results. Descriptions of Dutch Protestant cannibalism—Dryden, for instance, accuses the Dutch at Amboyna of ingesting the body fat of their English victims—were never particularly effective as a form of pro-Stuart propaganda. The Whigs adapted the stock images of English Civil War propaganda much more successfully, not only to condemn James II's reign, but to construct an overarching condemnation of absolutist philosophy. The Whig figure of the cannibal father exhibited the worst excesses of the demonic Irishman—he was a rapist and a consumer of human flesh—and, like the demonic Irishman, he was rendered Other by his acts of fearsome excess. John Locke explicitly linked the absolute monarch with the discourse of New World savagery. He warns his reader against the dangers of absolutism in England by condemning the behavior of the tyrannical king of Peru. As that king was all powerful, Locke warns ominously, he could not be stopped from "beg[etting] Children on purpose to Fatten and Eat them."[103] The cannibal father makes himself frighteningly foreign through his combined acts of rape and cannibalism, overstepping himself so far as to become indistinguishable from the "savage" king of Peru. Such rhetoric represented a powerful argument on behalf of contractual monarchy and a potent justification of the Glorious Revolution. Here, then, is the use of rape and cannibal imagery as a means of Othering, one that justifies the subjugation of a vile and antisocial enemy.

The popularity of rape imagery in seventeenth-century propaganda can finally be explained by its conjoint powers as an emotional weapon and a political tool. Frequently intertwined with the language of cannibalism, contagion, savagery, and monstrosity, images of rape were designed in a variety of ways to redirect readerly revulsion into political action. Depictions of rape served both as a shorthand for the ills plaguing the nation and as a call to arms, one frequently coupled with an appeal to English chivalric masculinity. G. S., author of *A Briefe Declaration Of The Barbarous And inhumane dealings of the Northern Irish Rebels*, for instance, has taken pen to paper on behalf of innocent women and children and hopes "to Excite the English Nation to relieve our poor Wives and Children, that have escaped the Rebels savage crueltie."[104] He also begs England to "send aid of men, and means forthwith to quell their boundlesse insolencies."[105] Rape is both a reason for and a spur to social and political change.

This is not to suggest that representations of rape remained static during the latter half of the seventeenth century. As political circumstances shifted and changed, authors altered and adapted the tropes of sexual violence to serve different political ends. My analysis of Restoration representations of rape thus begins in chapter 1 with the early years of the Restoration, when dramatic depictions of rape were few and devoted to rehabilitating the monarchy from two decades of horrifically violent parliamentary attacks. The specter of Cavalier violence, an all-too-common theme throughout the propaganda of the Civil Wars and Interregnum, haunted both the politics and drama of the 1660s as authors sought to unwrite, erase, and replace the memory of the debauched Cavalier with the more positive figure of the chivalric knight suffering nobly for king and country. As a result, a struggle to redeem the Cavaliers and recast the Roundheads as the ultimate societal villains underlies much of the drama of the period. Theatrical depictions of sexual violence produced throughout the 1660s redirect accusations of rape, murder, and tyranny onto the defeated parliamentary faction. While only three plays produced between 1660 and 1669, the Earl of Orrery's *The Generall* (1662), Thomas Porter's *The Villain* (1664), and Edward Howard's *The*

Usurper (1664), actually feature scenes of rape or attempted sexual assault, each play contrasts Cavalier honor and fidelity with Roundhead treachery and sexually violent aggression. Each author draws on the atrocity propaganda of the Civil War tracts to demonize the Puritans and reestablish the moral righteousness of royalism. It is not the rightful king's supporters, the plays argue, but the illegitimate Roundhead faction that brings sexual violence, property destruction, and finally popery to the realm.

In 1673, the future James II refused to take Anglican communion, stepping down from his position as Lord High Admiral of the Navy and publicly acknowledging his long-rumored conversion to Roman Catholicism. Occurring in the midst of the already unpopular Third Anglo-Dutch War, James's announcement fed a growing popular discomfort with royal policy and a concomitant fear of the growth of Catholic power at court. Set in this context, chapter 2 argues that treatments of onstage rape in the first half of the 1670s mirrored the growing divide within the culture between those who would support Charles II's anti-Dutch policies and those who feared the spread of popery and French-style absolutism. The chapter begins by examining John Dryden's 1673 play *Amboyna, or the Cruelties of the Dutch to the English Merchants*. A work of pro-royalist propaganda, the play foregrounds evil, demonic Dutchmen while emphasizing the comparative harmlessness of French Catholics. Dryden's Dutch commit rapes upon English liberties and English trade along with English women. Like Orrery, Porter, and Howard, then, Dryden displaces atrocity imagery onto a hated foreign Other, justifying in contrast Stuart foreign policy and suggesting that ties of mutual religion should not be the sole determining factor in the construction of international loyalties.

While Dryden uses the tropes of Civil War propaganda to defend the royal court from charges of corruption, contemporaneous plays by Elkanah Settle, Thomas Shadwell, and Aphra Behn offer a more critical look at court culture. In both Settle's *Love and Revenge* (1675) and Shadwell's *The Libertine* (1675), the world stands on the brink of societal collapse. For Settle, that disintegration stems from aristocratic male abdication of social and political responsibility, enabling the rise of overly powerful and toxic females. Reconfiguring the trope of the poisonous Catholic bride into an attack on Charles's poisonous Catholic mistresses, Settle condemns the continued presence of powerful Catholic women at court, along with the effeminizing effects of court libertinism. Shadwell, meanwhile, resurrects the image of the debauched Cavalier to condemn aristocratic male sexual excess. Shadwell's Don John has rejected patriarchal structures in his pursuit of pleasure, a path that ultimately leads him to death, destruction, and most damningly, Catholic ritual. Through Don John, Shadwell decries both the sexually violent immorality of libertine behavior and the fearsome specter of French Catholic influence at court. The chapter concludes with a look at Aphra Behn's *The Rover,*

Part I (1677), which, while more positive in its reading of the court than either *Love and Revenge* or *The Libertine*, is still profoundly critical of aristocratic male behavior. *The Rover*'s Cavaliers are both romantic heroes, faithful and true to their exiled king, and sexually violent exploiters of innocent women. In Behn's play, the trope of the debauched Cavalier is resurrected, if tempered, reflecting the extent of the playwright's political ambivalence on the eve of the Popish Plot.

In 1683, Algernon Sidney was executed for his role in the Rye House Plot, leaving behind his seminal work, *Discourses concerning Government*. A response to Sir Robert Filmer's recently published *Patriarcha: Or The Natural Power Of Kings*, Sidney repeatedly refers to the story of Lucrece in an effort to define the limits of monarchical authority. A king who proves a tyrant by sexually abusing his subjects, Sidney suggests, loses the right to rule. Such a view contrasts powerfully with Filmer's representations of the Lucrece myth; while Filmer acknowledges the horror of Lucrece's fate, he consistently asserts that political rebellion is a greater sin than rape. Taken together, Sidney and Filmer reveal the centrality of the Lucrece myth to contemporary debates over the nature and limits of monarchical authority. For Sidney, sexual violation reveals the limits of a subject's contractual authority, while for Filmer, it proves only the need for continued obedience.

The treatment of Lucrece as a medium for negotiating political philosophies is also apparent in the drama of the period. My third chapter therefore takes as its central focus John Wilmot, Earl of Rochester's *The Tragedy of Valentinian* (first performed in 1684, but written significantly earlier) and Nathaniel Lee's *Lucius Junius Brutus* (1680), two contemporaneous plays that offer very different dramatic treatments of the rapist monarch and the Lucrece myth. While such representations would become much more prevalent after the Glorious Revolution, already by 1684 Rochester's *Valentinian* treats sexual violence as a justifiable reason for rebellion. Valentinian has licensed his overthrow with his attack on a virtuous subject, and Rochester regards the resulting regicide as the inevitable, albeit regrettable, conclusion to Valentinian's bad behavior. In contrast, Lee's *Lucius Junius Brutus* suggests that rebellion against a violent monarch will not necessarily lead to a better form of governance. Lee's Brutus is a propagandist who manipulates the memory of Lucrece, selfishly commingling the imagery of rape with the threat of cultural contagion to garner support for his rebellion. Brutus's authority as a politician is predicated on his effacement of Lucrece's memory, while the stability of his government rests upon the need for violent spectacles of suffering. The resulting parliamentary government is both stagnant and cruel, a new form of tyranny to replace the old. The contrast between Rochester's treatment of the Lucrece myth and Lee's thus demonstrates the extent to which images of sexual violation were used to mediate political philosophies. In both cases, the plays reveal the moral impact of rape rhetoric on both the private individual and the public domain and trace the shift from private morality to public concern embedded in the myth of Lucrece.

The combination of sexually violent imagery with instances of cannibalism was, as we have seen, common in both English Civil War and Exclusion Crisis–era propaganda tracts. Images of cannibalism were particularly widespread between the Popish Plot and Glorious Revolution as authors both emphasized the horrors of civil war and depicted the ways in which parents and children turn on and destroy one another in an age of civil strife. Disruptions to parent-child relationships implicit in the concept of civil war manifest themselves as the monstrous births produced by rape and as acts of intrafamilial cannibalism, perpetrated in Tory propaganda by disobedient and ungrateful children, in Whig tracts by that absolutist monster, the cannibal father. Chapter 4 begins by examining images of rape, flesh eating, and familial conflict in a group of Popish Plot and Exclusion Crisis–era plays, Lee's *Lucius Junius Brutus* (1680) and *Mithridates, King of Pontus* (1678), along with Thomas Otway's *Venice Preserv'd* (1682) and John Crowne's *Thyestes* (1681). In all of these plays, parents and children have become toxic to each other, and in each case, the combination of rape and cannibalism reflects the collapse of societal boundaries and symbolizes the place of the diseased individual family in the context of the diseased body politic. Evil and parricidal Queen Tullia of Lee's *Lucius Junius Brutus*—both a murderous child and the play's poisonous Catholic bride—personifies the danger that children may pose to their parents in an era of civil strife. In contrast, Lee's Mithridates, Otway's Priuli, and Crowne's Atreus all emerge from their texts as deadly fathers who symbolically rape their own daughters and destroy rather than nurture their progeny. Atreus in particular becomes the monster lurking at the heart of the nation, the poisonous patriarch who, instead of nurturing his realm, will see it turn to chaos and despair. What all of these plays suggest is that the disruptions to parent-child relationships fomented by political strife and manifested in acts of rape and cannibalism undermine the nation's foundations and leave the world destabilized and ill.

Contrasted with the underlying political pessimism that characterizes the works of Lee, Otway, and Crowne is Edward Ravenscroft's *Titus Andronicus* (performed 1678, published 1687), which offers a very different interpretation of intrafamilial cannibalism. Although the play was initially written during the Popish Plot hysteria, it was not published until some years later, in the wake of the Rye House Plot, the death of Charles II and accession of James II, and the execution of the Duke of Monmouth. While the plays of Otway, Lee, and Crowne all end with societal disintegration, Ravenscroft's play uses the act of cannibalism to reestablish appropriate societal boundaries. The play begins with an invasion via rape; it ends with the elimination of social toxins via ingestion. The power of the Goths is finally neutralized as

Tamora and Aron literally consume their children out of existence. The cannibal father becomes, perversely, a symbol of renewed cultural stability, reflecting Ravenscroft's persistent loyalty to the Stuart line.

In my final chapter, I turn to the treatment of rape in the Williamite theater and examine the trope of the ravished monarch. In the aftermath of the Glorious Revolution, Williamite propagandists continued to disseminate images of Catholics and Tories as rapists and cannibals, even as Jacobite propagandists accused their enemies of "ravishing" their king. The political use of the male rape victim of course predated the events of the Glorious Revolution. In his 1680 anti-Catholic polemic, *The Female Prelate*, for instance, Elkanah Settle used the trope of male rape to discredit the Catholic Church; the Duke of Saxony becomes a victim of Pope Joan's lust, suggesting that male bodies, too, are vulnerable to acts of popish sexual excess. In the aftermath of the Glorious Revolution, Settle returned to this theme in *Distress'd Innocence* (1690); although the play purports to be apolitical, it uses the rhetoric of male rape to protest indirectly the events of the Glorious Revolution. When the play's innocent hero is stripped of his titles and honors, the other characters speak of him as they would a victim of sexual assault. Like James II, he has been unjustly ravished of his rightful position, suggesting that to take the throne by force is a violation of both the individual's bodily rights and the larger body politic.

Dramatists who supported the Glorious Revolution likewise employed the image of the male rape victim, in their case to justify the rightness of revolt. Just as the playwrights of the 1660s sought to displace accusations of rape onto the parliamentarians, Whig authors of the 1690s used images of sexual violence to rehabilitate the image of William and Mary. The chapter concludes with readings of Nicholas Brady's *The Rape* (1692), Mary Pix's *Ibrahim* (1696), and John Crowne's *Caligula* (1698). For Pix and Crowne, the rapist monarch ravishes his masculine subjects politically and economically, transforming the disenfranchised male into a victim of sexualized assault. While Sidney and Locke use images of female victims to protest absolutism, Pix and Crowne encode the consequences of tyranny in the violence done to men. Brady, meanwhile, displaces the rhetoric of male rape onto the play's villains. Like the playwrights of the 1660s, Brady defines the rapist as the enemy of the current political regime, redeeming in contrast the image of the seated monarch. To trace the treatment of the male rape victim onstage, then, is to gain a more nuanced understanding of postrevolution political and theatrical rhetoric.

There is, of course, a danger in reading acts of physical violation as acts of metaphoric or allegorical violence. To do so is potentially to engage in what Lynn A. Higgins and Brenda R. Silver term the "obsessive erasure . . . of sexual violence against women."[106] When critics read rape allegorically, Higgins and Silver warn, they privilege a "masculine perspective premised on men's fantasies about female sexuality" and contribute to a contemporary culture of "rape and rapability."[107] When rape is transformed into an artistic and allegorical symbol, it comes to "exis[t] as a context independent of its occurrence as discrete event."[108] It is, however, the very unseen presence of sexual violation in Restoration literature and culture that this book aims to explore. While some plays foreground the physicality of the act of rape in the eroticized spectacle of the actress's violated form—the titillating promise of sexual situations and naked female flesh could certainly help to attract an audience—they also transform that very real pain into social and political metaphors. Rape victims in these texts are both suffering victims and moral/political symbols, revealing the extent to which depictions of sexual violence both mirrored and shifted with the major political upheavals of the later seventeenth century.

NOTES

1. *A Bloody Tragedie, Or Romish Maske. Acted by five Iesuites, and sixteene young Germaine Maides* (London, 1607), b4r.
2. Ibid., c1r.
3. Ibid., b4v. For discussion of the anti-Catholic polemicist tendency to sexualize the confessional, see Stephen Haliczer, *Sexuality in the Confessional: A Sacrament Profaned* (Oxford: Oxford University Press, 1996).
4. *A Bloody Tragedie*, c1v.
5. Ibid., c2r.
6. Ibid., d1v.
7. Ibid., d3r.
8. Ibid., b3r.
9. In the early 1620s, the future Charles I considered marrying a Spanish Catholic princess, causing widespread outrage in England.
10. Although contemporary tracts numbered as many as three hundred thousand among the dead, modern historians think two thousand deaths a more likely number. For historical treatments of the Irish Rebellion, see Raymond Gillespie, "The End of an Era: Ulster and the Outbreak of the 1641 Rising," in *Natives and Newcomers: Essays on the Making of Irish Colonial Society, 1534–1641*, ed. Ciaran Brady and Raymond Gillespie (Bungay: Irish Academic Press, 1986), 191–213; Keith J. Lindley, "The Impact of the 1641 Rebellion upon England and Wales, 1641–5," *Irish Historical Studies* 18, no. 70 (1972): 143–76; Arthur F. Marotti, *Religious Ideology and Cultural Fantasy: Catholic and Anti-Catholic Discourses in Early Modern England* (Notre Dame: University of Notre Dame Press, 2005); and James Morgan Read, "Atrocity Propaganda and the Irish Rebellion," *Public Opinion Quarterly* 2, no. 2 (1938): 229–44.
11. Trinity College Dublin MS 818, fols 055r–056v: 877. For further descriptions of the carnage, see Trinity College Dublin's online archive of the 1641 depositions: http://1641.tcd.ie/index.php.
12. Trinity College Dublin MS 839, fols 038r–039v: 1365.
13. Trinity College Dublin MS 826, fols 239r–239v: 1921.
14. John Foxe, *Foxe's Book of Martyrs* (Blacksburg: Wilder Publications, 2009), 271. Popularly referred to as the *Book of Martyrs*, Foxe's work was initially published under the title *Actes and Monuments of these latter and perillous dayes, touching matters of the Church.* For readings of Foxe's impact on English culture, see Patrick Collinson, Arnold Hunt, and Alexandra Walsham, "Religious Publishing in England 1557–1640," in *The Cambridge History of the*

Book, Volume IV, 1557–1695, ed. John Barnard and D. F. McKenzie (Cambridge: Cambridge University Press, 2002), 29–66; William Haller, *The Elect Nation: The Meaning and Relevance of Foxe's Book of Martyrs* (New York: Harper & Row, 1963); and Raymond D. Tumbleson, *Catholicism in the English Protestant Imagination: Nationalism, Religion, and Literature* (Cambridge, Cambridge University Press, 1998).

15. Foxe, *Acts and Monuments*, 271.

16. *A Bloody Battell: Or the Rebels Overthrow, and Protestants Victorie* (London, 1641), a4r.

17. James Salmon, *Bloudy Newes from Ireland* (London, 1641), a3v.

18. *The Bloudy Persecution of the Protestants in Ireland* (London, 1641), av4.

19. For discussion of sodomy rhetoric in anti-Catholic discourse, see Peter Lake, "Antipopery: The Structure of a Prejudice," in *Conflict in Early Stuart England: Studies in Religion and Politics 1603–1642*, ed. Richard Cust and Ann Hughes (London and New York: Longman Group, 1989), 75.

20. *The Manner of the Burning the Pope in Effigies in London On the 5th of November, 1678* (London, 1678), 8.

21. *A Bull Sent By Pope Pius To encourage the Traytors in England, pronounced against Queen Elizabeth, of ever glorious Memory* (London, 1678), 1.

22. *A Caution To All True English Protestants, Concerning the Late Popish Plot* (London, 1681), 10.

23. *A Scheme Of Popish Cruelties Or A Prospect of what wee must Expect under a Popish Successor* (London, 1681), 1.

24. Ibid.

25. *An Abstract of the Bloody Massacre in Ireland* (Scotland, 1700), 23–24.

26. *The Kings Maiesties Speech On the 2. Day of December, 1641* (London, 1641), a1r.

27. Tristram Whetcombe, *The Rebels Turkish Tyranny in their march Decem. 24, 1641* (London, 1641), a1r.

28. Salmon, *Bloudy Newes from Ireland*, a1r.

29. John Dennis, *Original Letters, Familiar, Moral, and Critical*, 2 vols. (London, 1721), 1:63.

30. Ibid.

31. Jean Marsden, "Rape, Voyeurism, and the Restoration Stage," in *Broken Boundaries: Women & Feminism in Restoration Drama*, ed. Katherine M. Quinsey (Lexington: University of Kentucky Press, 1996), 186.

32. Elizabeth Howe, *The First English Actresses: Women and Drama 1660–1700* (Cambridge: Cambridge University Press, 1992), 45.

33. Derek Hughes, "Rape on the Restoration Stage," *The Eighteenth Century* 46, no. 3 (2005): 227.

34. Susan J. Owen, *Restoration Theatre and Crisis* (Oxford: Clarendon Press, 1996), 175. For an expansion of this argument, see also Susan J. Owen, "'He that should guard my virtue has betrayed it': The Dramatization of Rape in the Exclusion Crisis," *Restoration and Eighteenth-Century Theatre Research* 9, no. 1 (1994): 59–68.

35. Emily Detmer-Goebel, "The Need for Lavinia's Voice: *Titus Andronicus* and the Telling of Rape," *Shakespeare Studies* 29 (2001): 77. For more on Early Modern rape law, see John Hamilton Baker, *An Introduction to English Legal History* (London: Butterworths, 1979); Nafize Bashar, "Rape in England between 1550 and 1700," in *The Sexual Dynamics of History: Men's Power, Women's Resistance*, ed. The London Feminist History Group (London: Pluto Press, 1983), 28–42; Miranda Chaytor, "Husband(ry): Narratives of Rape in the Seventeenth Century," *Gender and History* 7, no. 3 (1995): 378–407; Shani D'Cruze, "Approaching the History of Rape and Sexual Violence: Notes towards Research," *Women's History Review* 1, no. 3 (1993): 377–97; Lorraine Helms, "'The High Roman Fashion': Sacrifice, Suicide, and the Shakespearean Stage," *PMLA* 107, no. 3 (1992): 554–65; and Marion Wynne-Davies, "'The Swallowing Womb': Consumed and Consuming Women in *Titus Andronicus*," in *The Matter of Difference: Materialist Feminist Criticism of Shakespeare*, ed. Valerie Wayne (Ithaca: Cornell University Press, 1991), 129–51.

36. *Statutes of the Realm*, Stat. Westm. Prim., *3 Edw. I*, c. 13, 1275.

37. *Statutes of the Realm*, Stat. Westm. Sec., *13 Edw. I*, c. 34, 1285.

38. J. B. Post, "Ravishment of Women and the Statutes of Westminster," in *Legal Records and the Historian: Papers Presented to the Cambridge Legal History Conference, 7–10 July 1975, and in Lincoln's Inn Old Hall on 3 July 1974*, ed. J. H. Baker (London: Swift Printers, 1978), 153.

39. Ibid., 158.

40. T. E., *The Lawes Resolutions of Womens Rights: Or, the Lawes Provision for Women* (New York: Garland Publishing, 1978), 382.

41. Ibid., 384.

42. William Shakespeare, *Titus Andronicus*, in *The Norton Shakespeare*, ed. Stephen Greenblatt et al. (New York: Norton, 1997), 371–434, 1.1.408–9. Further references to *Titus Andronicus* are from this edition and will be cited parenthetically in the text by act, scene, and line number.

43. Helms, "'The High Roman Fashion,'" 557.

44. T. E., *The Lawes Resolution*, 402.

45. Carolyn Sale, "Representing Lavinia: The (In)Significance of Women's Consent in Legal Discourse of Rape and Ravishment and Shakespeare's *Titus Andronicus*," in *Women, Violence, and English Renaissance Literature: Essays Honoring Paul Jorgensen*, ed. Linda Woodbridge and Sharon Beehler (Tempe: Arizona Center for Medieval and Renaissance Studies, 2003), 10.

46. J. D. Gammon attributes this shift to developing notions of individuality and individual psychology: J. D. Gammon, "Ravishment and Ruin: The Construction of Stories of Sexual Violence in England, c. 1640–1820" (PhD diss., University of Essex, 2001).

47. *A barbarous and inhumane Speech Spoken by the Lord Wentworth, Sonne to the late Earle of Straford* (London, 1642), a4r.

48. Charles Blount, *An Appeal From the Country To the City, For the Preservation of His Majesties Person, Liberty, Property, and the Protestant Religion* (London, 1679), 2.

49. Anti-Catholic tracts frequently blamed the Catholics for the destruction caused by the Great Fire; see John Kenyon, *The Popish Plot* (London: Phoenix Press, 1972), and John Miller, *Popery and Politics in England, 1660–1688* (Cambridge: Cambridge University Press, 1973).

50. *An Abstract Of The Unnatural Rebellion And Barbarous Massacre Of The Protestants In the Kingdom of Ireland, In the Year 1641* (London, 1689), 3.

51. Ibid., 5.

52. Wiliam Lilly, *The Dangerous Condition of the United Provinces Prognosticated* (London, 1672), 2.

53. Robert Ferguson, *A Brief Account of some of the late Incroachments and Depredations of the Dutch upon the English* (London, 1695), 2.

54. Charles Blount, *King William and Queen Mary Conquerors* (London, 1693), a3r.

55. James Tyrrell, *Patriarcha non Monarcha. The Patriarch Unmonarch'd* (London, 1681), 27.

56. Susan Brownmiller, *Against Our Will: Men, Women and Rape* (New York: Bantam, 1975), 14.

57. Karen Bamford, *Sexual Violence on the Jacobean Stage* (New York: St. Martin's, 2000), 9.

58. John Wilmot, Earl of Rochester, *Lucina's Rape Or The Tragedy of Valentinian*, in *The Works of John Wilmot, Earl of Rochester*, ed. Harold Love (Oxford: Oxford University Press, 1999), 133–231, 2.2.87–93. Further references to *The Tragedy of Valentinian* are from this edition and will be cited parenthetically in the text by act, scene, and line number.

59. Bamford, *Sexual Violence*, 61.

60. John Dryden, *Albion and Albanius*, in *The Works of John Dryden*, ed. Vinton Dearing, 20 vols. (Berkeley: University of California Press, 1976), 15:1–55, 1.1.51–60. Further references to *Albion and Albanius* are from this edition and will be cited parenthetically in the text by act, scene, and line number.

61. According to James Winn, Dryden used such imagery throughout his career: *"When Beauty Fires the Blood": Love and the Arts in the Age of Dryden* (Ann Arbor: University of Michigan Press, 1992), 256.

62. Ibid., 257.
63. William Shakespeare, *The Rape of Lucrece*, in *The Norton Shakespeare*, ed. Stephen Greenblatt et al. (New York: Norton, 1997), 635–82, ll. 1743–44. Further references to Shakespeare's *The Rape of Lucrece* are from this edition and will be cited parenthetically in the text by line number.
64. A true Son of the Catholick Apostolick Church, *A Catholick Pill To Purge Popery* (London, 1677), 2.
65. Luke Beaulieu, *Take heed of Both Extremes Or, Plain and useful Cautions Against Popery, And Presbytery* (London, 1675), a2v.
66. Anthony Horneck, *The Honesty of the Protestant, And Dishonesty of the Popish Divinity* (London, 1681), 150.
67. John Nalson, *The Project of Peace, Or, Unity of Faith And Government* (London, 1678), 2.
68. John Oldham, *The Jesuits Justification* (London, 1679), 1.
69. *A Gratulatory Poem On The Just And Piovs Proceedings Of The King and Parliament Against The Papists* (London, 1674), 1.
70. Benjamin Keach, *Sion in Distress: Or, The Groans Of The Protestant Church* (London, 1681), 9.
71. Ibid., 1.
72. Ibid., 3, 4.
73. Ibid., 6.
74. Ibid., 7.
75. Ibid., 25.
76. *A Nest of Nunnes Egges, strangely Hatched* (London, 1680), 1.
77. Ibid.
78. Katherine Eisaman Maus argues that such conflicts also reflected the theatrical desire to cast first Rebecca Marshall and Elizabeth Boutell and later Elizabeth Barry and Anne Bracegirdle in oppositional roles: "'Playhouse Flesh and Blood': Sexual Ideology and the Restoration Actress," *ELH* 46, no. 4 (1979): 595–617.
79. Allison Shell, *Catholicism, Controversy and the English Literary Imagination, 1558–1660* (Cambridge: Cambridge University Press, 1999), 31. For further discussion of the Church's seductive power, see Carol S. Wiener, "The Beleaguered Isle: A Study of Early Jacobean Anti-Catholicism," *Past and Present* 51 (1971): 27–62.
80. *Battering Rams Against Rome's Gates* (London, 1641), 1, 2.
81. Frances Dolan, *Whores of Babylon: Catholicism, Gender, and Seventeenth-Century Print Culture* (Ithaca and London: Cornell University Press, 1999), 39.
82. *An Abstract of the Bloody Massacre in Ireland*, 11.
83. *An Abstract of Some few of those Barbarous, Cruell Massacres and Murthers, of the Protestants, and English* (London, 1662), 5.
84. *News from the Sessions House* (London, 1689), 3.
85. *A Collection of Certain Horrid Murthers in Several Counties of Ireland* (London, 1679), 9.
86. See, for instance, Leah S. Marcus, "John Milton's *Comus*," in *A Companion to Milton*, ed. Thomas N. Corns (Oxford: Blackwell, 2001), 232–45. For discussion of *Comus*'s political undertones, see Cedric Brown, *John Milton's Aristocratic Entertainments* (Cambridge: Cambridge University Press, 1985), and Christopher Hill, *Milton and the English Revolution* (London: Faber and Faber, 1977). For discussion of the masque's sexual content, see Beth Bradburn, "Bodily Metaphor and Moral Agency in *A Masque*: A Cognitive Approach," *Milton Studies* 43 (2004): 19–34; James Broaddus, "'Gums of Glutinous Heat' in Milton's Mask and Spenser's *Faerie Queene*," *Milton Quarterly* 37, no. 4 (2003): 205–14; William Shullenberger, "Girl Interrupted: Spenserian Bondage and Release in Milton's Ludlow Mask," *Milton Quarterly* 37, no. 4 (2003): 184–204; and Catherine Thomas, "Chaste Bodies and Poisonous Desire in Milton's Mask," *Studies in English Literature 1500–1900* 46, no. 2 (2008): 435–59.
87. John Milton, *The Riverside Milton*, ed. Roy Flannagan (Boston: Houghton Mifflin, 1998), 109–71, ll. 679–81. Further references to *Comus* are from this edition and will be cited parenthetically in the text by line number.

88. Henry Bullinger, *A Confutation Of the Popes Bull which was published more than two yeres agoe against Elizabeth the most gracious Queene of England, Fraunce, and Ireland* (London, 1572), *3r.

89. Samuel Harsnett, *A Declaration of egregious Popish Impostures* (London, 1603), a2v.

90. *The English Pope* (London, 1643), 21. For discussion of images of Circe in Catholic literature, see Erica Veevers, *Images of Love and Religion: Queen Henrietta Maria and Court Entertainments* (Cambridge: Cambridge University Press, 1989).

91. *A Bloody Tragedie*, c1v.

92. Dolan, *Whores of Babylon*, 131–35. For readings of Henrietta Maria's position in the English court, see Malcolm Smuts, "Religion, European Politics and Henrietta Maria's Circle, 1625–41," in *Henrietta Maria: Piety, Politics and Patronage*, ed. Erin Griffey (Burlington: Ashgate, 2008), 13–38, and Michelle Anne White, *Henrietta Maria and the English Civil Wars* (Burlington: Ashgate, 2006).

93. *A Copie of the King's Message sent by the Duke of Lenox* (London, 1644), 6.

94. *Battering Rams*, 1.

95. *The Kings Maiesties Speech*, a2r.

96. *Battering Rams*, 1.

97. Ibid., 2.

98. Maggie Kilgour, *From Communion to Cannibalism: An Anatomy of Metaphors of Incorporation* (Princeton: Princeton University Press, 1990), 83.

99. Horneck, *The Honesty of the Protestant*, 55.

100. Lindley, "The Impact of the 1641 Rebellion," 146.

101. *The Manner of the Burning the Pope*, 4.

102. Dolan, *Whores of Babylon*, 36.

103. John Locke, *Two Treatises of Government*, ed. Peter Laslett (Cambridge: Cambridge University Press, 1960), 200.

104. G. S., *A Briefe Declaration Of The Barbarous And inhumane dealings of the Northerne Irish Rebels* (London, 1641), title page.

105. Ibid.

106. Lynn A. Higgins and Brenda R. Silver, eds., *Rape and Representation* (New York: Columbia University Press, 1991), 2.

107. Ibid.

108. Ibid., 3.

Chapter One

Rape and the Rehabilitation of Royalist Identity, 1660–1665

The anonymously authored pamphlet, *A Blazing Starre seen in the West* (1642), tells the story of a Devonshire virgin who left her friends and relatives on the evening of Monday, November 14, 1642, to return to her father's house. Her "Friends and Kinsfolkes . . . were importunate to have her stay all night," not wanting her to travel the roads alone.[1] They remind the girl that "there were so many deboyst Covaliers [sic] abroad, so that they could not passe securely in the day time, much less in the night," but the girl decides to risk the journey anyway, not wanting to worry her father with her absence.[2] She immediately begins to regret her decision when it "grew very darke, so that she could scarce discerne her hand" before her face, and her fears are further compounded when she "heard the noyse of a Horse galloping towards her, at which she beganne to be affraid."[3] Luckily the rider, Ralph Ashley, is a family friend who suggests accompanying her for protection on the road. She accepts his offer, "partly by her knowledge of his supposed friendship to her father, and partly by her desire to get home without any further danger."[4]

Unfortunately for the girl, Ralph Ashley is insincere in his avowed desire to protect her. Instead, "the Devill strait furnished him with a device to obtaine his wicked purpose," and once she is securely installed on his horse, he rides off the road, and "went about to ravish her, taking a grievous oath that no power in heaven or earth could save her from his lust."[5] With human aid seemingly beyond reach, the young woman calls out to God for succour: "O Lord God of Hosts, tis in thy power to deliver me, help Lord or I perish."[6] God hears the virgin's prayer; although Ashley "tooke a great oath swearing God Damme-him, alive or dead he would injoy her," God sends out a "streame of fire strucke from the Comet, in the perfect shape, and exact resemblance of a flaming Sword, so that he fell downe staggering."[7] Proof of

God's wrath notwithstanding, the severely wounded Ashley refuses to repent for his crime, cursing instead "the perverseness of that Roundheaded-whore" whom he blames for his injuries.[8] Finally, "he died raving and blaspheming to the terrour and amazement of the beholders," while the girl recovers fully from her injuries, remaining ever virtuous in the face of suffering.[9] After her deliverance, "the very first words that she spake were these, Lord thou art Iust in thy Judgments and mercifull in the midest of thy justice, wherefore I beseech the [sic] let not this sinne be imputed to his Charge, in the day of Judgment."[10] She prays for Ashley's soul, offering compassion where he showed none.

God's personal intervention in the young woman's affairs both confirms her personal worth and reveals the political leanings of the Divine. While women often faced dangers when travelling the roads alone at night, the girl's friends and later her father emphasize that times are especially treacherous because there are "so many Cavaliers abroad."[11] Clearly they have good reason for concern; as the title page informs the reader, Ashley is "a deboyst Cavalier" whose politics motivate at least in part his sexually violent act.[12] He refers to the young woman as a "Roundheaded-whore," suggesting that his hatred of her (and her father's) political position outweighs his allegiance to his old friend.[13] To be a royalist is to abandon all claim to decency, empathy, or loyalty, and thus when God strikes Ashley down, He is not only aiding an innocent girl but revealing His support for the parliamentarian faction of the English Civil Wars. The tract provides a "fearefull example to al [Ashley's] fellow Cavaliers"; royalists should read of his horrible fate and repent, both of their personal sins and of their political choices.[14]

The introduction to this volume detailed the popularity of the demonic Irishman trope in English Civil War propaganda. This chapter explores the related tropes of the debauched Cavalier and his malignant consort, the poisonous Catholic bride, and traces their afterlife in the rape plays of the early Restoration theater. According to Deborah G. Burks, negative images of Cavaliers abounded during the years of the English Civil Wars: "royal and royalist men appear as rapacious, violent abusers of the innocent citizens of the English nation."[15] After the Restoration, playwrights continued to resurrect the imagery of the propaganda tracts, now using scenes of rape not to condemn but to honor the king. While only three plays of the 1660s actually staged scenes of sexual violence, each is interested in rehabilitating the monarchy from two decades of parliamentary attacks. The Earl of Orrery's *The Generall* (1662) is both the first heroic drama and the first play to use rape to redeem the memory of the Cavaliers. Orrery displaces the violence of the debauched Cavalier onto the parliamentary faction, accusing Cromwell's supporters of the worst sorts of sexually violent atrocities and improving by proxy the image of the royalist. He also constructs a discourse of rape and royalism that will be expanded upon and developed over the next forty years.

Subsequently, Thomas Porter's *The Villain* (1664) and Edward Howard's *The Usurper* (1664) adopt a similar technique to establish their own royalism, albeit *The Usurper* more explicitly, *The Villain* only in passing. Howard will also resurrect the rhetoric of the anti–Henrietta Maria tracts, engaging with the discourse of the poisonous Catholic bride to dismiss fears about the king's Catholic mistresses and new Catholic queen. In all of these plays, the discourse of sexual violence is the discourse of political controversy, while the combination of sexual atrocity and dramatic pathos reflects the depth of the theater's involvement with the world of political propaganda.[16]

POLITICAL PROPAGANDA IN THE 1640S: THE TROPE OF THE DEBAUCHED CAVALIER

The tale of rape and divine retribution that began this chapter incorporates many of the recurring tropes of English Civil War parliamentarian propaganda. *A Blazing Starre*'s Roundhead maid is an innocent woman wronged by Cavalier excess. She is obedient to her father, devout in her worship of God, and forgiving and merciful in her treatment of her assailant. Ralph Ashley, by contrast, is violent and sacrilegious. The shepherds who find the wounded Ashley are initially astounded to hear him "blaspheming, and belching forth many damnable imprecations," and he later dies entirely unrepentant, "raving and blaspheming to the terrour and amazement of the beholders."[17] The tract thus concludes with a moral that is also a political warning: "Reader heare is a president for all those that are customary blasphemers, and live after the lusts of their flesh, especially all those Cavaliers which esteem murder & rapine the chiefe Principalls of their religion, for doubtlese this is but a beginning of Gods vengeance for not onely he, but they, and we, and all of us, except we repent; we shall all likewise perish."[18] The Cavaliers as a party are, like Ashley, blasphemous, lustful, and violent. They are rapists and murderers who commit atrocities against innocent parliamentarians, reject the true faith, and worship only their own perverse desires.

Another anonymously authored tract, *A New Mercury, called Mercurius Problematicus* (1644), offers a "brief Character of a Cavalier of these times," enumerating the many destructive qualities of the royalists:

> A Cavalier of these times, appears like a burning Beacon; which makes all men expect some approaching mischief. He tells you, he fights for the King and his lawes, yet obeys none, but stands upon his own prerogative: For Rapine is his Vocation, and Murther his Recreation; imbruing his hand in the bloud of his Country with as much delight, as if *Beati-bellifaci* were the truest Motto. If Common Prayers be suppressed, his devotion is almost silenced; for he hath but one prayer for himself, and a very short one, but that I confesse is

> often in his mouth, and continually in his actions, which is *God dam him.* He loves his King as he doth his Whore, expressing to both a feigned fidelity, onely to satisfie his unlawfull appetities, which being done, he regards both alike. If he conquer any man that appears religious, it is argument enough to give no quarter, but minse him into Attomes: And he shewes his greatest contrition when at any time he lets a *Roundhead* escape unkilled, for he never repents heartily, but of that sinne. He beleeves there is no such way to know a good subject, as drinking a health to the Parliaments confusion; Nor any such Traitor as he which denies it.[19]

The tract rehearses the litany of complaints leveled against the royalists throughout the period. Cavaliers are violent beasts who rape virtuous women and murder innocent men. They are whoremongers and drunkards who speak sacrilege and lack true religion. They rejoice in their cruel treatment of the Roundheads and claim loyalty to the king but eschew true fidelity to any but themselves. In fact, by treating their king as they would a common whore, they feminize their ruler and undermine the strength of the monarchy they claim to support.

Such accusations returned again and again throughout the period as parliamentarian propagandists sought to delegitimize royalist politics. According to George Lawrence, the Cavaliers would frequently "drink a health to the confusion of the Gospell of Iesus Christ"; they would "drink, and be drunk, and whore, and be damnd, and will not be beholding to God to save us," an oath that Lawrence labels "unparalleld blasphemy, contrary to the principles of Nature, Reason, and Religion."[20] Threats of violence frequently accompanied such instances of drunken blasphemy. The royalist speaker of *The Wicked Resolution Of The Cavaliers* (1642), for instance, proposes the following toast: "My brave companion and Cavalier, let us drink courageously that we may kill the Divell and all his regiment of roundheads."[21] Another 1642 pamphlet, *A wonderfull And Strange Miracle*, describes how Andrew Stonsby, a Cavalier, demanded a "Sea of Drinke, that Leviathan-like he might swill himselfe to death in his owne Ellement."[22] Stonsby couples his desire for drink with a desire for sex—he wishes for "ten Legions of Whores"—and concludes with a Satanic toast.[23] "I beginne a health to the Devill," he avows, frightening the onlooking crowd: "the rest of his company though they were steeped in Wine, began to shrinke back."[24] Stonsby is punished for his sacrilege when the devil comes to claim him, but even while dying, he refuses to repent: "they found the miserable wretch layd groveling on the ground, raving and blaspheming, and so he continned [sic] for the space of a day and a night, and afterward died raging and blaspheming against God, and cursing the *Roundheads*."[25] As in *A Blazing Starre,* the Cavalier of *A wonderfull And Strange Miracle* is instantly punished for his blasphemy, but even proof of divine displeasure cannot dissuade him from his sacrilege.

In many of the tracts, Cavalier fondness for drink leads to alcohol-induced property damage. The author of *Strange, true, and lamentable NEWES from Exceter* [sic] (1643) describes how the royalist army "went into some Cellars where was plenty of wine, and beere, drank what their gormandising guts would hold, and let the rest run about the house . . . moreover they breake the Covenant which was made, in every respect, the very first hour that they entered the City and fell to plundering, pillaging, robbing, stealing, cutting and slashing."[26] The royalists are implacable in their hatred of the Roundheads and constantly seek to destroy both their persons and their goods. According to Lawrence, "A great Company of Cavalliers comming to plunder a Town, they swore, that they would robbe, and slay all the *Roundheads* in the Towne."[27] *The Insolency and Cruelty of the Cavaliers* (1643) similarly describes "the plundering and pillaging of Winslow, and Swanborne, and diverse other townes in the Counties of Buckingham, and Hartford," and it enumerates the goods stolen from various Roundhead country squires.[28] *Terrible Newes From York* (1642) lists "the barbarous Actions of the Cavaliers at *Yorke,* in plundering the houses, seizing the goods, and imprisoning the persons of those Citizens that refuse to contribute money to maintaine a War against the Parliament, having already plundered above twenty Citizens houses."[29] The Cavaliers are accused of "cutting . . . purses, breaking of houses, and pillaging the same, and sundry other Out-rages; as calling for things and not paying a farthing for it."[30] In some cases, they abandon all pretense of lawful behavior and become common thieves. One group of soldiers reportedly took a tailor and his servants hostage in his home, "each man drawing his sword and . . . vowing to kill him, if he told them not where his Gold was."[31]

Since for the royalists of the parliamentary pamphlets "no death was bad enough for Round-heads," no treatment too outré, the Cavaliers also attack their women, both a form of property crime and an outrage against English manhood.[32] Accounts of sexual violence pervade the propaganda tracts. *A perfect Declaration of The Barbarous and Cruell practices committed by Prince Robert, the Cavalliers, and others in his Majesties Army* (1642) details how royalist soldiers "spoyled his Majesties good subjects, and many were murthered and barbarously used, ravishing of women, and bloudily killing others, not sparing those that were great with child, nor pittying poore little infants."[33] *The Wicked Resolution Of The Cavaliers* (1642) reprints a speech supposedly "Made by a Cavalier to one of his Dammee Companions": "we desire nothing but to cut throats, take purses, ravish maids, plunder houses, murder Roundheads, defie the Parliament, and like Phaeton, set all the world on fire."[34] William Cartwright, author of the Roundhead tract, *The Game at Chesse*, directly links property crime with sexual assault. The Cavaliers, he writes, only pretend loyalty to the king while maltreating the truly loyal parliamentarian faction. They "invade the Subjects Estates and

Persons that continue firme in their Allegiance to the King and the white *Knights* [the Parliament], plundering their Houses, and inforcing their wives and daughters to their lusts."[35] The royalist army, he complains, "hath produced so many blacke and bloody effects in this Kingdome, and so many plunderings, rapines and murthers, that the beauteous face of this pleasant Land is bestained and bedewed with blood; the Inhabitants thereof beaten and terrified out of their peaceful dwellings, their goods dispoyled and taken away."[36]

Antiroyalist tracts of the 1640s also link the violence of the debauched Cavalier with that of the demonic Irishman. John Goodwin's *Anti-Cavalierisme*, for instance, demands "the suppressing of that Butcherly brood of Cavaliering Incendiaries, who are now hammering England, to make an Ireland of it."[37] George Lawrence even more explicitly connects Cavalier excess—drunkenness, whoremongering, sexual violence, and blasphemy—with Catholic sacrilege. Comparing the Cavaliers to the biblical Midianites, Lawrence writes,

> They were uncleane both by bodily and spirituall uncleannesse. . . . We put *spirituall* and *bodily uncleannesse* together, because one seldome goes without the other. As for *bodily uncleannesse,* we will not accuse them how many they abused; you may take that *ex concessio* themselves . . . that they would Whore, Drinke, and be Damned, wherefore if they doe not whore, at least they lie both which Sinnes God will judge; yet we cannot but give you the Report of the Country, of two *Cavalliers* who ravished one *Maide* while another stood by and held the Horses: of 7. [sic] more, who abused another, before shee could be released from them; besides the many Rapes and Chamber-Adulteries, which we leave to the All-seeing Eyes and Revenging Hand of Iustice, and as for *Spirituall Uncleannesse,* which is Idolatry, that cannot be free from their Campe, having so many *Papists* and prophane ones in their unhallowed and *Pseudo-Catholique* Army.[38]

Lawrence deftly shifts between the physical violence of rape and the spiritual evils of blasphemy and Catholicism. The sexual and the religious are linked as two forms of uncleanness, while uncontrollable sexual aggression functions as a natural extension of Catholic idolatry among the "Popish, and evill affected Cavaliers."[39]

In all of these tracts, the authors make an implicit appeal to the good men of England to stand up against royalist tyranny and to protect their wives, children, and goods from harm. Implicit in such warnings is the fear that English Catholics will erupt in a massacre to rival the carnage of the 1641 Irish rebellion; by recalling the tales of Irish violence, the tracts tap into popular fears of "a Catholic enemy whose aim is the total annihilation of Protestantism."[40] An increase in crime, they insist, is the direct byproduct of Catholic plotting within the realm. Left to flourish, the Catholics will "slay our fathers, ravish our mothers, plunder our houses, spoil our goods, and utterly deprive us of all outward comforts."[41] Thus in the words of *Anti-Cavalierisme*, "You are to stand up in defence of your Lives, your Liberties, your Estates, your Houses, your Wives, your Children, your Brethren, and that not of this Nation only, but of those two other Nations likewise united under the same government with this, in the defence of those Religious and faithfull Governours, that Honourable Assembly of Parliament."[42] All good Protestants must fight against the combined forces of "the Papists and bloud-thirsty Cavaliers," must defend "the King [and] the Rights and Privilidges of Parliament, against all malignant Parties, both Papists and Cavaliers."[43] The debauched Cavalier becomes for the English the domestic ally of the demonic, blood-thirsty Irishman, and together those evil men "would subject our Roiall King under the Popes Supremacy, and so ensnare us under a Tyrant."[44]

The anti-Cavalier and anti-Irish tracts share a mutual vocabulary of violent atrocity. That Charles I and Henrietta Maria were commonly known to be soliciting Catholic (and even Irish Catholic) support for the royalist cause further reinforced the widespread fear that no Protestant man, woman, or child would be safe from the joint violence of Cavalier and Catholic. *The Dammee Cavalliers Warning Piece* complains, "how often have they appointed our men for the swords & slaughter, our wives & daughters for Rapes and Adulteries, & after to cruell murther, our children to have been dashed in pieces against the stones in the streets, as too many have Been in *Ireland,* our cities to have been fired about our eares, and all our wealth to be a prey for them."[45] *A Powerfull, Pitifull, Citi-Full Cry* decries the "plundering Cavaliers, who neither have respect to sex nor age, the gray head, nor the harmlesse babes but burn, destroy, rob, plunder, pillage all without any mercy or pity."[46] These men "plunder, pilladge, ravish, and doe what they please."[47] They maltreat women and the elderly, "throwing [a] grave minister with his aged wife downe the staires."[48] They are especially cruel to children: "such infants as we, have had their braines dashed out against the stones, or posts of houses, tost up and down upon the points of their pikes."[49] And like the Irish of the 1641 tracts, they target pregnant women. One pamphlet describes the investigation into the murder of a woman "shot under the back into the belly, being very great with child, and within a Month or five weeks of the time of her delivery."[50]

If the Cavaliers are linked with the Irish Catholics by their acts of rape and plunder, they are also connected by the shared imagery of vampirism and cannibalism. Royalist armies are alternately labelled "bloudy minded Cannibals,"[51] "malignant and bloud-sucking Cannibals,"[52] "bloud sucking Chavaliers,"[53] and "bloud-thirsty Cavaliers."[54] Such comments serve both to remind Protestant audiences of the supposed horrors of transubstantiation and to render the Catholics and Cavaliers jointly Other. "Self-fashioning is achieved in relation to something perceived as alien, strange, or hostile," Stephen Greenblatt writes. "This threatening Other—heretic, savage, witch, adulteress, traitor, Antichrist—must be discovered or invented in order to be attacked and destroyed," thereby determining the contours of English national identity.[55] Accordingly, the propaganda tracts transform the Cavaliers into a monstrous Other against which only the Roundheads may be judged English and worthy. One tract goes so far as to suggest that "bondage under the Turk is humanity and mercy" compared to the "slavery" and "tyranny of the Cavaliers."[56] Writing of the worst of the anti-Irish atrocity pamphlets, Raymond Tumbleson argues that their aim is to "stigmatize a people as so vile and degraded that all measures are justified against them and ruthless ones are necessary."[57] By linking the Cavaliers to an array of English cultural enemies, the anti-Cavalier tracts participate in a similar ideological project. The Cavaliers and the Catholics are worse than the cruelest of foreign enemies, justifying their final annihilation.

REDEEMING THE CAVALIERS: ORRERY'S *THE GENERALL*

In the decade following the Restoration, it fell to royalist authors to dismantle Roundhead political culture and rewrite the image of the monarchy for the new generation. As such, the theater became an important source of political activism. Nancy Klein Maguire explains,

> Since Charles II recognized the propaganda value of the theater, and relished drama personally, nearly all of the new playwrights were politicians who became playwrights either to gain or to enhance their political credibility. Whether triumphant after twenty years of fidelity to the Stuart cause or hopeful that they could blot out their Cromwellian allegiances, the playwrights, like other Royalists, defended the traditional power-structure in an attempt to rehabilitate themselves and their culture. In tragicomic rituals reenacting regicide and restoration, they promoted kingship in the new circumstances by exonerating themselves of the execution of Charles I while celebrating the restoration of his son.[58]

Roger Boyle, Earl of Orrery, was one such playwright who wrote to rehabilitate both the monarchy and his own reputation. Initially a friend to both Charles II and Oliver Cromwell, Orrery (then Lord Broghill) finally supported Cromwell in the civil wars, becoming a trusted advisor to the Lord Protector and urging him to accept the crown: "Rather than go to prison for supporting Charles II's cause, Orrery himself served during the Interregnum on Cromwell's cabinet, was elected to Parliament, and urged Cromwell to become king."[59] As he became disillusioned with the Interregnum government, he began to work for Charles's return. While his plan was abandoned in favor of General George Monck's, he was instrumental in ensuring the success of the Restoration, for which Charles forgave his earlier disloyalty and awarded him the title of Orrery.

After the Restoration, Charles and Orrery remained on good terms, and it was apparently at Charles's behest that Orrery authored his first play, *The Generall*. In a letter to the Duke of Ormonde, Orrery explains, "When I had the honour and happiness the last time to kiss His Majesty's hand, he commanded me to write a play for him . . . and therefore, some months after, I presumed to lay at his majesty's feet a tragic-comedy, all in ten-feet verse and rhyme . . . because I found his majesty relished rather the French fashion of writing plays than the English."[60] Charles made his request in late 1660, and the play premiered under the title *Altemera* at the Dublin Theatre in the fall of 1662. Charles was pleased with the play and threw his support behind it, writing to Orrery, "I will now tell you, that I have read your first play, which I like very well, and doe intend to bring it upon the Stage, as soone as my Company have their new Stage in order, that the Seanes may bee worthy the words they are to sett forth."[61] The play finally premiered at Drury Lane with the King's Company on September 14, 1664. Samuel Pepys, who saw the play two weeks later on September 28, was not impressed: "so we saw, coming late, part of *The Generall,* my Lord Orrery's (Broghill) second play; but, Lord, to see how no more, either in words, sense, or design, it is to his *Harry the 5th* is not imaginable, and so poorly acted, though in finer clothes, is strange."[62] While *Altemera*, the earlier version, is no longer extant, Orrery apparently made few revisions to the text, making *The Generall* both the first newly authored play of the Restoration to feature a scene of sexual violence and the first play of the period written in rhymed heroic couplets. Throughout the play, Orrery uses rape as a central component of his political project and, as we shall see, constructs many of the tropes that will define the rape play for the remainder of the century.

On the surface, *The Generall* presents a straightforward dramatic allegory of the events of the Interregnum and Restoration. The play begins in the aftermath of the evil unnamed king's usurpation of the throne from the rightful ruler, Melizer. According to army commander Thrasolin,

> Melizer shou'd by right possesse the throne.
> Nor is't lesse true, that man who rules us now
> Is both a Tirant and usurper too,
> For when Evender I fight did fall,
> The Monster was the Armies Generall,
> And when the Royall Melizer hee shou'd
> Have Crown'd as being first Prince of the bloud,
> Hee seiz'd on him, and by his boundlesse pow'r
> Made him close prisoner in the fatall Tower,
> Where still our lawfull king hee has deteyn'd.[63]

As a result, the kingdom has fractured, with some nobles choosing to support (and purchase power within) the new regime; Olerand, another commander, admits that "Hee lately bought that Office hee possess't" (4.2.69). Meanwhile, other nobles, including the virtuous Lucidor, have been labelled rebels for their continued loyalty to the true king. The usurper excuses his crime by attempting to redefine the concept of divine right: "What ever crymes are acted for a Crowne," he explains, "The Gods forgive, when once they put it on" (4.1.27–28). Whoever holds the throne has the right to rule, he argues, or else God would not have allowed him to succeed in his pursuit of power. Merit and might, he goes on to claim, and not birth legitimize the rightful monarch.

By the end of the play, however, the correct king has been restored to his position by a coalition of army commanders. Memnor announces, "Your Subjects, Sir, from whose Campe now I came, / Have sent mee to acquaint you in their name / Their Joy, that in your Lawfull throne you sitt. / To their true sovereigne gladly they submitt" (5.1.399–402). Meanwhile, the usurper is struck down by the true king, a dramatic fantasy of punishment and reconciliation that replays the events of the Restoration with a more satisfactory outcome. According to Jonathan Scott, the early years of the Restoration "entailed a process of grieving, and of struggle between forgetting and memory."[64] As part of that struggle, royalists had to accept the fact that Cromwell was never punished for his crime, that he was only defeated by natural death. *The Muses Joy For the Recovery of that Weeping Vine Henrietta Maria* (1660), for instance, complains that Cromwell "Gasp't in his bed *too late*, and yet *too soon*" since he did not "*live* to *Hang* and suffer for his sin."[65] Likewise, in *A Third Conference Between O. Cromwell And Hugh Peters* (1660), Peters's ghost comments that Cromwell "had the luck to die in your bed, and to have a pompous Funeral with all Prince-like solemnities (never to be paid for!)."[66] After the Restoration, a rash of effigy burnings took place as people "avoided the issue of their own compliance and accommodation with the Cromwellian regime."[67] Thomas Rugge describes one such scene: "in Westminster a very great fiere was made, and on top of the fier they put old Oliver Cromwell and his wife in sables, theire pictures lifely made like them in life, which was burnt in the fire, and State armes."[68] Such displays culminated in January 1661 when Charles II ordered the exhumation of Cromwell's corpse:

> On 30 January 1661, the anniversary of the execution of Charles I, the bodies of Oliver Cromwell, Henry Ireton, and John Bradshaw were exhumed from their graves in Westminster Abbey, dragged to Tyburn on hurdles, and hanged before a crowd of thousands. At sunset, the bodies were taken down, decapitated, and buried in a pit under Tyburn, while the heads were placed on spikes atop Westminster Hall.[69]

According to Laura Lunger Knoppers, the "disinterment of Cromwell was intended as a solemn display of justice and punishment," although as she points out, by punishing Cromwell so publicly, the king returned him to the center of public discourse once more.[70] Perhaps even more problematically than Knoppers notes, the spectacle also served as a reminder that true justice—the punishment of Cromwell's living form—did not and would never occur. There is a limit to a king's authority, and he cannot command Cromwell back to life that he may sentence him to death.

It is here that the stage offers a salve to a nation's guilty conscience. While Charles II and the English people had to content themselves with exhuming and humiliating Cromwell's earthly remains, Orrery's King Melizer defeats the usurper onstage. In the play's climactic scene, Melizer prevents the usurper from committing suicide: "Thy deaths a debt my hand alone must pay. / Had I allow'd what now thou wouldst have done, / Thou hadst usurp'd my vengeance, as my crowne" (4.6.436–38). That Melizer defeats the usurper so easily proves both his potency and God's support for his cause. While Thrasolin says somewhat ironically of the usurper that "I call him King, because hee fills the throne" (1.4.333), Clorimun recognizes that Melizer joins merit with right and that both are displayed in his easy victory over the false king. Melizer's "virtues are soe great, his right soe good, / Hee should bee King by choice as well as bloud" (3.2.207–9). As Mita Choudhury explains, "The king's 'right' gives him the 'legitimacy' to rule, a right/legitimacy that the usurper does not have."[71] The end of the play thus reestablishes the primacy of divine right; the person marked by birth to rule is also the most qualified for and deserving of the position.

If the usurper is punished, his supporters are redeemed. Olerand has purchased his position within the new government but renounces it when Clorimun returns to the fight and it appears the rebellion may succeed. According to Cratoner, Olerand

> privately brought mee to Clorimun,
> Where Olerand protested before mee
> Hee wou'd this night sett him at Libertie.
> The Generall too vow'd hee'd noe more deferre
> By open force to Restore Melizer,
> Which hee noe longer cou'd esteeme unjust,
> Th'usurper having freed him of his trust. (4.2.73–79)

Clorimun, like Monck and Orrery, initially fights for the usurper but ultimately is recalled to virtue and supports his king in an act of reunion and reconciliation. All those who profited under tyranny gladly rejoin the royalist fold; even the common people renew their loyalty and recognize they have been at fault: "Since in a Tyrants cause wee prosper'd soe, / In the true Kings our Swords shou'd Wonders doe. / On the wrong side wee know how wee can fight. / Let's prove now wee can doe it on the right" (4.2.92–95). Unity reigns as Melizer promises amnesty and mercy for all: "Past faults I'le never to Remembrance bring, / For which the word I give you of your king" (5.1.411–12). The play concludes with a reference to the 1660 Act of Indemnity and Oblivion as the country revels in the goodness of its lawful monarch.

Several critics have analyzed Orrery's political and personal intentions in crafting *The Generall*. According to Nancy Klein Maguire, "Orrery . . . used playwriting to rehabilitate himself politically, but in modern terms, his self-indicting autobiographies were also his psychotherapy. Orrery, probably unconsciously, used playwriting to work through his own political history, particularly his obsession with the regicide."[72] Kathleen Lynch concurs, calling the play "a kind of medicine for the soul. His conscience was eased, his monarch (he must have hoped) reassured by his successive portraits of a distinguished general reluctantly serving a usurper and joyfully thereafter bringing in the rightful king."[73] Yet to read *The Generall* against the backdrop of the English Civil War–era antiroyalist pamphlets is to recognize the extent to which Orrery deliberately engaged with the long-standing tropes of Roundhead propaganda. The play, like the tracts, uses sexual morality to negotiate political movements, and it is in the treatment of sex and sexual violence that Orrery's celebration of royalism becomes most clear. First and foremost, as the tyrant is a usurper, he is also a rapist, one who eagerly attempts to force Altemera into sex. The tyrant will claim Altemera's body without consent as he unlawfully conquered the nation, and the play continually reinforces the link between imperial conquest and sexual violence. When Mora, Altemera's stronghold, is conquered, Filadin remarks, "When townes are conquer'd by the force of Warre, / Walls first are storm'd and then the Women are" (2.2.257–58). Similarly, when defeat is assured, a Page counsels Altemera, "Fly, Madam, Fly, or else you are undone; / The Towne is now possesst by Clorimun" (2.4.371–72). Sexual violence and military conquest are treated as extensions of one another, and both prove the usurper's baseness and corruption.

To attack Altemera is, metaphorically speaking, to attack the nation; she functions as a stand-in for the English/Sicilian state, and thus the health of her body reflects more broadly the health of the country. That the usurper has committed a horrible crime becomes terribly apparent when Altemera begins to wither away and die under his cruel control: "I perceive a palenesse in her Lipps," the usurper complains, "And her triumphant Eyes are in an Ecclipse. / The bright Virmillion from her Cheekes is fledd, / And death beginns to reigne where beauty did" (4.6.383–86). Altemera's decline mirrors the damage caused by the usurpation, and only with the return of the true king can she be restored to health and prosperity. Importantly, one of Melizer's first acts as king is to bestow his consent for Altemera's long-desired marriage to Lucidor: "And, Lucidor, since you to armes did fly / But to preserve your mistresse Chastitie, / As soone as arte and time your Mistresse cures, / By sacred nuptiall Rites shee shall be yours" (5.1.389–92). Melizer reasserts his control over the kingdom by asserting his right to approve Altemera's matrimonial (and sexual) choices. He affirms himself as a ruler to the nation by first functioning as a ruler to Altemera.

According to Staves, Orrery's use of rape anticipates the political culture of the Exclusion Crisis and Glorious Revolution. Perhaps more urgently, it looks backward to the political culture of the English Civil Wars. In depicting the false king as a cruel rapist, Orrery transforms the trope of the debauched Cavalier into the trope of the debauched usurper. Sexual violence and sexual excess in the play are solely associated with the tyrant and his supporters. Clorimun, like the false king, is in love with Altemera, and as he initially fights on the usurper's side, he is also initially willing to commit an act of violence to slake his desire. "I renounce virtue, I am all but Love" (3.2.46), he tells Altemera. Fortunately, Clorimun proves his virtue by resigning Altemera to Lucidor, thus avoiding the usurper's fate.

> Your scorning death in mee such greifs had bred,
> I wish'd you rather Lucidors than dead.
> Why shou'd not I, since Life againe you have,
> Performe that which will keep you from the Grave,
> And save your life now at as high a Rate
> As I would lately have redeem'd it at? . . .
> You must be either death's or Lucidors,
> Be his then, Madame. (5.1.337–42, 350–51)

Clorimun's return to sexual virtue correlates with his return to political virtue. He will not follow the tyrant's lead and become a rapist, nor will he fight any longer to preserve the usurper's rule: "The tyrant then forc'd you to that sad fate; / What was his sinne, why shou'd I immitate?" (5.1.343–44). Personal morality follows political morality, reaffirming the royalist insistence that true virtue (both personal and political) lies with the monarch, not the leaders of the interregnum government.

The behavior of the other army commanders also reflects the parallel between political and sexual behavior. Thrasolin, Monasin, and Filadin are interesting figures, insofar as they accede to the new government, even as they attempt to undermine it from within. Neither fully traitor nor fully loyal to Melizer, they occupy a politically liminal space characterized by opportunism rather than principle. Monasin and Filadin in particular are willing to fight for the usurper, accepting positions in the new king's army. As their political allegiances are shifting and groundless, so, too, are their romantic impulses unfixed and disloyal. In act 2, they pause to comment on the women of their acquaintance, criticizing them for being too chaste or too loose, too old or too intelligent. Monasin calls Daphnis "a witt, reads books, / And her words are more hansome than her looks. / That woman's brought to an unhappy passe / When her tongue is the best part shee has" (2.2.163–66). He mocks Cloris, who "vainly hopes her Lovers to persuade / By her discretion, now her beauties fade" (2.2.185–86). Cratoner calls Amanta "old enough ugly to be, I knowe; / And young enough too long to live soe too" (2.2.177–78). Filadin criticizes Calione for thinking too much of herself: "I prais'd her body, and shee prais'd her soule" (2.2.200), while Cratoner confirms that "Love enters at the Eye, not at the Eare" (2.2.210). The men celebrate their catty gossip as a way to strike a blow against female falsity: "Since they will have us tell lyes to their face, / Yet, when their backs be turn'd, let truth take place" (2.2.231–32). They also insist upon the evils of marriage. Cratoner calls marriage "needlesse, for if Love Comands / Their hearts to Joyne, they need noe nuptiall bands" (2.2.144–45), while Monasin protests the "artificiall" bands of marriage (2.2.153) and Filadin the "horrid Chaines" of matrimony (2.2.155).

This scene has, to date, received little critical attention, perhaps because it seems wholly inappropriate to the overarching tone of the play, a scene torn from a sex comedy and inserted into a heroic drama. I want to suggest, however, that Orrery includes this scene not just to provide comic relief, but to associate the usurper's opportunistic followers with the negative aspects of Cavaliering. Unlike the usurper, these men are not rapists, but their wit, flippancy, unchastity, and rejection of matrimonial mores bespeak their sexual corruption and underscore their accompanying political untrustworthiness. Their words also recall some of the more flippant Cavalier carpe diem lyrics, among them Sir John Suckling's famous pronouncement, "Out upon it, I have lov'd / Three whole days together; / And am like to love three more, / If it prove fair weather."[74] While not violent like the usurper himself, Thrasolin, Monasin, and Filadin embody one aspect of the debauched Cavalier—sexual profligacy—here displaced onto those men of questionable loyalty. According to Stephen Flores, "Heroic faithfulness—to one's king, kin, class, lover, or spouse—functions as a metaphor and a formula for solidarity, for a social and political order constituted by a public recognition of one's allegiance to the court and to the upper classes and the values necessary to their hegemony."[75] When working at least partially for the usurper's camp, the men lack fidelity, sexual or otherwise, associating the usurping faction, the parliamentary faction, with libertinism. Tellingly, the men make no more such comments after returning to the royalist fold. After the Restoration, they speak only of honor and decry the wickedness of mankind.

If the usurper's men speak the language of Suckling, Lucidor speaks the language of Richard Lovelace. Lucidor, named a rebel for his continued loyalty to the crown, evinces no interest in Cavalier sexual excess, instead remaining ever loyal to his love for Altemera. When he leaves her, he does so honorably, because he must fight for personal glory. Echoing Lovelace's famous lines from "To Lucasta, Going to the Wars," "I could not love thee, Dear, so much / Loved I not honour more,"[76] Altemera complains that

"Though you love mee, yett you love glory more" (1.2.235). "I can forgive you all thinges," Altemera tells Lucidor, "But leaving mee, and leaving mee for Warre" (1.2.206–7). In response, Lucidor both proclaims his eternal love for Altemera and defends his love of honor, the only thing he values beyond her:

> Hee, Madam, that is destin'd unto you,
> Must needes bee destin'd unto Triumphes too.
> The Justice of the Gods is sure too high
> Your care to give mee, and their owne deny.
> I have your Love, and in your Quarrell fight:
> That makes itt duty, this makes itt delight.
> In your just Cause all dangers I despise.
> My Sword shall bee resistlesse as your Eyes. (1.2.250–57)

What the play does, then, is subtly to divide the negative aspects of Cavaliering, the sexual excess characteristic of Suckling's poetry, from the positive pursuit of honor for self, king, and country represented in Lovelace's. Lucidor becomes the answer to the debauched Cavalier, the positive figure of the royalist that stands in contrast to the corruptions of the false king and his men.

PORTER, HOWARD, AND THE TROPE OF THE DEBAUCHED USURPER

On October 18, 1664, Thomas Porter's *The Villain* premiered in London. One of the first hits of the newly reopened theaters, *The Villain* pokes fun at aspects of *The Generall* (previously circulating in manuscript) while borrowing elements of *Othello* for presentation on the contemporary stage.[77] *The Villain* is not an explicitly political play; while the main characters are soldiers, their romantic travails are never linked to an overarching political plot. Yet Nancy Klein Maguire suggests that contemporary audiences might have imaginatively connected Maligni, the play's Iago/vice figure, with Oliver Cromwell: "a theatre-goer in the 1660s might also have seen a connection between Maligni and Cromwell. The typical epithet for Cromwell in Restoration plays and other publications was 'monster' . . . Porter uses the term for Maligni."[78] As Maligni is also the play's attempted rapist, Porter, like Orrery, displaces the rhetoric of sexual violence onto a stand-in for the lord protector. Maligni, like Orrery's king, attempts an act of sexual usurpation, stealing a woman who does not belong to him, perhaps an oblique glance at Restoration politics.

It is not until Edward Howard's *The Usurper* (1664), however, the third and final play of the decade to feature a scene of sexual violence, that the rhetoric of rape is employed in its most fully developed and explicitly political form. Expanding on the tropes first constructed by *The Generall*, *The Usurper* offers the clearest dramatic engagement with Roundhead propaganda. Like Orrery, Howard treats his play as a political act, a form of effigy burning and a way to witness the execution of the tyrant. Howard has "rais'd a bold Usurper up, to Fall," and if the audience will only support the play's continued success, the nation may watch the horrid criminal punished over and over on a nightly basis:

> Faith let him live, if but to dye agen.
> His Crime was horrid, and it is not fit,
> One death of the Usurper Expiate it:
> Let him dye often, He's content that way,
> Still to be punish'd, so you'l spare the Play.[79]

Certainly, as Harold Love has suggested, Howard here refers to the exhumation of Cromwell's corpse: "*The Usurper* was designed to appeal to the same unpleasant streak in the royalist mentality that was responsible for the exhumation and mutilation of the Protector's body, unctuously alluded to in its closing lines."[80] Yet Howard is also describing a *dramatic* act, transforming the play into a glorious extension of that earthly punishment. Howard celebrates his own royalism—the play represents "a Record of all such Loyalty; / That after long Contests, did safely bring, / Subjects to Rights, and to his Throne our King" (72)—and honors the theater's ability both to punish the guilty and to reform the immoral: "The Moral use of Plays, does make us know / Actions, which virtues Raise, and vice lay Low: / Teaching the Bad, though even dead, to fear / They may be Reviv'd, to be punish'd here" (72). To die is not the worst fate; even the dead must fear posthumous resurrection on the public stage, a thought that must give any evildoer pause. The usurper himself may die, but his image will live on night after night to be punished before a patriotic and royalist theater-going populace.

As is true of *The Generall*, regret over Cromwell's peaceful end permeates Howard's play. In act 3, Damocles the Usurper (Cromwell) asks his faithful henchman, Hugo (Hugh Peters), what the people are saying about him. The people, Hugo reports,

> Say, you are but an Usurper, and though you
> Have the luck to dye in your Bed; nay, and may
> Have the liberty to stinke in your Grave,
> Yet they hope before they dye to make it a
> Holiday, and see you hang'd after all this, to
> The great Comfort of the Nation. (33)

To Howard's great regret, Cromwell was lucky enough to die in his bed and did not provide solace to the nation with the spectacle of his rightful execution. Thus the play offers the royalist comfort that historical circumstances did not afford. Damocles, like Orrery's usurper, will be confronted and overthrown by the rightful government, the senators he has ordered assassinated and the king, Cleander, whom he unfairly replaced. While Orrery's tyrant dies quickly, shamed by recognition of his wrongdoing, Damocles is both unrepentant and subject to a much lengthier onstage punishment. Damocles is taunted—"who durst confine me thus, and give me / Such saucy Language," he complains (69)—and stripped of his authority, and when he finally dies by his own hand, he faces the inevitability of eternal punishment for his crimes. "My eyes grow dim o'th'sudden," he exclaims, "'Tis a trouble / Now to look upwards: Heaven's a great way off, / I shall not find the way i'th'dark" (70). He may evade earthly punishment, but God has seen and judged his actions.

Damocles is condemned to hellfire, a conclusion that mirrors the treatment of Cromwell in many of the early Restoration royalist tracts. *A Parly Between the Ghosts of the Late Protector, and the King of Sweden, At their Meeting in Hell* (1660), for instance, opens with Oliver Cromwell "taking Tobacco in the great Divills own Closet," and concludes with a graphically scatological vision of his eternal punishment.[81] One of Satan's henchmen "came presently and stopp'd his mouth with Cow-dung, as Bakers stop their Ovens, and so he was delivered to another Officer, who instantly Chained him before the General pissing place next the Court Door, with a strict charge, that nobody that made water thereabouts, should pisse any where, but against some part of his body."[82] Such a punishment is not only deserved but necessary, as even Satan must worry about the security of his throne; in *The Case is Altered. Or, Dreadful news from Hell* (1660), the ghost of Cromwell tells his wife that he hopes to "usurp a power from the Devil."[83] Thus *Hells Higher Court of Justice* (1661) offers another vision of punishment and restraint: Cromwell will

> be bound
> Within a red-hot throne and one [sic] his head
> A burning Crown about him shall be spread,
> Robes furred with brimstone that they still may be
> Marks of his late Usurped Soveraignity.[84]

He will be tormented for all time with the symbols of his undeserved office.[85]

In forcing Damocles to confront the reality of hellfire, *The Usurper* draws upon the themes of early Restoration propaganda. Like these tracts, *The Usurper* offers audiences the opportunity to deny Cromwell a peaceful death and eternal reward, royalist justice finally served. Damocles says jokingly, "when their Breath / Is spent, their Heirs may take up their quarrel / And kill me in a Chronicle; where they shall read / That all their Fathers were my slaves" (34). While Damocles laughs, his words describe Howard's project; the play will kill the usurper in a chronicle to atone for the nation's failure to execute him in real life. And the "comfort" of such a spectacle is available to the nation on a nightly basis, if only audiences are patriotic enough to support the play with their attendance.

To rehabilitate the image of the monarchy successfully, Howard must, like Orrery, overcome twenty years' worth of parliamentary attacks. A precedent for such defenses did exist among English Civil War propaganda pamphlets, although they are few in number compared with the deluge of anti-Cavalier sheets. *The Cavaliers Catechism* (1647) presents a dialogue between a Cavalier and a suspicious questioner who recites the litany of charges: the Cavaliers are "all most infamous Livers, Atheists, Epicures, Swearers, Blasphemars [sic], Drunkards, Murderers, and Ravishers, and (at the least) papists."[86] The Cavalier proceeds to deny all such charges, proclaiming, "To these and the like scandalous aspersions, I will only say thus, (in briefe Sir) that as I cannot excuse all of our Party (no more than you can all of yours) so I cannot but in Conscience (according to my ability) be bound to defend & vindicate the Major part of us from such malitious, and fraudulent Calumniations."[87] The author of *The Noble Cavalier Caracterised, And A Rebellious Caviller Cauterised* also defends the royalist faction by separating the good and just actions of the Cavaliers from the evil acts of an unrelated faction, the Cavillers: "The *Caviller* is a Rascall, whether he swim, go, or ride; the *Cavalier* dares fight and be valiant, obey Law, and serve for his Soveraigne, his Countrey, for the true Religion established, for the Lawes, for the Subjects Liberty, for the Rights and Priviledges of Parliament, and for the peace."[88] Like Orrery, the author of the tract separates the negative aspects of the Cavalier ethos from the positive, disavowing the unsavory behavior of some. He also links the Cavalier faction with the protection of the true Protestant faith, disrupting the connection between royalism and so-called popish tyranny.

Not surprisingly, defenses of royalism became more intense in the months directly preceding the return of Charles II. One 1660 tract, *The Black Book Opened*, presents a dialogue between a "Noble Cavalier" and a "Select number of those Pure refined, Diabolical Saints called (by the most Loyal Subjects) KING-KILLERS."[89] No longer are the Cavaliers linked with brutality and bloodshed and the parliamentarians with loyal opposition. Instead the Cavaliers become "Noble," while the aging Roundheads reveal themselves to be inveterate and implacable in their disloyalty. Despite the fact that "all Nations for a King do cry," one man insists, "Id'e rather dye in a ditch, then live to see a King."[90] Still, he recognizes that he has committed a displeasing act in the eyes of God: "I should count it a good step in my way to Heaven, could I as *Pilate* wash my hands clear from the guilt of that bloody and unparallell'd murther."[91] Horrified by the crowd of unrepentant Roundheads, the Cavalier finally exclaims in anger, "Villains have you swallowed up the precious blood of a Martyred Father, and subverted the Laws of his Kingdoms, and now do you aim at a Sons blood too, will your Hell Govern'd hearts delight in nothing but sentencing Kings, and Butchering Loyal Subjects? Is no pitty in you?"[92] The Cavalier's rhetoric here inverts the accusations of Roundhead propaganda; the Cavalier is noble, upstanding, and true, both to his king and to his faith. The Roundheads, in contrast, are violent parricides, unnatural children who have rebelled against father, king, and God. They have also metaphorically ingested the blood of their king, an act of implied vampirism (and perhaps, by extension, Catholicism).

The Black Book Opened represents an early attempt to respond to parliamentarian propaganda in the lead-up to the Restoration, and other tracts published after Charles's return follow suit. The Cromwell of *A Third Conference between O. Cromwell and Hugh Peters* tells his henchman that "the lust of ruling caused me to tumour to such a monstrosity, that nothing could gratifie my desires, but Rapines and Murders"; as is the case with Orrery's usurper and Howard's, lust for illicit rule leads to lust for illicit sex.[93] Meanwhile, John Gauden, author of *Cromwell's Bloody Slaughter-house* (1660) calls the Roundheads "bloodthirsty and deceitfull."[94] They are "ravening Wolves" who have metaphorically cannibalized their own monarch: "can nothing satiate your cruel Appetites and Hydropick thirst, but only the flesh and blood of our King?"[95] Gauden calls the Roundheads the "impudent Ravishers both of Church and State."[96] They have been guilty of "unavoidable Tyranny, unsatiable Rapine, and cruel Oppression," and they have tricked the English people into complicity with their horrifying corruption: "You would have us all to pledge you in that horrible draught of the King's bloud, which you have greedily drank; to approve and abet your execrable villainies."[97]

The Usurper adopts similar rhetoric in its defense of royalism. Like the Cavaliers of the propaganda sheets (and like Orrery's Monasin, Filadin, and Cratoner), Damocles's men are sexually lascivious. Hugo, his chief supporter, has cuckolded much of the senate. Referring to the senators that survived Damocles's purge, Hugo tells Damocles, "Those that remain are your own Creatures, Sir, / And most of 'em my Cuckolds, their Wives, / Shall bear me witness" (14).[98] Meanwhile Damocles, like Orrery's king, is a rapist, and metaphorically speaking, a source of infection in the nation. Driven mad with lust for the virtuous Libyan Queen Timandra, mistress to the rightful king, Damocles attempts to rape her: "I wo'not leave," he insists, "Till I have made thee leprous and unfit / For any mans Embrace" (62). His sexuality will disease Timandra, rendering her unsuitable for other company. She concurs: "I could not hope a Life here / Without Stain to my Honour" (53). The rape will be a blot and an infection, destroying her from within.

Initially, Damocles uses the image of the rape victim to describe the state of the nation at the conclusion of the late wars and to celebrate the stability of his rule. He addresses the

> Grave, honour'd Gentlemen,
> True Patriots and Preservers of your Country,
> Whose Bosome was late panting, and her Cheek
> Pale with the loss of Blood, the Punick Sword
> Had Ravish'd from her. (10)

According to Damocles, the recent uprising has sexually victimized the nation, and he uses the language of ravishment to lament war-induced property loss. Even as Damocles claims to heal the wounded nation, however, he is also the poisonous corruption at its heart. Cleanthe, the king's sister, explains, "his very Name / Carries a secret poison in the Breath," and the damage he does to female bodies encodes the damage he has done to the nation (45). The attempted rape of Timandra metaphorically represents another form of usurpation, as Damocles appropriates a second piece of property that rightfully belongs to Cleander. His lust for empire is linked with his lust for Timandra, connecting the desire for illicit and unwelcome sex with the desire for illicit and unwelcome rule. The image of Timandra's body violated and diseased thus performs the same function as the image of the dying Altemera, insofar as both symbolize the tragic consequences of the usurper's presence in England/Sicily. It is only with the return of the true king that Timandra and the nation can thrive once more. Cleander proclaims that he "hath no Ambition, but / To Repair his sad and bleeding Country, / And that the Laws, after so many Stromes, / May run in their own free and ancient Channel" (66).

While Damocles never engages in any literal acts of vampirism onstage, Howard, drawing on the rhetoric of the royalist tracts, also invokes the trope of blood drinking to taint him. The play, like the propaganda tracts, shifts between forms of atrocity, merging the image of the rapist with that of the vampire. Cleander, disguised as a Moor, confronts Damocles:

> Keep those Bugs
> Upon thy Brow to fright tame Fools, and such
> As born from Worms do Crawl about thy Court,
> And lick the dusty Pavements: Snakes that live
> And lap the blood of Innocents. (54)

Cleander likens Damocles's followers to vampiristic snakes who feed upon the blood of martyrs. Later, Timandra accuses Damocles himself of vampiristic tendencies. When she learns that Hiarbas, her Moorish servant (Cleander in disguise), is to be put to death, she begs her manservant "This favour, when Hiarbas with his Blood / Hath satisfied the Thrist [sic] of Damocles, / That you would bring me word" (60). Timandra and Cleander embody virtue in distress, while the parliamentarian forces are linked, however tenuously, with Catholic excess. In contrast, Howard emphasizes Cleander's virtue and mercy, linking him with Charles II. Like Orrery's Melizer, Cleander offers forgiveness and absolution to the nation: "There shall be an Indemnity for those / Whose frailty, and not malice, made 'em Act / Under the Tyrant" (70), he decrees, another reference to the Act of Indemnity and Oblivion. Cleander's mercy, like Charles's, proves his fitness to rule: "Mercy becomes a King," Cleomenes explains approvingly, "which as it flows / Upon your Enemies, should have a free / Stream to your Friends" (71). Damocles revels in blood while Cleander displays his forbearance.

HOWARD'S *THE USURPER* AND THE TROPE OF THE POISONOUS CATHOLIC BRIDE

As Howard glorifies Cleander/Charles II, he also works to restore the reputation of royalist women. Throughout the English Civil War propaganda sheets, the figure of the debauched Cavalier was linked not only with the demonic Irishman, his political ally, but with the corrupting influence of the poisonous Catholic bride, tainting all royalist women with the specter of popery. Catholic women, propaganda tracts imply, are naturally dangerous and bloodthirsty, all too willing to abandon feminine decorum to commit acts of horrific violence against Protestants. Foxe's *Acts and Monuments*, for instance, describes how Irish Catholic women joyfully participated in the carnage of the 1641 Rebellion: "Even the weaker sex themselves, naturally tender to their own sufferings, and compassionate to those of others, have emulated their robust companions in the practice of every cruelty."[99] Aristocratic Catholic women, however, are more adept in anti-Catholic tracts at concealing their murderous impulses. Rather than acting out violently, they choose instead to insinuate themselves by way of marriage into the circles of court power. Often outsiders by birth as well as religion, such women seek to corrupt their Protestant husbands, poison their morality and honor, and ultimately instigate the rapes of English Protestant women and the massacres of English Protestant men. Attacks on royalist Catholic women centered in the 1630s and 1640s on the figure of Queen Henrietta Maria, who became a lightning rod for criticism, fear, and mistrust. Henrietta Maria was a target of hatred before she ever set foot on English soil. Her refusal to attend her own coronation, coupled with her very public mourning performances for English Catholic martyrs, only solidified her reputation as a dangerous outsider who had been granted too much access to the inner circles of government.[100] As Charles I grew closer to his wife, the danger embodied in the queen became even more urgent, since many worried that her influence would lead Charles away from the Church of England. Widely portrayed as "uncrowned, foreign speaking, emotionally remote, offensively behaving above her gender station by performing in court plays, and ardently Catholic,"[101] the queen was also accused of "incensing the King to this dissention with . . . his Parliament."[102] Throughout the 1640s, then, Roundhead authors justified rebellion by positioning themselves as Charles's saviors. They were determined, they claimed, to save the king from the poisonous "Pests and Vipers"—his wife and chief advisors—who surrounded him and sought to lead him astray.[103] *Englands Miserie* (1642), written by a "Well-wisher to His King and Countrey," blames "these Machivillians (or rather matchlesse-villains) that professe themselves to be friends, when indeed they are fiends" for Charles's failure to heed the will of the Parliament.[104] The author insists that the king is taking bad advice from a collection of "flattering *Achitophel*-Cavaliers, proud ambitious Prelates, and blood-suck-thirsting Church Papists," chief among them, his vampiristic wife.[105]

The reaction to the release of Charles and Henrietta Maria's letters following the Battle of Naseby (1645) encapsulates the cultural anxieties centered on the queen. After capturing Charles I's letters in the battle, the parliamentary government swiftly printed and publicized their contents in a collection entitled *The King's Cabinet opened*. The Parliament insisted upon the authenticity of the letters, going so far as to establish a public exhibition open to anyone who might wish to verify the king's handwriting. The existence of such a collection is inherently voyeuristic; as the title advertises, the Parliament has opened the doors to the king's innermost sanctum and provided intimate access to the details of his private dealings with his wife. According to the collection's editors, "it were a great sin against the mercies of God, to conceale those evidences of truth, which hee so graciously (and almost miraculously) by surprizall of these Papers, hath put into our hands."[106] These monstrous truths are twofold: that Charles had been "seduced out of his proper sphere" by bad advisors and evil counselors, and even more upsettingly, that he was allowing his wife an unprecedented, highly inappropriate level of control over his political choices.[107] According to the editors,

> It is plaine, here, first, that the Kings Counsels are wholly managed by the Queen; though she be of the weaker sexe, borne an Alien, bred up in a contrary Religion, yet nothing great or small is transacted without her privity & consent. . . . The Queens Counsels are as powerfull as commands. The King professes to preferre her health before the exigence, and importance of his owne publick affaires.[108]

It is the king's uxoriousness as much as his seemingly popish leanings that angers the editors; that Charles allows himself to be subservient to his own wife, that he welcomes and even encourages her political counsel bespeaks his failings as a ruler and underscores the degree to which the Parliament must save the king from himself. Henrietta Maria embodies the dangerous triad of bad counselor, monstrous seductress, and popish infidel leading the country to inevitable destruction.

For many parliamentarian propagandists, then, the outbreak of the civil wars was the inevitable, albeit regrettable, result of Henrietta Maria's position in the kingdom. Asked "Whence did these unnaturall broyles spring and arise," the author of *The English Pope* (1643) attributes the realm's turmoil to the "poisonous tongues" of the pope and his female servants at court.[109] Henrietta Maria, the author suggests, appeared harmless as a young bride, but her presence enabled the insidious growth of Catholic political strength: "Whilst the Queene was verie young, and the plot of our Hierarchists not fully ripe, the Babylonish Mysteries were not fit to be revealed: and yet even in those times, the work went on darkly and insensibly."[110] In the privacy of the bedchamber, such pamphlets insist, Henrietta Maria works tirelessly and seductively to bend her husband to the pope's will. According to *The Great Eclipse of the Sun, Or, Charles His Waine* (1644),

> The King being in full Conjunction with this *Popish Plannet,* the Queen, hee was totally eclipsed by her Counsell, who under the Royall Curtaines, perswaded him to advance the Plots of the Catholikes, under the colour of maintaining the *Protestant Religion.* Ordinary women, can in the Night time perswade their husbands to give them new Gowns or Petticoates, and make them grant their desire; and could not Catholick Queen *Mary* . . . by her night discourses, encline the King to Popery and make him believe that he had no true obedient subjects, but Catholicks.[111]

Henrietta Maria's sexuality produces her political power; her access to Charles's innermost chambers ensures that her proposals will be heard, in the form of a curtain lecture if not in a more formal capacity.

While many authors blame Henrietta Maria for the nation's civic unrest, the author of *The English Pope* blames an older poisonous Catholic woman for Henrietta Maria's presence in England. It was at the urging of Catholic Mary Villiers, Countess of Buckingham and mother to Charles I's favorite, George Villiers, Duke of Buckingham, the tract claims, that Charles elected to take a Catholic bride:

> And now when three Kingdomes are under the subjection of one Prince, who is under the subjection of one lustfull, rash, young Favourite, and that Favourite solely at the devotion of his vitious, opprobrious, mischievous mother, and that mother a meere Votaresse to Rome, utterly forfeited, resigned, and sold to

> the commands of Jesuites: When our miserable Nations are in this ridiculous, preposterous posture of government, who can wonder that a Spanish or French Match for our Prince should be designed?[112]

The Countess of Buckingham is the first Catholic woman to "inebriate or debosh" the king's "understanding."[113] That Charles elected to marry Henrietta Maria is evidence of her success.

Ultimately, the relationship between Charles and Henrietta Maria leads to demonic conception and monstrous pregnancy. The author of *The English Pope* writes, "This violent sharp malady, of which we labour so distressedly at this present, began to seize the vitals of this State, long before its violence appeared."[114] Here the tract's author adopts the rhetoric of maternal monstrosity to condemn the wars; civil strife is itself a form of grotesque and unnatural progeny. Henrietta Maria, meanwhile, is an "indulgent . . . nursing mothe[r] to the Roman Church," one whose womb brings forth the horrors of civil war, both the culmination of her popish plot and a powerful example of deviant Catholic procreation.[115] Subsequently, her presence poisons the wombs of innocent Protestant mothers and gives rise to a generation of monstrous and murderous offspring. One of the speakers of *A Mappe of Mischiefe* (1641) complains that because of Henrietta Maria, "my wombe might beare a Monster of all mortalls, one whose delight is to cherish trecheries, never thinking of God or goodnesse. This is that Mortall that will not stick to shed the blood of Infants, nay to act any wickednesse whatsoever, and must it be my hard fortune to bee troubled with these things."[116]

Both a monstrous mother and an ideological source of disease, Henrietta Maria functions throughout propaganda culture as a pestilence tainting both king and country. *A Mappe of Mischiefe* explicitly adopts the language of contagion to describe the queen's effect upon the kingdom. As "E," the personification of England, celebrates Henrietta Maria's departure, "V," embodiment of the Dutch United Provinces, laments her arrival on foreign shores.[117] V begs God for deliverance from Henrietta Maria's "pestilentious filth which will else infect me and mine with sore contagions."[118] England, meanwhile, celebrates her newfound freedom from poisonous Catholic disease: "Faith my heart is so merry because that I shall be eased of a burthen under which I have a long time groaned . . . why Sister wouldst thou have me to be sad, because I am suddenly to be rid of a plague," she asks.[119] Henrietta Maria is an infection in the kingdom, and one who will finally cause the individual English subject to be "drowned in . . . blood."[120] Implicit in such constructions of the queen is the fear that she will spur the king to acts of brutality against his own people; he will be "carried on by evil councellours to shed the blood of his subjects . . . and all because they would not be slaves, or put on fetters being born unto freedom."[121] She will also propel her husband and his army to "ravish Wives and Virgins, to fire mens Barnes, and to destroy the Graine," and at her behest, the king will permit his armies to "plunder and take away all they can finde," including the unwilling bodies of English women.[122] "[M]urther, rapine, lamentation" will spread throughout the land, finally linking acts of sexual violence with Catholic female perversity.[123] Henrietta Maria will "have her stroke againe, and then we are in a worse condition," left to the mercy of debauched Cavaliers, demonic Irishmen, and papal tyranny.[124] The anti–Henrietta Maria tracts thus reveal the extent of Roundhead anxiety over the queen's power, an anxiety conveyed through overlapping tropes of atrocity: rape, murder, vampirism, and maternal deviance.

After the Restoration, Royalist authors, of course, advanced a more sympathetic view of Henrietta Maria. The 1660s witnessed the publication of numerous pamphlets celebrating her life and goodness. The author of *The Muses Joy* names the queen a "living Martyr,"[125] while John Dauncey insists that the queen has been unjustly slandered by her enemies: "This illustrious and thrice *Noble* Princess hath not had the least *share* in this ill *humour* of the *times,* whilest the *basely* imployed *industry* and *disingenuity* of some men hath endeavoured to represent her under a black Cloud of *guilt,* who never knew how to wear other than a pure, white and Angel-like Vest of Innocency."[126] Edmund Waller celebrated her return to and repairs of Somerset House by praising her "Frugality" (undoubtedly a response to the rumors of her financial profligacy), "Bounty," and "Genius," all the while proclaiming her "Constant to *England* in [her] love."[127] She is lionized in her capacity as a mother and shown alternately rejoicing in Charles's success and mourning the loss of her other children, Henry and Mary. In a 1660 poem mourning the death of Henrietta Maria's daughter Mary, a young John Wilmot refers to the "great Queen . . . that in mighty wrongs an Age have spent," and offers consolation that in the loss of her daughter, her "sigh's have an untainted guiltlesse breath."[128] The author of *The Muses Joy* meanwhile prays that she "never *weep* again, / Unless it be for *joy* she once had *pain,* / That once her *blest Womb* with a *Charls* did teem, / Should both a Crown *Inherit* and *Redeem.*"[129] Here the monstrous womb of *The English Pope* is reimagined as a blessed and holy place, while Henrietta Maria herself is treated as the best and most natural of mothers. The queen finds joy in her son's triumph—"all my joy / Is in this Gracious King," she insists in one ballad, an implicit reminder that her happiness is tied to the continued health of England and Charles II's success as king.[130]

Not all of the English population was willing to accept the newly positive image of the queen mother, however. When in 1660 rumors of Henrietta Maria's return to English soil began to circulate, one contemporary laborer supposedly exclaimed,

> That Queene Henrietta Maria was not the Queene of England, and that he (the said Edward Bilton) would never acknowledge her for a Queene, and that she was a traytour and had been the cause of all this mischief (meaning the late warres in England), and that if shee (Henrietta Maria) should come into England, she would breed nothing but sects and scisms, and if anyone would rise, hee would bee the second man to venter [sic] both life and estate to keepe her forth.[131]

Despite Samuel Pepys's offhand comment that Henrietta Maria was "a very little plain old woman, and nothing more in her presence in any respect nor garb than any ordinary woman," she was still feared by many and blamed by others for the destruction of the innocent martyr, Charles I.[132] Indeed, suspicions of the queen continued to run high throughout the decade. Henrietta Maria's repairs to Somerset House, the former seat of her Catholic court circle, induced some to post "placards calling for the 'extirpation of popery'" at her palace.[133] Meanwhile, the May 1662 arrival of another foreign Catholic queen, the Portuguese Catherine of Braganza, at least initially resurrected the concern that foreign wives could gain too much political and personal access to the body of the king.

In Howard's *The Usurper*, therefore, the play's use of rape imagery underscores the degree to which Howard is conscious of the anxieties surrounding Henrietta Maria and Catherine. To allay fears about each queen's powers and goals, Howard reworks the story of Shakespeare's *Titus Andronicus*, a play in which a poisonous foreign bride brings rape and destruction to her adopted land. *The Usurper* begins in the wake of Damocles's usurpation of the throne, as Dionysius, Damocles's son, returns triumphant from the wars in Africa. Dionysius brings with him the fair Queen Timandra, whose kingdom he has successfully conquered. Imprisoned as spoils of war, the queen serves as a symbol of Sicilian might and tangible proof of Dionysius's skill in battle. Shakespeare's *Titus Andronicus* also begins with a foreign queen brought in chains from periphery to center as a symbol of martial prowess; the presence of the Gothic Queen Tamora, like that of the African Queen Timandra, displays Roman imperial power. In both plays, the queen brings with her a Moorish servant with whom she has a preexisting romantic/sexual relationship, and each servant is ultimately taken into the service of the king. Timandra pleads for her servant, Hiarbas, as Tamora pleads for Aaron; Timandra begs Damocles, "I only pray, / This noble Moor, whose Fate hath suffer'd much / In mine, may have a part in your high Favour / And Freedome" (23). Enamored of the queen, Damocles grants Hiarbas both his freedom and his favor: "Sir, you have it" (23), he promises.

In both Shakespeare's *Titus Andronicus* and Howard's *The Usurper*, the foreign queen captures the eye of the domestic ruler. In the case of Shakespeare's Saturninus, the ruler is attracted both to Tamora's exotic beauty—Tamora "dost overshine the gallant'st dames of Rome" (1.1.314)—and to the fact that she is not a Roman woman. Having been rejected by Lavinia, "Rome's rich ornament" and embodiment of upstanding Roman womanhood, Saturninus views Tamora as the antithesis of Romanness (1.1.52). He therefore invites the outsider into his inner sanctum and grants her access through marriage both to his body natural and to the Roman body politic. Likewise, Timandra's beauty fascinates and obsesses Damocles; though she weeps, he exclaims, she "looks fair as doth the Face of Day" (20), and he later comments on her "Angelique form" (21). He then uses the rhetoric of courtly love both to mitigate her resentment of captivity and to seduce her to his will. "Your [sic] are Queen Timandra still," he tells her, "and let me tell you / So far from being a Prisoner, that you have made / Your self a Conquest" (20). She has enslaved him with the power of her beauty—"I change the name of King to be your Servant" (23), he tells her, and suggests that her conquest avenges her country's defeat. "A Victory of me, by those fair Eyes; / So that what Spoil my Souldiers made within / Your Kingdom, you have Reveng'd this very minute / By making me the Conquerour, your Captive" (20). He then seeks to court Timandra, ostensibly with the intent to marry: "The Crown you wear, / If you but smile shall have a double Lustre, / And call to it another bright Companion; / This Island to Obey you" (21).

Ultimately, however, the plays begin to diverge, and their differences are significant to an understanding of Howard's project. Shakespeare's Tamora is only too happy to marry into the Roman imperial family, the better to effect her revenge and destroy Rome from within. In contrast, Timandra has been treated honorably by her captors, telling Damocles, "Your Son hath us'd me honourably, abating what / The Laws of War oblige him too" (20). Timandra's sadness stems from the indignity of her position, "A Queen, Your Prisoner" (20), and later, from the danger Damocles poses to her person, but she recognizes that she has been treated respectfully and in accordance with the rules of war. As such, she does not enter the kingdom with the sole intent of wreaking vengeance, and she has no desire to join herself with the hated Damocles. When Damocles proposes, she rejects him outright, telling him, "this shadow [her body] / You have in your pocession [sic], but my Soul / Can never be your Captive" (21). She remains steadfast in her fidelity to Hiarbas/Cleander, refusing Damocles and proclaiming the sanctity of her love. Timandra tells Hiarbas,

> I promis'd
> My love to you with such devotion,
> As with our last Breath gives up our Souls
> To Heaven: And those that dare lay Violence
> Upon our mutual Vows shall Reap the fruit
> Of nothing but their Sins. (24)

Tamora, by contrast, is all too willing both to marry and to cuckold the emperor, while her feelings for Aaron are predominantly sexual. Aaron comments that "Venus govern[s] your desires" (2.3.30), while Tamora herself suggests that she and Aaron "may, each wreathed in the other's arms, / Our pastimes done, possess a golden slumber" (2.3.25–27).

Additionally, while Tamora seeks to sow discord in Rome, Timandra tries to prevent the outbreak of factionalism and discord. Despite her obvious indifference, Timandra's beauty attracts both Damocles and Dionysius; father and son become romantic rivals, culminating in Dionysius's death at his father's hand. Sensing the misery that will result when son is pitted against father, Timandra intercedes on Dionysius's behalf: "Sir, I intreat, your Son may not, for his / Civilities to me, meet with your Anger" (23). Timandra is a conciliator who tries, even in captivity and defeat, to bring peace to the nation, and when she finally marries Hiarbas, now revealed to be the rightful King Cleander, the union is a cause for celebration. Unlike Tamora, whose marriage into the circles of power leads to rape, mutilation, and cannibalism, Timandra's marriage brings about the restoration of order and a nation and monarchy set to rights. Timandra emerges from the play as an anti-Tamora, her mirror image and her opposite, a foreign queen who seeks to reconcile rather than divide. In this way, Timandra represents the royalist response to and dismissal of the trope of the poisonous Catholic bride. A victim of the debauched usurper's attempted sexual assault, Timandra is virtuous, loving, and true, suggesting that England should rejoice at, and not fear, the presence of its own foreign queens. Neither Henrietta Maria nor Catherine of Braganza is a Tamora. Instead, both women are Timandras, faithful and loyal sources of peace and prosperity in their adopted land. The play invokes the tropes of the anti–Henrietta Maria tracts only to undermine and reject their lines of assault.

As we shall see in greater detail in chapter 4, the *Titus* plot as it was employed in the later seventeenth century would allegorize the dangers posed by allowing foreigners, and in the case of Restoration England, the Catholics, too much access to political and social authority. The story of the sexually enthralling foreign queen who encourages the rape of the innocent domestic martyr would represent an extremely useful allegory for authors afraid of the foreign presence in the realm. Tamora uses her sexual power over the king to achieve a dangerous and destructive degree of power, using rape as a weapon to undermine the nation she so despises. For Howard, however, the foreign queen is not a threat, but an ideal companionate mate. *The Usurper* thus unwrites the story of *Titus Andronicus*, depicting a foreign queen who brings peace, not discord, to the kingdom. As Howard displaces the image of the debauched Cavalier onto Cromwell and his men, he also denies any dangers posed by Henrietta Maria and Catherine of Braganza, those potentially poisonous Catholic brides.

CONCLUSION

While only three plays of the 1660s actually feature scenes of rape or attempted sexual assault, all three invoke critically the memory of Oliver Cromwell, and two of the three use scenes of sexual violence as an opportunity for extended political allegory. To read such scenes of sexual violence in the context of the long-standing propaganda pamphlet war, therefore, is to come to a new understanding of the ideological work such scenes performed within their own social contexts. For authors of the 1660s, rape scenes were designed to reaffirm the power of the monarchy and divorce the royalist faction from the popular tropes of the debauched Cavalier and poisonous Catholic bride. As we shall see in the next chapter, however, growing fears of the Catholic presence in England, coupled with the Duke of York's public conversion to Catholicism, led to a very different treatment of rape in the 1670s. If the Earl of Orrery and Edward Howard rejected the trope of the debauched Cavalier, playwrights of the 1670s would embrace it once more, resurrecting the rhetoric of English Civil War propaganda to express their own discomfort with royal policy. The treatment of dramatic rape mirrors the culture's developing uneasiness with the state of contemporary politics.

NOTES

1. *A Blazing Starre seen in the West at Totneis in Devonshire* (London, 1642), a2r.
2. Ibid., a2v.
3. Ibid.
4. Ibid., a3r.
5. Ibid., a3r, a3v.
6. Ibid., a3v.
7. Ibid., a3v, a4r.
8. Ibid.
9. Ibid.
10. Ibid., a4v.
11. Ibid., a2v.
12. Ibid., a1r.
13. Ibid., a4r.
14. Ibid., a1r.
15. Deborah G. Burks, *Horrid Spectacle: Violation in the Theater of Early Modern England* (Pittsburgh: Duquesne University Press, 2003), 282. Burks offers a trenchant analysis of violent imagery in Jacobean theater along with the works of Cavendish, Dryden, and Behn.
16. It is here that my argument differs most fundamentally from those of Jean Marsden and Elizabeth Howe. While rape scenes undoubtedly titillated, the sexual assaults staged in the 1660s are brief and not at all explicit; playwrights are more interested in exploring the political dimensions of rape imagery than in exploiting the spectacle of the actress's physical form.
17. *A Blazing Starre*, a4r.
18. Ibid., a5r.
19. *A New Mercury, Called Mercurius Problematicus* (London, 1644), a3v–a4r.
20. George Lawrence, *The Debauched Cavalleer: Or the English Midianite* (London, 1642), 4.

21. *The Wicked Resolution Of The Cavaliers* (London, 1642), 1.

22. John Hadfred, *A wonderfull And Strange Miracle or Gods Just Vengeance against the Cavaliers* (London, 1642), 3.

23. Ibid.

24. Ibid., 5.

25. Ibid., 5–6.

26. William Warren, *Strange, true, and lamentable Newes from Exceter, And other parts of the Western countreyes* (London, 1643), a3v.

27. Lawrence, *The Debauched Cavalleer*, 5.

28. *The Insolency and Cruelty of the Cavaliers* (London, 1643), title page.

29. *Terrible Newes From York* (London, 1642), title page.

30. *University Newes, Or, The Unfortunate proceedings of the Cavaliers in Oxford* (London, 1642), a3r.

31. *A great Robbery in the North, Neer Swanton in Yorkshire* (London, 1642), 2.

32. *A True and Perfect Relation Of A victorious Battell Obtained against the Earl of Cumberland And his Cavaliers* (London, 1642), 7.

33. R. Andrews, *A perfect Declaration of The Barbarous and Cruell practices committed by Prince Robert, the Cavalliers, and others in his Majesties Army* (London, 1642), a2r.

34. *A Wicked Resolution of the Cavaliers*, 1, 2.

35. William Cartwright, *The Game at Chesse* (London, 1643), 7.

36. Ibid., 4.

37. John Goodwin, *Anti-Cavalierisme, Or, Truth Pleading As well the Necessity, as the Lawfulness of this present War* (London, 1642), title page.

38. Lawrence, *The Debauched Cavalleer*, 7. For discussion of contemporary depictions of Cavalier army camps, see Robin Clifton, "The Popular Fear of Catholics during the English Revolution," *Past & Present* 52 (1971): 37.

39. *The Protestation And Declaration of the Popish, and evill affected Cavaliers* (London, 1642), title page.

40. Ethan Howard Shagan, "Constructing Discord: Ideology, Propaganda, and English Responses to the Irish Rebellion of 1641," *Journal of British Studies* 36, no. 1 (1997): 9.

41. *A Powerfull, Pitifull, Citi-Full Cry, of Plentifull Children, And their Admirable, lamentable Complaint* (London, 1643), a2v.

42. Goodwin, *Anti-Cavalierisme*, 5.

43. Thomas Kittermaster, *A Wonderfull Deliverance Or Gods abundant mercy in preserving from the Cavaliers the towne of Draiton In the County of Hereford* (London, 1642), a3r.

44. *A Powerfull, Pitifull, Citi-Full Cry*, a2v.

45. *The Dammee Cavalliers Warning Piece, In a view on the Prophecy of the Prophet Obadiah* (London, 1643), 3.

46. *A Powerfull, Pitifull, Citi-Full Cry*, a3r.

47. Ibid., a3v.

48. A Gentleman of good quality, *True Intelligence From The West: Or A true Relation of the desperate Proceedings of the Rebels, and Cavaliers gathered together at Angry-Fisherten in Wilt-shire* (London, 1647), 3.

49. *A Powerfull, Pitifull, Citi-Full Cry*, a2v–a3r.

50. *An exact and true Relation of A most cruell and horrid Murther committed by one of the Cavaliers, on A Woman in Leicester* (London, 1642), 4.

51. A Gentleman of good quality, *True Intelligence from the West*, 5.

52. *Nocturnall Occurrences Or, Deeds Of Darknesse: Committed, By the Cavaleers in their Rendezvous* (London, 1642), a2r.

53. I. H., *A briefe Relation, Abstracted out of severall Letters, of A most Hellish, Cruell, and Bloudy Plot against the City of Bristoll* (London, 1642), a2v.

54. Kittermaster, *A Wonderfull Deliverance*, a3r.

55. Stephen Greenblatt, *Renaissance Self-Fashioning: From More to Shakespeare* (Chicago and London: University of Chicago Press, 1980), 9.

56. *A True Relation Of two Merchants of London, Who were taken prisoners by the Cavaliers* (London, 1642), a3v.

57. Tumbleson, *Catholicism*, 89.

58. Nancy Klein Maguire, *Regicide and Restoration: English Tragicomedy, 1660–1670* (Cambridge: Cambridge University Press, 1992), 3.

59. Stephen P. Flores, "Orrery's *The Generall* and *Henry The Fifth*: Sexual Politics and the Desire for Friendship," *Eighteenth Century: Theory and Interpretation* 37, no. 1 (1996): 56.

60. Orrery, cited in F. W. Payne, "The Question of Precedence between Dryden and the Earl of Orrery with Regard to the English Heroic Play," *Review of English Studies* 1, no. 2 (1925): 174. For discussion of the play's authorial history, see also William S. Clark, "Further Light upon the Heroic Plays of Roger Boyle, Earl of Orrery," *Review of English Studies* 2, no. 6 (1926): 206–11, and W. S. Clark, "The Earl of Orrery's Play *The Generall*," *Review of English Studies* 2, no. 8 (1926): 459–60.

61. Charles II, cited in Kathleen M. Lynch, *Roger Boyle, First Earl of Orrery* (Knoxville: University of Tennessee Press, 1965), 147.

62. Samuel Pepys, *The Diary of Samuel Pepys*, ed. Robert Latham and William Matthews, 11 vols. (Berkeley: University of California Press, 1970–83), 5:281–82.

63. Roger Boyle, Earl of Orrery, *The Generall*, in *The Dramatic Works of Roger Boyle*, ed. William S. Clark II, 2 vols. (Cambridge: Harvard University Press, 1937), 1:101–64, 1.1.33–42. Further references to *The Generall* are from this edition and will be cited parenthetically in the text by act, scene, and line number.

64. Jonathan Scott, *England's Troubles: Seventeenth-Century English Political Instability in European Context* (Cambridge: Cambridge University Press, 2000), 24.

65. John Crouch, *The Muses Joy For the Recovery of that Weeping Vine Henrietta Maria* (London, 1660), a3r.

66. *A Third Conference Between O. Cromwell And Hugh Peters In Saint James's Park* (London, 1660), 2.

67. Laura Lunger Knoppers, *Constructing Cromwell: Ceremony, Portrait, and Print, 1645–1661* (Cambridge: Cambridge University Press, 2000), 173.

68. Thomas Rugge, *The Diurnal of Thomas Rugg, 1659–1661*, ed. William L. Sachse, Camden Third Series (London: Royal Historical Society, 1961), vol. 91, no. 90.

69. Knoppers, *Constructing Cromwell*, 182.

70. Ibid.

71. Mita Choudhury, "Orrery and the London Stage: A Loyalist's Contribution to Restoration Allegorical Drama," *Studia Neophilologica* 62, no. 1 (1990): 45.

72. Maguire, *Regicide and Restoration*, 258–59. For further discussion of Orrery's dramatic motivations, see Tracey E. Tomlinson, "The Restoration English History Plays of Roger Boyle, Earl of Orrery," *Studies in English Literature 1500–1900* 43, no. 3 (2003): 559–77.

73. Lynch, *Roger Boyle*, 159. For similar views, see Susan Staves, *Players' Scepters: Fictions of Authority in the Restoration* (Lincoln: University of Nebraska Press, 1979), and John Kerrigan, "Orrery's Ireland and the British Problem," in *British Identities and English Renaissance Literature*, ed. David J. Baker and Willy Maley (Cambridge: Cambridge University Press, 2002), 197–225.

74. Sir John Suckling, "Out upon It!" in *The Norton Anthology of English Literature*, 8th ed., ed. Stephen Greenblatt et al., 2 vols. (New York: Norton, 2006), 1:1681, ll. 1–4.

75. Flores, "Orrery's *The Generall*," 58.

76. Richard Lovelace, "To Lucasta, Going to the Wars," in *The Norton Anthology of English Literature*, 8th ed., ed. Stephen Greenblatt et al., 2 vols. (New York: Norton, 2006), 1:1682, ll. 12–13.

77. For analysis of *The Villain's* relationship to *The Generall*, see Maguire, *Regicide and Restoration*.

78. Ibid., 68.

79. Edward Howard, *The Usurper: A Tragedy* (London, 1668), 72. Further references to *The Usurper* are from this edition and will be cited parenthetically in the text by page number.

80. Harold Love, "State Affairs on the Restoration Stage, 1660–1675," *Restoration and Eighteenth-Century Theatre Research* 14, no. 1 (1975): 3.

81. *A Parly Between the Ghosts of the Late Protector, and the King of Sweden, At their Meeting in Hell* (London, 1660), 5.

82. Ibid., 17.
83. *The Case is Altered. Or, Dreadful news from Hell* (London, 1660), 6.
84. *Hell's Higher Court of Justice* (London, 1661), d2r.
85. For other depictions of Cromwell in Hell, see Abraham Miles, *The last farewel of three bould Traytors* (London, 1661), and Anthony Sadler, *The Subjects Joy For The Kings Restoration, Cheerfully made known in A Sacred Masque* (London, 1660).
86. *The Cavaliers Catechisme* (London, 1647), 3.
87. Ibid., 4.
88. John Taylor, *The Noble Cavalier Caracterised, And A Rebellious Caviller Cauterised* (Oxford, 1643), 1.
89. *The Black Book Opened, Or Traytors Arraigned and Condemned by their own Confession* (London, 1660), 1.
90. Ibid.
91. Ibid.
92. Ibid.
93. *A Third Conference*, 6.
94. John Gauden, *Cromwell's Bloody Slaughter-house* (London, 1660), 1.
95. Ibid., 1–2.
96. Ibid., 7.
97. Ibid., 65, 71–72.
98. Royalist propaganda also accused both Cromwell and Peters of lechery; in *A Third Conference*, for instance, Peters acts as Cromwell's bawd.
99. Foxe, *Acts and Monuments*, 269.
100. Only fifteen at the time of her marriage, Henrietta Maria had been "exhorted by her mother, her confessor and Pope Urban VIII to demonstrate her commitment to her faith and proselytize on its behalf" (Smuts, "Religion, European Politics," 15), a task she undertook both with enthusiasm and a lack of political finesse.
101. Ibid., 29.
102. Cartwright, *The Game at Chesse*, 6.
103. *The Key To The Kings Cabinet-Counsell* (London, 1644), 6.
104. *Englands Miserie, If Not Prevented by the speedie remedie of a happie union between His Maiestie and this Parliament* (London, 1642), 1.
105. Ibid. For similar rhetoric, see also Robert, Earl of Warwicke, *A Most Worthy Speech, Spoken by the Right Honourable Robert Earle of Warwicke* (London, 1642).
106. Thomas May, Henry Parker, and John Sadler, *The Kings Cabinet opened* (London, 1645), a3r.
107. Ibid.
108. Ibid., g2r.
109. *The English Pope*, 2, a4r.
110. Ibid., 12.
111. *The Great Eclipse of the Sun, Or, Charles His Waine* (London, 1644), 3.
112. *The English Pope*, 7.
113. Ibid., 21.
114. Ibid., 12.
115. Ibid., 4.
116. *A Mappe of Mischiefe, Or A Dialogue Betweene V. and E. concerning the going of Qu. M. into V* (London, 1641), 2–3.
117. The initial "V" likely refers to the V in "Verenige" from "Republiek der Zeven Verenigde Nederlanden," the Dutch name for the United Provinces. Henrietta Maria sailed from England to Holland in February of 1642, tasked with raising money for the royalist cause.
118. *A Mappe of Mischiefe*, 3.
119. Ibid., 6.
120. Ibid., 5.
121. Ibid., 4.
122. Warwicke, *A Most Worthy Speech*, 4, 5.
123. *The English Pope*, 12.

124. *The Reformed Malignants* (London, 1643), 1.

125. *The Muses Joy*, a2v.

126. John Dauncey, *The History Of The Thrice Illustrious Princess Henrietta Maria de Bourbon, Queen Of England* (London, 1660), a5v.

127. Edmund Waller, *Upon Her Majesties new buildings at Somerset-House* (London, 1665), 1.

128. John Wilmot, Earl of Rochester, "To her Sacred Majesty," in *Epicedia Academiae Oxoniensis, in Obitum Serenissimae Mariae Principis Arausionensis* (Oxford, 1660), g1r.

129. *The Muses Joy*, a3v.

130. *The Queens Lamentation* (London, 1660), 1.

131. Royal Commission on Historical Manuscripts, *9th Report, Part I*, Manuscripts of the West and North Ridings (London, 1883), 326.

132. Pepys, *The Diary of Samuel Pepys*, 1:299.

133. Caroline M. Hibbard, "Henrietta Maria (1609–1669) ," in *Oxford Dictionary of National Biography* (Oxford University Press, 2004), accessed February 10, 2011, doi: 10.1093/ref:odnb/12947.

Chapter Two

Rape and the Roots of Discontent, 1666–1677

In June 1667, the Dutch fleet, led by Admiral Michiel Adriaenszoom de Ruyter, sailed up the Thames and the Medway, catching the English navy largely unawares. The attack was disastrous for the British, culminating in the loss of multiple naval vessels, including the highly symbolic *Royal Charles*. In his poem *The Last Instructions to a Painter*, Andrew Marvell describes the attack using the language of rape and accuses the Dutch of unlawfully and nonconsensually penetrating British territory:

> When aged *Thames* was bound with Fetters base,
> And *Medway* chast ravish'd before his Face,
> And their dear Off-spring murder'd in their sight;
> Thou, and thy Fellows, held'st the odious Light.
> Sad change, since first that happy pair was wed,
> When all the Rivers grac'd their Nuptial Bed;
> And Father *Neptune* promis'd to resign
> His Empire old, to their immortal line![1]

De Ruyter, "the Ravisher" (l. 758), has reduced the Thames (and by extension, England) to the status of an impotent old man unable to prevent the violation of his wife and murder of his children. Drawing on a long-standing tradition of anti-Dutch propaganda, Marvell condemns the Dutch as cruel and violent ravishers of innocent women and nations. England, the poem suggests, has been penetrated and poisoned by Dutch treachery, "a humiliation for the English, a violation of the natural order, and an index to the sickness of the court which allowed it to happen."[2]

If England is maltreated by the Dutch, it is the fault of her rulers that she could be so violated; the debauchery of Charles II and his entourage have led to the redirection of funds from military defense to the maintenance of parasitic courtiers and mistresses.[3] At the same time, the royal court has become too accepting of sexual violence. Even as Charles laments the maltreatment of the Medway, for instance, he orders the pardon of John, Viscount Mordaunt, a longtime royalist supporter and accused rapist impeached by the Parliament, licensing Mordaunt's actions and setting him free to rape again: "Now *Mordaunt* may, within his Castle Tow'r, / Imprison Parents, and the Child deflowre" (ll. 349–50). Charles himself is also rendered sexually predatory. At the end of the poem, a personified female England comes to Charles in the guise of a rape victim, naked, humiliated, despairing:

> There, as in the calm horrour all alone,
> [Charles] wakes and Muses of th' uneasie Throne:
> Raise up a sudden Shape with Virgins Face,
> Though ill agree her Posture, Hour, or Place:
> Naked as born, and her round Arms behind,
> With her own Tresses interwove and twin'd:
> Her mouth lockt up, a blind before her Eyes;
> Yet from beneath the Veil her blushes rise;
> And silent tears her secret anguish speak. (ll. 889–97)

Rather than feeling pity, Charles is aroused by the sight of England's naked sufferings, "unable to distinguish between matters of state and erotic fantasy."[4] Instead of offering his kingdom sympathy, comfort, and justice, he initiates more unwelcome sexual contact:

> The Object strange in him no Terrour mov'd:
> He wonder'd first, then pity'd, then he lov'd:
> And with kind hand does the coy Vision press,
> Whose Beauty greater seem'd by her distress;
> But soon shrunk back, chill'd with her touch so cold,
> And th' airy Picture vanisht from his hold. (ll. 899–904)

Charles's natural pity for his kingdom's suffering gives way to thoughtless desire, his lechery leading him to attempt another outrage upon the nation.[5] The poem thus intimates, in Margarita Stocker's words, that "vitiation from within has exposed England to her vitiation from without."[6]

The Last Instructions to a Painter ends with a warning to Charles II: he must reform his court or risk another civil war with resultant regicide. After ravished England flees, Charles comes face to face with the ghosts of his murdered ancestors, his father, Charles I, and his grandfather, Henry IV of France (Henrietta Maria's father).

> Shake then the room, and all his Curtains tear
> And with blue streaks infect the Taper clear:
> While, the pale Ghosts, his Eye does fixt admire
> Of Grandsire *Harry*, and of *Charles* his Sire.
> *Harry* sits down, and in his open side
> The grizly Wound reveals, of which he dy'd.

And ghastly *Charles*, turning his Collar low,
The purple thread about his Neck does show:
Then, whisp'ring to his Son in Words unheard,
Through the lock'd door both of them disappear'd. (ll. 915–24)

The ghosts warn Charles against placing too much faith in untrustworthy advisors—"His Fathers Ghost too whisper'd him one Note, / That who does cut his Purse will cut his Throat" (ll. 937–38)—but Charles does not heed the warning.[7] Instead, he decides on the Earl of Clarendon's fall and turns for comfort to his unfaithful mistress, the Duchess of Cleveland, and his deceitful counselors, the Earl of Arlington and Sir William Coventry. Charles recognizes the true natures of his closest courtiers:

Through their feign'd speech their secret hearts he knew;
To her own Husband, *Castlemain*, untrue.
False to his Master *Bristol*, *Arlington*,
And *Coventry*, falser than any one,
Who to the Brother, Brother would betray. (ll. 931–35)

He will not "trus[t] himself to such as they" (l. 936), yet he does not banish them from his inner circle. Instead, he allows them to feed on him like a group of vampiristic leeches. Marvell describes Charles's entourage as "His minion Imps that, in his secret part, / Lye nuzz'ling at the *Sacramental* wart; / Horse-leeches circling at the Hem'roid Vein" (ll. 495–97). The leeches feed on Charles's blood, alternately an image of vampiristic and scatological consumption, and a form of perverse breast-feeding. Charles is feminized both in his capacity as a monstrous mother giving suck to parasitic children and in his unwillingness to privilege the concerns of a suffering nation over the desires of his body. Here is Rochester's satirical comment, "His sceptre and his prick are of a length, / And she may sway the one who plays with th' other," taken to its most horrific conclusion, a world where kingly abdication of responsibility enables foreign invasion and societal collapse.[8]

Charles II's simultaneous hypersexuality and effeminate abdication of authority—what Barbara Riebling calls the "emasculation of dissolute desire"—combine to create a royal court populated with dangerously poisonous and overly powerful women.[9] The Duchess of Cleveland, for instance, already famous for her many infidelities, has become masculine both in her expansive desires and in her pursuit of her chaste male servant.

Great Love, how dost thou triumph, and how reign,
That to a Groom couldst humble her disdain!
Stript to her Skin, see how she stooping stands,
Nor scorns to rub him down with those fair Hands . . .
But envious Fame, too soon, begun to note
More gold in's Fob, more Lace upon his Coat. (ll. 81–84, 97–98)

Although Castlemaine wishes she could attract her servant using the traditionally desirable characteristics of femininity—youth and virginity—she must instead stoop to wooing him with forward advances and offers of financial advancement, "a humiliation of the King's mistress and of the King himself."[10] Meanwhile, Frances Stuart has garnered real political power by gaining the affection of the king. Marvell writes, "The *Court* in Farthing yet it self does please, / And female *Stewart* rules there, *Rules the four Seas*. / But Fate does still accumulate our Woes, / And *Richmond* here commands, as *Ruyter* those" (ll. 761–64). Marvell here puns on the fact that Frances Stuart appeared as the figure of Britannia on British coins and medals to suggest that Charles II is fatally ruled by his women.

Perhaps most striking, however, is Marvell's condemnatory description of Anne Hyde, wife of James, Duke of York. In one of the poem's most mean-spirited portraits, Marvell describes the duchess as a hypocrite who acts whorishly before marriage and pretends prudishness afterward: "She perfected that Engine, oft assay'd, / How after Childbirth to renew a Maid. / And found how Royal Heirs might be matur'd / In fewer months than Mothers once indur'd" (ll. 52–55). She is disgusting in appearance and déclassé in manner: "Paint her with Oyster Lip and breath of Fame, / Wide Mouth that Sparagus may well proclaim: / With Chanc'lor's Belly, and so large a Rump" (ll. 61–63). She is also potentially dangerous; like a hag performing alchemical experiments (or the ridiculous Margaret Cavendish), she develops a scientific knowledge that comes perilously close to a cultivation of the black arts. A "Philosopher beyond *Newcastle's* Wife," she studies "how a mortal Poyson she may draw, / Out of the cordial meal of the *Cacao*" (ll. 50, 67–68). Marvell insinuates that Hyde will use this newly learned expertise with poison to murder Lady Denham, her husband's mistress; she is "painted as a sorceress brewing poison in an attempt to murder her sexual rival."[11] And she finally represents another manifestation of perverse maternity; the duchess gives birth unnaturally quickly (less than two months after her marriage to James), she cannot keep her male children alive, and her breasts contain the cancerous growth that will kill her: "in her soft Breast Loves hid Cancer smarts" (l. 74). Her ability to give life is perverted into a source of toxicity and death.

The Last Instructions to a Painter encapsulates many of the antiroyalist tropes that would pervade the propaganda and drama of the early 1670s. As the excitement and optimism of the early Restoration faded, destroyed by plague, fire, and naval defeat, authors increasingly began to question the wisdom of a court more obsessed with libertine pleasures than with responsible governance. This discomfort is reflected in the many writings of the period in which men disavow their responsibilities to protect and defend, becoming instead sexually violent and untrustworthy.[12] Simultaneously, their women grow poisonous as they are afforded too much power within a collapsing patriarchal hierarchy; male failure permits the growth of female evil. Such anxieties pervade early 1670s propaganda, as the trope of the poisonous Catholic bride is reconfigured into the trope of the poisonous Catholic mistress, while the ghosts of murdered fathers appear to offer futile warnings of oncoming destruction.

Of course, not all writers were so skeptical of Charles II's court, and the conflict between pro- and increasingly antimonarchical viewpoints plays out both in contemporaneous political tracts and in the dramatic treatment of sexual violence. This chapter therefore examines the often conflicting and contradictory treatment of rape in the early 1670s. The chapter begins with an analysis of John Dryden's 1673 play, *Amboyna, or the Cruelties of the Dutch to the English Merchants*. A work of royalist propaganda designed to foment support for the increasingly unpopular third Anglo-Dutch War (1672–1674), *Amboyna* treats rape in much the same way as Orrery's *The Generall* or Howard's *The Usurper*. Throughout the play, Dryden deploys the atrocity tropes so common to English Civil War propaganda, in this case to target not the Irish, the Catholics, or even the Roundheads, but the villainous and lecherous Dutch. Dryden replaces the tropes of the demonic Irishman and debauched usurper with the trope of the demonic Dutchman, implicitly rehabilitating the court's Catholic faction and rallying the country behind Charles II's war.

Contrasting with Dryden's anti-Dutch, pro-royalist propaganda is the equally virulent anti-Catholicism that characterizes the contemporaneous plays of Elkanah Settle and Thomas Shadwell. Settle and Shadwell would later become famous as passionate supporters of Whig exclusion policy, but even in the years preceding the Popish Plot, both Settle's *Love and Revenge* (1675) and Shadwell's *The Libertine* (1675) criticize an increasingly libertine court, linking its libertinage with its tolerance for French absolutism and Catholic excess. In both plays, male obsession with debauchery precipitates societal collapse. As in Marvell's *Last Instructions*, the ghosts of murdered fathers offer warnings to reform, only to be ignored in the pursuit of more and greater pleasure. For Settle as for Marvell, male abdication of responsibility enables the violence of treacherous females who, in the absence of male control, become literal poisoners and figurative sources of social toxin. Settle thus develops the imagery of the poisonous Catholic mistress to condemn the dangerous combination of aristocratic masculine abdication of responsibility and unchecked Catholic female malice. Shadwell, in contrast, focuses on the problem of male sexual deviance, transforming the trope of the debauched Cavalier into the new trope of the debauched libertine. All of England, Shadwell suggests, is at risk from the destructive consequences of the libertine's protonihilist and self-destructive drive for pleasure, a warning to the court to reform. The chapter concludes with a reading of Aphra Behn's *The Rover, Part I* (1677), a play that fully encapsulates the extent of the era's political uncertainty. In Behn's play, the positive aspects of the Cavalier—Lovelace's chivalry and heroism—and the negative—Suckling's inconstancy and vice—are no longer separated from one another as in Orrery's *The Generall* or displaced onto a political enemy. Instead, they are combined in the play's putative heroes, reflecting the period's profound ambivalence toward royalist behavior on the eve of the Popish Plot.

DRYDEN'S *AMBOYNA* AND THE TROPE OF THE DEMONIC DUTCHMAN

Although anti-Catholic pamphlets remained in circulation throughout the 1660s and early 1670s, they are, generally speaking, not as collectively violent or as focused on atrocity as the pamphlets of the previous or subsequent periods. Tracts accusing Catholics of rape, torture, and cannibalism, while still available, were temporarily less common than academic criticisms of Catholic doctrine and liturgical practice.[13] Such a change in tenor may be attributed in part to the harsh licensing restrictions put in place after the Restoration and perhaps in part to a general cultural optimism about the future of the English government. By the mid-1670s, however, the humiliating failure of the Second Anglo-Dutch War combined with the popular rumor that Catholics ignited the 1666 Great Fire of London and the open presence of Catholics in the highest echelons of the court led to a new explosion of anti-Catholic sentiment. According to *A Relation Of The Most Material Matters Handled In Parliament Relating To Religion, Property, And The Liberty Of The Subject* (1673), for instance, the House of Commons was extremely concerned with "the extraordinary increase of Popery and prevalency of that Faction at Court" and had begun to fear, "and not without Grounds: The Ruine of the Protestant Interest" at court.[14]

Of particular interest to anti-Catholic polemicists was the progress of Charles II's foreign policy. The loss of the Second Anglo-Dutch War, coupled with a growing sentiment that Catholic France and not the Protestant Netherlands represented the most pressing political threat, decreased popular support for the new war. Rumors regarding the contents of the secret Treaty of Dover and the passage of the unpopular Declaration of Indulgence also fanned the flames of discontent, as Charles II's public support for seemingly pro-Catholic policies convinced many members of the public that the king was playing a secret and potentially disastrous foreign policy game. According to Steven C. A. Pincus,

> The third Anglo-Dutch war proved to be a time in which two rival interpretations—the one claiming that the republican Dutch, the other that the absolutist French, were seeking universal monarchy—could be tested. . . . The political

> developments of 1672 . . . invalidated the claims that the Dutch were seeking universal dominion, while strengthening the belief that Louis XIV coveted the throne of Charlemagne. This shift in popular sentiment took on added significance when Charles II and his government attempted to evade demands for peace. Political moderates as well as their more radical brethren became convinced that court corruption was preventing England from going to war with France and allying with the United Provinces, that the government was conducting a private foreign policy.[15]

Pincus argues that anti-Catholic sentiment grew out of a fear of French military strength: "The panic about popery grew out of fears of a French universal monarchy, rather than the other way around."[16] These fears were greatly augmented in 1673, when the future James II's Catholicism became a matter of public record, leading many to believe that Charles was focusing on war with the Dutch Protestants to obfuscate the growing and insidious power of the court Catholics. "From peace with the French and war with the Dutch . . . *Libera nos, Domine*," one anonymous satirist wrote.[17]

It is in this context that John Dryden wrote *Amboyna* (1673), a deliberate act of political propaganda that demonizes the Dutch and defends the alliance with the French. Drawing on the techniques of the 1660s rape plays, Dryden, like Howard and Orrery, traffics in atrocity to glorify the British monarchy. Dryden dedicates the play to the Catholic Lord Clifford and complains in the prologue that England traditionally placed too much emphasis on ties of mutual religion: "The dotage of some Englishmen is such / To fawn on those who ruine them; the Dutch. / They shall have all rather than make a War / With those who of the same Religion are."[18] The Dutch, Dryden claims, have publicly shamed England on the world stage, yet "Cuckold like," the Englishman "loves him who does the Feat" (prologue 12). Mutual Protestantism, he suggests, has insulated the Dutch from well-deserved retribution, and to emphasize the dangers of placing too much faith in the bonds created by the Protestant religion, he invokes the memory of the English Civil Wars: "What injuries so'er upon us fall, / Yet still the same Religion answers all: / Religion wheedled you to Civil War, / Drew English Blood, and Dutchmens now wou'd spare" (prologue 15–18). Dryden blames the outbreak of the Civil Wars on the failure of religious tolerance and suggests that to continue in intolerance—that is, to privilege Dutch Protestantism over French Catholicism—is to court disaster. Such rhetoric seeks to justify both Charles II's foreign policy and the much-maligned Declaration of Indulgence.

To stir up enmity against the Dutch and foment support for Charles's unpopular war, Dryden revives the tale of the Amboyna massacre, a staple of seventeenth-century anti-Dutch propaganda. Historically, the massacre occurred in 1623, when a Japanese mercenary confessed under torture to a plot by the British East India Company to oust the Dutch Vereenigde Oost-Indische Compagnie (the Dutch East India Company) from their shared trading post at Amboyna. According to Dutch records, the English merchants, led by Gabriel Towerson, also confessed to the scheme under torture and thus on March 9, 1623, ten Englishmen were executed for their participation in the supposed plot. Tracts condemning the Dutch for their actions began to circulate in England as early as 1624 and persisted throughout the century.[19] Roundhead propagandists in particular encouraged the spread of such material as a way to justify Oliver Cromwell's war with the Dutch (1652–1654). *A True Relation Of The Unjust, Cruel, And Barbarous Proceedings against the English at Amboyna In the East-Indies* (1651), for instance, informs its reader that the massacre was an act of utmost cruelty, a horrifying act before God:

> To take away any mans life without due course of Justice, though it be with the greatest civility and easiness of death that could be, is a crime which God hath denounced murder, and will visit accordingly; but to heighten and multiply a death with all the previous Tortures that a passionate Diabolical malice can invent, cruelty inflict, or the frame of mans body undergo, is so far from being manly or Christian, that it is beyond savageness and bestiality, and approaches that accursed frame of spirit that had plundged himself into, who sits in the seat of darkness.[20]

The author reminds the English people that the massacre finally went unpunished and that Charles I did not bother to seek justice for England or her gloriously martyred dead:

> In King Charles's time the business was not stirred in, he had too great designs at home, than to preserve our Honour, or remedy our injuries abroad; but now since that yoak of Kingship is taken off our necks, me thinks we should like men, whose shackles are taken off them while they are asleep, leap up nimbly, and make use of our Liberty. It were the most irrational thing in the World to think of forgiving of them, who, though they received assistance from us in their greatest affliction and lowest miserie, have refused not onely to assist us now, when their case is ours, but have been more than neutral against us, jealous, it should seem, that their way of Government, which they have so grown and thriven under, should have the same effects with us.[21]

It fell to Oliver Cromwell to do what the weak and careless monarch would not, to punish the Dutch finally and irrevocably for their bloodthirsty cruelty. Underlying such claims to patriotism was parliamentary anger at the United Provinces' refusal to recognize the nascent English republic, along with its continued financial support for Charles II and his exiled court.[22] To the tract's author, Dutch persistence in aiding the banished Cavaliers is a sign of continuing ingratitude toward England; as many tracts remind the reader, England helped to free the Netherlands from the shackles of Spanish rule, yet the Dutch favor those who would oppress England in turn.

Throughout the anti-Dutch pamphlets, authors employ images of atrocity identical to those found in the anti-Catholic and anti-Cavalier tracts. One 1652 pamphlet describes the tortures inflicted on the English at Amboyna in painstaking detail. To force a confession, one man is waterboarded—"they poured the water softly upon his head, until the cloth was full up to his mouth and nosti's [sic], so that he could not draw his breath, but he must suck in the water."[23] Another is tormented with fire: "they burnt him with lighted Candles in the bottom of his feet, until the fat dropt out the Candles. . . . They burnt him also under the elbows; likewise in the palm of his hands; they moreover burnt his arm-holes, till his intrails might be seen."[24] The fascination with entrails made visible by torture recalls the descriptions of the Irish Rebellion discussed in the introduction to this study, bespeaking the repetitive and overlapping nature of propaganda culture. Anti-Dutch polemicists draw on the same pool of atrocity imagery as their anti-Catholic enemies; the demonic Dutchman, like his Irish and Cavalier brethren, revels in rape, torture, and dismemberment, and poses a true threat to British national security.

After the Restoration, similar accounts of the "Cruel, Inhumane and Ingrateful" Dutch circulated during the years of the Second and Third Anglo-Dutch Wars (1665–67 and1672–74, respectively).[25] As in the 1641 Irish massacre tracts, anti-Dutch pamphlets of the period demonize their enemies by trafficking in the language of cannibalism. Demonic Dutchmen are referred to as "Bloody Butchers"[26] and accused of having "Roasted Men alive."[27] Stories of atrocities committed on the island of Poleroon are revived, in which the Dutch are accused of hiring Japanese mercenaries to murder men, women, and children: "the Out-cry in the Streets was terrible, Men, Women, and Children being cut in pieces, and the Town a Shamble of dead persons."[28] Demonic Dutchmen are also rapists; the inhabitants of the Banda Islands are described as begging the English for protection from the Dutch "whose practice it was, daily to exact upon them, and to murther them at their pleasures, and to abuse their Wives whiles themselves were inforced to look on, and not dare in the least to resist them."[29] The Dutch are murderers and sadists, ravishers and cannibals, a distant, fearsome Other, news of whose ill deeds distracts from deficiencies in contemporary English foreign policy.

According to Robert Markley, "Dryden rushed *Amboyna* to the stage to stir up popular resentment against the Dutch as England prepared to wage yet another war against the United Provinces, this time in league with the French."[30] To that end, the anti-Dutch pamphlets offered Dryden a fertile range of preexisting images upon which to draw. Dryden's Dutch are hypocritical, mercenary, and corrupt. They appear trustworthy in public only to turn on their supposed friends in private. The Fiscal, for instance, counsels Harman Junior to pretend friendship to Towerson since, he explains, "your Father, underhand, may do a mischief, but 'tis too gross above board"

(2.1.144–45). They are ungrateful in the extreme, both personally and politically. Harman Junior quickly forgets that Towerson "reliev'd me from the Pirats, and brought my Ship in safety off" (1.1.178–79), while his father dismisses England's role in saving the Netherlands from Catholic Spain. Van Herring, a Dutch merchant, is initially loath to attack English factories as the English "have preserv'd [our throats] from being cut by the *Spaniards*" (1.1.49–50). The Fiscal concurs, insisting, "We can never forget the Patronage of your *Elizabeth*, of famous memory; when from the Yoke of *Spain*, and *Alva's* Pride, her potent Succors, and her well tim'd Bounty, freed us, and gave us credit in the World" (1.1.231–34). Unfortunately, such favors ultimately mean nothing to the Dutch characters, driven as they are by mercenary greed. They "incarnate a pure commercial interest that excludes all forms of faith, justice, and reciprocity."[31]

In comparison with the vile Dutch, Dryden's Catholics look quite good. Spanish Catholic Perez proves much more honest than his Dutch employers, and he demonstrates the innate sense of honor that they lack. Here Dryden breaks with a long-standing tradition of anti-Spanish propaganda. As far back as the 1550s, authors spread tales of the so-called Black Legend of Spain, stories of Spanish atrocities committed against the native inhabitants of the Americas, along with stories of Spanish violence against Jews and Moors in Spain and against Protestants (the Dutch in particular) elsewhere on the European continent.[32] Such tracts describe the Spanish as barbarous, merciless, and cruel, all too eager to commit acts of rape, torture, murder, and infanticide. In Philip Wayne Powell's words, "The basic premise of the Black Legend is that Spaniards have shown themselves historically to be *uniquely* cruel, bigoted, tyrannical, obscurantist, lazy, fanatical, greedy, and treacherous."[33] According to Bartolomé de las Casas, whose 1552 treatise *The Spanish Colonie* was first translated into English in 1583, the Spanish reveled in the torture of the innocent, noble "savages" under their governance. Enumerating the evil deeds of a Spanish captain in Guatemala, de las Casas exclaims, "O howe many poore children hath hee made fatherlesse Orphans, howe many men and women widowers and widowes, bereeving the [sic] also of their childre [sic]! How many adulteries, whoredoms and rapes, hath he been the cause of. . . . Howe many anguishes and calamities by him have nombers suffered."[34]

Other treatises accused the Spanish of committing atrocities against the Dutch. Willem Baudartius, for instance, accused the Spanish Duke of Alba and his soldiers of having "threatened, struck, robbed, plundered, [and] raped the women and young daughters" of the Netherlands.[35] Baudartius accuses the duke of treating Dutch women as spoils of war: "Many beautiful, rich women who were taken from their husbands . . . he gave to his Soldiers . . . to satisfy their lusts and their goods for their thievery."[36] As is true of acts of sexual violence in the English Civil War tracts, Baudartius connects "rape, theft, and other acts of violence," suggesting "that he sees rape both as a violent act and a property crime against Netherlandish men—both of which signal Spanish depravity."[37] Similar accounts spread throughout the Netherlands during the years of the Dutch Revolt, as William of Orange encouraged the spread of anti-Spanish propaganda to foment political support for his rebellion.[38] They also circulated in English translation. George Gascoigne, for instance, condemned Spanish atrocities in his 1576 treatise, *The Spoyle of Antwerp*. A witness to Spanish violence against the Dutch, Gascoigne writes,

> I may not passe over with sylence, the wylfull burning and destroying of the stately Townehouse & all the monuments and records of the Citie: neither can I refraine to tel their shamful rapes & outragious forces presented unto sundry honest Dames & Virgins. It is a thing too horrible to rehearse, that the Father and Mother were forced to fetche their yong [sic] daughter out of a cloyster . . . & to bestow her in bed betweene two Spaniards, to worke their wicked and detestable wil with her.[39]

The Spanish have committed unspeakable acts against innocent Protestants, Gascoigne suggests, necessitating English intervention in Dutch affairs (the very intervention for which Dryden's Dutch are entirely ungrateful).

To read anti-Spanish tracts alongside anti-Irish, anti-Catholic, antiroyalist, and anti-Dutch documents of the period is to recognize the repetitive nature of early modern propaganda culture. Stories of rape, murder, and infanticide cross national and religious boundaries with ease and are swiftly refocused from one enemy to the next in successive periods of social unrest. Drawing on a communal pool of atrocity imagery, therefore, Dryden's *Amboyna* overwrites the Black Legend of Spain with tales of the demonic Dutchman. While Dryden's Dutch are inexorably cruel, the Spanish, embodied in the character of Perez, are ultimately harmless and even likable. Here, Dryden attempts to diminish and redirect popular anti-Catholic animus, reminding his audience that the Catholics—French, Spanish, and Irish alike—pose no threat in comparison to the treacherous Dutch. Unlike the Fiscal, Perez fully recognizes Towerson's obvious and innate worth: "he's a brave and worthy Gentleman, I wou'd not for the wealth of both the *Indies*, have had his Blood upon my Soul to answer" (3.2.132–34). Granted, Perez is not above mercenary motives; he refuses the commissioned killing only when he discovers that Towerson intended "as a testimony of [his] gratitude for [Perez's] honourable Service to bestow on him five hundred English pounds" (3.2.9–11). Yet there are lines of honor that Perez, a Spanish Catholic, won't cross even for money, lines that the Dutch Fiscal cannot or will not recognize. Respect for Towerson's good qualities even prompts Perez finally to fight on the side of the English, suggesting that the Catholics represent a lesser threat to English national interests. At the same time, Perez is rendered largely impotent and therefore safe, in sharp contrast to the Dutch sexual threat. While Perez is loyal to his unfaithful wife, the Dutch revel in cuckolding and sexual violence. They "are of a Race that are born Rebels, and live every where on Rapine" (4.4.50–51), and the Fiscal reminds Harman Junior that he can commit rapes with impunity: "Is not your Father Chief? Will he condemn you for a petty Rape?" (4.4.53–54). The Dutch thus become, like the Cavaliers and Catholics of the English Civil War tracts or the Spanish of the Black Legend, a source of infection and illness. Ysabinda complains that "the foul speckled stains" left on her body by the rape are "ne'r to be washed out, but in my death" (4.5.38, 39).

Several critics read Ysabinda as the allegorical embodiment of India threatened by Dutch imperialism. Bridget Orr, for instance, calls Ysabinda "a synecdoche for the possession of Amboyna."[40] That no rapes are reported in the original Amboyna documents certainly helps to substantiate such a reading. To read these texts alongside the tropes of older atrocity narratives, however, is to reveal how Dryden adopts the rhetoric of rape both to deflect criticisms of the court onto a foreign threat and to reinforce the necessity of Charles's military campaign. Ysabinda's broken and abused body represents not only the destruction of the colonial nation, but more importantly, the damage that England has suffered (and will continue to suffer) at Dutch hands. Towerson complains that the Dutch have treated the English as imperial subjects rather than partners in the colonial enterprise: "We are not here your Subjects, but your Partners," he tells Harman Senior, "and that Supremacy of power you claim, extends but to the Natives, not to us: dare you, who in the *British* Seas strike Sayl, nay more, whose Lives and Freedome are our Alms, presume to sit and judge your Benefactors?" (5.1.266–70). The English have ceded their position of authority to the Dutch, the colonizers becoming the colonized in India. Ysabinda's death, like Altemera's decay, thus symbolizes the damage done to the English nation as the Dutch usurp English property, humiliate English men, and degrade them to the status of natives.

By the end of the play, the Dutch are revealed to be more savage than "savages," as their acts of rape and sexual excess morph into acts of torture and finally, implied cannibalism. Harman tells his servant, "Boy, take that Candle thence, and bring it hither, I am exalted, and wou'd light my Pipe just where the Wyck is fed with *English* Fat" (5.1.364–66). Van Herring concurs: "So wou'd I; oh the Tobacco tasts Divinely after it" (5.1.367). The Dutch light their pipes on fire fed by English body fat, an ingestion of English flesh. Such cannibal imagery is new to Dryden's play; it does not appear in any of the Amboyna massacre tracts, reflecting Dryden's insistence that the Dutch are worse than any Catholic enemy, Spanish, Irish, or French. Finally, after deploying the rhetoric of rape, torture, and cannibalism against the Dutch, Dryden concludes by linking them with the Roundheads. The Dutch, like the English Civil War parliamentarians, have overthrown their lawful sovereign and for that act alone cannot be trusted. Beaumont exclaims, "Wee'l shame your Cruelty; if we deserve our Tortures, 'tis first for freeing such an infamous Nation, that ought to have been slaves, and then for trusting them as Partners, who had cast off the Yoke of their lawful Soveraign" (5.1.165–68).[41] To overthrow a seated monarch is a sin far worse than continued adherence to Rome. *Amboyna* thus participates in the same ideological project as *The Generall* and *The Usurper*: Dryden adopts the language of atrocity propaganda to discredit a hated foreign Other and then links that Other with the memory of Roundhead regicidal violence. Charles II's foreign policy is redeemed in contrast, as Dryden distances the king (and by extension, the French Catholics) from Dutch ingratitude, Dutch lasciviousness, and Dutch cruelty.

MALE LIBERTINISM AND THE POISONOUS CATHOLIC MISTRESS: 1670S PROPAGANDA

By the mid-1670s, the anti-Dutch, pro-royalist sentiment exemplified by Dryden's *Amboyna* was being drowned out by a virulent and progressively dominant cultural strain of anti-Catholicism. The performance of Dryden's *Amboyna* therefore marks a turning point in the treatment of onstage rape, the last play of the decade to use sexual violence to glorify the monarchy. Offstage, meanwhile, a growing number of anti-Catholic tracts began to circulate, once again likening the Catholics to a plague that would destroy the nation with domestic unrest. Popery is "such a Plague" that seeks "with dangerous Errours to Infect the mind."[42] William Lloyd concurs: "We say as a man that hath the Plague may live, but not by the Plague; so Popery being the bane of Christianity, and enmity to mans salvation, those that are saved among them, must be saved from Popery, not by it."[43] Catholics seek only to pour "our poison upon the earth," and undermine Protestant governments.[44] Other tracts recall the list of English kings deposed by Catholic treachery, as papists revel in the "Bloody Wars we have raised, the horrid Treasons we have Fomented, the cruel Massacres we have caused through Bohemia, England, France, and Germany of old, and in Ireland, and Vallies of Piedmont of a later date."[45] The memory of the Irish massacre is again invoked, in which "300000 were murdered, whose Blood stands still upon the score: which Cruelty, as former Ages cannot parallel, so future Ages will hardly believe."[46] George Fox enumerates Catholic atrocities committed against Protestants: "One was wrackt unto a Wheel, and beat with a Bulls Pizzle. One hanged, and her Skin fleyed off. One bound about a Globe, and her Skin fleyed off her Head and Face. One had had his Tongue cut out. One broken in a Mortar. One bound to a Pillar, his Head downward, and roasted. One fryed in a Pan. The Mother whipt, and her Dugs pulled off."[47] He concludes with a list of specifically Irish atrocities, including acts of Irish sexual violence:

> As for the Protestant Ministers whom they surprised, their Manner was first to strip them, and after bind them to a Tree or Post, where they pleased, and then to ravish their Wives and Daughters before their Faces (in Sight of all their merciless Rabble) with the basest Villains they could pick out, after they hanged up their Husbands and Parents before their Faces, and then cut them down before they were half dead, then quartered them, after dismembred them, and stopped their Mouthes therewith.[48]

In many of the tracts, Catholics are once more likened to vampires and cannibals. Fox invites his reader to contemplate how the Catholic Church "has been drunk with the Blood of Saints and Martyrs."[49] The speaker of *A Passionate Satyr Upon a Devilish Great He-Whore That lies yonder at Rome* wonders, "Must We, Canibal like, eat up our God, / Or else must We not in Heaven have aboad?"[50] Meanwhile, the author of *The Character of a Papist* insists that the Catholics believe "the Host in an instant Metamorphosed (or if you will) transubstantiated into very Flesh and Blood, Which is no sooner made, but forthwith they devour it, which raises a Question, Whether a Cannibal or Papist, be the rankest Flesh eater, since the former eats only Mans Flesh, the later [sic] that of his God."[51] The tract ends with a song emphasizing the cannibalistic aspects of the Eucharist:

> A Wafer the Priests Charm's into a God,
> If you will believe it you may.
> And so it becomes true Flesh and Blood,
> The clean contrary way,
> Oh! the clean contrary way.
> Then into your mouth he puts it all raw,
> If you will believe it, you may,
> Which surely will bleed if that you it Chew,
> The clean contrary way,
> Oh! the clean contrary way.[52]

For many anti-Catholic polemicists, religious error is linked with sexual hypocrisy, as priests are revealed to be notorious cuckold makers: "Must all Men be blind that open their Eyes, / That Priests may do what they please with their Wives?" *A Passionate Satyr* asks.[53] *A Catholick Pill to Purge Popery* (1677) describes the sins of sexually incontinent popes:

> Pope John the thirteenth was an Adulterer, and an incestuous person, Being found Without the City with another mans wife, he was wounded of her husband, that within eight days after he died. . . . Pope Sixtus the fourth

> erected at Rome a Stews of double abominations, not only of women, but also of men. . . . Alexander the sixth committed incest with his own daughter. . . . Innocentius the eighth had divers bastards, and boasted of them.[54]

Frequently, such attacks on the Catholic faith are linked with criticisms of court libertinism, as libertine behavior is treated as a byproduct of Catholic excess. Charles has surrounded himself with Catholic priests, whores, and sycophants, people who seduce him from the path of virtue and poison him politically, religiously, and sexually. In the words of John Ayloffe's "Britannia and Raleigh" (1674–75),

> A colony of French possess the court;
> Pimps, priests, buffoons I'th' privy-chamber sport.
> Such slimy monsters ne'er approach'd a throne
> Since Pharoah's reign, nor so defil'd a crown.
> I'th'sacred ear tyrannic arts they croak,
> Pervert his mind, his good intentions choke . . .
> Thus fairy-like the King they steal away,
> And in his place a Louis changeling lay.[55]

The toxic presence of the court Catholics has led both to Charles's sexual gluttony and to his pro-French foreign policy.

As criticisms of court Catholicism became more common and pointed, the image of the poisonous Catholic bride—an image initially tied to the memory of Queen Henrietta Maria—was replaced in the late 1660s with the image of the poisonous Catholic mistress.[56] Like Henrietta Maria before her, the poisonous Catholic mistress (the Duchesses of Cleveland and Portsmouth most commonly) used her sexual access to the king to influence and control his political choices.[57] The author of "The Royal Buss" (1675) calls the Duchess of Portsmouth an "incestuous punk" who has "Made our most gracious Sovereign drunk," and accuses her of poisoning the entire nation:

> The Devil take her for a whore!
> Would he had kiss'd ten years before,
> Before our city had been burn'd,
> And all our wealth to plagues had turn'd;
> Before she'd ruin'd (pox upon her!)
> Our English name, blood, wealth, and honor.[58]

Nell Gwyn is, ironically, praised, both because she is the "Protestant whore," and because she does not aspire to a position of political authority.[59] The author of the clandestine satire "Nell Gwynne" (1669) comments,

> Hard by Pall Mall lives a wench call'd Nell.
> King Charles the Second he kept her.
> She hath got a trick to handle his p—,
> But never lays hands on his sceptre.
> All matters of state from her soul she does hate,

And leave to the politic bitches.[60]

Nell is an acceptable mistress insofar as she does not attempt to parlay sexual access into political power.

Mary of Modena, James's Catholic wife, also came in for her share of criticism, as the thought of another well-placed, influential Catholic woman caused widespread discomfort. According to Andrew Marvell,

> For his Royal Highness to marry the Princess of Modena, or any other of that Religion, had very dangerous consequences: That the minds of his Majesties Protestant subjects will be much disquieted, thereby filled with infinite discontents and Jealousies. That his Majesty would thereby be linked into such a foraine Alliance, which will be of great disadvantage and possible to the Ruine of the Protestant Religion. That they have found by sad experience how such marriages have always increased Popery, and incouraged Priests and Jesuits to pervert his Majesties subjects: That the Popish party already lift up their heads in hopes of his marriage: That they fear it may diminish the affection of the people toward his Royal Highness, who is by bloud so near related to the Crown: That it is now more than one Age, that the subjects have lived in continual apprehensions of the increase of Popery, and the decay of the Protestant Religion: Finally that she having many Kindred and Relations in the Court of Rome, by this means their enterprises here might be facilitated, they might pierce into the most secret Counsels of his Majesty, and discover the state of the Realm.[61]

Mary of Modena becomes the figurative ravisher of her husband, penetrating the domestic sphere physically and ideologically, a simultaneous invasion of the public sphere as well as the domestic.

Clandestine satires aside, direct and open criticisms of the royal mistresses and court women in the period were relatively few. Licensing restrictions prevented open condemnations of the court, and thus the majority of satirical poems circulated secretly in manuscript, only to be published years later in the collections of *Poems on Affairs of State*.[62] I want to suggest, however, that implicit criticisms of the court women can be found in the resurrected stories of treacherous and sexually violent Catholic women that pervade the published anti-Catholic tracts. Alongside stories of the Irish massacre, authors also revived the story of the St. Bartholomew's Day massacre of Paris (1572), focusing especially on the role of Catherine de Medici, the queen mother, in spurring on the carnage. Another manifestation of the poisonous Catholic bride (or widow in Catherine's case), Catherine de Medici encourages her son to order acts of violence against Protestant men and her subjects to commit acts of sexual violence against Protestant women. According to *Popish Policies and Practices Represented in the Histories of the Parisian Massacre* (1674), the queen is "by her own nature and proper design enclined" to promote "the utter ruine of the Protestants by a total slaughter."[63] When the king, her son, balks at arranging the massacre, Catherine, along with the king's evil counselors, manipulates and shames him into action:

> The Queen fearing lest the King [her son], whom she thought she did observe still wavering and staggering at the horridness of the enterprise, should change his mind, comes into his Bed chamber at midnight, whither presently Anjou, Nevers, Biragus, Tavannes, Radesianus, and after them Guise came by agreement. There they immind [sic] the King, hesitating, and after a long discourse had to and fro, upbraided by his Mother, that by his delaying he would let slip a fair occasion offered him by God, of subduing his enemies. By which speech the King finding himself accused of Cowardise, and being of himself of a fierce nature, and accustomed to bloud-shed, was inflamed, and gave command to put the thing in execution. Therefore the Queen laying hold of his present heat, lest by delaying it should slack, commands that the sign which was to have been given at the break of day should be hastened.[64]

The queen takes advantage of her son's weakness, poisoning his mind and manipulating him into condoning Catholic "slaughters and rapines."[65] The text foregrounds the image of Catherine de Medici as the poisonous instigator of sexually violent horror, and she later becomes a literal poisoner; as the margin note reminds the reader, the king "died in less than two years after of a Bloudy-flux, proceeding, as was suspected, from poison given him by the procurement of his Mother and Brother."[66] In Catherine de Medici, the figure of the poisonous Catholic bride merges with the figure of the unnatural, monstrous mother who destroys her own progeny. Similarly deviant mothers abound in the tracts of the period, with the Church itself as the ultimate exemplar of maternal monstrosity. Alternately "the Mother of Harlots, and Abomination of the Earth,"[67] the "Mother of the Fornications of the Earth,"[68] and the "Mother of . . . Idolatry,"[69] the Church gives birth to a constant stream of evil plots. In *News from Rome*, the pope asks the devil for help with the Church's "most holy design which we have so long been Midwifing into the World"; without Satan's help, the plot "is likely to prove Abortive and fatally Miscarry."[70]

Equally revealing of the contemporary political climate is the sudden burst of interest in the story of Donna Olimpia Maidalchini (1591–1657), recently deceased sister-in-law of and mistress to the late Pope Innocent X. Born in 1591 to a tax collector father and minor noblewoman mother, Olimpia evinced a strong personality and sense of personal ambition from a young age. When her father decreed that Olimpia, then fifteen, would save her family money by joining a convent, Olimpia refused to give her consent, causing a minor scandal within the world of Viterbo, Italy. Her father was finally forced to acquiesce to her demands, and she subsequently married twice, first at the age of seventeen to wealthy landowner Paolo Nini, and after his death, to the nobleman Pamphilio Pamphili. Only twenty-one years old, Donna Olimpia was closer in age to her brother-in-law, thirty-eight-year-old Gianbattista Pamphili (the future Innocent X) than to her much older husband. Olimpia and Gianbattista quickly became inseparable, prompting gossip that the two were involved in an incestuous affair. According to Eleanor Herman, Olimpia's modern biographer, the birth of Olimpia's first surviving son and heir caused many to wonder whether Gianbattista, and not Pamphilio, "might be the father of the bouncing baby boy."[71] As Gianbattista's primary confidante and advisor, Olimpia was instrumental in overseeing his election first to the position of papal nuncio, and later, after the death of her husband, to the office of pope. Now a rich widow and presumed by all to be Innocent's lover, Olimpia became the most powerful woman in Rome, restricting access to the pope and determining the distribution of papal favors. With the exception of a three-year estrangement during which Olimpia left the city, she remained the most powerful woman in Rome until Innocent's death in 1655. The succeeding pope, Alexander VII, opened an investigation into the legalities of her dealings under Innocent, but she died of the plague in 1657 before any conclusions could be reached.

Although Donna Olimpia has been largely ignored by modern historians, the pope's "dependence on" her is, to this day, described as "the great blemish on [Innocent's] pontificate" in the *Catholic Encyclopedia.*[72] References to Donna Olimpia also appear regularly in the tracts of the 1670s. According to Alexander Cooke, author of *A Present for a Papist: Or The Life and Death Of Pope Joan* (1675), Donna Olimpia's influence within the Church hierarchy, along with the story of Pope Joan, proves that the Church is corrupt and unfit: "If matters then have gone thus at Rome, (the people there having been most intollerably abused, not only by this Female Pope, Donna Olympia, Sister in Law and overruling Miss to Pope Innocent the Tenth, and others of the like Masculine Gender) what hopes of Infallability?"[73] The story of Olimpia's life was first translated into English in 1666 in a tract entitled *The Life Of Donna Olimpia Maldachini, Who Governed the Church during the Time of Innocent the X*, a tract that ran through multiple editions between 1666 and 1678. Throughout the tract, Donna Olimpia is depicted as an unnatural wife, unfaithful, incestuous, and cruel. Initially married to the pope's brother, she uses her sexuality to control her brother-in-law: "She, who desired nothing more than the exercise of . . . power, freely bestowed her affections, the more to oblige [the pope] to an absolute surrender of himself. Thus the more he submitted his will to Donna Olimpia, the more love she heaped upon him."[74] Donna Olimpia, like Henrietta Maria and Charles II's mistresses, uses the power of her sexuality to gain inappropriate and unfair access to the body politic. The tract complains that the pope's power is "subjected to the frail disposal of a woman."[75] The pope is unmanned, controlled by the whims of a dangerous and unnatural woman. Finally, she becomes so indispensible to the pope that he tells her in a letter, "Remote from you I am like a Ship without a Rudder, left to the sole mercy of Fortune."[76] The tract's publication of Pope Innocent's letter recalls the publication and contents of Charles I's letters to Henrietta Maria in *The King's Cabinet opened*, proving that the pope, like the late monarch, was uxoriously and dangerously susceptible to feminine wiles. Leti complains that former popes may have fornicated, but if a pope "admitted [a mistress] into his Bed, she entred not into his Councils."[77] In contrast, Pope Innocent "presented Donna Olimpia not only with his heart and affections, but with his hand, person, and dominion; without restraint, limit, or respect: and it is most assuredly true, that never any King gave so much power to his Wife, nor any Queen Regent commanded her Councels with so much authority as Donna Olimpia had usurped unto her self both over Pope, Councel, and People."[78]

If Donna Olimpia is a bad counselor and sexual threat, she is also another manifestation of the monstrous and sexually violent mother. When her young granddaughter is reluctant to consummate the marriage Donna Olimpia has arranged for her, Donna Olimpia insists that the new husband force his unwilling bride—by today's standards, an instance of marital rape. Only twelve years old at the time of the marriage, Olimpiucchia shamed her grandmother with her behavior on her wedding day: "Olimpiucchia raced up to her old bedroom and locked the door. The wedding guests could hear her loud sobs echoing through the walls. . . . She shrieked that she knew what her husband expected of her that night . . . and she wanted no part of it."[79] When her attempts to reconcile the girl to the marriage fail, Donna Olimpia "dragged her into a carriage and took her to the Palazzo Barberini [her husband's residence] herself. . . . The ambassador of Mantua wrote, 'The grandmother took her there almost violently one evening.'"[80] The marriage was subsequently consummated, presumably against Olimpiucchia's will and much to Donna Olimpia's relief. Donna Olimpia thus reinforces her own power by suborning, and indeed commissioning, an act of rape against her own flesh and blood. Simultaneously, driven by ambition and an extreme thirst for power, she refuses to educate her son and heir, lest he attempt to replace her as the head of the family: "She neglected the Education of her Children, especially of her Son: for fear it might waken his spirits a little, to a future disturbance of her absolute power over the house of Pansilio."[81] She also attempts to thwart her son's matrimonial ambitions. When Prince Camillo, Olimpia's son, resigns his cardinalship in favor of marrying Olimpia Aldobrandini, Princess of Rosana, Olimpia Maidalchini forces the pope to banish him and his bride from the city: The pope "held a two hours conference with Donna Olimpia, to resolve what was to be done in this case. The result of which was, that the Prince Camillo and his Lady, should be banished from Rome. Upon which the Orders were brought him to depart, to the amazement of all."[82] The common people are amazed that a mother could treat her son so unfairly, as are the members of the papal court. "The Court wondered most at these two particulars, in the banishment of Prince Camillo. The first was to see a Pope so besotted with a Woman, as to punish his Nephew for having directed his love to a Princess of equal quality to himself. Who could but admire to see a Pope given over to the excess of an aspiring woman, who governed Church, State, Court, and Pope himself with a high hand: and at the same time become so cruel to his only Nephew, for appropriating with the love of so noble a Lady, so considerable a Patrimony to the house of Pansilio!"[83]

Leti's tract sets up the two Olimpias as inverse images of each other, a real-life analogue to such dramatic pairings as Settle's Fredigond and Aphelia, Lee's Tullia and Teraminta, and Ravenscroft's Tamora and Lavinia. As is common in the drama of the period, Leti's work juxtaposes an evil, lecherous mother against an innocent young bride victimized by the elder woman's ambitious excess, and thus, as we shall see, sheds new light on the many similar pairings appearing contemporaneously on the British stage. Such a portrayal was not, in fact, historically accurate. According to other accounts, Olimpia Aldobrandini was hardly a complete innocent. When Olimpia's son Camillo first met his future wife, she was already married to Prince Paolo Borghese. She married Camillo in 1647, less than a year after the death of her husband and despite his mother's objections. Princess Olimpia also evinced a personality as strong as her mother-in-law's; according to Herman, "It was a cruel irony that Camillo, who had married the princess to get away from the domination of his bossy mother, now found himself dominated by a bossy wife. In fact, appearances aside, the two Olimpias were remarkably similar; both were ambitious, strong, and far smarter than he, and neither would ever let him forget it."[84] Donna Olimpia was apparently jealous of Princess Olimpia's youth and beauty and particularly worried that she would usurp the pope's affections and act as a rival "in the disposal of the Pope, at least limit her in part if not in the whole."[85] The two Olimpias remained enemies and rivals their entire lives, only reconciling just before the elder Olimpia's death. The degree to which Leti renders the elder Olimpia monstrous and the younger Olimpia the embodiment of virtue in distress, however, reflects the degree to which he hopes to demonize and discredit Maidalchini. Within the context of English political culture, the tract also serves to remind readers of the evils perpetrated by poisonous Catholic mistresses, both domestically and abroad.

The frequent repetition of the Donna Olimpia story in tracts of the period suggests that the pope's mistress functioned as a stand-in for all the Catholic wives and mistresses who could not safely or directly be publicly accused. She also personifies the dangerous consequences of a world in which women are not effectively policed, a world in which men privilege the pursuit of sexual pleasure over religious devotion or effective governance. The world that emerges from the propaganda tracts of the late 1660s and early 1670s, then, is quite similar to the view of the court proffered in Marvell's *The Last Instructions to a Painter*. The pursuit of libertine pleasure has created a realm in which patriarchy has begun to crumble. In its place are effeminate rulers, violent debauched libertines, and poisonous and destructive women. It is in this context that we must read and understand Settle's *Love and Revenge* and Shadwell's *The Libertine*, two plays in which male abdication of responsibility leads to societal collapse. For Settle, as for Marvell and the Donna Olimpia authors, that abdication licenses the spread of female poison and eventually the disruption of lines of inheritance through rape and Catholic monstrosity. Shadwell meanwhile transforms the figure of the debauched Cavalier into the figure of the debauched libertine. The tropes of English Civil War propaganda are altered to suit the concerns of a new generation, demonstrating the link between aristocratic pursuit of pleasure, the acceptance of erroneous and harmful Catholic doctrine, and finally protonihilist destruction.

MALE ABDICATION, FEMALE POISON: SETTLE'S *LOVE AND REVENGE*

Elkanah Settle's *Love and Revenge* (1675), an adaptation of William Heminge's little-known Caroline play, *The Fatal Contract* (c. 1633), depicts a royal court very similar to that of Marvell's *The Last Instructions to a Painter*. Drawing on material from earlier Jacobean plays—*Hamlet*, *Othello*, and *The Revenger's Tragedy* most clearly[86]—the play reveals the problems that ensue when patriarchy collapses and women are allowed too much social and sexual authority. The play begins in the wake of a series of horrifically violent acts. The fair Chlotilda has been raped by Crown Prince Clotair, and in an attempt to avenge her violation, Chlotilda's family murdered an innocent man, Clotair's uncle and brother to Queen Fredigond. Subsequently, Fredigond avenged her brother's death with the murders of Chlotilda's entire family, save two absent brothers, Dumain and Lamot, and Chlotilda herself, who is missing and presumed dead. Dumain explains,

> For in the high displeasure of that Queen
> All our Posterity was doom'd, some felt the Wheel,
> Some Wrackt, some Hang'd, others empaled on Stakes;
> And had not we been then in *Wittenburgh*
> We had added to the number of the Dead.[87]

When Dumain and Lamot return to the kingdom, they have every motivation in the world to seek vengeance, to punish both the violation of their sister and the death of their father. That the brothers were away at Wittenberg during these tragic events constructs an imaginative parallel between Dumain and Lamot and Shakespeare's Hamlet, also away in Wittenberg during his father's murder and mother's subsequent remarriage. Dumain and Lamot, however, have no interest in assuming the role of avenger. When Queen Fredigond offers them a place at court, they disclaim the need for revenge, only too glad to accept personal advancement instead. Lamot tells his brother,

> We'l take the gracious offer of the Queen.
> She's Princely, Vow'd our Friend; besides, what ill
> Can we expect from her, who might have sent
> Her murdering Ministers, and slain us here,
> Had She intended foul play? No, She's Noble. (5)

Despite their assertions at the end of the play that there is honor in vengeance, that "This Revenge / Is an Estate to the Family; 'twill make / The *Dumane* race immortall" (72), they take no part in seeking that glorious revenge, in clearing their family's name, or in seeking redemption for their sister's reputation. Male abdication of responsibility thus becomes evident from the earliest moments of the play.

Other male characters likewise fail in their duties as avengers. Crown Prince Clotair is a rapist, but he is also son to an unfaithful mother and murdered father. Still, he repeatedly privileges his sexual conquests above his duty to his family name and personal honor. As he leaves his mother's side to rendezvous with (and potentially rape) Aphelia, he acknowledges that he should be more concerned with his duty to his parents.

> My Father dyed but now; his Fate calls down
> For thoughts of Vengeance, and my tender breast
> Should be with dreams of piety possest:
> With thoughts of Blood and Death, of Funeral Beds,
> Of Martyr'd Monarchs, and of Traytors heads;
> A Mother's Tears, and walking Fathers Ghost,
> Disturb'd i'th'other world, for what in this was lost. (15)

The play alludes to Hamlet's father's ghost—another specter doomed to walk the world and lament what he has lost—to emphasize both Clotair's responsibility to his father and his refusal to act as Hamlet does. Despite his father's death just hours before, Clotair chooses to seek out Aphelia (whose name, of course, invokes the memory of *Hamlet*'s Ophelia), insisting, "These should I think on; but to night sleep sorrow: / For Love to night, and for Revenge to morrow . . . It is not Ghosts, but Lovers walk by Night" (15, 16). Love, for Clotair, is far more important than revenge.

The memory of Hamlet's father's ghost is invoked a second time in a scene that blends elements of Shakespeare's *Hamlet* with elements of Middleton's *The Revenger's Tragedy*. To further her own revenge, Chlotilda (now living disguised as the Moorish Nigrello) sends Clotair to his mother's chambers, hoping that Clotair will catch Fredigond with her lover, Clarmount. Like *The Revenger's Tragedy*'s Lussurioso, also sent to his mother's chambers by the avenger, Vindice, Clotair runs to his mother's room, and as in *The Revenger's Tragedy*, the revenger's plan goes awry. Instead of catching his mother in the sexual act, Clotair encounters what he believes is his father's ghost. When Fredigond realizes that her tryst is about to be discovered, she tells Clarmount, "in my Closet / Lyes th'Habit that my Husband wore last Night / When he was Poyson'd; put on that, and . . . / Make up the form of the dead King" (25). Later, when Clotair enters her chamber, she invents an elaborate ghost story designed to convince her son that his father's discontented spirit walks abroad:

> Oh Son,
> Such horrid Apparitions
> Have I beheld, have quite unwitted me:
> Your Fathers Ghost most terribly frightful
> Has thrice this dismal Night appear'd to me:
> In his right hand he bore a shining Cup,
> Which to his mouth he rais'd with looks so gay,
> As if he drank a health to some young Bride.
> The aiery Potion drank, strait in a fume
> He threw the seeming Goblet to the ground,
> And with an alter'd look assumed a paleness
> More death-like then the frost, his Age and Cares
> Made him in Life-time wear: To Heav'n he pointed,
> Thrice did he cry, Revenge; and at that word
> Sprang through the Roof which now stands bare to Heav'n,
> Where he did rain down Fire which here you see. (25–26)

Thus when Clotair encounters the disguised Clarmount, he believes he is confronting his father's ghost, and his reaction bespeaks both fear and guilt for having prioritized sex with Aphelia over duty to his father's memory:

> My Fathers form exactly, who could think
> The Devil were so good at Picture-drawing,
> Pray Heav'n he be not Ceremonious; for
> I find my self but ill provided for
> A Complement. If it be Injuries,
> Break open Monuments, and disturb the Dead:
> I'le see thy rights perform'd. If thou desirest
> To be appeas'd with Blood, Blood thou shalt have:
> Or if that's not enough, I'le build thee Temples.
> Thou shalt have Altars, humane Sacrifices.
> Do but depart; thy presence does not please me,
> Thou art not Company for Flesh and Blood. (26)

In Heminge's original text, Clotair encounters what he believes is his *brother's* ghost, not his father's. In a substantially less descriptive passage, Fredigond tells him, "O my Son, such horrid apparitions full of dread / Have I beheld, have quite unwitted me; / Thy brothers Ghost, young *Clovis* Ghost in armes / Has thrice appear'd to me this dismall night."[88] That Settle chooses to substitute old King Childrick's apparition for Clovis/Lewis's bespeaks the symbolic power of *Hamlet* as a backdrop to the text. As a good son, Clotair should drop everything to avenge his father; in Hamlet's words, "thy commandment all alone shall live / Within the book and volume of my brain / Unmixed with baser matter."[89] Instead, Clotair continues to value his interactions with and desire for Aphelia over his responsibility to his father. In this, Clotair's behavior is also reminiscent of Charles II's in *Last Instructions to a Painter*. Instead of heeding his (supposed) father's political warning, he chooses mistress over patriarch and goes on to plot another act of sexual violence.

Despite Lewis's eventual status as the hero of the play, he, too, privileges love over revenge. Like Clotair, Lewis chooses mistress over father, insisting that his duty to Aphelia outweighs his duty to the late king. "This process of a Fathers Death, has rowz'd / My Soul, and shew'd me Horrors in a shape / Too terrible to enter Loyal hearts" (32), he exclaims, yet finally concludes, "My Resentments / Of my wrong'd Fathers death a while must pause, / I'le Right a Kings, but first a Mistress's Cause" (33). Unfortunately, his protection proves insufficient as Aphelia is repeatedly sexually menaced and Lewis fails to best his brother in a duel. What the play dramatizes, then, is the systematic failure of men as patriarchs and avengers as they privilege sexual desire over duty. Clotair in particular emerges from the play as another manifestation of the debauched Cavalier (now libertine), sexually violent, dangerously impetuous in his appetites, and ultimately unconcerned with the effectual functioning of the government. Indeed, it is Clotair's failure to offer appropriate leadership that finally leads to the play's tragic ending, reminding the spectator that a libertine king does not pride himself on stable governance.

As is the case in Marvell's *Last Instructions*, male abdication of responsibility permits the rise of feminine evil. Queen Fredigond functions as the play's poisonous Catholic bride; like Catherine de Medici and Donna Olimpia, she is both sexually violent and a monstrous mother, yet her behavior is predicated on her husband's and son's disinclination to police her sexuality. Dumain and Lamot specifically criticize old King Childrick for failing to lock his wife away from the world and prevent her from straying: "Were I the King . . . / Before the Wanton and hot-blooded Queen / Should have the License to be suspected, / I'de lock her up, and house her like a Silk-worm" (3). Childrick's failure to prevent his wife's adultery is finally punished by his murder at the hands of the woman he has neglected to restrict. Still,

Clotair has no interest in regulating his mother's behavior after his father's death. While Hamlet and Lussurioso are tormented by the possibility of their mothers' unchastity, Clotair remains dismissive:

> I find the sin of Lust is not so Capital.
> My Father but last Night by Poyson Dyed,
> And I at the same time by Lust inflamed,
> Left the concern due to a Fathers Murder,
> To flye into a Mistresses embrace.
> I but a Father lost; and by that loss
> I gain'd a Throne: She lost a King and Husband,
> And with that loss a Crown: Yet Love had power
> To make her losses, King and Crown forget,
> And the next Night flye to a Lovers Arms.
> Why then should I be troubled; when my sin
> (If it be one) runs in my Blood. (29)

Fredigond's lack of concern for her husband's death, Clotair argues, excuses his own failures, and thus he is not bothered by evidence of her extramarital sexual desires. Too late he realizes that such sexual freedom has the potential to destroy the fabric of society; left unchecked, female infidelity leads to female violence.[90] According to Fredigond, "I once was a Kind Wife and Pious Mother. / But now my Husband, and my Sons must dye . . . / Almighty Love this wondrous Change has made, / A Love that has my hopes of Heav'n betray'd" (8). Because she desires Clarmount beyond honor and reason, she ignores the bonds of matrimony and the blood ties of maternity to ensure her lover's rise to power:

> For my *Clarmount*,
> My best-lov'd *Clarmounts* sake, Husband and Sons
> Are Clouds betwixt my Love and Me: and all
> The tyes of Blood, and Nature are too small
> To check what Love resolves. (8)

The freedom to sin sexually afforded by her son's neglect renders Fredigond cruel and merciless, and once outside the systems of masculine control, she grows ever more dangerous.

Clotair's failures to control his mother's behavior are twofold: he does not restrict her sexually, and perhaps more importantly, he forces her to avenge her brother's death on her own, as he is himself uninterested in vengeance. Fredigond's villainous acts reflect not only her unfettered lust and ambition—in an act reminiscent of Donna Olimpia's treatment of Olimpiucchia, she arranges the rape of Chlotilda to further her lover's rise to power and her own—but the fact that she must accept the role of avenger within the play's world. Just as Chlotilda must punish her own rape, Fredigond must punish her brother's murder alone: "Their Parents waded in my Brothers blood," she says of Chlotilda's relatives, "For which I'le be reveng'd on all their Race" (5, 6). The position of female avenger is, however, a particularly fraught one. Although prompted by necessity, the pursuit of vengeance requires a woman to abandon her femininity and become in the process a threatening monster. For Fredigond, that monstrosity results in poisonous tendencies and the abandonment of the domestic roles of wife and mother. Nigrello calls her a "Monster-Woman," the product of an "Adulterate Race" (15), while Lewis tells her,

> Adulterate Woman, shame of Royalty;
> I blush to call thee Mother, yes to think it.
> Whilst I reflect upon thy tainted blood,
> I doubt the pureness of my own. The spring head
> Defiled, who knows but the under stream may be
> Corrupted. (70)

Her actions have also infected the nation. Nigrello speaks of the "bleeding Kingdo[m]" wounded by Fredigond's actions (31), while Lamot imagines the medical cure necessary to restore the body politic to rights: "The Ulcerous State is ripe, and we must launce it" (54). Clotair calls his mother's adulterous desires "the base Canker" that "spreads through Families" (78), a species of toxin that dilutes and corrupts familial blood. Fredigond thus becomes a horrifying sexual abomination. Aphelia, being led into sexual peril by Nigrello, asks, "Into what Labyrinth do you lead me, Sir?" (17), linking Fredigond with the mythological Pasiphaë, whose sexual deviance prompted bestiality and grotesque birth. Clotair meanwhile becomes the Minotaur, the monstrous byproduct of Fredigond's deviance and the physically present danger menacing Aphelia.

Throughout *Love and Revenge*, therefore, Settle subtly reminds his viewer that a king obsessed with pleasure can be easily manipulated by evil and poisonous women. Such themes were not new to Settle's oeuvre; he began employing the trope of the poisonous Catholic bride as early as 1673 in his hit play, *The Empress of Morocco*. In that play, Settle juxtaposes the treachery of the murderous and lustful queen mother, Laula, against the virtue and bravery of her daughter and daughter-in-law, the young queens Morena and Mariamne. In *The Empress of Morocco*, Settle implicitly links the figure of the poisonous old queen with the figure of Henrietta Maria (and by extension, Charles II's Catholic mistresses), indicating that by the time of *The Empress of Morocco*, Settle was already warning against the dangers of unfettered Catholic female power. According to Anne Hermanson:

> In the highly-charged political decade which was rapidly moving toward the Popish Plot and Exclusion Crisis, the devil of the evil woman is used . . . politically. The Empress of Morocco was probably first produced in July 1673. Certainly, Settle had a place in court when he wrote and produced the play, and he was writing from the perspective of an "insider". By this time,

> Charles's new French mistress, Louise de Keroualle, was in a position of power at court and only a month away from becoming a duchess. James had publicly acknowledged his Catholicism and was slated to marry the Catholic Princess, Mary of Modena. For a Protestant like Settle, the 'feminine' threat—not only from within, the form of Catholic women at court, but also in the 'female' body of the Catholic Church—was already eating away at the stability of the state. Settle's evil Queen Mother reflects on former times when other conniving queen mothers were seen to be threatening stability: in particular, the Queen Mother Catherine de Médicis. Like Catherine de Médicis, Charles II's own mother Henrietta Maria tried desperately to control her son's political affairs. Her Catholic (thus nefarious) influence over her husband Charles I remained in people's minds.[91]

Like the court's controlling wives and mistresses, Laula is a source of disease festering at the heart of the nation. She literally kills with poison and metaphorically destroys the virtuous. "I begin to think your Mothers Heart / Has Poyson in't," Crimalhaz tells Mariamne insultingly, and he refers to Laula's "Poyson'd Breath"; she is the toxin in his veins that will finally destroy him.[92]

Settle's decision to adapt *The Fatal Contract* bespeaks a similar political project. Although the queen mother had been dead for several years by the time of *Love and Revenge*, Settle's decision to adapt Heminge's play revived the discourse of Henrietta Maria, still lingering in people's minds and made continually relevant through attacks on Donna Olimpia and Catherine de Medici. Heminge's play was originally acted by Henrietta Maria's acting troupe, the queen's Men, immediately linking the play with the hated queen. Fredigond, like Henrietta Maria, is described as eclipsing the king, a frequent insult, as we have seen, in the English Civil War tracts. "She is the Greater Light, the King a Star, / That only shines but through her Influence" Lamot says (4)—an image echoed by Lewis, who remarks of his mother's influence on the kingdom, "How is thy worth Ecclips'd" (69). Like Henrietta Maria, Fredigond is also an actress: "How did I act the Mother?" she asks Clarmount, and brags that she wept for her son "as an Actor in a Play would do" (23). And like Henrietta Maria, Fredigond enjoys watching plays and attends the "Masques and Revelling" (4). Most importantly, she is sexually monstrous and corrupts her husband with her deviance. Here Settle has altered the content of the original play. Settle depicts old King Childrick as a chaste and virtuous man, unlike Heminge's Childrick, who maintained a secret grotto where he coupled with his illicit conquests. Heminge's queen resolves to rendezvous with her lover in the place "where *Childrick* kept his Concubine" (3.3.225). Not so, Settle's Childrick, who keeps the same grotto as a spot for prayer and devotion. Settle's Fredigond directs Nigrello to the place where "Childrick oftentimes retired, / When fits of piety (rest his soul) / Took him ith'head" (48). Fredigond's sexual corruption is offset by Childrick's restrained piety, and she works to poison his virtue, even as she cuckolds and humiliates him. Lamot finally attributes the army's state of disarray to Fredigond's evil influence:

> In good old *Childricks* raign, before his Queen
> Had taught him Revels, and untaught him War,
> Before her wanton Lust had sheathed his Sword,
> To give her treacherous Poyson, pow'r of death;
> I knew that they had valour, and a cause
> To shew it in. (52)

Fredigond uses her sexuality to mislead the king and draw him from the righteous path. The play thus recalls traditional accusations against Henrietta Maria, Catherine de Medici, and Donna Olimpia, along with the new concerns inspired by Mary of Modena and Charles II's mistresses.

Underlying *Love and Revenge* is therefore a fundamental anxiety about the political threat posed by unchecked female power, an anxiety embodied in the juxtaposition of Fredigond and Aphelia, the monstrous mother and the innocent virgin she menaces. Between these two extremes falls Chlotilda/Nigrello, neither chaste nor whorish, yet who, like Fredigond, becomes monstrous as a result of masculine failure. At least initially, Chlotilda is as much Fredigond's victim as she is Clotair's, since it is Fredigond who arranges for her rape. That Clotair rapes Chlotilda only at his mother's behest further underscores his masculine inadequacies; despite his standing as crown prince, he cannot compel Chlotilda's submission and only "succeeds" with her sexually because of his mother's intervention. Yet Chlotilda does not remain a victim for long. Working against the tradition of the seventeenth-century rape play in which the rape victim's suicide is an anticipated certainty, Chlotilda does not immediately resign herself to death. As Carol A. Morley points out in relation to Heminge's Crotilda, she "imitates neither classical prototypes, such as Lucrece and Virginia, nor contemporary variant inversions, such as Shakespeare's Lavinia or Fletcher's Lucina."[93] Instead, Chlotilda must seek her own justice, a quest motivated by male failure; Chlotilda cannot play Lucrece if there is no Collatine or Brutus to avenge her sufferings. In consequence, Chlotilda becomes monstrous, arranging a rape for Clotair as Fredigond once did. The queen and her victim become equally poisonous doubles of each other, with Chlotilda's blackface disguise externalizing both the "stain" of the rape and the darkness of her now corrupted nature. Early in the play, Aphelia expresses sympathy for Philomel: "Poor Ravisht *Philomel*, thy Lot was ill / To meet that Violence from a Brother" (18). Of course Philomel, the rape victim-avenger, is an infanticidal murderess who suborns cannibalism. Like Philomel, Chlotilda is also associated with images of grotesque eating; planning the rape of Aphelia, she exclaims,

"Oh admirable Villainy! Revenge / Does feed on Ruine" (13). Revenge, here Chlotilda, will feed on ruin, Aphelia, imaginatively cannibalizing her and her sad fate.

Love and Revenge thus juxtaposes the poison of the two female avengers, Fredigond and Chlotilda, against the virtuous purity of Aphelia and creates a happy ending predicated on the restoration of patriarchal authority. Such a happy ending for Settle is made possible by the fact that he sanitizes much of Heminge's more shocking and graphic imagery.[94] In Heminge's play, Crotilda very clearly follows the trajectory of the Jacobean revenger who becomes the thing he hates. As Fredson Bowers argues in his landmark study, *Elizabethan Revenge Tragedy*, the revenger, "though inherently good," becomes "warped and twisted to abnormality by the intolerable stress of his almost impossible situation."[95] Charles A. and Elaine S. Hallett concur: "By the end of most revenge tragedies, there seems to be no way the revenger could go on living. He has committed atrocities that equal and in some cases even surpass those of his antagonist, and if justice requires the villain's death, it also requires the revenger's."[96] Crotilda first reveals her extraordinarily sadistic streak when she tortures Fredigond and her lover, Landrey (Heminge's version of Settle's Clarmount). First she taunts their starving bodies with the sight of food and then, in a punishment recalling Vindice's treatment of *The Revenger's Tragedy*'s Duke, poisons Fredigond, gags her, and forces her to watch the culmination of the revenge plot: "I will be bold to gag your Ladyship; / I'l leave a peeping hole through which you shall / See sights, shall kill thee faster than thy poison" (5.2.138–40), Crotilda promises, echoing Vindice's "If he but wink . . . Let our two other hands tear up his lids / And make his eyes, like comets, shine through blood."[97] Crotilda also enacts her sadistic desires on Aphelia. She plays the Iago to Clotair's Othello, and, in the play's most shocking and ethically dubious moment, mutilates Aphelia's innocent body. According to Heminge's stage directions, "they bind [Aphelia] to the Chair, the Eunuch much sears her breast" (5.2.262).

All of these acts of violence are excised from Settle's text. While Settle's Nigrello does order the death of the queen, she does not herself perform the task, nor does she revel in violence to the extent of her Heminge counterpart. This is not to suggest that Settle's Nigrello/Chlotilda is entirely free from the taint of sadism. Settle's Chlotilda is offered numerous opportunities to exact her revenge, but like Hamlet, who declines to kill Claudius at his prayers—"And am I then revenged / To take him in the purging of his soul, / When he is fit and seasoned for his passage?" Hamlet demands (3.3.84–86)—Chlotilda wants to ensure not just death, but eternal damnation for the queen. Knowing that Fredigond is planning to order several murders, Chlotilda declines to save Fredigond's future victims. Rather, she explains, these new crimes "will add / More weight to her Damnation, and more edge / To my Revenge" (10). She reiterates this sentiment when she arranges for Fredigond's assignation with Clarmount:

> Should I prevent her Lust this second time,
> Before the third she may repent, and so
> May save her Soul which my Revenge would damn:
> Yet I'le prevent her, and contrive it so
> She shant repent, nor shall Hell lose a Subject. (49)

Still, at the end of the play, Chlotilda's desire for vengeance fails her as the glory of kingship overwhelms. She cannot punish her rapist without raising her hand against her king: "I cannot strike him," she laments. "Oh relenting heart! / What Awe hangs on the brow of Majesty. / Faint heart! A Man so long, and now turn Woman / In the last action of my Life" (81). The ending obviously reflects the ideologies of the post-Restoration era, where the glory of the king's body politic outweighs the sins of Clotair's body natural. Chlotilda begs her brothers to "Call not these Ruines Treason, but Revenge" (82); that is to say, she insists that she is taking action not against the body politic, but against Clotair's body natural alone, "A satisfaction due to an Injur'd Lady" (82). Still, it is in abandoning her final revenge and renouncing the power of her disguise that Chlotilda becomes virtuous once more: "For all my other Scenes of Cruelty," she announces, "I put on my own Sex agen to dye" (82). She resigns her final vengeance to the keeping of her male relatives, and safe in the knowledge that the men will take up her cause and use her martyred memory to shore up the new regime, she seeks death. Thus Chlotilda is reincorporated into the civic realm, her monstrousness banished and her memory put to a less threatening political use. Equilibrium is attained as poisonous and sexualized women are driven from a remasculinized realm. In this way, the play offers a subtle warning to Charles II and his courtiers, who must school their behavior or risk destruction. When the men spend too much time indulging their libertine proclivities and not enough time policing their women, they enable monstrous females to poison the political sphere. Charles II must, *Love and Revenge* urges, reclaim his position of masculine authority and rescue the nation from feminine poison. The realm can yet be saved, but the monarch first must recognize the peril.

THE DEBAUCHED LIBERTINE AND THE FAILURE OF FEMALE REVENGE: SHADWELL'S *THE LIBERTINE*

At first glance, Elkanah Settle and Thomas Shadwell may seem an odd pairing, given Shadwell's vitriolic remarks about Settle both in *Notes and Observations on the Empress of Morocco* (1674) and in the preface to *The*

Libertine. Shadwell criticizes Settle for being a "rough hobbling rhymer" and roundly insults him as a dramatist: "some may write that in three weeks, which he cannot in three years."[98] Such vitriol stems at least in part from professional competition and Shadwell's apparent suspicion that Settle was poaching on his territory. After all, both *Love and Revenge* and *The Libertine* were written for the Duke's Company, and both are dedicated to William Cavendish, Duke of Newcastle.[99] While such a dedication may have been intended to shore up Settle's royalist credentials—Settle praises Newcastle's "Sacred principles of Honour, that . . . were thought fit to be precepts for an Heir to a Crown" (sig. a4r)—Shadwell clearly viewed that dedication as a professional discourtesy and a threat.[100] In many ways, however, Shadwell's *The Libertine* represents a companion piece to Settle's *Love and Revenge*. Like Settle, Shadwell invokes the memory of *Hamlet* and creates in his play another female avenger; unlike Settle, Shadwell proceeds to deconstruct that trope. Rather than becoming a source of social poison as in *Love and Revenge*, Shadwell's female avenger is powerless in the face of male libertine excess. As we shall see, societal disintegration here stems not from masculine impotence and feminine evil, but from debauched libertine excess and Catholicism.

The ghosts of murdered fathers pervade Settle's *Love and Revenge*, as the allusions to Shakespeare's *Hamlet* underscore the play's masculine failures. In Settle's play, however, it is the *idea* of ghosts that matters; unlike in *Hamlet*, no supernatural events actually occur onstage. Not so in Shadwell's *The Libertine*, where in act 2, Don John comes face to face with his father's ghost: "Repent, repent of all thy villainies," the ghost demands (2.3.84); "My clamorous blood to heaven for vengeance cries. / Heaven will pour out his judgements on you all" (2.3.85–86). While Clotair and Lewis abandon their duties to their father's memory, they do at least acknowledge that a responsibility exists. Don John, in contrast, disclaims any allegiance to his father, not because he is obsessed with love, but because he is himself his father's murderer: "Farewell; thou art a foolish ghost," he tells his father. "Repent, quoth he. What could this mean? Our senses are all in a mist sure" (2.3.92–93). Don Lopez concurs, calling the specter a "silly Ghost" and insisting that "I'll no sooner take his word than a whore's" (2.3.100–101). Despite Don John's initial similarities to Hamlet—early in the play, he describes "the fond fantastic thing, called conscience, / Which serves for nothing but to make men cowards" (1.1.4–5), echoing Hamlet's assertion that "conscience does make cowards of us all" (3.1.85)—Don John mocks his father's ghost, symbolizing his rejection of the entire system of patriarchal culture and inheritance.[101]

Because Don John is a murderer, there is no one left to avenge his father's death, reflecting the play's overwhelming lack of effective revengers. Octavio cannot avenge his dishonored love, Maria, since he is instantly killed by

Don John and his men. Nor can her brother offer succour, as he, too, is instantly defeated. "'Sdeath! A man in my sister's chamber! Have at you, villain" (1.2.11–12), the unnamed brother exclaims as Don John runs at him. "O villain, thou hast killed my brother, and dishonoured me," Maria cries with no help of rescue (1.2.15). Likewise, both Don Francisco, father to Clara and Flavia, and their respective unnamed fiancés fail to avenge their women and their own dishonor. Don Francisco attacks his daughters rather than the truly guilty Don John—"I will revenge my self on these" (4.1.187), he says—and then is almost instantly killed, while "the two Bridegrooms are hurt" in the scuffle (4.1.191). Even Don Pedro, Duke and father to the nation, goes to his grave unpunished. "I run him through the lungs as handsomely, and killed him as decently, and as like a gentleman as could be," Don John brags (1.1.108–10); "The jealous coxcomb deserved death; he kept his sister from me. Her eyes would have killed me if I had not enjoyed her, which I could not do without killing him" (1.1.110–12). Like Don John's father, the father to the nation finds no living champion, and his epitaph memorializes the fact that his death went unavenged: "Here lies Don Pedro, governor of Seville, barbarously murdered by that impious villain, Don John, 'gainst whom his innocent blood cries still for vengeance" (4.3.5–7). Don John disrupts both the system by which men protect their female relatives and the integrity of the nation-state; the system of masculine honor in the play is fatally broken by his libertine excess.

The inability of men to seek and achieve effective revenge stems at least in part from the failure of societal controls to police male behavior adequately. If Settle's play advocates that men regulate female desires and behavior, for Shadwell it is the men who must be restrained. To that end, Shadwell offers two competing definitions of "nature," one Hobbesian in construction and the other proto-Lockean.[102] The proto-Lockean view is best epitomized by the shepherds whose masque Don John interrupts and destroys. Living in Edenic bliss, the shepherds occupy a state of nature associated with pastoral innocence, a world that can be destroyed only by fallen "art."

> Second Nymph: In humble cottages we have such contents
> As uncorrupted nature does afford,
> Which the great, that surfeit under gilded roofs,
> And wanton in down beds, can never know.
> First Shepherd: Nature is here not yet debauched by art;
> 'Tis as it was in Saturn's happy days.
> Minds are not here by luxury invaded. (4.2.13–19)

Nature in this construction must be protected from corruption by the societal forces of organized religion and a repressive state, a position echoed by Maria in her lament against Don John. According to Maria, "More savage cruelty reigns in cities than ever yet in desarts among the most venomous serpents and remorseless ravenous beasts could once be found. So much has barbarous art debauched man's innocent nature" (2.2.36–40). Unfortunately, Maria's innocence, like that of the shepherds, cannot withstand the force of Don John's cruel and violent art. In Michael Alssid's words, "John literally silences forever the singer of traditional, romantic illusion."[103]

Contrasting with this viewpoint is the Hobbesian view advocated by Don John, in which human nature is driven by "the darkest extreme of libertinism," in essence, unrestricted id.[104] "Nature" in this construction must be restrained by the necessary mechanisms of church and state, here named "sense" and "rationality" and decried by Don John. The libertines complain,

> Don John: My business is pleasure: that end I will always compass, without scrupling the means. There is no right or wrong, but what conduces to, or hinders pleasure . . .
> Don Antonio: We live the life of sense, which no fantastic thing, called Reason, shall control.
> Don Lopez: My reason tells me I must please my sense.
> Don John: My appetites are all I'm sure I have from heaven, since they are natural; and them I always will obey. (1.1.124–26, 128–32)

Reason wars with the brutish concupiscence and violence of nature in its untouched form, revealing, as many critics have noted, the extremity and emptiness of the libertine ethos. In Aaron Jaffe's words, the play "unflinchingly excoriates both the social implications of libertine doctrines and practices and their misappropriation of Hobbesian ideas and language."[105] If the state protects the shepherds from violence, to Don John it offers nothing but unwelcome, unnatural, and unfair restraint.

In the end, it is Don John's view of nature that wins out; the shepherds' paradise is destroyed as the state fails in its duty to control and restrain the dark desires of the libertine id. Don Francisco privileges his duty to his guests over his duty as a magistrate, with fatal consequences for all concerned: "My house has been your sanctuary, and I am obliged in honour not to act as a magistrate, but your host. No violence shall here be offered to you" (4.1.157–59), he promises just before Don John destroys his household. The governor, too, is at fault, as he falls prey to his son's violent impulsivity. When Don Pedro's murder goes unavenged, it represents the unfortunate result of a society whose rulers have failed to govern and contain effectively and whose most virile members embrace the proto-Sadeian and orgiastic violence of nature rather than the social controls and safety of patriarchal governance. As Cynthia Lowenthal writes, the libertines descend into a world "composed of nothing but this kind of repetition, a numbing sameness of activity that never satisfies," and necessitates ever larger acts of violence.[106]

That the men fail in their duties as avengers necessitates, for Shadwell as for Settle, that women seek their own retribution. Shadwell's Maria parallels Settle's Chlotilda/Nigrello; both women are victims of rape, and both women have seen their loved ones brutally murdered in their quest for justice. Subsequently Maria, like Chlotilda, dresses as a man (albeit not one in blackface) in order to pursue justice: "I am ashamed of these soft tears, till I've revenged thy horrid murder" (2.2.21–22), she promises her dead lover, and tells Flora, "Inspired by my just rage this arm shall teach you wonders. I'll show you now what love with just revenge can do" (2.3.2–3). As in *Love and Revenge*, the existence of the female avenger reflects the failure of patriarchal structures. Maria must avenge Octavio, as there is no one left to avenge either her lover or her suffering. She laments, "the honour of mankind is gone with thee," and plans that "When I have revenged my dear Octavio's loss, I then shall die contented" (3.2.531, 533–34). For Settle, as we have seen, such a move is profoundly disconcerting, as it transforms the raped woman from innocent victim to poisonous monster. At first glance, Shadwell would seem to offer a similar view of the female avenger; after all, Maria uses vampiric imagery to describe her revenge, saying, "I will revel in his blood. O I could suck the last drop that warms the monster's heart" (2.2.23–24). Ultimately, however, Shadwell's play undermines dramatic expectations entirely. While Maria's story initially seems integral to the overarching plot, she is not strong enough to make a lasting impact on Don John. While the audience might expect her, perhaps along with Leonora, Don John's cast mistress, to engage in a final act showdown with the libertines, both women are unceremoniously killed just two acts later and long before the play's final denouement.[107] Maria announces dramatically, "This is the villain who killed the lover of Antonio's Sister, deflowred her, and murdered her Brother in his own house" (4.1.109–10). Receiving no support from Don Francisco, she cries out: Octavio's "ghost, and all the rest whom he has barbarously murdered, will interrupt your quiet. They'll haunt you in your sleep. Revenge, revenge!" (4.1.143–45). Unfortunately, her pleas go for naught, as she dies attempting to save Don Francisco and his daughters. Rather than portraying Maria as a source of toxin, it is Don John who becomes poisonous; he literally compels Leonora to drink from a poisoned cup, precipitating her death. "Y'have drunk the subtlest poison that Art e'r yet invented" (3.2.609–10), Don John tells Leonora. She responds, "Thou hast murdered the only creature living that could love thee" (3.2.614).

What *The Libertine* therefore traces is the failure of the Philomel narrative to achieve a lasting or significant revenge. Maria is not Fredigond or Chlotilda, and she does not represent a significant threat to the play's world. At the same time, the play dismisses out of hand the efficacy of the Lucrece narrative. For Settle, order can be restored only when Nigrello/Chlotilda commits suicide, that is to say, when dangerous Philomel can be reconfigured into unthreatening Lucrece. Shadwell, in contrast, never makes such a move. When Shadwell's women attempt to play the part of Lucrece, their efforts are either dismissed or ignored. In act 2, Don John complains that contemporary women are no longer interested in preserving their purity through suicide. "There's ne'er a Lucrece nowadays; the sex has learnt more wit since" (2.1.323–24), he says, echoing Cavalier poet Thomas Carew's vision in his poem "A Rapture" (published 1640). Carew imagines a perfect world, wherein

> The Roman Lucrece . . . reads the divine
> Lectures of love's great master, Aretine,
> And knows as well as Laïs how to move
> Her pliant body in the act of love.
> To quench the burning ravisher, she hurls
> Her limbs into a thousand winding curls,
> And studies artful postures.[108]

In a perfect state of nature, Carew suggests, a world without a restrictive concept of honor, even the chaste Lucrece would indulge sexually without shame. Don John likewise assumes that in his ideal state of nature, women would have no interest in restricting sexual expression or in refusing any man who wishes to sample their charms. He rejects the concepts of virtue and honor, insisting, "There's nothing good or ill, but as it seems to each man's natural appetite" (2.1.336–37). Of course, Don John's claims are undermined just six lines later, when a nameless woman stabs herself rather than submit to his assault: "No, monster; I'll prevent you" (2.1.343), she says as she dies. Unfortunately, her self-sacrifice is in vain; it has no effect on the libertines' behavior, nor does it motivate the crowd to action on her behalf. The nameless woman dies in an ethical vacuum where she, like Don John's numerous other victims, will finally go unavenged.

Lucrece fails. Philomel fails. And Don John's proto-Sadeian world finally descends into nihilism, where the only end point to his behavior is self-annihilation. He becomes the victim of his own excess, while the play denies its audience the comforting proof of effective social justice. In the end, moreover, his libertinism is linked with the dangers of Catholicism. In the final moments of Don John's life, the ghosts of his victims offer the libertines "four glasses full of blood" (5.2.47). The message is clear: the act of vampirism represents the culmination of all other bad acts, the true moment of no return. The Catholic Eucharist becomes the demonic black hole at the center of the play, an act so monstrous that even Don John recoils from it: "'Sdeath, do you mean to affront us," Don John demands as the libertines "throw the glasses down" (5.2.64, 63).[109] Unchecked hedonism leads directly to Catholicism and finally eternal damnation. Thus Shadwell's *The Libertine*, like Settle's *Love and Revenge* and Marvell's *The Last Instructions to a Painter*, offers a warning to the court to reform its excessive—and dangerously Catholic—ways before it is too late, before society is damaged beyond recognition and the courtiers can expect nothing but hellfire and destruction to result.

CONCLUSION: BEHN'S *THE ROVER, PART I* AND POLITICAL AMBIVALENCE ON THE EVE OF THE POPISH PLOT

The plays examined in this chapter all use images of rape to express their political opinions, and they become increasingly critical of the monarchy as the decade progresses. It is, however, Aphra Behn's *The Rover, Part I* (1677) that best encapsulates the political ambivalence of the period, at once idealizing and criticizing the court circle. One of the last plays to stage a rape attempt before the outbreak of the Popish Plot, *The Rover* has also received the most critical attention. While Behn was undoubtedly a Tory playwright, critics have split over her play's political message and the extent of her support for the royalist cause. Maureen Duffy, for instance, calls the play "her most outright and positive celebration of those cavalier childhood heroes," "good propaganda" for "rallying the faithful when the first romance of the king's return had worn thin and the country was again divided into factions."[110] Adam Beach likewise calls the play "Behn's most daring expression of Royalism"; the play "acknowledges concerns about the raging sexuality of the Stuart court," even as it encourages the viewer to treat libertine exploits with a "spirit of both carnival and forgiveness."[111] In Beach's reading, Hellena serves as the model "for the perfect Stuart subject, a person who is desperately attracted by the very outrageousness of Cavalier sexuality."[112] Ann Marie Stewart concurs: "Behn embraced not only Charles's politics, but also the romping sexual fun at the palace. . . . [H]er depiction of sexual licentiousness on the stage reflects her politics, particularly in a character like Willmore. Libertinism as a cultural movement was a sexual liberation for women and men."[113] Other critics, however, have read the play's scenes of sexual violence as a sustained criticism of the libertine ethos, a philosophy that fundamentally endangers the women it claims to liberate. Susan J. Owen calls the play "as profound a questioning of libertinism as is to be found in any other Restoration comedy,"[114] while for Dagny Boebel, Willmore and Blunt are ultimately indistinguishable in their acts of gendered violence: "Willmore and Blunt think and act in nearly identical ways. Behn's text . . . performs a carnivalesque displacement by exposing both Whigs and Tories, Puritans and Cavaliers, as upholders of a violent, hierarchical gender ideology."[115]

I am not interested in re-covering such well-trod ground here. Instead, I want to suggest that *The Rover*'s ambivalence toward Willmore, its simultaneous attraction to and repulsion from his behavior, combines both aspects of the political discourse examined in this chapter. Throughout the play, the Cavaliers are simultaneously lionized and demonized. Here is not, as in the case of Orrery and Howard, a full-scale defense of royalism, but rather a more measured response to the figure of the libertine courtier. On the one hand, Belville and Willmore are extremely attractive characters, dashing, brave, and loyal to their true king. Both have sacrificed position, estate, and homeland to follow Charles II to the continent. Belville in particular is reminiscent of Orrery's Lucidor, insofar as he is honorable in battle and chivalrous in his protection of Florinda, for which he won her love. Florinda explains, "I knew him at the siege of *Pamplona*, he was then a Colonel of *French* horse, who when the Town was Ransack't, Nobly treated my Brother and my self, preserving us from all Insolences; and I must own, (besides great Obligations) I have I know not what, that pleads kindly for him about my Heart, and will suffer no other to enter."[116] In these lines, Belville seemingly embodies the Lovelacian conception of Cavalier honor so prominent in Orrery's *The Generall*. By the same token, Blunt, the character who has most clearly rejected the political ethos of royalism, is hypocritical, rapacious, and sexually violent, perhaps a throwback to the anti-Roundhead plays of the early 1660s. Belville describes Blunt's character in harshly negative terms: He is "of an *English* Elder Brother's humour, Educated in a Nursery, with a Maid to tend him till Fifteen, and lyes with his Grandmother till he's of Age: one that knowes no pleasure beyond riding to the next Fair, or going up to *London* with his right Worshipful Father in Parliament-time" (1.2.268–73, 275–76). Blunt himself celebrates his lack of political honor, praising his own foresight in refusing to join with the Cavaliers and lose his estate: "Gentleman, You may be free, you have been kept so poor with Parliaments and Protectors, that the little Stock you have is not worth preserving—but I thank my Stars, I had more Grace than to forfeit my Estate by Cavaliering" (1.2.44–47). When he attacks Florinda, therefore, Blunt functions as another manifestation of the debauched Roundhead so common a decade earlier.

Behn, unlike Orrery, however, does not cleanly divide the honorable and romanticized characteristics of the Lovelacian Cavalier from the dishonorable characteristics of the Suckling libertine. Belville is the play's romantic hero, but he is perfectly happy to commit acts of senseless and gendered aggression, commenting offhandedly about his willingness to smash the windows of Angellica Bianca's house: "Are we to break her Windows?" he asks Willmore (3.1.85–86). Meanwhile, Willmore, the titular Rover, is both loyal to his king and disloyal to his female conquests.[117] He is attractive and witty but also sexually violent and lacking in morals. As Jonas DeRitter points out, his treatment of Florinda is actually identical to Blunt's: both assume that because she is not noble (or apparently a virgin), she must be available for sex, no matter her consent or lack thereof. He asks Florinda, "why at this time of Night was your Cobweb Door set open dear Spider—but to catch Flyes?" (3.5.160–61). Later, Blunt tells Florinda, "I will kiss and beat thee all over; kiss, and see thee all over; thou shalt lye with me too" (4.5.612–13), and is then joined by Frederick in an attempted gang rape. DeRitter calls the similarity "perhaps the most powerful criticism of Behn's title character."[118]

While Willmore's behavior never rises to the level of Don John's atrocity, Shadwell's play might have resonated in the minds of *The Rover's* audience; both plays feature a pair of sisters desperate to escape the patriarchal prison surrounding them (in Shadwell's case, Clara and Flavia seek sexual adventure apart from marriage, while Hellena seeks sexual adventure apart from the nunnery).[119] Clara's picture attracts Don John as Angellica Bianca's attracts Willmore. "Have you seen my picture?" Clara asks Don John (3.2.406). He responds, "And lov'd it above all things I ever saw, but the original" (3.2.407).[120] Similarly, when Willmore steals Angellica's portrait, he tells her, "I saw your Charming Picture and was wounded; quite through my Soul each pointed Beauty ran" (2.1.225–26).

Ultimately, Willmore is a more attractive version of Don John, one whose self-serving pursuit of more and greater pleasure is tamed and reabsorbed into the matrimonial economy. In Willmore, Behn offers her audiences a modified form of the debauched libertine; even as she romanticizes Cavalier behavior, she exposes the dark and frightening underside of the libertine ethos, refusing the comfortable division of good Cavaliering from bad "Cavilling" common ten years prior. What *The Rover* offers, then, is a qualified form of the warning underlying *Love and Revenge* and *The Libertine*. The court stands on the brink of a precipice: it must either reform, reincorporating itself back into the hierarchy of normative values, or risk oncoming destruction. As we shall see in the next chapter, however, the ambivalence and unease of the 1670s soon exploded into the intense fear and anger of the Popish Plot and Exclusion Crisis. Just a few months after the first performance of *The Rover, Part I*, depictions of sexually violent atrocity returned with a vengeance in both the propaganda and the drama, and this time without the comfort of a happy ending.

NOTES

1. Andrew Marvell, *The Last Instructions to a Painter*, in *The Poems and Letters of Andrew Marvell*, ed. H. M. Margoliouth, 2 vols. (Oxford: Clarendon Press, 1971), 2:147–72, ll. 743–50. Further references to *The Last Instructions to a Painter* are from this edition and will be cited parenthetically in the text by line number.

2. Warren L. Chernaik, *The Poet's Time: Politics and Religion in the Work of Andrew Marvell* (Cambridge: Cambridge University Press, 1983), 203.

3. Annabel M. Patterson points out that the "funds already granted" for naval upkeep "had not . . . been spent on the war, but on maintaining the court's luxury and debauchery": *Marvell and the Civic Crown* (Princeton: Princeton University Press, 1978), 159. For further historical background, see also Michael Seidel, *Satiric Inheritance: Rabelais to Sterne* (Princeton: Princeton University Press, 1979), 140.

4. Steven N. Zwicker, "Lines of Authority: Politics and Literary Culture in the Restoration," in *Politics of Discourse: The Literature and History of Seventeenth-Century England*, ed. Kevin Sharpe and Steven N. Zwicker (Berkeley: University of California Press, 1987), 245.

5. Zwicker, by contrast, does not read this figure as a rape victim, commenting instead on her "coldness": "Virgins and Whores: The Politics of Sexual Misconduct in the 1660s," in *The Political Identity of Andrew Marvell*, ed. Conal Condren and A. D. Cousins (Brookfield, VT: Scolar Press, 1990), 104. See also James Turner, who describes the "palpable frigidity of this Britannia-figure": "The Libertine Abject: The 'Postures' of *Last Instructions to a Painter*," in *Marvell and Liberty*, ed. Warren Chernaik and Martin Dzelzainis (New York: St. Martin's, 1999), 242.

6. Margarita Stocker, *Apocalyptic Marvell: The Second Coming in Seventeenth Century Poetry* (Athens: Ohio University Press, 1986), 172.

7. Barbara Riebling calls this encounter "a *de causibus* warning: change your ways or risk being killed by your people": "England Deflowered and Unmanned: The Sexual Image of Politics in Marvell's 'Last Instructions,'" *Studies in English Literature 1500–1900* 35 (1995): 152. For a similar reading, see A. D. Cousins, "The Idea of a 'Restoration' and the Verse Satires of Butler and Marvell," *Southern Review* 14, no. 2 (1981): 131–42.

8. John Wilmot, Earl of Rochester, "A Satyr on Charles II," in *Restoration Literature: An Anthology*, ed. Paul Hammond (Oxford: Oxford University Press, 2002), 38–39, ll.11–12.

9. Riebling, "England Deflowered," 142.

10. Zwicker, "Virgins," 97.

11. Riebling, "England Deflowered," 140.

12. Here I agree with Harold Weber that sexual desire represents a "potentially subversive force" that "generates the collapse of conventional hierarchies": *Paper Bullets: Print and Kingship under Charles II* (Lexington: University Press of Kentucky, 1996), 93–94.

13. See, for instance, William Fenner, *Four Select Sermons Upon Several Texts of Scripture* (London, 1668), and William Penn, *A Seasonable Caveat Against Popery* (London, 1670).

14. *A Relation Of The Most Material Matters handled In Parliament Relating To Religion, Property, And The Liberty Of The Subject* (Netherlands, 1673), 9. This pamphlet describes at length the parliamentary proceedings leading up to Charles II's abandonment of the Declaration of Indulgence in exchange for financial support for the war.

15. Steven C. A. Pincus, "From Butterboxes to Wooden Shoes: The Shift in English Popular Sentiment from Anti-Dutch to Anti-French in the 1670s," *Historical Journal* 38, no. 2 (1995): 335. For further analysis of the Second and Third Anglo-Dutch Wars, see also Alvin D. Coox, "The Dutch Invasion of England: 1667," *Military Affairs* 13, no. 4 (1949): 223–33; Susan Iwanisziw, "Tortured Bodies, Factionalism, and Unsettled Loyalties in Settle's Morocco Plays," in *Staging Pain, 1580–1800: Violence and Trauma in British Theater*, ed. James Robert Allard and Matthew R. Martin (Burlington: Ashgate, 2009), 111–36; Paul Seaward, "The House of Commons Committee of Trade and the Origins of the Second Anglo-Dutch War, 1664," *Historical Journal* 30, no. 2 (1987): 437–52; and Steven C. A. Pincus, "Popery, Trade and Universal Monarchy: The Ideological Context of the Outbreak of the Second Anglo-Dutch War," *English Historical Review* 107, no. 422 (1992): 1–29.

16. Pincus, "Butterboxes," 351.

17. "A Litany," in *Poems on Affairs of State: Augustan Satirical Verse, 1660–1714*, ed. George deF. Lord, 7 vols. (New Haven: Yale University Press, 1963), 1.190, ll. 1, 3.

18. John Dryden, *Amboyna, or the Cruelties of the Dutch to the English Merchants*, in *The Works of John Dryden*, ed. Vinton A. Dearing, 20 vols. (Berkeley: University of California Press, 1994), 12:1–79, prologue 5–8. Further references to *Amboyna* are from this edition and will be cited parenthetically in the text by act, scene, and line number.

19. For the earliest examples of Amboyna massacre tracts, see *Newes out of East India: Of the cruell and bloody usage of our English Merchants and others at Amboyna* (London, 1624); John Skinner, *A True Relation Of The Unjust, Cruell, And Barbarous Proceedings against the English at Amboyna In the East-Indies* (Saint-Omer, 1624); and Robert Wilkinson, *The Stripping of Ioseph, Or The crueltie of Bretheren to a Brother* (London, 1625).

20. *A True Relation of the Unjust, Cruel, and Barbarous Proceedings against the English at Amboyna In the East-Indies* (London, 1651), *4v.

21. Ibid., *5v–*6r.

22. For discussion of the English Commonwealth's relationship with the Dutch government, see Simon Groenveld, "The English Civil Wars as a Cause of the First Anglo-Dutch War, 1640–1652," *Historical Journal* 30, no. 3 (1987): 541–66. For discussion of the circumstances surrounding the First Dutch War, see Jonathan Israel, "Competing Cousins: Anglo-Dutch Trade Rivalry," *History Today* 38 (1988): 17–22, and J. E. Farnell, "The Navigation Act of 1651, the First Dutch War, and the London Merchant Community," *Economic History Review* 16, no. 3 (1964): 439–54. For discussion of military tactics during the Dutch Wars, see M. A. J. Palmer, "The 'Military Revolution' Afloat: The Era of the Anglo-Dutch Wars and the Transition to Modern Warfare at Sea," *War in History* 4, no. 2 (1997): 123–49.

23. *A Memento for Holland: Or A True and Exact History of the most Villainous and Barbarous Cruelties used on the English Merchants residing At Amboyna in the East-Indies* (London, 1652), 18.

24. Ibid., 19.

25. *A True and Compendious Narration; or (Second Part of Amboyney)* (London, 1665), a2r.

26. Ibid., 4.

27. *The Grand Abuses Stript and Whipt* (London, 1672), 1.

28. Robert Codrington, *His Majesties Propriety, And Dominion on the British Seas Asserted* (London, 1672), 138.

29. Ibid., 142.

30. Robert Markley, *The Far East and the English Imagination, 1600–1730* (Cambridge: Cambridge University Press, 2006), 159.

31. Shankar Raman, *Framing "India": The Colonial Imaginary in Early Modern Culture* (Stanford: Stanford University Press, 2002), 203.

32. For discussion of the genesis of the Black Legend, see Margaret R. Greer, Walter D. Mignolo, and Maureen Quilligan, eds., introduction to *Rereading the Black Legend: The Discourses of Religious and Racial Difference in the Renaissance Empires* (Chicago: University of Chicago Press, 2007), 2.

33. Philip Wayne Powell, *Tree of Hate: Propaganda and Prejudices Affecting United States Relations with the Hispanic World* (Albuquerque: University of New Mexico Press, 1971), 11. As Powell points out, the accuracy of the accounts that shape the Black Legend has been hotly debated. For further historical analysis, see Benjamin Keen, "The Black Legend Revisited: Assumptions and Realities," *Hispanic American Historical Review* 49, no. 4 (1969): 703–19.

34. Bartolomé de las Casas, *The Spanish Colonie, Or Briefe Chronicle of the Acts and gestes of the Spaniardes in the West Indies, called the newe World* (London, 1583), f1r.

35. Willem Baudartius, *Morghen-wecker der vrye Nederlantsche Provintien*, translated in Amanda Pipkin, "'They were not humans, but devils in human bodies': Depictions of Sexual Violence and Spanish Tyranny as a Means of Fostering Identity in the Dutch Republic," *Journal of Early Modern History* 13 (2009): 243.

36. Ibid.

37. Ibid.

38. For discussion of William's propaganda techniques, see René Van Stipriaan, "Words at War: The Early Years of William of Orange's Propaganda," *Journal of Early Modern History* 11, no. 4/5 (2007): 331. For historical analysis of the Dutch Revolt, see Peter J. Arnade, *Beggars, Iconoclasts, and Civic Patriots: The Political Culture of the Dutch Revolt* (Ithaca: Cornell University Press, 2008); Graham Darby, ed., *The Origins and Development of the Dutch Revolt* (New York: Routledge, 2004); Geoffrey Parker, "The Origins of the Dutch Revolt," *History Today* 34, no. 7 (1984): 17–21; and Herbert Rowan, "The Dutch Revolt: What Kind of Revolution?" *Renaissance Quarterly* 43, no. 3 (1990): 570–90.

39. George Gascoigne, *The Spoyle of Antwerp. Faithfully reported, by a true Englishman, who was present at the same* (London, 1576), c1v. For further analysis of Gascoigne's treatise, see Linda Bradley Salamon, "Gascoigne's Globe: *The Spoyle of Antwerp* and the Black Legend of Spain," *Early Modern Literary Studies* 14, no. 1, special issue 18 (2008): 7.1–38.

40. Bridget Orr, *Empire on the English Stage, 1660–1714* (Cambridge: Cambridge University Press, 2001), 158. For discussion of comparable tropes in plays of the New World, see also Markley, *The Far East*, and Heidi Hutner, *Colonial Women: Race and Culture in Stuart Drama* (Oxford: Oxford University Press, 2001).

41. By the time of Dryden's *Amboyna*, the Dutch had already restored William to power following the 1672 lynching deaths of Johan and Cornelis de Witt. Given that the English, too, had overthrown and restored a king, Dryden is condemning the Dutch for crimes the English perpetrated in their own country.

42. *A Gratulatory Poem*, 1.

43. William Lloyd, *Papists No Catholicks: And Popery No Christianity* (London, 1677), 5.

44. *A Letter From The Devil To The Pope And His Prelates* (London, 1670), 2.

45. *News from Rome* (London, 1680), 3. See also William Denton, *The Burnt Child dreads the Fire* (London, 1675); Henry Foulis, *The history Of Romish Treasons and Usurpation: Together With A Particular Account Of many gross Corruptions and Impostures In the Church of Rome* (London, 1671); and G. C., *Popish Plots And Treasons From the beginning of the Reign of Queen Elizabeth* (London, 1676).

46. *Speculum Papismi: Or, A Looking-Glass for Papists Wherein They may see their own sweet Faces* (Cambridge, 1669), i1r. For further references to the Irish massacre, see *Popery Absolutely Destructive to Monarchy* (London, 1673), and *A Short Memorial Of The Most Grievous Sufferings Of The Ministers Of The Protestant Churches In Hungary* (London, 1676), 2.

47. George Fox, *The Arraignment And Condemnation of Popery* (London, 1675), 167. Fox continues in this vein for five pages.

48. Ibid., 192.

49. Ibid., 6.

50. *A Passionate Satyr Upon a Devilish Great He-Whore That lives yonder at Rome* (London, 1675), 2.

51. *The Character of a Papist* (London, 1673), 4.

52. Ibid., 7–8.

53. *A Passionate Satyr*, 2.

54. A true Son, *A Catholick Pill*, 75.

55. John Ayloffe, "Britannia and Raleigh." in *Poems on Affairs of State: Augustan Satirical Verse, 1660–1714*, ed. George deF. Lord, 7 vols. (New Haven: Yale University Press, 1963), 1:228–36, ll. 25–30, 33–34. The poem provides a warning of future revolt should Charles's behavior continue unchecked. For further criticisms of Charles's mistresses, see "The King's Vows" in *Poems on Affairs of State: Augustan Satirical Verse, 1660–1714*, ed. George deF. Lord, 7 vols. (New Haven: Yale University Press, 1963), 1:159–62; "On the Prorogation," in *Poems on Affairs of State: Augustan Satirical Verse, 1660–1714*, ed. George deF. Lord, 7 vols. (New Haven: Yale University Press, 1963), 1:179–84; John Lacy, "Satire," in *Poems on Affairs of State: Augustan Satirical Verse, 1660–1714*, ed. George deF. Lord, 7 vols. (New Haven: Yale University Press, 1963), 1:425–28; and Andrew Marvell, "Upon his Majesty's being made Free of the City" in *Poems on Affairs of State: Augustan Satirical Verse, 1660–1714*, ed. George deF. Lord, 7 vols. (New Haven: Yale University Press, 1963), 1:237–42.

56. This is not to suggest that Henrietta Maria's exploits were entirely forgotten. *Popery Absolutely Destructive to Monarchy* reminds the reader that Henrietta Maria flouted English laws by praying for Catholic martyrs in England (*Popery Absolutely Destructive*, 112–13). Several years later, Andrew Marvell would blame Henrietta Maria for Charles II's initial alliance with the French and for the debacle of the Second Anglo-Dutch War: *An Account of the Growth Of Popery And Arbitrary Government in England* (Amsterdam, 1677).

57. For discussion of the royal mistresses' power at court, see James G. Turner, *Libertines and Radicals in Early Modern London: Sexuality, Politics, and Literary Culture, 1630–1685* (Cambridge: Cambridge University Press, 2002), and Sonya Wynne, "The Mistresses of Charles II and Restoration Court Politics," in *The Stuart Courts*, ed. Eveline Cruickshanks (Gloucestershire: Sutton, 2000), 171–90.

58. "The Royal Buss," in *Poems on Affairs of State: Augustan Satirical Verse, 1660–1714*, ed. George deF. Lord, 7 vols. (New Haven: Yale University Press, 1963), 1:263–5, ll. 65, 66, 23–28.

59. Derek Parker describes this famous anecdote as follows: "Driving through London streets crowded with merrymakers celebrating the anniversary of the accession of Queen Elizabeth I, [Gwyn] was booed under the impression that she was [the Duchess of Portsmouth], leaned out the window of her carriage, and shouted, 'Be still friends—I am the *Protestant* whore!'" *Nell Gwyn* (Gloucestershire: Sutton, 2000), 157.

60. "Nell Gwynne," in *Poems on Affairs of State: Augustan Satirical Verse, 1660–1714*, ed. George deF. Lord, 7 vols. (New Haven: Yale University Press, 1963), 1:420, ll. 1–6.

61. Marvell, *Account*, 43–44.

62. For discussion of licensing restrictions and the circulation of clandestine satire, see George deF. Lord, introduction to *Poems on Affairs of State: Augustan Satirical Verse, 1660–1714*, 7 vols. (New Haven: Yale University Press, 1963).

63. Edward Stephens, *Popish Policies and Practices Represented in the Histories of the Parisian Massacre; Gun-powder Treason; Conspiracies Against Queen Elizabeth And Persecutions Of The Protestants in France* (London, 1674), 21.

64. Ibid., 27.

65. Ibid., 49.

66. Ibid., 27.

67. *A Protestant Catechisme for Little Children, or Plain Scripture against Popery* (London, 1673), 14.

68. Gilbert Burnet, *The Mystery of Iniquity Unvailed* (London, 1673), 2.

69. Ibid., 24.

70. *News from Rome*, 5.

71. Eleanor Herman, *Mistress of the Vatican: The True Story of Olimpia Maidalchini: The Secret Female Pope* (New York: William Morrow, 2008), 71.

72. Michael Ott, "Pope Innocent X," in *The Catholic Encyclopedia* (New York: Robert Appleton, 1910), accessed April 20, 2011, http://www.newadvent.org/cathen/08020b.htm.

73. Alexander Cooke, *A Present for a Papist: Or The Life and Death Of Pope Joan* (London, 1675), a3v. For other mentions of Donna Olimpia, see *The Burning of the Whore of Babylon, As it was Acted, with great Applause* (London, 1673), 3.

74. Gregorio Leti, *The Life Of Donna Olimpia Maldachini, Who Governed the Church during the Time of Innocent the X* (London, 1666), 8.

75. Ibid., 25.

76. Ibid., 9.

77. Ibid., 69.

78. Ibid., 70.

79. Herman, *Mistress of the Vatican*, 325.

80. Ibid., 332.

81. Leti, *The Life Of Donna Olimpia Maldachini*, 13.

82. Ibid., 39–40.

83. Ibid., 45–46.

84. Herman, *Mistress of the Vatican*, 309.

85. Leti, *The Life Of Donna Olimpia Maldachini*, 43.

86. Heminge's frequent allusions to earlier plays have since earned him the reputation of a plagiarist. For criticisms of his work, see Joseph Quincy Adams Jr., "William Heminge and Shakespeare," *Modern Philology* 12, no. 1 (1914): 51–64; Fredson Thayer Bowers, "The Stabbing of a Portrait in Elizabethan Tragedy," *Modern Language Notes* 47, no. 6 (1932): 378–85; and Anne Hargrove, introduction to *The Fatal Contract*, by William Heminge (Kalamazoo: Medieval Institute Publications, 1978).

87. Elkanah Settle, *Love and Revenge: A Tragedy* (London, 1675), 5. Further references to *Love and Revenge* are from this edition and will be cited parenthetically in the text by page number.

88. William Heminge, *The Fatal Contract*, in *The Plays and Poems of William Heminge*, ed. Carol A. Morley (Madison: Farleigh Dickinson University Press, 2006), 303–89, 3.1.38–41. Further references to *The Fatal Contract* are from this edition and will be cited parenthetically in the text by act, scene, and line number. Settle changes the name of Clotair's brother from Clovis to Lewis.

89. William Shakespeare, *Hamlet*, in *The Norton Shakespeare*, ed. Stephen Greenblatt et al. (New York: Norton, 1997), 1659–2090, 1.5.102–4. Further references to *Hamlet* are from this edition and will be cited parenthetically in the text by act, scene, and line number.

90. In Anne Hermanson's words, "a sexually aggressive woman is an evil aberration of normal womankind and becomes infinitely more dangerous the more privileged her position": Anne Hermanson, "Monstrous Women in Aphra Behn's *Abdelazer* and Elkanah Settle's *The Empress of Morocco*," in *Aphra Behn (1640–1689): Le Modèle Européen*, ed. Mary Ann O'Donnell and Bernard Dhuicq (Entrevaux, France: Bilingua GA Editions, 2005), 31. Hermanson is writing of Settle's *The Empress of Morocco*, but her words are equally applicable to *Love and Revenge*.

91. Ibid., 30–31.

92. Elkanah Settle, *The Empress of Morocco. A Tragedy* (London, 1687), 47.

93. Carol A. Morley, introduction to *The Plays and Poems of William Heminge*, by William Heminge (Madison: Farleigh Dickinson University Press, 2006), 291.

94. Settle frequently excises Heminge's risqué jokes and acts of overt violence, changes that Morley attributes to his need to conform to the morality of the Restoration era (Ibid., 247).

95. Fredson Bowers, *Elizabethan Revenge Tragedy* (Princeton: Princeton University Press, 1940), 278.

96. Charles A. and Elaine S. Hallet, *The Revenger's Madness: A Study of Revenge Tragedy Motifs* (Lincoln: University of Nebraska Press, 1980), 11. Many critics have written on the treatment of revenge in Jacobean tragedy and on the revenger's tendency to become the thing he hates. See, for instance, Catherine Belsey, *The Subject of Tragedy: Identity and Difference in Renaissance Drama* (London: Methuen, 1985), and Anne Pippin Burnett, *Revenge in Attic and Later Tragedy* (Berkeley: University of California Press, 1998). For discussion of historical understandings of revenge and vengeance, see Ronald Broude, "Revenge and Revenge Tragedy in Renaissance England," *Renaissance Quarterly* 28, no. 1 (1975): 38–58, and Lily B. Campbell, "Theories of Revenge in Renaissance England," *Modern Philology* 28, no. 3 (1931): 281–96. For the relationship between revenge, politics, and theatricality, see Annalisa Castaldo, "'These were spectacles to please my soul': Inventive Violence in the Renaissance Revenge Tragedy," in *Staging Pain, 1580–1800: Violence and Trauma in British Theater*, ed. James Robert Allard and Matthew R. Martin (Burlington: Ashgate, 2009), 49–56, and Darryl Grantley, "Masques and Murderers: Dramatic Method and Ideology in Revenge Tragedy and the Court Masque," in *Jacobean Poetry and Prose: Rhetoric, Representation and the Popular Imagination*, ed. Clive Bloom (New York: St. Martin's, 1988), 194–212. For revenge tragedy as a response to Reformation changes in religious and funereal customs, see Thomas P. Anderson, *Performing Early Modern Trauma from Shakespeare to Milton* (Burlington: Ashgate, 2006); Huston Diehl, *Staging Reform, Reforming the Stage: Protestantism and Popular Theater in Early Modern England* (Ithaca: Cornell University Press, 1997); Thomas Rist, "Religion, Politics, Revenge: The Dead in Renaissance Drama," *Early Modern Literary Studies* 9, no. 1 (2003): 1–20; and Thomas Rist, *Revenge Tragedy and the Drama of Commemoration in Reforming England* (Burlington: Ashgate, 2008). For revenge tragedy as a response to Elizabethan and Jacobean politics, see Eileen Allman, *Jacobean Revenge Tragedy and the Politics of Virtue* (Newark: University of Delaware Press, 1999), and Stephen Mullaney, "Mourning and Misogyny: *Hamlet*, *The Revenger's Tragedy*, and the Final Progress of Elizabeth I," *Shakespeare Quarterly* 45, no. 2 (1994): 139–62.

97. Thomas Middleton, *The Revenger's Tragedy*, in *English Renaissance Drama: A Norton Anthology*, ed. David Bevington et al. (New York: Norton, 2002), 1297–1370, 3.5.203–5.

98. Thomas Shadwell, *The Libertine*, in *Four Restoration Libertine Plays*, ed. Deborah Payne Fisk (Oxford: Oxford University Press, 2005), 1–85, preface, ll. 30, 34–35. Further references to *The Libertine* are from this edition and will be cited parenthetically in the text by act, scene, and line number.

99. F. C. Brown attributes Shadwell's attack to professional jealousy over the success of Settle's *The Empress of Morocco*: *Elkanah Settle: His Life and Works* (Chicago: University of Chicago Press, 1910), 12–13. Given that Settle was "one of the most commercially successful dramatists of the 1670s," professional jealousy is certainly not implausible: Don-John Dugas, "Elkanah Settle, John Crowne and Nahum Tate," in *A Companion to Restoration Drama*, ed. Susan J. Owen (Malden: Blackwell, 2001), 378. For a discussion of Dryden's role in creating the *Notes and Observations*, see also Roswell G. Ham, "Dryden versus Settle," *Modern Philology* 25, no. 4 (1928): 409–16, and Anne Doyle, "Dryden's Authorship of *Notes and Observations on the Empress of Morocco* (1674)," *Studies in English Literature 1500–1900* 6, no. 3 (1966): 421–45. For discussion of Settle's response to such attacks, see Maximillian E. Novak, introduction to *The Empress of Morocco and Its Critics*, by Elkanah Settle (Berkeley: Augustan Reprint Society, 1968).

100. For discussion of the relationship between Shadwell and his patrons, see Harold Love, "Shadwell, Flecknoe and the Duke of Newcastle: An Impetus for *MacFlecknoe*," *Papers on Language and Literature* 21, no. 1 (1985): 19–27, and Harold Love, "Shadwell, Rochester, and the Crisis of Amateurism," *Restoration* 20, no. 2 (1996): 119–34.

101. Don John's pleasures are forbidden by all aspects of the patriarchal authority system. In Oscar Mandel's words, "Don Juan the sensualist does find himself opposed, not only by injured fathers, husbands, and fiancés, but by the Law and God": *The Theatre of Don Juan: A Collection of Plays and Views, 1630–1963* (Lincoln: University of Nebraska Press, 1963), 18. As such, he works to destroy the system that would restrict him.

102. For further discussion of the Hobbesian elements of Shadwell's *The Libertine*, see Helen Pellegrin, introduction to *Thomas Shadwell's The Libertine: A Critical Edition* (New York and London: Garland, 1987); Raman Selden, "Rochester and Shadwell," in *Spirit of Wit: Reconsiderations of Rochester*, ed. Jeremy Treglown (Oxford: Basil Blackwell, 1982); Thomas B. Stroub, "Shadwell's Use of Hobbes," *Studies in Philology* 35, no. 3 (1938): 405–32; Dale Underwood, *Etherege and the Seventeenth-Century Comedy of Manners* (New Haven: Yale University Press, 1957); and Christopher J. Wheatley, *Without God or Reason: The Plays of Thomas Shadwell and Secular Ethics in the Restoration* (Lewisburg: Bucknell University Press, 1993).

103. Michael Alssid, *Thomas Shadwell* (New York: Twayne, 1967), 126. See also H. Gaston Hall, who suggests that in destroying the shepherds' paradise, Don John undermines conceptions of both the pastoral ideal and chivalric masculinity: "Dom Juan: Personnage Europeen Du XVIIe Siecle," in *Horizons européens de la literature française au XVIIe siècle*, ed. Wolfgang Leiner (Tübingen: Narr, 1988), 139–47.

104. Alssid, *Thomas Shadwell*, 108.

105. Aaron Jaffe, "Seditious Appetites and Creeds: Shadwell's Libertines and Hobbes's Foole," *Restoration* 24, no. 2 (2002): 56. For a similar reading, see Robert D. Hume, who suggests that Don John's bad acts depict libertine philosophy in its most outrageous and exaggerated form: *The Rakish Stage: Studies in English Drama, 1660–1800* (Carbondale: Southern Illinois University Press, 1983), 174. In such a world, "Chaos, the ultimate seventeenth-century horror, would reign": Arthur Gerwirtz, *Restoration Adaptations of Early 17th Century Comedies* (Washington, DC: University Press of America, 1982), 88.

106. Cynthia Lowenthal, *Performing Identities on the Restoration Stage* (Carbondale: Southern Illinois University Press, 2003), 160.

107. The extreme and senseless violence of *The Libertine* has led multiple critics to treat the play as a comedy rather than a serious tragedy. See, for instance, Laura Brown, *English Dramatic Form, 1660–1760: An Essay in Generic History* (New Haven: Yale University Press, 1981); Robert D. Hume, *The Development of English Drama in the Late Seventeenth Century* (Oxford: Clarendon Press, 1976); and Don R. Kunz, *The Drama of Thomas Shadwell* (Salzburg: Institut Für Englische Sprache Und Literatur, 1972). Ian Spink calls the play a "burlesque": "Purcell's Music for 'The Libertine,'" *Music and Letters* 81, no. 4 (2000): 522. Meanwhile, Rose Zimbardo comments on the bleakness of "the total vision of the play": *A Mirror to Nature: Transformations in Drama and Aesthetics, 1660–1732* (Lexington: University Press of Kentucky, 1986), 125.

108. Thomas Carew, "A Rapture," in *The Norton Anthology of English Literature*, 8th ed., ed. Stephen Greenblatt et al., 2 vols. (New York: Norton, 2006), 1:1672–75, ll. 115–18.

109. Writing of Jacobean revenge tragedies, Huston Diehl explains, "By confronting their readers with the violent, grotesque, and absurd implications of transubstantiation, [authors] aggressively seek to denaturalize Roman Catholic beliefs in the nature and efficacy of the Mass" (Diehl, *Staging Reform*, 114). Shadwell, too, renders such beliefs ridiculous and, with Don John's demise, moves beyond ludicrousness to monstrosity.

110. Maureen Duffy, *The Passionate Shepherdess: Aphra Behn, 1640–89* (London: Jonathan Cape, 1977), 153.

111. Adam R. Beach, "Carnival Politics, Generous Satire, and Nationalist Spectacle in Behn's *The Rover*," *Eighteenth-Century Life* 28, no. 3 (2004): 2, 3.

112. Ibid., 7.

113. Ann Marie Stewart, "Rape, Patriarchy, and the Libertine Ethos: The Function of Sexual Violence in Aphra Behn's 'The Golden Age' and *The Rover, Part I*," *Restoration and Eighteenth-Century Theatre Research* 12, no. 2 (1997): 26–27. For similarly positive readings of Behn's politics, see Nancy Copeland, *Staging Gender in Behn and Centlivre* (Burlington: Ashgate, 2004); Janet Todd, *The Sign of Angellica: Women, Writing and Fiction, 1660–1800* (New York: Columbia University Press, 1989); and Melinda Zook, "Contextualizing Aphra Behn: Plays, Politics, and Party, 1679–1689," in *Women Writers and the Early Modern British Political Tradition*, ed. Hilda Smith (Cambridge: Cambridge University Press, 1998), 73–93.

114. Susan J. Owen, "'Suspect my loyalty when I lose my virtue': Sexual Politics and Party in Aphra Behn's Plays of the Exclusion Crisis, 1678–83," in *Aphra Behn*, ed. Janet Todd (New York: St. Martin's, 1999), 62. Owen also discusses Behn's ambivalence to Willmore and libertinism in two later works: "Drink, Sex and Power in Restoration Comedy," in *A Pleasing Sinne: Drink and Conviviality in Seventeenth-Century England*, ed. Adam Smyth (Rochester: D.S. Brewer, 2004), 127–39, and *Perspectives on Restoration Drama* (Manchester: Manchester University Press, 2002). For other critical views of Willmore, see Turner, *Libertines and Radicals*, and Anita Pacheco, "Rape and the Female Subject in Aphra Behn's 'The Rover,'" *ELH* 65, no. 2 (1998): 323–45.

115. Dagny Boebel, "In the Carnival World of Adam's Garden: Roving and Rape in Behn's *Rover*," in *Broken Boundaries: Women & Feminism in Restoration Drama*, ed. Katherine Quinsey (Lexington: University Press of Kentucky, 1996), 59.

116. Aphra Behn, *The Rover, Part I*, in *The Works of Aphra Behn*, ed. Janet Todd, 7 vols. (Columbus: Ohio State University Press, 1995), 5:445–521, 1.1.45–49. Further references to *The Rover, Part I* are from this edition and will be cited parenthetically in the text by act, scene, and line number. The threat of rape underlies this passage. Although Florinda's town was ransacked, Belville kept her person safe, likely protecting her from the sorts of sexual violence that accompany political defeat in plays like *The Generall*. That Florinda says she will "suffer no other to enter" also has sexual resonance; she will not let men other than Belville invade her body as they did her town.

117. As Jacqueline Pearson points out, to behave as a libertine is a political act, demonstrating allegiance to the court faction. See Jacqueline Pearson, *The Prostituted Muse: Images of Women & Women Dramatists, 1642–1737* (New York: St. Martin's, 1988), 152.

118. Jonas DeRitter, "The Gypsy, *The Rover*, and the Wanderer: Aphra Behn's Revision of Thomas Killigrew," *Restoration* 10, no. 2 (1986): 84, 86.

119. See also Kaufman, who uses Don John to offset Willmore: Anthony Kaufman, "'The Perils of Florinda': Aphra Behn, Rape, and the Subversion of Libertinism in *The Rover*, Part I," *Restoration and Eighteenth-Century Theatre Research* 11, no. 2 (1996): 13–14.

120. Don John would doubtless have been attracted to Clara and Flavia without the added enticement of either beauty or a painted advertisement, given that they are (a) female and (b) engaged to be married. The use of the painting as advertisement, however, is explored in much greater detail in both *The Rover* and its source play, Thomas Killigrew's *Thomaso*. For discussion of Aphra Behn's revisions of Killigrew's *Thomaso*, see DeRitter, "The Gypsy," and Todd, *The Sign of Angellica*. For discussion of the relationship between portraiture, commodification, and female sexuality, see Ashley Brookner Bender, "Moving Miniatures and Circulating Bodies in Aphra Behn's *The Rover*," *Restoration* 31, no. 1 (2007): 27–46; Nancy Copeland, "'Once

a Whore and Ever'? Whore and Virgin in *The Rover* and Its Antecedents," in *Early Women Writers: 1660–1720*, ed. Anita Pacheco (London: Longman, 1998), 149–59; and Elin Diamond, "*Gestus* and Signature in Aphra Behn's *The Rover*," in *Early Women Writers: 1660–1720*, ed. Anita Pacheco (London: Longman, 1998), 160–82.

Chapter Three

Lucrece Narratives: Rochester, Lee, and the Ethics of Regicide

On December 7, 1683, Algernon Sidney was beheaded for treason. During his arrest for participation in the Rye House Plot, authorities discovered a copy of his unfinished manuscript, *Discourses concerning Government*. An answer to Sir Robert Filmer's *Patriarcha: Or The Natural Power Of Kings* (1680), the *Discourses* argues on behalf of contractual monarchy and insists that the people have the right to overthrow a tyrannical king.[1] Throughout the text, Sidney makes repeated reference to the story of Lucrece, using Tarquin as a classical example of a king who earned his overthrow. Tarquin, Sidney writes, "by his insolence, avarice and cruelty, brought ruin upon himself and his family."[2] Tyrannical monarchs corrupt their people; through "the violence of tyranny all good order was overthrown, good discipline extinguished, and the people corrupted," leaving the Romans no choice but to "recove[r] their liberty by expelling Tarquin."[3] Indeed, in the case of such a ruler, the people have a responsibility to rebel:

> When Hannibal was at the gates, or any other imminent danger threatened them with destruction; if that magistrate had been drunk, mad, or gained by the enemy, no wise man can think that formalities were to have been observed. In such cases every man is a magistrate; and he who best knows the danger, and the means of preventing it, has a right of calling the senate or people to an assembly. The people would, and certainly ought to follow him, as they did Brutus and Valerius against Tarquin.[4]

For Sidney, the rape of Lucrece offers a powerful example of the negative effects of monarchical tyranny, while the tale of Tarquin's overthrow functions as a medium for negotiating conflicting political and social philosophies.

Other writings of the period also use the rape of Lucrece to justify monarchical deposition. The author of *Sir Edmund Berry Godfrey's Ghost* (1679), for instance, suggests that a monarch led astray by Catholic priests and mistresses would ultimately earn the same fate as Tarquin. The ghostly speaker accuses the court of being "with luxury o'ergrown," and condemns Charles II for his fondness for the Duchess of Portsmouth: "Each night you lodge in that French siren's arms, / She straight betrays you with her wanton charms . . . / Imperial lust does o'er your scepter sway, / And, though a sov'reign, makes you obey."[5] Recalling the ending of Marvell's *The Last Instructions to a Painter,* the poem suggests that the presence of Catholic mistresses, courtiers, and priests has poisoned the royal court and turned the king into a lecherous and sexually violent tyrant. The author then compares Charles II to Tarquin, reminding the Stuart monarch of his precursor's demise.

> Rome ne'er to such a glorious state had grown
> Had not luxurious Tarquin there been known;
> A single rape was deem'd such a disgrace
> They extirpate his odious name and race
> Though he from Tuscan Kings did succour crave,
> Yet they with arms pursu'd him to his grave.[6]

The poem concludes with a warning to Charles, instructing him to banish his priests and change his sexual behavior or risk becoming a hated English Tarquin:

> Trust not in prelates' false divinity,
> Who wrong their princes, shame their deity . . .
> Repent in time and banish from your sight
> The pimp, the whore, buffoon, Church parasite;
> Let innocence deck your remaining days
> That after ages may unfold your praise.[7]

If Charles II continues in his current ways, he will license his overthrow, as did Tarquin before him.

Depictions of rape as a justification for political revolt would become, as we shall see in chapter 5, much more common in the aftermath of the Glorious Revolution. Speaking of theater of the 1690s, Derek Hughes writes, "Rape was now a justification of extreme political action: a means of focusing attention on the supremacy of private rights over tyrannical power, even when wielded by a legitimate, hereditary monarch."[8] In the early 1680s, however, such sentiments were both rare and dangerous; Sidney was executed at least in part for the ideas expressed in his *Discourses*. Instead, allusions to Lucrece were more often employed by proponents of divine right ideology to protest the idea of contractual monarchy and to discredit the concept of democratic government. Sir Robert Filmer, for instance, does not deny in his *Patriarcha* that what happened to Lucrece was horrible, but he argues that her death did not create a right to rebel. In the case of uprisings against "the insolencies of tyrants," Filmer argues that republicans "propound a remedy far worse than the disease."[9] The people cannot be trusted with self-governance, and Filmer is quick to point out that the rape of Lucrece did not actually lead to democracy. Contrasting the experience of the Athenians, who, "for the love of their Codrus changed their government" with that of the Romans, who rebelled "out of Hatred to their Tarquin," Filmer points out that "neither of them thought it fit to change their state into a democracy."[10] Civil wars, he claims, are not "occasioned by the tyranny of any prince," but by "the wantonness of the people."[11] Monarchical overreach in the private sphere does not license political rebellion.

The conflict between Sidney's treatment of the Lucrece myth and Filmer's reflects both the central political conflict of the day and the continued contemporary resonance of that story. The pathos-laden tale of Lucrece's painful violation and subsequent tragic death offered a powerful corrective to the concept of unchecked sovereign authority, privileging personal autonomy and the rights of the individual over the fulfillment of libertine monarchical desires. Tory authors thus attempted to counter the overwhelming emotional power of the Lucrece narrative in several ways. One pseudonymous author, H. P., attempted to discredit Lucrece sexually, insinuating that she invited the "rape" and only committed suicide when her plan to gain political power fell through:

> *Lucrece* the Chast, the Fair, of Noble blood
> Would not be buss'd for all that's good,
> She would not truckle to her Loves decree,
> She would not kiss, poor heart, not she.
> Bravely the Noble *Doxy* strove,
> Though at last forc'd to pay her Tax of Love.
> When the lascivious Scene was Done,
> And the Slut saw she was not made a Queen,
> She tore her Hair and dainty Quoif,
> With a sharp Ponyard ended all the strife,
> And quickly did the little job of life.[12]

Collatine, meanwhile, is not a wronged husband seeking justice for his wife, but a jealous dupe:

> A Snivelling Peer that lov'd his Spouse too well,
> Rather than be a Cuckold would rebell;
> For's Country's sake he thought it was no sin:

For well knew he
That Petticoat and Property
With the same Letters did begin.[13]

While such sordid actions do not inherently warrant rebellion, the common people, those "*Roman* Bullies," seize any opportunity to rise up, an experiment with democracy that fails:

For this the *Roman* Bullies seiz'd his Crown,
For this they threw the mighty Lecher down,
And in his stead two Consuls fill'd the Chair,
Almanack Kings that lasted by a Year:
They and their Senate all reform'd anew
From Cit and Bumkin to the Nobler Crew.
The Alphabet it self was crost,
The Letters that made *Rex* were lost
And *S. P. Q.* did Rule the Roast;
At last their Civil Wars made such a stir,
They were forc'd to accept the Kingly Power
A Monarch of three Syllables an Emperour.[14]

H. P. rewrites the story of Lucrece to undermine the heroism of all involved. Tarquin is still a violent lecher, but his violence is encouraged by a power-hungry Lucrece who is all too willing to cuckold her husband in exchange for power. Collatine is an uxorious fool who would rather cry rape than acknowledge his own social humiliation. And the political revolution fostered by the rape is itself a failure, as the incapable republican government is quickly replaced by the more stable empire.

Other Tory tracts discredit the story of Lucrece by linking the rebellion against Tarquin with the Roundhead rebellion against Charles I. According to the Nonconformist speaker of "A Summons from a True Protestant Conjurer to Cethegus' Ghost, To Appear September 19, 1682" (1682),

Brutus was brave, and his impulse divine,
When first from Rome he chas'd the royal line;
And something like't we did, ere forty-nine.
But those blest reformation days soon pass'd,
And Charles' return our blooming hopes did blast.[15]

To praise the rebellion under Brutus is intellectually to ally with the Roundheads who martyred their innocent king. Conversely, underlying the Tory dismissal of the Lucrece narrative is the suggestion that to depose a seated monarch is a uniquely Catholic practice. As we have already seen, numerous anti-Catholic tracts of the early 1670s offered a roster of monarchs unseated by Catholic treachery. Tracts of the late 1670s and early 1680s frequently followed suit, depicting the Jesuits as proponents of contractual monarchy. The Jesuit speaker of *A Popish Political Catechism* (c. 1685), for instance, argues that a "Magistrate by his Miscarriages abdicates himself from being a

Magistrate, and proves a Robber instead of a Defender."[16] He goes on to define a tyrant as one who "rules tyrannically, converting all things to his own use, while he contemns and neglects the publick good, afflicts his Subjects contrary to Law, spoiling them of their Goods, robbing them of their Lives, or perverting them in their Religion."[17] In the case of a tyrant, the Jesuit speaker argues, the people are absolved of their oaths and have the right (and indeed the responsibility) to overthrow their king. The rape of Lucrece, he goes on to claim, provides a sufficient and just reason to depose Tarquin: "By what Authority did Rome abrogate the Authority of Tarquin, and drove him, his Wife and Children into Banishment? Tarquin's Invasion of the Bed of Collatinus gave a sufficiently just Cause."[18] The pamphlet thus aligns the rhetoric of contractual monarchy, the rhetoric of Sidney's *Discourses*, with Catholic treachery.

The battle between those who would affirm the divine power of hereditary monarchy and those who would establish limits to monarchical power unfolded through contemporary treatments of the Lucrece myth. A similar set of conflicts also appears in the drama of the period, as authors use Lucrece narratives to negotiate reactions to the events of the Popish Plot and Exclusion Crisis. This chapter takes as its focus John Wilmot, Earl of Rochester's *The Tragedy of Valentinian* (performed in 1684 but written much earlier) and Nathaniel Lee's *Lucius Junius Brutus* (1680), two plays that recreate the story of Lucrece in markedly different ways and mirror the conflict between Sidney's treatment of the myth and Filmer's. Rochester's *Valentinian* strongly implies that the rape of Lucina provides sufficient justification for regime change; acts of sexual violence offer, to return to Hughes's phrase, "a justification of extreme political action."[19] In contrast, *Lucius Junius Brutus* is highly suspicious of Brutus's rise to power; Brutus's political success is predicated on the effacement of Lucrece's memory, while the actions of his republican conspirators are as violent as those of the royalists. Monarchical overthrow does not heal the realm and may indeed lead to even worse forms of societal oppression, suggesting that acts of sexual violence do not necessarily excuse acts of political violence.

At the same time, Rochester and Lee are both interested in the process of propaganda making on a metatheatrical level and, in particular, in the place of the Lucrece story in the broader realm of political rhetoric. The late 1670s and 1680s saw a resurgence of sexually violent pamphlets, as authors demonized Catholics, defended their king, or warned against the miseries of renewed civil war. Female bodies are sacrificed in these tracts to broader political and social ends, natural bodies becoming victims of the need for change in the body politic. Authored in such an atmosphere, *Valentinian* and *Lucius Junius Brutus* both trace the development of the propagandist who traffics in atrocity to effect political change. While vastly different characters on the surface—one a ravished innocent, the other a feigned madman—both

Rochester's Lucina and Lee's Brutus recognize the political power of sexually violent imagery, and each harnesses that force to foster rebellion. Disempowered sexually by Valentinian's superior physical strength, Lucina reasserts herself as a political martyr in the aftermath of her rape. Lucina becomes Lucrece through her suicide, killing herself into spectacle because she knows that her death will destroy Valentinian's perceived authority. Meanwhile Brutus rises to power through his canny exploitation of rape imagery, manipulating the memory of Lucrece to gather support for his rebellion. The propagandist's treatment of the Lucrece story thereby reveals the author's political intentions. As Lucina is a sympathetic victim-propagandist, *Valentinian* supports the overthrow of the corrupt king. Lee's Brutus, in contrast, like his new government, is devious, opportunistic, and corrupt. Taken together, then, what *Valentinian* and *Lucius Junius Brutus* offer is a meditation on the nature and ethics of sexually violent propaganda, along with an extended exploration of the limits of monarchical authority.

ROCHESTER'S *VALENTINIAN* AND THE LIMITS OF MONARCHICAL AUTHORITY

Scholars have been unable to establish conclusively the authorial history of Rochester's *Valentinian*. Probably written in the late 1670s before illness restricted Rochester's activities—James William Johnson, Rochester's modern biographer, dates Rochester's initial decision to revise Fletcher's *Valentinian* to 1676—the play was later edited for publication by unknown hands and finally performed in 1684, four years after Rochester's death.[20] Like many plays of the period, Rochester's tragedy comments on contemporary politics. Critics have, for instance, frequently linked the Emperor Valentinian's sexual excess with Charles II's. According to J. Harold Wilson, "the poet intended Valentinian as a portrait of Charles II" while "his own personality was reflected in the character of Maximus, the philosophical-minded favorite of the Roman emperor."[21] Larry Carver concurs, writing that the emperor was "evidently meant to be a satirical portrait of Charles II."[22] Harold Love, in contrast, takes a more measured approach to the parallel, suggesting that Valentinian is not a direct "portrait of Charles II or of James, though there might be a kind of veiled hint of what things would be like if James ever became king. What Valentinian and Charles had in common was an insatiable appetite for sex; but Charles was not, as far as is known, a sadist or a rapist, nor was he bisexual."[23]

Whatever Rochester's actual intent, the play was authored in an era of great political contention, begun after the Duke of York's public conversion, revised amid the turmoil of the Popish Plot, and performed after the resolution of the Exclusion Crisis. Throughout the play, Rochester analyzes the rhetorical structure of political conflict and negotiates the relationship between private language and individual morality, private language and political action. As we have seen, seditious speech could represent a real and present threat to a sitting monarch; rumors and innuendo about a king's personal failings, coupled with criticisms of governmental policy, could undermine a regime in dangerously pressing ways. Charles II himself was clearly aware of the dangers of unfettered speech, first passing the Licensing of the Press Act in 1662 and, ten years later, ordering the suppression of seditious talk. According to a 1672 proclamation, "great and heavy Penalties are Inflicted upon all such as shall be found to be spreaders of false News, or promoters of any Malicious Slanders and Calumnies in their ordinary and common Discourses."[24] Seditious words, Charles complains, "Incite and Stir up the People to hatred or dislike of the Person of his Majesty, or the Establisht Government," and therefore must be banished from the realm.[25] Underlying such a proclamation is the belief that negative political speech may poison the individual subject against his monarch, a view proffered in Rochester's *Valentinian* by the Roman general Aecius. Acutely aware of the political danger posed by seditious language, Aecius uses the rhetoric of contagion to describe the social impact of antimonarchical propaganda. The "exponent of divine right in the play," Aecius abhors even the suggestion of punishing the emperor's bad acts.[26] To Aecius, disloyal words are equivalent to treasonous deeds; hence he arrests Pontius for speaking seditiously. Maximus initially defends Pontius to his friend, asking Aecius to "Pray consider what certaine ground you have" (4.1.23–24). Aecius responds,

> What Grounds?
> Did I not take him preaching to the Souldiers
> How lazyly they liv'd, and what dishonour
> It was, to serve a Prince so full of Softness!
> These were his very words Sir. (4.1.24–28)

Pontius's words, not his deeds, are his crime, and Aecius has caught him in the act of (speaking) treason. The danger, of course, is that Pontius's discontent will spread among the troops and thereby grow into full-scale rebellion. Pontius, he claims, is one "whose infection / Has spread it self like poyson through the Army / And cast a killing Fogg on fair allegeance!" (4.1.43–45). Political dissension in this construction is an infection and a poison, a contagious miasma that destroys the listener's civic virtue.

Pontius's words condemn him—"All your language / Makes but against you Pontius" (4.1.97–98), Aecius insists. Such is his preoccupation with dangerous language that Aecius forces Maximus, too, to proclaim his linguistic innocence—"I soe [sic] no danger in my words" (1.1.79), Maximus promises, despite his disdain for Valentinian's policies and actions. Later, when

Maximus does attempt to rebel, Aecius refers to his former friend as "that lost Wretch / Whose breast is poyson'd with soe vile a purpose" (5.1.9–10); the desire for rebellion is reimagined as a species of toxin. Simultaneously, however, Aecius believes that foul and infectious words have corrupted the emperor, turning him away from his duty to the kingdom. When Proculus succeeds in turning Valentinian against Aecius, his most faithful friend and ally, Aecius threatens Proculus:

> Look to't, when ere I draw this sword to punish
> You and your grinning Crew will tremble, Slaves,
> Nor shall the Ruin'd World afford a corner
> To shelter you, nor that poor Princes Bosome,
> You have invennom'd and polluted soe. (5.1.44–48)

Aecius imaginatively transforms Proculus's words, like Pontius's, into an insidious infection. To hear bad language is to invite corruption, the same fear underlying the treatment of Catholic mistresses and advisors in contemporary anti-Catholic discourse. Just as the Catholic religion may "disperse / Into weak Souls [its] poisonous influence," antimonarchical ideologies may disease both the army and the populace.[27]

The language of contagion, applied by Aecius to the political sphere, is also applied to what at first appears to be a very private battle of wills between Lucina and Valentinian. From the beginning of the text, the pair is locked in a battle for sexual supremacy that is also, by extension, linguistic. Just as Aecius believes that ill speech can corrupt politically, Valentinian hopes that he can use seductive and pernicious language to destroy Lucina's virtue and convince her to succumb. Thus Lucina is constantly importuned, not only by Valentinian, but also by his bawds and their wives, whose express purpose is to tempt Lucina into sexual transgression. Grown sick of their promises and threats, Lucina exclaims against their poisonous speech. "Tempt me no more," she insists to Phorba:

> If any of your Ancesters
> Dyed worth a Noble deed—that would bee cherished—
> Soul-frighted with this black infection,
> You would run from one another to Repentance
> And from your guilty eyes drop out those Sins
> That made ye blinde and Beasts. (2.1.52–57)

Like Aecius, Lucina perceives of language as an infection—in her case, a very personal form of plague—and she resolves to avoid the occasion for vice.

Because the other characters also believe in the power of language as poison, they doubt the strength of Lucina's continued resistance. Despite Lucina's harsh dismissals, Phorba will not leave Lucina alone with her virtuous thoughts. "In Conversation," she says instead, "Doubts are resolv'd, and what sticks near the conscience / Made easy and allowable" (2.1.36–37). For Phorba, conversation functions as a moral panacea, a salve to a guilty conscience. The bawds need only talk enough and Lucina will feel justified to succumb. Phorba therefore insinuates that Lucina's resistance will wane: "how shee blushes," she points out to Ardelia. "And what flowing Modesty runnes through her / When wee but name the Emperour" (2.1.80–82). The insinuation that Lucina's blush signifies her secret willingness underscores an inherent faith in the power of sexual propaganda. One word, the name of the emperor, is enough to arouse Lucina's blushes, creating a transgressive thrill that prefigures her eventual and inevitable sexual lapse.

Maximus, too, displays an inherent faith in the power of seduction and a concomitant distrust of his wife's fidelity. Outwardly, Maximus denies that self-interest drives his hatred of Valentinian:

> Mistake mee not dearest Aecius:
> Doe not believe that through meane jealousy
> How far the Emperour's Passion may prevaile
> On my Lucina's thoughts to our dishonour,
> That I abhorre the person of my Prince . . .
> I am concern'd for Rome, and for the World. (1.1.134–38, 145)

Implicit in Maximus's protestation of civic-mindedness, however, is the fear that Lucina may succumb, that Valentinian may invade his wife's body along with her thoughts and that he himself will be dishonored. Despite Lucina's obvious virtue, Maximus does not fully trust her strength.

The play thus questions the extent to which Lucina is tempted by Valentinian's ardent pursuit, and in passages new to Rochester's adaptation, Lucina actually appears to acknowledge her illicit interest in the emperor: "Ah, cease to tempt those Gods and Vertue too!" she begs Valentinian (1.1.187), and puts him off by insinuating that in future, he will not be so rebuffed. When Valentinian tries to grab her, she promises to reconsider his suit: "Hold Sir, for mercys sake: / Love will abhor whatever force can take. / I may perhaps perswade my selfe in time / That this is duty which now seemes a Crime" (1.1.285–88). Given the circumstances in which Lucina speaks, this promise appears at first glance to be a feint: Lucina would say anything to avoid Valentinian's physical assault. In act 3, however, Rochester's additions suggest that Lucina's conscience may in fact be at odds with her desire. When Lucina wanders away from the court into a grove, Marcellina and Claudia, her women, perceive her wanderlust as evidence of temptation: "But Claudia," Marcellina says, "why this sitting up all night / In groves by purling streames? this argues heat, / Great heat and vapours, which are maine corrupters!" (3.3.7–9). Throughout the play, Lucina has been marked by her coldness; Chylax calls her a "Cake of Ice" (2.2.114), while Balbus describes her as "Cold as Christall, / Never to bee thaw'd" (2.2.43–44). That she now experiences heat suggests that, at least in the eyes of her women, she has not been immune to the emperor's charms.

In the same act, Lucina privately acknowledges her susceptibility to Valentinian's illicit attractions:

> The Emperour!
> Unwonted horrour seizes mee all o're
> When I but heare him nam'd: sure tis not hate
> For though his impious Love with scorne I heard
> And fled with Terrour from his threatning Force
> Duty commands mee humbly to forgive
> And blesse the Lord to whom my Lord does bow;
> Nay more methinks hee is the gracefull'st man,
> His words so fram'd to tempt, himself to please,
> That tis my wonder how the Powers above,
> Those wise and carefull Guardians of the good,
> Have trusted such a force of tempting charmes
> To Enemys declar'd, of Innocence. (3.1.30–42)

Marcellina's diagnosis of Lucina's heat is not, in fact, altogether unfounded. Lucina is torn between fear of physical assault, understanding of her civic duty to the emperor, and a much more fearsome recognition of her own weakness. Lucina may have, as she claims, a "conscience" (2.1.157), but her admission in the grove presents the possibility that she may actually be susceptible to the sexual and polluting force of his language and that her desire may one day overpower her will. Lucina's fear of Valentinian is motivated at least in part by a fear of her own reaction to his beauty and his words, along with a fear that she may indeed one day justify "That this is duty which now seems a Crime" (1.1.228).

If seductive language may poison Lucina's virtue, the play initially suggests that Lucina's virtuous language may instead redeem Valentinian. When the emperor proclaims his love for Lucina, he cites her virtue as one of her primary attractions: "Your beauty had subdu'd my heart before— / Such Vertue could alone enslave mee more" (1.1.270–71). Later, he suggests that her chastity is so alluring that it threatens to render him chaste as well. Using the language of infection, Valentinian insists,

> Before my dazl'd Eyes coud you now place
> A thousand willing Beautyes to allure
> And give mee lust for every loose embrace,
> Lucina's Love my vertue would secure;
> From the contagious charme in vain I fly,
> That seiz'd upon my heart, and may defye
> That great preservative Variety. (1.1.311–17)

Itself a form of contagion, Lucina's virtue is also possibly the antidote to the filth of Valentinian's daily routine. Like Settle's Clotair, who is temporarily redeemed by Aphelia, Valentinian will, he avers, take Lucina's example of virtue to heart and reform. Ardelia exclaims, "If any thing redeeme the Emperour / from his wild flying Courses, this is shee! / Shee can instruct him if yee mark; shee is wise too" (2.1.62–64). Language, when properly employed, has the capacity to reform as well as destroy.[28]

Valentinian and Lucina thus represent two opposing sources of infectious language, and the play treats them both as authors, one telling a tale of corruption, the other one of redemption. What emerges from their conflict is a battle for linguistic and dramatic control that represents a wider battle for personal and public order. As part of his faith in the power of his imperial speech, Valentinian describes himself as an author; in Marina Hila's words, "language and spectacle" are the "twin pillars of the emperor's political power."[29] Valentinian cites his linguistic power when, early in the play, he complains of Lucina's rejection: "Gods! Why was I markt out of all your Brood / To suffer tamely under mortall Hate? / Is it not I that do protect your shrines? / Am author of your Sacrifice and prayers?" (1.1.167–70). As emperor, Valentinian names himself the author of the nation, a sentiment Maximus echoes angrily: "Why is this Author of us?" he demands (1.1.74). While Maximus's description of the emperor as author is original to Fletcher's play, Valentinian's similar self-description is Rochester's addition, emphasizing the link between author*ship* and author*ity*. Valentinian encodes power in linguistic terms; his right to author his nation's prayers to the gods (and implicitly, to put words in Lucina's mouth) is the sign of his imperial prerogative.

Finally, however, Valentinian's narrative of seduction fails, as Lucina is not truly susceptible to linguistic corruption. As a result, Valentinian employs a different form of narrative, one in which he succeeds with her by force. Sexual violence becomes Valentinian's art, a script he pens to express his power over Lucina and by extension, his kingdom. In Peter Byrne's words, "She assumes the role of an audience, he of playwright and producer."[30] Valentinian orchestrates the rape scene in minute detail:

> You see the Appartment made very fine
> That lies upon the Garden, Masques and Musick
> With the best speed you can, and all your Arts
> Serve to the highest for my Masterpiece
> Is now on foot. (3.2.52–56)

The rape is Valentinian's "Masterpiece," his greatest work of art; it is "intended to engage her aesthetically on the same emotionally transformative level as if she were responding to a theatrical performance."[31] That he arranges the music, the scenery, and even the blocking of the rape emphasizes the artificiality and theatricality of the sexual assault.

In the climactic scene of the play, a scene entirely original to Rochester, Valentinian rapes Lucina offstage while a troupe of dancers rehearses an upcoming masque onstage. Valentinian has specifically ordered the masque to detract attention from the rape:

> 'Twill serve to draw away
> Those listning fooles who trace it in the Gallery;
> And if (by chance) odd noises should bee heard,
> As womens Shricks [sic], or soe, say tis a Play
> Is practicing within. (4.2.191–95)

Valentinian has facilitated a sadistically witty moment of dramatic irony: as Lycinias comments, it's a "merry pranck" to stage the rape of Lucrece during the rape of Lucina (4.2.196). As the dancing-masters rehearse, some of the true Lucina's suffering breaks through the performance: "Blesse mee," Lycinias exclaims, "the Lowd shricks and horrid out cryes / Of the poor Lady! Ravishing d'yee call it? / She roares as if she were upon the racke" (4.2.9–11). Lucina's screams merge with the rehearsal for the masque, emphasizing the link between Valentinian's sexual violence and theatricality. The rehearsal onstage substitutes for the "real" performance within the bedchamber, a work of the emperor's conscious authorship, though a work that cannot publicly be staged. Valentinian's script, his masterpiece, becomes his ultimate expression of imperial power and authorial privilege; he has achieved his goal of having Lucina while she is yet chaste.

If the rape functions as an expression of authorship, the rape's immediate aftermath would initially seem to confirm Valentinian's vision of his narrative. When Lucina calls for vengeance, vowing, "As long as there is life in this Body / And breath to give me words, I'le cry for Justice" (4.4.3–4), Valentinian insists on her powerlessness—"Justice will never hear you," he boasts, "I am Justice" (4.3.5)—and he insists that his voice carries the ultimate authority: "Know I am farre above the faults I doe / And those I doe I'me able to forgive" (4.4.87–88).[32] Moreover, he taunts Lucina for her linguistic impotence: she lacks sufficient "credit in the telling it" to overcome his version of events (4.4.90). Lucina, Valentinian brags, is utterly helpless: "Your Husband cannot help you, nor the Soldiers: / Your Husband is my Creature, they my weapons" (4.4.94–95). In keeping with Valentinian's script, Lucina acknowledges that he has effectively rewritten her identity. "Gods," she mourns:

> what a wretched thing has this man made mee

> For I am now noe Wife for Maximus,
> Noe company for women that are virtuous,
> No Family I now can claime or Country,
> Nor name but Caesars Whore. (4.4.42–46)

Valentinian has effaced Lucina's reputation, her family, and even her name. His actions have renamed her; she is no longer Lucina, but "Caesar's whore," her identity now existent only insofar as she bears relation to the emperor.

Valentinian rapes Lucina to satisfy the demands of his physical body, but it is here in the aftermath of sexual violence that the distinction between private and public, body natural and body politic, breaks down and the play's political leanings emerge. The private battle of wills between Lucina and Valentinian and their conflicting stories of chastity and cuckoldry are never only of individual consequence. Within a royal court, sexuality is always imbued with political significance. For Lucina, her encounters with and rejections of Valentinian are initially private. Not so for Valentinian, who, as emperor, recognizes her refusals as both a private rebuff and a political danger. As a divinely appointed ruler, Valentinian should, he insists, see a direct, one-to-one correspondence between his words and his subjects' actions. He brags of his powers to Lucina:

> Have I not Pretors through the spacious Earth
> Who in my name doe mighty Nations sway,
> Injoying rich Dominions in my right?
> Their temporary Governments I change,
> Divide or take away, as I see good,
> And this they think noe Injury nor shame. (1.1.212–17)

Valentinian commands and the world reacts accordingly. By refusing Valentinian, however, Lucina transforms him, the ruler and author of Rome, from emperor to slave: "Alas," he complains,

> All Power is in Lucina's Eyes.
> How soone could I shake off this heavy Earth
> Which makes mee little lower than your selves
> And sitt in Heav'n an Equall with the first,
> But Love bids mee pursue a Nobler Aime,
> Continue Mortall, and Lucina's Slave. (1.1.177–82)

Valentinian imagines himself (briefly and disingenuously) as Lucina's slave, a frightening, albeit temporary, rhetorical disempowerment. As is true for Settle's Clotair, Valentinian's inability finally to command Lucina's willing submission becomes a sign of political weakness, tangible proof of the limits to his divine authority. If he cannot force one woman's submission, he cannot hope to command the armies of imperial Rome. Lucina's personal narrative of fidelity conflicts with and threatens to overpower Valentinian's own linguistic and political mandate.

Finally Valentinian assaults Lucina rather than look weak before his kingdom, a powerful expression of his absolutist philosophy. Paradoxically, however, the rape becomes the source of his disempowerment, the moment when the private acts of private bodies become irrevocably public and political, and when personal suffering is transformed into a justification for regicide. In 1675, Settle's Chlotilda could not punish the king for his private act of violence lest she instead harm the body politic. In 1684, Rochester's Lucina dramatizes the new strain of political thought encapsulated in Sidney's *Discourses*, one that not only licenses but obligates the people to oppose a tyrannical king. The clash between Valentinian and Lucina therefore underscores a broader clash in political ideologies. Valentinian approaches his authority from a Filmerian perspective, perfectly confident in his absolute and unquestioned authority over his subjects. In fact, however, his power is revealed to be untenable, tyrannical, and false, as the play finally propounds a contractual conception of rulership more reminiscent of Sidney's work than Filmer's. Lucina functions both as the symbol of suffering created by monarchical overreaching and as the agent of the emperor's overthrow; in the aftermath of her rape, she becomes a very different sort of author, one who uses her rape as a form of political propaganda. Before the assault, Lucina attempts to enhance the emperor's individual morality, an essentially private affair. After the rape, she tells a story of monarchical tyranny and becomes the infection Aecius fears. Early in the play, Balbus threatens Lucina with physical violence. He reports:

> I askt her
> After my many offers, walking with her,
> And her many downe denyalls, How
> If the Emperour growne mad with love should force her:
> She pointed to a Lucrece that hung by,
> And with an angry looke that from her Eyes
> Shot Vestall Fire against mee, she departed. (2.2.87–93)

By gesturing, albeit silently, to the painting of Lucrece, Lucina promises her allegiance to that older narrative, a script powerful enough to unseat kings. If Valentinian will play the rapist, Lucina will play Lucrece, in the context of imperial politics a true political threat.

In attempting to dissuade Valentinian from rape, Lucina warns him that sexual assault will forever taint her, body and soul: "I will become so leprous / That yee shall Curse mee from yee" (4.2.150–51), she promises. She will become "A Plague to Roome, and Blott to Cesars fame!" (1.1.203). In most plays, the victim of sexual assault bears the "stain" of that attack alone. Lucina, however, insists that Valentinian will also be infected by the contagion he transmits. She will be ruined, but her blood will be forevermore on Valentinian's hands. That Lucina chooses to use the word "Blot" underscores the conflict between narratives. She is his victim, but she rhetorically transforms herself into an error of his penmanship. After the rape, Valentinian himself becomes the toxin, a blot not only on her fame, but on the reputation of the empire:

> the Empire,
> In which thou livest a strong continu'd surfeit
> Like poyson will disgorge thee, good men raze thee
> From ever being read again—
> Chast wives, and fearfull maids make vows against thee. (4.4.14–18)

She labels Valentinian a poison, a contaminant that good people will avoid, and thus like the Romans of Sidney's *Discourses*, who, as we have seen, "recove[r] their liberty by expelling Tarquin," demands a public, political punishment for his private act of violence.[33] If Valentinian rewrites Lucina's identity by renaming her "Caesar's whore" (4.4.46), he also enables Lucina to rename him in turn. Deferring to the narrative of Lucrece for the second time in the play, Lucina curses the emperor: "The sins of Tarquin be remembered in thee" (4.4.60), she cries. She may be no better than a "glorious whore" (4.4.66), but she likens Valentinian to a notorious and executed tyrant. This label will prove more powerful than Valentinian's bragging pronouncements about his own power. His author(ity) is not powerful enough to avoid the denouement of Lucrece's story and Tarquin's fate.

Lucina initially expresses her virtue silently with her gesture toward Lucrece's painting. She finally expresses her fidelity both to her husband and to Lucrece's narrative with her suicide, the ultimate expression of chastity. Rochester's version of the play emphasizes the pathos of Lucina's death, extending the description of her final moments by twelve lines. Fletcher's description of Lucina's suicide is somewhat abrupt. According to Claudia,

> When first she enter'd
> Into her house, after a world of weeping,
> And blushing like the Sun-set, as we saw her;
> Dare I, said she, defile this house with whore,
> In which his noble family has flourish'd?
> At which she fel, and stird no more. (3.1.364–69)

Rochester's Claudia continues:

> At this she fell—Choakt with a thousand sighs;
> And now the pleas'd expiring Saint
> (Her dying Lookes, where new borne Beauty shines
> One opprest with Blushes), modestly declines,
> While death approacht with a Majestick grace,
> Proud to looke Lovely once in such a face.
> Her Armes spread to receive, her wellcome guest,
> With a glad sigh, she drew into her Breast.
> Her Eyes then languishing tow'rds Heav'n she cast
> To thanke the powers that death was come at last;

And at th' approach of the Cold silent God
Ten thousand hidden Glories rusht abroad. (4.4.345–56)

This highly descriptive account of Lucina's death contrasts with the terse announcement of Fletcher's original text. As when she points to the painting of Lucrece, Lucina does not speak. Instead, she gestures, she looks, she blushes, and she sighs, emphasizing the thematic importance of her suicide; she receives death as she would a welcome lover, with open arms and glad sighs, a sharp contrast to her fervent rejection of the emperor. By welcoming death into herself, she effaces the trace of Valentinian's lust and reasserts control over her own body. Appropriately enough, the moment of Lucina's death, the moment when she wrests final and permanent control of the narrative away from Valentinian, is itself reduced to narrative (in this case, Claudia's). The rape and Lucina's response to the rape emerge as two opposing, if equally unstageable, masterpieces.

The Tragedy of Valentinian indicates that Lucina finds power in Lucrece's script, and thus Rochester edits Lucina's final meeting with Maximus to suggest that the suicide is the product of her will alone. In both versions of the play, Maximus and Aecius immediately read the fate of the now ravished Lucina on her body: "Already in thy tears I've read thy wrongs" (4.4.127), Maximus laments, treating her body as a text to be read and interpreted. Only in Fletcher's original script, however, does Maximus view Lucina's suicide as a foregone conclusion. When Fletcher's Lucina first expresses an intent to kill herself, Maximus praises her virtue: "Farewell thou excellent example of us," he tells her, "Thou starry vertue, fare-thee-well, seeke heaven, / And there by Cassiopeia shine in glory, / We are too base and dirty to preserve thee" (3.1.157–58). Rochester, by contrast, excises these lines, focusing instead on Maximus's love and concern for his wife. "[T]hese lipps / Tast not of ravisher," he promises (4.4.142–43), while Aecius urges Lucina to live and "draw from that wilde man [Valentinian] a sweet repentance" (4.4.172). The sight of Lucina's ravaged body will, he insists, offer a corrective to and a penance for the corrupt ruler.

Subsequently, Rochester excises Maximus's lengthy speech requiring Lucina's death: "she must not live" (3.1.156), he concludes in Fletcher's script. For Fletcher, Lucina commits suicide at her husband's urging as well as her own behest. Certainly, Rochester's Maximus is hardly a perfect husband by modern standards; despite his initial affirmation that the rape was not Lucina's fault, he later becomes anxious, doubting her fidelity if she does not kill herself: "The Emperour / is young and handsome, and the woman flesh, / And may not these two couple without scratching" (4.4.272–74), he asks bitterly. Such comments momentarily recall the depiction of Lucrece from H. P.'s *A Satyr Against Commonwealths*, and the fear that Lucina may, like H. P.'s Lucrece, have cried rape to conceal adultery. Yet Maximus expresses his doubts only after Lucina has left the stage and is out of earshot. The decision to die is Lucina's own, one that establishes her merit both as a wife and as a catalyst for political change; she claims suicide as both her duty and her desire: "The Tongues of Angells cannot alter mee" (4.4.187), she avers. No words can change Lucina's fate nor alter the course of her narrative. Her death is her final act of will and authorship, and one that finally strips Valentinian of his authority.

In choosing death, Lucina recognizes her own presence and power as spectacle. It was, of course, Lucina's physical beauty that initially inspired Valentinian's sexual interest, but if her visual appeal leads to her destruction in life, she offers a very different sort of spectacle in death. By martyring herself, Lucina accepts her role as a public theatrical spectacle; in essence, she kills herself into art to deconstruct the text that Valentinian has scripted and transforms herself into the ultimate form of antimonarchical propaganda. The sight of Lucina's body, borne throughout the town, will, as Sidney suggests, inspire widespread outrage and provide the impetus for political change in Rome. In this, Rochester implies that the spectacle of rape, when dramatically performed and effectively harnessed, will spread treasonous contagion throughout the kingdom and poison men's minds against their government. The rhetoric of rape and contagion is therefore never only of individual concern, and *The Tragedy of Valentinian* exposes the process by which a private, sexual crime becomes a public, political act.

In the end, Valentinian is overthrown by his people as the rape of Lucina provides sufficient justification for his deposition, leaving Maximus to mourn his own loss: "Lead me to Death or Empire which you please / For both are equall to a Ruin'd man . . . / Sorrows soe just as mine must never end / For my Love ravish'd and my murder'd Friend" (5.5.253–54, 266–67). Significantly, Rochester has chosen to end his play a full act before the original source text. In Fletcher's earlier version, Maximus gladly marries Valentinian's widow and becomes equally tyrannical before his own eventual overthrow. According to Hila, "Maximus duplicates his predecessor's faults as soon as he has succeeded to the throne, which suggests that there is something fundamentally wrong with the ideological underpinnings of political power, including the doctrine of divine right."[34] Fletcher's text also suggests that regicide cannot be tolerated.[35] Any man who kills a king will be punished by God with his own harsh demise. In contrast, not only does Rochester's Maximus go unpunished, but his takeover of the throne is a cause for celebration.[36] Meanwhile, liberty from tyranny is made possible by Lucina's decision to transform her own body into an effective form of antimonarchical propaganda. Rochester once again emphasizes the move toward a contractual understanding of monarchy and produces a treatment of the Lucrece narrative dangerously reminiscent of Algernon Sidney's.

LEE'S *LUCIUS JUNIUS BRUTUS* AND THE DANGERS OF REVOLT

Although Rochester's *Valentinian* justifies the overthrow of a violent monarch, it was Nathaniel Lee's *Lucius Junius Brutus* that proved the more immediately controversial; the play was suppressed after only three nights for "very Scandalous Expressions & Reflections vpon ye Government."[37] Critics have speculated that the censors may not have actually read the play, that the language of royalism and republicanism alone may have made them sufficiently nervous to inspire a preemptive suppression. Antony Hammond writes, "It is clear from the wording that the Chamberlain was acting upon a complaint, not first-hand knowledge, and that he had not troubled to verify the objections to the play."[38] That said, the play's depiction of the royalists is far from complimentary and certainly could have raised concerns. At the center of *Lucius Junius Brutus* lies a royalist black mass in which human sacrifice and blood drinking are performed onstage: as a "busie Commonwealths' Man," symbol of parliamentary government, is displayed crucified upstage, priests distribute goblets "fill'd with Blood & Wine" that the royalists may drink the blood of human sacrifice and grow strong.[39] Brutus will later condemn the conspirators, his own sons among them, calling them "Sons of Murder, that get drunk with blood" (4.1.241). In the context of the Exclusion Crisis, this scene is central to any pro-Whig reading of the play, as royalism is here linked with Catholic vampirism and perversity. As in the English Civil War tracts, acts of rape escalate into instances of blood drinking, dark parodies of the Catholic Eucharist that align the royalists with the most pernicious and terrifying aspects of libertine and Catholic excess.

The scene of blood drinking notwithstanding, however, *Lucius Junius Brutus* defies a straightforwardly antiroyalist, anti-Catholic reading. For all that Brutus condemns the royalists for their perversity, he has himself participated in a vampiristic act; at Brutus's insistence, Lucrece's avengers seal their pact by kissing her knife, tasting the blood of Lucrece's self-sacrifice to cement their oath. Brutus says,

> Behold, you dazled Romans, from the wound
> Of this dead Beauty, thus I draw the Dagger,
> All stain'd and reeking with her Sacred blood,
> Thus to my lips I put the Hallow'd blade,
> To yours Lucretius, Collatinus yours, . . .
> kiss the Ponnyard round. (1.1.434–39)

Brutus's use of Lucrece's knife is a less obvious but no less definite act of blood drinking than that of the royalists. It is also an addition of Lee's imagining. According to Livy, the Lucrece story's source text, Brutus "put the knife into Collatinus's hands, then passed it to Lucretius, then to Valerius"; at no point in Livy's narrative do they kiss the bloodied weapon.[40] That Brutus, like his hated son, participates in an act of vampirism suggests that the republicans may be no better than the royalists they replace.

For both Lee's royalists and republicans, the spectacle of human suffering plays a fundamental role in the transfer and affirmation of political authority. Brutus in particular recognizes that female sacrifice leads to political consequences, and he argues for the necessity of human sacrifice to ensure stability in the wake of a rebellion. Brutus tells the Senate,

> It has been found a famous truth in Story,
> Left by the ancient Sages to their Sons,
> That on the change of Empires or of Kingdoms,
> Some sudden Execution, fierce and great,
> Such as may draw the World to admiration,
> Is necessary to be put in Act
> Against the Enemies of the present State. (5.2.6–12)

For a nation to stand, a display of violence is essential; the spectacle of suffering is needed to channel the power of the multitude. He continues,

> Had Hector, when the Greeks and Trojans met
> Upon the Truce, and mingled with each other,
> Brought to the Banquet of those Demy-Gods
> The Fatal head of that illustrious Whore;
> Troy might have stood till now. (5.2.13–17)

The death of Helen would have united the Greeks and the Trojans and averted an unnecessary war. Commonly depicted as a rape victim,[41] Helen is useful to Brutus only in death, worthy only insofar as she can cement political bonds between men. Similarly, Brutus is eager to exploit the sins of Tarquin's body natural to reshape the contours of the Roman body politic, and he will use Lucrece as he encourages Hector to use Helen: as a necessary sacrifice. In this, Brutus's use of Helen and Lucrece mirrors the use of rape in propaganda as described throughout this study. Here is female physical suffering stripped of its personal impact and transformed into a public symbol to be fought over and debated by men. The individual woman's trauma is a cause for celebration if it leads to masculine advancement or political change.

Fully aware of the political ramifications of Lucrece's death, Brutus quickly and callously harnesses the political power of her narrative to effect his rise to power: "Leave me to my work, my Titus," he tells his son, "For from this Spark a Lightning shall arise / That must e're Night purge all the Roman Air" (1.1.278–80). Brutus does not admit to personal ambition but rather constructs himself as a "social and moral surgeon," come to "cure the ailing body politic."[42] Titus, too, conceives of his father as a doctor, aiding the nation in its recovery: "My Father, like an Æsculapius / Sent by the Gods, comes boldly to the Cure; / But how, my Love? by violent Remedies" (2.1.445–47). Certainly, Brutus's Rome is in need of healing; throughout the play, Lee foregrounds imagery of contagion and illness, with the sexually corrupt acts of the Tarquin family serving as the primary agents of infection. Lee's Lucrece laments her "dishonored blood" in the aftermath of her rape (1.1.392), while Teraminta, the bastard daughter of the king, carries the "natural Contagion" of the Tarquin line (1.1.220). As such, her marriage to Titus can only be a "detested Epithalamium" and "polluted Rit[e]" (1.1.212, 214). In the "slimy joys" of consummation (1.1.216), Teraminta will pollute her lover via contact with her poisonous blood (as her half-brother, Tarquin, does to Lucrece).[43] Later, upon the exposure of the royalist counterplot, Brutus describes his sons' complicity using the imagery of disease: his sons are "two Villains lurking in my blood" (4.1.226). The realm of Rome itself has grown ill, and thus Titus encourages Teraminta to forsake "this Contagious Air" for his embrace (3.3.67). The filth of Tarquin's evil and years of misrule have poisoned the land and given rise to a series of monsters. The members of the Tarquin family are described as the "Monster[s] of Mankind" (1.1.355), while Fabritius claims that the mob has become a "strange blunder-headed Monster" (2.1.32). Brutus admits that he has "act[ed] deformity in thousand shapes" (1.1.118), while infection threatens to spill over the bounds of the fictional world—the play's prologue describes the proliferation of infectious wit, a form of "malice" that "poyson[s] half the house" (prologue, 10). The blood of the theater, like the blood of the nation, has grown corrupt.

In creating a Rome poisoned by sexual corruption, Lee follows two earlier versions of *The Rape of Lucrece*, Shakespeare's poem of 1594 and Thomas Heywood's drama of 1608, both of which depict rape as a form of disease, a poison that infects, distorts, and destroys both the victim's blood and the marrow of her society. According to Shakespeare's Lucrece, her body has become "spotted, soiled, corrupted" and "blemished" (ll. 1172, 1175), her blood "stained" and "tainted" by Tarquin's assault (ll. 1181, 1182). Heywood's Lucrece concurs: she has been "stain'd, polluted, and defil'd," her body "soil'd with lust-burn'd sinne."[44] In both adaptations, the rape has engendered a wider atmosphere of societal illness. Shakespeare's Lucrece curses the "rotten damps" (l. 778), "poisonous clouds" (l. 777), and "unwholesome breaths" of "hateful, vaporous and foggy night" (ll. 778, 771); nature itself spreads contagion and disease. Likewise, Heywood's Brutus says that Tarquin's ill deeds have infected the larger realm of Rome: "The state," he claims, "is full of dropsie and swollen big / with windie vapors" (b1r).

According to Lee's Brutus, the sexual excesses of the Tarquin family—the rape of Lucrece and illegitimacy of Teraminta—both reflect and create the contagion that pervades the realm. Here again we see the shift from private sexuality to public concern illuminated in Rochester's *Valentinian*, with bloodletting in acts of political violence a potential means of purgation. While Lucrece's body becomes, as Brutus terms it, a "Public Wound" (2.1.152), Titus's abused body will "heal" that "wounded freedom" with his execution (4.1.524). Throughout the play, characters insist that suffering will serve as a means to redemption. Lucrece's "dishonor'd blood" becomes "chast blood" in the wake of her suicide (1.1.392, 442), at least according to Brutus. Similarly, Titus must, Brutus claims, "bleed before People" to reaffirm the strength of the republic (4.1.528). Titus accepts the necessity and benefit of the blood purge as a requirement for social and personal redemption. He tells his father, "I hope the glorious Liberty of Rome, / Thus water'd by the blood of both your Sons, / Will get Imperial growth and flourish long" (5.2.168–70), and he resigns himself to the status of sacrificial victim. He will "make [Brutus] reparation" for his disloyalty with death (4.1.456). Even at the expense of his own existence, Titus masochistically insists on redeeming himself through flagellation and the public shedding of blood. "My constant sufferings are my only Glory" (4.1.528), he boasts, and he dreams of a Rome run red with redemptive blood: "Ere yet she can be well," Titus avers, Rome "must purge and cast, purge all th'infected humors / Through the whole mass, and vastly, vastly bleed" (2.1.448–50).

Shakespeare and Heywood also offer the possibility of violent bloodletting as a means to purge the nation and restore social order. Heywood's Brutus promises to "pierce" the "windie vapors" of the state, "to purge th'infected blood, bred by the pride / of these infested bloods" (b1r), while in Catherine Belling's words, Shakespeare's poem "culminates . . . in Lucrece's purificatory suicide: with a knife, she makes herself bleed."[45] Lucrece's "chaste blood," rendered free from taint by the ritual of bloodletting, provides the impetus for the successful overthrow of the Tarquins, thereby righting the political realm. Heywood, too, concludes with an image of restoration in the wake of a blood purge: "After so much effusion and large washe / Of Roman blood, the name of peace is welcome" (k2v), he writes. The state has been redeemed from tyranny, and according to Belling, "The body politic can now begin to heal."[46]

In Lee's play, however, despite his protestations of civic altruism, Brutus's interest in redemptive bloodletting exposes the depths of his personal ambition and his canny understanding of the political power of Lucrece's self-sacrifice. Brutus gladly exploits the emotional impact of Lucrece's suffering, transforming her private experience into a public spectacle that reveals the effectiveness of sexual violence as a form of political propaganda. In the process, Brutus effaces the memory of Lucrece in a thoroughly unsettling manner. Rochester's *Valentinian* foregrounds both the tension leading up to the rape and its psychological aftermath; Valentinian does not assault Lucina until the end of act 4, unlike his counterpart in Fletcher's play, who accomplishes his design at the end of act 2. In contrast, Lee's play does not focus on the rape. As his title implies, Lee's interest lies in the political ramifications of the assault and in Brutus's rise to power; Lucrece's story ends as Brutus's begins. Like Rochester's Lucina, Brutus takes control of the political narrative and parlays an act of private sexual violence into public political power. But while Rochester's Lucina controls her own narrative, Lee's Brutus takes control of Lucrece's story. He gains power through her suffering, and his success hinges on his ability to manipulate and redirect to his own benefit the public's emotional response to her death.

Lee's Lucrece, like Rochester's Lucina, demands vengeance for her suffering in a pathos-laden scene: "All that I ask you now," she begs,

> is to Revenge me;
> Revenge me Father, Husband, Oh revenge me:
> Revenge me, Brutus; you his Sons revenge me;
> Herminius, Mutius, thou Horatius too,
> And thou Valerius; all; revenge me all:
> Revenge the Honor of the Ravish'd Lucrece. (1.1.407–12)

Lucrece's appeal is potent, leading some critics to assume that Brutus must himself be moved. Sue Owen, for instance, argues that Brutus is motivated to rebellion not by ambition, but by a desire to avenge the wronged Lucrece: "Brutus is capable of political opportunism, but it would be wrong to see him as 'exploiting' the rape of Lucrece. Lucrece's own dramatic rendering of her wrongs, demands for revenge, and noble suicide make such an interpretation unworkable. Brutus is not motivated by self-interest."[47] I would argue, however, that Brutus's interest in Lucrece's sufferings is negligible. Before Lucrece's suicide, before he has even received confirmation of her attack, Brutus has already begun to anticipate his assault on the Tarquin family. Brutus had long despised the Tarquins; according to Livy, King Tarquin confiscated Brutus's property and ordered the execution of his brother:

> Now Brutus had deliberately assumed a mask to hide his true character. When he had learned of the murder by Tarquin of the Roman aristocrats, one of the victims being his own brother, he had come to the conclusion that the only way to save himself was to appear in the king's eyes as a person of no account. . . . Accordingly he pretended to be a half-wit and made no protest at the seizure by Tarquin of everything he possessed.[48]

Although Lee's characters never discuss Brutus's past onstage, his hatred for the Tarquins forms an openly acknowledged backdrop to the play's events. Brutus has forsaken personal reputation and social standing to await the optimal opportunity for revenge, and he praises his own powers of patience and endurance:

> O, what but infinite Spirit, propt by Fate,

For Empire's weight to turn on, could endure
As thou hast done, the labours of an Age,
All follies, scoffs, reproaches, pities, scorns,
Indignities almost to blows sustain'd,
For twenty pressing years, and by a Roman? (1.1.112–17)

Brutus has concealed his true nature from the world and for twenty years has been unable to "Disclose the weighty Secret of my Soul . . . to my dearest Friend, / To my own Children, nor my bosome Wife" (1.1.129, 127–28). He insists that his masquerade proves his civic virtue; his "infinite Spirit" has sustained him that he might eventually preserve Rome from destruction. Still, underlying Brutus's claim to righteousness is a drive for power and the "self-interest" that Owen denies. For years, Brutus has been feigning madness while awaiting his opportunity to strike, and when he hears about the rape, he knows that his moment has come. Thus he callously rejoices over Lucrece's downfall. In public, Brutus will lament; in private, his celebration of Lucrece's sufferings belies his apparent grief: "[F]rom the blackness of young Tarquin's Crime / And Fornace of his Lust," he tells his son,

the virtuous Soul
Of Junius Brutus catches bright occasion,
I see the Pillars of his Kingdom totter:
The Rape of Lucrece is the midnight Lantorn
That lights my Genius down to the Foundation. (1.1.272–77)

The rape of Lucrece represents a grand opportunity. Tarquin's crime of lust has unsettled the kingdom and allowed Brutus to avenge his own sufferings.

To achieve his revenge most effectively, Brutus co-opts the power of Lucrece's image, gradually replacing her sufferings in the public imagination with his own. In his first soliloquy, Brutus displays a rhetorical tendency to marginalize Lucrece. He begins by relaying the news of her assault:

Occasion seems in view; something there is
In Tarquin's last abode at Collatine's:
Late entertain'd, and early gone this morning?
The Matron ruffled, wet, and dropping tears,
As if she had lost her wealth in some black Storm! (1.1.94–98)

Brutus's description of Lucrece continues for fifteen lines; from there, he abruptly transitions to a litany of his own sufferings. Lucrece is a "pattern," he claims, "For all succeeding Wives. O Brutus! Brutus! / When will the tedious Gods permit thy Soul / To walk abroad in her own Majesty, / And throw this Vizor of thy madness from thee?" (1.1.107, 108–11). Brutus moves from a lamentation of Lucrece to a self-lamentation literally in the middle of a line. For the remaining twenty-six lines of the soliloquy—nearly twice as many lines as he devoted to Lucrece—Brutus does not mention her again, further undermining his claim to selflessness. His real passion comes through in his self-pitying display, while his interest in Lucrece is, from the earliest moments of the play, linked with his desire for personal advancement.

In the grief and confusion following Lucrece's death, Brutus emerges as a leader, and he calls for violent political action:

> Swear, and let all the Gods be witnesses,
> That you with me will drive proud Tarquin out,
> His Wife, th'Imperial Fury, and her Sons,
> With all the Race; drive'em with Sword and Fire
> To the World's limits, Profligate accurst:
> Swear from this time never to suffer them,
> Nor any other King to Reign in Rome. (1.1.444–50)

Tellingly, Brutus never explicitly demands the punishment of Sextus Tarquin, the rapist. Instead he demands the banishment of Tarquinius Superbus, the king, and Tullia, his much-despised wife.[49] Tarquin himself appears merely as an afterthought, an undifferentiated member of the royal family. That Brutus does not seek to punish the guilty party suggests that vengeance is not Brutus's true goal. Rather, he obfuscates the real problem, manipulating the crowd into confusing political rebellion with private vengeance.[50] By the end of Brutus's speech, Lucrece has been forgotten, now irrelevant to the tide of political upheaval. Brutus has perpetrated what Joyce MacDonald calls "the reduction of the body of Lucrece to the status of that public wound."[51]

If Brutus marginalizes Lucrece, the members of her family are all too eager to follow suit; unlike the suicide of Rochester's Lucina, which gives her momentary control, the suicide of Lee's Lucrece is brushed aside, even by her closest relatives. In act 2, Collatine becomes disenchanted with his inability to advance in Brutus's new regime, and, like Settle's Dumain and Lamot, he pledges his allegiance to the royalist faction. Despite his promise to avenge Lucrece not one act prior, he begins to fight alongside and even socialize with the friends of his wife's rapist. Brutus tells Valerius:

> I have intelligence of [Collatine's] Transactions,
> He mingles with the young hot blood of Rome,
> Gnaws himself inward, grudges my applause,
> Promotes Cabals with highest Quality,
> Such headlong youth as, spurning Laws and manners,
> Shar'd in the late Debaucheries of Sextus,
> And therefore wish the Tyrant here again. (3.1.106–12)

Collatine's lack of fidelity to his wife's cause is, on one level, shocking—how could the bereaved husband of act 1 transform so rapidly into the cynical, libertine courtier of act 3 with nary a thought for his wife's memory?[52] On another level, however, the shift is indicative of the play's overall trajectory: having served her political function, Lucrece herself is no longer important to the play's characters. When her memory no longer advances Collatine, he is more than prepared to switch his allegiance to the opposing side.

The experience of the rape victim is thus effaced, redirected by men who would transmute suffering into power, while her death is avenged merely as a demonstration of Brutus's power as orator. What emerges from the play is not, as in Rochester's *Valentinian*, the triumph of Lucina/Lucrece over her attacker, but the triumph of Brutus as a master rhetorician. From the earliest parts of the play, Brutus demonstrates a talent for harnessing the emotional and propagandistic power of language and spectacle. He uses his oratorical skills to his advantage in his dialogue with the Roman mob, threatening the crowd with an imaginary omen. "What, art thou blind?" he asks the crowd; "[W]hy, yonder, all o'fire; / It vomits Lightning; 'tis a monstrous Dragon" (1.1.318–19). No such dragon exists—one peasant complains, "For my part, I saw nothing" (1.1.333). Yet he is soon cowed into submission by the force of the mob: "Down with him, knock him down," Vinditius threatens, and the peasant capitulates: "Mercy: I did, I did" see the dragon, he insists, "a huge monstrous Dragon" (1.1.336).[53] To Victoria Hayne, Brutus's rhetorical skill points to a larger discomfort with the nature and role of language in Restoration society: "the play participates in a cultural suspicion of language widespread in the late seventeenth century. That conflict is directed toward building distrust of Brutus's eloquent oratory."[54] It also reflects a specific discomfort with the political power of language and with the propagandist's ability to create action from words. The play's world will ultimately be controlled by Brutus's rhetoric. At the beginning of the play, Brutus has been posing as a fool, a man whose words disturb and amuse but, generally speaking, whose language is not valued. Fabritius and his courtier friends, for instance, seek out Brutus to "divert ourselves" with "the impertinence of a Fool" (1.1.143, 145). As he gains in political authority, however, Brutus simultaneously gains in linguistic force, with multiple characters commenting on the power of his speech. According to Vinditius, only Brutus has ever succeeded in moving him to tears: "O, Neighbours, oh! I bury'd seven Wives without crying" (2.1.167), he exclaims (however disingenuously), and until Brutus's eulogy for Lucrece, "I never wept before in all my life" (2.1.168). Subsequently, characters begin to praise Brutus's godlike power. In the wake of Brutus's speech, Valerius insists, "O Brutus, as a God, we all survey thee" (2.1.236), while Tiberius, Brutus's second son, complains that the Roman people treat Brutus "Like Jove when follow'd by a Train of Gods" (3.1.5). Later, Valerius, speaking for the Roman Senate, deifies Brutus still living: "[W]hy, he's no more a man; / He is not cast in the same Common mould . . . / He looks and talks, as if that Jove had sent him" (5.1.8–9, 11).

Brutus finally emerges as a god among the Roman people because he succeeds in manipulating them where others have consistently failed, and Brutus both accepts and encourages the belief in his own divinity.[55] As the play concludes, Brutus requests peace and prosperity for the new republic:

> Let Heav'n and Earth for ever keep their bound,
> The Stars unshaken go their constant Round;
> In harmless labour be our steel employ'd,
> And endless peace thro all the World enjoy'd,
> Let every Bark the Waves in safety Plough,
> No angry Tempest curl the Ocean's brow;
> No darted flames from Heav'n make Mortals fear,
> Nor Thunder fright the weeping Passenger. (5.2.197–84)

It is worth contrasting Brutus's speech here with Valentinian's. In the wake of Lucina's suicide, Valentinian proclaims his power over nature:

> The world is my creature;
> The Trees bring forth their Fruit, when I say Summer;
> The wind that knows no limits but its wildness,
> At my command moves not a Leaf: The Sea,
> With his proud mountain-waters envying Heav'n,
> Where I say still, runs into chrystal mirrors. (5.2.21–26)

Valentinian insists that he can control the weather, that he can stop the winds and halt storms; unfortunately, his power is undermined by his inability to speak Lucina back to life and by his political impotence in the aftermath of the rape. Brutus expresses similar desires to Valentinian's—prosperity and an end to discord and storms—but unlike Valentinian, he achieves those goals; the play theoretically concludes with the restoration of order in the new republic.[56] Thus while Brutus does not directly proclaim his power over nature—he displaces the power onto the gods to whom he prays—the impact of his speech is to emphasize his control and accomplishment, even at the expense of his own blood.

Valentinian is a linguistic failure: as Hila writes of Fletcher's emperor, "his rhetoric is subjective and limited rather than absolute."[57] Valentinian cannot reanimate the dead, nor can he retain control of his personal narrative. In contrast, while Brutus cannot speak Lucrece back to life, he does speak her back to purity. While Lucrece initially bemoans her "dishonored blood" after the suicide (1.1.392), Brutus renames it "chast Blood" and "Sacred blood" (1.1.442, 436). Seemingly, Lucrece's death has restored her purity and removed Tarquin's infection from her veins. Both Lucrece's impurity and her subsequent redemption are, however, imaginative constructs. Lee's Tarquin attacks and injures Lucrece, but he does not leave behind a physical spot or literally contaminate her blood. As we have already seen, Shakespeare's *The Rape of Lucrece* literalizes the taint, Lucrece's blood flowing from her wounds in two distinct streams. The "black" blood "that false

Tarquin stained" separates from "some of her blood still pure and red" (1743–44).[58] The evil of the rape has a tangible and visible effect upon the body of the victim. In contrast, only one type of blood issues from the veins of Lee's Lucrece. She may feel herself tainted, but unlike Shakespeare, Lee provides no evidence that the feeling is anything more than a psychological belief. His Lucrece is spotted because she claims herself to be so, and when Brutus pronounces her chaste once more, she is redeemed not because she has killed herself, but simply because Brutus has announced her redemption. Brutus thus claims control of Lucrece's body along with her narrative; that Lucrece's family accepts his pronouncement confirms the power of his oratory.

Subsequently, the image of Lucrece becomes one of Brutus's most pointed propagandistic weapons, and he will summon her "ghost" three times during the course of the play. First, in order to cement the loyalty of the republican faction, Brutus paints a vivid picture of her ghost, who (he claims) warmly approves of his plan for vengeance: "Oh, methinks I see / The hovering Spirit of the Ravish'd Matron / Look down; She bows her Airy head to bless you, / And Crown th'auspicious Sacrament with smiles" (1.1.452–55). Lucrece supports and encourages their actions, Brutus insists; therefore, those actions must be right and good. Given Lucrece's dying plea for revenge—"Revenge me; Oh Revenge, Revenge, Revenge," she begs (1.1.421)—it is likely that Lucrece would indeed have approved of Brutus's plan. Yet her "appearance" onstage is entirely imaginative. In Victoria Hayne's words, "No phantom appears on stage; it exists entirely in Brutus's language."[59] Lucrece has become a fictional construct, a character in Brutus's rhetorical arsenal to be summoned at his will.

In act 1, Brutus describes the ghost of Lucrece to foment political discontent among the aristocracy; he again summons her spirit to sway the common people: "Behold she comes, and calls you to revenge her," he tells the public, brandishing Lucrece's knife.

> Her Spirit hovers in the Air, and cries
> To Arms, to Arms; drive, drive the Tarquins out.
> Behold this Dagger, taken from her wound,
> She bids you fix this Trophee on your Standard,
> This Ponnyard which she stab'd into her heart,
> And bear her Body in your Battels front. (2.1.212–17)

The image of Lucrece, coupled with the threat of aristocratic violence—Brutus promises the city will be filled with "Rapes, Adulteries, / The Tiber choak'd with Bodies" should Tarquin reclaim his throne (2.1.221–22)—is enough to sway the people to his side and create widespread support for the new republic. Finally, Brutus summons the image of Lucrece to manipulate his son's behavior. To prevent Titus from consummating his illicit marriage to Teraminta, Brutus once more brandishes Lucrece's knife and demands his son's obedience. "[O]n this, / This spotted blade, bath'd in the blood of Lucrece," he says, "I'll make thee swear on this thy Wedding night / Thou wilt not touch thy Wife (2.1.345–47). If Brutus himself is not truly moved by Lucrece's suffering, he is profoundly aware of her power as a symbol. Thus he forces his son to swear obedience not merely on Lucrece's knife, but on her soul: "Swear too, and by the Soul of Ravish'd Lucrece, / Tho on thy Bridal night, thou wilt not touch" Teraminta (2.1.399–400). Brutus's tactic is effective. Just as he is able to manipulate Lucrece's family and the Roman mob, he is able to compel his son's submission: "I swear," Titus capitulates, "ev'n by the Soul of her you nam'd, / The Ravish'd Lucrece, Oh th' Immortal Gods! / I will not touch her" (2.1.401–2). Lucrece's greatest power lies in her weight as a symbol, while Brutus's power lies in his ability to harness that significance to his own ends.

Eventually, Brutus moves to channel popular love for Lucrece into love for (and obedience to) himself. Initially, when Brutus demands vengeance, he pledges to fight "For Chastity, for Rome, and [Lucrece's] violated Honor" (1.1.429). Brutus will again speak of violation and demand vengeance late in the text, but this time, the nation of Rome, not Lucrece, plays the role of victim: "I swear the Gods have Doom'd thee to the grave" (4.1.496), he tells Titus after discovering and foiling the royalist counterplot. "The violated Genius of thy Country / Rears his sad head, and passes Sentence on thee" (4.1.497–98). The country as a whole has been assaulted, and Brutus mourns the "assaulted Majesty of Rome" (5.2.35). Then the rhetoric shifts once more; it is not Lucrece, not Rome, but Brutus himself, who has been violated: "O rise, thou violated Majesty" (4.1.561), Titus begs his father, "Rise from the Earth; . . . I now submit to all your threatn'd vengeance" (4.1.562, 564). Now Brutus has been assaulted, has suffered as Lucrece once suffered. Rome has been ravished by the royalist plot and Brutus, as a metonymic stand-in for Rome, has replaced Lucrece as the primary victim of the crime. Brutus encourages such an identification, co-opting the country's sympathy for the ravished Lucrece; he (and by extension Rome, with which he is inextricably linked) has become the victim of royalist excess, while the virtuous Roman matron, once a catalyst for change, lies forgotten.

To examine Lee's Brutus is to disclose the growth of the propagandist and the process by which the image of rape becomes a political weapon. Such a process is not necessarily positive for Lee. Unlike Rochester, for whom Lucina's victory in death over Valentinian is a cause for celebration, Lee evinces a profound suspicion of Brutus's verbal skills. And unlike Rochester, Lee does not celebrate the tyrant's overthrow, expressing instead a much more Filmerian suspicion of political change. Filmer, as we have seen, argues that to oust a legitimate monarch is to invite new forms of political corruption, "a remedy far worse than the disease."[60] Lee's play likewise concludes with the unsettling notion that Brutus's new government is as tyrannical as the one it replaced. Brutus, of course, insists that he has set the world back to rights. In this new world, he claims, "endless peace" will be "thro all the World enjoy'd" (5.2.200), and "No dreadful Comets threaten from the Skies, / No venom fall, nor poys'nous Vapors rise" (5.2.207–8). Owen concurs, "Lee leaves us, ultimately, not with a nightmare, but with the transcendence of nightmare through human effort."[61] Yet does he really? If Brutus's tactics are suspiciously unsavory, so, too, is the government of his nascent republic. On the one hand, Brutus offers freedom through republicanism from the arbitrary law and personal favoritism of monarchy.[62] However, Tiberius praises these same things as the benefits of aristocratic rule:

> Remember this in short. A King is one
> To whom you may complain when you are wrong'd;
> The Throne lies open in your way for Justice:
> You may be angry, and may be forgiven.
> There's room for favor, and for benefit,
> Where Friends and Enemies may come together,
> Have present hearing, present composition,
> Without recourse to the Litigious Laws;
> Laws that are cruel, deaf, inexorable,
> That cast the Vile and Noble altogether;
> Where, if you should exceed the bounds of Order,
> There is no pardon: O, 'tis dangerous,
> To have all Actions judg'd by rigorous Law. (2.1.8–20)

Staves calls this speech "a monarchist argument contrasting the mercy prerogative affords with the harshness of impersonal law."[63] What Brutus condemns as arbitrariness, the royalists celebrate as the opportunity for social mobility through patronage—Fabritius, for instance, has risen from the position of a servant to the position of a favored courtier—and compassion before the law.

No less ethically dubious, of course, is Brutus's treatment of his favorite son. In the case of Lucrece's suicide, bloodletting does purge contagion, Lucrece's "dishonored" blood becoming "chaste" blood and "sacred" blood after her death (1.1.392, 442, 436). When Brutus condemns his son to execution, however, the efficacy of the purge is not as clear. Titus believes himself tainted by his association with the royalist plot—he describes himself as "Black . . . with all my guilt upon me" (4.1.403)—but his self-sacrifice does not necessarily redeem. According to Valerius, Titus is tainted not by his involvement with the treasonous plot, but rather by the act intended to reclaim him:

> But see, O Gods, behold the Gallant Titus,
> The Mirror of all Sons, the white of Virtue;
> Fill'd up with *blots*, and writ all o're with blood,
> Bowing with *shame* his body to the ground;
> Whipt out of breath by these Inhuman Slaves! (5.1.33–37, emphasis mine)

The ostensibly purifying whipping has done as much damage to Titus as the initial act of disloyalty. Titus's body, once white with innocence, has been blotted not by his crimes, but by the mark of the lictor's lash. The punishment yields degradation, not catharsis, while Brutus himself emerges a "God of Blood" and "more Tyrannical than any Tarquin" (5.1.103, 116). In transforming Titus into a second Lucrece, he also becomes, perversely and incestuously, the play's second violator. Critics who argue on behalf of *Lucius Junius Brutus*'s Whiggish leanings frequently praise Brutus's stoic nobility in sacrificing his children for the greater societal good. Laura Brown, for instance, writes, "Brutus can be consistently heroic because his merit is everywhere and always tied to his republican virtue."[64] Yet Brutus uses his son as he uses Lucrece—to cement the new regime—creating a structural parallel between the two characters and replaying Lucrece's violation in Titus's form. Multiple moments in the text reinforce the parallelism between Lucrece and Titus. Brutus describes Lucrece, mourning the rape "as if she had lost her wealth in some black Storm!" (1.1.98); Valerius uses similar language to describe Titus's whipping: "How fares this noble Vessel, that is rob'd / Of all its Wealth" (5.2.188–89), he wonders. Both the sexual assault and the whipping are described in terms of lost property. Similarly, just as Lucrece laments her lost honor, "blot[ted]" "with the Blood of Tarquin" (1.1.358), Titus speaks of "my blotted honor" (4.1.469). Titus becomes the play's second Lucrece, Brutus's contemporary Helen, and the sacrifice necessary to realize Brutus's political design.

For some critics, the parallel between Teraminta and Lucrece is more obvious than that of Titus and Lucrece, since both female characters are brutally attacked, Lucrece by an unscrupulous noble, Teraminta by an unscrupulous republican mob. Titus describes Teraminta's appearance after her assault:

> Ha! my Teraminta!
> Is't possible? the very top of Beauty,
> This perfect face drawn by the Gods at Council,
> Which they were long a making, as they had reason,
> For they shall never hit the like again,
> Defil'd and mangled thus! What barbarous wretch
> Has thus blasphem'd this bright Original? (5.1.53–59)

Like Lucrece, she has been defiled, her beauty attacked and soiled. Thus Julie Ellison sees Teraminta as a second victim of a sexualized attack: "In the last act, as in the first, the broken body of a violated woman is the somatic sign of republican rigor. The suicide of Lucrece catalyzed the republican victory over Tarquin at the beginning of the play. At the end, Teraminta enters disheveled and wounded after being tormented (in effect, raped) by 'the mob,' to which she is twice vulnerable, as a member of the tyrant's family and as an illegitimate member of that family."[65] The parallelism between Teraminta and Lucrece certainly emphasizes the parallels between the two political parties. The mob replaces Sextus Tarquin as a defiler of women, perpetrating the very act that initially aroused its rebellious ire. Yet the play also makes quite clear that Teraminta has *not*, like Lucrece, been sexually assaulted; she has emerged from her encounter with the mob with virginity intact. She will subsequently plead for Brutus's mercy "By all these wounds upon my *Virgin* breast" (5.2.130, emphasis mine). The preservation of Teraminta's chastity emphasizes Brutus's deliberate complicity in the construction of a sacrificial victim for the greater political good. He has "avenged" one victim by creating another.[66]

Throughout the text, Brutus feminizes his son in anger, calling him "fond, young, soft, and gentle" (2.1.381) and demanding that he "shake this soft, effeminate, lazy Soul / Forth from thy bosom" (1.1.229–30). Later, when Teraminta laments her husband's sufferings, she imagines breast-feeding from his abused and broken body. Gazing at Titus's flayed and bloodied form, Teraminta says that she has come

> to pant my last,
> To wash thy gashes with my Farewel tears,
> To murmur, sob, and lean my aking head
> Upon thy breast, thus like a Cradle Babe
> To suck thy wounds and bubble out my Soul. (5.1.83–87)

Citing these lines, Joyce MacDonald calls Titus "hermaphroditic" and writes, "That Titus offers to nourish his lover with his heart's blood also points to the inherent disorder of the masculine body that Brutus would reorganize and rededicate to manhood."[67] What has gone entirely unnoticed by critics, however, is the striking religious subtext of the moment. Titus's act of breast-feeding directly recalls the image of Christ lactating blood familiar from medieval Catholic iconography. Drawing on 1 Peter's assertion that people, "As newborn babes, desire the sincere milk of the word,"[68] medieval writers frequently "called the wound in Christ's side a breast. . . . Over and over again in the fourteenth and fifteenth centuries we find representations of Christ as the one who feeds and bleeds. Squirting blood from wounds often placed high in the side, Christ fills cups for his followers just as Mary feeds her baby."[69] A tradition of such imagery also existed in seventeenth-century English literature. Richard Crashaw's epigram to Luke 11, *Blessed be the paps which Thou hast sucked*, for instance, explicitly employs the image of a maternal and lactating Christ: "Suppose he had been Tabled at thy Teates, / Thy hunger feels not what he eates: / Hee'l have his Teat e're long (a bloody one) / The Mother then must suck the Son."[70] Lee draws on this iconographic tradition and on the image of Christ's bloody teat when Titus imaginatively nourishes his wife with his sacrificial blood. When Teraminta imagines "suck[ing]" on Titus's wounds, she imagines an act of vampirism transformed by Christian iconography into Eucharistic ritual. Given the play's overwhelming anti-Catholicism—when confronted with literal blood drinking in the royalist conspirator's black mass, Vinditius says, "if a man can't go to Heaven, unless your Priests eat him, and drink him, and roast him alive; I'll be for the broad way, and the Devil shall have me at a venture" (4.1.126–29)—it may seem strange that the play's "most virtuous and attractive characters—the Romeo and Juliet of the piece" would themselves engage in a Catholic-style ritual.[71] Here nonetheless is Eucharistic imagery and blood drinking associated not with black mass and sadism, but with Titus's self-sacrificial heroism, certainly complicating the anti-Catholicism of the play. It also challenges again the ethics of Brutus's justice; as a second Lucrece, Titus provides another broken and effeminized body through which power can be affirmed. As a Jesus figure, he dies for the sins of a diseased society and a power-crazed father.

Teraminta's speech marks the third in a series of blood-drinking rituals that merge the image of the monarchy with the image of the commonwealth and recall the chaos and upheaval of civil war. Teraminta, perhaps the most innocent victim in the second half of the play, criticizes Brutus for his cruelty and coldness toward his progeny; she calls her husband the "God-like Son / Of an inhuman barbarous bloody Father" (5.1.51–52). Teraminta comes to despise Brutus, and thus she rewrites the story of Titus's birth: "A wretch so barbarous never could produce thee" (5.1.70), she tells him; "Some God, some God, my Titus, watch'd his absence, / Slipt to thy mothers bed and gave thee to the World" (5.1.71–72). In act 1, Titus tries to free Teraminta from the stain of her parentage by reimagining the circumstances of her conception: "A God thy Father was, a Goddess was his Wife" (1.1.45), he insists, denying her father's paternity. In act 4 the play comes full circle, and Teraminta does the same for her husband, thereby constructing a parallel between the two fathers and suggesting that Brutus is just another Tarquin, another tyrant to take the place of the first. While Brutus initially calls Tarquin a "monster," Teraminta finally accuses Brutus of possessing a "monstrous nature" (5.2.155).[72] Tiberius, too, castigates his father, telling him to "Enjoy the bloody conquest of thy Pride, / Thou more Tyrannical than any Tarquin" (5.1.115–16). Tiberius speaks from his own thwarted ambition, of course, but he speaks truth in this. Brutus, like his royalist counterparts, harnesses the power of human, sexualized suffering and turns his son into an unjustly executed martyr, becoming in the process a "God of Blood" (5.1.103). Thus a true catharsis is impossible for the Roman republic. Brutus may have purged the realm of aristocratic misrule, but he has established a new tyranny in its place.[73] The murder of Titus, while strong enough to cement the empire, cannot heal a public wound first created by Sextus Tarquin and then exacerbated by Brutus's merciless justice.

CONCLUSION

In the end, Lee presents a very different treatment of the Lucrece myth from Rochester's, one more reminiscent of Filmer's *Patriarcha* than Sidney's *Discourses*. Unlike Rochester's *Valentinian*, which finally celebrates the emperor's removal from office, Lee leaves his audience with the specter of a new tyranny to replace the old. Political rebellion does not bring an end to suffering, but instead invites new forms of corruption, violence, and decay. Meanwhile, the sympathetic propaganda of Rochester's Lucina is replaced by the opportunistic propaganda of Lee's Brutus, a form of rhetoric associated not with liberation from tyranny but with an illegitimate and repressive regime. Despite the contemporary censoring of the play, then, Lee offers a critical view of both republican governance and the unethical motivations of those who would transform acts of private violence into public action. As we shall see in the next chapter, however, the political cannot be cleanly separated from the personal. As the Exclusion Crisis itself represented a conflict within a single family, the language of paternalism transformed all civil unrest into acts of intrafamilial violence. Underlying many of the plays in the period is a fear of familial collapse engendering broader societal destruction. Authors combine the rhetoric of rape with cannibalism to question the nature of familial and parental responsibilities in an age of extreme civic unrest.

NOTES

1. According to Jonathan Scott, "the polemical intention of the *Discourses* was to refute Sir Robert Filmer's *Patriarcha*": *Algernon Sidney and the Restoration Crisis, 1677–1683* (Cambridge: Cambridge University Press, 1991), 203–4. Scott has provided the fullest modern discussion of Sidney's life, works, and intellectual legacy. See also Jonathan Scott, *Algernon Sidney and the English Republic, 1623–1677* (Cambridge: Cambridge University Press, 1988).
2. Algernon Sidney, *Discourses concerning Government*, ed. Thomas G. West (Indianapolis: Liberty Classics, 1990), 543.
3. Ibid., 342.
4. Ibid., 328–29.
5. "Sir Edmund Berry Godfrey's Ghost," in *Poems on Affairs of State: Augustan Satirical Verse, 1660–1714*, ed. Elias F. Mengel, 7 vols. (New Haven: Yale University Press, 1963), 2:7–11, ll. 30–31, 34–35.
6. Ibid., ll. 84–89.
7. Ibid., ll. 92–93, 100–103.
8. Hughes, "Rape," 232–33.
9. Sir Robert Filmer, *Patriarcha and Other Writings*, ed. Johann P. Sommerville (Cambridge: Cambridge University Press, 1991), 33.
10. Ibid., 26, 27.
11. Ibid., 34.
12. H. P., *A Satyr Against Common-wealths* (London, 1684), 5.
13. Ibid., 4–5.
14. Ibid., 5.

15. "A Summons from a True Protestant Conjurer to Cethegus' Ghost, To Appear September 19, 1682," in *Poems on Affairs of State: Augustan Satirical Verse, 1660–1714*, ed. Howard H. Schless, 7 vols. (New Haven: Yale University Press, 1963), 3:263–66, ll. 11–16.

16. *A Popish Political Catechism: Or, A View of the Principles of the Synagogue of Antichrist, concerning the Power of Kings* (London, 1685), 2.

17. Ibid., 2–3.

18. Ibid., 4.

19. Hughes, "Rape," 232.

20. James William Johnson, *A Profane Wit: The Life of John Wilmot, Earl of Rochester* (Rochester: University of Rochester Press, 2004), 206. Harold Love, in contrast, dates the play to early 1675: "The Rapes of Lucina," in *Print, Manuscript & Performance*, eds. Arthur F. Marotti and Michael D. Bristol (Athens: Ohio State University Press, 2000), 208. For discussion of the play's publication history, see Lucyle Hook, "The Publication Date of Rochester's *Valentinian*," *Huntington Library Quarterly* 19, no. 4 (1956): 401–7.

21. J. Harold Wilson, "Satiric Elements in Rochester's *Valentinian*," *Philological Quarterly* 16 (1937): 41. Wilson likens Valentinian's pursuit of Lucina to Charles II's pursuit of Frances Stuart. Likewise, Wilson calls Charles II an "actual prototype" for Rochester's Valentinian": "Rochester's *Valentinian* and Heroic Sentiment," *ELH* 4, no. 4 (1937): 266.

22. Larry Carver, "Rochester's *Valentinian*," *Restoration and Eighteenth Century Theatre Research* 3, no. 1 (1989): 25.

23. Harold Love, "Was Lucina Betrayed at Whitehall?" in *That Second Bottle: Essays on John Wilmot, Earl of Rochester*, ed. Nicholas Fisher (Manchester: Manchester University Press, 2000), 188. For a contrasting view of Rochester as Valentinian, see Peter Byrne, "'Where Appetite Directs': Tragic Heroism's Recovery in Rochester's *Valentinian*," *Pacific Coast Philology* 40, no. 1 (2005): 158–77.

24. Charles II, *A Proclamation To Restrain the Spreading of False News, and Licentious Talking of Matters of State and Government* (London, 1672), 1.

25. Ibid.

26. Marina Hila, "'Justice shall never heare ye, I am justice': Absolutist Rape and Cyclical History in John Fletcher's *The Tragedy of Valentinian*," *Neophilologus* 91, no. 4 (2007): 746.

27. *A Gratulatory Poem*, 1.

28. For more negative readings of Lucina, see Byrne, "'Where Appetite Directs,'" along with Arthur Colby Sprague, *Beaumont and Fletcher on the Restoration Stage* (Cambridge, MA: Harvard University Press, 1926).

29. Hila, "'Justice shall never heare ye,'" 753.

30. Byrne, "'Where Appetite Directs,'" 160.

31. Ibid.

32. See also Kirk Combe, who reads this exchange as a condemnation of the falsity of divine right ideology: *A Martyr for Sin: Rochester's Critique of Polity, Sexuality, and Society* (Newark: University of Delaware Press, 1998), 137.

33. Sidney, *Discourses*, 342.

34. Hila, "'Justice shall never heare ye,'" 749.

35. Some critics have read more ambivalence into Fletcher's attitude toward tyrannicide; see, for instance, Philip J. Finkelpearl, *Court and Country Politics in the Plays of Beaumont and Fletcher* (Princeton: Princeton University Press, 1990). For other readings of the politics of Fletcher's *Valentinian*, see Rebecca W. Bushnell, *Tragedies of Tyrants: Political Thought and Theater in the English Renaissance* (Ithaca and London: Cornell University Press, 1990); Sandra Clark, *The Plays of Beaumont and Fletcher: Sexual Themes and Dramatic Representation* (New York: Harvester Wheatsheaf, 1994); and Robert Y. Turner, "Responses to Tyranny in John Fletcher's Plays," *Medieval and Renaissance Drama in England* 4 (1989): 123–41.

36. In this, my argument differs fundamentally from Jeremy Webster's; Webster argues that Rochester sympathizes with a monarch "torn between national duty and personal desire": *Performing Libertinism in Charles II's Court: Politics, Drama, Sexuality* (New York: Palgrave Macmillan, 2005), 140.

37. William Van Lennep, ed., *The London Stage, 1660–1800*, 5 vols. (Carbondale: Southern Illinois University Press, 1960), 1:293.

38. Antony Hammond, "The 'Greatest Action': Lee's *Lucius Junius Brutus*," in *Poetry and Drama, 1570–1700: Essays in Honour of Harold F. Brooks*, eds. Antony Coleman and Antony Hammond (London: Methuen, 1981), 175.

39. Nathaniel Lee, *Lucius Junius Brutus*, in *Works*, ed. Thomas B. Stroup and Arthur L. Cooke, 2 vols. (New Brunswick: Scarecrow Press, 1954), 4.1.28, 4.1.104. Further references to *Lucius Junius Brutus* are from this edition and will be cited parenthetically in the text by act, scene, and line number.

40. Livy, *Ab Urbe Condita*, trans. B. O. Foster, 14 vols. (Cambridge, MA: Harvard University Press, 1970), 1:83.

41. Shakespeare's *The Rape of Lucrece*, for instance, explicitly refers to Helen as a rape victim.

42. J. M. Armistead, "The Tragicomic Design of *Lucius Junius Brutus*: Madness as Providential Therapy," *Papers on Language and Literature* 15 (1979): 48.

43. Victoria Hayne points out the difference between Brutus's and Titus's descriptions of the impending consummation: "'the pangs of bliss' or 'slimy joys'": "'All Language Then Is Vile': The Theatrical Critique of Political Rhetoric in Nathaniel Lee's *Lucius Junius Brutus*," *ELH* 63, no. 2 (1996): 344.

44. Thomas Heywood, *The Rape of Lucrece. A True Roman Tragedie. With the severall Songs in their apt places, by Valerius, the merrie Lord amongst the Roman Peers* (London, 1608), h3v. Further references to *The Rape of Lucrece* are from this edition and will be cited parenthetically in the text by page number.

45. Catherine Belling, "Infectious Rape, Therapeutic Revenge: Bloodletting and the Health of Rome's Body," in *Disease, Diagnosis, and Cure on the Early Modern Stage*, eds. Stephanie Moss and Kaara L. Peterson (Burlington: Ashgate, 2004), 121.

46. Ibid., 125.

47. Sue Owen, "'Partial Tyrants' and 'Freeborn People' in *Lucius Junius Brutus*," *Studies in English Literature 1500-1900* 31, no. 3 (1991): 473.

48. Livy, *Ab Urbe Condita*, 80.

49. For discussion of Lee's Tullia, see chapter 4.

50. Antony Hammond provides a useful commentary on Brutus's Machiavellian tendencies, his "confusion of ends and means" (Hammond, "The 'Greatest Action,'" 181).

51. Joyce MacDonald, "Public Wounds: Sexual Bodies and the Origins of State in Nathaniel Lee's *Lucius Junius Brutus*," *Studies in Eighteenth-Century Culture* 32 (2003): 232.

52. In contrast, Livy does not place Collatine among the ranks of the conspirators. He writes, Collatine "resigned the consulship and went into voluntary exile at Lavinium, taking with him everything he possessed" (Livy, *Ab Urbe Condita*, 91).

53. Vintidius's creation of false omens may offer a comment on the political culture of the late 1670s. As John B. Rollins points out, the year 1678 "would see two lunar and three solar eclipses: astrologers delighted in assigning the most malign of interpretations to these events": "Judeo-Christian Apocalyptic Literature and John Crowne's *The Destruction of Jerusalem*," *Comparative Drama* 35, no. 2 (2001): 215.

54. Hayne, "'All Language,'" 343.

55. According to Gerald Parker, the power of Brutus's language enables his acts of cruelty: "'History as Nightmare' in Nevil Payne's *The Siege of Constantinople* and Nathaniel Lee's *Lucius Junius Brutus*," *Papers on Language and Literature* 21, no. 1 (1985): 15. Owen, by contrast, is less suspicious of Brutus, arguing that the mob's reaction reveals the legitimacy of Brutus's cause (Owen, "Partial Tyrants," 471). See also Richard Brown, who comments on the strength of Brutus's oratory: "Heroics Satirized by 'Mad Nat. Lee,'" *Papers on Language and Literature* 19 no. 4 (1983): 385–401.

56. According to Livy, a series of wars subsequently plagued the new republic. Lee, however, ignores this historical fact, leaving his audience with a feeling of restoration, safety, and peace.

57. Hila, "'Justice shall never heare ye,'" 756.

58. For further analysis of disease imagery in Shakespeare's poem, see Belling, "Infectious Rape."

59. Hayne, "'All Language,'" 345.

60. Filmer, *Patriarcha*, 33.

61. Owen, "Partial Tyrants," 478.

62. Many critics have commented on Lee's negative depiction of the royalists. Owen, for instance, writes, "The royalists are associated with tyranny, ambition, lust, greed, lawlessness, and Catholicism. While Brutus hopes and prays for peace, they revel in bloodshed" (ibid., 472). In contrast, she claims, Brutus's government looks positively just.

63. Staves, *Players' Scepters*, 245. In this, Lee's language closely follows Livy's: "A king, they argued, was, after all, a human being, and there was chance of getting from him what one wanted rightly or wrongly; under a monarchy there was room for influence and favour; a king could be angry and forgive; he knew the difference between an enemy and a friend. Law, on the other hand, was impersonal and inexorable. Law had no ears" (Livy, *Ab Urbe Condita*, 92).

64. L. Brown, *English Dramatic Form*, 76. See also Frances Barbour, who describes Lee as "consistently anti-divine-right and anti-Tory": "The Unconventional Heroic Plays of Nathaniel Lee," *Studies in English* 20 (1940): 116. Other critics profess fondness for the character of Brutus—Antony Hammond calls him "the man of fierce and passionate principle" (Hammond, "The 'Greatest Action,'" 178), while John Loftis defends the "deserved execution" of Titus and Tiberius: introduction to *Lucius Junius Brutus*, by Nathaniel Lee (Lincoln: University of Nebraska Press, 1967), xxii.

65. Julie Ellison, *Cato's Tears and the Making of Anglo-American Emotion* (Chicago: University of Chicago Press, 1999), 35.

66. See also MacDonald, "Public Wounds," for whom the replacement of Lucrece with Titus reflects the banishment of the feminine.

67. Ibid., 238.

68. 1 Pet. 2:3.

69. Caroline Walker Bynum, "The Body of Christ in the Later Middle Ages: A Reply to Leo Steinberg," *Renaissance Quarterly* 39, no. 3 (1986): 427.

70. Richard Crashaw, "Luke 11. Blessed be the paps which Thou hast sucked," in *The Complete Poetry of Richard Crashaw*, ed. George Walton Williams (Garden City: Anchor Books, 1970), 14, ll. 1–4.

71. J. M. Armistead, *Nathaniel Lee* (Boston: Twayne, 1979), 38.

72. J. Peter Verdurmen concurs: "through [Titus and Teraminta], Lee projects the anguish, paralysis and victimization that Brutus, as the controller of their world, makes unavoidable": "*Lucius Junius Brutus* and Restoration Tragedy: The Politics of Trauma," *Journal of European Studies* 37, no. 2 (1995): 83.

73. See also G. Wilson Knight, who is equally critical of Brutus's new republic: *The Imperial Theme: Further Interpretations of Shakespeare's Tragedies Including the Roman Plays* (London: Oxford University Press, 1931).

Chapter Four

Rape and the Cannibal Father, 1678–1687

In 1679, Protestant Dissenter-turned-Anglican William Allen made an impassioned plea to Protestant Nonconformists, begging them to eschew separatism and return to the Anglican fold: "I would now with a still small Voice speak Peace and Harmony," he tells his reader, "perswade to Unity and Conformity, and Brotherly Love and Affection. . . . I would bring Balm to your Wounds and Ease to your Griefs of Separation."[1] Allen, like Nathaniel Lee's Brutus, positions himself as a doctor come to heal the realm of schism, but in this case, he will do so through peaceful reunification rather than bloodletting: "I come not . . . with Launcets and Razers, to cut and break up the Wounds, or with Probes and Pledgets to search or keep them open; the Wounds of Division and Separation have been sufficiently handled by able and skilful Chirurgions, and now is the time, if ever, to apply a Cataplasm and healing Plaister."[2] Underlying Allen's call to unity is a fear of Roman Catholic deviousness and a belief that the pope will foster divisions within the Protestant Church that he may overtake and destroy it. Working through the pope, Satan will infect the English people with "the Poyson of Pride, of Ambition, of Luxury and Ease, and of false Doctrine. By this means he set them at Variance with one another, the Children against the Father, the Father against the Children."[3] Allen reminds his reader that all good Protestants have "one Father God" and "one Mother the Church," and thus wonders, "Why . . . this Separation?"[4]

Central to Allen's rhetoric is an image of the English Protestant nation as a single family, with monarch and church as parents. He tells his Nonconformist readers that he speaks to them "as a Friend, as a Brother" because they are all one family under God and king.[5] The Dissenters must "Return like the lost Prodigal Son to the Father of your Country, and into the Bosom of your Mother."[6] He reminds his reader that "the fifth Commandment, *Honor your Father*," also reaches "to your King the Father of his Country."[7] In rebelling against the established church, the Dissenters prove themselves both privately disobedient and publicly treasonous. They represent "a means of the great increase of *Popery* in this Land" and are the worst sorts of "Unnatural and Disobedient Sons."[8] As they defy their father the king, they sexually dishonor their mother, the Anglican Church: "They bespatter her Reputation, they fling dirt in her Face, they endeavor to pollute her Garments, they would render her Odious, Papistical, Ridiculous; they call her Whore and compare her with *Babylon*."[9] Finally, driven by popish plots and treachery, they devour their mother in an act of perverse cannibalism: The Catholic Church will "make you like Vipers, to gnaw asunder the Womb of your Mother, and to eat your way to Separation thorow [sic] her bowels."[10] Cannibal imagery provides a vocabulary for discussing political and religious conflict and divisiveness within the Protestant family.

Allen is not alone in deploying the discourse of cannibalism in his tract. Entwined images of rape, vampirism, and cannibalism, central to the propaganda pamphlets of the English Civil Wars, again pervade anti-Catholic works between the years of the Popish Plot and the Glorious Revolution. *A Bull Sent by Pope Pius* (1678) describes the Catholics as those who "Murder'd their Kings, and Thrones laid desolate" and who "Are flesh'd with slaughter, drunk with steeming blood."[11] They speak with "polluted Lips,"[12] "eat" their Lord "Carnally,"[13] and are guilty of having "plotted against the Blood, Life, and Estates of the Innocents, in Fathering High Treason upon them."[14] They engage in "Poysons, Rapes," and "Massacres" and insist that "Kings are Usurpers" who must be overthrown.[15] As in the English Civil War tracts, the Catholics are accused of committing horrible acts of sexual violence and infanticide, one tract describing how "Women were Ripped up alive, young Children dashed against the Pavement, Embrio's torn from the bleeding Womb, Hoary Hairs stained with Blood, Churches Robbed, Houses Fired, Women Ravished, Virgins Deflowred, and then Murthered with the most exquisite torment."[16] They defile their Lord through the ceremony of the Eucharist: "I will not here put you in mind of the strange absurdities that must follow from this Doctrine of Transubstantiation, *viz.* that Christ, when he did eat and drink in this Sacrament, must have eaten his own flesh, and that the Apostles must have eaten his body."[17] And they support a Church that is "an Association of Monsters, and a Den of Cannibals," filled with "Injustice, Rapine, and Cold-blooded Murder."[18]

The connections between rape, cannibalism, and familial strife are also foregrounded in Baptist preacher Benjamin Keach's 1679 poem, *Sion in Distress: Or, The Groans of the Protestant Church*. As I explained in the introduction to this study, Keach presents an Anglican Church, Sion, that has been symbolically ravished by the evil Catholic Whore of Babylon. Sion expresses herself with "deep and piercing sobs," and with utmost pathos describes her victimization at the hands of that "*Babylonish Whore*, / Big with a Bastard" and that "*Brutish Whore*! Of *Cannibals* the worse."[19] Here once again we see the propagandistic tendency to juxtapose two women, one martyred, the other monstrous, to dramatize the conflict between religions. Unlike the loving Sion, the Catholic Church is a truly horrible mother, one who teaches her "tender Children to infringe the Law"[20] and encourages her offspring to commit horrible acts of violence: "From Mothers Womb" they will "tear the heart / Of Unborn-Infants; they'll deflour, / Then rip her up in half an hour."[21] Such children delight in disrupting familial relations by forcing wives and children to turn on husbands and fathers. Writing of the Irish massacre, Keach exclaims:

> They made *poor wives* with *husbands blood* to spill,
> And trembling Youths, their aged Parents kill.
> They forc'd the Son to stab his dearest Mother,
> And then one Brother to destroy the other.
> Some they put fast in Stocks, then teach a Brat
> To ripe them, and make Candles of their Fat.
> How many Virgins did they Ravish first?
> Then with their hearts-blood quench their eager Thirst.[22]

The Catholic Church is the ultimate monstrous mother who glories in the creation of unnatural children. She is also explicitly a vampire, and one who sends her children to "*gore* my *Sides* and spoil my *Interest*," to "rend, to tear, and make a spoil of me."[23] Anti-Catholic tracts of the late 1670s and 1680s thus link depictions of rape and cannibalism with disruptions to family structure. Whig authors often accused the Catholic Church of insidiously seeking to turn family members against one another, both on the macrocosmic level of the English Protestant Church fracturing into sects and on the microcosmic level of the individual family. Priests are accused of committing acts of incestuous rape: "A Sisters Ravishment is held no Sin, / With their own Offspring, some have wicked been."[24] Meanwhile the pope orders a

> Nursing Mother sent
> Unto our Church, with this intent,
> Not to be kind to it, but rather
> T'orelay the Babe, and kill the Father:
> 'Tis he, grand Patron of Confusion,
> Who works in Houses Dissolution:
> 'Tis he who, true Arch-Rebel Monger,
> 'Gainst elder Brother sets the younger.[25]

Underlying all of these representations is the fear that Catholicism will destroy families and set children against their parents and one another.

Set in this context, this chapter explores the prevalence of rape and cannibal imagery as metaphors for political and religious disruptions in the drama and propaganda of the late 1670s and 1680s. Between the years of the Popish Plot and Glorious Revolution, combined descriptions of sexual violence and flesh eating encoded a constellation of anxieties surrounding the appropriate relationship between father and child, subject and monarch. For anti-Catholic polemicists, the Church represented a terrifying source of familial angst, one that encouraged children to replace obedience to their fathers (and, by extension, their monarch) with obedience to the pope. Catholic children in these pamphlets represent a source of profound anxiety; they must always be watched lest they turn on and cannibalize their parents. While Tory tracts often downplayed the harmful aspects of the Catholic Church, they, too, employed the rhetoric of the cannibal child, in this case to protest in microcosm the evils of political rebellion. Such tracts frequently demonized the Duke of Monmouth and blamed the period's civic unrest on Monmouth's poisonous ambition to consume his father. In contrast, in a third strain of cannibal rhetoric, Whig polemicists adopted combined images of rape and flesh eating to demonize monarchical absolutism. The evils of disobedient children are dwarfed in many Whig tracts by the far more terrifying acts of the cannibal father, the depraved patriarch who rapes his daughters-in-law before ingesting his sons in a show of brute force. A warning against the dangers of allowing any one man too much power, the sexually violent cannibal father offers a powerful rhetorical corrective to absolutist philosophy. In all of these cases, acts of rape and flesh eating join to interrogate the appropriate role of the father within the family and, by extension, of the monarch within the nation.

As Tim Harris has suggested, contemporary propagandists on all sides of each political divide employed similar language in attacking their enemies, an observation thoroughly borne out in the decade's treatment of rape and cannibal imagery.[26] To examine the political writings of the late 1670s and 1680s is to uncover the repertoire of common tropes that anti-Catholic polemicists and Catholic supporters, Whigs and Tories alike, all shared to depict political and familial atrocity. Onstage, fears of Catholic violence, disobedient children, and paternal overreach overlap and blend nearly to the point of collapsing into one another, often complicating straightforwardly partisan readings of individual dramas. Disrupted parent-child relationships, frequently encoded in the language of rape and cannibalism, are nearly universal in the rape plays of the period. After a broad look, then, at the figurative mayhem in the tracts and plays of these decades—murder, incest, poison, cannibalism, and repeated rapes—the chapter proceeds with a glance back at Lee's *Lucius Junius Brutus*, along with analyses of Thomas Otway's *Venice Preserv'd* (1682) and Lee's earlier play, *Mithridates, King of Pontus* (1678). In each of these texts, relationships between parents and children have disintegrated, undermining the security of the body politic. Rather than honoring their parents and protecting their children, the parent-child pairs in these plays are poisonous to each other. Children have become "Villains lurking in my blood" for Lee's Brutus (4.1.226), while the language of rape and/or cannibalism figures forth the diseased individual family in the context of the diseased body politic.

The chapter then turns to John Crowne's *Thyestes. A Tragedy* (1681) and Edward Ravenscroft's *Titus Andronicus* (performed in 1678, published in 1687), two plays that contain literal acts of flesh eating.[27] In both cases, rape and parental cannibalism occur as effects of the collapse of familial and societal boundaries that normally preserve the integrity of the political nation. Thyestes's opening act of incestuous rape precipitates the royal family's decline, while Atreus expresses his parental and monarchical authority through acts of murder and forced cannibalism. Atreus becomes the monstrous parent lurking at the heart of the nation, the cannibal father who destroys his realm instead of nurturing it, and he is fundamentally convinced that as king, he has the absolute right to do so. Despite the fact that Atreus is never punished for his foul deeds, the play condemns his behavior with a vision of oncoming disaster. In the persons of Agamemnon and Menelaus, the play foreshadows the endless fighting and dishonorable deaths of the Trojan War, along with the final collapse of the House of Atreus precipitated by Tantalus's and Atreus's cannibalistic atrocities. Belying Crowne's ostensibly Tory politics, therefore, the play registers a fundamental discomfort with the prospect of monarchical absolutism as symbolized by the House of Atreus's toxic familial interactions.

Ravenscroft, in contrast, uses the image of the cannibal father to restore social boundaries and return the nation to rights. While the play was adapted in 1678 as an allegory of the Popish Plot, it was not published until 1687, in the run-up to the Glorious Revolution. While *Thyestes* condemns the cannibal father, *Titus Andronicus* encodes its author's Tory faith in an absolutist philosophy. Throughout the play, Ravenscroft reveals his terror, not of internal disruptions to the family, but of infiltration and disruption from without. Aron's baby and the mutilated Lavinia become twin sources of concern, the products of racial or cultural miscegenation and the results of the foreign infiltration of the Roman homeland. Evidence of sin made visible, Lavinia and the baby are disruptive in life, and thus their deaths at their own fathers' hands are perversely comforting. Aron consumes his child out of existence, while Lavinia is swallowed by her mother Earth, enacting the erasure of instability and corruption. *Titus* concludes with a fantasy of the reestablishment of political boundaries and the reaffirmation of national identity, both of which are conducted through the act of cannibalism. Parental cannibalism thus emerges from the play as a cure for societal ills, underscoring Ravenscroft's Tory absolutism and praise for James II's new government. England has been stabilized as *Titus*'s Rome has been stabilized, the treachery of foreign outsiders banished and peace finally restored.

THE EXCLUSION CRISIS AND THE POLITICS OF FAMILIAL COLLAPSE

In many anti-Catholic propaganda tracts, authors accuse the Catholic Church of transforming parents into monsters and children into fiends. Familial relationships disintegrate as individuals privilege allegiance to their church over duty to one another. The Church has "absolved children from honouring their indigent Parents," and worse still, "not only natural Parents, but Kings."[28] Catholics honor their "Ghostly DADS," that is, their priests, before their own blood and nation.[29] They also maltreat their mothers; the Catholic priest "Cares not what dirt he throws in his own Mothers Face."[30] In essence, the Catholic hierarchy, "of which the *Pope* is *Father* and *Head*, and *Rome* the *Mother* and *Nurse*" replaces correct and rightful parents in both the personal and the public spheres.[31] It creates a generation of children, which, when it "were fledg," will "peck out the Eyes of [its] Dam."[32] One 1679 tract, *The Popes Down-fall, At Abergaveny*, literalizes this danger in graphic terms when it relates the story of the parricidal John Kirby. According to the tract's author, Kirby, "being a Papist . . . consequently delighted more in the Blood of a Protestant, though it were of his own Father, then the downfall of the Pope."[33] As such, he becomes the figurative devourer of his own father: "The young Proselyte having the Pope in his belly, had a greater Stomach for Blood and Revenge then for Victuals, and long'd more for a cut of his Father's Throat then the mutton."[34] He then performs a real act of physical violence. When his father attempts to reconcile his son to the Church of England, Kirby refuses to listen and obey: "the Son instead of submitting quietly to the Fatherly Correction, snatcht up the Dish, threw it at his Fathers Head, and therewith dasht out his Brains; [his sister] crying out her Father was kill'd, he answered no, his holy Father was alive."[35] Kirby allows the pope to supplant his biological father in his affections and respect, to horrifying and violent consequences.

Anti-Catholic tracts were not, of course, alone in discussing disruptions to familial structure. As Rachel Weil points out, on both sides of the political divide, "Tracts and treatises during the exclusion crisis wound up being saturated with commentary on the family."[36] The Whig preoccupation with popish treachery and disruptions to familial structure provoked by the pope and his minions was mirrored on the Tory side by a preoccupation with disobedient children who would destroy their parents to satisfy their own ambitions. As the doctrine of patriarchalism transformed all forms of political strife into instances of familial rebellion, "the fear of disorder, expressed through metaphors of familial chaos, was the Tories' strongest polemical card."[37] According to Filmer,

> If we compare the natural duties of a father with those of a king, we find them to be all one, without any difference at all but only in the latitude or extent of them. As the father over one family, so the king, as father over many families, extends his care to preserve, feed, clothe, instruct and defend the whole commonwealth. His wars, his peace, his courts of justice and all his acts of sovereignty tend only to preserve and distribute to every subordinate and inferior father, and to their children, their rights and privileges, so that all the duties of a king are summed up in an universal fatherly care of his people.[38]

As Gordon J. Schochet explains, Filmer had "inextricably united his argument for divine right of kings with patriarchal authority."[39] To disobey the monarch, then, was not only to commit an act of treason, but to violate the fifth commandment.[40]

Contemporary discussions of the child's duty to his father and the subject's to his king inevitably reflected upon the central political crisis of the day, the conflict of leadership within the Stuart family. Joyce Green MacDonald writes, "At its heart, the Exclusion Crisis was a failure of reproductive biology."[41] It also threatened to turn father Charles against son Monmouth and brother Charles against brother James, presaging, fearsomely, a return to the familial chaos of civil war. Thus while Whig discourse condemned the toxic Catholic child, Tories focused instead on the fractious relationship between James Scott, Duke of Monmouth, and his father and uncle. According to Toni Bowers, "Contemporaries were used to imagining the bastard prince as a kind of walking paradox—the personification of all that was lovely and heroic as well as all that was despicable, ungodly, and treasonous."[42] While Whig tracts praised Monmouth for his "Virtue," "Worth," and "beauteous Mind," Tory tracts treated the Duke as a dangerous, parricidal usurper, a Protestant analogue to the Catholic John Kirby.[43] The author of *A Second Remonstrance by way of Address From The Church of England* asks,

> Can we imagine a Person, who has no *Religion* but Debauchery, will be a fit Instrument to Protect or Establish *Truth* and *Piety*? Can we imagine, He, who never sought any thing but his own *private Ends,* will have any generous thoughts for the *Publick*? Can we imagine, He who *Plotted* the death of a *tender* and a *Royal Father,* and prefer'd the Lives of those *Conspirators,* (who seduced him, before the safety of the *King & Kingdom,*) has any sence of *Piety, Honesty* or *Religion* in him?[44]

Monmouth is described as an ungrateful child, "Unworthy of his Prince, whose tender care / For him did every Day and Hour appear."[45] He has "soar'd with *Icarus* in too high a Sphere, / Ungratefully Conspiring to Ensnare / His Royal Father, and his Uncle too."[46] And in fostering a rebellion, he has forced other fathers and children to turn on one another. Because of his ambition, "Parents have lost all the sense and tenderness of Nature; and Children, all the Sentiments of Duty and Obedience; the Eternal Laws of Good and Just, the Laws of Nature and of Nations, of God and Religion, have been violated; Men have been transformed into the cruelty of Beasts, and into the Rage and Malice of Devils."[47] As such, the author of *The Countreys Advice* begs him to "Think on the guiltless Blood you hourly spill / Where Brother Brother, Father Son does kill."[48] Rebellion against the rightful patriarch leads only to "Treason, Murther, Rape, and Misserie [sic]."[49] Monmouth himself is a sexually violent monster; he "Delights in Sin,"[50] and according to *The Young Bastards Wish, A Song*, proclaims, "next I'll Debauch the sweet Wife of my Friends, / And ravish ten Sisters where none dare contend: / Each Night a true Virgin shall come to my Bed / If false the next Morning I'll cut off her Head."[51] In such tracts, Monmouth serves as the latest manifestation of the debauched Cavalier, sexually violent, dishonorable, and untrustworthy. A "hopeful parricide," he is also overly ambitious and will destroy his father and his king to gain a crown, first through his participation in the Rye House Plot and later through his aborted invasion attempt.[52]

Images of destructive children also pervade the theater of the period. In Lee's *Lucius Junius Brutus*, for instance, children are consistently described as a threatening source of social toxicity. Initially Brutus's favorite child—"I love thee more than any of my Children" (2.1.278), Brutus says—Titus taints himself first through contact with Tarquin's blood due to his illicit marriage to Teraminta and later through his complicity in the royalist plot. Brutus comes to see his sons as a form of disease lurking within his own body, a pollutant that will enervate and destroy him. Titus and Tiberius become "two Villains lurking in my blood" (4.1.226), and Brutus weeps "To see his Blood, his Children, his own Bowels / Conspire the death of him that gave'em being" (4.1.288–89). Children represent not futurity, but death, and Brutus will turn on and execute his own flesh and blood rather than allow such disease to fester.

The potential for children to become fatal threats to their parents is most powerfully underscored in *Lucius Junius Brutus* by the unseen presence of King Tarquin's queen, Tullia. A formidable character in Heywood's earlier play, which begins before the uprising that made Tarquin king, Tullia exists in Lee's play only offstage. Nonetheless, Tullia's memory pervades the play, recalling once again the accusations leveled throughout the 1670s at Henrietta Maria, Donna Olimpia, and the Duchesses of Cleveland and Portsmouth, and representing another dramatic manifestation of the poisonous Catholic bride. Richard Brown directly links the mob's hatred of Tullia with Lee's dislike of Charles II's foreign women: "In Brutus, Tarquin's 'furious queen,' Tullia, allied with the conniving priesthood, suggests Charles's entanglements with Catholic and foreign women who were thought to endanger English security, that is, his Portuguese queen, Catherine, his favorite sister, Henriette, who lived in France, and his French mistress, the Duchess of Portsmouth."[53] Unlike earlier poisonous Catholic brides Fredigond and Laula, Tullia does not appear onstage, but she remains a potent and destructive figure nonetheless. It is only due to her intervention, for instance, that Titus joins the rebel faction. Teraminta reveals, "the Queen has Sworn to end me . . . / both [her priests] have Commission / To stab me in your presence, if not wrought / To serve the King" (3.2.106–9). By threatening Teraminta's life and forcing Titus to rebel, Tullia's actions drive the play's denouement, indirectly provoking Titus's execution and Teraminta's death.

It is also Tullia who stimulates the worst of the mob's anger due to her horrifying treatment of her own father. Vinditius rouses the mob practically to a public lynching by reminding them of Fabritius's complicity in the death of the previous king, Tullia's father, whom she helped her husband depose. Fabritius describes his rise to power, first as Tullia's coachman and later as her courtier and pimp: "I was at first the Son of a Car-man, came to the honor of being Tullia's Coachman, have been a Pimp, and remain a Knight at the mercy of the People" (2.1.116–18), he explains. Vinditius then questions Fabritius about his involvement in the regicide:

> Vinditius: Answer me then. Was not you once the Queen's Coachman?
> Fabritius: I was, I was.
> Vinditius: Did you not drive her Chariot over the Body of her Father,
> the dead King Tullus?
> Fabritius: I did, I did: tho it went against my Conscience. (2.1.96–100)

The callousness and cruelty of the murder enrage the crowd, and thus Brutus employs the same story to foment popular support for his rebellion. He recalls the king's

> past Crimes,
> The black Ambition of his furious Queen,
> Who drove her Chariot through the Cyprian Street
> On such a damn'd Design, as might have turn'd
> The Steeds of Day, and shock'd the starting Gods,
> Blest as they are, with an uneasie moment. (2.1.174–79)

Tullia has committed an act of regicide that is also literally a parricide. Driven by an unfeminine and threatening ambition, she has unrepentantly destroyed her father to gain a throne.[54] Brutus subsequently begs the people, "Drive Tullia out, and all of Tarquin's Race" (2.1.227). Ostensibly the actions of Tarquin, the rapist, have ignited Brutus's rebellion, but only Tullia's deeds are abhorrent enough to warrant special mention. Tullia emerges from the text as an anti-Lucrece, the monster woman who destroys her blood rather than sacrifice for it. Allied as she is with the play's royalist, implicitly Catholic faction, she also represents a dramatic female version of John Kirby from *The Popes Down-fall, At Abergaveny*. Her story, like Kirby's, encapsulates the danger that children pose to their parents. Tullia rises to power by treading both literally and figuratively on the body of her father, an action Tiberius replicates in his own quest to depose Brutus. The children are locked in a mortal battle for supremacy over their parents, echoing at once a Whiggish fear of Catholic excess and a Tory rejection of Monmouth's ambition.

While Brutus's children threaten their father, Brutus proves no less dangerous than they, for he oversees the execution of his sons. Fears of murderous children are thus tempered in many plays and tracts by an equally pressing fear of toxic, poisonous parents. In some tracts, parental evil is the by-product of Catholic malice; if the Church can convince a child to murder his sire, it can also prevail on parents to destroy their offspring. The dangers that Catholic parents pose to their children had long pervaded pamphlet culture. Catherine de Medici, as we have seen, was depicted as a literally poisonous Catholic mother, insofar as she supposedly poisoned her son to satisfy her ambition. Likewise, the Catholic mother of *A rare Example of a virtuous Maid in Paris* (1674) functions as a parental analogue to John Kirby; where Kirby kills his innocent Protestant father, this mother kills her innocent Protestant daughter. Upset by her daughter's religious dissent, the ballad's mother reveals the girl's heresy first to her extended family and then to the Parisian authorities:

> With weeping and wailing,
> her mother then did go,
> To assemble her Kinsfolks,
> that they the truth may know,
> Who being then assembled,
> they did this maiden call,
> And put her into prison,
> to fear her there withal.[55]

Finally, a judge orders the girl's execution and the mother repents, but too late to save her child. The poem thus suggests that Catholic parents are as untrustworthy as Catholic children. It also reveals the extent to which civic unrest and religious dissension transform the domestic sphere into a fraught and dangerous space, subject to horrifying acts of violence.

More often, however, depictions of murderous parents reflect a broader Whig discomfort with tyrannical fathers as symbols of absolute monarchy. As we saw in chapter 3, some Whig theorists argued that the rapist monarch earned his overthrow, a concept directly countered in Bohun's Preface to Filmer's *Patriarcha*. According to Bohun, wives, children, and servants never have the right to rebel against their patriarch. He acknowledges that opponents of patriarchal theory invoke the right to self-defense to defend rebellion, asking, "Suppose the Father of a Family in the state of Nature should in a mad or drunken fit go about to kill or maim himself, or one of his innocent Children, can any body think this were rebellion against the Monarch of the Family for his Wife to rescue her innocent Child or self out of his hands by force, if she could not otherwise make him be quiet?"[56] Even in such a case, Bohun concludes, the subordinate has no right to rebel, as society would be torn apart by the rupture of revolt: "What horrible confusion must this introduce into all Societies to give Inferiours a power to judge their Superiours mad or drunk, and thereupon to resist and oppose them with force."[57] Subjects may use persuasion to sway their patriarch—"Wives, Children, and Servants that are dutiful have ways to appease their *Monarchs*"—but they may not lay hands on him.[58] As Bohun points out, the consequences of rebellion, of unleashing an anarchic mob, are far more detrimental than the consequences of a single child harmed. Thus even a rapist or murderous monarch cannot be stopped. Bohun poses the question, "Must I sit still and suffer my throat to be cut, my Estate ruined, my Wife ravished, and not dare in any case to defend my self till God is pleased to interpose, and that in an Age in which Miracles are Ceased?"[59] Yes, he replies, as political upheaval

> can onely serve to fill the World with Rebellions, Wars, and Confusions, in which more thousands of Men and Estates must of necessity be ruined, and Wives Ravished and murthered in the space of a few days, than can be destroyed by the worst Tyrant that ever trod upon the Earth amongst his own Subjects in the space of many years, or of a whole life.[60]

The life of the individual child or subject is worth less than the health of the body politic. To depose a sexually violent king is to expose many more unfortunate innocents to mob violence.

In contrast to Bohun, Whig political philosophers of the period were extremely interested in defining the limits of parental—and by extension, monarchical—authority. The father's role is to nurture, not destroy, his progeny, these authors rebut. According to Rachel Weil, "The idea that the family exists for the benefit of children (rather than for the benefit of fathers, or the keeping of order) became so deeply rooted in the writings of Whig thinkers that it was assumed rather than defended."[61] A child, James Tyrrell argues, does not have to submit uncritically, even unto death, to an unfit ruler. Tyrrell writes, he "would be glad to know where and how God hath given this Absolute power to Fathers over their Children, and by what Law Children are tyed to an Absolute Subjection or Servitude to their parents. . . . I see no divine Charter in Scripture of any such absolute despotick power granted to *Adam* or any other Father."[62] The father has no right to kill his offspring: he "has no more right over the Life of his Child than another man; being as much answerable to God if he abuse this Right of a Father, in killing his innocent Son, as if another had done it."[63] Instead, it is the father's responsibility to care for and protect that child: "in his Children he is chiefly to design their good and advantage, as far as lies in his power, without ruining himself."[64] If the father becomes violent, the children have the right to self-defense: "it is lawful for the Children to hold, nay binde their mad or drunken Parents, in case they cannot otherwise hinder them from doing mischief, or killing either themselves, their Mothers, or Brethren."[65] For Tyrrell, a father gives life but may not cause death; the "danger of fathers injuring their children is greater than that of children becoming over-enthusiastic about their own rights."[66] If a father proves unfit to rule, he may morally be stopped, stripping "away [Filmer's] biblical support for the father's power of life and death."[67]

Although John Locke did not publish his *Two Treatises of Government* until 1690, the text grew out of the political climate of the 1680s, and it articulates a concept of fatherhood highly relevant to a discussion of that decade. Taking the concepts of divine right and paternal authority to their furthest conclusions, Locke suggests that the doctrine of absolutism licenses any number of societal evils, up to and including infanticide and cannibalism. Such parental behavior is entirely unacceptable, as evidenced by God's wrath at the Canaanites, who sacrificed their children in religious ceremonies:

> They shed innocent bloud even the bloud of their sons and of their daughters when they sacrificed unto the Idols of Canaan. . . . The Land was polluted with bloud, therefore was the wrath of the Lord kindled against his people in so much that he abhorred his own inheritance. The killing of their Children, though it were fashionable, was charged on them as innocent bloud, and so had, in the account of God, the guilt of murder, as the offering them to Idols had the guilt of Idolatry.[68]

As we saw in the introduction to this volume, Locke also condemns the people of Peru, who "begot Children on purpose to Fatten and Eat them."[69] Although for Locke, upstanding Englishmen should reflexively recoil from such "savage" acts, cannibalism functions as the reductio ad absurdum of absolutist rhetoric. Should you allow a father unlimited authority over his children or a king unlimited power over his subjects, you tacitly permit them to commit even cannibal atrocities. Locke continues,

> Be it then as Sir Robert says, that Anciently, it was usual for Men to sell and Castrate their Children. . . . Let it be, that they exposed them; Add to it, if you please, for this is still greater Power, that they begat them for their Tables to fat and eat them: If this proves a right to do so, we may, by the same Argument, justify Adultery, Incest and Sodomy, for there are examples of these too, both Ancient and Modern; Sins, which I suppose, have their Principal Aggravation from this, that they cross the main intention of Nature, which willeth the increase of Mankind, and the continuation of the Species in the highest perfection.[70]

Tyrrell also invokes the image of cannibalism (in this case, of animals eating their young) to describe an imbalanced relationship between parents and children: "all Animals are determin'd by Nature, to prosecute and endeavour the Common Good of their own Species."[71] Once they have children,

> they love and defend, as part of themselves, unless some unusual Distemper intervene, which may sometimes disturb or change these natural Propensions; as when Sows or Rabbets [sic] eat or destroy their young ones; which happening but seldom, is rather to be accounted among the Diseases of the Brain, or Distempers of the Appetite, than to be ascribed to their natural State or Constitution.[72]

Locke's absolutist cannibal father thereby contrasts with the Catholic or ambitious cannibal child; the child who would destroy his parent is mirrored in the parent who would devour his young.

STAGING INTRAFAMILIAL CONFLICT: OTWAY AND LEE

Conflicts between destructive parents and poisonous children play out on the stage as a way for authors to engage with contemporary political movements. If Lee's Tullia and Tiberius represent murderous children, Brutus is all too eager to murder his children to cement his own power. A similar conflict structures Thomas Otway's *Venice Preserv'd*, as Otway invokes the language of rape to describe intrafamilial conflict and condemn a father who declines to protect his child. In marrying Jaffeir, Belvidera has disobeyed her father, Priuli, who views her elopement as a form of theft. "You stole her from me, like a Thief you stole her, / At the dead of night," he accuses Jaffeir.[73] He also treats the marriage as a form of disease, an infection in his body:

> But then, my onely child, my daughter, wedded;
> There my best bloud runs foul, and a disease
> Incurable has seiz'd upon my memory,
> To make it rot and stink to after ages.

Curst be the fatal minute when I got her. (5.1.5–9)

As a result of Belvidera's marriage, Priuli has grown jealous and vindictive, becoming what Philip Harth terms "an inhumane father."[74] First, he curses his child with poverty and barrenness—"A steril Fortune, and a barren Bed, / Attend you both" (1.1.53–54)—and then he uses his political authority to order the removal of all her worldly possessions.[75] According to Derek Hughes, Pierre transforms "the removal of the bed into a metaphor of the prostitution of Jaffeir's marriage."[76] I would suggest, however, that Pierre actually describes the confiscation using the language of rape, or in William H. McBurney's words, "the domestic variant of the national rape."[77] He calls the soldiers who perform the confiscation "The sons of public Rapine" (1.1.234), and he explicitly sexualizes the removal of Jaffeir and Belvidera's bed:

> The very bed, which on thy wedding night
> Receiv'd thee to the Arms of *Belvidera*,
> The scene of all thy Joys, was violated
> By the course hands of filthy Dungeon Villains,
> And thrown amongst the common Lumber. (1.1.245–49)

Belvidera's reaction to the loss also implicitly suggests sexual assault. She "came weeping forth, / Shining through Tears" (1.1.258–59). Thus when Pierre and Jaffeir swear vengeance, their actions recall Lucrece's death scene in Lee's *Lucius Junius Brutus*. Pierre invokes the image of Belvidera's sufferings to manipulate Jaffeir as Brutus does his supporters. Pierre tells Jaffeir,

> Man knows a braver Remedy for sorrow:
> Revenge! the Attribute of the Gods, they stampt it
> With their great Image on our Natures; dye!
> Consider well the Cause that calls upon thee:
> And if thou art base enough, dye then: Remember
> Thy *Belvidera* suffers: *Belvidera!* (1.1.286–91)

Jaffeir, like Brutus's companions, swears allegiance on the life of the violated woman (in this case, Belvidera), and promises, like Collatine, "I will revenge my *Belvidera's* Tears!" (1.1.255).

Even before the play's first act of actual sexual violence, then, Belvidera has already been metaphorically and financially ravished by her own father. Priuli has violated his duty to protect his daughter, figuratively raping her and sowing in the process illness and rebellion in the realm. From the beginning of the play, parent/child relationships have become fundamentally corrupt—this is a world "Where Brother, Friends, and Fathers, all are false" (1.1.253)—and they grow worse as the play continues. Jaffeir acknowledges that open rebellion will force him to confront and potentially harm the father (in-law) he should honor. He tells his co-conspirators, "if you think it worthy / To cut the Throats of reverend Rogues in Robes, / Send me into the curs'd assembl'd Senate; / It shrinks not, tho I meet a Father there" (3.2.220–23). Later, his willingness to use Belvidera as collateral to ensure his position among the conspirators is described in the language of corrupt parenthood. Jaffeir characterizes himself as his wife's child, not her husband: "every moment / I am from thy sight, the Heart within my Bosom / Moans like a tender Infant in its Cradle / Whose Nurse had left it" (3.2.17–20). Belvidera extends the simile, representing her husband as a toxic child who brings destruction to the mother who gave him life:

> I fear the stubborn Wanderer will not own me,
> 'Tis grown a Rebel to be rul'd no longer,
> Scorns the Indulgent Bosom that first lull'd it,
> And like a Disobedient Child disdains
> The soft Authority of *Belvidera.* (3.2.22–26)

Just as Jaffeir will commit parricide against Priuli, he will also commit matricide (metaphorically speaking) against his wife.[78]

As Belvidera aligns herself with the wronged parent in her conversation with Jaffeir, she also treats rebellion as a very great evil for both family and state. She tells Jaffeir,

> Murder my Father! Tho his Cruel Nature
> Has persecuted me to my undoing,
> Driven me to basest wants; Can I behold him
> With smiles of Vengeance, butcher'd in his Age?
> The sacred Fountain of my life destroy'd?
> And canst thou shed the blood that gave me being?
> Nay, and be a Traitor too, and sell thy Country? (3.2.155–61)

Here we see Otway's Tory politics in play in ways less explicit than the crude sexuality of the Nicky-Nacky scenes: Rebellion against an individual parent is as horrifying and unacceptable on the local level as political revolt. Jaffeir is contemplating both an act of treason against the state and an act of treason within the family, and both are worthy of condemnation. The righteousness of Jaffeir's actions is further undermined by the fact that Priuli's "rape" of Belvidera is always metaphorical and is, indeed, primarily financial. Such an assault pales before the sexual violence of Renault, which is real and physical and which threatens to transform Belvidera into a latter-day Lucrece. In the aftermath of Renault's attempted assault, Belvidera explicitly invokes the Lucrece myth:

> the old hoary Wretch, to whose false Care
> My Peace and Honour was intrusted, came
> (Like *Tarquin*) gastely with infernal Lust.
> Oh thou *Roman Lucrece*!
> Thou could'st find friends to vindicate thy Wrong;
> I never had but one, and he's prov'd false. (2.1.5–10)

The conspirators and not the senators play the role of Tarquin, suggesting that rebellion and not obedience leads to true misery. Subsequently, her description of mother/child suffering as a consequence of civil war recalls the ever-present imagery of the Irish Rebellion. She laments

> the poor tender lives
> Of all those little Infants which the Swords
> Of murtherers are whetting for this moment;
> Think thou already hearst their dying screams,
> Think that thou seest their sad distracted Mothers
> Kneeling before thy feet, and begging pity
> With torn dishevel'd hair and streaming eyes,
> Their naked mangled breasts besmeard with bloud. (4.1.48–55)

Rebellion against father and rebellion against country are dangerously equivalent, and both lead to devastating suffering and carnage.[79]

Venice Preserv'd has, of course, rightly been read as an allegory of the Popish Plot and treated, often alongside Dryden's *Absalom and Achitophel*, as an example of the most virulent Tory propaganda. According to John Robert Moore, "It is against the party of Shaftesbury that every line of contemporary satire in *Venice Preserv'd* is directed."[80] Harry Solomon likewise calls the play "court propaganda designed to discredit inflammatory Whig rhetoric and to win moderate Whigs to the Tory cause,"[81] while David Bywaters explains that the play "presents a consistent and thorough attack on the Whigs, on the City they misgoverned, and on the plot they manipulated to their ill purposes."[82] Certainly, the "double assault on Shaftesbury" in Renault and Antonio, along with the internal corruption of the conspiratorial faction, suggests the rightness of Tory loyalty.[83] I would agree with Jessica Munns, however, that "the play cannot be reduced to a mere piece of Tory Whig-bashing."[84] The degradation of parent-child relationships in the play produces an anxiety that defies a monolithic political reading, adopting aspects of both Tory and Whig political propaganda. The failure of parent-child relations has sparked the rebellion, with intractable fathers and disobedient children equally to blame for societal destruction. Thus while Priuli and Belvidera reconcile, albeit too late to save her life, the play ends with Priuli's advice to fathers to be less unforgiving: "bid all Cruel Fathers dread my Fate" (5.1.539). As in the world of *Lucius Junius Brutus*, the parents and children have grown toxic to one another, with fathers ravishing daughters and sons seeking to murder their sires. While *Lucius Junius Brutus* urges bloodletting as a cure for disobedience, however, *Venice Preserv'd* ends instead with a plea for intergenerational tolerance and understanding—an understanding that goes beyond political leanings—as a preferable alternative to the bloodshed of civil and intrafamilial war. Parents and children (along with subjects and their kings) must finally and irrevocably put aside their differences for the sake of peace, both in the individual household and in the wider realm.[85]

The conflict between destructive parents and poisonous children is also apparent in Lee's earlier *Mithridates*, as the discourse of disrupted parent-child relationships combines with the discourse of rape and cannibalism. Jealous of his son Ziphares's relationship with the beautiful Semandra, and angered by Ziphares's greater popularity with the common people, King Mithridates comes to distrust and despise his son. When the crowd celebrates Ziphares's martial success, Mithridates bitterly fumes, "Perish the Bodies that went forth to meet him, / A prey for Worms, to stink in hollow ground. / O, Viper! Villain! not content to take / My Love, but Life! wilt thou unthrone me too?"[86] In his anger, Mithridates constructs a parallel between two forms of perceived property crime, one personal, the other political; because he believes that Ziphares has usurped his rightful mistress, Mithridates assumes that an attempt on his throne will soon follow. He thus renames civil war "Bosom-war" (50), suggesting that for Lee, as for the propaganda authors, civil war divides the national family against itself. Implicit in this image is also the belief that children are a part of their parents, and that for the child to turn on the father is to become an infection conspiring against the will and health of the whole. Like *Lucius Junius Brutus*'s Brutus, Mithridates treats his children as diseased limbs which must be excised that he might survive. Confronted with the true personal and political treachery of his younger son, Pharnaces, Mithridates exclaims, "Pharnaces, / I'll cut thee off, as an infectious limb" (53). Ziphares, meanwhile, becomes his father's figurative rapist—"Die, die, thou Ravisher of my Repose" (35), Mithridates commands—and finally the cannibal that consumes him out of existence. Although eating imagery is initially employed positively to describe Ziphares's gratitude to his father—he promises that he will "devour your hands with Filial dearness" (25)—it later encodes parricidal impulses. Like William Allen's Catholic children who devour their own mother's womb, Ziphares becomes his father's "Bosom-wolf" who vampiristically "laps my dearest blood" (33).

While Mithridates is threatened by his children, he proves just as deadly to his progeny. Pharnaces complains that his father has stolen his mistress and Ziphares's, echoing Mithridates's claim that such a usurpation cannot be tolerated. "She knew my love, before she saw my Father" (16), he says of Monima, his beloved. "For in the Plunder I first lighted on her: / Tho afterwards he took my beauteous spoil, / As now he does my Brothers" (16). Pharnaces insists that Mithridates, despite being father and king, does not have the right to intrude on his subject's (or his son's) rightful property. Recalling Algernon Sidney's rhetoric of rape and tyranny, Pharnaces argues that in turning sexual tyrant, Mithridates has licensed his own overthrow. The king further oversteps himself when he rapes Semandra. In the aftermath of the assault, she likens him to "a Dragon in his Den," an "Aspic" and a "Baslis[k]" (46), suggesting that he has become a poisonous monster that disfigures his victim. "The temper of her Soul is quite infected," Ziphares complains. "The catching Court-disease, / Has spotted all her white, her Virgin Beauties" (44). Ziphares has confused the stain of rape with the stain of infidelity, but Semandra has been metaphorically spotted nonetheless, disfigured by contact with Mithridates's poisonous soul. Finally, the king poisons his own children to death: "Blame not the guiltless," he tells Archelaus, "for by me he's poyson'd: / By this inhumane Tyrant, Monster, Parricide; / By me the Drugs were mixt, and dol'd about / To my unhappy Children" (76). The play judges this act truly horrible. Earlier, Semandra had warned Mithridates against taking such action, horrified that he might "design [Ziphares's] Death, . . . / reap the Bloody Harvest of his own Life, / And, Atreus-like . . . feed on [his] own Bowels" (22). As the children feed vampiristically on their parent, the father metaphorically ingests the flesh of his progeny.

At the end of the play, Ziphares and Semandra dream of a utopian paradise in which positive parent-child relationships are possible. Semandra prays that

> we'll be wedded too
> In th'other World; our Souls shall there be mixt:
> Who knows, but there our joys may be compleat?
> A happy Father, thou; and I, perhaps,
> The smiling Mother of some little Gods. (74)

Such a happy realm is impossible in the world of *Mithridates*. The "bleeding Country" has not yet healed from Mithridates's tyranny and the Roman takeover (68). Indeed, when the Romans invade the town, Pharnaces begs Pompey to "mow off hoary Heads, hurl infants puling / From the lug'd breast, kill in the very Womb: / To Beauties cries be deaf" (66). In imagery once again reminiscent of the English Civil War tracts, Pharnaces rejoices to see pregnant women assaulted and parental relationships destroyed in the womb. The destruction of parent-child relationships emerges as both the cause and the product of civil war. It also reflects both Whig fears of the poisonous parent and Tory fears of the destructive child, locked in a battle for political and social supremacy.

CROWNE'S *THYESTES* AND THE HORRORS OF THE CANNIBAL FATHER

While Lee's *Lucius Junius Brutus* and *Mithridates* and Otway's *Venice Preserv'd* all contain images of inappropriately violent parents, depictions of the cannibal father appear most literally in John Crowne's *Thyestes* and Edward Ravenscroft's *Titus Andronicus*, two plays that include actual acts of intrafamilial cannibalism. As we shall see, Ravenscroft uses images of cannibalism to discredit Whig philosophy and reinforce the rightness of unlimited monarchical authority. Crowne, in contrast, offers a scathing criticism of Tory ideology and an argument against absolutist rhetoric. Despite the fact that at the time of *Thyestes* Crowne was making a living as a Tory playwright, the play promotes a political philosophy more akin to Locke's or Tyrrell's than Bohun's or Filmer's.[87] In 1681, the year Crowne published *Thyestes*, two prior adaptations of the play were already in circulation. Jasper Heywood's *The Seconde Tragedie of Seneca entituled Thyestes faithfully Englished* (1560) offered a fairly literal translation of the Latin text and was, as critics have suggested, particularly influential on later Elizabethan dramatists, including Shakespeare.[88] More closely contemporaneous with Crowne was John Wright's *Thyestes A Tragedy, Translated out of Seneca* (1674), also a relatively faithful translation, although it is attached to his satirical *Mock-Thyestes, in Burlesque*. Unlike these earlier authors, Crowne does not offer a direct translation of the text, and his changes to the work ultimately bespeak his concerns with the state of contemporary politics. Most obviously, the play contains many broad moments of traditional anti-Catholicism. The prologue begins by referring to the contemporary political climate, as Crowne ironically links theatrical skill with the tricks of Roman Catholic prelates: "To day like cunning Romish Priests we try / If we can awe you, with an antient lye," he writes, playing on the traditional antitheatrical association of Catholicism with the stage.[89] He reiterates that association in the epilogue when he commands the audience, "But pray let Poets live, for they no ways / Offend you with damn'd Plots, but in their Plays" (56). Crowne highlights the distinction between the honest living he earns as a playwright and the pope's false living earned by playing on people's credulity and fear. Priests "invade the Poet's Property" (60), while Crowne is, he claims, "like the Pope" insofar as they both "regard not much your praise, / He Tickets sells for Heaven, and we for Plays" (prologue). Crowne will use theater to entertain and enlighten; the pope will use a very different sort of theatrical art to dupe and confuse.

Anti-Catholicism also filters into the play proper in Philisthenes's lengthy, by now clichéd tirade against Atreus's priests. In lines original to Crowne's adaptation, Philisthenes claims that priests are always liars, for it is their “Trade to lye, you live by lies” (42). “You Cheats,” he calls them, “you Murderers, you Quacks of Hell, / You keep mankind diseas’d to vend your Drugs” (42). They are, he continues, sexually lascivious and untrustworthy: “You keep the Keys of Womens Chambers too, / And let men have what share in ’em you please: / When you deliver up a Marriage Lock, / You still reserve a Key for your own use” (43). They care more about monetary gain than spiritual welfare; should the king swear allegiance to “th’ infernal Gods, / For money you wou’d aid their hellish Vows, / And curse all honest men that wou’d not aid. / Religion’s made by you a Lottery book” (43). They corrupt the king with their evil ways and poison the nation: “The King was cur’d of his disease, Revenge. / And you have sold him some Religious lye, / Has poyson’d him with Cruelty again” (42). And finally they become the king’s court-appointed murderers: “ever while you live call Priests,” Philisthenes complains bitterly, “If you wou’d have a solemn murder done” (46).

Of even more concern to the play’s world, however, and a greater threat than that posed by the priests (who are, after all, only acting at Atreus’s behest), is the collapse of familial relationships precipitated by an act of fatherly overreach, and a disruption of boundaries between Self and Other. Crowne’s *Thyestes* begins in the aftermath of two horrifying familial tragedies: Tantalus’s murder and roasting of his son, Pelops, and Thyestes’s incestuous rape of Aerope, his brother Atreus’s loyal wife. From the earliest moments of the text, the play diverges from its Roman predecessor, as the Aerope of earlier versions deceived her husband willingly. Seneca’s Atreus complains that

> Wife and kingdom, he
> took both. Our ancient
> symbol of power
> he took by deceit. . . .
> The traitor
> dared something huge, he
> took my wife to help,
> he took my ram. . . .
> No part of the family is free
> from traps. My wife is
> corrupted.[90]

Crowne’s Aerope, by contrast, is the victim of her brother-in-law’s illicit lust, and she protests her innocence throughout the play: Aerope tells Atreus, “I have ever been your faithful Wife, / And ne’re deserv’d to lose that glorious Name” (27). Thyestes himself will later admit to the rape: “I ravish’d her, and Hell did ravish me” (40). Thyestes usurps Atreus’s wife’s body along with his throne, two forms of property crime that enrage and madden the king.

Atreus does not, unfortunately, believe his wife when she tells him she was raped. He expects that, like her Senecan counterpart, she slept with his brother willingly, an act of consensual incest rather than rape. When Aerope becomes distressed at the sight of Thyestes, Atreus can only interpret her anxiety as desire: "the Whore commits / Incest in fancy with the Villain here, / Before my Face: The very sight of him / Has got her Spirit big with Insolence" (39–40), he says, treating their mutual gaze as a species of illegitimate sexual contact. Aerope continues to protest her blamelessness—"I never yet dissembled with the King" (27)—and she insists that if her body is stained, her fundamental being remains pure and untouched. "The Heavens are not so spotless as my Soul. . . . Yet am I thought a Strumpet, nay a lew'd / Incestuous monstrous Strumpet!" (23). Her body, she explains, is like a ruined building—"You build new Palaces on broken Walls" (28), she tells her husband when it appears he might forgive her—but it houses a spotless soul. She also separates her whorish form from pure spirit, calling herself "A shining Strumpt and a tatter'd Wife" and "a hot flaming whore" (25). Aerope thus emerges from the text as a unique character in the annals of Restoration drama: a rape victim who wants to live. Unfortunately, her failure to play Lucrece and kill herself undermines her claims to virtue, and she is forced to spend the play fighting, finally unsuccessfully, against the ideological pressures demanding her death.

While *Thyestes* begins in the recent aftermath of an incestuous rape, it also begins in the distant aftermath of an act of parental cannibalism, fundamentally entwining three discrete evils. In the play's opening scene, Megara the Fury taunts the ghost of Tantalus as he watches what has become of his house. She tells him that as the original cannibal father, he has cursed his family to suffer from "Incest, Treason, Blood" (1), and points out that Atreus has become fatally poisonous: "Nature's diseas'd and scar'd at his approach; / Trees shed their Leaves, as poyson'd men their Hair" (2). She also attributes the evil natures of Atreus and Thyestes to Tantalus's fault: they are "The greatest proof of *Tantalus* his blood" (8). Tantalus therefore laments the effect that his actions have had on his progeny. "Return me to my dark dire Prison in Hell" (2), he begs, rather than be forced to watch the coming destruction. He knows that punishment for his sins will be visited on his descendants and that he has been the prime mover of the disease that now pervades the kingdom.

Atreus, too, knows that the world has grown ill, that he, like Settle's Fredigond and Chlotilda, has both been poisoned and become poisonous: "My gaping aking wounds can ne're be cur'd" (4), he tells his servant. He has been undone by his father's misdeeds, his brother's treachery, and his wife's supposed lust, and he has been consumed by a "Feaver of Revenge" (10). In contrast, Thyestes laments his own complicity in bringing the world to such a state: "How cou'd I carry such a load of sin / And feel no pain?" he wonders (30). To rape Aerope, he realizes, was to poison her, disfigure her beyond recognition, and engender a social sickness that cannot be eluded. "I was the first that brought / Incest and Treason to my Brother's Court / From my own self came all my Villainy" (30). Unlike Atreus, Thyestes does not consider his sin inborn, the inescapable consequence of his father's actions. Rather, he wonders whether his environment may have proven toxic, leading him to villainy: "Perhaps I felt no sin, because I liv'd / In the'Element of sin, my Brother's Court" (30). Drawing on the Chorus of the original play's valorization of simple living over court life—"When my days have passed / without clatter, / may I die / old and ordinary," the chorus prays—Thyestes abjures the dangerous intrigue and complexity of the court and argues that even the best of men may grow corrupt when inexorably poisoned by the atmosphere of the court.[91] In this, Crowne subtly invokes the trope of the debauched Cavalier/libertine, accusing the court, however obliquely, of the same sorts of evil deeds that pervade Shadwell's play or Settle's.

Ultimately, however, the twin evils of rape and cannibalism merge in the play's world to infect future progeny, destroy the sanctity of parent-child relationships, and transform all pregnancies into monstrous births. Fear of maternal monstrosity permeates the text, with Atreus in particular growing obsessed with dangerous mothers; because his wife has been (involuntarily) unfaithful, Atreus cannot trust in the paternity of his children and he treats them as potential monsters disfiguring his household. He tells Antigone, "By heavens, thy Mother was so rank a Whore, / That it is more than all the Gods can tell / What share of thee is mine" (5). His wife, he explains, is worse than monstrous:

> Why in her stead was I not doom'd to love
> Some gastly, grim, devouring, Hellish Fury;
> Whose Hairs were Serpents and her breath a plague;
> Whose Bones were Gibets, and her Nerves Iron Chains;
> Whose Eyes were Comets, and her Voice was Thunder;
> Whose Teeth were Hooks all gor'd with humane blood;
> Whose Flesh and Blood was a devouring bog,
> Compounded of all poisons in the world?
> In her abhor'd embrace I had not found
> So many Deaths and Hells as I do now. (6)

Atreus refers to his children by Aerope as "these damn'd incestuous Brats / . . . the irruptions of a burning Whore" (5), while his own mental torment, "this hellish mind / Was the creation of that cursed woman" (6). Meanwhile, he has also grown monstrous in his hatred and has begun to destroy the family line. "Oh I am mad, I burn" (9), he exclaims. "Furies with flaming brands are in my breast: / Their Snakes with their own poyson almost burst; / And every Vein o' mine contains a Snake" (9). Like Settle's Fredigond, his blood has been tainted, suggesting that for Crowne, the figure of the poisonous Catholic bride has been supplanted by the even more destructive figure of the cannibal father. In such a world, a world where "Brother whor'd Brother's Wife" and "Brother depos'd Brother from his Throne" (1), poison is everywhere, so widespread as to make snakes proud. Megara triumphs,

> Let me have Murders, such as all my Snakes
> May rear themselves to see, and hiss Applause.
> The Father eat the Nephew he begot;
> The Bastard Nephew go out of the World,
> A way more horrid than he came into it. (2)

Even nature has sickened to the point that it can only breed monstrosity. Megara tells Tantalus,

> Let the vast Villainy of thy damn'd Race
> Reach, and confound the Heavens; make the night
> Engender with the Day; the groaning Day
> Bring forth Gygantick darkness at full Noon,
> Such as for hours may pluck the Sun from Heaven.
> At this black Feast, I'le let thee be a Guest,
> Devour thy fill in quiet, when thy Cup
> Flowes with the Blood of thy incestuous Race,
> Nothing shall dare to snatch it from thy Lips. (2)

In imagery reminiscent of William Allen's and Benjamin Keach's contemporary propaganda tracts, Megara combines references to nature's decay with images of inappropriate parentage, monstrous children, and a cannibalistic banquet, finally foreshadowing the play's denouement. In such a society, only monstrous births are possible.

For the world of *Thyestes*, as for the worlds of *Mithridates* and *Lucius Junius Brutus*, the toxin that poisons the kingdom is precipitated at least in part by the collapse of familial boundaries and by parental inability to treat children as entities separate from themselves. When Thyestes rapes Aerope, he commits an act of incest, an act that fundamentally damages the boundary between Self and Other; at least on the sexual level, family members are meant to remain Other. Once that first boundary is breached, others begin to falter. Thyestes, for instance, imagines himself committing an act of incest with his native land. Upon seeing his homeland again for the first time in years, he exclaims,

> Oh! wondrous pleasure to a banish'd man!
> I feel my lov'd, long look'd for Native Soyl;
> My former Incest (horrid to be nam'd)
> Gave me not greater pleasure, than this new
> Innocent Incest with my Mother Earth. (35)

Although this second instance of incest is purely metaphorical, it reflects the way in which Thyestes continues to sexualize familial relationships. He is altogether unable to separate his personal desires from the familial Other.

The collapse of familial boundaries extends to the play's parent-child relationships. Some critics have disparaged Crowne's addition of the love plot, arguing that Crowne included it to pander to Restoration audience tastes: according to Arthur Franklin White, "The taste of Crowne's time demanded a 'love-interest' in tragedy."[92] Thematically, however, the love plot is crucial to the play, as it reflects the extent of the societal collapse precipitated by rape and culminating in cannibalism. Like Thyestes, Atreus cannot discern the boundary that should separate parents from children. Because Philisthenes is Thyestes's offspring, Atreus views him as an extension of his hated father, and equally as poisonous. Philisthenes initially tries to distance himself from his father's ill deeds. When Thyestes laments that "Thou wilt derive unhappiness from me, / Like an hereditary ill disease," Philisthenes insists, "Sir, I was born when you were innocent, / And all the ill you have contracted since, / You have wrought out by painful penitence" (31). He has not been compromised by his father's actions. Atreus, however, does not agree and first uses Philisthenes as bait to snare Thyestes, then kills him in retribution for his father's crimes. Atreus explains his reasoning to a defiant Philisthenes:

> Philisthenes: Why have you order'd me to be thus bound?
> Atreus: To dye.
> Philisthenes: For what?
> Atreus: Thou art *Thyestes* Son.
> Philisthenes: That's not my fault.
> Atreus: But a damn'd fault of his,
> To dare to multiply his cursed self,
> And send a filthy and incestuous Stream
> To poyson all the Ages of the World;
> But here it stops. (44)

For Atreus, Philisthenes is indistinguishable from his father, a copy of Thyestes's original and a poisonous waste product to be destroyed. He cannot conceive of Philisthenes as an independent entity apart from his father and thus treats him as fair game in the battle between brothers: "I cannot wound thy Father, but through thee" (45), he tells Philisthenes.

Likewise, Atreus cannot separate his daughter, Antigone, from himself and his own will. While Atreus is initially suspicious of Antigone's parentage, it quickly becomes clear that she is his flesh and blood and that as such, he can only view her as an extension of himself. As is the case with Lee's Brutus and Mithridates, who are shocked to realize that their children can be their enemies, Atreus firmly believes that his daughter is a copy of himself, his will, hers. Thus he is blindsided by her supposed treachery, that she dared to love without consent the man Atreus bid her wed. He complains,

> Oh! my murder'd hopes!
> I thought this Maid
> Had Vertues wou'd support our failing House;
> I thought o' her side I was thunder proof,
> And she's as false as any of our Race,
> A Traytress to her Father and her King. (52)

Antigone's love for Philisthenes is the ultimate betrayal: "Hast thou abus'd me so?" Atreus demands (52). She has proven herself Other by her love—"She's none of mine" (52), he subsequently tells Thyestes—and when her life is no longer worth anything to him, he tries to kill her. This is not merely a father punishing his daughter for matrimonial disobedience; rather, Atreus is stunned to realize that any boundary exists between the two, that Antigone is Other and not Self, that she has an interiority he cannot predict and control (insofar as she has obeyed the letter but not the spirit of his commands).

In response, Antigone spends the majority of the play seeking to undermine and flee the imposition of her father's will. In pledging herself to Philisthenes, she seeks to deepen an interiority that marks her as separate from, as Other than, her father's Self. In response to Atreus's demand, "How durst thou, Traytress, love my Enemy," Antigone responds, "He had more worth than all our Race besides, / None of our Race did e're deserve to live, / But this sweet Youth, and me for loving him" (52). She and Philisthenes alone, Antigone insists, deserve to live and thrive, for they have not been tainted by the sins of their fathers; indeed, she claims that in direct opposition to their parents, "Our warring Fathers never ventur'd more / For bitter hate, than we for innocent Love" (14). Antigone seeks, like *Lucius Junius Brutus*'s Titus and Teraminta or *Mithridates*'s Ziphares and Semandra, to divorce herself from her father and avoid the poison in his family line. She replaces Atreus with Peneus in her affection: "I'le be disposed of, *Father*, as you please" (14, emphasis mine), she tells him, calling Peneus father and agreeing to submit to his will rather than Atreus's. In the end, Antigone outsmarts her father, definitively asserting her will through suicide. Antigone will not wait to die by her father's hand (as does Lavinia in Ravenscroft's *Titus Andronicus*), but instead performs her death on her own initiative. She tells Atreus, "I have so wounded my obedience, / By loving that dear Youth without your leave, / That 'tis too weak to hold my mighty grief, / Which forces me to dye without your leave" (53). As she has loved without Atreus's permission, she will die without his permission. In this, Antigone's death thematically mirrors that of *Valentinian*'s Lucina, who dies in a final expression of force. The suicidal gesture is self-denying, but a gesture of will nonetheless, and in direct contrast to the treatment of poisonous children in

Tory propaganda, her disobedience is celebrated. As in Rochester's *Valentinian*, resistance to an unfit ruler is both necessary and good, and Antigone is heroic in her quest to defy an evil father and monarch.

Contrasting with Antigone is her lover Philisthenes who, unlike Antigone, is less keen to reinforce boundaries within the family; where she replaces and distances, Philisthenes adopts and combines. He honors his connection to his own father, calling himself "One you may trust, / half your own self" (31), and he later celebrates the reunification of his fractured family. Indeed, he is all too willing to accept Atreus as the "Father of my Father" (19) and to make Atreus's will his own. Atreus becomes, at least temporarily, a second father to Philisthenes: "Sir, I wou'd call you,—cou'd I speak for Tears, / Father,—and giver of my best new life" (21). Appropriately then, while Antigone proves her autonomy with her suicide, Philisthenes becomes literally one with his father through the act of cannibalism. Several critics have worked to establish a theoretical understanding of cannibalism both as a physical reality and as a metaphorical construct. For Jeff Berglund, to ingest another human being is to collapse definitively the boundaries of Self and Other and to absorb the Other into one's own being:

> Consumption by another collapses identity boundaries: in being consumed, *You* become *Me*, *I* become *You-Me*. Figuratively, cannibalization threatens one's sense of integrity. Being cannibalized makes one estranged from one's familiar self/selves. In sum, cannibalization makes the familiar unfamiliar. At the same time it threatens to make the unfamiliar familiar. It erases difference through the collapse of boundaries. This fear of losing one's self to another alien culture is also the force responsible for projecting cannibalistic behavior onto others, in what I have referred to as a classic moment of "Othering."[93]

Philisthenes merges with his father through ingestion, the Other becoming the Self, and once Thyestes learns the truth, he is loath even to kill himself, "Lest I in my own bosom stab my Son" (50). Thyestes's child has become a physical part of him, causing Atreus to triumph, "Confusion I have in thy bowels made" (50). Initially, Thyestes breached the boundary between brothers with his unlawful rape. Atreus tells Thyestes, "Thou with my Children wou'dst have treated me, / But that thou wert afraid they were thy own / Incestuous Bastards all" (51). The rape makes Atreus's children indistinguishable from Thyestes's (and renders Antigone's relationship with Philisthenes potentially also incestuous); the two brothers cannot be told apart as parents. Now Atreus, in the ultimate expression of monarchical will, punishes his brother by forcing him to merge with his own son. The evils sown by rape/incest are reaped in the act of cannibalism—the physical realization of all such inappropriate commingling.

At the end of the play, Thyestes dies, murdered by Aerope, his initial victim. As in Settle's *Love and Revenge*, no one has been willing to avenge Aerope's suffering. She begs Atreus, "Not as you are my Husband, but my King . . . / To bring my innocence into the light" (39), but her husband is deaf to her suit. Thus Aerope must become Philomel, taking her moment of revenge and resigning herself to the suicide that will finally prove her innocence. She stabs Thyestes, exclaiming,

> This for the loss of my dear Husband's Love:
> This for the loss of my dear Daughter's Life:
> This for the ruin of my honest Name:
> This for my Life I am about to lose.
> Now I have done my self this little right,
> I can with comfort dye! (54–55)

Aerope then dies while Atreus, despite his evil acts, lives on. Atreus has taken revenge at the expense of family and nation and become the dramatic embodiment of Locke's cannibal father (albeit one who forces other fathers to eat their young, rather than indulging in cannibal acts himself). The banquet represents to Atreus a combined assertion of imperial and fatherly prerogative, a prerogative reaffirmed by the play's lack of poetic justice. Atreus will not be punished for his crimes, indeed cannot be punished in a society where monarchical will is absolute.

This is not to suggest that Crowne finally approves of Atreus's actions. Despite Atreus's belief in his absolute authority, the state of nature at the end of the play exhibits the extent to which he has overstepped and underscores the play's closing political message. Aerope announces, "I was with my two little pretty Sons . . . / When of the sudden, with a thousand groans, / The Air brought forth a monstrous Shade, as black / As Hell had vomited a Lake of Pitch" (54). As Atreus has led both House and nation to more and greater suffering, nature has given birth to its own monstrosity. Meanwhile, the audience is left with the knowledge that Atreus's sons will inherit the throne only to suffer the carnage and destruction of the Trojan War. Peneus prophesies that

> Prince *Agamemnon*, Oracles agree,
> Shall lay a glorious Empire in the Dust,
> And *Menelaus* be the chiefest Cause.
> But yet no Oracle did utter this
> Without ill-boding sounds. (7)

One of these children will, like his father, be condemned to the shame of an unfaithful wife. The other will, like his father, become a monstrous parent in his own right, murdering a daughter in the quest for bloody revenge. Here, then, is the Whig fear of absolutism made horrifyingly literal, belying Crowne's Tory politics and revealing the extent to which patriarchal overreach is a fearsome thing indeed. The play's grotesque carnage offers a warning against unfettered absolutist philosophy; rape and cannibalism merge with monarchical tyranny to precipitate political and social destruction.

DEFENDING ABSOLUTE MONARCHY: RAVENSCROFT'S *TITUS ANDRONICUS*

Turning now to Ravenscroft's adaptation of *Titus Andronicus*, the last play of the period to feature a scene of parental cannibalism, we find a very different treatment of the cannibal father. Although *Titus Andronicus* is perhaps the most famous play of the period to feature a scene of onstage flesh eating, it represents in many ways a deviation from the other plays examined in this chapter. First, the play was published almost a decade after its initial performance, an unusually long interval for the period. That the play was resurrected for publication in the lead-up to the Glorious Revolution underscores Ravenscroft's political project. To glorify James II and reassure audiences that the kingdom has been purged of disruptive foreign influences. To that end, images of parental cannibalism in the play bespeak not societal and familial corruption, but as we shall see, the comforting banishment of that corruption. Additionally, unlike the other plays examined in this chapter, *Titus Andronicus* offers an uncritically positive view of monarchy and treats intrafamilial cannibalism as a way to achieve social stability, not attack it. The play begins with a fulsome dedicatory panegyric of James II that clearly establishes Ravenscroft's Tory credentials. He calls James "a Prince whose personal Virtues render him Great, not only by Nature Endow'd, but by Experience taught; a Prince whose Life from his Cradle to his Coronation, was spent in the School of Virtue; and every Action, whilst a Subject, was a Noble Lesson for succeeding Princes to Learn and imitate."[94] Ravenscroft praises the continuation of legitimate monarchical succession, honors James for his virtue in suffering, and celebrates his triumph over his foes. He then traces the line of Stuart kings and praises their individual virtues: "Live, My Lord, in the Service of a Prince whose Descent cannot be parallel'd, if we but turn back our thoughts to the Monarchs of his Race, that have rul'd the English Scepter: The first was James the Learned, the next Charles the Pious, the third Charles the Mercyfull, and now Reigns JAMES the Warlike and the Just" (dedication ll. 37–42). Ravenscroft explicitly juxtaposes Charles II with James II and considers their individual merits as rulers. As Charles was known for his mercy, James will be remembered for his justice.[95]

Titus Andronicus begins when racial, religious, and political foreigners, the Goths, gain entrée into Rome. For Ravenscroft, as was the case with Edward Howard in *The Usurper*, the presence of outsiders at the heart of the Roman Empire initially bespeaks Roman triumph and imperial might. Tamora and her sons have been captured and brought back to the city as trophies of war, and they provide evidence of Titus's superior Roman martial prowess. Tamora even acknowledges that she was "brought to *Rome*, To Beautify thy Triumphs" (1.1.43–44). Despite the Roman military victory, however, parent-child relationships have been destablized in the aftermath of the war with the Goths. First, Titus has ordered the murder of Tamora's son in retribution for his own lost children. Later, when his son disobeys his orders, he willingly becomes his child's executioner, explaining, "My sons would never so dishonour me" (1.1.291). As happens to Lee's Titus and Ziphares, the disobedient child quickly earns the punishment of the treasonous. The successful conclusion of the foreign war does not settle—and indeed, creates—turmoil as father turns on son and brother wars with brother.

The disruptions within the Roman family are further exacerbated when Tamora marries into the imperial clan, effecting an invasion and takeover from within. Saturninus is sexually attracted to Tamora, and thus he inappropriately elevates her status as prisoner.[96] He tells her, "Madam tho' chance of war has brought you here, / You come not to be made a scorn in *Rome*, / Princely shall be your usage Every way" (1.3.95–97). Later, after being shamed before the nation with the loss of Lavinia, Saturninus marries Tamora in a deliberate rejection of Roman women. The archetypal Roman maiden, "*Romes* bright Ornament" (1.1.51), Lavinia has rejected Saturninus, and thus he hastens to make Tamora "Empress of Rome" instead (1.1.51). For Naomi Conn Liebler, Tamora's absorption into the Roman world suggests a redefinition of Roman identity: "Tamora and her sons, former prisoners of war, are absorbed into Roman (or neo-Roman) identity, and the distinction of 'Roman' from 'non-Roman' is no longer persuasive, no longer even possible. Tamora's empowerment enables her to avenge her son's death, but she does so as a new-made Roman."[97] I would argue, in contrast, that Tamora cannot and never does become Roman. Even as he promises to make her his empress, Saturninus still refers to Tamora as "thou Majestick *Goth*" (2.1.34); her ethnic identity is not forgotten or abandoned when she marries, and her presence persists in symbolizing the destructive intrusion of ethnic outsiders into Rome.[98] In postcolonial terms, the periphery has invaded the homeland and will work to destroy it from within.

To accomplish fully their destructive aims, the Goths engage in three acts of illicit sexuality: an exogamous marriage, a sexual assault, and an extramarital, interracial affair. Each of these acts emphasizes the dangers of political invasion—of allowing foreign Others too much access to and control of the domestic Self—and contributes to the disruption of relationships between parents and children. Unlike Timandra of Howard's *The Usurper*, Ravenscroft's Tamora functions as an archetypal poisonous Catholic bride, a violent and sexually alluring foreigner who is also a "blot and Enemy to our general Name" (3.1.186). That "polluted Empress" (5.3.50), along with her sons and fearsome lover, will infect the nation from within and unsettle the foundations of Roman society.[99] Much like Settle's Fredigond, Tamora subsequently encourages a rape. When Chiron and Demetrius assault Lavinia, rape simultaneously represents an attack on Lavinia as individual, on Lavinia as Titus's child, and on Lavinia as symbol for the Roman nation.[100] In destroying Lavinia's beauty, Chiron and Demetrius are simultaneously striking blows at Lavinia, at Bassianus, at Titus, and at the Rome that has defeated them and paraded them through the streets in disgrace. Lavinia's body becomes a contested site, her suffering, the symbol of Rome's (and by extension, England's) political woes. Underscoring Ravenscroft's depiction of Lavinia, however, is his wider concern that alien influences will infiltrate, penetrate, dismember, and destroy the homeland. To rape Lavinia, Aron explains, is to "make Invasion on a Princes right" (2.1.284). The rape serves as a metaphor for inter- and intranational conflict. Sexual violence, that is, represents another species of imperial conquest, while Lavinia becomes the unfortunate victim of a clash in nationalities, a vessel to be broken in service of revenge. Her body is polluted both by the rape—she "passes beyond the verge of exogamy when she is raped by her father's enemies"—and by the possibility that she has conceived an illegitimate (and hence monstrous) child.[101] Such a baby would disrupt the Andronicus family lineage, destroy Lavinia's value as a potential Roman mother, and represent a horrifying hybrid of Roman and Goth.

At the same time, the rape of Lavinia is treated as a perversely cannibalistic act, linking the acts of rape, vampirism, cannibalism, and ultimately, Catholic ritual. When Aron manipulates Chiron and Demetrius into attacking Lavinia, he compares the act of sex to the act of eating. Sharing a woman, he tells them, is much like sharing a meal: "How stand your Eager appetites affected? / Wou'd each have her all, all to himself, / And not allow the other to breakfast with him?" (2.1.311–13). Ravenscroft draws on Shakespeare's hunting imagery—"What, hast thou not full often struck a doe / And borne her cleanly by the keeper's nose?" (1.1.593–94), Demetrius asks, comparing the act of rape to the act of poaching—and merges it with the image of feasting: "You intend her then but for a running-Banquet, / A snatch or so, to feed like men that go a hunting" (2.1.316–17), Aron says.[102] These words prefigure the banqueting scene at the end of the text, when human bodies are literally consumed. They also blend the rape of Lavinia with Eucharistic ritual. When the Goths imagine feeding on her body, they transform her, perversely, into the Host; she becomes the sacrificial victim in a deviant and unholy Mass.

Ultimately, however, a hybrid child will be produced not by Lavinia's body, but by Tamora's, and Ravenscroft thereby constructs an imaginative parallel between Lavinia's rape and Tamora's interracial transgression. More so than for Shakespeare, the specter of miscegenation in Ravenscroft is meant to enrage and sicken. Shakespeare's Tamora gives birth to her child during the course of the play, in the interval between acts 3 and 4, and its existence represents primarily a political threat. The nurse tells Aaron, Chiron, and Demetrius, "She is delivered, lords, she is delivered" (4.2.62). According to the nurse, the child represents "Our empress' shame and stately Rome's disgrace" (4.2.61), not merely because the child is Aaron's, but because Tamora would gladly pass off the child as Saturninus's heir. As a result, Royster names the child "a foreign invader . . . the product of Tamora's and Aaron's transgression against Saturninus's authority, and, by extension, a transgression against Rome."[103] The child offers proof of Tamora's infidelity and represents the haunting possibility of illegitimacy diverting appropriate lineal descent.

In contrast, the baby in Ravenscroft's play is not the product of an extramarital affair, nor does Tamora intend it as a potential claimant to the throne. The nurse tells Chiron and Demetrius that Tamora "in Secret / . . . was deliver'd after your Royall Father dy'd" (5.1.12–13). Tamora bore the child in the interval between the death of her Gothic husband and her marriage to Saturninus, so when Chiron insists (following Shakespeare's original) that his mother will "dye by the Emperours rage" should the baby be discovered (5.1.79), his fear is provoked not by Tamora's adultery but by her "monstrous" interracial desire. The child's very existence motivates the characters to murderous rage. According to Anthony Gerard Barthelemy, "the disgust over the adultery, the miscegenation, and the actual blackness of Aron and the child exceeds greatly anything found in Shakespeare's *Titus Andronicus*."[104] In both Shakespeare's and Ravenscroft's versions of the play, the child is described as "Black and loathsome" (5.1.12), "black / and dismall" (5.1.29–30), "Accursed" (5.1.32), and "foul and black" (5.1.51). Ravenscroft adds several other, even more powerfully negative descriptions of the baby, calling it "this black brat, / This Babe of darkness" (5.3.138–39), and "the Hellish infant" (5.3.178). The child represents a powerful shame and a threat to Roman culture. Thus Aron will taunt his listeners, calling the child "That Little thing where *Moor* and *Goths* combin'd" (5.3.220), knowing that its mere mention will appall the Roman establishment. Tamora, the poisonous Catholic bride, has given birth to an infectious monster child. The corrupt blood made possible by Lavinia's rape manifests itself in the birth of Aron's baby.

Taken together, Tamora's marriage, the rape of Lavinia, and the birth of the biracial child symbolize the infiltration and corruption of Rome through illicit forms of sexuality. If Lavinia is contaminated by her encounter with

Chiron and Demetrius, sexual contact with Aron is also treated as a form of staining. Bassianus tells Tamora, "Believe me Madam, your Swarthy *Cymerion* / Has made your Honour of his bodies hue, / Black, Loathsome, and Detested" (3.1.78–80). The pollution of Aron's skin color, he claims, bleeds onto and taints Tamora. Later, Lucius imagines Aron as a suffocating sickness: "What dost avail to call thy self a Sun, / That art so muffl'd in black clouds, / The steams that rise from blood, hang round thee like a fog" (5.3.77–79). Aron's skin is the contagious and poisonous miasma of ill health, the disease infecting the empire, the illness festering in the heart of the nation. The poison of rape merges ideologically with the infectious dangers of racial and ethnic impurity.

Ravenscroft's play thus begins with the penetration of the Other into the homeland, underscoring the author's anxiety about the Catholic presence in England. Rome (and, by extension, England) has allowed dangerous influences to fester within its boundaries. The result of such reverse colonization[105] will be a bloodied, wrecked, and dismembered nation (via Lavinia) or monstrous unions and horrific hybrid births (via Tamora). For the rest of the play, however, Ravenscroft works to overcome and banish these threats to the nation. While the play initially stages acts of sexual corruption through rape and miscegenation, it also works to expel these toxins, first by exposing and later by digesting the threat, literally and figuratively. The specter of the outsider is banished from the city, "a visible purgation of evil from Rome," and a fantasy of national purity reestablished.[106] Shakespeare's play, by contrast, concludes with an image of international union, as the Goths band together with the Andronici to fight Saturninus and his hated queen. According to Shakespeare, Lucius joins with the Gothic army. In David Willbern's words, "The Andronici were rejected by the city they shed blood to defend, and both take revenge on that city by joining with the enemy from whose attacks they once protected her."[107] Lucius promises his father, "Now will I to the Goths and raise a power, / To be revenged on Rome and Saturnine" (3.1.300–301). Later, Saturninus learns that Lucius has become the "general of the Goths" (4.4.68) and hears from Emilius that

> The Goths have gathered head, and with a power
> Of high-resolved men bent to the spoil
> They hither march amain under conduct
> Of Lucius, son to old Andronicus,
> Who threats in course of this revenge to do
> As much as ever Coriolanus did. (4.4.62–67)

Although the Goths were once Titus's mortal enemies, they join with the Andronici to help overthrow the tyrant. For Virginia Mason Vaughan, such cooperation represents the "triumph of the colonized people and the establishment of a new Rome" that invites and privileges commingling.[108] Shakespeare's play concludes with "a loss of racial and cultural purity," as Roman and Goth unite in mutual dislike of Saturninus and Tamora and a newly hybridized Roman state emerges.[109]

No such union occurs in Ravenscroft's text. In his note to the reader, Ravenscroft promises to correct the imperfections of Shakespeare's play, which he describes as "rather a heap of Rubbish than a Structure" ("To the Reader," ll. 12–13).[110] In having his Lucius join with Titus's former legions, Ravenscroft corrects one such perceived flaw: why should the Goths betray their queen for the hated Andronicus family? Ravenscroft's Lucius instead finds support amongst Titus's old regiment:

> The old Legions too by *Titus* late brought home,
> Without the City make their Randevouze;
> Within the People cry Revenge aloud,
> Revenge for the wrong'd *Titus* and his slaughter'd Sons.
> To them the Army Ecchoes with Loud shouts,
> Long live Lucius Emperour of Rome. (5.1.197–202)

Saturninus concurs, acknowledging, "He is the darling of the Souldiers, / Him they did hope should be *Romes* Emperour" (5.1.204). For Ravenscroft, the Goths remain the external enemy driven to destroy Rome and do not transform into a friendly, unified populace.

Ravenscroft's desire to avoid cultural mixing is also apparent in his treatment of Aron's capture. In Shakespeare's play, Aaron is betrayed by a Goth, one of Lucius's soldiers, who captures Aaron out of loyalty to his commander. The Gothic soldier privileges his duty to the Roman Lucius over his ethnic and national identity. Ravenscroft's Aron is also betrayed by a Goth, but for revenge. Aron has murdered a nurse, wife of the Goth who captures him:

> The Nurse that only knew this secret deed—
> This morning dy'd, but with her parting breath
> Declar'd the secret to my Wife her frend.
> And bid her bear this issue to the *Moor*—
> Who wou'd reward her for't—and so he did:
> For she no sooner had perform'd the trust,
> But he his dagger struck into her heart,
> And Bore away the Child in's Arms.—
> I was not then far off, and knew it well.
> And therefore follow'd him with these my friends.
> Seiz'd him in flight, and bring him bound to you. (5.3.37–47)

The Goth comes upon Aron not accidentally as in Shakespeare—Shakespeare's Goth explains, "suddenly / I heard a child cry underneath a wall. / I made unto the noise" (5.1.23–25)—but in a deliberate act of vengeance. He is a renegade Goth, a defector, not a member of a sympathetic Gothic army. Thus Ravenscroft's play maintains the national boundaries that Shakespeare's play elides.

Most notably, however, Ravenscroft reaffirms national integrity through the digestion both of Lavinia and of Aron's child, those lingering twin specters of cultural corruption. Lavinia's shamefully dismembered body is removed from sight and entombed within the vault of the Andronici. She is, in essence, swallowed by the womb-like earth, imaginatively paralleling the ingestion of Aron's baby. "Like the Earth thou has swallow'd thy own encrease" (5.3.158), Titus tells Aron, directly connecting the deaths of Lavinia and the baby as two perversely cannibalistic moments.[111] Meanwhile the Goths are definitively destroyed. As the architect of evil and the physical embodiment of diseased Otherness, Aron receives the harshest punishment. Ravenscroft's Lucius decrees that Aron shall be both tortured and burned. "It was decreed he should expire in flames, / Around him kindle streight his Funeral Fire. / The Matter is prepar'd, now let it blaze: / He shall at once be burnt and Rack'd to death" (5.3.270–73). Aron is not only executed, but incinerated, his threatening physical body reduced to ashes. At the same time, it is not enough for Tamora merely to kill her child; Aron tells his captors, "She has out-done me in my own Art— / Out-done me in Murder—Kill'd her own Child. / Give it me—I'le eat it" (5.3.232–34). Ravenscroft's Aron cannibalizes his son, reabsorbing the baby into his own being and destroying any trace of its physical existence.[112] Ravenscroft's revision thus demonstrates his almost hysterical revulsion at the idea of the baby and, by extension, his revulsion for the concept of miscegenation. The baby must be ingested and then the physical body of Aron himself burned out of existence for order to be reestablished. In another variation of Lee's Roman blood purge, the infected must bleed and the source of contagion be destroyed before the social order can reassert itself.[113]

When Aron ingests his child, then, his act of violence represents, perversely, the reaffirmation of Roman sovereignty and the reestablishment of racial purity. As we have already seen, the act of cannibalism, like the acts of rape and miscegenation, combines the Self with the Other in ways that disrupt both the individual and the polis. For the Romans to engage in cannibalism would be to participate in another instance of threatening cultural mixing. Ravenscroft therefore emphasizes that cannibalism is a Gothic act. While the Romans compel the Goths to feed on one another, they do not themselves partake of human flesh or allow the Goths into their own bodies by ingesting them. Rather than disrupt the boundary of Self and Other, the acts of cannibalism in Ravenscroft's *Titus Andronicus* work to reaffirm separation. Aron and Tamora eat their own children, reabsorbing Goth into Goth and dividing the foreign Other from the Roman Self. The baby's threatening presence is destroyed as it is ingested by the parent who gave it life, consuming and thereby banishing the specter of Otherness from the political realm. Here, then, the cannibal father serves to reaffirm rather than attack national sovereignty. In sharp contrast to Crowne's *Thyestes*, where acts of cannibalism presage societal destruction, Ravenscroft's *Titus Andronicus* celebrates the rejuvenation of Roman strength, as acts of forced cannibalism shore up the ruling regime rather than undermine it.

In the end, the grotesque and graphic acts of violence that conclude Ravenscroft's *Titus Andronicus*—torture, infanticide, cannibalism—are also perversely comforting; the play completes its ideological trajectory with the reaffirmation of Roman national integrity and the eradication of any and all lingering signs of personal, racial, religious, and territorial rape. Beginning with infiltration by the Other, the play concludes with the reassertion of Roman control, allegorically an image of Protestant reunification and the expulsion of Catholic (Gothic) poison. If Crowne concludes with a fearsome and destructive act of paternal overreach, Ravenscroft offers instead a fantasy of boundaries reestablished and the xenophobic pleasure of national, familial, and racial purity renewed. This is not, as in the case of Howard's *The Usurper*, a vision of the homeland improved by foreign and feminine influences, but, in essence, a fantasy of ethnic blood purge with cannibalism as the terrifying yet reassuring culmination. Taken together, *Titus Andronicus* and *Thyestes* unequivocally demonstrate how the entwined imagery of rape, disease, and cannibalism underscores anxieties surrounding familial integrity and the sanctity of boundaries as England headed into the Glorious Revolution, while nonetheless stressing alternatives—two opposite sets of possibilities—for an end to the period's political unrest.

CONCLUSION

To examine the propaganda and drama of the late 1670s and 1680s is to realize the fluidity and universality of rape and cannibal imagery in the writings of the period. Whig and Tory, anti- and pro-Catholic polemic all invoke the rhetoric of intrafamilial cannibalism to protest political enemies. Similar crossovers persisted after the Glorious Revolution, as Whigs and Tories continued to employ conflicting yet broadly overlapping forms of atrocity narrative to attack their enemies. As we shall see in chapter 5, in the aftermath of the Glorious Revolution, images of destructive familial relationships merged with the rhetoric of male violation. While Whig supporters of William and Mary used rape imagery to defend the overthrow of tyrants, Tory supporters of James treated William and Mary as the poisonous ravishers of their own father. Fears of the cannibal father were thus subsumed by the no less strategically terrorizing figure of the father-as-victim.

NOTES

1. William Allen, *A Friendly Call, or a Seasonable Perswasive to Unity* (London, 1679), 3.
2. Ibid., 4.
3. Ibid., 8.
4. Ibid., 9, 10.
5. Ibid., 2
6. Ibid., 51.
7. Ibid., 53.
8. Ibid., 59, 40
9. Ibid., 40.
10. Ibid., 45.
11. *A Bull Sent by Pope Pius*, 1.
12. *A Seasonable Memento, For all that have Voyces in the Choyce of A Parliament* (London, 1681), 1.
13. *The Rise and Fall Or Degeneracy Of The Roman Church* (London, 1680), 14.
14. *A Memorial of the Late and Present Popish Plots* (London, 1680), 4.
15. Oldham, *The Jesuits Justification*, 1.
16. Oates, *A Balm*, 18. For similar commentary, see also AntiPapist, *Fair Warning To take heed of Popery* (London, 1679); Thomas Barlow, *Popery: Or, The Principles & Positions Approved by the Church Of Rome* (London, 1683); Lewis Du Moulin, *A Short and True Account Of The Several Advances The Church of England Hath made towards Rome* (London, 1680); and Titus Oates, *A Balm presented to these Nations, England, Scotland, and Ireland* (London, 1680).
17. Horneck, *The Honesty of the Protestant*, 62.
18. *Salus Britannica: Or, The Safety Of The Protestant Religion* (London, 1685), 3.
19. Keach, *Sion in Distress*, 3, 6, 7.
20. Ibid., 25.
21. Ibid., 85.
22. Ibid., 96–97. For other contemporary representations of the Irish and Parisian massacres, see also *A Short Disswasive From Popery, And From Countenancing and Encouraging of Papists* (London, 1685); Ezerel Tonge, *Jesuitical Aphorismes* (London, 1679); and James Ussher, *Bishop Ushers Second Prophesie Which He delivered to his Daughter on his Sick-Bed* (London, 1681).
23. Keach, *Sion in Distress*, 4.
24. *News from Rome*, 3.
25. *The Common-Hunt, Or, The Pursute of the Pope* (London, 1679), 3. Similarly, the author of *The horrid Popish Plot Happily Discover'd* points out that the city of Rome was founded on an act of fratricide: "*Rome's* Founder by a *Wolf* ('tis said) was nurs'd, / And with his *Brother's blood* her Walls at first / He cemented": *The horrid Popish Plot Happily Discover'd* (London, 1678), 1.
26. Tim Harris articulates usefully the lack of political coherence underpinning Restoration political culture: "This rhetoric was not used solely by the whigs in the context of the popish plot. From the early 1660s, and throughout Charles II's reign, we find concerns being expressed about the security posed by authorities to people's 'lives, liberties and estates' by nonconformist groups protesting against religious persecution. The exclusionist whigs employed this rhetoric, I shall argue, fully aware of the very powerful resonance it had for nonconformists. What is interesting, however, is that for the nonconformists the greatest threat to liberty seemed to come not so much from an absolutist crown, which at times showed itself willing to use its prerogative powers to secure toleration, but from parliament. What has never been noticed is that the tories also used this rhetoric quite extensively during the early 1680s; they were eager to portray themselves as the true defenders of English liberties guaranteed by law, but for them the threat to liberty and property was posed by the whig and nonconformist

challenge to the government in church and state": "'Lives, Liberties and Estates': Rhetorics of Liberty in the Reign of Charles II," in *The Politics of Religion in Restoration England*, ed. Tim Harris, Paul Seaward, and Mark Goldie (Cambridge: Basil Blackwell, 1990), 218–19.

27. Derek Hughes calls the proliferation of dramatic cannibal imagery "a sign of the deep trauma accompanying the Popish Plot and Exclusion Crisis": "Human Sacrifice on the Restoration Stage: The Case of *Venice Preserv'd*," *Philological Quarterly* 88, no. 4 (2009): 368.

28. William Lloyd, *Seasonable Advice To All Protestant People Of England* (London, 1681), 20.

29. Mercurius Hibernicus, *A Pacquet Of Popish Delusions, False Miracles, and Lying Wonders* (London, 1681), a4r.

30. *The Pharisee Unmask'd* (London, 1687), 6.

31. Monsieur Jurieu, *Le Dragon Missionaire: Or, The Dragoon Turn'd Apostle* (London, 1686), 14.

32. Gilbert Coles, *A Dialogue Between A Protestant and A Papist* (Oxford, 1679), a3r.

33. *The Popes Down-fall, At Abergaveny* (London, 1679), 5.

34. Ibid., 5–6.

35. Ibid., 6.

36. Rachel Weil, *Political Passions: Gender, the Family and Political Argument in England 1680–1714* (Manchester: Manchester University Press, 1999), 23.

37. Rachel Weil, "The Family in the Exclusion Crisis: Locke versus Filmer Revisited," in *A Nation Transformed: England after the Restoration*, ed. Alan Houston and Steve Pincus (Cambridge: Cambridge University Press, 2001), 122.

38. Filmer, *Patriarcha*, 12.

39. Gordon J. Schochet, *Patriarchalism in Political Thought: The Authoritarian Family and Political Speculation and Attitudes Especially in Seventeenth-Century England* (New York: Basic, 1975), 139.

40. As both early modern and contemporary critics of Filmerian theory have pointed out, Filmer entirely ignores the role of the mother in raising children. For modern readings of the treatment of women in seventeenth-century political theory, see Melissa A. Butler, "Early Liberal Roots of Feminism: John Locke and the Attack on Patriarchy," *American Political Science Review* 72, no. 1 (1978): 135–50; Margaret J. M. Ezell, *The Patriarch's Wife: Literary Evidence and the History of the Family* (Chapel Hill and London: University of North Carolina Press, 1987); Carole Pateman, *The Sexual Contract* (Stanford: Stanford University Press, 1988); Gordon Schochet, "The Significant Sounds of Silence: The Absence of Women from the Political Thought of Sir Robert Filmer and John Locke (or, 'Why can't a woman be more like a man?')," in *Women Writers and the Early Modern British Political Tradition*, ed. Hilda L. Smith (Cambridge: Cambridge University Press, 1998), 220–42; and Mary Lydon Shanley, "Marriage Contract and Social Contract in Seventeenth Century English Political Thought," *Western Political Quarterly* 32, no. 1 (1979): 79–91.

41. Joyce Green MacDonald, "'Hay for the Daughters!' Gender and Patriarchy in *The Misery of Civil War* and *Henry VI*," *Comparative Drama* 24, no. 3 (1990): 196.

42. Toni Bowers, "Behn's Monmouth: Sedition, Seduction, and Tory Ideology in the 1680s," *Studies in Eighteenth Century Culture* 38 (2009): 17.

43. *A Congratulatory Poem on the Safe Arrival of His Grace James Duke of Monmouth at Utretch, on Saturday Sept. 27. 1679* (London, 1679), 1. For other representative laudatory depictions of Monmouth's virtues, see also *Englands Darling, Or Great Brittains Joy and hope on that Noble Prince James Duke of Monmouth* (London, 1681); *Englands Happiness Restored, Or A Congratulation Upon the Return of his Grace James Duke of Monmouth* (London, 1679); *Valiant Monmouth Revived* (London, 1684); and J. F., *Englands Lamentation For The Duke of Monmouth's Departure* (London, 1679).

44. *A Second Remonstrance by way of Address From The Church of England to both Houses of Parliament* (London, 1685), 2.

45. *Perkin's Passing-Bell, Or The Traytors Funeral* (London, 1685), 1.

46. Ibid.

47. *Absalom's Conspiracy; Or, The Tragedy of Treason* (London, 1680), 1.

48. *The Countreys Advice To the Late Duke of Monmouth, And Those in Rebellion with Him* (London, 1685), 1.

49. Ibid., 2.

50. *Monmouth Degraded. Or James Scot, the little King in Lyme. A Song* (London, 1685), 1.

51. *The Young Bastards Wish, A Song* (London, 1685), 1.

52. Matthew Prior, "Advice to the Painter," in *Poems on Affairs of State: Augustan Satirical Verse, 1660–1714*, ed. Galbraith M. Crump, 7 vols. (New Haven: Yale University Press, 1963), 4:44–49, l. 25. It is, of course, this very sort of depiction Dryden attempted to guard against in *Absalom and Achitophel* when he depicted the duke "as a victim of seduction" by bad counselors (Bowers, "Behn's Monmouth," 23). For discussion of Monmouth's role in the Rye House Plot, see Zook, "Contextualizing Aphra Behn," along with Richard L. Greaves, *Secrets of the Kingdom: British Radicals from the Popish Plot to the Revolution of 1688–1689* (Stanford: Stanford University Press, 1992); Ronald Hutton, *Charles II: King of England, Scotland, and Ireland* (Oxford: Clarendon Press, 1989); and J. R. Jones, *The First Whigs: The Politics of the Exclusion Crisis 1678–1683* (London: Oxford University Press, 1961). For general discussion of Monmouth's life, see Bowers, "Behn's Monmouth," along with Robin Clifton, "James II's Two Rebellions," *History Today* 38, no. 7 (1988): 23–29; Peter Earle, *Monmouth's Rebels: The Road to Sedgemoor* (London: Weidenfeld & Nicolson, 1977); Mark Goldie, "Contextualizing Absalom: William Lawrence, the Laws of Marriage, and the Case for King Monmouth," in *Religion, Literature, and Politics in Post-Reformation England, 1540–1688*, ed. Donna Hamilton and Richard Strier (Cambridge: Cambridge University Press, 1996), 208–30; Stephen A. Timmons, "Executions Following Monmouth's Rebellion: A Missing Link," *Historical Research* 76, no. 192 (2003): 286–91; and J. N. P. Watson, *Captain-General and Rebel Chief: The Life of James, Duke of Monmouth* (Boston: Allen & Unwin, 1979).

53. R. Brown, "Heroics Satirized," 45. That Tullia is linked with the explicitly vampiristic royalists furthers the connection between her character and the royal court's Catholic women.

54. Livy describes Tullia's treatment of her father's body as follows: "The story goes that the crazed woman, driven to frenzy by the avenging ghosts of her sister and husband, drove the carriage over the father's body" (Livy, *Ab Urbe Condita*, 72). While Livy's Tullia defaces her father's corpse in a frenzy of fear, Lee's Tullia does so in a display of purposeful disrespect.

55. *A rare Example of a vertuous Maid in Paris* (London, 1674), 1.

56. Edmund Bohun, "A Preface to the Reader," introduction to *Patriarcha: Or The Natural Power Of Kings*, by Sir Robert Filmer (London, 1685), f7v.

57. Ibid., f8r.

58. Ibid., f8r–f8v.

59. Ibid., a3v.

60. Ibid., a4v.

61. Weil, "The Family," 114. Weil links this new understanding of the family with changing attitudes toward child-rearing in the later seventeenth century. See, for instance, J. H. Plumb, "The New World of Children in Eighteenth-Century England," *Past and Present* 67 (1995): 64–95, and Lawrence Stone, *The Family, Sex and Marriage in England 1500–1800* (New York: Harper & Row, 1979).

62. Tyrrell, *Patriarcha non Monarcha*, 9–10.

63. Ibid., 18.

64. Ibid., 17.

65. Ibid., 23.

66. Weil, *Political Passions*, 61.

67. James Daly, *Sir Robert Filmer and English Political Thought* (Toronto: University of Toronto Press, 1979), 67.

68. Locke, *Two Treatises of Government*, 201.

69. Ibid., 200.

70. Ibid., 201. As Weil points out, this is actually a deliberate misreading of Filmer's theory: "Reliance on a ludicrously stereotyped version of Filmer gave the whigs an illusion of clarity and unity (*we* do not eat our children)" (Weil, *Political Passions*, 43).

71. James Tyrrell, *A Brief Disquisition Of The Law of Nature* (London, 1692), 66.

72. Ibid., 67.

73. Thomas Otway, *Venice Preserv'd*, in *Restoration Drama: An Anthology*, ed. David Womersley (Oxford: Blackwell, 2000), 465–502, 1.1.49–50. Further references to *Venice Preserv'd* are from this edition and will be cited parenthetically in the text by act, scene, and line number.

74. Philip Harth, "Political Interpretations of *Venice Preserv'd*," *Modern Philology* 85, no. 4 (1988): 356.

75. Priuli uses his political power to wage a private battle, conflating "sex and politics": Debra Leissner, "Divided Nation, Divided Self: The Language of Capitalism and Madness in Otway's *Venice Preserv'd*," *Studies in the Literary Imagination* 32, no. 2 (1999): 22.

76. Derek W. Hughes, "A New Look at *Venice Preserv'd*," *Studies in English Literature 1500–1900* 11, no. 3 (1971): 441.

77. William H. McBurney, "Otway's Tragic Muse Debauched: Sensuality in *Venice Preserv'd*," *Journal of English and Germanic Philology* 58, no. 3 (1959): 390.

78. In contrast, Pat Gill argues that the men of *Venice Preserv'd* are feminized, not infantilized: "Revolutionary Identity in Otway's *Venice Preserv'd*," in *Illicit Sex: Identity Politics in Early Modern Culture*, ed. Thomas DiPiero and Pat Gill (Athens: University of Georgia Press, 1992), 245.

79. Similar imagery appears in John Crowne's 1680 adaptation of Shakespeare's *Henry VI*, *The Misery of Civil War, a Tragedy*. In that play, a return to civil war unleashes roving bands of brutish soldiers who rob, ravish, and kill innocent citizens.

80. John Robert Moore, "Contemporary Satire in Otway's *Venice Preserv'd*," *PMLA* 43, no. 1 (1928): 168.

81. Harry M. Solomon, "The Rhetoric of 'Redressing Grievances': Court Propaganda as the Hermeneutical Key to *Venice Preserv'd*," *ELH* 53, no. 2 (1986): 289. See also Bessie Proffitt, who aligns Venice with the Whore of Babylon and the Catholic Church: Bessie Proffitt, "Religious Symbolism in Otway's *Venice Preserv'd*," *Papers on Language and Literature* 7, no. 1 (1971): 26–37.

82. David Bywaters, "Venice, Its Senate, and Its Plot in Otway's *Venice Preserv'd*," *Modern Philology* 80, no. 3 (1983): 245–57. For other readings of the play's political content, see Michael DePorte, "Otway and the Straits of Venice," *Papers on Language and Literature* 18, no. 3 (1982): 254, and Roswell Gray Ham, *Otway and Lee: Biography from a Baroque Age* (New York: Greenwood Press, 1931).

83. Ellison, *Cato's Tears*, 41. For a reading of gender roles and the Nicky-Nacky scenes, see Danielle Perdue, "The Male Masochist in Restoration Drama," *Restoration and Eighteenth-Century Theatre Research* 11, no. 1 (1996): 10–21.

84. Jessica Munns, "'Plain as the light in the Cowcumber': A Note on the Conspiracy in Thomas Otway's *Venice Preserv'd*," *Modern Philology* 85, no. 1 (1987): 56. Several critics have disputed the reading of the play as allegory. See, for instance, Philip Harth, "Political Interpretations," along with Ronald Berman, "Nature in *Venice Preserv'd*," *ELH* 36, no. 3 (1969): 529–43; Z. S. Fink, *The Classical Republicans: An Essay in the Recovery of a Pattern of Thought in Seventeenth-Century England* (Evanston: Northwestern University Press, 1945); and Gerald D. Parker, "The Image of Rebellion in Thomas Otway's *Venice Preserv'd* and Edward Young's *Busiris*," *Studies in English Literature 1500–1900* 21, no. 3 (1981): 389–407.

85. According to Jack D. Durant, the English people should also realize the differences between Priuli and Charles II: "Their political father, wholly unlike Priuli, loves and protects them": "'Honor's Toughest Task': Family and State in *Venice Preserved*," *Studies in Philology* 71, no. 4 (1974): 502. Under such a king, the people have no reason to rebel.

86. Nathaniel Lee, *Mithridates, King of Pontus, A Tragedy* (London, 1678), 36. Further references to *Mithridates* are from this edition and will be cited parenthetically in the text by page number.

87. Although Crowne's father was a parliamentarian during the English Civil Wars, his son did not share those politics after 1660. For biographical information, see Arthur Franklin White, "John Crowne and America," *PMLA* 35, no. 4 (1920): 447–63, and Arthur Franklin White, *John Crowne: His Life and Dramatic Works* (Cleveland: Western Reserve University Press, 1922).

88. For Jasper Heywood's biography, see Joost Daalder, introduction to *Thyestes*, by Jasper Heywood (New York: Norton, 1989). See also Shivaji Sengupta, "Biographical Note on John Crowne," *Restoration* 6, no. 1 (1982): 26–30.

89. John Crowne, *Thyestes. A Tragedy* (London, 1681), prologue. Further references to *Thyestes* are from this edition and will be cited parenthetically in the text by page number.

90. Lucius Annaeus Seneca, *Thyestes*, trans. Caryl Churchill (London: Nick Hern Books, 1995), 9.

91. Ibid., 16.

92. White, *John Crowne*, 122.

93. Jeff Berglund, *Cannibal Fictions: American Explorations of Colonialism, Race, Gender, and Sexuality* (Madison: University of Wisconsin Press, 2006), 9. Modern anthropologists differentiate between anthropophagy, "the actual consumption of human flesh," and cannibalism, a symbolic construct associated with sorcery, savagery, and the monstrous: Gananath Obeyesekere, *Cannibal Talk: The Man-Eating Myth and Human Sacrifices in the South Seas* (Berkeley: University of California Press, 2005), 14. This book refers to acts of anthropophagy as cannibalism since they are designed to render monstrous Catholic ritual. For further anthropological discussion, see William Arens, "Cooking the Cannibals," in *Consuming Passions: Food in the Age of Anxiety*, ed. Sian Griffiths and Jennifer Wallace (Manchester: Manchester University Press, 1998); Mark P. Donnelly and Daniel Diehl, *Eat Thy Neighbor: A History of Cannibalism* (Gloucestershire: Sutton, 2006); Peter Hulme, "Columbus and the Cannibals," in *The Post-Colonial Studies Reader*, ed. Bill Ashcroft and Gareth Griffiths (London: Routledge, 1995); and Frank Lestringant, *Cannibals: The Discovery and Representation of the Cannibal from Columbus to Jules Verne* (Berkeley: University of California Press, 1997).

94. Edward Ravenscroft, *Titus Andronicus, or The Rape of Lavinia*, in *Shakespeare Adapatations from the Restoration*, ed. Barbara A. Murray (Madison: Fairleigh Dickinson University Press, 2005), 1–88, dedication ll. 23–28. Further references to *Titus Andronicus* are from this edition and will be cited parenthetically in the text by act, scene, and line number.

95. That Ravenscroft dedicated the play to the Catholic Earl of Arundel also reflects his Tory loyalties.

96. While the marriage is inappropriate from Ravenscroft's perspective, the Romans actually encouraged intermarriage with conquered peoples.

97. Naomi Conn Liebler, *Shakespeare's Festive Tragedy: The Ritual Foundations of Genre* (London: Routledge, 1995), 146.

98. As Sid Ray points out, "Saturninus's sexual attraction to Tamora obscures his sense of duty . . . and causes him foolishly to place the enemies of Rome too near the heart of its power": "'Rape, I fear, was the root of thy annoy': The Politics of Consent in *Titus Andronicus*," *Shakespeare Quarterly* 49, no. 1 (1998): 33. See also Emily Bartels, who views the marriage as provoking a "breakdown of distinctions between 'ours' and 'theirs'": "Making More of the Moor: Aaron, Othello, and Renaissance Refashionings of Race," *Shakespeare Quarterly* 41, no. 4 (1990): 443.

99. While the image of Tamora as the "blot and enemy to our general name" (2.2.182) is original to Shakespeare's text, the view of Tamora as "polluted" is Ravenscroft's addition. In part, this corruption results from Tamora's illicit contact with Aaron, as blackness was frequently viewed as a "natural infection" and "infection of blood": Sujata Iyengar, *Shades of Difference: Mythologies of Skin Color in Early Modern England* (Philadelphia: University of Pennsylvania Press, 2005), 8, 9.

100. The association between Lavinia and Rome dates back to Virgil's *Aeneid*. For discussion of the play's classical antecedents, see Sara Eaton, "A Woman of Letters: Lavinia in *Titus Andronicus*," in *Shakespearean Tragedy and Gender*, ed. Shirley Nelson Garner and Madelon Sprengether (Bloomington: Indiana University Press, 1996), 54–74; Aparna Khastgir, "Endings as *Concordia Discors*: *Titus Andronicus*," *Studia Neophilologica* 73 (2001): 36–47; Robert S. Miola, *Shakespeare's Rome* (Cambridge: Cambridge University Press, 1983); and Molly Easo Smith, "Spectacles of Torment in *Titus Andronicus*," *Studies in English Literature 1500–1900* 36 (1996): 315–31.

101. Helms, "'The High Roman Fashion,'" 558.

102. Ravenscroft constructs another parallel between sexuality and cannibalism when Titus's sons, Quintus and Martius, are lured to Bassianus's body with the promise of sexual gratification. "O Love! How I do long to taste thy Banquet! / And revel with the fair Inviters" (3.1.215–16), Quintus exclaims at the thought of sexually available women, echoing both the final banquet and Aron's suggestion that Chiron and Demetrius "feed" on Lavinia (2.1.316).

103. Francesca T. Royster, "White-Lined Walls: Whiteness and Gothic Extremism in Shakespeare's *Titus Andronicus*," *Shakespeare Quarterly* 51, no. 4 (2000): 449.

104. Anthony Gerard Barthelemy, *Black Face, Maligned Race: The Representation of Blacks in English Drama from Shakespeare to Southerne* (Baton Rouge: Louisiana State University Press, 1987), 99.

105. I have taken this term from Stephen D. Arata's influential essay on imperialism in nineteenth-century fiction. Arata defines the "narrative of reverse colonization" as one in which "the colonizer finds himself in the position of the colonized, the exploiter becomes exploited, the victimizer victimized. Such fears are linked to a perceived decline—racial, moral, spiritual—which makes the nation vulnerable to attack from more vigorous, 'primitive' peoples": "The Occidental Tourist: *Dracula* and the Anxiety of Reverse Colonization," *Victorian Studies* 33, no. 4 (1990): 623. Jack D'Amico's work identifies a similar fear underlying early modern representations of race, a similarity that justifies the adoption of a term first coined for the late Victorian mindset. See Jack D'Amico, *The Moor in English Renaissance Drama* (Tampa: University of South Florida Press, 1991).

106. Ayanna Thompson, *Performing Race and Torture on the Early Modern Stage* (New York: Routledge, 2008), 63.

107. David Willbern, "Rape and Revenge in *Titus Andronicus*," *English Literary Renaissance* 8, no. 2 (1978): 176.

108. Virginia Mason Vaughan, "The Construction of Barbarism in *Titus Andronicus*," in *Race, Ethnicity, and Power in the Renaissance*, ed. Joyce Green MacDonald (London: Associated University Press, 1997), 182.

109. Ibid., 172.

110. Ravenscroft's estimation of Shakespeare's play persisted well into the twentieth century. T. S. Eliot famously termed the play "one of the stupidest and most uninspired . . . ever written": *Selected Essays* (New York: Harcourt, 1964), 67. Paul Cantor likewise calls *Titus* "obviously an immature work": *Shakespeare's Rome: Republic and Empire* (Ithaca: Cornell University Press, 1976), 211.

111. Several critics have commented on the womb-like nature of the pit containing Bassianus's body. Willbern argues that the pit "is both womb and tomb, and vagina" (Willbern, "Rape and Revenge," 171). Likewise, Wynne-Davies calls the pit a "'swallowing womb' (239) that links female sexuality to death and damnation" (Wynne-Davies, "The Swallowing Womb," 135).

112. See also Thompson, who argues that "the black body becomes digestible in that it is transformed into something consumable" (A. Thompson, *Performing Race and Torture*, 64). In contrast, the baby's fate in Shakespeare's play is never specified. Note that Ravenscroft also excises Shakespeare's white-appearing biracial baby; no hybrid child will linger at the edges of the text to threaten the newly reconstituted Roman Empire.

113. See also Imtiaz Habib, who employs medical terminology to describe the execution of Shakespeare's Aaron: "The 'cure' of Aaron will also thus be the 'cure' of the state": "Elizabethan Racial Medical Psychology, Popular Drama, and the Social Programming of the Late-Tudor Black: Sketching an Exploratory Postcolonial Hypothesis," in *Disease, Diagnosis, and Cure on the Early Modern Stage*, ed. Stephanie Moss and Kaara L. Peterson (Burlington: Ashgate, 2004), 98.

Chapter Five

Rape in the Aftermath of Revolution: Images of Male Rape, 1688–1699

On November 5, 1688, William, Prince of Orange, landed at Torbay and set foot on English soil. The date of the Prince's landing was doubly significant, being both the eighty-third anniversary of the defeat of the Gunpowder Plot and the centennial anniversary of the destruction of the Spanish Armada. William had come, his supporters claimed, to free England from the bonds of papal tyranny, and he was welcomed by multiple tracts that celebrated him as England's savior. According to one anonymous author, "His injur'd Peoples woes too well he knew, / Too well he saw, and seeing felt 'em too . . . / He came to drive and purge the guilty Land."[1] According to Craig Rose, "There is no doubt that King William's supporters genuinely believed their hero to be a heaven-sent deliverer," and thus they rallied behind his cause and, they later claimed, drove out the hated James with only minimal bloodshed.[2] Thomas Yalden's *On The Conquest Of Namur* (1695) suggested that God had blessed William and made him invincible to James's forces: "A thousand Deaths and Ruines round him fled, / But durst not violate his Sacred Head; / For Angels guard the Prince's Life and Throne."[3] A "Song" set "To the tune of 'Lilli burlero'" (1688) likewise exulted, "The pillars of Popery now are blown down. / One thousand, six hundred, eighty and eight; / Which has frighted our Monarch away from his crown, / One thousand, six hundred, eighty and eight."[4] Such treatments of William helped to construct what Steven Pincus calls the Whig view of the revolution: "bloodless, consensual, aristocratic, and above all sensible," the view that has largely persisted until the present day.[5] In this interpretation, "the English people rose up all across the land to overthrow a despotic king and . . . they were justified in doing so."[6]

Recently, historians have begun to challenge the Whig myth of the so-called Glorious Revolution. Again, according to Steven Pincus, historians "have underplayed how much violence pervaded everyday life in England itself. In 1688 and after, England as well as Scotland and Ireland—and then much of Europe—were plagued by battles, rioting, and property destruction. . . . There were no great set-piece battles in England in 1688–89. There was, however, a good deal of violence involving James's army and what remained of his militia."[7] Pincus continues, "The Revolution of 1688–89 was neither aristocratic nor bloodless. Nor was it consensual."[8] Revisionist views of the revolution notwithstanding, the long triumph of the Whig perspective bespeaks both the success of Whig policies in the eighteenth century and the skill with which William and his supporters manipulated the available media of the time. Unlike James II, who largely eschewed propagandizing techniques, William clearly understood the value of laudatory propaganda to the maintenance of a stable regime. As a result, Elaine McGirr writes,

> Tories left the field open for Whigs to exploit the aesthetic and ideological overlap of the art dedicated to the king, the character attributed to him, and the religion confessed by him. The Whigs inverted and burlesqued the heroic's charged language and characters in order to attack James, his religion, and his alleged predilection for tyranny, cruelty, and arbitrary sway. Given that the Tories did not promote an effective countermodel, the Whig characterization of James and his policies went largely unchallenged.[9]

Unlike James, William encouraged (and in many cases, commissioned) pamphlets to promulgate his favored conception of current events, and, as Lois G. Schwoerer explains, conducted an "intensive campaign of propaganda . . . throughout the months of the Revolution."[10] He even brought his own printing press with him to England and moved rapidly to respond to unfavorable depictions, not only with censorship and prosecutions, but with his own counterpropaganda.[11]

Despite their efforts to drown out and suppress unfavorable representations of their regime, William and Mary could never fully stem the tide of Jacobite publications. Book burnings and prosecutions of Jacobite printers and authors notwithstanding, propagandists continued to condemn William and Mary for being ungrateful, murderous children, monstrous, illegitimate monarchs, and the figurative ravishers of James II and the nation. Such works often sexualized the act of usurpation, treating James as a victim of sexual assault and warning upstanding Englishmen against future attacks on their own persons and livelihoods. Central to such tracts is a discourse of male rape that uses the pathetic figure of the ravished monarch to protest political rebellion. This chapter therefore begins with an analysis of 1690s propaganda tracts, glancing first at Whig rhetoric before turning to the trope of the ravished monarch, the wretched victim of his children's ambitious ire.

The chapter then turns to the drama of the period, examining the prevalence of male rape victims on the 1690s stage. Such imagery was not entirely new to the postrevolutionary era. In the immediate aftermath of the Restoration, for instance, John Dryden praised Charles II's mercy in *Astraea Redux*, "that same mildness, which your father's crown / Before did ravish"[12] likening the regicide to an act of rape. Several years later, in Elkanah Settle's 1680 anti-Catholic polemic, *The Female Prelate: Being the History of the Life and Death of Pope Joan*, the Catholic Church commits a sexual assault on the Duke of Saxony through the body of Joanna Angellica. Although the play does not explicitly call Saxony's experience a rape, it creates a clear parallel between Angeline's bed-trick ravishment and Saxony's, who, like his wife, dies as a Lucrece figure to prove the dangers of Catholic tyranny. After 1688, however, the trope of the male rape victim becomes much more common, both in the propaganda tracts and onstage. Thus the chapter compares Settle's *The Female Prelate* with his first postrevolutionary work, *Distress'd Innocence: or, The Princess of Persia* (1690). Unlike *The Female Prelate*, *Distress'd Innocence* purports to be apolitical, but it uses the image of the male rape victim subtly to protest William and Mary's accession to the throne. Like James, the honest and honorable Hormidas has been unjustly ravished of his rightful position. His sexualized suffering protests his political disenfranchisement, revealing Settle's developing Jacobite loyalties in the aftermath of the revolution.

Settle was not alone in employing tropes of sexual violence to comment on political events. As Derek Hughes explains, rape plays of the late 1690s frequently sought to justify the events of the Glorious Revolution: a "noticeable number of them authorized regicide, even when the slaughtered monarch was a legitimate ruler. . . . Rapist legitimate rulers could simply be killed."[13] Colley Cibber's *Xerxes: A Tragedy* (1699) offers perhaps the clearest example of what Hughes is describing. According to the virtuous Aranthes, "'Tis not who Reigns, but who Reigns well is King," suggesting that the rapist monarch earns his overthrow.[14] The plays examined in the second half of this chapter, however—John Crowne's *Caligula* (1698), Mary Pix's *Ibrahim, The Thirteenth Emperour of the Turks* (1696), and Nicholas Brady's *The Rape: Or, The Innocent Imposters* (1692)—all use rape imagery to justify the revolution in slightly different ways. While Crowne and Pix use images of female rape to discredit sitting monarchs, they also present their audiences with men who have been politically and economically ravished. Valerius Asiaticus and Amurat, like Julia and Morena, become the victims of sexualized aggression, starkly demarcating the limits of monarchical power. The violated male body, for Crowne and Pix as for Settle, encodes the dangers of tyranny and offers a powerful impetus for regime change. In contrast, it is the villain of Brady's *The Rape* who espouses the rhetoric of male rape. Brady's evil Genselaric makes the specious claim that he has been ravished of his rightful position and titles, even as he proves himself unfit for those titles because of his acts of sexual assault. By reassigning the language of male ravishment to his villain, Brady implicitly aligns Jacobite rhetoric with tyranny and violence. At the end of the century, then, we have come full circle: as authors of the 1660s displaced accusations of rape onto their villains to redeem Charles II and his court, Brady displaces accusations of male rape onto his villain, rehabilitating by contrast the rule of William and Mary.

WARRING WORDS: PROPAGANDA IN THE 1690S

As part of their campaign to win the allegiance of their new subjects, William and Mary commissioned and encouraged the spread of anti-Catholic propaganda, reviving the by now all-too-familiar litany of Catholic evils to shore up their regime. As in decades past, Catholics are accused of whoredom, idolatry, cannibalism, and sedition. Catholicism is "a Religion Bloody, Damnable, Trayterous, Blind and Blasphemous,"[15] while the Catholics are "guilty of heinous Sins . . . Unrighteousness, Malice, Drunkenness, Murder, and especially . . . Whoredom, and all manner of Uncleanness, even Sodomy it self not excepted."[16] The Church is filled with "*Thieves*, *Whoremongers*, and *Idolaters*,"[17] and the Whore of Babylon is "never so satisfied, as when she can make her self Drunk with the Blood of the Saints."[18] Her very voice is poisonous: from "her Mouth she Rain'd a poys'nous foam,"[19] and thus "'Tis very difficult nay, almost impossible, for a man to be of the *Roman* Church, and not have his Principles Vitiated, and his Morals Depraved by her."[20] The author of *The Pope in a Passion* also links Catholic poison with Catholic cannibalism: "The Papists are Cruel, for they that eat Gods / Must needs have strong Stomachs, and likewise the odds, / They'll poison your Pulpits, and whip you with Rods."[21]

Other tracts resurrected stories of the French and Irish massacres. *Popish Treachery* (1689) describes how French Catholics tortured Protestants:

> They basted their Naked Legs with scalding Grease, or boyling Oyl. Others they made to hold red hot Coals in their Hands; burnt the soals of their Feet; tore the Hair from their Beards, and Nails from their Fingers . . . they beat and bruis'd the Men, and made the Women suffer a thousand indignities. They would often [take] them separately into Chambers, to torment them, but so as they might hear each other cry; and every one in suffering, suffering for themselves, and for the rest of their Family, which they either saw in torments, or heard the crys thereof.[22]

In Ireland, "Women great with Child have been hanged up, and their Bellies ripped open, that the Infant has dropped out, and been thrown into a Ditch," while others were "boiled alive in Cauldrons" and still others "driven through the Streets naked; and if, through weakness, they kept not their pace, they were pricked forward with Spears and Swords."[23] According to the Catholic speaker of *News from the Sessions-House*, the Irish Catholics "committed the most barbarous and execrable Murthers, Villanies, sparing neither Man, Woman, or Child, ripping up Women with Child, ravishing chast Matrons, drowning, putting to the Sword, &c, many thousands of innocent Protestants."[24] Such descriptions mingled with stories of new atrocities committed by Irish forces in Dublin during the years of the revolution. According to Lord Massarene, "The rapines, assaults, robberies and outrages of the papists committed daily upon the Protestants increase."[25] Stories of old enormities thus combined with new to emphasize the continued and pressing Irish Catholic threat.

As stories of atrocity were promulgated, so were depictions of Catholic disruptions to the family. George Walker describes how the Catholics forced mothers to "throw their own Children into the Water; Wives to hang their own Husbands; Children to hang up their own Parents," thus destroying familial relationships with instances of compelled intrafamilial violence.[26] The Catholic Church was accused of encouraging Protestant children to forsake the fifth commandment. *News from the Sessions-House* accuses the personification of "Popery" of declaring "that Children of his Religion owe not Obedience to their Parents."[27] Meanwhile, Catholic women are again accused of birthing monstrosities. In the revolutionary years, images of unnatural motherhood were frequently linked with rumors of the so-called warming-pan scandal, the rumor (propagated in part by the future Queen Anne) that Mary of Modena had not given birth to her son James, but had instead smuggled him into the birthing chamber on a warming pan as a false Catholic heir.[28] One satirist of the period mockingly wrote, "As I went by St. James', I heard a bird sing, / 'Of certain the Queen has a boy in the spring.' / But one of the chairmen did laugh and did say, / 'It was born overnight and brought forth the next day.'"[29] Another satirist writes, Mary "was made the lawful mother / Of tiler's children's youngest brother, / Who was begot, or born, or made, / A Prince of Wales in masquerade."[30] That the child may have been "made" rather than "born" bespeaks its status as a potentially demonic interloper threatening the kingdom. It also reflects the association of Catholicism "with a kind of monstrous motherhood that deprived men of their paternal rights."[31] The general thrust of these tracts was to insist that taking the oath to William amounted to an act of national and individual self-preservation. Without William and Mary, the English would see "the Destruction of our People, the utter Consumption of our Estates, the burning of our Houses, the Ravishing of our Wives and Daughters, the Extirpation of

Families by Sword or Halter, and the utter Ruining our Cities, Towns and Villages."[32] Faced with such a horrible future, Whig authors had no choice but to offer "thanks to Heaven" that "a softer and gentler Coronation Glory, Oblation and Gift, not Rapine and Violence encircled that Brow."[33]

Contrasting with Whig anti-Catholicism, however, was an equally virulent strain of Jacobite anti-Williamite rhetoric that William and Mary never fully succeeded in repressing. Paul Monod explains, "The government could do little more than harass booksellers and printers; even capital punishment was not enough to suppress Jacobite publicists."[34] If anti-Catholic tracts compared the Battle of the Boyne (1690) with the defeat of the Irish Rebellion, Jacobite propagandists "collapsed the Glorious Revolution into the Civil War, equating the dour William of Orange with Oliver Cromwell."[35] Other authors focused critically on William's Dutch blood, resurrecting tales of the demonic Dutchman. According to Rose, "The King's Dutchness was a theme to which Jacobite writers returned again and again."[36] Some authors recalled Dutch treachery at Amboyna, glorifying the memories of the Second and Third Anglo-Dutch Wars and reminding English readers that the Dutch had never repented for their long-ago crime:

> In the Reign of King *Charles* the Second, their Old Reckoning for their Pranks at *Amboyna,* enflam'd by fresh and continual Encroachments upon our *East-India* Traffick, compell'd that Peaceful Prince to humble them by Two several Wars; and yet the late and present Proceedings with us on that side the World do sufficiently shew, That for their Injustice they may indeed be *Punished,* but they can never find in their Hearts to *Repent.*[37]

The author of *The State-Prodigal his Return* (1689) further suggests that Dutch behavior is no better than Irish:

> They take what they will, and pay what they will, with Oaths and blows into the bargain. The Army of King James, in his whole Reign, never committed so many Riots, Batteries and base Murthers, as your Dutch-men in a Years time. Among the rest, think upon that Action of running their Swords through a poor Child in a Cradle, to be revenged of the Mother, for hindring them from Killing the Father.[38]

Meanwhile, Robert Ferguson complains of the "Encroachments, Rapines, and Robberies of the Dutch" and suggests that the nation has placed itself in grave danger by allowing the United Provinces too much control over and access to English trade.[39] The Dutch have gloried in the "Ravishment of Ancient Freeholds and Inheritance from divers of the Subjects of these Dominions,"[40] and will "commit Rapine upon our Liberties" if allowed to control the English government.[41]

Ferguson co-opts the language of rape to describe the negative consequences of political and economic disputes. Depictions of the demonic Dutchman were also, however, occasionally linked with Jacobite attacks on William III's rumored homosexuality. For anti-Williamite polemicists, William's supposed affairs with his Dutch favorites served both as proof of his Dutch sexual "perversion" and as a warning to the nation that William would violate male bodies as he violated the nation. One anonymous satirist asks, "If a willy Dutch Boar for a rape on a Girle / Was hang'd by the Laws approbation / Then what does he merit that Buggers an Earl / And ravish's the whole nation?"[42] According to Paul Hammond, clandestine satires of William's sexuality use "the trope of sodomy as a parodic form of sex . . . to enforce the idea that William is a mere travesty of a king."[43] They also frequently criticize William's preference for his male Dutch courtiers, "young men who monopolize his attention politically and sexually," recalling criticisms of Charles II's powerful mistresses.[44] At the same time, such satires reinforce a view of the Dutch as violent rapists who commit physical as well as economic crimes against the English. As Marvell writes of Charles II in *The Last Advice to a Painter*, William turns a blind eye to the rape committed by one of his fellow Dutchmen because he is too busy indulging his own sexual proclivities. That William's tastes run to men allows the satirist to depict him as a real threat to his people; he may be willing to sodomize his male subjects physically even as he ravishes the nation economically.

Mary II also came in for her share of criticism in the Jacobite press, starkly contrasting with the image of the queen propagated by her supporters. Williamites praised Mary for being both the perfect wife, submissive, loyal, domestic, and kind, and the perfect queen; indeed a "greater number of sermons, elegies, and medals appeared to memorialize Mary's death than that of any other monarch."[45] The Mary of Williamite tracts combines "Female Sweetness" with "Courage Masculine."[46] Within her, "Contrasting contrarieties agreed, / Humble submission and supremacy."[47] She lacks political ambition—"she was always grieved at the occasion of taking the Government, and as glad to resign it"[48] —and prefers virtuous domestic industry to licentious court intrigue:

> She took [her court] Ladys off from that Idleness, which not only wast their time but exposes them to many temptations, and engaged them to work; She wrought many hours a day her self, and had her Maids of honour and Ladys working about her: And whereas the female part of the Court had been in the former reignes subject to much just scandal, She has freed her Court so entirely from all suspitions.[49]

Mary is a model for wives and "a true tender Nursing Mother to the best of Churches."[50] While personally childless, Mary nurtures her nation and her church, in sharp contrast to Mary of Modena's deceptive maternity and the Whore of Babylon's monstrous motherhood. Such images were intended to placate a nation nervous about governmental upheaval and Dutch invasion; as Tony Claydon writes, such treatments of Mary "did much to soothe fears that the crown had fallen into the hands of a foreigner."[51] Even though William was a foreigner, Mary's perfections as a loyal English wife underscored the fundamental rightness of the popular revolt.

Unlike the much-lauded queen of Williamite tracts, the Jacobite Mary was an undutiful child who had destroyed her father to gain a throne. Here the rhetoric of the poisonous child so important to the propaganda of the 1680s comes directly to bear on depictions of the seated monarchs. Writing of Mary, Charlwood Lawton asks Archbishop Tillotson to "*study the fifth commandment*."[52] He goes on to complain that Mary "has partaken with *Thieves* and *Liars* against her own *Father*; *She* is a Receiver of what has been *by them* from him *wrongfully* taken away."[53] In other tracts, Mary is not just a disobedient thief, but an unrepentant parricide. One 1689 poem, "The Female Parricide," likens Mary both to *King Lear's* Goneril and to Tullia of the Lucrece myth, making her the worst sort of unnatural daughter:

> Oft have we heard of impious sons before,
> Rebelled for crowns their royal parents wore;
> But of unnatural daughters rarely hear
> 'Til those of hapless James and old King Lear.
> But worse than cruel lustful Goneril, thou!
> She took but what her father did allow;
> But thou, more impious, robb'st thy father's brow.
> Him both of power and glory you disarm,
> Make him, by lies, the people's hate and scorn,
> Then turn him forth to perish in a storm.
> Sure after this, should his dead corpse become
> Exposed like Tarquin's in the streets of Rome,
> Naked and pierced with wounds on every side,
> Thou wouldst, like Tullia, with triumphant pride
> Thy chariot drive, winged with ambitious fire,
> O'er the dead body of thy mangled sire.[54]

Arthur Mainwaring's *Tarquin and Tullia* (1689) also resurrects the story of Tullia to criticize William and Mary. Mainwaring writes,

> This King removed, th'assembled states thought fit
> That Tarquin in the vacant throne should sit,
> Voted him regent in their senate house,
> And with an empty name endowed his spouse—
> The elder Tullia, who (some authors feign)
> Drove o'er her father's corpse a trembling wain.

But she, more guilty, numerous wains did drive,
To crush her father, and her King, alive;
In glad remembrance of his hastened fall
Resolved to institute a weekly ball;
She, jolly glutton, grew in bulk and chin,
Feasted on rapine and enjoyed her sin.[55]

In such poems, William and Mary become the real-life analogues of the "Villains lurking" in the blood of Lee's Brutus. They are ungrateful, deceitful children who have committed "the ultimate act of filial impiety,"[56] and they have founded a "Government raised by Parricide and Usurpation, entered into by Violation of [William's] own Declaration, supported by the Overthrow of all our Laws Sacred and Civil, and the Perjury of the Nation."[57] Clearly such representations bothered Mary; as Schwoerer points out, performances of *King Lear* were banned during her lifetime.[58]

At the same time, the invocation of the Tullia story reflects the centrality of rape imagery to Jacobite propaganda as well as Williamite. Just as anti-Catholic polemicists warned against popish rapes and massacres, early Jacobite writers insisted that political rebellions would lead only to violence and suffering. Ferguson complains that the mob is too easily manipulated by stories of Irish atrocity: "The very Mob, whom by fictitious Lyes and Falshoods, of a few Irish being every where burning Houses and cutting Throats, [William of Orange] decoyed and enflamed into an insolent and brutal Rage against their Rightful King, and who became the Ladder unto, and the great Pillars of his Throne."[59] Once unleashed, the anarchic crowd threatens the safety of every man, woman, and child in England. In overthrowing their lawful king, the common people have learned that they need not obey any law: "Men might lawfully rob Temples, and plunder Banks and Exchequers, upon the Motive and Design of discharging their Debts. . . . Nay they may virtuously murther their Parents, deflower Maids, and ravish their Sisters, upon the Inducement and in order to the End of getting into Possession of Estates."[60] England will thus become a victim of sexual violence; the country is a "Rose so virgin white before, / Now blusing [sic] with the stain of Gore."[61] The nation's maiden innocence will be destroyed by the violence of revolt.

In overthrowing their rightful king, the English people have "prostitute[d] their Liberties" to the wealthy yet dangerous Dutch and "defac'd the Purity of" the nation with the act of overthrow.[62] As in Dryden's *Albion and Albanius*, where the English Civil Wars are likened to an act of marital infidelity, the Glorious Revolution is treated as evidence of sexual corruption. Some authors applied the language of rape directly to descriptions of usurpation: as Howard Erskine-Hill notes, Jacobite principles "found early expression in the polemical and sensational image of rape, in both senses."[63] As we saw in the introduction to this study, Charles Blount laments the execution of

Charles I, during which the king's "Crown, as well as his Life" were "most unjustly ravished from him."[64] Likewise, Ferguson describes acceptance of William and Mary's reign as a rape upon Anglican principles,

> because the very Things they did, plainly interfered with the whole Religion which they professed and owned. And there was such an outragious Rape committed by [the Revolution] upon their Principles, and such an open deflouring of the Chastity, which their Church had hitherto preserved in point of Allegiance to Lawful and Rightful Monarchs, that were it not that great Multitudes of that Communion both preserved their own Innocency, and have loudly condemned the Crime of their own quondam Brethren and Fellow members; their whole Church would forever lye under the same Blot and Infamy.[65]

The Church has been ravished by revolutionary ideology, while James II has been ravished of his rightful throne. The king in this construction is the victim of sexual assault, while the English people are spotted and stained by their own violent acts. Similar descriptions appear in discussions of James's actions in fleeing London. Crucial to establishing William and Mary's legitimacy was proving that James had voluntarily abdicated his throne, and the debate over James's political actions was likened in satirical tracts to a debate over his sexual virtue.[66] Was James a chaste matron taken by force, likening usurpation to rape? Or was he a licentious whore who voluntarily forfeited his chastity, linking abdication with promiscuity? One circulating broadside described James as a virgin female who suffered a horrible gang rape, only to be declared a whore by the Parliament: "She's made a mere whore by the vow of our state, / Cause surely her maidenhead did she abdicate." [67] James is at once a king wronged by his evil daughter, Tullia, a man implicitly raped by his homosexual Dutch son-in-law, and a Lucrece figure himself, the victim of a sexualized political assault.[68] The image of James as ravished monarch therefore represented an important tool in the Jacobite propaganda arsenal.

By likening James to a rape victim, Jacobite tracts undoubtedly feminize and shame him, even as they protest his maltreatment. At the same time, they reflect the unseen presence of male rape victims both in the political discourse and the theater of the period. Such rhetoric was not, of course, new. Indeed, a glance back at Elkanah Settle's infamous Exclusion Crisis–era play, *The Female Prelate*, is instructive for understanding the treatment of male rape onstage after 1688. The decade's "most virulent piece of propaganda on behalf of the Whigs,"[69] Settle's play uses acts of sexual violence to demonize the Catholic Church and demonstrate the effects of "tyranny in association with popery . . . with its arbitrary judgments, expropriations, rapes, tortures, and murders."[70] To that end, the play concludes with a dire warning about the dangers of an unchecked Catholic Church:

Oh, Romans, you will live to see that day
When from your Roofs your Daughters will be dragg'd,
Their Virgin Innocence abused with dust,
And thus brought home a lamentable Spectacle.
Thus shall your Wives and Daughters all be ravished,
Dishonour'd, Poyson'd.[71]

Echoing the bloodiest of the anti-Catholic propaganda sheets, the Duke of Saxony insists that no woman shall be safe from Catholic violence. If even Angeline, the chaste Duchess of Saxony, can suffer a horrifying violation at the hands of a prelate, lower-class women will have no hope of escaping sexual abuse:

If this dear Beauty, born of Noble Blood,
By Wedlock planted in a Prince's Bosom,
Could not escape from Treason, Rapes and Death,
How shall your Wives, your Daughters and your Sisters,
To whom no Awe, nor Guard makes difficult approach.
Be safe; no, I presage they shall be prostituted all,
Defiled, abused, torn up with impious lust. (67)

Saxony hopes his story will act as a warning to the Roman nation; the people must curb the excesses of the Catholic Church and the tendency of cardinals to "place themselves above the law" or witness their families destroyed by the excesses of unchecked prelatic lust.[72]

As in many of the anti-Catholic propaganda tracts we have examined thus far, Catholic tyranny leads to the sexual violation of innocent females and enables the growth of overly powerful and destructive women. According to J. Christopher Warner, in the late seventeenth century, tales of Pope Joan provided "a straight-forward personification of monstrous female lust and ambition. She is a symbol of Rome, the Whore of Babylon, as well as a jab at Charles II's much-hated mistress, the Duchess of Portsmouth."[73] The treatment of female monstrosity in the play—Joanna's female monstrosity—underscores the continuities between Settle's various dramatic works. Pope Joan is heir to Settle's earlier monstrous women, a new incarnation of *The Empress of Morocco*'s Laula and *Love and Revenge*'s Fredigond. Although critics have generally overlooked the continuities between *The Female Prelate* and *Love and Revenge*, both plays begin with a son who must avenge his murdered father against a poisonous woman who has long concealed her calumny. "I had a Father, / Whose Blood, whose Royal Blood is unrevenged" (2), Saxony tells his wife. According to Saxony, his father was "most basely poysoned: / Nay, poysoned by a Priest, his savage Confessor. / That cursed Slave that fed upon his Smile" (2). Joanna, the old duke's murderer, is figuratively a cannibal in Saxony's description, and one who has grown toxic in her monstrosity. Characters refer to Joanna's "black Blood" and "invenomed Breath" (7, 13). Saxony, meanwhile, calls her a "Hellish Fiend" who left a "Sulphorous Brand . . . burning in my Father's Heart" (12), a "Monster" (7), and an "incarnate Devil" (52). In *Love and Revenge*, Fredigond's monstrosity stems from an inappropriate sexual drive, the failure of men to police her actions, and a desperate need to avenge the death of her brother. Joanna's monstrosity originates in her inappropriate access to male spheres of knowledge, transforms into an inappropriate sexual drive, and culminates in the need to avenge her status as cast mistress to the old Duke of Saxony. Joanna has found intellectual and social freedom as Cardinal John. She describes her education:

> As many Languages as *Romes* proud Hills
> My Virgin Nonage spoke. As many Arts and Sciences
> As the famed Stagyrite studied to inspire
> The Conqueror of the Universe, were mine.
> So far I fadom'd into Books, Men, Manners,
> Reasons, Religions; I could take all Forms:
> The perfect Christian, or complete Philosopher;
> To Nature, or to Natures God at pleasure:
> Dispute on both sides, and on both sides vanquish. (26)

Joanna's cross-dressed disguise thus affords her both intellectual and physical freedom; she gains access to her (initially) beloved duke through the supposed sanctity of the confessional. John "won so far my Royal Father's Favour" that "His Ear, his Hand, his Soul was all his own" (11). In this, Craig M. Rustici explains, Settle "hyperbolically illustrates the dangerous intimacy between confessor and penitent" and emphasizes Joanna's status as a snake coiled at the heart of the kingdom.[74] She will "twine within that Royal Princes Heart" and spread her malice and disease throughout the land (11).

Because Joanna has rejected the "normal" female way of life—Owen points out that Joanna's cross-dressing "emphasizes [her] monstrosity"—images of maternity are disrupted throughout the play.[75] According to Joanna, "So fair I stood for the world's awful Thunderer, / Wits Goddess from my Brain already born" (26). Joanna replaces her "natural" ability to mother children with the unnatural birth of wit. While she has been sexually active, there is no evidence until the end of the play that she has ever conceived a child (ultimately she is betrayed by her female body when her miscarriage offers proof of her gender). Instead, she gives birth to horrifying plots and ideas, praising her "fertile Brain" (9), not her fertile body. Later, she describes her attraction to Saxony: "Gorged with the Fountain, for the Stream I thirst. / And teeming with the'unnatural Monster burst" (32). Joanna "teems" with unnatural desire and, like *Titus Andronicus*'s Chiron and Demetrius, compares sexual experience to a gluttonous and monstrous banquet. Meanwhile, the Church itself, supposedly the great mother who nurtures her people, is a corrupt whore. Saxony initially praises his late father's religious virtue, saying that the old duke "was a constant Catholick, / His Faith and

Life incorporate, his Principles / Suck'd in from Rome's own Breast" (16). Unfortunately, the people cannot suck salvation from a poisonous teat. Instead, they will be "Profaned and sullied by a Whore, a Syren" (71), their souls endangered by the Church's venom. Joanna's femininity thus forms an integral part of Settle's condemnation of the Catholic Church, and it offers concrete proof of the need for a Protestant, masculine alternative to corrupt female excess.

Contrasting with Joanna is the Duke of Saxony, son to a murdered father and husband to a ravished wife. If the character of Joanna incorporates aspects of Settle's earlier Fredigond, Saxony is the more honorable heir to *Love and Revenge*'s Chlotair and Lewis. A virtuous son, Saxony insists upon his familial duty and invokes, like Clotair, the memory of King Hamlet's ghost. "I had a Father, A Prince so Excellent, so truly Noble, / Too good for this base world" (2), Saxony says, language that "recalls to us Hamlet's praise of Old Hamlet." [76] It is not enough for God to punish his father's murderer, Saxony claims: "Blood requires blood" (3). Although Angeline questions her husband's continued pursuit of vengeance after so many long years—"seven long years have past, / And in that time the mourning Robe should sure / Be quite worn out" (2)—Saxony insists that a child's responsibility to his father's memory never fades. "Never, my *Angeline.* / Methinks I've still that poysoner in my eye" (2). Subsequently, in a climactic scene of the play, Saxony literally encounters his father's ghost; according to the stage directions, on the night of the bed trick, "The Ghost of the old Duke of Saxony rises with a burning Taper in his hand" and "touches a train of fire above him, which immediately writes upon the Wall, in Capital letters in a bloudy fire, the word MURDER; which continues burning some time" (50). In *Love and Revenge*, Nigrello stages a fake fire to expose Fredigond and Clarmount, while Fredigond stages the ghost of Childrick to avoid suspicion. *The Female Prelate* replays these events and literalizes them. The heretics light an actual fire to drive out the hated pope, and Saxony encounters the embodied specter of his father. Ultimately, however, Saxony proves as poor a revenger as Chlotair and Lewis. Already he has waited seven years to effect his vengeance, but when he finally goes to act, he learns that in a world where the Catholic Church reigns supreme, secular rulers are powerless before the whims of the prelacy. Saxony insists that the Church has no right "To judge a King, and doom a Soveraign Head" (17), but he cannot overpower the Church hierarchy or succeed in bringing his revenge plot to fruition. [77]

Because the Church is so powerful, Saxony fails to avenge his father and protect his kingdom. Next, he fails to save his wife from sexual violence. Angeline, the fair lady to Joanna Angellica's dark, is raped, prompting her to compare her suffering to Lucrece's and Philomel's:

> Ravisht! Oh ruine, fate, destruction, Death!

These Eyes, these Lips, oh Heav'ns, this sacred Bosom,
Once the blest Throne of thy transported Joys,
Made a loath'd Monsters Prey! But oh ye Powers,
This is not half my Scene of Woe! Alas,
The bleeding *Lucrece* and the mourning *Philomel*
Could plead as much as this: But I am a wretch
A thousand times more monstrously deform'd.
Oh my vast Wounds! (62)

Saxony attempts to ignite the power of the Lucrece myth and use his wife's death as the impetus for political change—"Revenge my Wrongs, and this fair Martyrs Blood" (70), he begs—but the common people are not moved by the sight of her suffering. "Burn him, burn him, burn him" (70), they say of Saxony instead. Although Saxony compares himself to Mark Antony, come to eulogize Julius Caesar's unjust death, he finds instead, as Rustici notes, that the "Romans have degenerated from their ancient virtue. Catholicism's mercenary spirituality has infected their consciousness and eroded their self-reliance."[78] Saxony is no Lucius Junius Brutus, and Angeline is a failed Lucrece. Like the unnamed shepherdess of Shadwell's *The Libertine*, whose suicide goes entirely unheeded, Angeline's death means nothing in the ethical vacuum created by popery. Angeline will not bring change with her suicide, and after she is gone, Catholic treachery will fester indiscriminately and unchecked.

Although Angeline did not consent to sex with Lorenzo, seventeenth-century English law would have been unlikely to define her experience as a rape. After all, she bears no wounds and offered no resistance. Still, Angeline views herself as the victim of sexual violence, her experience made all the worse because she did not resist. Angeline laments,

When to my fatal Bed th'Adulterer came,
But oh that hour be blotted from eternity!
I harmless, languishing, expecting Innocence,
Met the foul Traytour, kist, embraced him, loved him,
Around his neck my longing arms I threw;
For I was kinde, and thought, my Lord, 'twas you.
Oh horrour, horrour, unexampled horrour! (63)

Angeline expresses her anguish with the vocabulary of rape: she is spotted, stained, and poisoned, a "sullied bloated thing" and a "polluted Monster" (62), and she wants to kill herself to remove the taint. She must seek "Death's kind hand," which "wipes all my stains away" (64), because she has no other way to establish her innocence.

Since Angeline views herself as a victim of sexual violence, the parallels between Angeline's experience and Saxony's suggest that her husband, too, has been sexually assaulted. There is little difference between Angeline's encounter with Lorenzo and Saxony's with Joanna Angellica. Both have been the victim of bed tricks, believing that they were making love to their spouses when in fact they were unwittingly committing adultery. They describe their experiences in similar terms: while Angeline calls herself a "sullied bloated thing" (62), Saxony laments his "bloated Soul" (59). Like Angeline, Saxony sees himself as having been poisoned, his marriage bed polluted by the extramarital contact: "Horrour unspeakable!" Saxony cries (53), recalling Angeline's "horrour, unexampled horrour!" (63). "What Monster has this night slept in my arms?" He continues,

> Not Christian slaves, wrapt up in Pitch, and light
> Like burning Tapers to the Savage *Nero*,
> Not *Hercules* in his invenom'd shirt,
> Nor *Lucifer* at his first plunge in Hell,
> Felt half the Fires my raging Entrails swell. (52)

Like Angeline, Saxony immediately plans to commit suicide, thereby proving his love and purity: "My *Angeline* / Has been my first, and Death's my second Bride" (58), he cries. Despite the fact that the characters never refer to Saxony's encounter as a rape, he has been violated by Joanna's actions, and in the same way as his wife. When he dies, he does so not just to avenge Angeline, but because he is a rape victim in a Restoration tragedy, where rape victims must die for order to be reestablished. Saxony becomes the play's second Lucrece, another violated, martyred body to display to the mob, and his death is just as ineffectual. Joanna is defeated not by Saxony, but by her own traitorous female body. What *The Female Prelate* finally suggests, then, is that the Catholic Church violates men as well as women. Saxony's rape by Joanna Angellica symbolizes both the sexual dangers posed by the Church and the individual loss of political and economic autonomy inherent to living in a Catholic kingdom. Even as Settle threatens women with physical violation at the hands of lascivious and out-of-control priests, he suggests that men will suffer disempowerment and emasculation at the hands of the prelacy. Saxony cannot protect his kingdom, his wife, or even his own body from the calumnies of the Church.

ARTICULATING JACOBITE SYMPATHIES: SETTLE'S *DISTRESS'D INNOCENCE*

The tropes of male ravishment employed by *The Female Prelate* became much more common in the wake of the Glorious Revolution as images of male rape enabled authors subtly to comment on contemporary politics. Settle himself returned to such themes in his 1690 *Distress'd Innocence: Or, The Princess of Persia*, a play that expresses its Jacobitism in the language of male rape. Settle is, of course, best known for the virulent Whig anti-Catholicism that characterizes *The Female Prelate*, but he was not in fact committed to his Whig politics. According to Don-John Dugas, "Settle became a creature of politics during the 1680s, devoting his creative energies to one thing: ingratiating himself with whomever was in power. To further this end, he wrote confessionals explaining his change of political allegiance, lauding high-placed Tories in verse, and wrote tracts attacking prominent Whigs."[79] By 1690, Settle had alienated both sides of the political divide: his violent support of anti-Catholic policy in *The Female Prelate* and the pope-burning pageants had angered Tories, while his subsequent recantation of those beliefs alienated the Whigs. Thus in the preface to *Distress'd Innocence*, Settle expresses his intent to leave politics behind and write only for general amusement and entertainment:

> [W]ith what shame must I look back on my long Ten Years silence. Alas, I was grown weary of my little Talent in Innocent *Dramaticks*, and forsooth must be rambling into *Politicks*: And much I have got by't, for, I thank 'em, they have undone me. And truly when impertinent Busy Fools in my little post, in the name of Frenzy must aspire to State-Champions, though their Pens are drawn even on the Right side, they deserve no better Fate. . . . And now, after all my repented Follies, if an Unhappy Stray into Forbidden Grounds . . . may be permitted to return to his Native Province, I am resolved to quit all pretensions to State-craft, and honestly sculk into a Corner of the Stage, and there die contented.[80]

On the surface, *Distress'd Innocence* is not a political work in the vein of *The Female Prelate*. Instead, as Robert Hume writes, "Heroic pathos is the keynote" to the play; "Hormidas and Cleomira mingle pathos and nobility . . . Mrs. Barry exults in vengeance; Mrs. Bracegirdle suffers."[81] The play's contents, however, belie the claim that Settle is no longer interested in engaging the political sphere. As we shall see, *Distress'd Innocence* draws on and develops the tropes of *The Empress of Morocco*, *Love and Revenge*, and *The Female Prelate*, along with the discourse of the male rape victim, to consider the impact of political usurpation on the nation and the individual.

In the course of *Distress'd Innocence*, Cleomira, wife of the righteous general Hormidas, nephew of the king, is raped by the evil and ambitious Otrantes at the command of King Isdigerdes. Because Hormidas is envied far and wide, Otrantes and his compatriots view the rape of Cleomira as a form of homosocial punishment for Hormidas. "I'le stab thee through thy *Cleomira's* heart" (34), Otrantes tells Hormidas, suggesting that he will dishonor the husband by assaulting the wife. Later, access to Cleomira's body (now revealed to be royal) is equated with access to political authority. Otrantes will seek her hand to place himself closer to the line of succession. Cleomira is thus violated by two father figures, Otrantes, whom she has regarded as an uncle, and Isdigerdes, the king who should protect her but who instead orders and sanctions the rape. Isdigerdes links his authority to rule with Otrantes's ability to rape. He rages over his "impotent Revenge" and tells Otrantes, "If thou dost not win her, / Say I'm a Girl, and my weak Infant Vengeance / More worthy of a Rattle than a Scepter" (29). The king, like Otrantes, seeks to disenfranchise the innocent Hormidas through ill-treatment of his wife. Cleomira subsequently emerges from her experience as yet another ruined female vessel, and she joins the long tradition of Lucrece figures in seeking death. Isdigerdes explicitly compares Cleomira to Lucrece as he plans the rape: "This Vertue, my coy *Lucrece*, shall not guard thee" (29). After the assault, Cleomira views herself as poisoned and poisonous; like *Thyestes*'s Aerope, she becomes "Lovely Ruins" (44), a "bleeding *Lucrece*" tainted by a "Scorpion Wound" that "has stung so deep / That all the Scorpions Blood can never cure" (46, 47). She then dies both to proclaim her innocence and because she has no reason left to live.

Contrasted with the martyred Cleomira is the ambitious Orundana, and the two form another variation of Settle's virtuous woman / villainous woman pairings. Initially, the two women seem quite similar, as both have been victimized by the fathers in their lives and by the same baby-swapping trick. Orundana has been unfairly elevated to the status of princess, while Cleomira, the true princess, was raised as a foundling and pauper. Any parallels between the two women, however, subsequently break down. While Cleomira is raped, Orundana becomes a rapist. Like Fredigond and Joanna Angellica, Orundana has grown poisonous from her time spent at court, and her ambition drives her to destroy potential opponents to her throne. She speaks poisonous language to her (supposed) father, Isdigerdes, spreading rumors about Hormidas to discredit him politically. Hormidas calls the slanders "foul-mouth'd Falsehood, and invenom'd Malice," and begs the king to "Hear not this fowl polluting Calumny" (7). Like Joanna Angellica, Orundana also becomes an unnatural mother, overseeing the birth of plots, rather than children: "Let me embrace thee for this pregnant Mischief," she tells Rugildas, when he plans to disgrace Hormidas. "The great *Minerva* from the brain of *Jove* / Was not a Birth like this" (12). Most damningly, Orundana encourages the rape of Cleomira to protect her own position. In the lead-up to the assault, Cleomira begs Orundana for mercy, calling out to her as Lavinia calls to Tamora and using the language of natural motherhood to spark Orundana's sympathy:

> Snatch the Poor Lamb from the Wild Ravenous Wolves,
> And give him to a Longing Mothers Arms.
> Oh Royal Virgin, Love will one day make
> Thee a blest Mother too, and then thou'lt feel
> A Tender Mother's Love. (27)

Cleomira is herself a mother, and she attempts to melt Orundana with the rhetoric of motherhood, but, as is also the case for Lavinia, to no avail. Orundana has become unnatural, her fertility redirected from the positive force of childbirth to the negative birth of plots.

Despite her willingness to use sexual assault as a political weapon, Orundana ironically speaks of herself as a rape victim. She compares the loss of political authority to the experience of sexual violation and names herself a Philomel who must take revenge. She keeps her ears open for reports of challenges to her authority because

> Id'e have my Wrongs alarum'd in my Ears,
> Repeated oftner than my very Prayers;
> It whets my Vengeance keen, the Edge wou'd rust else.
> She who wou'd sing Revenge must play the watchful *Philomel*;
> Hold the sharp pointed Thorn against her Breast
> To keep her Ayres awake. (3)

Orundana refers in these lines to Philomel's power as a singer and nightingale; however, the sexually violent content of the text suggests that Orundana is worried that she, too, will be ravished, with ravishment here used to denote a form of property crime. Like James II, she will be ravished of what she believes is her rightful throne. Cleomira and Orundana thus emerge from the text both as parallels and as polar opposite types of rape victim; one has suffered physical assault, while the other equates political disenfranchisement with physical violation.

Just as Orundana uses sexual assault to represent the loss of political position, the play treats Hormidas as yet another type of rape victim. Like *The Female Prelate*'s Duke of Saxony, Hormidas uses sexual violence as a metaphor for political disruptions. As nephew to the king, Hormidas should be second in line to the throne, but a suspicious Isdigerdes strips him of his titles and relegates him to the status of stable boy. In expressing pity for Hormidas's situation, the other characters use sexually tinged speech. Hormidas, like Crowne's Aerope and Settle's Angeline, becomes a ruined building; Theodosius calls him "Thou Royal Ruines" (23). He also laments the "drowing [sic] Deep in which thou'rt swallow'd" and insists that he will "Hoist thy sunk Glories, and weigh up thy Ruins" (24, 25).[82] That Cleomira is also referred to as a ruin in the wake of her rape underscores the sexualizing of Hormidas's political state. Hormidas himself eroticizes political disenfranchisement when he begs the king to "Unplume me, rifle me, degrade me . . . / Be kind, and strip me naked" (7). Hormidas has been ravished, poisoned, diseased, and stained. His reputation, like that of a rape victim, has been besmirched; the slanderers, he says, have sought to "blacken my fair Truth" (9), and although he claims that he still possesses his "fair spotless Truth" (23), Cleomira agrees that his "unspotted Faith" has been "blemisht" (9). Hormidas also refers to Otrantes as the "Unpunisht Ravisher of all my Honours" (24), and he warns Cleomira that his "Infectious Ruine" may blemish her as well (26). His political disenfranchisement becomes a source of social toxin, infecting Hormidas metaphorically and the nation politically. Meanwhile, in treating a faithful servant so unfairly, by ravishing Hormidas metaphorically as he orders the rape of Cleomira physically, Isdigerdes, like Valentinian, stains himself and the reputation of his rule. He will finally lament his behavior, saying, "Oh, poor *Hormidas*! Were the ravish'd Coronets / Torn from thy Brow for Chaplets for this Villain? / Oh the mistaken Favours of the Crown!" (54). He will later proclaim both Hormidas and Cleomira "Spotless as a new born Day" (56), and he will blame his priests for "Religious Sacrilege" and "Rapines" (56), but too late to restore either to life. Nor can he punish the true villains. Rugildas tells him at the last, "No, silly, credulous, and thoughtless King, / I am past thy spight" (60).

What I want to suggest, then, is that Settle's interest in the male rape victim, in *The Female Prelate*, a sign of Whig leanings and a warning against Catholic policy, becomes in *Distress'd Innocence* an expression of Jacobite sympathies. As in Jacobite propaganda, the act of usurpation is likened to the act of rape; to take the throne by force, even from a corrupt monarch, is a violation of both the body politic and individual bodies natural. Settle's subtle Jacobitism also finally manifests itself in the play's treatment of King Isdigerdes. Isdigerdes survives the play's final bloodbath and continues his rule unopposed (if perhaps chastened by his experiences), while the attempted usurpers prove themselves unfit to rule. The king oversteps himself both sexually and politically and places his faith in the wrong sorts of councilors, but his actions do not finally license his overthrow or offer justification for contractual rulership.

DEFENDING THE REVOLUTION: VARIATIONS ON THE TROPE OF MALE RAPE

Settle's *Distress'd Innocence* represents in many ways an aberration, as the majority of the rape plays of the 1690s sought to defend the events of the Glorious Revolution. Such a usage of rape imagery is perhaps most blatant in Colley Cibber's 1699 *Xerxes*, a play that explicitly articulates a contractual theory of monarchical governance.[83] According to Artabanus, the play's hero, "He that neglects the Regal Office, / Should be compell'd to lay it down; / And we who feel the smart of that neglect, / Are only proper Judges, where to place it" (21). A ruler is only a ruler so long as he is fit to rule, and his right stems from his merit, not his birth: "I ha' no King, 'tis Merit, not a

Crown / That makes a King" (18), Mardonius insists. Meanwhile, Aranthes claims that rebellion in certain circumstances is not only permissible, but necessary:

> That Loyalty's Dishonorable,
> That bids me bear Dishonour: When Subjects
> Are no more the Carc of Kings, we then
> Have only left the Laws of Nature to Protect us,
> And Nature tyes us all to Self Defence. (19)

In attempting to rape an innocent woman (Artabanus's wife), Xerxes oversteps his authority sufficiently to prove himself unfit to rule, thereby necessitating his eventual overthrow.

From the beginning of the play, Xerxes has gone mad, celebrating victories that were actually defeats and insisting upon the boundless depths of his personal power. He accepts unironically and uncritically the sycophantic Cleontes's rhetorical insistence upon his divinity—Cleontes calls him "Thou Deity Ador'd! Immortal *Xerxes*" (6)—a sentiment he echoes at the end of the play, even in the face of death. "My Words have more than Power of common Kings" (45), he insists. Yet Xerxes, like Valentinian, ultimately faces the limit to his personal rule. When he demands that his minions resurrect the dead victims of his torture—"By Heav'n I'll have 'em Rackt to Life again!" (25)—he learns that even a king has no dominion over death. Like Crowne's Atreus, he also discovers that his subjects have an interiority that he can neither control nor compel. He can rape Tamira's body—indeed, he views the violation of a chaste woman to be the most exquisite form of pleasure, "a Joy for Gods to taste" (33)—but Tamira's mind and heart are her own. Thus she refuses to reveal Artabanus's hiding place, saying she has hidden him "in my Heart, / Where you, nor yours can enter to remove him" (25). Xerxes subsequently attempts to access that otherwise guarded interior via rape. He exclaims, "In her unwilling Ears I'll pour such Tales / Of Loose Desire, her very Soul shall feel the Rape" (29). Like Major Oldfox of Wycherley's *The Plain Dealer*, who threatens to ravish the Widow Blackacre "through the ear, lady, the ear only,"[84] Xerxes commits aural rape in an attempt to reach the untouched soul of Tamira's being.[85] Tamira, however, reminds him that although he may torture her body, her true being remains untouched: "Now satiate thy Rage, strip off my trembling Flesh, / And when thou'st Piece-meal torn these frailer Limbs away, / Still shalt thou leave unmov'd a naked Mind / Erect to Heaven" (27).

Tamira finally avoids Xerxes's assault by feigning wantonness, but it is also too late for his rule, as his cruel actions have unleashed the power of the mob. Mardonius enumerates the reasons for rebellion:

> Your Liberties infring'd, your Rights destroy'd,
> Your antient Glory sunk in Sloth and Tyranny;

Your Ransack'd Houses, and exhausted Treasure,
Your Tender Virgins, and your Wives deflower'd,
The publick Wrongs, and poor *Tamira's* Rack,
Are Stings too venom'd, not to swell Resentment. (40)

Once unleashed, the vengeance of the mob is as violent and threatening as any act perpetrated by Xerxes. Tamira, like Lee's Teraminta, is attacked by the crowd, her child threatened by people who would treat it as spoils of war: "The Child's my lawful Plunder, and I will keep it" (41), says a member of the rabble. In this, the play offers a qualified endorsement of rebellion; a king must rule well without violating the rights of his subjects—here, as in earlier plays, symbolized by the monarchical act of rape—yet the cost of revolution is high. Thus Mardonius warns,

Let Kings and jarring Subjects hence be warn'd,
Not to oppress, or drive Revenge too far:
Kings are but Men, and Men by Nature err;
Subjects are but Men, and cannot always bear.
Much shou'd be born before Revenge is sought:
Ever Revenge on Kings is dearly bought. (48)

The play contains both a warning to the king to foreground his subjects' best interests and a warning against the rush to revolt.

Xerxes is characteristic of the treatment of rape in quite a few of the plays of the 1690s. As Susan Staves explains, in numerous works, "Elaborate debates over lineage, history, and primogeniture have now given way to the idea of a utilitarian contract between sovereigns and subjects. If the sovereign brings harm to his subjects, he is deposed with a minimum of revolutionary guilt; if he confers benefits on them, they reward him with loyalty."[86] Thus in play after play, the audience is presented with a rapist ruler whose overthrow is treated as both right and good. William Mountfort's *The Injur'd Lovers: Or, The Ambitious Father* (1688), George Powell's *Alphonso King of Naples* (1690), and Charles Gildon's *The Roman Brides Revenge* (1696) all feature "Imperial Ravisher[s]" who must be deposed for the good of the nation.[87] Powell's play in particular stresses that merit is more important than birth in determining the right to rule. Although Cesario is not a nobleman, he has earned the right to marry the king's daughter because he "does deserve her: / H'as bravely fought, and bravely conquer'd for her."[88] Contrasted with the brave Cesario is the corrupt King Alphonso, who finally must abdicate for the good of the kingdom. He tells his successor, "when the Royal Helm is in thy hand, / Oh let my Wrack thy warning Seamark stand, / Shun but my Guilt" (47), reflecting his acknowledgment of his crimes against the country and his recognition that he has effectively lost his right to rule. Other playwrights continue to use rape to demonize the Catholics: John Bancroft's *King Edward the Third, With the Fall of Mortimer, Earl of March* (1690) features a sexually violent Catholic bishop whose power is sustained by Queen Isabella, the play's poisonous Catholic bride, while Powell's adaptation of John Fletcher's *Bonduca: Or The British Heroine* (1695) features a Roman invasion leading to multiple rapes and eventual deaths. In all of these cases, the suffering of female bodies offers a straightforward justification for contractual views of monarchy.

Other Whig plays of the period use images of rape in a less conventional manner; they adopt the rhetoric of male ravishment to mock and dismiss the tenets of Jacobite discourse and legitimate William and Mary's regime. At first glance, John Crowne's *Caligula* (1698) closely resembles Cibber's *Xerxes* in its politics. Dedicated to Henry Sidney, Earl of Romney, brother to the executed Algernon Sidney and one of William's principal commanders at the Battle of the Boyne, the play depicts yet another tyrannical monarch who must be dethroned for the good of the nation. According to Annius Minutianus, the emperor "has Vices I abhor to name; / They cover me with everlasting shame."[89] He takes credit for military victories he has not earned and has committed incest with his own sister: "He whored her on the Bridal Night" (5). Caligula, like Valentinian and Xerxes, believes in the absolute power of his authority and his unbounded ability to do as he pleases without mercy or restraint. He complains to Valerius Asiaticus, "Must I give reasons, Sir, for my Decrees? / I may do what I please, with whom I please. / Perhaps I burn proud Towns, and slaughter Men, / Only to please my humour, Sir—what then?" (9). Caligula believes himself to be a god, a belief first substantiated by Vitellius, who describes him as "Caesar, of Gods, the greatest and the best" (6), and later confirmed when he receives his "Image wrought in gold" (16), a graven image of himself for the people to worship. As a god, Caligula also refuses to be ruled by his parliament. He says, "I'll have no Guardians, I'm at Age to reign; / What my Birth gave, my Courage shall maintain. / I will endure no Partners in my Throne, / I'll govern as I please, and rule alone" (15). Caligula's callous treatment of his subjects and disgusting sexual excess are thus linked with his propensity for absolutism.

Of course, Caligula is not a god, but merely a "Ravisher of beauteous Wives, / Of Virgins, Realms, Religions, Laws, and Lives" (49). His monarchical overreach is reflected in his rape of Julia, the chaste wife of Valerius Asiaticus. Initially, Valerius counsels his wife to leave the court, a place infected with the "scent of Lust and Blood" (25). He warns her that she has

> vertues that [Caligula] slights,
> And Rapes and Rapines, are his high delights.
> He loves to make all Nature feel his force;
> Rivers he Ravishes, and turns their course . . .
> He scorns the Pleasure he can gain with ease. (24)

Caligula displays his power over all the world through acts of sexual force. At the same time, Valerius Asiaticus applies the rhetoric of rape to his own sufferings. First, he complains that the "Emperors Bawds ravish'd my Wife away" (38), ravishment here referring to Julia's abduction rather than her physical violation. In the aftermath of her rape, he also insists,

> New Giants have bound *Jove,* so he lies still,
> And lets this filthy Tyrant take his fill
> Of Whoredom, Blood, Rapes, Incest, what he will.
> Had *Caesar* ravish'd from me all my Lands,
> Bottomless treasures, numberless commands,
> But to thy beauty never had approach'd,
> Had left me thee unblemish'd, and untouch'd;
> My heart is so devoted to thy love,
> I wou'd not have chang'd happiness with *Jove.* (39)

Julia has been physically assaulted, but her unlawful abduction represents a ravishment of the husband as well as a rape of the wife. Later, Valerius views himself as blemished by Julia's assault. He demands revenge, that he may, "with [Caligula's] blood wash all my spots away" (39). Valerius thus transforms Julia's physical sufferings into a manifestation of his own wrongs, an appropriation of rape discourse to describe male political and economic suffering. For Crowne as for Settle in *The Female Prelate*, the male rape victim suffers due to a tyrannical and overreaching ruler (in this case, the king rather than the Catholic Church). This is not the Jacobite rhetoric of the ravished king unfairly dethroned, but the ravished subject disenfranchised by absolutist tyranny.

The figure of the male rape victim appears more prominently in Mary Pix's *Ibrahim*. Despite Constance Clark's claim that "It is hard to discern what Pix's political leanings were," the play clearly treats monarchical sexual tyranny as a justification for revolution.[90] Ibrahim, like so many other monarchs discussed in this study, has come to overestimate the extent of his authority. Like Valentinian, Ibrahim has grown soft and effeminate in his tastes, forgoing war in pursuit of pleasure:

> The great Forefathers of this degenerate Man,
> Instead of treading on *Persian* Carpets,
> Trod upon the Necks of *Persian* Kings;
> Whilst now (curs'd reverse of time) softness and ease,
> Flatterers and Women, fill alone our Monarch's Heart;
> Women enough to undo the Universal World
> Are here maintain'd, whose useless hundreds
> Are with such a train of Pride and Luxury,
> That Eyes before ne'er saw, nor can endless words describe.[91]

What's worse, he has begun to overstep himself economically, confiscating merchant goods for his harem's use and attacking the fundamental rights of his subjects to control their property:

> Wou'd you believe it? the Vultures deckt in Painted Plumes,
> So eager are for their vain trappings,
> That soon as a Merchant Ship salutes the Port,
> His Goods are seiz'd, and brought to the *Seraglio*
> Without Account, Value, or Justice. (2)

Like Caligula, Ibrahim speaks the language of absolutism:

> . . . absolute I'll be, or, cease to Reign!
> That easie King, whose People gives him Law,
> Flatters himself with Majesty and awe;
> The Royal Slave the daring rout commands,
> And force his Scepter from his feeble Hands. (32)

A monarch must rule alone, Ibrahim maintains, or else he is no better than a slave, and he may force any woman to his will, merging rape with the political philosophy of absolutism.

Contrasted with Ibrahim's faith in his own powers is a range of characters who seek to limit the monarch's authority. The Mufti, for instance, holds that the power of the throne does not entitle Ibrahim to defile women indiscriminately. He tells the king, "My Daughter is no Slave, and our holy Law / Forbids that you should force the free" (19). According to the Mufti, the "holy Law" supersedes the king's earthly authority and cannot be touched by royal prerogative. Morena herself insists that she owes allegiance to a higher authority than the king: "Holy, binding vows are past already / And horrid imprecations, which if I break, / Distraction, despair, eternal ruine / Straight will seize me" (23). She laments the existence of a king who could conceal an act of horrific violence behind a façade of political authority, leading Solyman to proclaim the need for revolt: "Nor / Shall I fear to purge the contagious / Veins of Majesty in such a cause" (30). The king does not have the right to rape, no matter how unfettered he considers his authority.

The trajectory of *Ibrahim* is such, then, that Morena must learn to disobey authority in the service of higher ideals. At the beginning of the text, even Amurat comments on the seriousness with which Morena views her duty to her father. "I know well, though her poor Slave shou'd suffer / A thousand wracks, she'd tread the rigid paths of Duty, / And let me die, rather than forefeit her obedience" (6), Amurat explains in act 1.[92] By the end, however, she disobeys, choosing to kill herself and gain everlasting fame rather than obey her father's injunction to live. She tells him,

> My Father! draw near; forgive this
> First, last act of Disobedience!
> You taught me, Sir, that Life no longer

Was a good, then a clear Frame attended it;
My Dishonour Rings through the Universe—
Pardon my quitting it! (40)

The play is somewhat cautious of the idea of political rebellion—as in *Xerxes*, the revolt unleashes a frightening and uncontrollable mob that is not necessarily preferable to the hated monarch:

Who can express the Terrours of this dismal Night!
The mad *Janizaries* up, and raging for Revenge,
Put private Broils upon the publick score,
Murder and Rapine, with Fury uncontroll'd
Raging through the City, and make the Devastation
Horrible, the mangled *Visier* they have
Piece-meal torn. (38)

Still, Morena's decision to rebel against her father and die is treated with approbation. Amurat calls her "once my / Living Mistress, now my dead Saint" (41). Rebellion under certain circumstances is preferable to the alternative of everlasting shame.[93]

Amurat, beloved by Morena, dies along with her—dual victims of Ibrahim's excess. As the pair loved each other in life, they die together as parallel figures.[94] Ibrahim is not, however, the play's only villain; indeed, he is arguably not even the play's worst villain. It is not Ibrahim's death, also at play's end, that signals the play's climax, but rather the death of Sheker Para, Ibrahim's primary mistress and bawd, an Eastern variation on the poisonous Catholic bride. It is Sheker Para who both hatches the rape plot and encourages its completion. According to the Mufti, "that vile Woman . . . with the Visier, / Joins to ruin *Ibrahim*" (2). Sheker Para represents the dark foil to Morena's virtuous light, continuing the tradition of creating parallel and opposing female figures. Like Settle's Fredigond, Sheker Para also urges her lover to softness and vice: "To charm my Monarch is the only study and / Business of your Slave," she promises, "and to that end, / Twenty fair Virgins whom yet your Eyes ne'er saw, / I have pick'd and chosen from a thousand, / And set in order for your view" (4). She later encourages Ibrahim's sexually violent tendencies both to increase her political power and to obtain the object of her sexual desires. She is proud that "the Sultan gives me greater Privilege / Than ever Woman had in the Ottoman Court" (5), and would rise ever higher.

Just as Fredigond wants Clarmount and Joanna Angellica desires the Duke of Saxony, Sheker Para lusts after the virtuous Amurat. As a result, Amurat is feminized in his interactions with the king's mistress. When she propositions him, Amurat's defenses are those of a woman; he blushes and turns pale, he refuses and attempts to flee: "heedless and cold he flew / From my Embrace" (13), Sheker Para complains. "Awe me not with thy blushes" (13), she tells him, and accuses him of having ice water in his veins, a turn of phrase generally applied to women who refuse. *Valentinian*'s Lucina, for instance, is described as a "Cake of Ice" (2.2.114), while Achmet comments on the "stoick vertue" that "rules in" Amurat's "cold Icy Veins" (5). Sheker Para, like Valentinian, also thinks that Amurat's refusals have undermined her claim to political power; as male monarchs discover in other plays, she cannot hope to command an empire if she cannot command Amurat's sexual submission:

> Have I seen Scepter'd Slaves kneeling
> At my feet, forgetting they were Kings,
> Forgetful of their Gods, calling alone on me;
> Passing whole days and hours as if measur'd
> With a Moment's Sand, and now refus'd
> By a Curst Beardless Boy! (13)

Amurat is a boy, not a man, feminine both in his hairlessness and his chastity.

Amurat will not actually be raped in Pix's *Ibrahim*. Nor will he become, like Settle's Duke of Saxony, the victim of a bed trick. Yet in constructing Amurat as an effeminate analogue to Morena, Pix evokes the image of the male rape victim once more. Before killing herself, Morena tells Ibrahim that "With dishevell'd hair, torn Robes, and / These bloody hands, I'll run thro' all thy Guards / And Camp, whilst my just complaints, compel rebellion!" (24); that is to say, Morena will play Lucrece, inspiring revenge before dying. The final death in the play is not Morena's, however, but Amurat's, and he refuses to take revenge against Sheker Para, choosing instead suicide over dishonor. Although she offers to let him "strike / Your Poynard to my Heart" (37), Amurat responds,

> The contaminated Blood shall never
> Stain the Sword of *Amurat*.
> Live! Detested Creature! Loaded
> With Shame and Infamy! Be it
> Thy Curse to live! Whilst
> Pointing Fingers, and busie Tongues
> Proclaim them. (37)

What Sheker Para offers Amurat is a revenge tinged with sadomasochistic sexual overtones; she will allow him to penetrate her in death as she could not compel him to do in life, an offer Amurat refuses. Instead he chooses suicide, another victim of the Sultan and Sheker Para's overreach. Like Morena, he lives as a chaste Lucina and dies a defiled Lucrece.[95] The man, like the woman, falls victim to monarchical tyranny and its radiating trails of destruction, presenting once more a justification for rebellion and regicide.

While some Whig plays co-opted the rhetoric of the male rape victim to illustrate the dangers of monarchical overreach for men, other plays employed this rhetoric to discredit Jacobite condemnations of James II's unfair ravishment. Derek Hughes has called Nicholas Brady's *The Rape* "a generally anomalous play,"[96] while Hume calls it "serious, pretentious, and overinflated."[97] Still, Brady's treatment of male rape in the play is quite revealing. His Williamite sympathies are already on display in the play's prefatory materials. Dedicating the play to Charles, Earl of Dorset and Middlesex (a champion of William's reign), Brady praises his services to the new government. Brady values Dorset's "true Affection to the Protestant Religion, and the English Liberties; Both of which were visibly struck at, and had infallibly been overturned, had not Providence made use of their present Majesties to rescue and relieve them."[98] God himself, that is, approved the overthrow of James II. When the play begins, the evil Genselaric is furious that the king has elected to wed his only son, Albimer, to Genselaric's beloved Eurione, daughter to the vanquished queen of the Goths. Genselaric subsequently rapes Eurione, yet ironically views himself as the one ravished. When he learns he cannot wed Eurione, he complains,

> Death to my hopes! he's fix'd unmoveably,
> And all my Wishes blasted: But shall I,
> Who nobly past through twenty rough Campaigns,
> Tamely look on, and see a puling Boy,
> A young effeminate Stripling, ravish from me
> A Mistress and a Crown! It must not be. (7)

Genselaric views Albimer as the only thing standing between himself and the achievement of his political and sexual ambitions. Thus when he talks of ravishment, he both expresses his irritation at the loss of property he believes to be rightfully his—ravishment in the older sense of property crime—and hooks into the rhetoric of male rape.

When King Gunderic officially decrees Eurione's engagement, Genselaric once again describes his experience in the language of sexual violence:

> How could I stand
> Thus tamely by, and see my panting Heart
> Pluck'd from my trembling Bosom fresh and bleeding
> By this inhumane King? Am I a Coward?
> Answer me, Friends, am I that wretched thing?
> I must be sure; I could not else look on
> And see the Tyrant ravish from my Soul
> All it holds dear and precious. (20)

Ironically, of course, it is only two scenes later that Genselaric becomes a rapist in fact. In one of the decade's more explicit stagings of sexual violence, "The scene draws, and discovers Eurione in an Arbour, gagg'd and bound to a Tree, her hair dishevel'd as newly Ravish'd, a Dagger lying by her" (25). According to Marsden, "The elaborately coded tableau carefully presents Eurione to the audience's gaze: Eurione's 'Ravish'd' hair becomes the symbol of her violation, the ropes and gag testify to her helpless state, and a dagger, the symbolic representation of her violation, lies by her side."[99] The scopophilic aspects of the play are undeniable, and they bespeak the use of female bodies as symbols of political unrest. Eurione has been diseased by her contact with Genselaric, and she will spend the remainder of the play anticipating her death: she cries, "here's she that was Eurione; / Now she is nothing but a loathsome Leprosie, / Which spread all o'er the Gothish Royal Blood, / Infects the Noble Race" (25). Yet her assailant, too, speaks of being assaulted, mirroring the behavior of Settle's Orundana, who also claims victimization. In *The Rape*, however, there is no innocent and "ravished" Hormidas to offset the ridiculousness of Gensalaric's claims. Instead, the language of property ravishment is placed into the mouth of a despicable, irredeemable villain, a tactic that ultimately works to discredit that rhetorical trope.[100]

What Brady offers, then, is a work ideologically similar in design to the rape plays of the 1660s. In those earlier works, accusations of rape were displaced onto the parliamentarian faction to absolve the royalist party of wrongdoing. Now, at the end of the century, Brady displaces the rhetoric of male rape onto the one who would destroy the nation. Those who deploy images of male ravishment—implicitly the Jacobite propagandists—represent the true threat to English women and English national stability. That the play concludes with the stabilizing marriage of a foreign royal son (Princess Valdaura, now revealed to be a man) to the domestic princess and heir to the throne (Prince Agilmond, secretly a female in disguise) also bespeaks the rightness of William and Mary's invasion. William and Mary will set England to rights as Valduara and Agilmond will restore their own realm. Meanwhile, Genselaric, despite his proclamations of victimhood, will suffer death by torture: "For me, I vow to keep / An Everlasting silence" (54), he says, his final words and refusal to speak reminiscent of Shakespeare's villainous Aaron. The male political rape victim is discredited, punished, and finally silenced.

CONCLUSION

By the end of the century, representations of rape had undeniably changed yet also come full circle. Images of sexual violence, used during the Civil Wars to discredit the monarchy and justify the regicide, returned in the early years of the Restoration, first to reinforce the rightness of monarchical rule, and later to delineate the limits of contractual monarchy. Although the targets of sexually violent propaganda shifted throughout the century, rape as a rhetorical tool remained remarkably static. Occupying a nebulous zone between crime against property and violation of the individual, acts of rape provided a consistent, emotionally charged set of tropes to guarantee some form of political response. An examination of the period's rape plays exposes the extent to which playwrights drew upon, responded to, and interacted with the offstage culture of political propaganda pamphlets. Scenes of dramatic sexual violence are designed not only to titillate and entice, but to engage with the wider political culture of the later seventeenth century, a culture often fluid and lacking in political coherence. Through an analysis of dramatic sexual assault, then, modern critics can recover a number of late-century struggles, including the place of the subject in both the individual family and the broader body politic, the negotiation of appropriate and inappropriate forms of sexual expression, and the battle against any and all sources of perceived cultural corruption, ranging from monarchical absolutism and court libertinism to foreign mistresses and, of course, that perennial threat, the Catholic Church.

NOTES

1. *The Murmurers. A Poem* (London, 1689), 2, 4.
2. Craig Rose, *England in the 1690s: Revolution, Religion and Wars* (Oxford: Blackwell, 1999), 20. See also Gerald Straka, who argues that contemporary politicians treated William's accession to the throne as another occasion of deliverance from Catholic tyranny: "The Final Phase of Divine Right Theory in England, 1688–1702," *English Historical Review* 77, no. 305 (1962): 642.
3. Thomas Yalden, *On The Conquest Of Namur, A Pindarique Ode. Humbly Inscrib'd To His Most Sacred and Victorious Majesty* (London, 1695), 10.
4. "Song to the tune of 'Lilli burlero,'" in *Poems on Affairs of State: Augustan Satirical Verse, 1660–1714*, ed. William J. Cameron, 7 vols. (New Haven: Yale University Press, 1963), 5:317, ll. 1–4.
5. Steve Pincus, *1688: The First Modern Revolution* (New Haven: Yale University Press, 2009), 5.
6. Ibid., 15.
7. Ibid., 254.
8. Ibid., 278. Pincus downplays the role of religion in provoking the revolution, arguing that James II moved too quickly to modernize the British state. For other readings of the Glorious Revolution, see John Carswell, *From Revolution to Revolution: England 1688–1776* (London: Routledge & Kegan Paul, 1973); Eveline Cruickshanks, *The Glorious Revolution* (Basingstoke: Macmillan, 2000); Graham Goodlad, "Before the Glorious Revolution: The Making of Absolute Monarchy?" *History Review* 58 (2008): 10–15; J. R. Jones, *The Revolution of 1688 in England* (London: Wiedenfeld & Nicolson, 1972); Bill Speck, "Religion's Role in the Glorious Revolution," *History Today* 38, no. 7 (1988): 30–35; Hugh Trevor-Roper, *Counter-Reformation to Glorious Revolution* (Chicago: University of Chicago Press, 1992); and John Van der Kiste, *William and Mary* (Gloucestershire: Sutton, 2003).
9. Elaine McGirr, *Heroic Mode and Political Crisis, 1660–1745* (Newark: University of Delaware Press, 2009), 102. McGirr argues that while James initially enjoyed popular support, he "did not press the advantage by having his proven propagandists mount heroic productions to divert his subjects and mythologize his rule" (Ibid., 102). In 1688 James did attempt to limit seditious speech, "but he was unable effectively to enforce this declaration": Lois G. Schwoerer, "Propaganda in the Revolution of 1688–89," *American Historical Review* 82, no. 4 (1977): 859.
10. Ibid., 847.

11. For discussion of William's printing press, see Schwoerer, "Propaganda."

12. John Dryden, "Astrea Redux," in *Restoration Literature: An Anthology*, ed. Paul Hammond (Oxford: Oxford Universiy Press, 2002), 23–32, ll. 258–59.

13. Hughes, "Rape," 232–33. In his earlier drama survey, Hughes also writes, "From mid-1696 onwards . . . there was an open season on rapist tyrants": Derek Hughes, *English Drama, 1660–1700* (Oxford: Clarendon Press, 1996), 430.

14. Colley Cibber, *Xerxes, A Tragedy* (London, 1699), 21. Further references to *Xerxes* are from this edition and will be cited parenthetically in the text by page number.

15. J. Gailhard, *Four Tracts* (London, 1699), 4:15.

16. Timothy Wilson, *A Seasonable Question, In A Sermon on Joshua 5.13* (London, 1690), 10.

17. B. H., *The Parliament of Bees. A Fable* (London, 1697), 1.

18. *Popish Treachery: Or, A Short and New Account of the Horrid Cruelties Exercised on the Protestants In France* (Edinburgh, 1689), 13.

19. Mr. Crown [John Crowne], *Daeneids, Or The Noble Labours of the Great Dean of Notre-Dame In Paris* (London, 1692), 5.

20. *Popish Treachery*, 12.

21. *The Pope in a Passion; Or, Bad News for England* (London, 1689), 1.

22. *Popish Treachery*, 8–9.

23. George Walker, *The Protestant's Crums of Comfort* (London, 1697), 98–99, 100, 101.

24. *News from the Sessions-House*, 3.

25. Massarene to Newdigate, cited in Pincus, *1688*, 273.

26. Walker, *The Protestant's Crums*, 100.

27. *News from the Sessions-House*, 2–3.

28. For discussion of the warming-pan scandal and Anne's role in fostering the rumors, see Edward Gregg, *Queen Anne* (London: Routledge & Kegan Paul, 1980), and Rachel Weil, *Political Passions*, 86–104.

29. Anonymous, "An Excellent New Ballad Called The Prince of Darkness, Showing how Three Nations may be Set on Fire by a Warming Pan," in *Poems on Affairs of State: Augustan Satirical Verse, 1660–1714*, ed. Wiliam J. Cameron, 7 vols. (New Haven: Yale University Press, 1963), 5:332, ll. 1–5.

30. Henry Mildmay, "The Progress," in *Poems on Affairs of State: Augustan Satirical Verse, 1660–1714*, ed. William J. Cameron, 7 vols. (New Haven: Yale University Press, 1963), 5:332, ll. 54–57.

31. Weil, *Political Passions*, 94.

32. Sir James Montgomery, *Great Britain's Just Complaint For Her Late Measures, Present Sufferings, And the Future Miseries She is exposed to* (London, 1692), 57.

33. *An Account of Mr. Blunts late Book, Entitled King William and Queen Mary Conquerors* (London, 1693), 6.

34. Paul Monod, "The Jacobite Press and English Censorship, 1689–95," in *The Stuart Court in Exile and the Jacobites*, ed. Eveline Cruickshanks and Edward Corp (London: Hambledon Press, 1995), 142. For discussion of the early Jacobites, see also Daniel Szechi, *The Jacobites: Britain and Europe, 1688–1788* (Manchester: Manchester University Press, 1994).

35. McGirr, *Heroic Mode*, 129. For further discussion of Civil War rhetoric in the Glorious Revolution, see also Rose, *England in the 1690s*, along with Paul Kléber Monod, *Jacobitism and the English People, 1688–1788* (Cambridge: Cambridge University Press, 1989).

36. Rose, *England in the 1690s*, 34.

37. *Englands Crisis: Or, the World Well Mended* (London, 1689), 1. Here the author rewrites history, offering the British a more favorable outcome to the Second and Third Anglo-Dutch Wars than is historically accurate.

38. *The State-Prodigal his Return; Containing a true State of the Nation. In a Letter to a Friend* (London, 1689), 4.

39. Robert Ferguson, *A Brief Account*, 56.

40. Ibid., 22.

41. Robert Ferguson, *A Letter to Mr. Secretary Trenchard, Discovering a Conspiracy against the Laws and ancient Constitution of England* (London, 1694), 7.

42. "Untitled," cited in Paul Hammond, *Figuring Sex between Men from Shakespeare to Rochester* (Oxford: Oxford University Press, 2002), 174.

43. Ibid., 181.

44. Ibid.

45. Lois Schwoerer, "Images of Queen Mary II, 1689–95," *Renaissance Quarterly* 42, no. 4 (1989): 743.

46. Henry Park, *Lachryme Sacerdotis. A Pindarick Poem Occasion'd by the Death Of that most excellent Princess, our late Gracious Sovereign Lady, Mary the Second, Of Glorious Memory* (London, 1695), 4.

47. Mr. Hume [Patrick Hume], *A Poem Dedicated to the Immortal Memory Of Her Late Majesty* (London, 1695), 7.

48. Daniel Defoe, *The Life Of That Incomparable Princess Mary, Our Late Sovereign Lady, Of ever Blessed Memory* (London, 1695), 60.

49. Cited in Rose, *England in the 1690s*, 42.

50. Thomas Bowber, *A Sermon Preached in the Parish-Church of St Swithin, London, March 10th, 1694/5* (London, 1695), 24.

51. Tony Claydon, *William III* (London and New York: Longman, 2002), 45. See also Weil, who suggests that elegies for Mary facilitated the posthumous transfer of authority to William (Weil, "Family," 115).

52. Charlwood Lawton, *A Letter formerly sent to Dr Tillotsen, and for Want of an Answer made publick* (London, 1748), 2:243.

53. Ibid. Other writers treated Mary's early death as a punishment for filial disobedience. See, for instance, Thomas Ken, *A Letter To The Author of a Sermon Entitled, A Sermon Preach'd At The Funeral Of Her late Majesty Queen Mary, Of ever Blessed Memory* (London, 1695).

54. "The Female Parricide," in *Poems on Affairs of State: Augustan Satirical Verse, 1660–1714*, ed. William J. Cameron, 7 vols. (New Haven: Yale University Press, 1963), 5:157, ll. 1–16.

55. Arthur Mainwaring, "Tarquin and Tullia," in *Poems on Affairs of State: Augustan Satirical Verse, 1660–1714*, ed. William J. Cameron, 7 vols. (New Haven: Yale University Press, 1963), 5:47–56, ll. 97–108.

56. Rose, *England in the 1690s*, 32.

57. Nathaniel Johnston, *The Dear Bargain. Or, A True Representation of the State of the English Nation under the Dutch* (London, 1690), 24.

58. Schwoerer, "Images," 735.

59. Robert Ferguson, *Whether the Parliament be not in Law Dissolved by the death of the Princess of Orange* (London, 1695), 56.

60. Robert Ferguson, *Whether the Preserving the Protestant Religion was the Motive unto, or the End, that was designed in the Late Revolution?* (London, 1695), 6.

61. Cited in Monod, *Jacobitism*, 65.

62. *Some Remarks upon our Affairs* (London, 1690), 2; *A Short History Of The Convention, Or, New Christened Parliament* (London, 1689), 1.

63. Howard Erskine-Hill, "Literature and the Jacobite Cause: Was There a Rhetoric of Jacobitism?" in *Ideology and Conspiracy: Aspects of Jacobitism, 1689–1759*, ed. Eveline Cruickshanks (Edinburgh: John Donald Publishers, 1982), 49.

64. Charles Blount, *King William and Queen Mary Conquerors*, a3r.

65. Ferguson, *Whether the Preserving*, 30–31.

66. For discussion of the controversy surrounding James's abdication, see George L. Cherry, "The Legal and Philosophical Position of the Jacobites, 1688–1689," *Journal of Modern History* 22, no. 4 (1950): 309–21; H. T. Dickinson, *Liberty and Property: Political Ideology in Eighteenth-Century Britain* (New York: Holmes and Meier, 1977); and J. P. Kenyon, *Revolution Principles: The Politics of Party, 1689–1720* (Cambridge: Cambridge University Press, 1977). For discussion of Jacobite beliefs, see also J. C. D. Clark, *English Society 1688–1832: Ideology, Social Structure and Political Practice during the Ancien Regime* (Cambridge: Cambridge University Press, 1985), 125.

67. "Untitled," in *Poems on Affairs of State: Augustan Satirical Verse, 1660–1714*, ed. William J. Cameron, 7 vols. (New Haven: Yale University Press, 1963), 5:59, ll. 17–18.

68. The suggestion that William had assaulted James also underlies Ralph Gray's 1689 "The Coronation Ballad, 11th April 1689." Gray calls William "An unnatural beast to his father and uncle" while mocking his inability to perform sexually with his wife: "The Coronation Ballad, 11th April 1689," in *Poems on Affairs of State: Augustan Satirical Verse, 1660–1714*, ed. William J. Cameron, 7 vols. (New Haven: Yale University Press, 1963), 5:43, ll. 57, 58.

69. J. Christopher Warner, "The Question of Misogynistic Polemic in Elkanah Settle's *The Female Prelate* (1680 and 1689)," *Restoration* 25, no. 1 (2001): 19.

70. Owen, *Restoration Theatre*, 128–29.

71. Elkanah Settle, *The Female Prelate: Being The History of the Life and Death of Pope Joan. A Tragedy* (London, 1680), 67. Further references to *The Female Prelate* are from this edition and will be cited parenthetically in the text by page number.

72. Owen, *Restoration Theatre*, 142.

73. Warner, "The Question of Misogynistic Polemic," 23. For the historical roots of the Pope Joan legend, see C. A. Patrides, *Premises and Motifs in Renaissance Thought and Literature* (Princeton: Princeton University Press, 1982), 152, and Clement Wood, *The Woman Who Was Pope: A Biography of Pope Joan, 853–855 A.D.* (New York: William Faro, 1931).

74. Craig M. Rustici, "Gender, Disguise, and Usurpation: *The Female Prelate* and the Popish Successor," *Modern Philology* 98, no. 2 (2000): 282.

75. Owen, *Restoration Theatre*, 174.

76. Warner, "The Question of Misogynistic Polemic," 26.

77. As Craig Rustici points out, "In Settle's view, no Catholic monarch was truly sovereign" (Rustici, "Gender, Disguise, and Usurpation," 281).

78. Ibid., 285.

79. Dugas, "Elkanah Settle," 383.

80. Elkanah Settle, *Distress'd Innocence: Or, The Princess of Persia. A Tragedy* (London, 1691), a3r–a3v. Further references to *Distress'd Innocence* are from this edition and will be cited parenthetically in the text by page number.

81. Hume, *Development of English Drama*, 400.

82. The image of Hormidas swallowed up by the deeps calls to mind the fate of *Titus Andronicus*'s Lavinia, finally swallowed up by the devouring earth.

83. To the extent that *Xerxes* has received any modern critical attention, it has been largely panned as a commercial and dramatic failure. See Leonard R. N. Ashley, *Colley Cibber* (New York: Twayne, 1965), and Helene Koon, *Colley Cibber: A Biography* (Lexington: University of Kentucky Press, 1986).

84. William Wycherley, *The Plain Dealer*, ed. Leo Hughes (Lincoln: University of Nebraska Press, 1967), 5.2.435–36.

85. Here Xerxes's behavior recalls that of Atreus in Crowne's *Thyestes*. It is not enough for Atreus to control his daughter's behavior; he also demands control over her interior thoughts and desires.

86. Staves, *Players' Scepters*, 100.

87. William Mountfort, *The Injur'd Lovers: Or, The Ambitious Father. A Tragedy* (London, 1688), 64.

88. George Powell, *Alphonso King of Naples. A Tragedy* (London, 1691), 36. Further references to *Alphonso King of Naples* are from this edition and will be cited parenthetically in the text by page number.

89. John Crowne, *Caligula. A Tragedy* (London, 1698), 4. Further references to *Caligula* are from this edition and will be cited parenthetically in the text by page number.

90. Constance Clark, *Three Augustan Women Playwrights* (New York: Peter Lang, 1986), 207.

91. Mary Pix, *Ibrahim, The Thirteenth Emperour of the Turks: A Tragedy* (London, 1696), 1. Further references to *Ibrahim* are from this edition and will be cited parenthetically in the text by page number.

92. While the developing relationship between Morena and Amurat at first appears illicit, it actually occurred beneath the watchful eyes of the Mufti. Morena does not love without her father's explicit or implied permission.

93. That the rape and death scenes were so explicitly violent—Margo Collins calls "the scene leading up to the rape . . . perhaps one of the most graphic of its kind"—likely contributed to the play's success: "Feminine Conduct and Violence in Mary Pix's She-Tragedies," *Restoration and Eighteenth-Century Theatre Research* 18, no. 1 (2003): 7. See also Jean I. Marsden, who calls the "brilliantly stylized rape scene, both titillating and graphic": "Mary Pix's *Ibrahim*: The Woman Writer as Commercial Playwright," *Studies in the Literary Imagination* 32, no. 2 (1999): 39.

94. In this, I think the play is more radical than Jacqueline Pearson would allow. Pearson criticizes "Pix's rather stereotypical view of women" and argues that the "polarisation of" Morena and Sheker Para "is conventional but vividly handled. Pix is not unconventional enough to allow the raped woman to survive or deny that she is 'polluted' (p. 38), though she goes as near as she dares" (Pearson, *The Prostituted Muse*, 177, 176). The construction of a male analogue to Morena is, however, a much more unconventional act. For a contrasting view of Pix, see Patsy S. Fowler, who argues that Pix's "plays contain significant feminist views": "Rejecting the Status Quo: The Attempts of Mary Pix & Susannah Centlivre to Reform Society's Patriarchal Attitudes," *Restoration and Eighteenth-Century Theatre Research* 11, no. 2 (1996): 49.

95. In this, my argument differs fundamentally from that of Margo Collins. For Collins, Amurat gains power over Sheker Para by "order[ing] her to live in infamy" (Collins, "Feminine Conduct," 8). I believe instead that Sheker Para's loss of power is equivalent to that of the rapist figures Ibrahim, Valentinian, Caligula, and Xerxes.

96. Hughes, "Rape," 232.

97. Hume, *Development of English Drama*, 401.

98. Nicholas Brady, *The Rape: Or, The Innocent Impostors* (London, 1692), a2r. Further references to *The Rape* are from this edition and will be cited parenthetically in the text by page number.

99. Marsden, "Rape," 191.

100. For a similar treatment of the male rape victim as villain, see also Charles Hopkins's *Boadicea Queen of Britain* (1697), where the rapist complains of his own "ravish'd Arms" and calls himself his victim's "Ravisht Lover": *Boadicea Queen of Britain. A Tragedy* (London, 1697), 21.

Works Cited

Adams Jr., Joseph Quincy. "William Heminge and Shakespeare." *Modern Philology* 12, no. 1 (1914): 51–64.

Allen, William. *A Friendly Call, or a Seasonable Perswasive to Unity*. London, 1679.

Allman, Eileen. *Jacobean Revenge Tragedy and the Politics of Virtue*. Newark: University of Delaware Press, 1999.

Alssid, Michael. *Thomas Shadwell*. New York: Twayne, 1967.

Anderson, Thomas P. *Performing Early Modern Trauma from Shakespeare to Milton*. Burlington: Ashgate, 2006.

Andrews, R. *A perfect Declaration of The Barbarous and Cruell practices committed by Prince Robert, the Cavalliers, and others in his Majesties Army*. London, 1642.

Anonymous. *Absalom's Conspiracy; Or, The Tragedy of Treason*. London, 1680.

———. *An Abstract of Some few of those Barbarous, Cruell Massacres and Murthers, of the Protestants, and English, in some parts of Ireland Committed since the 23, of Octob, 1641*. London, 1662.

———. *An Abstract of the Bloody Massacre in Ireland*. Scotland, 1700.

———. *An Abstract Of The Unnatural Rebellion And Barbarous Massacre Of The Protestants In the Kingdom of Ireland, In the Year 1641*. London, 1689.

———. *An Account of Mr. Blunts late Book, Entitled King William and Queen Mary Conquerors*. London, 1693.

———. *A barbarous and inhumane Speech Spoken by the Lord Wentworth, Sonne to the late Earle of Straford*. London, 1642.

———. *Battering Rams Against Rome's Gates*. London, 1641.

———. *The Black Book Opened, Or Traytors Arraigned and Condemned by their own Confession*. London, 1660.

———. *A Blazing Starre seen in the West at Totneis in Devonshire, on the fourteenth of this instant November, 1642*. London, 1642.

———. *A Bloody Battell: Or the Rebels Overthrow, And Protestants Victorie*. London, 1641.

———. *A Bloody Tragedie, Or Romish Maske. Acted by five Iesuites, and sixteene young Germaine Maides*. London, 1607.

———. *The Bloudy Persecution of the Protestants in Ireland, Being The Contents of severall Letters brought by his Majesties Post from Ireland, November the 21. 1641*. London, 1641.

———. *A Bull Sent By Pope Pius To encourage the Traytors in England, pronounced against Queen Elizabeth, of ever glorious Memory; shewing the wicked designs of Popery*. London, 1678.

———. *The Burning of the Whore of Babylon, As it was Acted, with great Applause, in the Poultrey, London, on Wednesday Night, being the Fifth of November last, at Six of the Clock*. London, 1673.

———. *The Case is Altered. Or, Dreadful news from Hell*. London, 1660.

———. *A Caution To All True English Protestants, Concerning the Late Popish Plot*. London, 1681.

———. *The Cavaliers Catechisme: Or, The Reformed Protestant catechising the Antichristian Papist, Malignants, Incendiaries, and other ill-affected Persons under the name of Cavaliers*. London, 1647.

———. *The Character of a Papist*. London, 1673.

———. *A Collection of Certain Horrid Murthers in Several Counties of Ireland. Committed since the 23. of Octob. 1641*. London, 1679.

———. *The Common-Hunt, Or, The Pursute of the Pope*. London, 1679.

———. *A Congratulatory Poem on the Safe Arrival of His Grace James Duke of Monmouth at Utretch, on Saturday Sept. 27. 1679*. London, 1679.

———. *A Copie of the King's Message sent by the Duke of Lenox*. London, 1644.

———. *The Countreys Advice To the Late Duke of Monmouth, And Those in Rebellion with Him*. London, 1685.

———. *The Dammee Cavalliers Warning Piece, In a view on the Prophecy of the Prophet Obadiah*. London, 1643.

———. *Englands Crisis: Or, the World Well Mended*. London, 1689.

———. *Englands Darling, Or Great Brittains Joy and hope on that Noble Prince James Duke of Monmouth*. London, 1681.

———. *Englands Happiness Restored, Or A Congratulation Upon the Return of his Grace James Duke of Monmouth, On Thursday night the 27th of this instant November 1679*. London, 1679.

———. *Englands Miserie, If Not Prevented by the speedie remedie of a happie union between His Maiestie and this Parliament*. London, 1642.

———. *The English Pope, Or A Discourse Wherein The late mysticall Intelligence betwixt the Court of England, and the Court of Rome is in part discovered*. London, 1643.

———. *An exact and true Relation of A most cruell and horrid Murther committed by one of the Cavaliers, on A Woman in Leicester, Billetted in her House*. London, 1642.

———. "The Female Parricide." In *Poems on Affairs of State: Augustan Satirical Verse, 1660–1714*, edited by William J. Cameron, 5:157. New Haven: Yale University Press, 1963.

———. *The Grand Abuses Stript and Whipt; Being an Account of some of the Injuries, Pride, and the insulting Insolences of the Hogen Mogen States of Holland*. London, 1672.

———. *A Gratulatory Poem On The Just And Piovs Proceedings Of The King and Parliament Against The Papists*. London, 1674.

———. *The Great Eclipse of the Sun, Or, Charles His Waine*. London, 1644.

———. *A great Robbery in the North, Neer Swanton in Yorkshire*. London, 1642.

———. *Hell's Higher Court of Justice: Or, The Trial of The three Politick Ghosts, Oliver Cromwell, King of Sweden, and Cardinal Mazarine*. London, 1661.

———. *The horrid Popish Plot Happily Discover'd*. London, 1678.

———. *The Insolency and Cruelty of the Cavaliers*. London, 1643.

———. *The Key To The Kings Cabinet-Counsell*. London, 1644.

———. *The Kings Maiesties Speech On the 2. Day of December, 1641*. London, 1641.

———. "The King's Vows." In *Poems on Affairs of State: Augustan Satirical Verse, 1660–1714*, edited by George deF. Lord, 1:159–62. New Haven: Yale University Press, 1963.

———. *A Letter From The Devil, To The Pope And His Prelates*. London, 1670.

———. "A Litany." In *Poems on Affairs of State: Augustan Satirical Verse, 1660–1714*, edited by George deF. Lord, 1:190. New Haven: Yale University Press, 1963.

———. *The Manner of the Burning the Pope in Effigies in London On the 5th of November, 1678*. London, 1678.

———. *A Mappe of Mischiefe, Or a Dialogue between V. and E. concerning the going of Qu. M. into V*. London, 1641.

———. *A Memorial Of The Late And Present Popish Plots, Published to refresh the Memories of all undepraved Englishmen, and thereby prevent the Ruine of this Nation, by disbelieving, or forgetting of them*. London, 1680.

———. *A Memento for Holland: Or A True and Exact History of the most Villainous and Barbarous Cruelties used on the English Merchants residing At Amboyna in the East-Indies, by the Netherland Governour and Councel there*. London, 1652.

———. *Monmouth Degraded. Or James Scot, the little King in Lyme. A Song*. London, 1685.

———. *The Murmurers. A Poem*. London, 1689.

———. "Nell Gwynne." In *Poems on Affairs of State: Augustan Satirical Verse, 1660–1714*, edited by George deF. Lord, 1:420. New Haven: Yale University Press, 1963.

———. *A Nest of Nunnes Egges, strangely Hatched, with the Description of a worthy Feast for Ioy of the Brood*. London, 1680.

———. *A New Ballad To the praise of James D. of Monmouth*. London, 1682.

———. *A New Mercury, Called Mercurius Problematicus. Proposing severall Problems; AND Resolving them by way of Quaere*. London, 1644.

———. *Newes out of East India: Of the cruell and bloody usage of our English Merchants and others at Amboyna, by the Netherlandish Governour and Councell there*. London, 1624.

———. *News from Rome, Or, A Dialogue Between His Holinesse And a Cabal of Cardinals At A Late Conclave*. London, 1680.

———. *News from the Sessions House. The Tryal, Conviction, Condemnation, and Execution of Popery, for High-Treason*. London, 1689.

———. *Nocturnall Occurrences Or, Deeds Of Darknesse: Committed, By the Cavaleers in their Rendezvous*. London, 1642.

———. "On the Prorogation." In *Poems on Affairs of State: Augustan Satirical Verse, 1660–1714*, edited by George deF. Lord, 1:179–84. New Haven: Yale University Press, 1963.

———. *A Parly Between The Ghosts Of The Late Protector, And The King of Sweden, At their Meeting in Hell*. London, 1660.

———. *A Passionate Satyr Upon a Devilish Great He-Whore That lives yonder at Rome*. London, 1675.

———. *Perkin's Passing-Bell, Or The Traytors Funeral*. London, 1685.

———. *The Pharisee Unmask'd: In A New Discovery Of The Artifices Used by Roman Catholic Priests To Convert Prisoners both at, and before the Time of Execution*. London, 1687.

———. *The Pope in a Passion; Or, Bad News for England*. London, 1689.

———. *Popery Absolutely Destructive to Monarchy*. London, 1673.

———. *The Popes Down-fall, At Abergaveny, Or A true and perfect Relation of his being carried through the Fair in a solemn Procession with very great Ceremony*. London, 1679.

———. *A Popish Political Catechism: Or, A View of the Principles of the Synagogue of Antichrist, concerning the Power of Kings*. London, 1685.

———. *Popish Treachery: Or, A Short and New Account of the Horrid Cruelties Exercised on the Protestants In France*. Edinburgh, 1689.

———. *A Powerfull, Pitifull, Citi Full Cry, of Plentifull Children, And their Admirable, lamentable Complaint*. London, 1643.

———. *A Protestant Catechisme for Little Children, or Plain Scripture against Popery*. London, 1673.

———. *The Protestation And Declaration of the Popish, and evill affected Cavaliers*. London, 1642.

———. *The Queens Lamentation*. London, 1660.

———. *A rare Example of a vertuous Maid in Paris*. London, 1674.

———. *The Reformed Malignants. Or, A discourse Upon the present state Of our affaires Betwixt a cavalier And a convert*. London, 1643.

———. *A Relation Of The Most Material Matters Handled In Parliament Relating To Religion, Property, And The Liberty Of The Subject*. Netherlands, 1673.

———. *The Rise and Fall Or Degeneracy Of The Roman Church, With A Lamentation for all Degenerate and Unregenerate Christians*. London, 1680.

———. "The Royal Buss." In *Poems on Affairs of State: Augustan Satirical Verse, 1660–1714*, edited by George deF. Lord, 1:263–65. New Haven: Yale University Press, 1963.

———. *Salus Britannica: Or, The Safety Of The Protestant Religion, Against all the present Apprehensions Of Popery Fully Discust and Proved.* London, 1685.

———. *A Scheme Of Popish Cruelties Or A Prospect of what wee must Expect under a Popish Successor*. London, 1681.

———. *A Seasonable Memento, For all that have Voyces in the Choyce of A Parliament.* London, 1681.

———. *A Second Remonstrance by way of Address From The Church of England to both Houses of Parliament.* London, 1685.

———. *A Short Disswasive From Popery, And From Countenancing and Encouraging of Papists*. London, 1685.

———. *A Short History Of The Convention, Or, New Christened Parliament*. London, 1689.

———. *A Short Memorial Of The Most Grievous Sufferings Of The Ministers Of The Protestant Churches In Hungary*. London, 1676.

———. *Some Remarks upon our Affairs*. London, 1690.

———. "Song to the tune of 'Lilli burlero.'" In *Poems on Affairs of State: Augustan Satirical Verse, 1660–1714*, edited by William J. Cameron, 5:317. New Haven: Yale University Press, 1963.

———. *Speculum Papismi: Or, A Looking-Glass For Papists Wherein They may see their own sweet Faces*. Cambridge, 1669.

———. *The State-Prodigal his Return; Containing a true State of the Nation. In a Letter to a Friend.* London, 1689.

———. "A Summons from a True Protestant Conjurer to Cethegus' Ghost, To Appear September 19, 1682." In *Poems on Affairs of State: Augustan Satirical Verse, 1660–1714*, edited by Howard H. Schless, 3:263–66. New Haven: Yale University Press, 1963.

———. *Terrible Newes From York.* London, 1642.

———. *A Third Conference Between O. Cromwell And Hugh Peters In Saint James's Park.* London, 1660.

———. *The Tragedy Of The Kings Armies Fidelity Since their entring into Bristol.* London, 1643.

———. *A True and Compendious Narration; Or (Second Part of Amboyney[sic]) Of Sundry Notorious or Remarkable Injuries, Insolences, and Acts of Hostility which the Hollanders Have Exercised from time to time against The English Nation in the East-Indies, &c.* London, 1665.

———. *A True and Perfect Relation of A victorious Battell Obtained against the Earl of Cumberland And his Cavaliers*. London, 1642.

———. *A True Relation of the Unjust, Cruel, and Barbarous Proceedings against the English at Amboyna In the East-Indies, by the Netherlandish Governour & Council there*. London, 1651.

———. *A True Relation Of two Merchants of London, Who were taken prisoners by the Cavaliers*. London, 1642.

———. *University Newes, Or, The Unfortunate proceedings of the Cavaliers in Oxford.* London, 1642.

———. "Untitled." In *Poems on Affairs of State: Augustan Satirical Verse, 1660–1714*, edited by William J. Cameron, 5:59. New Haven: Yale University Press, 1963.

———. *Valiant Monmouth Revived.* London, 1684.

———. *The Wicked Resolution Of The Cavaliers; Declaring Their malice and hatred to the Parliament the Commonwealth, and especially the City of London*. London, 1642.

———. *The Young Bastards Wish, A Song*. London, 1685.

AntiPapist. *Fair Warning To take heed of Popery*. London, 1679.

Arata, Stephen D. "The Occidental Tourist: *Dracula* and the Anxiety of Reverse Colonization." *Victorian Studies* 33, no. 4 (1990): 119–44.

Arens, William. "Cooking the Cannibals." In *Consuming Passions: Food in the Age of Anxiety*, edited by Sian Griffiths and Jennifer Wallace, 157–66. Manchester: Manchester University Press, 1998.

Armistead, J. M. *Nathaniel Lee*. Boston: Twayne, 1979.

———. "The Tragicomic Design of *Lucius Junius Brutus*: Madness as Providential Therapy." *Papers on Language and Literature* 15 (1979): 38–51.

Arnade, Peter J. *Beggars, Iconoclasts, and Civic Patriots: The Political Culture of the Dutch Revolt*. Ithaca: Cornell University Press, 2008.

Ashley, Leonard R. N. *Colley Cibber*. New York: Twayne, 1965.

Ayloffe, John. "Britannia and Raleigh." In *Poems on Affairs of State: Augustan Satirical Verse, 1660–1714*, ed. George deF. Lord, 1:228–36. New Haven: Yale University Press, 1963.

Baker, John Hamilton. *An Introduction to English Legal History*. London: Butterworths, 1979.

Bamford, Karen. *Sexual Violence on the Jacobean Stage*. New York: St. Martin's, 2000.

Barbour, Frances. "The Unconventional Heroic Plays of Nathaniel Lee." *Studies in English* 20 (1940): 109–16.

Barlow, Thomas. *Popery: Or, The Principles & Positions Approved by the Church Of Rome*. London, 1683.

Bartels, Emily. "Making More of the Moor: Aaron, Othello, and Renaissance Refashionings of Race." *Shakespeare Quarterly* 41, no. 4 (1990): 433–54.

Barthelemy, Anthony Gerard. *Black Face, Maligned Race: The Representation of Blacks in English Drama from Shakespeare to Southerne*. Baton Rouge: Louisiana State University Press, 1987.

Bashar, Nafize. "Rape in England between 1550 and 1700." In *The Sexual Dynamics of History: Men's Power, Women's Resistance*, edited by The London Feminist History Group, 28–46. London: Pluto Press, 1983.

Beach, Adam R. "Carnival Politics, Generous Satire, and Nationalist Spectacle in Behn's *The Rover*." *Eighteenth-Century Life* 28, no. 3 (2004): 1–19.

Beaulieu, Luke. *Take heed of Both Extremes Or, Plain and useful Cautions Against Popery, And Presbytery*. London, 1675.

Behn, Aphra. *The Rover, Part I*. In *The Works of Aphra Behn*, edited by Janet Todd, 5:445–521. Columbus: Ohio State University Press, 1995.

Belling, Catherine. "Infectious Rape, Therapeutic Revenge: Bloodletting and the Health of Rome's Body." In *Disease, Diagnosis, and Cure on the Early Modern Stage*, edited by Stephanie Moss and Kaara L. Peterson, 113–32. Burlington: Ashgate, 2004.

Belsey, Catherine. *The Subject of Tragedy: Identity and Difference in Renaissance Drama*. London: Methuen, 1985.

Bender, Ashley Brookner. "Moving Miniatures and Circulating Bodies in Aphra Behn's *The Rover*." *Restoration* 31, no. 1 (2007): 27–46.

Berglund, Jeff. *Cannibal Fictions: American Explorations of Colonialism, Race, Gender, and Sexuality*. Madison: University of Wisconsin Press, 2006.

Berman, Ronald. "Nature in *Venice Preserv'd*." *ELH* 36, no. 3 (1969): 529–43.

Bevington, David, et al., ed. *English Renaissance Drama: A Norton Anthology*. New York: Norton, 2002.

de Bévotte, Gendarme. *La Légende de Don Juan: Son Évolution Dans La Littérature Des Origines Au Romantisme*. Geneva: Slatkine Reprints, 1970.

Blount, Charles. *An Appeal From the Country To the City, For the Preservation of His Majesties Person, Liberty, Property, and the Protestant Religion*. London, 1679.

———. *King William and Queen Mary Conquerors*. London, 1693.

Boebel, Dagny. "In the Carnival World of Adam's Garden: Roving and Rape in Behn's *Rover*." In *Broken Boundaries: Women & Feminism in Restoration Drama*, edited by Katherine Quinsey, 54–70. Lexington: University Press of Kentucky, 1996.

Bohun, Edmund. "A Preface to the Reader." Introduction to *Patriarcha: Or The Natural Power Of Kings*, by Sir Robert Filmer, a1r–g4r. London, 1685.

Bowber, Thomas. *A Sermon Preached in the Parish-Church of St Swithin, London, March 10th 1694/5, Upon the Much Lamented Death of our Most Gracious Queen*. London, 1695.

Bowers, Fredson. *Elizabethan Revenge Tragedy*. Princeton: Princeton University Press, 1940.

———. "The Stabbing of a Portrait in Elizabethan Tragedy." *Modern Language Notes* 47, no. 6 (1932): 378–85.

Bowers, Toni. "Behn's Monmouth: Sedition, Seduction, and Tory Ideology in the 1680s." *Studies in Eighteenth Century Culture* 38 (2009): 15–44.

Boyle, Roger, Earl of Orrery. *The Generall.* In *The Dramatic Works of Roger Boyle*, edited by William S. Clark II, 1:101–64. Cambridge: Harvard University Press, 1937.

Bradburn, Beth. "Bodily Metaphor and Moral Agency in *A Masque*: A Cognitive Approach." *Milton Studies* 43 (2004): 19–34.

Brady, Nicholas. *The Rape: Or, The Innocent Impostors*. London, 1692.

Broaddus, James. "'Gums of Glutinous Heat' in Milton's Mask and Spenser's *Faerie Queene*." *Milton Quarterly* 37, no. 4 (2003): 205–14.

Broude, Ronald. "Revenge and Revenge Tragedy in Renaissance England." *Renaissance Quarterly* 28, no. 1 (1975): 38–58.

Brown, Cedric. *John Milton's Aristocratic Entertainments*. Cambridge: Cambridge University Press, 1985.

Brown, F. C. *Elkanah Settle: His Life and Works*. Chicago: University of Chicago Press, 1910.

Brown, Laura. *English Dramatic Form, 1660–1760: An Essay in Generic History*. New Haven: Yale University Press, 1981.

Brown, Richard. "Heroics Satirized by 'Mad Nat. Lee.'" *Papers on Language and Literature* 19, no. 4 (1983): 385–401.

Brownmiller, Susan. *Against Our Will: Men, Women and Rape.* New York: Bantam, 1975.

Bullinger, Henry. *A Confutation Of the Popes Bull which was published more than two yeres agoe against Elizabeth the most gracious Queene of England, Fraunce, and Ireland, and against the noble Realme of England.* London, 1572.

Burks, Deborah G. *Horrid Spectacle: Violation in the Theater of Early Modern England.* Pittsburgh: Duquesne University Press, 2003.

Burnet, Gilbert. *The Mystery of Iniquity Unvailed.* London, 1673.

Burnett, Anne Pippin. *Revenge in Attic and Later Tragedy*. Berkeley: University of California Press, 1998.

Bushnell, Rebecca W. *Tragedies of Tyrants: Political Thought and Theater in the English Renaissance*. Ithaca and London: Cornell University Press, 1990.

Butler, Melissa A. "Early Liberal Roots of Feminism: John Locke and the Attack on Patriarchy." *American Political Science Review* 72, no. 1 (1978): 135–50.

Bynum, Caroline Walker. "The Body of Christ in the Later Middle Ages: A Reply to Leo Steinberg." *Renaissance Quarterly* 39, no. 3 (1986): 399–439.

Byrne, Peter. "'Where Appetite Directs': Tragic Heroism's Recovery in Rochester's *Valentinian*." *Pacific Coast Philology* 40, no. 1 (2005): 158–77.

Bywaters, David. "Venice, Its Senate, and Its Plot in Otway's *Venice Preserv'd*." *Modern Philology* 80, no. 3 (1983): 256–63.

C., G. *Popish Plots And Treasons From the beginning of the Reign of Queen Elizabeth.* London, 1676.

Campbell, Lily B. "Theories of Revenge in Renaissance England." *Modern Philology* 28, no. 3 (1931): 281–96.

Cantor, Paul A. *Shakespeare's Rome: Republic and Empire*. Ithaca: Cornell University Press, 1976.

Carew, Thomas. "A Rapture." In *The Norton Anthology of English Literature*, 8th ed., edited by Stephen Greenblatt et al., 1:1672–75. New York: Norton, 2006.

Carswell, John. *From Revolution to Revolution: England 1688–1776.* London: Routledge & Kegan Paul, 1973.

Cartwright, William. *The Game at Chesse. A metaphoricall discourse shewing the present estate of this Kingdome*. London, 1643.

Carver, Larry. "Rochester's *Valentinian*." *Restoration and Eighteenth Century Theatre Research* 3, no. 1 (1989): 25–38.

Castaldo, Annalisa. "'These were spectacles to please my soul': Inventive Violence in the Renaissance Revenge Tragedy." In *Staging Pain, 1580–1800: Violence and Trauma in British Theater*, edited by James Robert Allard and Matthew R. Martin, 49–56. Burlington: Ashgate, 2009.

Chalmers, Hero. *Royalist Women Writers, 1650–1689*. Oxford: Clarendon Press, 2004.

Charles II. *A Proclamation To Restrain the Spreading of False News, and Licentious Talking of Matters of State and Government*. London, 1672.
Chaytor, Miranda. "Husband(ry): Narratives of Rape in the Seventeenth Century." *Gender and History* 7, no. 3 (1995): 378–407.
Chernaik, Warren L. *The Poet's Time: Politics and Religion in the Work of Andrew Marvell*. Cambridge: Cambridge University Press, 1983.
Cherry, George L. "The Legal and Philosophical Position of the Jacobites, 1688–1689." *Journal of Modern History* 22, no. 4 (1950): 309–21.
Choudhury, Mita. "Orrery and the London Stage: A Loyalist's Contribution to Restoration Allegorical Drama." *Studia Neophilologica* 62, no. 1 (1990): 43–59.
Cibber, Colley. *Xerxes, A Tragedy*. London, 1699.
Clark, Constance. *Three Augustan Women Playwrights*. New York: Peter Lang, 1986.
Clark, J. C. D. *English Society 1688–1832: Ideology, Social Structure and Political Practice during the Ancien Regime*. Cambridge: Cambridge University Press, 1985.
Clark, Sandra. *The Plays of Beaumont and Fletcher: Sexual Themes and Dramatic Representation*. New York: Harvester Wheatsheaf, 1994.
Clark, W. S. "The Earl of Orrery's Play *The Generall*." *Review of English Studies* 2, no. 8 (1926): 459–60.
Clark, William S. "Further Light upon the Heroic Plays of Roger Boyle, Earl of Orrery." *Review of English Studies* 2, no. 6 (1926): 206–11.
Claydon, Tony. *William III*. London and New York: Longman, 2002.
Clifton, Robin. "James II's Two Rebellions." *History Today* 38, no. 7 (1988): 23–29.
———. "The Popular Fear of Catholics during the English Revolution." *Past and Present* 52 (1971): 23–55.
Codrington, Robert. *His Majesties Propriety, And Dominion On The British Seas Asserted*. London, 1672.
Coles, Gilbert. *A Dialogue Between A Protestant And A Papist*. Oxford, 1679.
Collins, Margo. "Feminine Conduct and Violence in Mary Pix's She-Tragedies." *Restoration and Eighteenth-Century Theatre Research* 18, no. 1 (2003): 1–16.
Collinson, Patrick, Arnold Hunt, and Alexandra Walsham. "Religious Publishing in England 1557–1640." In *The Cambridge History of the Book, Volume IV, 1557–1695*, edited by John Barnard and D. F. McKenzie, 29–66. Cambridge: Cambridge University Press, 2002.
Combe, Kirk. *A Martyr for Sin: Rochester's Critique of Polity, Sexuality, and Society*. Newark: University of Delaware Press, 1998.
Cooke, Alexander. *A Present for a Papist: Or The Life and Death Of Pope Joan*. London, 1675.
Coox, Alvin D. "The Dutch Invasion of England: 1667." *Military Affairs* 13, no. 4 (1949): 223–33.
Copeland, Nancy. "'Once a Whore and Ever?' Whore and Virgin in *The Rover* and Its Antecedents." In *Early Women Writers: 1660–1720*, edited by Anita Pacheco, 149–59. London: Longman, 1998.
———. *Staging Gender in Behn and Centlivre*. Burlington: Ashgate, 2004.
Cousins, A. D. "The Idea of a 'Restoration' and the Verse Satires of Butler and Marvell." *Southern Review* 14, no. 2 (1981): 131–42.
Crashaw, Richard. "Luke 11. Blessed be the paps which Thou hast sucked." In *The Complete Poetry of Richard Crashaw*, edited by George Walton Williams, 14. Garden City: Anchor Books, 1970.
Crouch, John. *The Muses Joy For the Recovery of that Weeping Vine Henrietta Maria*. London, 1660.
Crowne, John. *Caligula. A Tragedy*. London, 1698.
———. *Daeneids, Or The Noble Labours of the Great Dean Of Notre-Dame In Paris, For the Erecting in his Quire a Throne for his Glory, and the Eclipsing the Pride of an Imperious, Usurping Chanter*. London, 1692.
———. *The Misery of Civil War*. In *Shakespeare Adaptations from the Restoration*, edited by Barbara A. Murray, 89–192. Madison: Fairleigh Dickinson University Press, 2005.
———. *Thyestes. A Tragedy*. London, 1681.

Cruickshanks, Eveline. *The Glorious Revolution*. Basingstoke: Macmillan, 2000.

Daalder, Joost. Introduction to *Thyestes*, by Jasper Heywood, x–xlv. New York: Norton, 1989.

Daly, James. *Sir Robert Filmer and English Political Thought*. Toronto: University of Toronto Press, 1979.

D'Amico, Jack. *The Moor in English Renaissance Drama*. Tampa: University of South Florida Press, 1991.

Darby, Graham, ed. *The Origins and Development of the Dutch Revolt*. New York: Routledge, 2004.

Dauncey, John. *The History Of The Thrice Illustrious Princess Henrietta Maria de Bourbon, Queen Of England*. London, 1660.

D'Cruze, Shani. "Approaching the History of Rape and Sexual Violence: Notes towards Research." *Women's History Review* 1, no. 3 (1993): 377–96.

Defoe, Daniel. *The Life Of That Incomparable Princess Mary, Our Late Sovereign Lady, Of ever Blessed Memory. Who departed this Life, at her Royal Pallace at Kensington, the 28th of December, 1694*. London, 1695.

de las Casas, Bartolomé. *The Spanish Colonie, Or Briefe Chronicle of the Acts and gestes of the Spaniardes in the West Indies, called the newe World*. London, 1583.

Dennis, John. *Original Letters, Familiar, Moral, and Critical*. 2 vols. London, 1721.

Denton, William. *The Burnt Child dreads the Fire*. London, 1675.

DePorte, Michael. "Otway and the Straits of Venice." *Papers on Language and Literature* 18, no. 3 (1982): 245–57.

DeRitter, Jonas. "The Gypsy, *The Rover*, and the Wanderer: Aphra Behn's Revision of Thomas Killigrew." *Restoration* 10, no. 2 (1986): 82–92.

Detmer-Goebel, Emily. "The Need for Lavinia's Voice: *Titus Andronicus* and the Telling of Rape." *Shakespeare Studies* 29 (2001): 75–92.

Diamond, Elin. "*Gestus* and Signature in Aphra Behn's *The Rover*." In *Early Women Writers: 1660–1720*, edited by Anita Pacheco, 160–82. London: Longman, 1998.

Dickinson, H. T. *Liberty and Property: Political Ideology in Eighteenth-Century Britain*. New York: Holmes and Meier, 1977.

Diehl, Huston. *Staging Reform, Reforming the Stage: Protestantism and Popular Theater in Early Modern England*. Ithaca and London: Cornell University Press, 1997.

Digby, Lettice. *A Full and True Account Of The Inhumane and Bloudy Cruelties Of The Papists To The Poor Protestants In Ireland In the year, 1641*. London, 1689.

Dolan, Frances. *Whores of Babylon: Catholicism, Gender, and Seventeenth-Century Print Culture*. Ithaca and London: Cornell University Press, 1999.

Donnelly, Mark P., and Daniel Diehl. *Eat Thy Neighbor: A History of Cannibalism*. Gloucestershire: Sutton, 2006.

Doyle, Anne. "Dryden's Authorship of *Notes and Observations on the Empress of Morocco* (1674)." *Studies in English Literature 1500–1900* 6, no. 3 (1966): 421–45.

Dryden, John. *Albion and Albanius*. In *The Works of John Dryden*, edited by Vinton Dearing, 15:1–55. Berkeley: University of California Press, 1976.

———. *Amboyna, or the Cruelties of the Dutch to the English Merchants*. In *The Works of John Dryden*, edited by Vinton A. Dearing, 12:1–79. Berkeley: University of California Press, 1994.

———. "Astraea Redux." In *Restoration Literature: An Anthology*, edited by Paul Hammond, 23–31. Oxford: Oxford University Press, 2002.

Duffy, Maureen. *The Passionate Shepherdess: Aphra Behn, 1640–89*. London: Jonathan Cape, 1977.

Dugas, Don-John. "Elkanah Settle, John Crowne and Nahum Tate." In *A Companion to Restoration Drama*, edited by Susan J. Owen, 378–95. Malden: Blackwell, 2001.

Du Moulin, Lewis. *A Short and True Account Of The Several Advances The Church of England Hath made towards Rome: Or, A Model of the Grounds upon which the Papists for these Hundred years have built their Hopes*. London, 1680.

Durant, Jack D. "'Honor's Toughest Task': Family and State in *Venice Preserved*." *Studies in Philology* 71, no. 4 (1974): 484–503.

E., T. *The Lawes Resolutions of Womens Rights: Or, the Lawes Provision for Women*. New York: Garland Publishing, 1978.

Earle, Peter. *Monmouth's Rebels: The Road to Sedgemoor*. London: Weidenfeld & Nicolson, 1977.

Eaton, Sara. "A Woman of Letters: Lavinia in *Titus Andronicus*." In *Shakespearean Tragedy and Gender*, edited by Shirley Nelson Garner and Madelon Sprengether, 54–74. Bloomington: Indiana University Press, 1996.

Eliot, T. S. *Selected Essays*. New York: Harcourt, 1964.

Ellison, Julie. *Cato's Tears and the Making of Anglo-American Emotion*. Chicago: University of Chicago Press, 1999.

Erskine-Hill, Howard. "Literature and the Jacobite Cause: Was There a Rhetoric of Jacobitism?" In *Ideology and Conspiracy: Aspects of Jacobitism, 1689–1759*, edited by Eveline Cruickshanks, 49–69. Edinburgh: John Donald Publishers, 1982.

Ezell, Margaret J. M. *The Patriarch's Wife: Literary Evidence and the History of the Family*. Chapel Hill and London: University of North Carolina Press, 1987.

F., J. *Englands Lamentation For The Duke of Monmouth's Departure: Reflecting on his Heroick Actions*. London, 1679.

Farnell, J. E. "The Navigation Act of 1651, the First Dutch War, and the London Merchant Community." *Economic History Review* 16, no. 3 (1964): 439–54.

Fenner, William. *Four Select Sermons Upon Several Texts of Scripture. Wherein The Idolatry, and Will-worship of the Church of Rome, is laid Open and Confuted, &c*. London, 1668.

Ferguson, Robert. *A Brief Account of some of the late Incroachments and Depredations of the Dutch upon the English*. London, 1695.

———. *A Letter to Mr. Secretary Trenchard, Discovering a Conspiracy against the Laws and ancient Constitution of England: With Reflections on the present Pretended Plot*. London, 1694.

———. *Whether the Parliament be not in Law dissolved by the Death of the Princess of Orange*. London, 1695.

———. *Whether the Preserving the Protestant Religion was the Motive unto, or the End, that was designed in the Late Revolution?* London, 1695.

Filmer, Sir Robert. *Patriarcha and Other Writings*, edited by Johann P. Sommerville. Cambridge: Cambridge University Press, 1991.

Fink, Z. S. *The Classical Republicans: An Essay in the Recovery of a Pattern of Thought in Seventeenth-Century England*. Evanston: Northwestern University Press, 1945.

Finkelpearl, Philip J. *Court and Country Politics in the Plays of Beaumont and Fletcher*. Princeton: Princeton University Press, 1990.

Fisk, Deborah Payne. Introduction to *Four Libertine Plays*, xi–xliv. Oxford: Oxford University Press, 2005.

Flores, Stephen P. "Orrery's *The Generall* and *Henry The Fifth*: Sexual Politics and the Desire for Friendship." *Eighteenth Century: Theory and Interpretation* 37, no. 1 (1996): 56–74.

Foulis, Henry. *The history Of Romish Treasons & Usurpations: Together with A Particular Account Of many gross Corruptions and Impostures In the Church of Rome*. London, 1671.

Fowler, Patsy S. "Rejecting the Status Quo: The Attempts of Mary Pix & Susannah Centlivre to Reform Society's Patriarchal Attitudes." *Restoration and Eighteenth-Century Theatre Research* 11, no. 2 (1996): 49–59.

Fox, George. *The Arraignment And Condemnation Of Popery*. London, 1675.

Foxe, John. *Foxe's Book of Martyrs*. Blacksburg: Wilder Publications, 2009.

Gailhard, J. *Four Tracts*. London, 1699.

Gammon, J. D. "Ravishment and Ruin: The Construction of Stories of Sexual Violence in England, c. 1640–1820." PhD diss., University of Essex, 2001.

Gascoigne, George. *The Spoyle of Antwerp. Faithfully reported, by a true Englishman, who was present at the same*. London, 1576.

Gauden, John. *Cromwell's Bloody Slaughter-house*. London, 1660.

A Gentleman of good quality. *True Intelligence From The West: Or A true Relation of the desperate Proceedings of the Rebels, and Cavaliers gathered together at Angry-Fisherten in Wilt-shire*. London, 1647.

Gerwirtz, Arthur. *Restoration Adaptations of Early 17th Century Comedies*. Washington, DC: University Press of America, 1982.

Gill, Pat. "Revolutionary Identity in Otway's *Venice Preserv'd*." In *Illicit Sex: Identity Politics in Early Modern Culture*, edited by Thomas DiPiero and Pat Gill, 239–55. Athens: University of Georgia Press, 1992.

Gillespie, Raymond. "The End of an Era: Ulster and the Outbreak of the 1641 Rising." In *Natives and Newcomers: Essays on the Making of Irish Colonial Society, 1534–1641*, edited by Ciaran Brady and Raymond Gillespie, 191–248. Bungay: Irish Academic Press, 1986.

Goldie, Mark. "Contextualizing Absalom: William Lawrence, the Laws of Marriage, and the Case for King Monmouth." In *Religion, Literature, and Politics in Post-Reformation England, 1540–1688,* edited by Donna Hamilton and Richard Strier, 208–30. Cambridge: Cambridge University Press, 1996.

Goodlad, Graham. "Before the Glorious Revolution: The Making of Absolute Monarchy?" *History Review* 58 (2008): 10–15.

Goodwin, John. *Anti-Cavalierisme, Or, Truth Pleading As well the Necessity, as the Lawfulness of this present War, for the suppressing of that Butcherly brood of Cavaliering Incendiaries, who are now hammering England, to make an Ireland of it*. London, 1642.

Grantley, Darryl. "Masques and Murderers: Dramatic Method and Ideology in Revenge Tragedy and the Court Masque." In *Jacobean Poetry and Prose: Rhetoric, Representation and the Popular Imagination*, edited by Clive Bloom, 194–212. New York: St. Martin's, 1988.

Gray, Ralph. "The Coronation Ballad, 11th April 1689." In *Poems on Affairs of State: Augustan Satirical Verse, 1660–1714*, edited by William J. Cameron, 5:43. New Haven: Yale University Press, 1963.

Greaves, Richard L. *Secrets of the Kingdom: British Radicals from the Popish Plot to the Revolution of 1688–1689*. Stanford: Stanford University Press, 1992.

Greenblatt, Stephen. *Renaissance Self-Fashioning: From More to Shakespeare*. Chicago and London: University of Chicago Press, 1980.

Greer, Margaret, Walter D. Mignolo, and Maureen Quilligan, eds. *Rereading the Black Legend: The Discourses of Religious and Racial Difference in the Renaissance Empires*. Chicago: University of Chicago Press, 2007.

Gregg, Edward. *Queen Anne*. London: Routledge & Kegan Paul, 1980.

Groenveld, Simon. "The English Civil Wars as a Cause of the First Anglo-Dutch War, 1640–1652." *Historical Journal* 30, no. 3 (1987): 541–66.

H., B. *The Parliament of Bees. A Fable*. London, 1697.

H., I. *A briefe Relation, Abstracted out of severall Letters, of A most Hellish, Cruell, and Bloudy Plot against the City of Bristoll*. London, 1642.

Habib, Imtiaz. "Elizabethan Racial Medical Psychology, Popular Drama, and the Social Programming of the Late-Tudor Black: Sketching an Exploratory Postcolonial Hypothesis." In *Disease, Diagnosis, and Cure on the Early Modern Stage*, edited by Stephanie Moss and Kaara L. Peterson, 93–112. Burlington: Ashgate, 2004.

Hadfred, John. *A wonderfull And Strange Miracle or Gods Just Vengeance against the Cavaliers*. London, 1642.

Haliczer, Stephen. *Sexuality in the Confessional: A Sacrament Profaned*. Oxford: Oxford University Press, 1996.

Hall, H. Gaston. "Dom Juan: Personnage Europeen Du XVIIe Siecle." In *Horizons européens de la literature française au XVIIe siècle*, edited by Wolfgang Leiner, 139–47. Tübingen: Narr, 1988.

Haller, William. *The Elect Nation: The Meaning and Relevance of Foxe's Book of Martyrs*. New York: Harper & Row, 1963.

Hallet, Charles A. and Elaine S. *The Revenger's Madness: A Study of Revenge Tragedy Motifs*. Lincoln: University of Nebraska Press, 1980.

Ham, Roswell G. "Dryden versus Settle." *Modern Philology* 25, no. 4 (1928): 409–16.

———. *Otway and Lee: Biography from a Baroque Age*. New York: Greenwood Press, 1931.

Hammond, Antony. "The 'Greatest Action': Lee's *Lucius Junius Brutus*." In *Poetry and Drama, 1570–1700: Essays in Honour of Harold F. Brooks*, edited by Antony Coleman and Antony Hammond, 175–85. London: Methuen, 1981.

Hammond, Paul. *Figuring Sex between Men from Shakespeare to Rochester*. Oxford: Oxford University Press, 2002.

Hargrove, Anne. Introduction to *The Fatal Contract*, by William Heminge, iv–xxii. Kalamazoo: Medieval Institute Publications, 1978.

Harris, Tim. "'Lives, Liberties and Estates': Rhetorics of Liberty in the Reign of Charles II." In *The Politics of Religion in Restoration England*, edited by Tim Harris, Paul Seaward, and Mark Goldie, 217–41. Cambridge: Basil Blackwell, 1990.

Harsnett, Samuel. *A Declaration of egregious Popish Impostures, to with-draw the harts of her Maiesties Subjects from their allegeance, and from the truth of Christian Religion professed in England, vnder the pretence of casting out deuills*. London, 1603.

Harth, Philip. "Political Interpretations of *Venice Preserv'd*." *Modern Philology* 85, no. 4 (1988): 345–62.

Hayne, Victoria. "'All Language Then Is Vile': The Theatrical Critique of Political Rhetoric in Nathaniel Lee's *Lucius Junius Brutus*." *ELH* 63, no. 2 (1996): 337–65.

Helms, Lorraine. "'The High Roman Fashion': Sacrifice, Suicide, and the Shakespearean Stage." *PMLA* 107, no. 3 (1992): 554–65.

Herman, Eleanor. *Mistress of the Vatican: The True Story of Olimpia Maidalchini: The Secret Female Pope*. New York: William Morrow, 2008.

Hermanson, Anne. "Monstrous Women in Aphra Behn's *Abdelazer* and Elkanah Settle's *The Empress of Morocco*." In *Aphra Behn (1640–1689): Le Modèle Européen*, edited by Mary Ann O'Donnell and Bernard Dhuicq, 25–32. Entrevaux, France: Bilingua GA Editions, 2005.

Heminge, William. *The Fatal Contract*. In *The Plays and Poems of William Heminge*, edited by Carol A. Morley, 309–89. Madison: Farleigh Dickinson University Press, 2006.

Heywood, Thomas. *The Rape of Lucrece. A True Roman Tragedie. With the severall Songs in their apt places, by Valerius, the merrie Lord amongst the Roman Peers*. London, 1608.

Hibbard, Caroline M. "Henrietta Maria (1609–1669) ." In *Oxford Dictionary of National Biography*. Oxford University Press, 2004–12. Accessed February 10, 2011. doi: 10.1093/ref:odnb/12947.

Hibernicus, Mercurius. *A Pacquet Of Popish Delusions, False Miracles, and Lying Wonders*. London, 1681.

Higgins, Lynn A., and Brenda R. Silver, eds. *Rape and Representation*. New York: Columbia University Press, 1991.

Hila, Marina. "'Justice shall never heare ye, I am justice': Absolutist Rape and Cyclical History in John Fletcher's *The Tragedy of Valentinian*." *Neophilologus* 91, no. 4 (2007): 745–58.

Hill, Christopher. *Milton and the English Revolution*. London: Faber and Faber, 1977.

Hook, Lucyle. "The Publication Date of Rochester's *Valentinian*." *Huntington Library Quarterly* 19, no. 4 (1956): 401–7.

Hopkins, Charles. *Boadicea Queen of Britain. A Tragedy*. London, 1697.

Horneck, Anthony. *The Honesty Of The Protestant, And Dishonesty Of The Popish Divinity, In A Letter To A Lady Revolted to the Church of Rome*. London, 1681.

Howard, Edward. *The Usurper, A Tragedy*. London, 1668.

Howe, Elizabeth. *The First English Actresses: Women and Drama 1660–1700*. Cambridge: Cambridge University Press, 1992.

Hughes, Derek. *English Drama, 1660–1700*. Oxford: Clarendon Press, 1996.

———. "Human Sacrifice on the Restoration Stage: The Case of *Venice Preserv'd*." *Philological Quarterly* 88, no. 4 (2009): 365–84.

———. "A New Look at *Venice Preserv'd*." *Studies in English Literature 1500–1900* 11, no. 3 (1971): 437–57.

———. "Rape on the Restoration Stage." *The Eighteenth Century* 46, no. 3 (2005): 225–36.

———. *The Theatre of Aphra Behn*. New York: Palgrave, 2001.

Hulme, Peter. "Columbus and the Cannibals." In *The Post-Colonial Studies Reader*, edited by Bill Ashcroft and Gareth Griffiths, 365–69. London: Routledge, 1995.

Hume, Mr. [Patrick Hume]. *A Poem Dedicated to the Immortal Memory of Her Late Majesty*. London, 1695.

Hume, Robert D. *The Development of English Drama in the Late Seventeenth Century*. Oxford: Clarendon Press, 1976.

———. *The Rakish Stage: Studies in English Drama, 1660–1800*. Carbondale: Southern Illinois University Press, 1983.

Hutner, Heidi. *Colonial Women: Race and Culture in Stuart Drama*. Oxford: Oxford University Press, 2001.

Hutton, Ronald. *Charles II: King of England, Scotland, and Ireland*. Oxford: Clarendon Press, 1989.

Israel, Jonathan. "Competing Cousins: Anglo-Dutch Trade Rivalry." *History Today* 38 (1988): 17–22.

Iwanisziw, Susan. "Tortured Bodies, Factionalism, and Unsettled Loyalties in Settle's Morocco Plays." In *Staging Pain, 1580–1800: Violence and Trauma in British Theater*, edited by James Robert Allard and Matthew R. Martin, 111–36. Burlington: Ashgate, 2009.

Iyengar. Sujata. *Shades of Difference: Mythologies of Skin Color in Early Modern England*. Philadelphia: University of Pennsylvania Press, 2005.

Jaffe, Aaron. "Seditious Appetites and Creeds: Shadwell's Libertines and Hobbes's Foole." *Restoration* 24, no. 2 (2002): 55–74.

Johnson, James William. *A Profane Wit: The Life of John Wilmot, Earl of Rochester*. Rochester: University of Rochester Press, 2004.

Johnston, Nathaniel. *The Dear Bargain. Or, A True Representation of the State of the English Nation under the Dutch*. London, 1690.

Jones, J. R. *The First Whigs: The Politics of the Exclusion Crisis 1678–1683*. London: Oxford University Press, 1961.

———. *The Revolution of 1688 in England*. London: Wiedenfeld & Nicolson, 1972.

Jurieu, Monsieur. *Le Dragon Missionaire: Or, The Dragoon Turn'd Apostle*. London, 1686.

Kaufman, Anthony. "'The Perils of Florinda': Aphra Behn, Rape, and the Subversion of Libertinism in *The Rover*, Part I." *Restoration and Eighteenth-Century Theatre Research* 11, no. 2 (1996): 1–21.

Keach, Benjamin. *Sion in Distress: Or, The Groans Of The Protestant Church*. London, 1681.

Keen, Benjamin. "The Black Legend Revisited: Assumptions and Realities." *Hispanic American Historical Review* 49, no. 4 (1969): 703–19.

Ken, Thomas. *A Letter To The Author of a Sermon Entitled, A Sermon Preach'd At The Funeral Of Her late Majesty Queen Mary, Of ever Blessed Memory*. London, 1695.

Kenyon, John. *The Popish Plot*. London: Phoenix Press, 1972.

———. *Revolution Principles: The Politics of Party, 1689–1720*. Cambridge: Cambridge University Press, 1977.

Kerrigan, John. "Orrery's Ireland and the British Problem." In *British Identities and English Renaissance Literature*, edited by David J. Baker and Willy Maley, 197–225. Cambridge: Cambridge University Press, 2002.

Khastgir, Aparna. "Endings as *Concordia Discors*: *Titus Andronicus*." *Studia Neophilologica* 73 (2001): 36–47.

Kilgour, Maggie. *From Communion to Cannibalism: An Anatomy of Metaphors of Incorporation*. Princeton: Princeton University Press, 1990.

Kittermaster, Thomas. *A Wonderfull Deliverance Or Gods abundant mercy in preserving from the Cavaliers the towne of Draiton In the County of Hereford*. London, 1642.

Knight, G. Wilson. *The Imperial Theme: Further Interpretations of Shakespeare's Tragedies Including the Roman Plays*. London: Oxford University Press, 1931.

Knoppers, Laura Lunger. *Constructing Cromwell: Ceremony, Portrait, and Print, 1645–1661*. Cambridge: Cambridge University Press, 2000.

Koon, Helene. *Colley Cibber: A Biography*. Lexington: University of Kentucky Press, 1986.

Kunz, Don R. *The Drama of Thomas Shadwell*. Salzburg: Institut Für Englische Sprache Und Literatur, 1972.

Lacy, John. "Satire." In *Poems on Affairs of State: Augustan Satirical Verse, 1660–1714*, edited by George deF. Lord, 1:425–28. New Haven: Yale University Press, 1963.

Lake, Peter. "Antipopery: The Structure of a Prejudice." In *Conflict in Early Stuart England: Studies in Religion and Politics 1603–1642*, edited by Richard Cust and Ann Hughes, 72–107. London and New York: Longman Group, 1989.

Lawrence, George. *The Debauched Cavalleer: Or the English Midianite*. London, 1642.

Lawton, Charlwood. *A Letter formerly sent to Dr Tillotsen, and for Want of an Answer made publick*. London, 1748.

Lee, Nathaniel. *Lucius Junius Brutus*. In *Works*, edited by Thomas B. Stroup and Arthur L. Cooke. New Brunswick: Scarecrow Press, 1954.

———. *Mithridates, King of Pontus, A Tragedy*. London, 1678.

Leissner, Debra. "Divided Nation, Divided Self: The Language of Capitalism and Madness in Otway's *Venice Preserv'd*." *Studies in the Literary Imagination* 32, no. 2 (1999): 19–31.

Lestringant, Frank. *Cannibals: The Discovery and Representation of the Cannibal from Columbus to Jules Verne*. Berkeley: University of California Press, 1997.

Leti, Gregorio. *The Life Of Donna Olimpia Maldachini, Who Governed the Church during the Time of Innocent the X*. London, 1666.

Liebler, Naomi Conn. *Shakespeare's Festive Tragedy: The Ritual Foundations of Genre*. London: Routledge, 1995.

Lilly, William. *The Dangerous Condition of the United Provinces Prognosticated, And Plainly Demonstrated, By Mr. William Lilly, In his Observations of that Comet which appeared in the Year of our Lord, 1652. And published in his annual Predictions in the Year 1654, &tc.* London, 1672.

Lindley, Keith J. "The Impact of the 1641 Rebellion upon England and Wales, 1641–5." *Irish Historical Studies* 18, no. 70 (1972): 143–76.

Livy. *Ab Urbe Condita*. Translated by B. O. Foster. Cambridge, MA: Harvard University Press, 1970.

Lloyd, William. *Papists No Catholicks: And Popery No Christianity*. London, 1677.

———. *Seasonable Advice To All Protestant People Of England*. London, 1681.

Locke, John. *Two Treatises of Government*. Edited by Peter Laslett. Cambridge: Cambridge University Press, 1960.

Loftis, John. Introduction to *Lucius Junius Brutus*, by Nathaniel Lee, i–xxiv. Lincoln: University of Nebraska Press, 1967.

Lord, George deF., ed. *Poems on Affairs of State: Augustan Satirical Verse, 1660–1714*. 7 vols. New Haven: Yale University Press, 1963.

Love, Harold. "The Rapes of Lucina." In *Print, Manuscript & Performance*, edited by Arthur F. Marotti and Michael D. Bristol, 200–214. Athens: Ohio State University Press, 2000.

———. "Shadwell, Flecknoe and the Duke of Newcastle: An Impetus for *MacFlecknoe*." *Papers on Language and Literature* 21, no. 1 (1985): 19–27.

———. "Shadwell, Rochester, and the Crisis of Amateurism." *Restoration* 20, no. 2 (1996): 119–34.

———. "State Affairs on the Restoration Stage, 1660–1675." *Restoration and Eighteenth-Century Theatre Research* 14, no. 1 (1975): 1–9.

———. "Was Lucina Betrayed at Whitehall?" In *That Second Bottle: Essays on John Wilmot, Earl of Rochester*, edited by Nicholas Fisher, 179–90. Manchester: Manchester University Press, 2000.

Lovelace, Richard. "To Lucasta, Going to the Wars." In *The Norton Anthology of English Literature*, 8th ed., ed. Stephen Greenblatt et al., 1:1682. New York: Norton, 2006.

Lowenthal, Cynthia. *Performing Identities on the Restoration Stage*. Carbondale: Southern Illinois University Press, 2003.

Lynch, Kathleen M. *Roger Boyle, First Earl of Orrery*. Knoxville: University of Tennessee Press, 1965.

MacDonald, Joyce Green. "'Hay for the Daughters!' Gender and Patriarchy in *The Misery of Civil War* and *Henry VI*." *Comparative Drama* 24, no. 3 (1990): 193–216.

———. "Public Wounds: Sexual Bodies and the Origins of State in Nathaniel Lee's *Lucius Junius Brutus*." *Studies in Eighteenth-Century Culture* 32 (2003): 229–44.

Maguire, Nancy Klein. *Regicide and Restoration: English Tragicomedy, 1660–1670*. Cambridge: Cambridge University Press, 1992.

Mainwaring, Arthur. "Tarquin and Tullia." In *Poems on Affairs of State: Augustan Satirical Verse, 1660–1714*, edited by William J. Cameron, 5:47–56. New Haven: Yale University Press, 1963.

Mandel, Oscar. *The Theatre of Don Juan: A Collection of Plays and Views, 1630–1963.* Lincoln: University of Nebraska Press, 1963.

Marcus, Leah S. "John Milton's *Comus.*" In *A Companion to Milton*, edited by Thomas N. Corns, 232–45. Oxford: Blackwell, 2001.

Markley, Robert. *The Far East and the English Imagination, 1600–1730.* Cambridge: Cambridge University Press, 2006.

Marotti, Arthur F. *Religious Ideology and Cultural Fantasy: Catholic and Anti-Catholic Discourses in Early Modern England.* Notre Dame: University of Notre Dame Press, 2005.

Marsden, Jean I. "Mary Pix's *Ibrahim*: The Woman Writer as Commerical Playwright." *Studies in the Literary Imagination* 32, no. 2 (1999): 33–44.

———. "Rape, Voyeurism, and the Restoration Stage." In *Broken Boundaries: Women & Feminism in Restoration Drama,* edited by Katherine M. Quinsey, 185–200. Lexington: University of Kentucky Press, 1996.

Marvell, Andrew. *An Account of the Growth Of Popery And Arbitrary Government in England.* Amsterdam, 1677.

———. *The Last Instructions to a Painter.* In *The Poems and Letters of Andrew Marvell*, edited by H. M. Margoliouth, 2:147–72. Oxford: Clarendon Press, 1971.

———. "Upon his Majesty's being made Free of the City." In *Poems on Affairs of State: Augustan Satirical Verse, 1660–1714*, edited by George deF. Lord, 1:237–42. New Haven: Yale University Press, 1963.

Maus, Katherine Eisaman. "'Playhouse Flesh and Blood': Sexual Ideology and the Restoration Actress." *ELH* 46, no. 4 (1979): 595–617.

May, Thomas, Henry Parker, and John Sadler. *The Kings Cabinet opened.* London, 1645.

McBurney, William H. "Otway's Tragic Muse Debauched: Sensuality in *Venice Preserv'd.*" *Journal of English and Germanic Philology* 58, no. 3 (1959): 380–99.

McGirr, Elaine. *Heroic Mode and Political Crisis, 1660–1745.* Newark: University of Delaware Press, 2009.

Middleton, Thomas. *The Revenger's Tragedy.* In *English Renaissance Drama: A Norton Anthology*, edited by David Bevington et al., 1297–1370. New York: Norton, 2002.

Mildmay, Henry. "The Progress." In *Poems on Affairs of State: Augustan Satirical Verse, 1660–1714*, edited by William J. Cameron, 5:332. New Haven: Yale University Press, 1963.

Miles, Abraham. *The last farewel of three bould Traytors.* London, 1661.

Miller, John. *Popery and Politics in England, 1660–1688.* Cambridge: Cambridge University Press, 1973.

Milton, John. *Of True Religion, Haeresie, Schism, Toleration, And what best means may be us'd against the growth of Popery.* London, 1673.

———. *The Riverside Milton.* Edited by Roy Flannagan. Boston: Houghton Mifflin, 1998.

Miola, Robert S. *Shakespeare's Rome.* Cambridge: Cambridge University Press, 1983.

Monod, Paul. "The Jacobite Press and English Censorship, 1689–95." In *The Stuart Court in Exile and the Jacobites*, edited by Eveline Cruickshanks and Edward Corp, 125–42. London: Hambledon Press, 1995.

———. *Jacobitism and the English People, 1688–1788.* Cambridge: Cambridge University Press, 1989.

Montgomery, Sir James. *Great Britain's Just Complaint For Her Late Measures, Present Sufferings, And the Future Miseries She is exposed to.* London, 1692.

Moore, John Robert. "Contemporary Satire in Otway's *Venice Preserv'd.*" *PMLA* 43, no. 1 (1928): 166–81.

Morley, Carol A. Introduction to *The Plays and Poems of William Heminge*, by William Heminge, 17–32. Madison: Farleigh Dickinson University Press, 2006.

Mountfort, William. *The Injur'd Lovers: Or, The Ambitious Father. A Tragedy.* London, 1688.

Mullaney, Stephen. "Mourning and Misogyny: *Hamlet, The Revenger's Tragedy*, and the Final Progress of Elizabeth I." *Shakespeare Quarterly* 45, no. 2 (1994): 139–62.

Munns, Jessica. "'Plain as the light in the Cowcumber': A Note on the Conspiracy in Thomas Otway's *Venice Preserv'd*." *Modern Philology* 85, no. 1 (1987): 54–57.

Nalson, John. *The Project of Peace, Or, Unity of Faith And Government, The only Expedient to Procure Peace, Both Foreign and Domestique*. London, 1678.

Novak, Maximillian E. Introduction to *The Empress of Morocco and Its Critics*, by Elkanah Settle, i–xix. Berkeley: Augustan Reprint Society, 1968.

Oates, Titus. *A Balm presented to these Nations, England, Scotland, and Ireland, To Cure the Wounds of the Bleeding Protestants, and open the Eyes of the deluded Papists, that are Ignorant of the Truth, &c*. London, 1680.

Obeyesekere, Gananath. *Cannibal Talk: The Man-Eating Myth and Human Sacrifices in the South Seas*. Berkeley: University of California Press, 2005.

Oldham, John. *The Jesuits Justification, Proving they Died as Innocent as the Child Unborn*. London, 1679.

Orr, Bridget. *Empire on the English Stage, 1660–1714*. Cambridge: Cambridge University Press, 2001.

Ott, Michael. "Pope Innocent X." In *The Catholic Encyclopedia*. New York: Robert Appleton, 1910. Accessed April 20, 2011. http://www.newadvent.org/cathen/08020b.htm.

Otway, Thomas. *Venice Preserv'd*. In *Restoration Drama: An Anthology*, edited by David Womersley, 465–502. Oxford: Blackwell, 2000.

Owen, Susan J. "Drink, Sex and Power in Restoration Comedy." In *A Pleasing Sinne: Drink and Conviviality in Seventeenth-Century England*, edited by Adam Smyth, 127–39. Rochester: D.S. Brewer, 2004.

———. "'He that should guard my virtue has betrayed it': The Dramatization of Rape in the Exclusion Crisis." *Restoration and Eighteenth-Century Theatre Research* 9, no. 1 (1994): 59–98.

———. "'Partial Tyrants' and 'Freeborn People' in *Lucius Junius Brutus*." *Studies in English Literature 1500–1900* 31, no. 3 (1991): 463–85.

———. *Perspectives on Restoration Drama*. Manchester: Manchester University Press, 2002.

———. *Restoration Theatre and Crisis*. Oxford: Clarendon Press, 1996.

———. "'Suspect my loyalty when I lose my virtue': Sexual Politics and Party in Aphra Behn's Plays of the Exclusion Crisis, 1678–83." In *Aphra Behn*, edited by Janet Todd, 57–72. New York: St. Martin's, 1999.

P., H. *A Satyr Against Common-wealths*. London, 1684.

Pacheco, Anita. "Rape and the Female Subject in Aphra Behn's 'The Rover.'" *ELH* 65, no. 2 (1998): 323–45.

Palmer, M. A. J. "The 'Military Revolution' Afloat: The Era of the Anglo-Dutch Wars and the Transition to Modern Warfare at Sea." *War in History* 4, no. 2 (1997): 123–49.

Park, Henry. *Lachryme Sacerdotis. A Pindarick Poem Occasion'd by the Death Of that most excellent Princess, our late Gracious Sovereign Lady, Mary the Second, Of Glorious Memory*. London, 1695.

Parker, Derek. *Nell Gwyn*. Gloucestershire: Sutton, 2000.

Parker, Geoffrey. "The Origins of the Dutch Revolt." *History Today* 34, no. 7 (1984): 17–21.

Parker, Gerald. "'History as Nightmare' in Nevil Payne's *The Siege of Constantinople* and Nathaniel Lee's *Lucius Junius Brutus*." *Papers on Language and Literature* 21, no. 1 (1985): 3–18.

———. "The Image of Rebellion in Thomas Otway's *Venice Preserv'd* and Edward Young's *Busiris*." *Studies in English Literature 1500–1900* 21, no. 3 (1981): 389–407.

Pateman, Carole. *The Sexual Contract*. Stanford: Stanford University Press, 1988.

Patrides, C. A. *Premises and Motifs in Renaissance Thought and Literature*. Princeton: Princeton University Press, 1982.

Patterson, Annabel M. *Marvell and the Civic Crown*. Princeton: Princeton University Press, 1978.

Payne, F. W. "The Question of Precedence between Dryden and the Earl of Orrery with Regard to the English Heroic Play." *Review of English Studies* 1, no. 2 (1925): 173–81.

Pearson, Jacqueline. *The Prostituted Muse: Images of Women & Women Dramatists, 1642–1737*. New York: St. Martin's, 1988.

Pellegrin, Helen. Introduction to *Thomas Shadwell's The Libertine: A Critical Edition*, by Thomas Shadwell, ix–xxxiii. New York and London: Garland, 1987.

Penn, William. *A Seasonable Caveat Against Popery. Or A Pamphlet, Entituled, An Explanation of the Roman-Chatholick* [sic] *Belief, Briefly Examined*. London, 1670.

Pepys, Samuel. *The Diary of Samuel Pepys*, edited by Robert Latham and William Matthews. 11 vols. Berkeley: University of California Press, 1970–83.

Perdue, Danielle. "The Male Masochist in Restoration Drama." *Restoration and Eighteenth-Century Theatre Research* 11, no. 1 (1996): 10–21.

Pincus, Steve. "From Butterboxes to Wooden Shoes: The Shift in English Popular Sentiment from Anti-Dutch to Anti-French in the 1670s." *Historical Journal* 38, no. 2 (1995): 333–61.

———. "Popery, Trade and Universal Monarchy: The Ideological Context of the Outbreak of the Second Anglo-Dutch War." *English Historical Review* 107, no. 422 (1992): 1–29.

———. *1688: The First Modern Revolution*. New Haven: Yale University Press, 2009.

Pipkin, Amanda. "'They were not humans, but devils in human bodies': Depictions of Sexual Violence and Spanish Tyranny as a Means of Fostering Identity in the Dutch Republic." *Journal of Early Modern History* 13 (2009): 229–64.

Pix, Mary. *Ibrahim, The Thirteenth Emperour of the Turks: A Tragedy*. London, 1696.

Plumb, J. H. "The New World of Children in Eighteenth-Century England." *Past and Present* 67 (1995): 64–95.

Post, J. B. "Ravishment of Women and the Statutes of Westminster." In *Legal Records and the Historian: Papers Presented to the Cambridge Legal History Conference, 7–10 July 1975, and in Lincoln's Inn Old Hall on 3 July 1974*, edited by J. H. Baker, 150–60. London: Swift Printers, 1978.

Powell, George. *Alphonso King of Naples. A Tragedy*. London, 1691.

Powell, Philip Wayne. *Tree of Hate: Propaganda and Prejudices Affecting United States Relations with the Hispanic World*. Albuquerque: University of New Mexico Press, 1971.

Prior, Matthew. "Advice to the Painter." In *Poems on Affairs of State: Augustan Satirical Verse, 1660–1714*, edited by Galbraith M. Crump, 4:44–49. New Haven: Yale University Press, 1963.

Proffitt, Bessie. "Religious Symbolism in Otway's *Venice Preserv'd*." *Papers on Language and Literature* 7, no. 1 (1971): 26–37.

Raman, Shankar. *Framing "India": The Colonial Imaginary in Early Modern Culture*. Stanford: Stanford University Press, 2002.

Ravenscroft, Edward. *Titus Andronicus, or The Rape of Lavinia*. In *Shakespeare Adapatations from the Restoration*, edited by Barbara A. Murray, 1–88. Madison: Fairleigh Dickinson University Press, 2005.

Ray, Sid. "'Rape, I fear, was the root of thy annoy': The Politics of Consent in *Titus Andronicus*." *Shakespeare Quarterly* 49, no. 1 (1998): 22–39.

Read, James Morgan. "Atrocity Propaganda and the Irish Rebellion." *Public Opinion Quarterly* 2, no. 2 (1938): 229–44.

Riebling, Barbara. "England Deflowered and Unmanned: The Sexual Image of Politics in Marvell's 'Last Instructions.'" *Studies in English Literature 1500–1900* 35 (1995): 137–57.

Rist, Thomas. "Religion, Politics, Revenge: The Dead in Renaissance Drama." *Early Modern Literary Studies* 9, no. 1 (2003): 1–20.

———. *Revenge Tragedy and the Drama of Commemoration in Reforming England*. Burlington: Ashgate, 2008.

Rollins, John B. "Judeo-Christian Apocalyptic Literature and John Crowne's *The Destruction of Jerusalem*." *Comparative Drama* 35, no. 2 (2001): 209–24.

Rose, Craig. *England in the 1690s: Revolution, Religion and Wars*. Oxford: Blackwell, 1999.

Rowan, Herbert. "The Dutch Revolt: What Kind of Revolution?" *Renaissance Quarterly* 43, no. 3 (1990): 570–90.

Royal Commission on Historical Manuscripts. *9th Report*, *Part I*, Manuscripts of the West and North Ridings. London, 1883.

Royster, Francesca T. "White-Lined Walls: Whiteness and Gothic Extremism in Shakespeare's *Titus Andronicus*." *Shakespeare Quarterly* 51, no. 4 (2000): 432–55.

Rugge, Thomas. *The Diurnal of Thomas Rugg, 1659–1661*, edited by William L. Sachse. Camden Third Series, vol. 91, no. 90. London: Royal Historical Society, 1961.

Rustici, Craig M. "Gender, Disguise, and Usurpation: *The Female Prelate* and the Popish Successor." *Modern Philology* 98, no. 2 (2000): 271–98.

S., G. *A Briefe Declaration Of The Barbarous And inhumane dealings of the Northerne Irish Rebels, and many others in severall Counties up-rising against the English, that dwelt both lovingly and securely among them*. London, 1641.

Sadler, Anthony. *The Subjects Joy For The Kings Restoration, Cheerfully made known in A Sacred Masque*. London, 1660.

Salamon, Linda Bradley. "Gascoigne's Globe: *The Spoyle of Antwerp* and the Black Legend of Spain." *Early Modern Literary Studies* 14, no. 1, special issue 18 (2008): 7.1–38.

Sale, Carolyn. "Representing Lavinia: The (In)Significance of Women's Consent in Legal Discourse of Rape and Ravishment and Shakespeare's *Titus Andronicus*." In *Women, Violence, and English Renaissance Literature: Essays Honoring Paul Jorgensen*, edited by Linda Woodbridge and Sharon Beehler, 1–27. Tempe: Arizona Center for Medieval and Renaissance Studies, 2003.

Salmon, James. *Bloudy Newes from Ireland, Or The barbarous Crueltie By the Papists used in that Kingdome*. London, 1641.

Schochet, Gordon J. *Patriarchalism in Political Thought: The Authoritarian Family and Political Speculation and Attitudes Especially in Seventeenth-Century England*. New York: Basic, 1975.

———. "The Significant Sounds of Silence: The Absence of Women from the Political Thought of Sir Robert Filmer and John Locke (or, 'Why can't a woman be more like a man?')." In *Women Writers and the Early Modern British Political Tradition*, edited by Hilda L. Smith, 220–42. Cambridge: Cambridge University Press, 1998.

Schwoerer, Lois. "Images of Queen Mary II, 1689–95." *Renaissance Quarterly* 42, no. 4 (1989): 717–48.

———. "Propaganda in the Revolution of 1688–89." *American Historical Review* 82, no. 4 (1977): 843–74.

Scott, Jonathan. *Algernon Sidney and the English Republic, 1623–1677*. Cambridge: Cambridge University Press, 1988.

———. *Algernon Sidney and the Restoration Crisis, 1677–1683*. Cambridge: Cambridge University Press, 1991.

———. *England's Troubles: Seventeenth-Century English Political Instability in European Context*. Cambridge: Cambridge University Press, 2000.

Seaward, Paul. "The House of Commons Committee of Trade and the Origins of the Second Anglo-Dutch War, 1664." *Historical Journal* 30, no. 2 (1987): 437–52.

Seidel, Michael. *Satiric Inheritance: Rabelais to Sterne*. Princeton: Princeton University Press, 1979.

Selden, Raman. "Rochester and Shadwell." In *Spirit of Wit: Reconsiderations of Rochester*, edited by Jeremy Treglown, 177–90. Oxford: Basil Blackwell, 1982.

Seneca, Lucius Annaeus. *Thyestes*. Translated by Caryl Churchill. London: Nick Hern Books, 1995.

Sengupta, Shivaji. "Biographical Note on John Crowne." *Restoration* 6, no. 1 (1982): 26–30.

Settle, Elkanah. *Distress'd Innocence: Or, The Princess of Persia. A Tragedy*. London, 1691.

———. *The Empress of Morocco. A Tragedy*. London, 1687.

———. *The Female Prelate: Being The History of the Life and Death of Pope Joan. A Tragedy*. London, 1680.

———. *Love and Revenge: A Tragedy*. London, 1675.

Shadwell, Thomas. *The Libertine*. In *Four Restoration Libertine Plays*, edited by Deborah Payne Fisk, 1–85. Oxford: Oxford University Press, 2005.

Shagan, Ethan Howard. "Constructing Discord: Ideology, Propaganda, and English Responses to the Irish Rebellion of 1641." *The Journal of British Studies* 36, no. 1 (1997): 4–34.

Shakespeare, William. *The Norton Shakespeare*. Edited by Stephen Greenblatt et al. New York: Norton, 1997.

Shanley, Mary Lydon. "Marriage Contract and Social Contract in Seventeenth Century English Political Thought." *Western Political Quarterly* 32, no. 1 (1979): 79–91.

Shell, Allison, *Catholicism, Controversy and the English Literary Imagination, 1558–1660*. Cambridge: Cambridge University Press, 1999.

Shullenberger, William. "Girl Interrupted: Spenserian Bondage and Release in Milton's Ludlow Mask." *Milton Quarterly* 37, no. 4 (2003): 184–204.

Sidney, Algernon. *Discourses concerning Government*, edited by Thomas G. West. Indianapolis: Liberty Classics, 1990.

Skinner, John. *A True Relation Of The Unjust, Cruell, And Barbarous Proceedings against the English at Amboyna in the East-Indies, by the Neatherlandish Governour and Councel there*. Saint-Omer, 1624.

Smith, Molly Easo. "Spectacles of Torment in *Titus Andronicus*." *Studies in English Literature 1500–1900* 36 (1996): 315–31.

Smuts, Malcolm. "Religion, European Politics and Henrietta Maria's Circle, 1625–41." In *Henrietta Maria: Piety, Politics and Patronage*, edited by Erin Griffey, 13–38. Burlington: Ashgate, 2008.

Solomon, Harry M. "The Rhetoric of 'Redressing Grievances': Court Propaganda as the Hermeneutical Key to *Venice Preserv'd*." *ELH* 53, no. 2 (1986): 289–310.

Speck, Bill. "Religion's Role in the Glorious Revolution." *History Today* 38, no. 7 (1988): 30–35.

Spink, Ian. "Purcell's Music for 'The Libertine.'" *Music and Letters* 81, no. 4 (2000): 520–31.

Sprague, Arthur Colby. *Beaumont and Fletcher on the Restoration Stage*. Cambridge, MA: Harvard University Press, 1926.

Staves, Susan. *Players' Scepters: Fictions of Authority in the Restoration*. Lincoln: University of Nebraska Press, 1979.

Stephens, Edward. *Popish Policies and Practices Represented in the Histories of the Parisian Massacre; Gun-powder Treason; Conspiracies Against Queen Elizabeth And Persecutions Of The Protestants in France*. London, 1674.

Stewart, Ann Marie. "Rape, Patriarchy, and the Libertine Ethos: The Function of Sexual Violence in Aphra Behn's 'The Golden Age' and *The Rover, Part I*." *Restoration and Eighteenth-Century Theatre Research* 12, no. 2 (1997): 26–39.

Stocker, Margarita. *Apocalyptic Marvell: The Second Coming in Seventeenth Century Poetry*. Athens: Ohio University Press, 1986.

Stone, Lawrence. *The Family, Sex and Marriage in England 1500–1800*. New York: Harper & Row, 1979.

Straka, Gerald. "The Final Phase of Divine Right Theory in England, 1688–1702." *English Historical Review* 77, no. 305 (1962): 638–58.

Stroub, Thomas B. "Shadwell's Use of Hobbes." *Studies in Philology* 35, no. 3 (1938): 405–32.

Suckling, Sir John. "Out upon It!" In *The Norton Anthology of English Literature*, 8th ed., edited by Stephen Greenblatt et al., 1:1681. New York: Norton, 2006.

Szechi, Daniel. *The Jacobites: Britain and Europe, 1688–1788*. Manchester: Manchester University Press, 1994.

Taylor, John. *The Noble Cavalier Caracterised, And A Rebellious Caviller Cauterised*. Oxford, 1643.

Thomas, Catherine. "Chaste Bodies and Poisonous Desire in Milton's Mask." *Studies in English Literature 1500–1900* 46, no. 2 (2008): 435–59.

Thompson, Ayanna. *Performing Race and Torture on the Early Modern Stage*. New York: Routledge, 2008.

Timmons, Stephen A. "Executions Following Monmouth's Rebellion: A Missing Link." *Historical Research* 76, no. 192 (2003): 286–91.

Todd, Janet. *The Sign of Angellica: Women, Writing and Fiction, 1660–1800*. New York: Columbia University Press, 1989.

Tomlinson, Tracey E. "The Restoration English History Plays of Roger Boyle, Earl of Orrery." *Studies in English Literature 1500–1900* 43, no. 3 (2003): 559–77.

Tonge, Ezerel. *Jesuitical Aphorismes; Or, A Summary Account Of The Doctrine Of The Jesuites, And some other Popish Doctors*. London, 1679.

Trevor-Roper, Hugh. *Counter-Reformation to Glorious Revolution*. Chicago: University of Chicago Press, 1992.

Tricomi, Albert H. "The Aesthetics of Mutilation in *Titus Andronicus*." In *Shakespeare and Language*, edited by Catherine M. S. Alexander, 226–39. Cambridge: Cambridge University Press, 2004.

A true Son of the Catholick Apostolick Church. *A Catholick Pill To Purge Popery*. London: 1677.

Tumbleson, Raymond D. *Catholicism in the English Protestant Imagination: Nationalism, Religion, and Literature*. Cambridge: Cambridge University Press, 1998.

Turner, James Grantham. "The Libertine Abject: The 'Postures' of *Last Instructions to a Painter*." In *Marvell and Liberty*, edited by Warren Chernaik and Martin Dzelzainis, 217–48. New York: St. Martin's, 1999.

———. *Libertines and Radicals in Early Modern London: Sexuality, Politics, and Literary Culture, 1630–1685*. Cambridge: Cambridge University Press, 2002.

Turner, Robert Y. "Responses to Tyranny in John Fletcher's Plays." *Medieval and Renaissance Drama in England* 4 (1989): 123–41.

Tyrrell, James. *A Brief Disquisition Of The Law of Nature, According to the Principles and Method laid down in the Reverend Dr. Cumberland's (now Lord Bishop of Peterboroughs) Latin Treatise on that Subject*. London, 1692.

———. *Patriarcha non Monarcha. The Patriarch Unmonarch'd*. London, 1681.

Underwood, Dale. *Etherege and the Seventeenth-Century Comedy of Manners*. New Haven: Yale University Press, 1957.

Ussher, James. *Bishop Ushers Second Prophesie Which He delivered to his Daughter on his Sick-Bed*. London, 1681.

Van der Kiste, John. *William and Mary*. Gloucestershire: Sutton, 2003.

Van Lennep, William, ed. *The London Stage, 1660–1800*. 5 vols. Carbondale: Southern Illinois University Press, 1960.

Van Stipriaan, René. "Words at War: The Early Years of William of Orange's Propaganda." *Journal of Early Modern History* 11, no. 4/5 (2007): 331–49.

Vaughan, Virginia Mason. "The Construction of Barbarism in *Titus Andronicus*." In *Race, Ethnicity, and Power in the Renaissance*, edited by Joyce Green MacDonald, 165–80. London: Associated University Press, 1997.

Veevers, Erica. *Images of Love and Religion: Queen Henrietta Maria and Court Entertainments*. Cambridge: Cambridge University Press, 1989.

Verdurmen, J. Peter. "*Lucius Junius Brutus* and Restoration Tragedy: The Politics of Trauma." *Journal of European Studies* 37, no. 2 (1995): 81–98.

Virgil. *The Aeneid*. Edited by H. E. Gould and J. L. Whiteley. London: Duckworth, 2007.

Walker, George. *The Protestant's Crums of Comfort*. London, 1697.

Waller, Edmund. *Upon Her Majesties new buildings at Somerset-House*. London, 1665.

Warner, J. Christopher. "The Question of Misogynistic Polemic in Elkanah Settle's *The Female Prelate* (1680 and 1689)." *Restoration* 25, no. 1 (2001): 19–34.

Warren, William. *Strange, true, and lamentable Newes from Exceter, And other parts of the Western countreyes shewing how cruelly the resolute Cavaliers have dealt with the inhabitants since the departure of that Right Noble Commander the Earl of Stamford*. London, 1643.

Warwicke, Robert, Earl of. *A Most Worthy Speech, Spoken by the Right Honourable Robert Earle of Warwicke*. London, 1642.

Watson, J. N. P. *Captain-General and Rebel Chief: The Life of James, Duke of Monmouth*. Boston: Allen & Unwin, 1979.

Weber, Harold. *Paper Bullets: Print and Kingship under Charles II*. Lexington: University Press of Kentucky, 1996.

Webster, Jeremy W. *Performing Libertinism in Charles II's Court: Politics, Drama, Sexuality*. New York: Palgrave Macmillan, 2005.

Weil, Rachel. "The Family in the Exclusion Crisis: Locke versus Filmer Revisited." In *A Nation Transformed: England after the Restoration*, edited by Alan Houston and Steve Pincus, 100–124. Cambridge: Cambridge University Press, 2001.

———. *Political Passions: Gender, the Family and Political Argument in England 1680–1714*. Manchester: Manchester University Press, 1999.

Wheatley, Christopher J. *Without God or Reason: The Plays of Thomas Shadwell and Secular Ethics in the Restoration*. Lewisburg: Bucknell University Press, 1993.

Whetcombe, Tristram. *The Rebels Turkish Tyranny in their march Decem. 24, 1641*. London, 1641.

White, Arthur Franklin. "John Crowne and America." *PMLA* 35, no. 4 (1920): 447–63.

———. *John Crowne: His Life and Dramatic Works*. Cleveland: Western Reserve University Press, 1922.

White, Michelle Anne. *Henrietta Maria and the English Civil Wars*. Burlington: Ashgate, 2006.

Wiener, Carol S. "The Beleaguered Isle: A Study of Early Jacobean Anti-Catholicism." *Past and Present* 51 (1971): 27–62.

Wilkinson, Robert. *The Stripping of Ioseph, Or The crueltie of Bretheren to a Brother*. London, 1625.

Willbern, David. "Rape and Revenge in *Titus Andronicus*." *English Literary Renaissance* 8, no. 2 (1978): 159–82.

Wilmot, John, Earl of Rochester. *Lucina's Rape Or The Tragedy of Valentinian*. In *The Works of John Wilmot, Earl of Rochester*, edited by Harold Love, 133–231. Oxford: Oxford University Press, 1999.

———. "A Satyr on Charles II." In *Restoration Literature: An Anthology*, edited by Paul Hammond, 38–39. Oxford: Oxford University Press, 2002.

———. "To her Sacred Majesty." In *Epicedia Academiae Oxoniensis, in Obitum Serenissimae Mariae Principis Arausionensis*. Oxford, 1660.

Wilson, J. Harold. "Rochester's *Valentinian* and Heroic Sentiment." *ELH* 4, no. 4 (1937): 265–73.

———. "Satiric Elements in Rochester's *Valentinian*." *Philological Quarterly* 16 (1937): 41–48.

Wilson, Timothy. *A Seasonable Question, In A Sermon on Joshua 5.13*. London, 1690.

Winn, James. *"When Beauty Fires the Blood": Love and the Arts in the Age of Dryden*. Ann Arbor: University of Michigan Press, 1992.

Wood, Clement. *The Woman Who Was Pope: A Biography of Pope Joan, 853–855 A.D.* New York: William Faro, 1931.

Wright, John. *Mock-Thyestes*. In *Thyestes A Tragedy, Translated out of Seneca. To which is Added Mock-Thyestes, in Burlesque*. London, 1674.

Wycherley, William. *The Plain Dealer*, edited by Leo Hughes. Lincoln: University of Nebraska Press, 1967.

Wynne, Sonya. "The Mistresses of Charles II and Restoration Court Politics." In *The Stuart Courts*, edited by Eveline Cruickshanks, 171–90. Gloucestershire: Sutton, 2000.

Wynne-Davies, Marion. "'The Swallowing Womb': Consumed and Consuming Women in *Titus Andronicus*." In *The Matter of Difference: Materialist Feminist Criticism of Shakespeare*, edited by Valerie Wayne, 129–51. Ithaca: Cornell University Press, 1991.

Yalden, Thomas. *On The Conquest Of Namur, A Pindarique Ode, Humbly Inscrib'd To His Most Sacred and Victorious Majesty*. London, 1695.

Zimbardo, Rose. *A Mirror to Nature: Transformations in Drama and Aesthetics, 1660–1732*. Lexington: University Press of Kentucky, 1986.

Zook, Melinda. "Contextualizing Aphra Behn: Plays, Politics, and Party, 1679–1689." In *Women Writers and the Early Modern British Political Tradition*, edited by Hilda Smith, 75–93. Cambridge: Cambridge University Press, 1998.

Zwicker, Steven N. "Lines of Authority: Politics and Literary Culture in the Restoration." In *Politics of Discourse: The Literature and History of Seventeenth-Century England*, edited by Kevin Sharpe and Steven N. Zwicker, 230–70. Berkeley: University of California Press, 1987.

———. "Virgins and Whores: The Politics of Sexual Misconduct in the 1660s." In *The Political Identity of Andrew Marvell,* edited by Conal Condren and A. D. Cousins, 85–110. Brookfield, VT: Scolar Press, 1990.

Index

About the Author

Jennifer L. Airey graduated summa cum laude from Brandeis University with a degree in English and American literature and subsequently earned her PhD from Boston University. She is currently assistant professor of English at the University of Tulsa, where she specializes in Restoration and eighteenth-century British drama. She has previously published articles on Wycherley and Dryden, and her article on the 1768 rape trial of Frederick Calvert, Lord Baltimore is forthcoming. Her scholarly interests include long eighteenth-century treatments of gender and sexuality, playhouse performance practice, and the relationship between British politics and the stage.

0 1341 1464567 1

To all those survivors who grew up with abuses—whether physical, mental, or sexual—and found the strength to overcome them in making themselves a better person.

AUTHOR'S NOTE

This novel is the revised edition of the original 2021 publication. It is a more in-depth, controversial tale of Rachael Anderson, who endured financial, social, and economic hardships while producing a large family. It tells how the family coped with the daily struggles and abuses that weathered most families. This story is considered a historical fiction. Names, characters, and incidences are based on the actual life of the author and are products of the author's imagination and are not to be construed as real. Any resemblance to actual events, locales, organizations, or persons, living or dead, is purely coincidental.

CONTENTS

FROM THE BEGINNING

The summer of 1952 beamed across the vast playground that lay alongside South Street. There were days Rachael escorted her two toddlers across the street, venturing into the neighborhood's amusement park. A chain-link fence encompassed the play world of metal swings, monkey bars, a seesaw, and a huge metal slide. From a year and a half's perspective, it touched the heavens. Nathan was too young climbing to the top. He crawled up halfway from the get-off point, made a turnaround, then slid down to where he began. Rachael stood watching her youngsters' enjoyment going from one amusement to another, finally settling on the swings to end the day.

Beth was a year older than her brother, having being born in Quincy, Illinois, in November 1949 to Clarence L. and Rachael M. Anderson. Rachael continued giving the slight pushes to the swings as her small ones giggled on their forward incline. Rachael watched their enjoyment while reminiscing of their earlier days.

Rachael remembered how Beth was shown as the darling child throughout the basin of Peoria, Illinois, where the Anderson clan lived. Clarence and Rachael had made their home in Kansas City, Missouri, and drove the many miles throughout the Illinois cornfields visiting Clarence's family in the farmlands of Macomb. In Rachael's mind, it didn't compare to the colonial settings of the Plymouth coast.

Rachael's family originated in Plymouth, Massachusetts, and was born to parents who could easily pass as her grandparents. Her mother, Sarah, was middle aged while her father, Milton, was on the threshold of his golden years. Rachael was born in Plymouth during May of 1929 and the only child to Milton and Sarah Manter, a period when the nation was facing its worst depression in history.

The depression hit everyone the hardest, with many losing their jobs and experiencing hard times. Hard times was no stranger to those living in the Manomet-Plymouth region. It was a couple of years after Rachael's birth that Milton developed severe arthritis in both legs, relying mostly on a cane to get about.

The Manters had little possessions, and their meager income wasn't enough to sustain a livelihood. They found refuge living with Milton's sister, Ethel Sampson, and her family on Manomet's Brook Road. Sarah was the main caretaker, utilizing her nursing skills in caring for the community.

Sarah was born not far from the Sampson homestead. Joshua and Martha Nickerson lived near the Manomet shores when they gave birth to Sarah in June of 1892. She was the second of three girls and a boy. The Nickersons' colonial-style home had limited accessories. It consisted of a hand pump at the kitchen sink, pulling water from the submersible well. They heated water on the stove and utilized an outhouse for relieving themselves. Bathing was primarily done by taking sponge baths since the house wasn't built with what was considered modern-day plumbing.

Milton was a generous man with an easygoing personality. He was mainly responsible for Rachael's upbringing during her formative years, allowing his daughter to do whatever she wanted for her own amusement. Sarah was the disciplinarian, making Rachael behave to her every word. Sarah believed in a quick switch of a stick, supporting her theory of not spoiling the child.

As Rachael was an only child, her neighborhood peers often posed as her surrogate siblings. She had a close relationship with one girl, Karen Adams, who lived several roads over. Both were similar yet different in nature. Karen was adventurous, wanting more out of life. She had dreams of leaving the Manomet farmlands and establishing a career in a big city. Rachael also had thoughts of experiencing life beyond her rural domain. She was flighty and flirtatious and wanted an exciting lifestyle. It was Rachael's peers that tried taming her social ethics during her elementary and adolescent years.

After graduation, Karen was invited to visit an aunt in Kansas City, Missouri. She thought this might be her ticket to the outside world. Karen told her best friend about the upcoming trip, sparking Rachael's interest in tagging along. There wasn't much of a career opportunity in the Manomet, Plymouth community. A girl usually married the first guy that came along that made her smile and produced a family. Rachael was ambitious and made it known to her parents she wanted to accompany Karen to Missouri. Sarah and Milton were reluctant but realized their daughter wasn't close to settling down and agreed to let Rachael travel to Kansas City for a short period. The permission hadn't left Sarah's mouth when Rachael was already packed.

She and Karen took the train from Plymouth to Boston, then transferred over for the train ride westward. It took a couple of days stopping at every major city along the plains. The train arrived in Kansas City, where Sonya Ethridge stood waiting at the station. She hugged her niece and welcomed Rachael to the city while driving the weary travelers to the Ethridge Victorian home. It was a massive house with large rooms that seemed to echo the inhabitants of past generations.

The days passed, and Sonya figured the girls had enough time to get settled and for them to start looking for a job. After all, it was the main reason for Karen's trip. Rachael was ready to explore her new surroundings. Sonya thought Rachael would be better off having something to do even if it was only temporary, keeping her out of mischief.

Both sat at the breakfast table sharing an occasional chuckle as they looked through the want ads of the local newspaper. Karen's outlook was more administrative while Rachael's was in waitressing or housekeeping.

The girls made several calls that followed with revealing interviews. Karen landed a secretarial position with Kansas City's Caterpillar Tractor Company. Days later, Rachael found a part-time job waitressing at a nearby diner. The jobs were just what the girls wanted and needed. It gave them the opportunity to meet and associate with people unlike those that lived on Manomet's Brook Road.

Many of Caterpillar's employees solicited the diner. Rachael worked during the lunch period, enjoying the banter and laughter of many of the blue-collar workers. Among those was a man named Clarence Anderson.

Clarence was a slender six footer with blue eyes and wavy brown hair. He was employed as an assembly line mechanic and a regular at the small diner. He caught the eye of Rachael Manter. He noticed her outgoing nature and her broad smile highlighting her oval face framed by her shoulder-length brown hair. Rachael's pleasant and flirtatious persona, coupled with her slender high-school looks, took every snide remark in stride. Waitressing suited her.

It wasn't long before Clarence would seat himself in Rachael's waitressing area. Their conversations became more personal with every cup of coffee. All Rachael could talk about with Karen was Clarence.

Sonya learned about Rachael's love interest and tried making her realize this was her first love and shouldn't take it seriously. She cautioned the young lady that there would be other loves in her life once returning to the East Coast in the fall.

Rachael, like Karen, couldn't see herself going back to the farm life in Manomet. She found herself a man and decided to pursue him. She started dating Clarence, wanting to know everything about him. She learned he was from Macomb, born in March of 1927, and the only son of three children born to Jesse and Hannah Anderson. Clarence had joined the naval reserves upon graduating high school and served two years of active duty during the end of World War II. He was accepted at a local college before being hired by Caterpillar Tractor. The pay was good and made his life in Kansas City.

By fall, the correspondence between Rachael and her parents went back and forth. It was time for Rachael to return home now that she had a taste of the outside world. Rachael wouldn't have any part of it. She was getting accustomed to the enjoyment of city life.

Rachael laid the foundation of her desires by announcing her marriage to Clarence. They set the date for Christmas Eve. Clarence was settled, yet his family was founded in Macomb on never-ending miles of cornfields and soybeans.

Sarah and Milton realized they no longer had any restraint over their daughter as they read the invitation of her upcoming wedding.

Sarah decided to call. "Hello, Rachael? How are you doing, dear?"

"I'm fine, Mom," came the response.

"I got your wedding announcement. Are you really serious about this wedding?" asked Sarah.

"Mom, of course I am. I love Clarence. He's everything I ever wanted. He's intelligent, caring, and is really down to earth. Besides, he has a good job and wants a family just as much as I do," replied Rachael enthusiastically.

"Rachael, you're young. You have your whole life ahead of you," Sarah said with a discouraging tone.

"Mom, this is what I want. Are you and Dad coming out?" asked the excited daughter.

"I'm planning on it. Is it all right if I stay where you are? Is there room?" asked Sarah.

"There's plenty for the both of you. When are you planning on traveling?" asked Rachael.

"It's just me, dear. Your father won't be making the trip because of his legs. I'm planning on taking the train out on the twenty-third. I don't want to leave your father alone too long. Is that all right with you?"

There was a slight pause before Rachael answered. "Sure, Mom, I'll arrange your visit on this end. Give my love to Dad."

"Okay, Rachael, I'll drop you a line before then. Take care of yourself, and hope to see you on the twenty-third," ended Sarah.

Rachael met her mother at the train station, giving her a hug and a kiss on her cheek. She was overwhelmed just seeing her mother at her side. Both seated themselves inside the car for the ride to Sonya's.

Sarah looked at her daughter smiling. "You're looking well, and I'm pleased you're able to take care of yourself. How's Karen doing?"

"She's doing okay and loves what she's doing," replied Rachael.

"How's your job holding up?" asked Sarah, making small talk.

"It's okay. I love meeting and talking to the different people that go there. How's Dad?" asked Rachael, changing the subject.

Sarah looked at her daughter. "He's holding his own. He misses you and is heartbroken that he couldn't make the trip to walk you down the aisle." Sarah continued, "Rachael, I know we've talked about this, but are you sure this is what you want? You're young. You have your whole life ahead of you. Why don't you put this whole thing aside and come back home with me? It'll give you time to think."

Rachael paused, then looked into her mother's eyes. "I want a new life. Manomet isn't for me. I like it here. There's so much to do and see. I love you, Mom, but I love Clarence too, and I want to raise a family."

Sarah tried unconvincingly to sway her daughter. The least she could do was help her with any last-minute arrangements for the wedding. Rachael was married at the Trinity Methodist Church in the evening of December 24, 1948. It was a small celebration, with only the immediate family attending.

Sarah rode the long train ride home staring out the window, thinking about her daughter's wedding. Sarah's eyes welled, recapturing the moment when the elder Mr. Anderson walked her daughter down the aisle, depriving Milton of being the proud father. The train continued while the disheartened mother looked out watching the landscape swiftly pass by.

Milton waited patiently for his wife's return. He wanted to know firsthand about his daughter's wedding. He rubbed his legs, cursing the chronic arthritis that gripped his muscles and prevented him from performing one of his proudest moments. Milton was the second of five children born to Caleb and Harriet Manter in Plymouth during October 1879. Like many of his generation, he graduated with an eighth-grade education with a background of farming.

The newlyweds stayed in Kansas City, often driving the occasional trip through the cornfield territory and arriving at the hidden hamlet of Macomb. Rachael got to know the Andersons with every visit. Clarence loved his town even though it wasn't for him. They stayed at the Andersons' farmhouse. From her bedroom, Rachael could see the miles of cornfields. Only a sprinkle of farmhouses and silos could be seen. The trees seemed to be corralled into the horizon. Rachael could only take so much of the rural countryside. It reminded her of the dirt roads she left behind less than a year earlier.

November of 1949, Clarence and Rachael gave birth to their first child, Elizabeth May Anderson. She was Rachael's pride and joy. Rachael had a family she could call her own. She could see her life getting more entangled with Clarence's hometown as time went on.

The Korean conflict headlined the nation's newspapers, and it was known that Clarence would be recalled to active duty. Rachael realized Clarence's departure, and there would be arrangements for her to stay at the Andersons among the acres of cornfields.

Rachael decided she needed to return to her native New England if she was to survive her husband's absence. Rachael convinced Clarence of a better life back in Plymouth. That spring, the young Anderson family packed what belongings they had and moved to the colonial shores with Rachael pregnant with her second child.

PLYMOUTH, MASSACHUSETTS

William and Flora Atwood looked forward to the arrival of their niece and her husband. The Atwoods had their home on South Street and made room for Rachael and her family. They owned a two-story house across from the large fenced-in playground that paralleled South Street. Flora was Sarah Manter's older sister. She married William Atwood the same year as her sister. William was a carpenter by trade and helped construct many of Plymouth's administrative buildings. Flora was a social butterfly and active in the community social circles.

The Atwoods loved traveling throughout the country, giving them no time for raising children. They earned enough money to buy a plot of land at Ellis Pond situated on Plymouth's outer edge. William built himself a small cottage as a retreat from Plymouth's flourishing environment.

A few doors down on South Street was the perfect home for sale. It was ideal for what Rachael and Clarence needed with a second child on the way. It was through the navy's programs that the young Andersons could purchase the place. They no sooner moved in when Clarence received orders to report to active duty, taking his place in the Korean conflict.

By the end of fall, Clarence was serving as a radioman second class on board an LST off the South Korean coast while Rachael was left pregnant with a newborn in her arms. Clarence provided his wife custody of the Ford car, giving her some independence. It wasn't enough. She approached her parents and convinced them to move in with her on South Street.

It was during the Christmas holiday when Nathan was born. Rachael's family dynamics was complete. She had a daughter and now a son. Rachael was glad having her mother around helping with the newborn. Her father was the ideal babysitter while both women left to do the shopping. It was the first of the year when Clarence was able to take time in returning home to see his newborn son.

He sent most of his money home for Rachael to pay the bills. She received additional help from her parents' Social Security checks. The Manters got her through the winter, and with spring on the horizon, Sarah felt it was time for her and Milton to find a place for themselves.

Sarah heard rumors of a family looking to care for their old matriarch and her estate. The Harold family lived on the north end of Plymouth in a two-story estate. The house was surrounded by five acres of flourishing lawns and flower gardens. Sarah knew the family and the matriarch, wasting no time answering the request. By summer, she and Milton had a few rooms they could call their own.

The Manters were given the ground floor of the estate. In return, they would care for the elder—cooking her meals, cleaning her second-floor living quarters, and taking care of the limited outdoor maintenance. A landscaper was hired to mow the lawns and keep the snakelike driveway clear during the winter months. If Sarah needed time for herself, she only needed to notify the family days in advance.

Rachael felt nervous driving her two toddlers while they sat in the back of the Ford. She preferred walking the mile and a half downtown. She prepared the baby carriage for the neighborhood stroll. The carriage was made of rugged steel, possessing an overpowering red leather hood with an extended metal scoop pan. It was perfect for placing those basic toiletries that comforted every infant. It was big enough to fit both children and the accessories for a casual walk along the shore.

Plymouth was a small colonial town established during the 1620s by Pilgrims belonging to the English Separatist Church at Leyden, Holland. They were sponsored and financed by the Merchant

Adventurers of London in colonizing themselves in English North America.

Its historic possessions attracted new occupants as the years passed. Its coastal shores invited a multitude of visiting motorboats, including fishing vessels that moored at the town's extended pier. The large pier jettisoned a short distance from the ornate large portico encasing the Plymouth Rock. The rock had been moved decades earlier when the rock's tourism increased. It had interfered with the fishing depot and novice fishermen hoping for a fresh supper's catch.

Accompanying the rock's portico stood two replicas of Pilgrim homes complete with thatched roofs. Alongside stood a replica of the fortress that protected the Pilgrims against the elements. Plymouth's coastal vista viewed miles of ocean water dotted with seasonal boats and nearby islands. Across the street stood Cole's Hill displaying historic statues and the large marble crypt that entombed the ancient bones of the original Pilgrims.

Rachael wheeled her carriage down South Street, turning on Sandwich and continuing along the waterfront. On one side were a couple of small independent parks with benches for the coastline sightseers. The sidewalk followed the curvature of the natural coast, passing Cole's Hill and the various Pilgrim monuments. A couple of white open-windowed trailers were strategically parked selling Pilgrim souvenirs, banners, postcards, and bottled soft drinks for the occasional tourist.

Rachael loved the waterfront. She grew up with the ocean bordering the town of Manomet. It provided a calmness to her soul. After spending a few hours among fellow wanderers, she wheeled the carriage back to her home. The walk did the threesome good. The salt air prepared them for a midafternoon nap.

Rachael managed the South Street dwelling with help from her mother and aunt. She loaded her two into the car for a day trip, driving along Manomet's Brook Road, where the remnants of Rachael's childhood and the Sampson homestead still remained.

She stopped at Clifton and Esther Michaels to say hello and get a glass of cold water for her younger two. The Michaelses were close friends of Sarah and Milton and played the part as Rachael's adopted aunt and uncle. Esther was a strong, forthright tall woman who projected herself monotonously. Clifton was the ideal retiree. His average height reflected a bald head and displayed the investment of many years of good eating. His presence was inviting, often emitting the aroma of cigar smoke. It was one of his enjoyable vices. An hour passed when Rachael loaded her toddlers and continued the drive on Brook Road, stopping at Aunt Ethel's for lunch.

Ethel Sampson lived on Brook Road all her life. She was Milton's younger sister and was born in the1890s. She was a small thin lady whose pleasantness radiated through her thin smile. She wore a simple dress and sported glasses that seemed to magnify her blue eyes. They served to highlight her gentle features. Ethel and her husband, Joseph lived alone now that their children had grown and were living on their own. Their homestead had been well preserved although its exterior was heavily weathered. The inside aired a distinct musty scent that reminisced throughout. The coolness of the nearby brook contributed to the mild dampness that embraced the house.

Ethel was finishing putting lunch together when Rachael arrived with her two kids. Milton's brother, Octavius, sat on the porch whittling away on a piece of tree limb. He had a slender build, and his weathered face sported a sun-bleached beard. Octavius involved himself in nautical enterprises and was a prominent figure in the operations of the area lighthouses. He was glad seeing his niece and her children. He accompanied them inside, where Ethel was already setting the table for eight. Rachael was curious who else was coming. Ethel invited Molly Baker and Katie Freeman. They were old family friends who hadn't seen Rachael in years. The luncheon brought back memories of days long passed.

Other days, the trips took Rachael driving to Ellis Pond visiting Uncle William and Aunt Flora. They owned a sheepdog named Teddy, after Teddy Roosevelt. William built the comfortable three-room cottage as a place to relax on those hot summer days. He constructed an outdoor charcoal pit made of cultivated stones, a picnic table, and a hammock that suited them. They often invited the surrounding socialites to stop by for a cool one and a dip in the pond. The Atwoods raised both white and gray rabbits. It was their hobby although they wouldn't say what happened to them after the summer season when the rabbit cages were emptied.

Rachael loved beaches, and Plymouth had its popular White Horse Beach. She remembered her earlier years when her parents spent a number of days basking in the sun. Rachael thought of all those seashells she gathered along its coastal shore. It was a warm summer day when Rachael gathered her children to spend a few hours enjoying the Atlantic shore. Rachael laid the large army blanket cornered with her shoes and stones preventing the ocean winds from blowing the blanket about. The salt air could be smelled as the ocean rolled its thrusting waves along the shore.

Rachael watched Nathan confront the oncoming waves. They were immense and continuously pounding the pristine white beach. Beth seemed brave enough to challenge the white suds rolling up along the beach shore. Nathan sat contently not far from his mother with a pail and shovel, making creative sand piles. Beth had to be watched constantly, having a tendency to wander off exploring. Today it was small oblong seashells that caught her interests.

It wasn't often Rachael made long, distant drives. When the moment arose, she made the long drive visiting Charles and Marie Baily. Marie was Sarah's younger sister, who married a businessman and produced a large family. Marie made no bones that her brood didn't provide her a moment's rest.

Rachael had a close relationship with her cousin Constance. She was the one Rachael grew up with over the phone. After Sarah finished talking with Marie, she'd let Rachael talk to Constance, sharing their innermost secrets of adventures and misgivings. Rachael's relationship with her cousin abruptly ended when Constance developed cancer that took her life. Her death devastated Rachael, leaving a void in her soul.

Mornings on South Street were no different from the daily occurrence of any other neighborhood. Folks went to work. Children were picked up by yellow school buses, echoing their loud vocals from within. Mothers cared for their young and tended to the housework. Some encountered the dairy truck delivering bottled milk, packages of butter, and tubs of cottage cheese. South Street had one of those delivery trucks driven by a slender crew-cut man named Tracy Booker.

Tracy lived a couple of streets over from South Street with his wife, Gloria, and two young sons. He made his rounds, stopping at the Anderson house delivering a couple of quarts of milk. Rachael met him at the doorway, getting the two glass bottles from his metal carryall. She spent time chatting away about her daily events. With Clarence gone, Rachael looked at Tracy as a neighborhood friend and a substitute for male companionship.

The fall of 1952 arrived. Rachael led her two into the playground running and jumping through the piles of leaves, creating mounds of laughter amongst the three of them. Beth was enrolled in nursery school at the Downy's converted storage building on the other side of town. Nathan made use of his well-discovered legs, making his mother chase him about the house. There were the short walks to Flora's house for morning coffee. She was prepared for Rachael's visit. She had a child's jigsaw puzzle comprising of a dozen large pieces. It amused Nathan putting it together as he chewed on one end while contemplating another.

Flora witnessed Rachael and the milkman sharing smiles and an occasional laugh while standing on the open bay porch.

Flora asked, "Who's the milkman you're talking to these mornings?"

Rachael responded, "Nobody. He's just the delivery guy saying hello."

Flora smirked. "Looks more than just a delivery guy. Looks like someone saying more than just hello."

"Come on, Aunt Flora. Don't make more of it than what it is," replied Rachael.

"Well, don't get yourself into something you can't handle. I've seen what can develop when you're not watching, and people are watching," Flora said sternly.

Afterward Rachael walked over to the playground with Nathan in hand. She sat thinking over her conversation with Aunt Flora while Nathan hobbled about on the beaten grass.

RENDEZVOUS

Rachael got her kids up and dressed for breakfast. Beth stood by the door waiting for George Downy, who drove her to nursery school. Nathan sat on the living room floor concentrating on his toy cars. Rachael kept an eye out the front window for the milk truck. She enjoyed meeting Tracy and their morning conversations.

On a particular morning, Rachael called Flora to see if she could watch Nathan while she went shopping. Her aunt always found time for her grandnephew. Rachael got Nathan dressed and hurriedly walked over to Flora's to drop him off. Rachael made her excuses and made it home in time before the delivery truck arrived. The milk truck made the brief stop, allowing Rachael to indiscreetly climb inside as it made the route down the side streets.

Flora watched the intervention from her living room window with the towhead at her side. The delivery truck returned in time, allowing Rachael to meet Beth from her day at preschool. When William was able, Flora had him follow the truck on its secret rendezvous, often making its way toward White Horse Beach. Those frequent occasions were temporarily halted when Clarence returned home for a week's leave.

Rachael began hearing the silent whispers about her among the neighbors. She tried reflecting them by having her parents over during the holidays. It coincided with the Harold family taking their matriarch home to enjoy the family get-together.

The new year came with the blistering winds off the Atlantic Coast. It fingered snowdrifts throughout Plymouth's network of streets. It seemed 1953 was off to a harrowing start. Rachael clung close to her children as they watched the snowflakes chaotically fall outside their living room window. It wasn't Rachael's main worry. She realized she had become pregnant, a pregnancy that shouldn't have happened.

Rachael thought long and hard about her present state, knowing she couldn't carry it to term. She had to find ways to lose what was growing inside her. She worked hard overexerting herself and pounded her stomach almost daily, hoping to release the attachment. She had to talk to someone and decided to find comfort in Flora.

After seeing Beth off to nursery school, Rachael embodied Nathan in winter clothes, making the short walk to Flora's. Her remarks weren't easy to swallow even when Rachael prepared herself for the degrading speech of "I told you so." It was afterward that Rachael wanted words of comfort on what to do next, but they never came. Flora could only make Rachael face the reality she had crossed the line of her idyllic navy life.

Rachael decided to consult her family doctor for prenatal care, then practiced the opposite in abusing herself. Despite her situation, Rachael continued meeting Tracy after making his deliveries. It meant rotating babysitters to watch Beth and Nathan.

Tracy worked on the dairy farm after his deliveries. He cleaned the manure troughs, then climbed into the hay lofts to feed the milking herd standing side by side in their stanchions. Rachael went with him a few times, purposely exerting herself to exhaustion.

It was late when Rachael collected her youngsters and nestled them into their beds. She decided to take a shower and climbed into the soft blankets for a night's sleep. The next morning, she awoke feeling stomach cramps. She hurried getting Beth dressed and fed before George Downy arrived. She called Flora to see if she had a few moments.

Rachael felt relieved that she showered the night before. It took Nathan a little while longer getting into his snowsuit and boots for the short walk to her aunt's house. Flora had the coffee pot brewing when Rachael arrived with her rosy-cheeked son. She saw that Rachael wasn't feeling right. Her stomach pains started to sharpen in the lower extremities. Suddenly she raced to the bathroom with Flora following, keeping a steady eye on Nathan. Within an hour, Rachael had lost the developing guilt within her. Flora called an ambulance, taking her niece to the hospital for her own protection.

Rachael spent the night at the hospital, ensuring there wasn't any complications. Flora managed to watch over her grandniece and grandnephew. William drove to the hospital, picking Rachael up and returning her home. During the ride, Rachael realized the seriousness of her ordeal and glad she kept her involvement with Tracy from her parents. She had to remain careful as Clarence was scheduled to be released from active duty in the upcoming fall.

Rachael knew the silent whispers were still channeling around South Street and needed to bring her friendship with Tracy out into the open. She convinced him to invite his wife in accompanying her to do some weekend shopping. Rachael thought just the sight of them would quell some of the rumors. She wanted the appearance that the Andersons and the Bookers were mutual friends.

It was late spring when Rachael pushed her carriage on the well-traveled sidewalk with the weathered cracks and growing moss along the divided seems. Nathan rode inside, preventing any time delay. Beth was able to keep up with her mother's pace. Rachael waited at the street corner, watching Gloria walk down the adjacent street. She looked like the typical housewife. Gloria was small framed, with her dark-brown hair weighing on her shoulders. A pair of semi-wing-tip eyeglasses highlighted her olive face accented with a determined look. Her everyday housedress was bookcased by her two spirited young boys. She held each of them by her hands, controlling their every move.

Rachael smiled. "Morning, Gloria. I hope I didn't interrupt your day. You see, I've only recently moved back to Plymouth, and I don't know too many people. Your husband has been kind enough to help me get to know the neighborhood and suggested I get to know you. I thought maybe a shopping trip might help. I hope you don't mind. What smart-looking boys you have."

Gloria gave a slight grin. "Morning, Mrs. Anderson. I have to admit I was a bit taken. Then again, I know what it's like being new to a neighborhood. I'm glad to meet you and your two children.

Maybe we can be friends. If you want, I know some stores that have a few good deals."

"Call me Rachael, please," said Rachael. "These are my two, Beth and Nathan. Beth just started nursery school. I really appreciate you doing this for me. It means a lot."

"Don't mention it. These two are Donald and Robert. They're my knights in shining armor," said Gloria, adding some levity to the situation.

The two mothers continued walking down Sandwich, then along Court Street's specialty stores. Rachael was careful conversing with Gloria, looking for any hint of how much the woman knew of her involvement with Tracy.

Rachael was thankful for the dip pan as it held the bulky shopping bags. She continued along South Street, with her two kids having left Gloria to walk down her street alone. Rachael arrived home, placing her children in bed for a nap, knowing it was a good afternoon.

By summer's end, the Harold matriarch had died, and her estate was put up for sale. The Manters needed a small apartment for themselves. For the time being, Rachael convinced them to move in with her until Clarence's arrival later that fall.

The faded leaves that shone brightly from their connected branches brought the evening of costumed witches and goblins. Sarah and Rachael prepared trays full of bundled treats. Sarah baked dozens of peanut butter cookies for the treaters while Rachael made popcorn balls. They laid out the decorative napkins, preparing each one with a small amount of candy corn, a couple of peanut butter cookies, and a small popcorn ball. Each napkin was carefully tied together with a seasonal ribbon. Milton sat on the porch with the overloaded tray and his cane by his side. He handed them to the tricksters willing to step up and approach him.

Rachael got Beth and Nathan dressed in costume and followed them door-to-door as they recited their learned line of trick or treat. The evening came to an end with the small containers of treats put away.

THE TURNAROUND

The Bremerton carrier group returned stateside, having completed a nine-month tour around the Korean peninsula. Clarence's Korean tour was over along with his active-duty commitment. Clarence was honorably discharged into the inactive reserves and couldn't wait to make the cross-country trek home. He made a stopover in Illinois for a couple of days, seeing his folks and family before making the flight home. He called Rachael, telling her of his plans and when to expect him. Clarence flew into Boston, catching the train to Plymouth.

Rachael waited at the station, leaving the children home with her parents. It would give her the opportunity to tell him how much she missed him and the support she received from the neighborhood. She'd mention the help she received from her parents, Aunt Flora, and Uncle William. She'd include Tracy and Gloria Booker and their two children. She'd tell how Gloria's husband, Tracy, the local milkman, occasionally checked on her welfare while making deliveries.

The train pulled into Plymouth alongside the A&P supermarket. Clarence stepped off, feeling glad to be home with the chaos of the overseas conflict behind him. He kissed his wife and couldn't wait to hug his children. He felt comfortable driving his old Ford while listening to Rachael's tales along the way.

It was late morning when Rachael drove along Cole's Hill with her arm extended with a pair of sunglasses. The police officer directing traffic quickly grabbed them with his white-gloved hands, easing the brilliant sunlight weighing on his eyelids. Clarence had been home for a few weeks, finding a job as a town cop. His shift was directing the traffic flow along the waterfront, with Rachael remembering her husband's forgotten sunglasses.

The frigid weather had arrived with 1954 on the horizon. The blizzard winds off the Atlantic brought colds and flu to many of the town's occupants. Many of the children at the Downy Nursery School had caught the mumps and chicken pox. Beth came down with the mumps while her brother broke out with chicken pox. They would spend most of their time in their bedrooms amusing themselves playing old maid and their favorite board game, Candyland.

Clarence made many friends working on the town's police force. One had a litter of pups, a mixture of German shepherd and collie. He thought a puppy would be a good addition for the kids. Clarence talked it over, and the kids were excited about having a puppy in the house. Rachael had second thoughts, knowing she would be the one tending to it. A week later, Clarence brought the female pup home as a Christmas present. They named it Patricia Doxanna, or Patty for short. Her development included features of a collie and the coloring of a shepherd.

The winter snows drifted like mountain ranges toppled by the endless train of snowplows. The neighborhood kids contested each other with snowball fights while bundled in their snowsuits with woolen tie-string caps. Sometimes they forged together, making decorative snowmen. Some stood on the sidelines like mechanical robots, unable to make those fluid arm movements that were bound by layered sweaters.

It was a new year, and 1954 started just as the previous had ended. Beth was on the later months of nursery school. In the fall, she would start first grade, with Nathan taking her place at nursery school. Rachael knew how timid her son was about things and thought enrolling him for the last semester with Beth. With her by his side, it would get him used to being around a lot of unfamiliar faces, and Beth would be a comfort should he feel nervous.

Rachael talked to George Downy about her son's shyness. George had little concern about Nathan's demeanor. He had been around kids of all sorts, and Nathan would blend in just like all the rest. For the remaining months, the sister and brother rode the Downy station wagon to the interacting nursery school.

The miniature school was divided into three eventful sections. One displayed a couple of round tables for young minds coloring pictures and making macaroni letter holders from paper plates and colorful garlands from strips of construction paper. Another was for the imaginative minds interacting with blocks, Lincoln Logs, and toy figurines. The final area was used for the last half-hour rest period, with the preschoolers lying on bath towels. The school's back end was enclosed by a chain-link fence, allowing the youngsters to run about releasing their bottled-up energy.

Clarence enjoyed working as a town cop, solving public outcries of family squabbles, petty crimes, and robberies. Rachael was left to her own devices on days when Clarence drove the Ford to work. She continued being friends with Gloria Booker, meeting her on walks into town for some window shopping. Their appearance gave assurances to the neighbors that theirs was a mutual friendship. Despite Rachael's maneuvering, she still took chances accompanying Tracy on his milk truck for their side-road endeavors. She returned home in plenty of time to meet her children. When Rachael had the car, she drove to Manomet visiting relatives and to her parents, who had moved to the northern outskirts of Plymouth.

Sarah found a vacancy in a two-story provincial house on the northern edge of Plymouth's business district. It was old and full of generational memories. The owners converted it into a half dozen studio apartments for the elderly. She and Milton were lucky to find one available. Each occupant was provided a large room, a small kitchenette, and a full bath. The first-floor occupancy was comfortable and affordable, meeting all their needs. The ornate structure sat back on Court Street with a well-manicured lawn in front. Sarah loved her new place and found it convenient to walk to the A&P and her favorite specialty shops even though the bus route passed her place daily.

The summer months brought the brow-sweating heat with little breeze from the ocean. With Beth and Nathan out of school,

Rachael found it difficult caring for her household. She found she was pregnant, knowing the child she carried wasn't Clarence's.

Rachael's infidelity still ran rampant through silent whispers among those on South Street. Peering windows watched as Tracy Booker entered the Anderson household on several occasions. On those days, Rachael made excuses of needing the car to visit her parents and dropped Clarence off at the police station. Rachael stayed home waiting Tracy's arrival. He'd stop by late mornings, and the couple made their way up the flight of stairs.

The precinct was slow, with Clarence deciding to take a few hours off. Instead of calling Rachael, he had his partner drop him off at home. He was surprised seeing the vehicle sitting in the drive. He entered the house as the sparsely dressed couple made a mad dash down the stairs.

Clarence stood awestruck. "What the hell?"

The couple raced around the staircase, heading toward the back door. Clarence reached out, trying to grab Tracy's arm. He escaped unscathed, leaving Rachael to face Clarence's wrath.

"What the fuck is going on?" demanded Clarence.

Rachael just stood silent, then, with a spark of rage, said, "It's over, Clarence. You might as well know now than hearing it off the streets. It's over. I don't love you. I haven't for quite a while. I can't stand the sight of you." Rachael continued, "I love Tracy, and that's all you need to know."

"What do you mean you love this guy? Who the hell is he anyway?" demanded Clarence.

"None of your business. I don't want to talk about it. I want you out of here. You hear me, Clarence. I want you out of here," yelled Rachael, feeling her heart pounding through her chest.

"What do you mean you don't want to talk about it? What about the kids? Do they know? How long has this thing been going on? Tell me, Rachael. Tell me!" shouted Clarence.

"Leave the kids out of it. I just want you out of here. None of this is your business," stormed Rachael.

"You're not getting away that easy, missy. This whole thing is my business. I'll go, but you haven't heard the last of this. I'll find out who this guy is, and then we'll see who's got who," Clarence ended in a rage.

Clarence ran up the stairs, throwing a few items in a suitcase as it sat upon the stirred-up bedsheets. He raced toward the front door, grabbing the car keys on the way out. He didn't travel far, stopping at the Atwoods and telling them of what had just happened.

Flora listened to all Clarence had witnessed. She called Rachael, and the harsh tones went back and forth to the ears of everyone in the room. The bickering seemed endless until Flora whispered to Rachael the final sentence that would keep her quiet. Rachael agreed to letting Clarence back into the house, if only a few days. It was a condition Rachael had to accept. Flora used the aborted pregnancy against her. Clarence returned to the place that was now a morgue and not the loving home he enjoyed.

The following days, the place became a series of shouting matches. Beth and Nathan eased down the staircase bearing witness to the skirmishes.

Rachael paused for only a second, shouting at her two, "Get back to your rooms, right now! Do you hear me?"

The constant yelling prompted Beth and Nathan into crying fits.

The cries were loud and pulsating, with Rachael reacting with the crack of the belt against the railing, yelling, "Both of you, stop crying, or I'll come up and give you something to cry about!"

Their shaken nerves prompted a series of bed wettings. It was soon afterward that Tracy's appearance to the Anderson home became commonplace.

Rachael drove Beth to Dr. Stewart's office to get vaccinated before attending school. She would be entering first grade at the elementary school a couple of blocks from the house. The state allowed children to enter first grade at four years with the realization they would turn five before the year ended.

Nathan nervously went through the motions at nursery school. The arguments ceased, and calmness encased the Anderson house. Clarence no longer walked through the entryway after his shift was over. The milkman's entrance was a mainstay. Some evenings, Rachael allowed Tracy to take her son to the dairy farm where he tended the herd. The barn was open ended, and the cows stood side by side in their stanchions. Tracy lifted Nathan into the hayloft, telling him to push down a few bales of hay. Tracy cleaned the manure trough and filled each feeding bowl with grain and slices of hay. A few hours passed when they arrived back on South Street.

The day came when George Downy dropped Nathan off at the provincial home on Court Street. Rachael thought it best for her son to stay with her parents during the divorce proceedings. Sarah reluctantly agreed to care of her grandson for a time. She made her daughter realized the burden she had created on everyone.

Milton and Sarah were early risers. Nathan, half awake, saw his grandmother crawl out of bed in her flowered pajamas. She grabbed her housecoat that draped over the chair beside the bed. Sarah motioned to Nathan to get up and wash his face and brush his teeth. She continued into the kitchen, cooking a pan of Cream of Wheat, a plateful of toast, and a kettle of hot water for their Postum.

Nathan finished washing and changed into his clothes for nursery school. Milton sat on the edge of the bed, grabbing his galvanized pitcher that sat on the floor in front of the dresser. He used it as his thunder jug during the night as his arthritic legs prevented him from getting to the bathroom in time. It was his routine to empty it come morning.

Sarah got the table ready with the three breakfast settings. Afterward she escorted Nathan to the building's alcove, where a small bench stood on each side welcoming its occupants. Both stood waiting for the Downy station wagon as their breaths penetrated the frigid air. Five minutes passed when the vehicle turned into the dirt driveway. George stepped out, opening the back door for Nathan. Sarah pushed him along, giving George a friendly wave. She watched as the wagon turned around and proceeded along Court Street.

Sarah returned to her kitchen as Milton finished his cup of Postum. She turned the television on for the morning news while she cleared the table and did the dishes. It was her turn to get dressed for the day. Sarah stood before the bathroom sink, staring at the portrait in the mirror. She saw herself with the gray-haired pigtail draped over her left shoulder. The evidence of time lay as facial lines about her face. Her rimless glasses highlighted her weary eyes. Sarah thought not of herself but of the predicament Rachael had brought upon herself.

She sighed, giving herself forty brushstrokes before knotting her hair into a presentable bun highlighted with a hairnet. After washing her face, she took the palm-sized cosmetic sand pad, scrubbing the hair stubs along her jaw. The final touch-up was a light coat of pancake. Sarah changed into one of her everyday dresses and was ready to meet the day.

Rachael stopped by her parents' place during the week and once on weekends. She checked on Nathan and took her mother shopping to help her along. It gave Sarah an opportunity to meet and get use to her new grandson, Kenneth, who was born days before Christmas. Nathan didn't know about his new brother, still wondering where he came from.

The two walked down the grocery aisles picking items that were on Sarah's shopping list.

Rachael paused, turning toward her mother. "Mom, I was wondering if you wouldn't mind watching Nathan a little while longer? It's just this whole divorce thing is getting to me. I've got Kenneth now, and Beth has been a great help."

Sarah stared at her daughter. "Rachael, I can watch him as long as you want. I have him sleeping on a cot. Don't you think he'd be better off being at Flora's place? She's only a few doors down with plenty of space. She could give Nathan his own room."

Rachael knew her mother was right. But Rachael didn't want to hear any more of her aunt's "I told you so" and lectures on the affair that shouldn't have happened, an affair that her mother knew little about.

Rachael's only response to the old woman was "I know, Mom, but you know Flora. She and Uncle William are always traveling about, and I'd feel better if Nathan was with you."

The two women continued down the aisles with hardly a word spoken.

THE TRANSITION

Nathan enjoyed being around his grandfather. Milton spent his time reading the *Old Colony* through his flesh-toned glasses and playing solitaire from the hidden deck in his pants pocket. He shared his card games with Nathan, teaching him rummy, war, slapjack, and various ways of solitaire. The most challenging was cribbage. The games taught Nathan confidence to think for himself. Milton showed Nathan how to tie his shoes and do a Winchester knot and became the primary male figure in Nathan's life.

Milton did his best sharing his basic knowledge with his grandson. Now an aged man in his seventies, Milton's arthritic legs became more chronic as the years passed. Old age had shrunk his youthful height of five feet, ten inches to somewhere around five feet, eight inches. He embellished a potbelly, aided by a bamboo cane that motioned with every step. Milton carried a small jackknife and a leather pouch befitting a man of his caliber. Within it lay a couple of dollars, a few coins, and a nail clipper.

Another game Nathan learned from his grandparents was store. The kitchen counter displayed a few spice containers and silverware as sale items. Pieces of paper with prices affixed to each item, along with paper money, taught Nathan the value of its buying power. Milton helped teach Nathan the difference between a penny, nickel, dime, quarter, and a dollar bill.

Sarah puttered with her housework while her two men amused themselves. She put her dustcloth away, leaving for a few moments to visit the other occupants in the building. She made the rounds checking on their health and welfare. She returned only to sit at her card table, piecing together a jigsaw puzzle usually comprising a thousand pieces. It took a few painstaking weeks putting it together, then she displayed it for a few days before tackling another in the same manner.

Flora often called her sister, keeping her informed of Rachael's escapades. Milton listened to his wife's conversations that seemed to be ongoing. He often interrupted her to get off the phone. Sarah just waved him off, motioning him to hush. The Manters had a following that stopped by on occasion. Nathan got familiar with the grown-ups, who assured him they were his relations. Joseph and Ethel Sampson and Flora and William Atwood, along with Clifton and Esther Michaels, made their frequent stops, catching up on the local gossip.

The school season was over, and the new season's greenery blanketed the countryside. The summer heat weaved around every structure and hardworking brow. The crickets buzzed their high notes with the flowing breeze. Tracy moved in with Rachael to help manage the household. It was time to have Nathan back, joining his brother and sister. The home Nathan was familiar with had changed. He got acquainted with his new brother and shared with Beth the time they were apart.

Nathan realized the milkman who stopped by delivering the milk bottles now lived under the same roof. His grandfather equipped Nathan the courage to be curious of his surroundings and the ability to face diversity despite displaying his shyness.

The house echoed the occasional rifts between Rachael and Tracy. Rachael had succeeded in gaining control of the house and the car. It was Gloria that wouldn't give Tracy a divorce. Tracy left his wife fending for herself and their two underage sons. Gloria's impulse was to pack up and return to Lynn, Massachusetts, where her family still resided. She rethought her dilemma, knowing that Tracy was responsible for her and their children. She was determined to get Tracy back or make his life miserable. She called Tracy every week for money. It bothered Rachael as she depended on Tracy to help with her household bills.

Rachael didn't have a job and couldn't work with three kids of her own. It would be months before her divorce would be finalized and she would start receiving the money for child support. The monthly payments on the house were more than she could afford.

Tracy quit the dairy job, finding an opening at Lyden's Printing Press just off the Route 3 exit ramp. He depended on Rachael to get him to and from work. Gloria kept Tracy's belongings in hopes he'd come to his senses and return. Rachael knew the only salvation for her situation was to sell the house and find a rental.

The house closed, giving Rachael little time to move. She went and pleaded with her aunt to let her live temporarily at Ellis Pond. Flora was hesitant but gave in, knowing Rachael needed a suitable place before the fall school season started. The cottage had one bedroom with a large living area. The futon could easily fold out into a double bed, and there was a reclining overstuffed chair that could be converted. The kitchen dinette was small but able to fit four or five people comfortably. The cottage had a half bath consisting of a sink and toilet. Bathing took turns in the kitchen. Rachael placed her furnishings in storage while she went about the Plymouth area looking at available rentals.

It was Clifton that led Rachael to a place in Kingston. He was in the real estate business before his retirement and was aware of Rachael's predicament. He used his influence to help his niece although what he did was out of love for Milton and Sarah. It was a three-bedroom home just off the main drag on Brightside Avenue. Rachael wasted no time signing the rental contract. The house would fit her needs now that she was pregnant with her fourth child.

KINGSTON

The moving van backed onto the Kingston driveway Friday morning. Rachael was anxious in getting the furnishings placed and making the house somewhat livable. She guided the movers through the kitchen side entrance and into placing her household effects to their respective rooms. The kitchen was large enough for her six-seater Coaster dinner table along with the appliances. It had a half bath in the rear. From the kitchen, a doorway led to a large living area that was divided into two separate rooms. The front room was arranged for watching television while the back staged the upright piano and a couple of lounging chairs. It gave Rachael a place to play and relax from the daily routines.

The front room sported the entrance door with a staircase leading to the upstairs bedrooms. The bedroom floor had a full bath at the head of the stairway, just like the previous house. There were three bedrooms, with Rachael and Tracy having the front, Beth and Nathan sharing the side, and Kenneth having his own.

School season was a few weeks away, and it was Nathan's turn to get vaccinated. Rachael had Tracy drive her son to the doctor's office. Dr. Stewart had Nathan sit on the examining table while preparing the needle for the inoculation. Nathan started whimpering as the needle point approached. Tracy braced him on his lower arms while the needle delivered the serum. He realized Nathan's weakness toward pain despite the strong facade the young lad presented.

Another lesson Rachael wanted Nathan to learn was to pee like a grown-up. Up to now, Nathan wasn't tall enough to stand before the toilet. Tracy decided to teach him on a Saturday when Rachael went grocery shopping. He watched her from the front window as she backed out of the driveway, then drove down the road with Kenneth and Beth in tow.

The timeliness couldn't be more perfect for Tracy to teach the small lad the lesson. He called Nathan, wanting to show him something in the bathroom. Nathan got up from watching cartoons and followed Tracy upstairs. He watched Tracy stand before the toilet, motioning for him to come closer. Tracy lifted the toilet seat, unzipped himself, and pulled out his penis. He placed his hand over Nathan's, placing both around his shaft. They stood there while Tracy peed into the bowl. After he finished, he stroked himself with Nathan's hand still holding on. Tracy smiled at the small boy and asked him to do the same.

Nathan just stood there with a blank look on his face. Tracy gently placed Nathan in front of the bowl and pulled down his pants. Tracy took Nathan's hand, placing it around his small genitals and told him to pee into the bowl. Nathan felt cold and nervous. He did what Tracy asked. After it was over, Tracy pulled the boy's pants up and told him to use his zipper to pull himself out. Tracy saw how shaken the boy was and let him return to watch television. As they descended the stairs, Tracy smiled, telling him not to tell his mother what they did; it was a guy thing.

Dawn broke through the horizon when Rachael got up, grabbing her housecoat from the bedpost. She walked out into the hallway.

"Beth, Nathan, time to get up and get ready for school."

Rachael peeked in Kenneth's bedroom, decided to let him sleep a little longer, and headed for the stairs. She heard the moans of the older two getting out of bed as she descended. They made their way to the bathroom, washed their face and hands, brushed their teeth, got dressed while their mother filled their cereal bowls with cornflakes, and prepared glasses of orange juice and a plate of toast.

Rachael prepared peanut butter and jelly sandwiches for their lunch, wrapping them in waxed paper, and neatly placed them with a thermos of milk in their decorative lunch boxes. The two finished eating and placed their bowls in the sink. There was a slight struggle in putting on their sweaters as they grabbed their lunch boxes.

Beth started second grade, with Nathan starting first. They left the house, making their way down the road. They met other zombielike kids on Mayflower Road, with Beth leading Nathan down the main street to catch the yellow school bus. It traveled only a mile or two before it came to a stop in front of a large school building. Nathan was confused, not knowing this stop was for second graders and above. He followed his sister off the bus before being redirected back on. First graders were taken across town to another stonelike building, where a classroom waited for them.

Rachael got herself dressed while Tracy finished breakfast. They got into the car with Rachael dropping her man off at the printing company. There were days she let Tracy take the car but found she needed it more. She knew Gloria was on her tail and didn't trust Tracy with the vehicle. He had a tendency of arriving home late on days when he drove.

Tracy called Gloria from work, telling her his new job, and provided her some support money for the boys. She made it her business to be at his job on Fridays collecting a few dollars. It was never enough. Gloria was convinced Tracy wasn't going to return to her and needed the support of her parents. She shared the whole affair and asked them to move to Plymouth. It would be hard to give up their Lynn apartment, a place they called home for over ten years. In the long run, it was for the best, knowing they were helping their daughter raise their two grandsons.

Flora kept tabs on the drama that swept the family. She had her social circle keeping her updated. She called Rachael to see if she needed anything. Rachael convinced her aunt she was all right and the kids were happy going to school.

Things weren't going well. Rachael had exhausted what little money she got from the sale of the house. The divorce wasn't finalized, and the support money she was counting on would have to wait. Rachael needed help, and the only person she could turn to was Clifton Michaels.

The elementary school for the first graders was small and constructed from rustic stones. It was over a century old and still maintained its soundness. The small class was given to Mrs. Hardy. She was an elderly woman with short gray hair befitting women her age. This was her last year teaching. She had her young students sitting in a circle, sharing thoughts and ideas with each other. They colored, had story time, and learned to print the alphabet.

Nathan was reluctant in grasping on how to read. Mrs. Hardy took time during coloring to give Nathan the special attention he needed by sounding out individual letters and melding those sounds into readable words. It took a lot of patience before Nathan was able to comprehend his teacher's motives.

Riding the school bus home released the harnessed energy that was suppressed during the six hours of learning. The route took the reverse from the morning ride, descending down the long driveway to the big school. The kids filed on the bus, including Beth. Their voices excitingly overpowered one another about their day's activities. It drove just short of a mile before coming to a stop and dropping the group off in front of Mayflower Road.

School days came and went with Beth and Nathan pretty much settled in their separate routines. There were times they arrived home seeing the car gone. Rachael left a note on the kitchen table allowing them to make a peanut butter sandwich and a glass of milk. She had gone shopping, sometimes with their grandmother and sometimes alone. The last line on the note read "Be good until I get back. Love, Mom." On shopping days, the two were on their own for about an hour. Rachael returned, stopping the car at the side door. She called for her two to help empty the trunk of grocery bags.

"Take the lighter ones and leave the heavier ones for me. I'll be right out," Rachael told her two as she gathered Kenneth and the diaper bag from the front seat.

Weekends were spent playing in the spacious yard or going over to friends. Nathan developed a friendship with a neighbor named Bobby. He lived on Mayflower Road's dead end. His house was surrounded by woods, and he invited Nathan over to play inside the wooded compound. The grounds were carpeted with pine needles that were paved into intricate roadways for playing trucks.

Soon the telephone sounded with the calling of their names from the front door. It was time for Nathan to go home. Going and returning from Bobby's for a four-and-a-half-year-old was an adventure. Walking the roadside wasn't all that hard. Nathan found the shortcut path through the woods that led to the far corner of his side yard. The house stood in clear view.

He made his way through the side door with everyone mingling about the kitchen. He saw his mother dishing the supper into serving bowls. Beth was already sitting at the table, with Kenneth in the wooden high chair drumming the tray with a miniature spoon.

Tracy sat strumming his guitar with a buddy from work. They sat around playing country music over a couple of beers.

Rachael motioned to Nathan. "Go wash your hands and face, then take your seat at the table."

He passed through the living room where Patty lay comfortable on the decorative carpet. Tonight the meal consisted of mashed potatoes, green beans, and meatloaf.

A middle-aged couple lived across the street farther down the road. The woman was a Sunday school teacher at the Plymouth Congregational Church and called Rachael asking if she was interested in joining the church. Rachael hadn't any interest but thought it would be a good time to introduce the biblical stories to Beth and Nathan.

Rachael went along, provided the woman drove the two children to and from Sunday school classes. Sunday morning, Beth and Nathan walked over to their neighbor's house, meeting the woman at her doorstep, then followed her into the car for the drive to the white steepled church in the heart of Plymouth. Sometimes they had no choice in staying for the church service. Going to church was the Sunday routine during the winter months. Rachael planned dinner in the early afternoon with the remaining day geared for relaxation.

Christmas brought on a different tone. It was the first time Tracy and Rachael celebrated Christmas together. Gloria called Lyden's Printing, hoping Tracy would spend time with his sons, but Tracy ignored her pleas. Rachael and her mother drove around Kingston finding a sidewalk vendor selling Christmas trees. The two managed to make it home, carefully removing it from the trunk and placing it in the corner of the front living room. Rachael waited until the following weekend to give her parents an opportunity to help decorate it.

A Santa's face was placed in Rachael's bedroom window, lighting up the jolly elf to the outsiders. Lighted candles were carefully placed in every window to display the holiday spirit.

The Lionel train set was carefully taken from its wrappings. It had a motorized engine and a red caboose running along the base of the decorated branches. A train station came complete with small costumed figurines and miniature pine trees dotting both sides of the tracks. It served as the cornerstone for the decorations displayed above it. The stockings were hung along the stairway wall just under the indented alcove, where a bright-red telephone sat.

Rachael told her children, when they awoke on Christmas morning, they could enjoy their stockings before breakfast. Each stocking was filled with a traditional apple, an orange, a bag of chocolate gold coins, a toothbrush, and a few small toy items.

The Christmas season echoed the music of noels sung by the two youngsters around the piano while their mother fingered each note. Christmas dinner was celebrated with the company of Milton and Sarah.

The Sunday school class performed a short play about the birth of Jesus. Church volunteers tediously sewed the costumes. The Sunday school children were dressed as angels singing carols of Jesus's coming. Rachael drove the family to witness her children's performance among other angelic members.

Winter continued, with Beth and Nathan rolling in the snow, making snowmen, and sliding down the small hill behind the house. School ran its usual course riding the school bus back and forth.

Rachael decided to teach Nathan to ride the public commuter bus from Kingston to Plymouth. The bus route drove by Milton and Sarah's provincial building and continued through the center of town. Rachael walked with Nathan the first couple of times to the bus stop. As the bus approached, she instructed her son to stick out his arm. The bus stopped, opening its door and revealing the welcoming driver. He gestured the young lad to step on board.

Nathan stepped up, then turned toward his mother as she reminded him, "Remember, your grandmother will meet you when it's time to get off."

The boy regained his confidence and took a window seat. The onlookers stared at the small boy, having their doubts.

Peeping out the window, Nathan saw the roadside buildings that looked familiar. He had traveled the same route in the car. Sarah stood at the corner, hailing the bus as it approached. The bus stopped, and Nathan gingerly walked to the front, stepping off into his grandmother's arms. She was so pleased that he did his first bus ride without any problems. He reminded her it was like riding the school bus but different. Nathan spent the rest of the day with her. It was evening when Rachael stopped by, retrieving him for the ride home.

The winter months were coming to an end. March began the spring weather along with the birth of Laura Jane. The crib was placed in Beth's room, with Nathan moving in with Kenneth. The responsibilities of raising a family continued to wear on Rachael. She realized, with each new child, she needed to reorganize her daily routine.

It was shortly after Laura's birth Rachael received notification of her divorce. She had to appear in court to settle on the child support. She thought over what her response would be as she knew Kenneth and Laura were Tracy's. She knew of the complications involved if she put Tracy's name on their birth certificates. Rachael wasn't true to herself on whether her relationship with Tracy would last.

To protect herself and to provide support for her four kids, Rachael had named their father as Clarence Anderson. She knew Clarence might dispute it, but Rachael had the upper hand being a woman who could display emotional and abusive wrought. Rachael submitted the four names, and the court approved the support.

The summer's heat penetrated the air when Rachael decided to enroll Beth in a swimming class at Kingston's Gray's Beach. She asked Nathan if he wanted to accompany his sister. He kept thinking of all those horseshoe crabs and jellyfishes that might take a hold and drag him away. Swimming lessons just wasn't what he wanted to do.

After dropping Beth off, Rachael continued driving, with Laura nestled in the front with Kenneth and Nathan sitting in the back. She visited Tracy at the printshop. He saw them drive in from behind his workbench window. He walked out, leaned in the passenger window, and chatted a few moments. Tracy mentioned that Gloria stopped by earlier asking for money. Nathan sat in the back seat looking up at the crew-cut former milkman. His hollowed brown eyes felt as if they were piercing one's inner soul. After a moment, he returned to the building.

The *Old Colony* printed the celebration of the *Mayflower II* arriving at Plymouth's coast during the summer months. England had built the *Mayflower* replica and sailed her maiden voyage across the ocean and into Plymouth's crowded harbor.

It was early evening when Rachael gathered her children for the drive to the historic event and found a side street to park the vehicle. Rachael carried Laura and took hold of Nathan's hand. Tracy carried Kenneth and the army blanket while Beth walked closely by her mother. The family followed the crowd down Leyden Road. They came to rest atop Cole's Hill, laying the blanket down for the kids. The townspeople were everywhere, arriving with picnic baskets, blankets, sweaters, and any other necessities to witness the event.

As darkness filled the sky, the ship appeared into the spotlights along the shore. *Mayflower II* was decked with vintage Pilgrims dressed in 1620-era costumes with their brown and black knickers, matching caps, and white blossom-sleeved blouses. The evening echoed the crowd's thunderous cheers roaring along the shoreline, with fireworks blaring into the sky while the band played a host of patriotic tunes. The celebration had waned, and soon darkness prevailed. It was under the starlit sky when the exhausted crowd made their way back to their cars toward home.

Rachael's relationship with Tracy became the topic of uncontrollable whispers among family and friends. Gloria continued vocalizing the fight for her husband's return with the surrounding neighbors. The decision to move far from Plymouth was the only answer if Rachael's family was to survive.

Rachael's situation wasn't unique as similar lives were duplicated in many households, often protected by family members and close friends behind closed doors. By summer's end, Rachael started packing to parts unknown. This time, the move would take them into one of the suburbs of Boston, Massachusetts.

WINTHROP

Tracy traveled outside the Boston suburbs investigating the prospects on a couple of shipping/receiving positions. In the interim, Rachael needed to call her aunt.

"Hi, Aunt Flora, it's Rachael. I'm calling to let you know Tracy and I are thinking about moving north, maybe around the Boston area. He's up there now looking at a few job openings. I was wondering if the kids and I could use the cottage again for a short while."

Flora wasn't all that surprised about the announcement. She could only respond with some curiosity.

"Really, Rachael? Tracy is job hunting around Boston? Why do you have to move, and why can't you stay where you are?"

"I don't want to renew the lease, and I might have to put most of the furnishings in storage until I find a new place to live," replied Rachael.

Fora sighed. "Rachael, why do you allow yourself to get into these predicaments? I don't mind you using the cottage, but you know as well as I do it isn't big enough for you and the kids. We tried that the last time, remember? Besides, you know William has cancer, and I can't leave him right now."

Rachael's voice changed into one of desperation. "Then what am I supposed to do? Tracy and I have been harassed by Gloria these past weeks, and I can't put up with it much longer. We've decided to move away, and I was hoping to count on you for help."

Flora had heard of Gloria's antagonistic bouts with her niece and Tracy through the gossip mill. She thought a moment, coming up with a compromise.

"I'm going to call your mother and see if she can help. I can take Nathan and Kenneth. Maybe your mother can take Laura for a time. Will that help?"

Rachael still needed a place for herself and Beth. "Is it okay if Beth and I stay at the cottage?"

Flora shook her head in disgust, pausing for a moment. "Okay, Rachael, you and Beth can use the cottage, but I don't want the place messed up. Do you understand?"

"Thanks, Aunt Flora. Thank you for doing me this favor. You don't know what it means," exclaimed Rachael.

Flora hung the phone down, knowing what her niece had gotten herself into. She decided to dismiss her own conclusions on the whole fiasco. She looked at her husband resting in his easy chair with Teddy laying beside him.

Flora called Sarah, getting everything settled. Sarah agreed making use of her cot once again. Rachael and Beth arrived at the cottage, making themselves comfortable, awaiting a call from Tracy.

Flora kept the boys at her house, putting both in one of her spare bedrooms. Nathan was given the responsibility of watching his brother. Kenneth, having discovered his legs, had Nathan chase him about the rooms. William continued resting in the living room while Flora continued with her housework. She kept watch on her husband, making sure he was comfortable and taking his meds. The boys' frolicking gave some levity to the watchful silence.

Tracy was familiar with Boston's north end, having grown up in Lynn. He hoped one day to return to his childhood town and was looking at job prospects surrounding the area. He interviewed for a few shipping and receiving positions just north of Boston and was ultimately hired by a company outside of Winthrop.

Tracy realized he was closer to his roots, remembering his early day of his youth and of his mother, Maude, and his estranged father, David Booker.

Tracy was born in Lynn in 1935 with his parents divorcing before Tracy knew of his father. His mother remarried, giving birth to a few more children. Over time, he became alienated from his family and found refuge within a troublesome neighborhood.

Tracy's life placed him in one compromising situation after another, leading him to drop out of school. He recalled those early days of traveling from one place to another trying to support himself. He didn't qualify to serve during the World War but was able to fill the positions of those that did. He worked himself south, marrying Gloria along the way. Tracy had a few family members still living in the Lynn area but had become estranged from them.

He quickly looked through the local newspapers for available rentals. After days of answering inquiries, Rachael and Tracy accepted a small second-floor apartment on Pauline Street in Winthrop.

Rachael had the movers pack up the Kingston furnishings with the selected necessities separated for the new apartment. They knew the apartment was temporary and had to make do. The movers arrived with the essentials that filled the four average-sized rooms. The landlords were an elderly couple living on the first floor. Rachael put the apartment together, then gathered her family for the long drive to their new and different surroundings.

The stairway climbed to a small hallway. Turning right was a bedroom for Beth and Laura. Adjacent to it was a living room where a convertible sofa bed stood for Rachael and Tracy. Down the hallway on the right was another bedroom for the two boys. Across was the bath. Continuing down was a large kitchen that was suitable for the table and chairs. There was a back door that led to a small porch and stairway descending to a fenced-in backyard. It was convenient for letting Patty out. On the other side of the fence stood a large earthen playground belonging to Winthrop's elementary school. The school was just a couple of doors down, making it easy for the two oldest to walk to school.

Rachael got everyone settled and started preparing for the school season. The first day of school was filled with mixed emotions. Rachael made the quick decision to send Beth and Nathan to school and register themselves. She got them up early, getting them fed and dressed. Rachael left Tracy to tend for himself as he needed to catch the early commuter bus for work.

She stood before her two oldest, handing Beth a folded note. "I want you to go to the principal's office and give them this note. It'll tell them where you and Nathan went to school and gives them my name, our address, and who to contact in case of an emergency."

Beth looked at her mother with complete understanding.

Rachael continued, "If the principal needs any more information, tell them to write me a note, and bring it home. Do you understand, Beth?"

Beth nodded, then looked toward her brother.

Rachael brushed the few pieces of lint off her daughter's shoulders, adding one more comment, "If they ask why your mother didn't bring you, tell them I had to stay home with your brother and sister."

Rachael didn't have a phone. It wouldn't be worth having one installed for the short period she had planned to live in the apartment. She knew the two would do what was asked since living in Kingston gave them the confidence Rachael expected. Beth nodded and took Nathan's hand for the short walk to the school.

It didn't take long for the officials to cipher through what these young children were relaying. They managed to understand the note's information. The principal escorted them to their respected classes. The second grade consisted of about thirty kids in rows of desks facing a wall of chalked blackboards. The teacher was Mrs. Bernard, a middle-aged woman having the patience of Job. Her method of teaching made everyone feel like they belonged and made the classwork a fun experience.

Nathan's class was split into different reading sections. Everyone read from the same book on different levels. The book *On Cherry Hill* featured the loveable characters of Dick, Jane, Sally, and Jake intertwined with stories of woodland creatures. Nathan's group had about six classmates taking turns reading various paragraphs. Mrs. Bernard enticed them to put feelings into their readings as if they were acting out the story line. Nathan tried imitating a forest animal when it came his turn to read. It brought smiles to his teacher and fellow readers. He was only outdone by another reader in the group. She was a small girl with short brown hair wearing a pleated dress. Her name was Julia Winters. While the group read, Mrs. Bernard put the rest of the class working on a worksheet of mathematical problems.

Nathan got to know Julia as both occasionally volunteered helping Mrs. Bernard after class. They wiped down the blackboards and clapped the erasers from the day's collection of chalk dust. Both walked home, with Julia leaving Nathan at his door. She continued around the corner where her family lived.

Adjacent to Pauline Street was Hermon Street. It was home to a Congregational church where Beth and Nathan started attending Sunday school. Rachael got the family up early, making sure Beth and Nathan had washed and dressed while cooking breakfast for the crew. As the two were about to leave, Rachael gave each a few cents for the offering and Beth an extra for the Sunday paper.

There was a drugstore at the street corner that sold a variety of sundries. It didn't take long before Beth and Nathan pirated the offering money for a candy bar while getting the paper. The chocolate bars were gobbled down in no time, taking baby steps getting home. Climbing the stairs, they smelled the aromatic cooking of the Sunday dinner. They changed into their everyday clothes, wanting to go outside and play.

Nathan followed his sister into the kitchen, where Rachael stood over the stove.

"Mom, is it all right for Nate and I go out and play in the schoolyard?"

"Not now. I want the both of you to help me get dinner ready. First I need the potatoes peeled and then the carrots," answered their mother.

"Peel potatoes and carrots?" Beth said, looking bewildered at her mother.

"Yes. Now get some newspapers and spread them on the table, and I'll show you two how to peel," instructed Rachael.

Beth went to the outer porch, grabbed a couple of sheets of old newspaper, and spread them on the table. Nathan watched as his mother placed the two vegetables on the paper. She showed them how to hold the peeler, then slowly peeled away the vegetable skin and placed the readied vegetables into a pan of water.

The two followed their mother's lead and completed their peeling assignment. Rachael followed through, putting the vegetable pans on the stove to cook.

Family time circled around watching television, playing in the schoolyard, or reading books. Their television had a small screen encased in a cherry-red cabinet. Two small doors protected the glass screen from any outside contact. They opened like window shutters when put into use.

The toys the kids played with in Kingston had been donated to the Salvation Army. Rachael felt they had outlived their usefulness. She preferred her children use their own creative imaginations for amusement. The older two found reading a book could hold one's imagination for only so long. More often, Beth and Nathan played with the neighborhood kids in the school playground. Rachael only had to call them from the back porch to get their attention.

Rachael was a traditionalist. She grew up having Wednesday spaghetti night, beans and franks on Saturdays, and a roast dinner on Sundays. Saturday evenings was bath night. Rachael filled the bathtub where it was safe enough for the kids. She got the two oldest taking their baths first.

When Nathan's turn came, Tracy was sitting on the sofa next to Rachael. He whispered to her he wanted to teach Nathan how to clean himself. Nathan was sitting in the soapy water when Tracy opened the door, letting himself in and closing it after him. He smiled down on the lad, telling him he was going to teach him another guy thing. Tracy stood before the tub, having Nathan stand before him. Nathan stood up, having the soapy water drain down on his naked body. He crossed his arms over his chest for temporary warmth. Tracy undid his pants, letting them carefully drop to the floor.

Tracy reached down for the facecloth and had Nathan take hold of it. He guided the boy's hand with the facecloth, cleaning around the head of his penis, then guided the small hand to clean all around the man's genitals. Tracy smiled, ensuring Nathan what he was doing was all right. Tracy had the boy do the same to himself. This time, Tracy guided Nathan's hand all around his small parts. Tracy quickly dried himself off, putting himself together and telling Nathan not to tell his mother what they just did. It was a guy thing.

Nathan finished and ran into his bedroom, putting on his pajamas. He and Beth sat on the living room floor watching the poor reception while their mother tended to Kenneth and Laura in the bathroom. Nathan looked up at Tracy from the corner of his eye. Tracy smiled, giving the boy a wink.

Winthrop was an accessible town. Everything was within walking distance. The library, church, and school were all within proximity. A couple of blocks stood a supermarket. The bulky carriage saved carrying the heavy grocery bags back to the apartment. A movie theater stood a couple of streets from the apartment, where Rachael could take her kids to see the latest Disney film.

Finances were tight, and the Ford had seen better days. The needed repair costs were more than what it was worth. Rachael decided to sell it as it was easier to pay for public transportation than maintaining the vehicle. Public transportation was available, even for traveling to the inner city.

Rachael began feeling the everyday stresses. Without a phone, her days were left with her two toddlers, with another on the way. She wrote letters upon letters, keeping the lines of communication flowing.

Flora had written of her loss of William. Cancer had taken over his body, and he succumbed that fall. Her high school friend Karen had established herself in Kansas City and was living on her own, having a male interest in her life. Ethel had lost her husband, Joseph, due to health issues. It didn't seem to be a good year from Rachael's perspective. She allowed her imagination to get the best of her. Her stress wasn't on her family but of Tracy. Rachael's worry was of Tracy calling Gloria. She suspected it because the money and his pay stub reflected it.

The holidays were approaching. The distance between the Winthrop apartment and Rachael's parents was more than a town away. It was a couple of hours drive. They always shared the Thanksgiving and Christmas holidays with their daughter and grandchildren. Rachael was planning on having them again this year, but without a vehicle, alternate arrangements had to be made.

Sarah found Clifton Michaels willing to drive them up for the holiday. Cliff hadn't seen his "niece" in months. It would give him an opportunity to see how Rachael was progressing.

Sleeping arrangements meant doubling up. Sarah bunked with Kenneth, and Milton doubled up with Nathan. Their room was the larger of the two bedrooms with bigger beds. Thanksgiving passed with Cliff arriving to take Sarah and Milton back home.

Rachael scanned through the Spiegel catalog's toy section. She called out to Beth and Nathan, asking them to pick two toys that they'd like Santa to bring them. Nathan asked for an Etch A Sketch and a board game. Beth asked for a Betsy Wetsy doll that was popular that year. A few weeks before Christmas, Rachael and Tracy bought a tree and placed it by the living room window. Rachael had only a couple of boxes of decorations and called everyone in the living room to make the tree festive.

A large box of cookies arrived from Hannah Anderson. Rachael was surprised of its arrival, wondering how she knew their Winthrop address. Hannah had to have Clarence's investigative help since the support checks were now being sent to the 8 Pauline Street address. Hannah didn't want her grandchildren to be forgotten or forget her and their father. Hannah hoped, during the holidays, Rachael might be a little sympathetic and allow the box of cookies. Hannah would continue to send a box for the next few years.

Rachael allowed the cookies and shared them with the family even though she had a bitter taste for the Andersons. She knew Clarence wouldn't be making any surprise visits with the divorce decree denying visitation rights. A week before Christmas, Rachael hinted she was going to make Beth's wish come true.

Rachael realized she needed help. Her baby was due to arrive and wanted her mother by her side. The kids arrived home from school when Rachael asked Beth to watch the place while she went to the corner store to make a call. Rachael dialed her mother on the public phone, convincing her to make the trip to Winthrop.

Sarah knew the Greyhound bus went from Plymouth to Boston. She called the bus company, learning she could catch the airport limo to Logan, then a commuter bus to Winthrop. It would be costly, but Rachael needed her to watch the kids while she delivered.

Sarah felt bad leaving Milton by himself for Christmas. She asked the neighbors to stop by seeing if he was all right. She notified Flora and Ethel of what she was about to do. It took a day's travel to make the trip. Rachael was overjoyed seeing her mother, and the grandchildren surrounded her with hugs and kisses.

Sarah got up early, putting on her housecoat and slippers. She made her way into the kitchen, exploring the cabinets and refrigerator. Sarah found what she needed to cook breakfast of oatmeal, toast, and hot chocolate. She noticed they were low on milk and made a pitcher containing a mixture of evaporated milk. Beth and Nathan were reluctant to try it, but their grandmother assured them it wasn't that bad. Beth tasted it, and it wasn't to her liking. Nathan thought differently, giving his smile of approval. To Sarah, oatmeal wouldn't be right without a couple of prunes thrown onto it. Nathan looked at the wrinkled lumps with disgust.

"What are these?" asked Nathan.

"They're prunes. They're good for you," replied Sarah.

"Yuck," spouted Nathan. "They don't look good."

He turned toward his sister, who looked at the wrinkled lumps in discontent. Sarah stood at the table, looking at her grandchildren with some resemblance of caring.

"Prunes are good for you. They have vitamins that'll make you grow big and strong. It's what your body needs. If you cut them up and mix them with the oatmeal, they'll taste better," explained their grandmother.

The two wanted them tossed but obeyed their grandmother by consuming the wrinkled lumps with their eyes closed. Sarah returned to the stove, fixing herself a bowl, when a mouse snuck out from under the counter, crossed her foot, and raced into the gap beside the refrigerator. Sarah was startled for a moment but said nothing. She wanted to avoid upsetting the two reluctant heads still reeling over the ordeal with the prunes. For the next couple of days, oatmeal with evaporated milk was the menu warming the bellies for the cold winter days. Sarah found time to let Patty out the back door. She seemed to be lost among the humans that sporadically walked around.

Rachael went into labor and was ambulanced to the Boston hospital. Sarah didn't see the crib in any of the rooms. It was still packed away in storage with the rest of the furnishings. The only reasonable thing to do was to create a makeshift crib from the baby carriage. She imagined that was what Rachael had in mind. The day before Christmas, Rachael arrived home with Beth's Betsy Wetsy. Her name was Gretchen Alice.

Sarah sat at the kitchen table drinking a cup of coffee. Rachael put the kids to bed for a nap and joined her mother with a hot cup.

Sarah looked at her daughter, sighing. "I don't know how you're keeping this place afloat, but you're doing okay." She tapped her fingers on the table in a rhythmic motion for a moment. "Can I ask you a question, Rachael? What are you doing, and what are you getting yourself into?"

"What do you mean, Mom?" asked Rachael, looking confused.

Sarah responded angrily, "I mean, you've got five mouths to feed cramped into this small apartment. You have a dog to care for. What's going on, and how many more kids are you planning on? That's what I mean."

Rachael looked bewildered, responding, "I know what I'm doing, Mom. Tracy is working and looking for a better job. This place is only temporary until we can find something better. We're doing okay. I know it looks bad, but it's not."

Sarah continued her examination, "What about the furnishings in storage? That's got to cost a pretty penny. What's Tracy got to say about all this?"

"He knows what's going on. I love Tracy, and I love my family. Everything is going to be just fine, you'll see," cried Rachael.

Sarah wasn't convinced. For the time being, she let Rachael play her game. Sarah wasn't sure how dedicated Tracy's role in all this was, especially knowing that his wife was acting with a vendetta back in Plymouth. She could see this family hitting a brick wall somewhere down the road. The next day, Sarah made the journey home hoping Milton was able to survive the week without her.

The new year started cautiously with Rachael becoming more temperamental. She realized her mother was right. The stress of five children in a small apartment became tiresome. She decided to have Beth and Nathan help with the housework. Rachael trained them to make their beds and pick up their rooms. They were taught to make the morning oatmeal, toast, and school lunches. Watching their grandmother gave them the confidence they could do it.

Rachael figured her two oldest were old enough to change a diaper. She took Gretchen and laid her on the couch, showing how to carefully unsnap the safety pins, remove the diaper along with any solid waste, and carefully replace it with a clean one. It was the first time Nathan saw the difference between a girl and a boy. The soiled diaper was taken to the bathroom, and the solids were dropped into the toilet. Rachael let them practice whenever Gretchen needed changing.

A radio stood on a kitchen shelf next to the entryway. It was turned on in the mornings, announcing the latest renditions of the weather and the local and national news. The morning cooks listened to Dave Maynard on WBZ out of Boston. He broadcasted newsworthy events about the city and the world.

President Dwight D. Eisenhower was proposing a new and more efficient highway infrastructure system in the way the nation traveled. It was needed because America's population had dramatically grown over the last decade.

The US Post Office followed suit and developed a zip code system in moving the mail more efficiently. It allowed the post office to assign postal numbers to certain areas of the country, state, and district.

The old Zenith television began losing reception, accompanied with a slight buzzing noise. One morning, Rachael turned it on, only to have it remain silent. The protective doors remained closed. It had survived the family since the days of South Street. Until it could be fixed or replaced, reading books led to the fabrication of the imagination.

The early months of the new year passed. It was time to look for a larger place, giving some relief to the landlords. They had heard the constant pitter-patter of footsteps going back and forth through their ceiling for months.

By early spring, Rachael was packed and ready to move. The rental truck was loaded, and during the early evening, it arrived at South Boston's East Third Street under a blanket of stars. Rachael and Tracy climbed out of the small moving van and unloaded the kids. They started moving the contents up the two flights of stairs to the third floor. Beth and Nathan took what they could carry, placing their objects in one of the larger rooms. With everyone exhausted, Rachael just told everyone to find a spot to sprawl out and go to sleep. The unpacking would be left for morning.

SOUTH BOSTON

The morning radiated through the windows of the large five-room apartment. Rachael woke on the living room floor with Gretchen nestled at her side using the rolled-up carpet as a pillow. She was unaware how the rest of the family weathered the night. The place was in total chaos with boxes and furnishings brought from Winthrop. The stored furniture would arrive later in the day. Rachael wanted everyone fed before tackling the wave of household effects. She sent Nathan to the corner store for a box of cereal, a carton of milk, and a loaf of Wonder Bread.

He ran down the two flights of stairs and opened the door, giving him his first glance of the neighborhood. He was in awe walking to the corner, examining every apartment building that lined both sides of the street. He was spellbound, wondering about the people who lived there and what were they like.

The corner store posed as a miniature supermarket. Food was shelved to the ceiling all the way around. Only jars and canned goods were shelved within arm's reach. Inside the entryway was a large glass enclosure that housed a multitude of penny candies. The old gray-headed proprietor came from the back room asking the lad what he wanted. Nathan watched the owner use a gripping pole to retrieve the cornflakes, then go over to a refrigerated crate and lift out a half gallon of milk. Along the front counter were shelves of various loaves, where Nathan handed over the loaf of Wonder Bread. Nathan paid for the bagged groceries and left the store amazed of what he just did.

He stood outside for a moment, noticing where he was standing. Nathan saw the street sign atop the metal pole. He was on the corner of East Third Street and P. The sign over the corner store read "Archie's General Store." Nathan retraced his steps, passing the parked cars one after another, back to the apartment.

Rachael had the table set with the cereal bowls and found the toaster in the box marked "kitchen items." Nathan arrived with the grocery bag and gave it to his mother. She called everyone around the table, and they took their assigned seats while she was rationing the cereal. Everyone sat cramped together around the dinner table. It was time to shop for an inexpensive table to add to her growing family. Nathan couldn't contain himself about his morning adventure. It didn't faze the toddlers but raised Beth's curiosity enough that she wanted to go out and explore.

Labeled boxes went to their respective rooms. Tracy took responsibility of putting the bed frames together accompanied with their related bureaus. The pots and pans were placed in the walk-in pantry. The small room had a built-in bureau with shelves lining the wall above it. The bureau made it easy placing the silverware and other cooking utensils in a standard order. Clothes boxes were the last items unpacked. The moving van arrived early in the afternoon, delivering the living room set, piano, more bureaus, nightstands, and boxes of various knickknacks that would have overwhelmed the Winthrop apartment.

Moving the furniture from the street to the third floor was cumbersome and exhausting. The piano wouldn't make the two flights of stairs. The movers found the only way to get it into the apartment was to erect a hoist on the roof and remove a window frame just below it. From the side alleyway, the creature was pulled up to the hollowed-out window and gradually pulled inside. With the frame back into position, the move was complete.

Rachael had everyone pulling their worth. Each was handed an item to place in one room or the other. She had all the emptied boxes and stuffing placed on the back porch. It took a day to put the apartment into some resemblance of order. The last thing was to fill a five-gallon can with kerosene from the small gas station two blocks away. Most everyone had kitchen stoves that ran on kerosene and kept a couple of five-gallon cans filled in their back rooms. The oil truck made its weekly rounds on Tuesday mornings. Today Tracy needed to make the trip so Rachael could cook the meals.

Saturday morning, Rachael needed to scope the neighborhood and find the school Beth and Nathan would be attending. She lowered the carriage down the two flights, making it comfortable for Gretchen. Rachael called the two oldest to accompany her on the stroll. Tracy stayed behind, looking after Kenneth and Laura.

The sky was a pristine blue without a cloud to be seen. The sun felt warm with each push of the carriage. A massive cement school stood on the corner of East Third and O. It was the South Boston Catholic Academy, a private school for those fortunate enough to be taught by stick-carrying nuns. It was enclosed in an asphalt playground protected by a chain-link fence.

Rachael wheeled the carriage block after block. A half hour passed when the entourage arrived at the Oliver H. Perry Elementary School on East Seventh Street. The majestic three-story red-brick building could be confused for any official city or district building. Its windows were large and spacious, requiring a hooked pole to unlatch and open for the fresh air to circulate. It was Beth and Nathan's new school, and they would register themselves come Monday morning to finish the remaining school year.

Monday arrived with the Beth and Nathan being woke by their mother's call around six. They staggered into the kitchen eating a bowl of cereal, then made a sandwich or two for lunch. They made their beds and spent the remaining time staring out the living room window, watching the neighborhood kids start their walk to school.

It was time to make their journey to school. Rachael got up and peered out the living room window. She watched her two walk along East Third Street until they disappeared around the corner. She noticed the sprinkle of kids uniformly dressed heading in the same direction.

Rachael had written a note with all the pertinent information she thought the school would need. Beth and Nathan made their way into the school asking for the principal's office. Nathan was amazed looking how high the ceilings were. They had a moment's wait when the principal came into view. Mrs. Kendell was not only the principal but the sixth-grade teacher. She greeted the new students, taking the note from Beth's hand.

Mrs. Kendell looked more than just a teacher. She was a tall woman who could easily be mistaken for a bank executive. Her dress was plain and professional without a single wrinkle. It was ornamented with a gold-leaf pin displayed above her left breast. Her hair was well coiffured with neither a strand out of place. She asked them their age, where they were from, and what their parents did for work. These were questions that verified what Mrs. Kendell discovered from the note. It took a few moments to fill out the registration forms on the new members. Afterward Mrs. Kendell smiled and escorted Beth to Mrs. McCrady's third grade and Nathan to Miss Lane's second-grade class.

The conservative appearance of the historic building matched the students' required dress. Casual clothes included skirts and blouses for girls and buttoned shirt and ties for boys. Those forgetting their ties sported a large paper bow tie as an act of humiliation. The day seemed long with school beginning at eight forty-five and remaining in session until two fifteen. The trail of kids leaving Oliver H. Perry simulated a trail of ants finding their way back to their nests.

The two arrived home feeling at ease, having walked the six-block journey. Beth pulled the mail from their designated box mounted within the entryway door. Both raced up the two flights of stairs, knocked on the front door, and was let in from the day's adventure. The door opened into a long, narrow hallway. The path led to the kitchen doorway on the left and the bathroom to the right. It was a typical bathroom with faded pastel-pink walls and an antiquated four-legged tub. Tracy's tall, narrow bureau stood against the wall behind the bathroom door. No one was allowed to look into any of the drawers, or they would risk the chance of getting whipped. Over the toilet was a sliding window, giving view to the entryway landing.

Against the kitchen wall stood a large kerosene stove that dominated the kitchen and dining area. A large bedroom stood adjacent to the right that became the girls' room. On the kitchen's back wall to the left was a roomy walk-in pantry. Opposite the pantry was a doorway leading to the back porch with a descending staircase. The back porch was lined with rows of clotheslines allowing the wash to hang out to dry. At the kitchen entrance was a doorway leading into another large room that became Rachael and Tracy's room. It was connected to the living room. Adjacent to the living room was a medium-sized bedroom that became the boys' room and opened back into the hallway.

The weekday routine began with the older two getting up half sleepy eyed and making their breakfast. Tracy got up, having found a job as a shipping clerk at a nearby company. Beth made school lunches from a choice of peanut butter and jelly, egg salad, bologna and cheese, or tuna fish. Nathan was old enough to take out the trash. The line of garbage cans stood in disarray alongside the building's alleyway. What time remained, Rachael let the two turn on the new portable TV to watch *Captain Kangaroo*. Tracy left moments before spending little time for breakfast. By eight twenty, it was time to leave for school. It was Rachael's signal to get up and tend to the smaller ones.

The second grade was located on the second floor on the south side of the building across from the fourth grade. Miss Lane was a tall, slender woman with short black hair styled in a princely bob. The last couple of months exposed the class to homonyms, synonyms, antonyms, and various clauses and phrases. The class was made up of about thirty kids having assigned seats according to size and gender.

The school day ended. The classes filed out to the end of the schoolyard. It was overcast with strong winds blowing in all directions, putting small twigs and seasoned leaves into flight. While the class waited to be excused, the entryway gate took a sudden swing and struck into Nathan's forehead. The classmates who surrounded him were startled by the blood. Miss Lane intervened, focusing on Nathan. She noticed his blooded eye and hurriedly escorted him into the school. Nathan was placed into the nearest chair, with Miss Lane handing him her handkerchief to hold against the wound. She quickened her pace to the teacher's lounge for a basin of cold water and paper towels.

Mrs. Kendell witnessed the proceedings from afar and raced to the boy's aid. Mrs. Kendell asked the boy if he knew his telephone number. Nathan replied his family didn't have a phone.

She continued with the next question, "What's your address and your neighbor's name?"

He looked up at the principal, "789 East Third Street. I think my mother mentioned the family living below us was Duran."

Mrs. Kendell went to the lounge, paged through the telephone book, and found the name and the correct address. She called, having them relay the message to Mrs. Anderson that her presence was needed. The neighbor agreed to watch Rachael's children while she raced to the school.

She arrived in a little over a half hour. After a moment's consultation, the school called a cab taking them to a doctor's office on the west end of East Broadway. She held her son while the doctor carefully sewed the flesh wound together. Three stitches were placed over Nathan's left eyebrow, then Rachael and Nathan walked the long trek home.

Nathan took the next day off, not putting pressure on the freshly sewn wound. Rachael wanted a morning walk around the neighborhood, asking Nathan if he would be all right by himself for about an hour. Nathan nodded, knowing he had the television to himself. She got the remaining three dressed and had them wait with Nathan. She lowered the vintage carriage down the two flights and gently pressed the blankets and pillow in their proper position. Rachael gathered the trio, placing Gretchen in the carriage with Laura sitting in front and Kenneth walking alongside. It was about the same time most mothers took their breaks, sitting on the steps, holding their morning coffee, or inhaling the first morning cigarette.

Rachael stopped and chatted with a few of the step warmers. It was her way of getting to know her neighbors. She strolled up one side and down the other before returning to her own front doorsteps. By late morning, the children were nestled around the television while their mother started rearranging her bedroom.

A large opening separated the parents' bedroom to the living room. Rachael thought of hanging a double-wide curtain to deter the traffic and allow for some privacy. The doorway at the adjacent wall led to the narrow hallway, creating the accessible traffic flow.

Rachael made her kids lunch before sending them to bed for an afternoon nap. She made herself comfortable on the couch to watch the first round of television soaps, starting with *Search for Tomorrow, Guiding Light, As the World Turns,* and *The Louise Day Show*. She got up, made herself a cold-cut sandwich, and continued with the *General Hospital* and *The Edge of Night.*

GROWING PAINS

Beth dished the vegetables into serving bowls while Nathan placed the dishes and silverware on the newly acquired dinner table. It was an inexpensive metal table that unfolded to accommodate the family members.

Tracy arrived home in time for supper. He had spent the past hour having a beer or two at the East Second Street Bar and Grill. The kids sat at their assigned seats as the family ate their simple meal of mashed potato, peas, and ground beef. The last child was excused from the table with the two oldest cleaning the aftermath and giving the table scrapes to Patty.

Rachael allowed the two outside to get acquainted with the neighborhood kids. Her instructions were to be within earshot of calling their names. The neighborhood was curious about Beth and Nathan, and after a few introductory questions, the two were accepted. The Costello family lived in a separate house between the three-story apartment buildings. The family consisted of Tony, Massy, Debra, and Mark. A couple of doors down lived the Burton family that included a son, Ed, who was a year ahead of Beth; a daughter, Susan, who was Nathan's age; and a younger son and daughter. There were other faces out and about that made up the neighborhood adolescence.

Rachael wanted to test her children's obedience and stuck her head out the living room window, calling their names. Within moments, they raced from the side of the apartment building. Rachael acknowledged their presence and was satisfied with their responses.

She added, "Time to come in."

The family's routine continued until school was let out for the summer. Beth was promoted to fourth grade and Nathan to third. Summer brought on more responsibilities for the two. Rachael had Nathan wash floors on his hands and knees as a mop and bucket wouldn't get the deep cleaning she had expected. Beth learned to do the wash using the family's Maytag washer and wringer. She made Beth pay close attention to the wringer as the clothes sometimes wrapped themselves around it. A connecting hose from the kitchen sink filled the washer's tub with the washer hose placed into the sink to empty it.

The clothes were hung row after row on the back porch. Each apartment had access to a clothesline that ran on a pulley from the porch to a centered telephone pole that stood on the end of the backyard. It was seldom used as the wind tangled the line, leaving the clothes dangling.

On weekends, Rachael wheeled Gretchen and one of her oldest grocery shopping. The vintage carriage continued its usefulness carrying the grocery bags back to the apartment. Rachael again rewarded her kids by letting them outside, provided they were within earshot. The summer heat often got unbearable, allowing the kids the three-block walk to Pleasant Beach. They placed their towels on the open sand and joined the multitudes in swimming and splashing in the Atlantic.

Marine Park ran adjacent to the beach, spreading out over three city blocks. It continued to the outer point called Castle Island. The park allowed for many picnickers to enjoy the cool evening breeze whispering from across the ocean. School bands often played popular show tunes at the park's gazebo from time to time. Rachael loved going to these events. She'd prepare by having Nathan retrieve the picnic basket and thermos from the pantry. Beth made enough peanut butter and jelly sandwiches to fill the hunger pangs. Rachael gathered everyone down at the entryway. Tracy steered the carriage down the two flights of stairs with the army blanket in tow. Rachael made sure the basket was packed with the sandwiches, paper cups and napkins, and the thermos filled with Kool-Aid. A Frisbee was packed to occupy the younger ones losing interest with the music.

The family walked the city blocks to Marine Park. They mingled with hundreds of other families that occupied blankets, listening to the nostalgic band tunes. Younger kids exercised their legs chasing each other or tossing the Frisbees back and forth. The patriotic and show tunes blared for over an hour before playing the last note. Families got up as if they themselves were an orchestrated event, folding their blankets and carrying their belongings for home.

Rachael trained Nathan to handle the carriage down the two flights and onto the sidewalk when she was in one of her shopping moods. Not everyone went, usually Kenneth or Laura, Gretchen, and Nathan making the trip. They'd walk downtown South Boston by way of East Third and O, crossing over and up the hill to Independence Square Park. The park's main attraction was a large water fountain that had weathered over the years. Its walkways jettisoned out toward the neighboring streets like octopus legs. Once through, they held on to one another, crossing East Broadway and continuing down to the Summer Street intersection.

East Broadway was lined with the multitude of various mom-and-pop stores that included a deli, a bakery, and a small hardware store. A couple of blocks stood a First National supermarket, where most everyone did their grocery shopping. Across the street was a barbershop, where Rachael decided Nathan could go for his trims. A short distance farther stood the South Boston Branch Library. Rachael had discovered the place on her earlier adventures. It was where she and Nathan exercised their literary fantasies. They continued along the city blocks on an incline, passing the rows of apartment buildings.

On the descending side, West Broadway intersected with Dorchester Street. West Broadway continued another mile, revealing even larger retail stores like Woolworths and the Five and Dime. There were individual clothing stores and shoe stores, including Buster Brown and Thom McAn. On the same stretch, the Broadway movie theater promoted the latest features. Both East and West Broadway were the hub for everyday shopping. Broadway led into Boston's upscale retail stores like Robert Hall, Filene's, and Jordan

Marsh displaying the latest fashions. To a seven-year-old, Nathan was awestruck with Downtown Boston and the Common.

The Boston Common was the jewel of Boston. The majestic park provided walkways pointing to many business districts that bordered its luscious garden-style vegetation. It showcased an elongated pond, where folks congregated in riding the iconic swan boats.

Most stores allowed carriages within their shopping walls while others preferred them outside. Nathan tended the carriage while his mother went in poring over the sale items. After shopping, the long walk home was tiresome and sometimes followed with the group hugging their pillows for an afternoon nap.

Nathan started the weekend getting up and walking to Archie's for the paper and a few items for breakfast. Tracy stood in his bathrobe cooking breakfast of bacon and eggs in the cast-iron skillet. Nathan returned in time to make the plateful of toast. Beth got Gretchen cleaned and placed her into the high chair. The kids left the table for their own amusement. Tracy and Rachael remained sipping their second cup of morning coffee.

Tracy leaned back, reading the paper with a lighted cigarette. He sported a pack of Lucky Strikes for his occasional smoke. It was accompanied with a glass of wine containing a raw egg that he swallowed in one great swoop. The old Zenith cabinet now served as his wine cabinet. Beth and Nathan labored washing the breakfast dishes and cleaning the kitchen while Tracy eyed Beth's growing figure.

It was after the Fourth of July when Rachael received a letter from Flora asking if Nathan could come and visit. Rachael remembered those earlier years when Flora had taken Nathan. Now that Uncle William had passed, she allowed Nathan to go down for a week. Rachael rode with Nathan on the transit bus to Tremont Street. Nathan got used to riding the bus with its many diverse people. They walked a couple of blocks to the Greyhound bus terminal. Rachael explained that someone would meet him at his grandmother's place. She bought her son a ticket and kissed him goodbye as he stepped onto the bus.

The bus pulled out of Boston, making side trips to the suburbs for a passenger or two before making the final trip down Route 3.

The Kingston exits came into view with the bus making a turnoff on the main connector leading into Plymouth. The bus crossed into the township with Sarah standing on the street corner waiting to flag the bus down. Flora arrived shortly afterward and was overjoyed seeing her grandnephew. He grabbed his suitcase and followed his grandaunt downtown, linking up with her neighbors Alan and Barbara Smyth for the return trip to Ellis Pond.

Having no place to unpack, Nathan lived in and out of his suitcase. Flora showed him how to convert the living room futon into a bed. She was an early riser, starting with a mile-long walk with Teddy. Flora loved her walks, having traveled networks of them over the years. Some mornings, she enticed Nathan to go with her on the winding trails.

Flora's kitchen stove ran on propane but was never used. It wasn't worth the upkeep since she only cooked for herself. She used a double hot plate for her meals. Flora's dining table was built replicating a restaurant's booth. The table was stationary with cushioned benches on each side. It was encased with a half wall, so those eating could peer into the living room. Flora cooked breakfast, delivering the two plates of eggs, bacon, toast, and cups of coffee. One of Flora's idiosyncrasies was making the toaster go through a cycle before inserting the bread. Afterward Nathan washed his face and hands while his grandaunt cleaned about her bedroom. Their positions swapped when one or the other had finished.

Flora loved showing her visitors off to the neighborhood, and Nathan was no different. The word spread that a new kid was staying at the Atwoods. Flora was accommodating and glad her grandnephew was making friends. A few stopped by for a game of cards with Nathan reciprocating at their homes. Flora left him to his own enjoyment of swimming in Ellis Pond. She periodically kept a distant eye watching his involvement with the other seasonal kids diving from the wooden raft. It was made of solid wood and anchored about fifty feet from the water's edge. Flora left an air mattress nearby in case Nathan needed it. Nathan wasn't an avid swimmer but had a preference for swimming underwater.

After hours of basking in the sun, Flora called Nathan to change out of his swimsuit. She was ready to take another walk with Teddy before cooking supper on the outdoor stove. The walk took them into the camping area that bordered the summer residents. They weaved all around the new trails. Flora was interested in seeing if the rumors were true that the campground owners had created a section for RVs. The duo walked about the campsites, giving the sidelined campers a smile and a heartwarming hello. The construction site suddenly came into view. Flora and Nathan were satisfied that the rumors were true and circled back to the beachfront.

Flora kept the supper simple with boiled potatoes, a vegetable, and a small roast. The outdoor barbecue pit took no time getting started. Lighting the crumpled newspaper and sticks produced the cooking temperature she needed. The mealtime chitchat was of home and the family gossip. Flora told Nathan she decided on selling her home on South Street. With William gone, the house was too much for her. She'd keep the cottage and was thinking about moving to the Cambridge area.

The Smyths had a home in Cambridge, and Flora knew of a cousin that still worked in the Boston area. She wrote to see if he'd like to go in on an apartment. Cambridge was central to all of Boston, and Flora would still live at the cottage during the summer. The new arrangements didn't faze Nathan. All that mattered was keeping the cottage that everyone loved. The two settled for the evening playing a few hands of cribbage before joining the Shufflers with their evening socials.

The week passed with Nathan feeling refreshed from the enjoyment of his newfound friends. The Smyths drove Flora and Nathan back to Plymouth, letting the grandnephew off at the bus depot. The vehicle continued on to the supermarket.

Nathan met his parents at the Greyhound terminal, then rode the transit bus back.

Rachael started quizzing him, "Did you have a good time?"

"Yeah, I'm getting better at swimming underwater." Nathan smiled.

"What did Flora have to say?" Rachael asked with a curious tone.

"Nothing much other than she was glad to see me. She still has Teddy, and we went on a few walks. Aunt Flora can do some long walks," Nathan stated with validity.

"What else did she do?" inquired Rachael.

"We just visited a few of the neighbors, then I went swimming. Other than that, I had a good time," replied Nathan, recapturing the visit in his mind.

Rachael looked at her son, still wondering if there was something else he wasn't telling her. Minutes passed, and the threesome arrived home, leaving Nathan to unpack. He arrived in time to help set the table for the traditional beans and franks that Beth had prepared.

Fall was around the corner, paving the way for another school season. Rachael had to manipulate school shopping, sizing for clothes, end-of-summer haircuts, book coverings, and everything else that went with it. Nathan needed a variety of bow and straight ties for his school's wardrobe. It was exhausting for Rachael making multiple trips to the stores getting everyone ready for school. She sat thinking everyone had what they needed when she envisioned the holiday season on the horizon.

She thought about her parents arriving and realized the need for another bed. Nathan had grown where his grandfather could no longer share a bed. Rachael decided on buying bunk beds for the boys, with Nathan taking the bottom and Kenneth on top. Nathan's metal headboard would be a spare with Kenneth's bed moved into the girls' room.

The first day of school led to passing out the lesson books. Nathan's class started with multiple columns of additions and subtractions with the introduction of problem-solving paragraphs, figuring out how many apples and oranges Sally or Sue had in the end.

With India ink and a quill pen, the class practiced penmanship, taking great care not to distort the written language. Left-handers looked like deformed cripples as they carefully printed so that their palms didn't smudge the freshly drawn letters. Nathan fell into this group, having been a southpaw all his life. Next was spelling, followed by a history lesson.

It was during this period Mrs. McCrady chose students to stand and read a paragraph or two. Children held their books close, concentrating on the scripted words, hoping to be overlooked by the teacher's scoping eyes. Reading before the class brought everyone's attention glued to the reader. Mrs. McCrady selected a student at random, who nervously read the three paragraphs before allowing another to endure the same humiliation.

There were three recesses throughout the day. Students eyed the clock as each one approached. After the third, it was difficult to teach the remaining lesson as the class became squeamish, waiting for the day to get over. Mrs. McCrady managed to get the last lesson taught with class participation before the final bell.

Suppertime brought Tracy home from work. Many times, Rachael looked for him from the living room window. She glanced across the street, where a spacious field stretched into East Second Street, then looked to the right where a fence crossed a vacant lot between the two apartment buildings. If he came from the field, he was returning straight from work. If he crawled through the broken fence boards, he came from the East Second Street Pub. His background was always a mystery to the kids. Beth and Nathan didn't know much about his past or where he worked. Rachael had told her kids that Tracy worked mostly as a longshoreman. Rachael knew Tracy's past, and the less said, the better.

When it came to give information about their father and his occupation, Beth and Nathan were told that their father was Clarence Anderson, who was a disabled vet. The neighborhood kids just naturally thought Tracy was Mr. Anderson and addressed him as such.

The pressures of the household and keeping Tracy focused on the family added to Rachael's stress. Her support check paid the rent and maybe a utility bill. Rachael depended on Tracy supporting the remaining bills. His frequent stops at the East Second Street Pub wasted the needed money on drinks for himself and his friends.

Rachael's frustrations toward Tracy carried over onto her two oldest. Tracy's attitude wasn't Rachael's only concern; she suspected the neighborhood kids were having a bad influence on her children.

She started questioning them of whom they played with and what was talked about every time they went out. Even their in-house mannerisms were toned. She capitalized on her children's usage of please and thank you, asking one of them to say the mealtime prayer.

Rachael's authoritarian tone didn't affect the smaller ones. Kenneth and Laura were busy instigating their own foolery. They often swayed in front of the television, preventing others from watching. Laura stood swaying once too many times for Nathan's patience. He got up and pulled her away, then slapped her bottom. She went crying to her mother, who returned with the belt. Nathan saw his mother head right toward him.

"Don't you ever touch these girls again. Do you hear me?" Rachael shouted while whipping the boy.

Nathan had all he could do to protect himself. The belt didn't end the punishment. Rachael couldn't wait to tell Tracy about the ordeal later that evening. His anxiety rose, wanting to teach Nathan a lesson, and called him into the kitchen.

"So you want to pick on kids smaller than you. Why not pick on someone your own size?" Tracy snapped. Tracy fell to his knees in front of the shaken lad. "Here, pick on me."

Nathan just stood there unable to move.

Tracy continued his intimidation, "Come on. Put up your fists."

The lad still didn't make a move.

Tracy grabbed the boy's hand and started jabbing it into the boy's chest. "Come on. Defend yourself. You're Mr. Tough Guy. You like picking on kids smaller than you!" shouted Tracy.

Nathan's nerves were shaken and started to weep.

"Why are you crying? I'm not hurting you. You are. You're hurting yourself," insinuated Tracy with a smile.

Tracy kept jabbing into the boy's chest before moving up and giving the lad a couple of belts in his face. The second belt caused the boy's lip to bleed with the cracking of the nose cartilage.

Tracy saw the blood beginning to flow, let go of the boy's hand, and ended the punishment. "Don't ever let me hear you striking any one of these girls again. Go wash up and get to bed. I don't want to hear another peep out of you."

Rachael stood on the other side of the room watching her son leave for the bathroom. She felt some satisfaction of what she just witnessed.

Nathan stood in the mirror seeing the blood run from his nose and over his split bottom lip and continue down his chin. He pressed a wad of wet toilet paper against the wound, hoping to make it stop. It was another five minutes before Nathan was able to leave the bathroom and crawl under his bedcovers.

Other antics from the ruthless duo were taking possessions and dismantling or breaking them "accidentally." Stiffer measures resulted with more lashings of the belt. Rachael thought the best place for it was on a nail by the kitchen stove as a constant reminder. Mandatory rules were put into place. Dishes had to be done and the kitchen cleaned within a half hour. Tracy sat timing the dishwashers while holding the belt in his hands. The older two had to get permission for just about everything. Even their friends had to meet with their mother's approval. Rachael's imaginations were straining the nerves of the older two. They were intimidated with fear, speaking only when spoken to.

Beth and Nathan continued their morning schedule. Nathan ran to Archie's for Tracy's morning paper while Beth made breakfast. Tracy got up putting on his bathrobe, making his way to the bathroom. He noticed Beth at the stove stirring the hot oatmeal. He gingerly walked up behind her, looking over her shoulder. Tracy leaned up against her, making a slight rubbing up and down on her buttocks. Beth felt him against her and felt her heart pulsating. She stood still, pretending he wasn't there in hopes he'd go away. He smiled and started to ask her if she liked what he was doing. The sound of Rachael tossing in the other room made Tracy move quickly into his bathroom routine.

Moments later, Nathan returned with the paper. He entered the kitchen, placing it on the table, and saw his sister putting the lunch sandwiches together. Everything appeared as if nothing had happened. School became a haven for the two. Getting permission to go to the library on various weekends gave some latitude to the calmness. Nathan read increasingly more to escape the disruptive reality that surrounded him.

The fall season brought the enchantment of Halloween. It was the family's first celebrated holiday since the days of Plymouth. Rachael knew she had to calm her temperament. She needed to have the children feeling comfortable with the grandparents arriving for the holidays. She allowed Beth and Nathan to go trick-or-treating and bought costumes that were sound and sensible. She dressed Nathan as a Dutch Boy and Beth, a mild version of a medieval princess.

The older two understood they had a little over an hour to trick-or-treat. They could travel among a group, staying on East Broadway, East Third, or East Second Street. Darkness arrived with Beth and Nathan heading down the two flights dressed for the night of deviltry. They went along the street going door-to-door, filling their bags with assorted candy. Within an hour, they were home with their just rewards.

November arrived with Beth turning nine. It was morning when Nathan headed down the hallway to the bathroom when Tracy walked up toward him. He stopped with a smile on his face. He placed his hand between Nathan's legs and started rubbing and placed Nathan's hand on his pants, pressing up and down, asking him if he liked it. Nathan froze, feeling his inner soul pulsating. After a moment, Tracy allowed him to pass. Nathan's mind was clouded, not knowing what to do or say. He pressed hard to put the episode out of his mind although Tracy's sly smirks made him remember.

The weekend before Thanksgiving, Rachael did the last-minute grocery shopping. She took Beth and Kenneth, with Gretchen in the carriage, leaving Laura and Nathan with Tracy behind. Tracy wanted Nathan to stay in case he had to go out. They sat watching the afternoon movie when Laura started dozing off. Tracy scooped her up, putting her in her bedroom for a nap. He returned and sat next to Nathan, placing his hand between Nathan's legs and started rubbing. Tracy unzipped his pants and placed Nathan's hand on his crotch, making him rub up and down. Nathan prayed for someone to come, unable to cry for help. He knew he'd get belted by putting up a fuss.

A few days passed when Rachael wanted him to go down to Plymouth to help his grandparents make the trip up for the holidays. A second breath hadn't left her mouth before he was ready to go. It meant taking a couple of school days off as Nathan rode the Greyhound bus to the provincial building. Milton's arthritis became more chronic, slowing his walking ability. Their ground-floor apartment made it easy for him to make the walk to the bus stop.

The day before Thanksgiving made early risers for the travelers. They got up, ensuring Milton had ample time walking to the bus stop, with Nathan and Sarah carrying the luggage. The bus arrived with the driver helping Milton get on board, placing him in the front seat. Milton hadn't anything to read and decided to bend the driver's ear with tales of his youth. Sarah and Nathan sat a couple of seats back. She noticed her husband's excitement of being on the bus knowing it was Milton's first bus ride since his youth. Sarah savored the moment yet strategized on the next move. Once at the terminal, the driver allowed the passengers to step out before helping Milton off.

The trio managed to walk to the front of the station. Nathan watched his grandfather while Sarah hailed a cab, riding the rest of the way to East Third Street. The hard part was about to begin, getting Milton up those two flights of stairs. It took time lifting one foot after another, pausing every third or fourth step. The second-floor landing gave some relief before reaching the top floor.

Thanksgiving went without any disruption or squabbling. The meal centered on a large turkey that Rachael washed, greased, stuffed, and placed in the oven during the wee hours of the morning. It was side dished by mashed potatoes and gravy, butternut squash, boiled onions, peas, stuffing, and cranberry sauce. Sarah made gravy from the turkey drippings. She mixed a couple of tablespoons of flour with milk, then poured it into the drippings, stirring constantly over a warm heat. The boiled gizzards, heart, and livers were diced and added into the gravy. Glasses of milk highlighted the kids' dishes while small glasses of wine for the adults. Milton settled for milk since he held steadfast on not drinking alcohol.

The table was set. Nathan was responsible for cracking the walnuts in half and hollowing them out. A raisin was placed in the bottom with a toothpick standing erect from it. Ship sails were attached to the toothpick, inscribing the name of the member, and were placed at their setting. It replicated the Pilgrims' first feast of Thanksgiving.

With everyone at the table and Gretchen in her high chair, a prayer was recited, and the dinner commenced without any interruptions. Afterward the members with overstretched stomach muscles huddled together in the living room watching the holiday movie. It was in CinemaScope or living black and white. Beth and Nathan took care of the aftermath, making sure everything was cleaned, wrapped, and put away. Even Patty's dish overflowed with leftovers.

Sarah took a few days during the first week of December to return to Plymouth. There were bills to be paid, and she wanted to ensure her place was safe and sound. Upon her return, she brought a bag full of various strips of cloth. Her new project was braiding strips together, then sewing the sides until they formed a braided rug. She did a couple of these as gifts for others throughout the year. She took a break from her tedious rug making and began mending the rips and holes of her grandchildren's clothes.

The winter weather left no resistance to the cold winds that blew from the Atlantic. The apartment's only heating source was the kitchen stove that kept the place somewhat warm. The inevitable chill could be felt in the front end of the place. Sarah and Rachael bought plastic window coverings with felt stripping to hold back the cold air. Clothes were dried in the kitchen on the upright wooden clothes dryer. Layers of newspapers were placed underneath, catching the drips.

Snow fell inches by the minute, leaving tall drifts as the ocean winds channeled through the hollowed streets. Drifts buried cars, making owners bundle up to shovel their vehicles to freedom only to find them later blocked by ambitious snowplows. The snowstorms brought on cabin fever. Everyone paired off playing one game or another. Nathan stayed close to his grandfather, playing cards or cribbage between going to school and doing chores. Milton didn't talk much but caught an eyeful of the household routine. Nathan, like his grandfather, wasn't a talker; but a lot was ingrained in his mind.

Sarah went with the adults shopping for a Christmas tree. They carried it the five blocks, then carefully placed it in the living room and secured it to the wall. The decorations came out with everyone taking part in bringing the tree to life. The Santa face took its place, lighting up the living room window. The final touch was the Lionel train running the never-ending track around the base. The detailed train station was carefully displayed on the living room mantle with layers of cotton batting simulating the season's snow.

Christmas was strained by the three birthdays. Gretchen turned one, Kenneth turned four, and Nathan turned eight. Rachael decided to divide their Christmas presents into birthday gifts. Nathan was reminded of that when opening his gift and accepted it with a grain of salt. Sarah contributed what she could during the holidays, knowing the hardships Rachael and Tracy were experiencing.

It was early evening before Christmas when Rachael gathered her brood before sending them to bed.

"I want everyone to know, if you get up early, you can have your stockings and play with any toy that isn't wrapped. Is that clear with everyone?"

All the heads nodded in the affirmative.

Rachael continued, "I want everyone to be as quiet as possible when you wake up. If I hear any squabbling, I'll have Santa take back your toys. Is that clear?"

Again the heads nodded, with a few mumbling, "Yes, Mom."

"Okay, now all of you get to bed, and I don't want to hear a peep out of you until morning," instructed their mother.

Santa's elves worked tirelessly during the late-night hours until the tree base was lost to mounds of presents. The predawn hour arrived to the awakened eyes of the anxious children. The amusement of the unwrapped toys allowed a couple of hours of well-deserved sleep to Santa's elves. It was after breakfast and the dishes were done that the family gathered in the living room.

The adults sat around the pile of presents.

Rachael called out, "Who wants to be Santa and hand out presents?"

She looked among the smaller set, picking Laura to play the role.

Laura picked up the first gift and studied the tag, trying to figure for whom it was intended.

Sarah knew she couldn't read and motioned to her granddaughter. "Bring it here, honey, and let's sound it out together."

Laura brought it over and, between them, sounded the name, then handed it to Gretchen.

One by one, the gift tag names were aided by an elf until Laura seemed to recognize the label. Laura stood wearing a large smile after the last gift was presented. She was proud of her accomplishment. The wrapping paper needed to be picked up before preparing the Christmas dinner. Sarah baked a couple of apple pies while Rachael prepared the ham with cloves and pineapple slices. The older ones peeled the vegetables. It was Thanksgiving all over again, with everyone sitting around the rest of the day.

New Year's was a few days off. Sarah wanted to get back to Plymouth. Rachael and Tracy accompanied her parents to the bus terminal, making sure they got on board the bus without any trouble. Arriving in Plymouth, the driver helped Milton off the bus. The apartment was only steps away. Sarah realized the difficulty the trip had on Milton, knowing it was his last bus ride.

School vacation and the preholiday routines came back into play. The kids were given permission taking the sleds to Marine Park for some fun. The park had a prominent downhill that provided mounds of sliding for those in the neighborhood. Those without sleds used waxed-bottom cardboard pieces. It wasn't long before the cold chill of the ocean penetrated the snowsuits, forcing many to return to the warmth of their abodes.

New Year's Eve arrived. Rachael sent the kids to bed early to avoid any crankiness later in the evening when the celebration counted. Around eleven, she awoke them to the sounds of Guy Lombardo and his orchestra playing a variety of show tunes until the dropping of the ball in Times Square. The band kicked off "Auld

Lang Syne," with viewers shouting, "Happy New Year!" Faint shouts from neighborhood windows could be heard echoing the same New Year wishes. Slowly everyone made their way back to bed. The new 1959 calendars were displayed on household walls everywhere.

THE NEW YEAR

New Year started with the traditional breakfast of bacon and eggs, toast, and hot chocolate. Rachael woke Gretchen for the morning breakfast, sitting her on a couple of thick catalogs in training her to sit upright at the table. She called Kenneth and Laura to get up and get ready for breakfast. It was one of the few meals the family sat together. The older two washed the dirty dishes and made sure all the kitchen surfaces were wiped down before the family gathered to watch the New Year's Day parade.

It was time to take the Christmas tree down. The empty boxes were brought from Rachael's closet, and the ornaments were removed one by one, each carefully placed into their containers. Only a few ornate decorations had their own special wrappings. It took most of the afternoon before the tree was carried down into the alleyway. There was little effort in putting together the holiday dinner as they mostly picked over the previous day's leftovers. New Year's Day remained laid-back without any fuss. Even Laura was content with herself sucking her thumb from a developed habit. A few sat at the table enjoying a board game of Careers. The day seemed so out of character, having the involvement and sharing the enjoyment of family before everyone crawled under the bed covers.

Saturday morning brought the younger ones sitting on the couch watching morning *Looney Tunes* cartoons. Rachael got up and went to the bathroom. Tracy sat at the kitchen table in his maroon-print bathrobe he received for Christmas. He sipped his coffee while reading the morning paper. A lighted cigarette rested in the ashtray. Nathan walked over to the living room corner bookcase looking for something to read. The curtains to his parents' room were open, giving a clear view into the kitchen.

Heading back, Nathan heard a loud psst. Looking toward the kitchen, he saw Tracy stand up, open his robe, and feel himself with one hand and beckoning him with the other. A chill brushed up Nathan's spine, and he ignored Tracy's desire. Moments later, Rachael came out with Tracy still sipping his coffee.

Nathan sat on his bed feeling his nerves vibrating. He was filled with worried emotions about Tracy's desires. The more he thought, the more Nathan felt he needed to talk to someone. Suddenly thoughts of all the repercussions raced through his head.

Who's going to believe an eight-year-old? What if it gets out to the cops? Will my parents get arrested? What will happen to us kids?

Nathan decided to ignore Tracy's advances and try to avoid being alone with him.

The early hours of a February morning rustled the sounds of footsteps and clothing being tossed. The wails of a baby's cry echoed throughout the place. The children awoke not knowing what to think or do while still in their beds. The front door opened and closed, then after a few moments, it repeated itself. Beth and Nathan got up peering out from their bedrooms. Tracy saw their prying eyes and shouted for everyone to stay in their rooms. The wails continued, catching everyone's wonder. It seemed to go for quite a while before there was a knock at the door and there were sounds of strange footsteps accompanied by the echoing of grown-up voices. Time lapsed a moment or two when the heavy footsteps sounded as they left through the outer door.

From his bedroom window, Nathan watched and waited to see what appeared from the front door overhang. The ambulance was parked right below his window. The commotion carried his mother in a chair wrapped in a sheet. The excitement traveled into silence. The wailing gone, and so was their mother. The older two had no choice but to go back to bed until dawn. Tracy had Beth stay home and watch the younger ones while he went to work.

The next morning was Lincoln's birthday. Beth got up and made breakfast. Nathan helped with the household chores, taking Patty out for her bathroom runs. Tracy stood by watching over everyone. As the day wore on, Tracy and Gretchen curled up on the couch watching a movie. Beth had broken out her paper dolls asking Nathan to play along with her on the living room carpet. Kenneth and Laura were amusing themselves playing a game in the girls' room.

All was peaceful when Tracy got a gleam in his eye asking Beth and Nathan into his bedroom.

Tracy stood before them, smiling. "Do you like playing house together?"

The two answered in unison, "Yes."

Tracy continued, smiling, "I'd like to see you pull down your pants."

Beth and Nathan stood startled, then looked at each other. They remained frozen, saying and doing nothing. Tracy waited, hoping to have them perform the sexual act. Nathan shook his head back and forth, not wanting to go through what was about to happen.

Minutes passed when Tracy replied with a wide grin, "It's okay. You can go back to playing."

Nathan's head again became clouded. His hands started shaking.

He wondered, *Why did Tracy want us to drop our pants*?

All he could think was Tracy wanted to rub between both their legs. One look at Beth told Nathan that Tracy was doing her just as he was with him.

Their refusal didn't affect Tracy. During the night, Nathan crept down the hallway to go to the bathroom. He approached the doorway, catching the outline of Beth leaving Tracy's room for her own. The thought of knowing his sister was in bed with Tracy worried Nathan. He peed and returned to his room, crawling under his blankets.

The weekend arrived with Rachael returning with a new baby girl. Abigail had been born in the apartment and now occupied the baby's crib. Her birth was a surprise to everyone. Rachael had only told her mother and Tracy. The shuffling of beds meant Abigail took the crib, Gretchen moved to the single bed, and Laura doubled up with Beth.

Months passed, bringing the trees into full bloom. The new season brought the occasional ring tapping at the door to the tune "Shave and a Haircut." Eileen Gordon was a neighbor who lived across the street with her husband, Kyle, and four children. She had two sons, Lawrence and Daven, and two young daughters, Rose and Camila. Apparently Nathan wasn't the only one looking out his window that cold morning watching his mother being lifted into an ambulance.

Eileen was a solid woman who possessed an outgoing demeanor who introduced herself on one of Rachael's outings. She popped over many mornings for coffee and a cigarette, sharing her compilation of family woes. There were very few people that would meet with Rachael's expectations. Eileen had succeeded in becoming one of them.

The older two arrived home from school, finding a gentleman sitting in the living room. Rachael introduced her two oldest to Pastor Robert Carter. He was going house to house trying to increase his flock at his Congregational church. Rachael was considering his proposal even though she already decided her two were going.

Saturday afternoon, Rachael loaded Abigail and Gretchen into the vintage carriage with Nathan walking alongside. They made the long track to locate the Congregational church. Rachael pushed the carriage along the city blocks of East Broadway to where it connected to Dorchester Street. She walked Dorchester one block, crossed over, and pushed the carriage uphill where the small English tutor church stood. It was quaint with rustic stones covered with ivy. Rachael knocked on the side door where the pastor and his family resided. The door opened, revealing the casually dressed pastor. After a few moments of conversing, Rachael and her troop started the journey home, stopping at the First National supermarket.

As they walked, Rachael looked over to her son. "What do you think about the church? Do you think you'll like it?"

Nathan looked at his mother. "It's not bad. I wouldn't mind going, but it's a long ways just to go to church."

"You won't have to walk all the time. You'll be taking the bus," assured his mother.

It was the first day attending Sunday school. Nathan woke and sat on the edge of his bed getting his head ready to face another day. He got dressed, making sure Beth was awake. He left the apartment, making his run to Mike's for the Sunday paper. His store took Nathan down East Third Street, rounding the corner at P Street, then up a block.

Beth made a pan of hot oatmeal for breakfast, then washed and dressed in her Sunday best. Rachael got up for a few moments, giving them the one-way bus fare and telling them the walk back would do them good. Nathan hurried changing his clothes and met Beth at the doorway. They walked to the bus stop at P and East Broadway, taking the Dudley Square bus to Dorchester Street and getting off at the first bus stop. They continued up a block, making their way into the church. They climbed to the second floor, where rows of long tables were arranged like picnic tables.

Each table represented a classroom. There was only a room for grades one through four as some grades required two tables. Fifth and six graders were placed in the church's enclosed alcoves that book cased both sides of the altar. Each grade was taught a certain section of the Bible's Old Testament. Teachers used felt figures on backgrounds to tell the lessons from the biblical fables. With the lessons over, Beth and Nathan made the long journey home.

On Sunday afternoons, the family frequented Pleasant Beach. Nathan became more daring wading into the Atlantic. He learned to swim the refreshing waters although his swims were mostly underwater. When the tide was out, beachgoers walked along the shoreline looking at the tiny air bubbles that spewed from spots along the ocean-drenched shore. The bubbles indicated clams, and folks dug them up by the pailfuls. Tracy and Rachael filled a pail and brought them home to steam.

Tracy filled the basin with water and placed it on the stove to boil. Rachael washed each clam, removing the sand from every crevice. The shells were dropped in the boiling water until every one sprung open. A stick of butter was melted in a saucepan ready for the tasty morsels. Rachael called Beth to join them. She was the seafood eater. Nathan followed just to watch. The three took turns taking a clam by the neck, dipping it in butter, then swallowing it whole. Nathan cringed just watching them.

"Want to try one?" asked Rachael, looking at her son's disturbing face.

"Naw, it looks like snots. How can you eat that?" asked Nathan.

"Easy," answered Beth.

She demonstrated, taking another clam, dipping it in butter, then slowly letting it drop into her mouth. It was enough to make Nathan leave the room, letting the three finish the bowl.

The heat from the summer mornings took Rachael and the kids spending time at the beach. They were left to their own temptations and the pounding waves. Rachael lay on the army blanket, tanning under the blaring sun. By noon, she packed the belongings and gathered everyone for the walk home for a quick lunch. Rachael returned in time to watch her TV dramas, still being her major form of entertainment.

By midsummer, Rachael enrolled her two oldest for a week of vacation Bible school. It would keep them occupied and off the streets. To Beth and Nathan, it was a continuation of Sunday school discussing Bible verses. Offsetting the Biblical lessons, the group assembled a few religious crafts that were mostly composed of simulated stained glass.

Karen Adams wrote asking if she could visit around the Labor Day weekend. She was anxious to see her high school friend after years of corresponding. The place went through a thorough cleaning. The woodwork that lined the lower half of the kitchen walls was scrubbed along the baseline. Beth and Nathan took old toothbrushes, getting down on their hands and knees removing the dirt that had built up along the floor's edge. They cleaned for hours before completing it by week's end.

It was the third week into August, and so was Nathan's scheduled trip to Ellis Pond. He looked forward to visit Ellis Pond knowing how relaxing it made him. Nathan was packed and rode the transit bus to the Greyhound terminal. The bus arrived in Plymouth with Flora waiting for Nathan's arrival. The grandparents had left for three weeks, visiting Milton's niece in Haverhill, Massachusetts.

After a quick hello kiss, they hurriedly walked to the other side of town meeting up with Alan and Barbara, who were loading their car with groceries.

Flora unlocked the door, where Teddy greeted them with a multitude of tail wags. Flora lived simply, relying on her friends and neighbors for getting about. She didn't have a phone, leaving outsiders to communicate through letters or the Smyths should an emergency arise. At the end of the season, Flora closed the place, traveling back to Cambridge to her small apartment she shared with her cousin Francis.

She unpacked the groceries as Nathan arranged his suitcase on a chair by the living room futon. He looked around the room like it was the first time. The marble-top table still had the rabbit-skin doily with a lamp sitting upon it. It sat alongside the window on the southern wall. A tall bookcase stood by the marble-top table. A stuffed pheasant stood on a chest, abutting the half walls that enclosed the dining booth. The Indian face carving on a coconut shell sat on the corner of the booth wall. On the pond side of the room stood a four-legged stand displaying the television.

A small oil stove sat next to it, overlooking the tranquil vista. A large multidesigned carpet covered the hardwood floor. Everything was where it had sat for years. Nathan took a deep sigh and changed out of his traveling clothes and into his shorts and T-shirt. He stood looking out the window. Just looking at the pond relieved a heavy weight from Nathan's shoulders, and he could feel the burden drain from his body.

Flora and Nathan spent a few moments catching up on family gossip and letting Nathan aware of the upcoming events around the pond. Flora was someone he felt comfortable sharing his inner thoughts although he couldn't bring himself to tell her about Tracy. Nathan thought of the devastation if it got back to his mother.

It was midafternoon when Nathan took his first swim of the day. A Red Sox game began broadcasting on the radio. Flora loved her Red Sox and enjoyed listening to every inning, whether on the radio or television. She cheered every home run from Carl Yastrzemski and Carlton Fisk.

The exercising walks continued both before breakfast and after supper. After Sunday morning's breakfast, Flora turned the television on and listened to Oral Roberts's Christian hour. It was her version of going to church. She believed in God and, like her sisters, wasn't an overly religious person. Later Flora put Teddy on a leash and, with Nathan alongside, walked about the neighborhood catching up on the local gossip.

Flora and Nathan made their way along the pond's parameter, stopping at the halfway zone where a chain-link fence protruded into the water's edge. The pond was split in half on both sides. Fencing was installed to identify the restrictive lines. One side of the pond was for private homeowners and the other for campers. Walking the roadside was the only way pond residents could shop at the small country store at the campground entrance.

At the fence line lived Flora's best friend, Martha. She was middle aged who, like others in earlier years, built her own home. She worked as a telephone operator for the town of Plymouth, whose job was connecting calls. On occasion, she intercepted calls from the owners of the Ellis Pond Campground and their teenage kids. She listened in, sharing the gossip with Flora. Nathan thought how humorous it was listening how these two ladies talked, catching bits and pieces of "She said what?" "No kidding," and "What did her father say?"

After spending a few minutes getting reacquainted, Flora and Nathan left Martha and made their way back. It was time to take the first dip of the day. Nathan managed to swim underwater to the raft, taking repetitive dives with each one more enjoyable than the previous. Tom and Gerard lived a couple of doors down and walked over, joining Nathan on the water-soaked raft. Flora remembered the air mattress, letting Nathan know it was available if he needed it.

The remainder of the week went on with more of the same before the time came to make the journey home. Barbara and Alan drove Flora and Nathan downtown to the bus stop. It took over an hour for the bus to arrive within the confines of South Boston.

Labor Day weekend was at the Andersons' doorsteps. Karen Adams flew in from Kansas City to Boston's Logan International

Airport. Rachael and Tracy took the transit bus, subways, and a taxi to the airway hub awaiting her arrival. Meanwhile, Beth and Nathan watched and fed the younger siblings supper. They tried keeping everyone emotionally harnessed, not presenting a state of chaos when the grown-ups returned.

Karen was Rachael's age and height but presented a slenderer figure. Her brown hair waved upon her shoulders, framing her face. Her makeup was of a working professional highlighted by a pair of slightly wing-tip eyeglasses. She carried a common suitcase along with a small conventional one for her cosmetics and hair rollers. She was staying the weekend before continuing down to Manomet to visit her family.

The kids had a few moments saying hello, with Karen catching up on everyone's events over the past years. Karen was promoted to a manager's position at Caterpillar and had traveled the states representing the company. She dated but hadn't decided to settle with anyone special. She was a career woman.

It was time for bed, with Gretchen sleeping in the boys' room. It left the single bed in the girls' for Karen. Beth and Laura remained doubled up with Abigail in the crib.

The next morning didn't deviate from the day's routine. Rachael and Tracy slept late. Money for the morning paper was usually left on the kitchen table. If not, Nathan got it out of Tracy's pants that hung on the bedpost. Nathan fished the change from Tracy's pocket, then walked out, crossing the street for Archie's. Walking past the apartment building where the Gordons lived, he noticed a few coins lying on the sidewalk. His eyes widened and quickly picked them up, stuffing them into his pocket. Nathan passed the tall picket fence that closed off a grassy field. The fence had a gap, leaving an opening for anyone to crawl through to a shortcut to the East Second Street Bar and Grill. Nathan made it to Archie's and returned with the morning paper. Rachael decided to get up upon hearing Nathan coming through the door.

She started breakfast with the smells of bacon starting a chain of rising sleepers. Karen rose from the girls' room, taking a seat at the table. She wasn't a breakfast person and settled for just coffee and toast. It took a while for the rest of the kids to finish. They placed their egg-stained dishes in the sink, then went back to their rooms to get dressed. Karen accompanied the younger ones in the living room watching Saturday-morning cartoons. It gave her a few moments to learn more about them. Late morning, Rachael and Tracy took her on a tour of the neighborhood.

The threesome walked toward the Atlantic shores.

Karen looked at her school chum. "Do you like Boston, Rachael? It seems like you were made for city life. I remember how you used to love Kansas City."

Rachael chuckled. "I remember those days. Do you still see some of the old timers?"

"I see a few. Most have gone on to other divisions or retired," responded Karen.

They stood at the corner across from Archie's. Tracy wanted to get a pack of cigarettes, leaving Karen and Rachael waiting on the corner.

Rachael asked the question she dared to ask in the correspondence with her school chum, "Have you ever heard from Clarence?"

Karen was surprised by the question. "No, but I heard that his father died. How are you holding up, Rachael?"

Rachael just smiled, saying, "I'm doing okay. I'm happy, and life couldn't be better."

"Are you managing? I mean, with all the kids. Do they like city life?" Karen asked.

"I admit it's tiresome sometimes, but Beth and Nathan are a great help. The kids love it here. There's so much to do with school, the beach, and plenty of playmates although I do worry about the older two being influenced by the neighborhood from time to time. Besides, Tracy has been supportive. I can't say I regret any of it…Oh, there's Tracy. Let's go down to the waterfront. I want to show you the ocean."

Karen knew Rachael was putting on a front. She placed her thoughts in the back of her mind and put her best face forward. She changed the subject by talking about her life in Kansas City. The threesome tracked on to the ocean shores.

The sun rose Labor Day morning, ending Karen's short weekend. Her bus was scheduled for early afternoon. Rachael and Tracy got dressed, ensuring everyone had breakfast. The aftermath was cleaned up, and by late morning, it was time for hugs and kisses from the remaining group. Tracy and Rachael accompanied Karen on the transit bus to Boston central. Karen got her ticket and gave the couple an enduring hug before boarding the bus.

Karen was glad seeing her old chum. She wondered if Rachael regretted the path she took. She thought Tracy was good company but not someone she'd settle down with. Karen stared out the window pondering more questions. She gave a big sigh, looking at the seats in front of her. Thoughts of her parents came to the forefront. Over the years, Karen flew to Providence, Rhode Island, to visit her family. This year was different.

School started early the next morning. Kenneth dressed for first grade and followed the trail of students making their way to the elementary school. Nathan's fourth grade was on the second floor across from the room where his first class took place upon moving to South Boston. The fourth-grade teacher was Mr. Mark Tomley. He was a younger man who looked every much like the typical family man. His rugged facial features could visualize him as someone who smoked cigars. Nathan was bewildered, not knowing what to expect as Mr. Tomley was his first male teacher.

That fall, Rachael wanted her son to join the Boys' Club. It stood a couple of blocks farther from the Congregational church on West Sixth Street. It was Saturday morning when he walked the distance. He filled out the forms and paid the annual fee, which was exactly what was given to him. A wooden card was made with his name engraved along with a membership number. It had to be presented every time Nathan came through the door.

The building included a spacious recreation room headed by a wall-to-wall stage. The room had four pool tables, a couple of Ping-Pong and card tables set up for games or puzzles. It had a library for those wanting to read, do homework, or just do craftwork. On the far end was a large gymnasium for playing basketball or any other indoor activity. There was a descending staircase that entered the basement leading to a few classrooms, an indoor swimming pool, and a well-equipped woodworking shop. After the tour, Nathan felt good about the place, then decided it was time to make the long walk home.

Sunday started its usual routine. Rachael had Nathan follow her to the side alley that was littered from one end to the other. The trash was thick with shovelfuls of food scraps loaded with maggots and paper waste from the tipped-over garbage cans. They were given the responsibility for keeping the alleyway cleaned in return for a reduction on the rent. Rachael raked, and Nathan shoveled most of the afternoon, filling every available garbage can.

Raking the alley gave some rewards. Soda bottles were trashed having a deposit value of two cents for smaller bottles and a nickel for the larger ones. The bottles gave Nathan some spending money on penny candy. Some of his favorites were bull's-eyes, Tootsie Rolls, Candy Buttons, and red licorice sticks. Archie had a small bookcase for used comic books. They caught Nathan's eye and went through them, singling out the Superman comics. They sold for ten cents with returns worth a nickel.

Rachael started developing poor circulation from being on her feet most of the day. Before bedtime, she lay on the couch, having one of the kids rub her legs and feet. Nathan often sat on the sofa's end, revitalizing her blood flow on a nightly basis. One advantage was staying up another half hour after the younger ones had gone to bed.

The calendar turned to November, bringing the holiday season with a rapping at the front door. On the other end was Doris Rines, who drove the grandparents up for the holidays. Rachael had the troop go down and help with the unloading. Doris and Nathan helped his grandfather lift his legs one after another up the two flights of stairs. It was sad to see Milton's legs become more crippling. His getting around grew more dependent on the use of his bamboo cane.

The Manters arrived early this year to help around the house. Rachael was hired part-time at Jordan Marsh's bargain basement. She worked the six weeks to offset the holiday costs. Rachael got up with Tracy, Beth, and Nathan, each taking turns washing in the bathroom.

Rachael got dressed, applied some facial makeup, then made her way to the Fourth Street bus stop. Makeup was something Rachael seldom used yet something Sarah seldom did without.

The kids completed their chores while Sarah cooked the meals. She kept busy sweeping the floors and dusting. Beth did the laundry, and Nathan washed the floors. Milton sat in the kitchen, playing solitaire or reading the *Boston Record American*. Most weekends, Nathan devoted most of his spare time at the Boys' Club. The club gave him a chance to meet new friends and enjoy some competitive games.

The club library was opened in the afternoon and closed during the supper hour. It reopened evenings, allowing those wanting to do homework and research. Nathan often took advantage of the library's evening hours. At closing time, the librarian asked the few inhabitants to help straighten the place by putting chairs back behind the tables and making sure the books and magazines were stored properly.

During the winter months, the Boys' Club sponsored various classes and posted them whenever they occurred. One class caught Nathan's interest. It was typing that met twice a week. He was apprehensive about asking his mother but got her approval. He made the three-mile walk during the nighttime to and from class.

It was a small class of about ten guys. Everyone was issued a typing book and started performing the finger exercises on the basic keys. Nathan's coordination needed improvement, along with his speed. When the class ended, Nathan knew he could operate a typewriter.

The Thanksgiving holiday lasted until the following Monday, when the nation returned to its daily routine. The new season became swollen with crowds of Christmas shoppers. Rachael had her son meet her at Jordan's.

Nathan rode the transit bus downtown to the Tremont subway. After three stops, the doors opened at Jordan's basement store. Rachael had about another hour to go, sending him up to the store's Christmas display of the Enchanted Village.

The Enchanted Village displayed a series of vintage stores and houses decked out in artificial snow and holiday decorations. Each building housed mechanical figures dressed in a Dickens costumes singing Christmas carols. It was the ultimate old-world dream for any child's imagination. Nathan met up with his mother, handing him a few bags for the journey home.

Weeks before Christmas, Rachael, Tracy, and Sarah did their annual venture of bringing home the Christmas tree. It took its prominent place in the living room corner. The decorations were hung with everyone taking turns placing the ornaments. A garland was hand strung from alternating popcorn and cranberries. The stockings were placed alongside the living room mantle. The Lionel train was put together, rounding the tracks over and over about the base of the tree. Rachael took her older two shopping at Woolworths, giving them a couple of dollars to buy gifts for their siblings.

Christmas arrived with the small ones parading around with their stockings and engulfing the candied contents. It was after breakfast and the aftermath was cleaned up that the assembly gathered in the living room with an appointed Santa to hand out gifts. It took a long while voicing the oohs and aahs when opening the wrappers and disclosing the personalized gift inside. The family consumed the baked ham and spent the remaining day relaxing while the winter cold swept across the snow-drifted streets.

Doris arrived and drove the grandparents back to Plymouth, putting everyone back in the preholiday routines. New Year's Eve did the traditional listening to Guy Lombardo. The stroke of midnight gave way to "Auld Lang Syne" wishing everyone a happy New Year, and the sleepy-eyed well-wishers slowly nestled back into their beds.

THE ADDITIONS

January of 1960 started a new decade. People's routine didn't change from any other. It was another time with more of the same. It was a year for more improvements.

Rachael realized the need for more room. She saw a picture in the *Home and Garden Magazine* how to convert the pantry into a small bedroom. First the dishes, bowls, cups, glasses, and silverware had to be relocated. Rachael thought about a wall cabinet and having it mounted on the kitchen wall abutting the girls' room.

She decided to start the refurbishing that deterred everyone's schedule. Beth and Nathan knew something was up. Every time their mother made changes, it was to accommodate someone else. The older two were shown how to prepare the kitchen walls for rewall-papering. The basin was filled with warm water. The sponges were soaked and wiped across the old wallpaper until it was easily scraped off.

The scraping continued when Rachael went shopping for the cabinet she had in mind. The cabinet arrived within days with the scraping just about finished. The familiar ring tap "Shave and a Haircut" sounded at the front door. It was Eileen making her late-morning stopover for coffee and a cigarette. She noticed the work in progress and offered to help apply the new wallpaper. Rachael showed off the new cabinet and told her to come back after lunch to start the wallpapering.

Beth made sandwiches for everyone while Nathan cleaned the debris along the wall base. Eileen returned with a pasting brush, ready to help hang the new print. It took most of the afternoon to paste and put the wallpaper in place. Tracy's arrival from work couldn't have timed it any better. His help was needed to secure the cabinet in place. Nathan, Beth, and Rachael held it in position while Tracy screwed it to the wall. The dishes and glassware were neatly placed within the new fixture. A two-drawer stand was placed below, housing the silverware and cooking utensils.

By morning, Rachael was anxious to start her project. She wheeled the carriage downtown purchasing a couple of wooden boards and hardware. She had Nathan saw one board into shelf dividers. The space between the wall and the utensil bureau was wide enough for a single bed. The measured boards were hammered along the wall and the side of the bureau. They supported the bed spring on three sides with a support leg on the open corner. A single mattress was found fitting the space like a glove. The shelving was painted white with blue dividers. In about a week, the transformation was finished, and Nathan had a room of his own.

Nathan's clothes were moved into the antiquated bureau. The shelving housed his books and trophy items. On the top shelf were a few used pots, platters, and a small teapot. Nathan found the teapot useful to hide his money. Rachael maintained her promise giving a dollar for every A and fifty cents for every B on the report card. He had about five dollars hidden. To accent a shelf, Rachael placed a large goldfish bowl. A small alcove in the back of the room housed a six-foot wooden chifforobe for hanging her son's clothes.

Next was upgrading the girls' room. Rachael refreshed the wood trim by painting it with the leftover white paint. There was enough to do the baseboards along the kitchen wall. The crowding in the girls' room needed to be resolved. Gretchen was moved into Kenneth's bedroom, leaving Beth and Laura in the double bed. Abigail was weaned into the single bed. It took a week to get the apartment back to normal.

Schools were instituting health checks on all its students. Childhood diseases like polio and tuberculosis (TB) headlined the nation. The medical field discovered they could issue the polio vaccine through a shot or a sugar cube. Oliver H. Perry School had inoculated the polio vaccine months earlier and was presently lining its students for the TB shots.

It was the fourth grade's turn for shots. Nathan stood in line along with the rest of his classmates. His physical was no different from anyone else. The nurse took a quick look at the back of the mouth, then checked the pulse and listened to the heart. A fine-tooth comb gently went through the hair, and finally the quick six-needled shot went into the forearm. The needle gun caught Nathan off guard, and his forearm was inoculated before he could say anything. He always had a fear for needles. The nurse seemed to detect a slight heart murmur on Nathan. She wrote a note on her medical notepad, making sure he handed it to his parents.

Nathan arrived home handing his mother the nurse's note. Rachael's face grew pale and looked at her son with some concern. She wrote her mother, wanting an appointment for the family doctor to look at Nathan during the February vacation. Nathan made the bus trip to Plymouth, not fully aware of the magnitude of his visit. Dr. Stewart's cold stethoscope didn't detect anything wrong and gave the boy a clean bill of health.

Milton and Nathan spent the next morning playing cribbage. They changed over to a game of dominoes, letting Sarah join in for a threesome. Ethel dropped by after lunch for a visit that surprised Nathan. Sarah spent a few moments getting the family updates before heading out to visit the neighbors. It was her way of giving Milton some private moments with his sister. Sarah asked Nathan if he wanted to accompany her, but Ethel insisted he stay. She hadn't seen him in quite a while.

Sarah left, and Milton's tone instantly changed while conversing with his sister. He voiced his inner emotions of not being content living where he was. He wanted to be closer to the shore. Ethel could only express her compassionate responses. He couldn't understand the changes that affected his life. The Manters' social security incomes could only afford the studio apartment. Their situation was no different from other seniors that inhibited the building. Milton couldn't comprehend the huge expense of living along the shoreline.

Ethel changed the conversation by turning her attention toward Nathan. She asked about the family, school, and his activities. There was always the question about Nathan's future ambitions, and he had always expressed his desire of becoming a teacher. Ethel always came across with a pleasant demeanor from her thin, frail body. Her face highlighted the thick lenses from her mousy brown hair. After they shared a few chuckles of family tales, Sarah returned, adding to the warmth of the room. Ethel never drove and had her niece taxi her about before returning to her Manomet home. The time came for Nathan to ride the bus north.

Expenses were mounting as the family grew. Rachael had to make the dollars stretch in giving her children the basics. Weekday suppers were modified consisting of a starch and a vegetable. The starch consisted mostly of a pasta or a potato variation. The potatoes were transformed to being either mashed, scalloped, or baked. Spaghetti with meat sauce helped provide a few meals among the children. The vegetable maintained a steady serving of carrots, peas, or string beans.

Rachael waited to eat when Tracy got home. She continued her routine of eating a cold-cut sandwich between her afternoon soaps. The next morning, the coffee table was laden with the stained dinnerware, pieces of steak bones, and dried out french fries.

March was the month South Boston specialized in celebrating Saint Patrick's Day. The majority of Boston's south end was Irish Catholics. It was the Saturday after Saint Patrick's that the city sponsored a morning parade. It marched along the bus route from East Broadway to East Fourth Street and continued all the way to Marine Park. It followed with a traditional breakfast at the American Legion on East Fourth Street.

Nathan watched the parade at the corner of O and East Fourth Street. He witnessed the stream of marching bands, listening to each musical orchestration among a sea of green hats and shamrocks. After the last ensemble paraded by, he followed the crowd to the Legion, where they served trays of egg and bacon sandwiches outside the entry doors. Nathan helped himself to a couple to munch on while walking home.

It was evening when everyone crawled under the covers for a night's rest when a peculiar rapping came at the door. Nathan lay awake trying to listen to the soft-spoken conversations from his parents' bedroom. In a moment, the door opened with a couple of policemen on the other side. They came to inform Tracy there was a warrant out for his desertion. A few lines conversed before the door closed, sending the policemen on their way. It was another puzzle piece Nathan retained in his head. He wasn't the only one wondering how the cops knew where they lived; Rachael and Beth lay in their beds wondering along with him.

The next morning, Eileen stopped over for coffee and a cigarette whining about her husband's laziness and her unresponsive older son.

Rachael tried to pay attention to what seemed to be Eileen's same bitches and moans. Rachael's mind was focused on the previous night's visitors. She could only think Tracy was talking to Gloria from work. Rachael wondered if he was sending her money while making her think he was wasting it on drinks at the pub.

She snapped back, focusing on Eileen who was still rambling. She listened a few more minutes while looking at her pregnant stomach, then Eileen suddenly stated she had to leave. Rachael called Laura to come with the hairbrush. While she waited, she rubbed her belly with visions of doubt racing through her head.

During April, Rachael left for the hospital and delivered a baby girl. Tracy told the household they had a new sister, Rebecca Eileen. In a few days, she occupied the emptied crib in the girls' room. Rachael wanted Eileen's name incorporated with Rebecca. Tracy thought his daughter's name should be from his family's side. After a couple of confrontations, Rachael sidestepped Tracy's request by officiating the birth certificate herself.

Rachael made it home in time for Easter. The mythical bunny made its arrival, leaving baskets filled with marshmallow chicks, jellybeans, chocolate eggs, and an Easter toy beside each bed. Large chocolate bunnies were left for Beth and Nathan.

Sunday saw its normal routine with the parents drinking coffee and reading the paper. The radio voiced Dave Maynard, who played the popular hits of rock and roll. Elvis Presley was the main headliner, surpassing crooners like Perry Como, Frank Sinatra, Patti Page, and Andy Williams.

Rachael prepared a ham, placing it in the oven. Her two oldest sat around the small dining table peeling potatoes and carrots. Sometimes there was the occasional onion. Rachael insisted they prepare it by holding the onion in one hand and chopping the surface with a knife in all directions to get the desired slices chopped. She knew the easier way of slicing the onion, then cutting them into cubes. Rachael wouldn't have it. She got the enjoyment of watching the onion juice squirt up and stinging the eyes of the beholder.

There wasn't any rush in getting anything done. The younger set relaxed in the living room watching television. While the dinner cooked, Nathan joined his siblings in the living room and found a seat in the overstuffed chair.

Rachael went into the bathroom to brush out her hair and splash a little water on her face. Tracy got up and crept into his bedroom. He saw a direct line to Nathan between the dividing curtains. He stood in the line of sight fondling himself at Nathan while others were hidden from the curtain. Nathan pretended not to notice the figure and continued watching television. Rachael came out of the bathroom and closed the dividing curtains while both reverted in getting dressed.

The birth of a new baby was usually followed a visit by Rachael's mother. This was no exception. Rachael sent Nathan up to O and Fourth Street to meet his grandmother. He stood on the corner when the bus came to a stop. Sarah stepped off, giving her grandson a hug.

"Hi, Gram," Nathan said while enduring the embrace.

"How are you doing, dear?" Sarah replied. "How's your mother and the new baby?"

"She's fine, and the baby is okay. How's Gramp?" Nathan asked.

"He's all right. He can live without me for a few days."

Nathan looked up at his grandmother and smiled.

"I bet it's getting crowded with the new baby?" inquired Sarah.

"Not really," Nathan stated. "I got my own room. Mom changed the pantry into my room. She put Gretchen in the bed that Gramp usually sleeps in. Guess you'll be sleeping in my old bed on the bottom bunk."

"What happened to the dishes and silverware?" inquired Sarah.

"Oh, that. Mom got a wall cabinet to put them in. It's on the wall outside the girls' room. You'll see," responded Nathan.

"I bet I will," Sarah said, sheepishly patting Nathan on the back of his shoulder.

The two kept walking until Sarah got to meet her seventh grandchild. Sarah spent the next few days helping her daughter around the house, doing the mending and ironing. Sarah was surprised how Rachael manage to fit everyone in the place. She could see the family outgrowing the apartment if the grandchildren kept coming at the rate they were.

Sarah found a chance to sit and look straight into her daughter's eyes. "Rachael, what on earth are you' doing? How many more children are you planning on? Can you understand you can't afford what you have now? Why did you decide on having another one? Is Tracy bringing home enough money to keep this place going?" asked Sarah with a soft but forthright tone to her voice.

Rachael could only respond, "I love my family, Mom. I've always wanted a large family. We're getting by, and if I have to, I'll get a full-time job. You'll see. It'll work out."

Sarah had her doubts, sitting upright in her chair. She heard this line before.

She got up, shrugging her shoulders and throwing her arms in the air. "Okay, Rachael, if you say so, but I still say you're getting in over your head."

Rachael felt she gave her mother answers to satisfy the moment, not letting her mother suspect Tracy's continued involvement with Gloria. She glanced at her mother, who was busily going through the backlog of dirty clothes and ironing.

Spring brought the ragman's weekly trips. Starting from spring to late fall, the ragman rode his large cart pulled by a broken-down hag up and down the lower parts of Southie. The neighborhood knew when he traveled East Third Street by his constant shouts of "Rags! Rags!" echoing throughout the neighborhood. It alarmed the inhabitants who had any bags of old clothing they wanted to sell. The ragman bought them according to their usefulness.

Rachael thought they might have a couple of bags. She had Nathan carry them down, waving for the ragman to stop. The unkempt figure climbed down from his cart, making a quick paw through the bags. He dragged them to the back of his cart, where he pulled out a scale with an attached hook. He weighed each bag, establishing the poundage, and gave Nathan a dollar for the lot. The ragman climbed back onto the weathered bench and continued his way down the street shouting rags.

From the sidelines, kids shouted snide remarks back toward him, "What does your mother wear?"

The ragman, trying not to react, again shouted, "Rags!" giving the sideliners a moment's chuckle.

CAMP FIRESIDE

Pastor Bob made another appearance at the Anderson household. He was recruiting young adults to attend summer camp in New Hampshire. His church was sponsoring a religious camp called Camp Fireside in the small town of Barrington. He told of the abundance of recreational activities and emphasized the fellowship with Christian children. It would be little to no costs for families wishing to send their kids. Rachael made no bones about having to make ends meet and didn't know if she could afford the camping costs.

Pastor Bob looked around, noticing the number of children, and gave Rachael assurances the church would cover the costs. She would only bear the expense of the necessities. She nodded, looking at her two oldest for approval. Beth and Nathan agreed to go for a week, scheduled for the later part of July. Once the church got their numbers, funds were raised to pay for the group.

Rachael lowered the carriage for an afternoon walk along the shoreline with Rebecca and Abigail. Nathan tagged along admiring the sail and motorboats bobbing in the ocean waves. The coastal walk followed alongside the L Street bathhouse. The huge green building sat along the shore with a fence line that extended down into the Atlantic. The bathhouse was walled, separating the men from the women, allowing each gender to bathe in the optional nude. Rachael wanted to know if they really did swim naked, asking Nathan to go in and check.

After confirming what she already knew, she encouraged Nathan to go swimming if he wanted. Nathan was totally thrown by her decision, wondering why she wanted him to swim around with a bunch of naked men. The thought of his mother's encouragement circled Nathan's brain, then he decided on dismissing it. They continued walking the big circle meeting up with East Broadway and making their way home.

Summer didn't excuse the oldest from their required summer reading. The school required two books to be read and book reports to be provided at the start of the school year. Beth wasn't an avid reader like her mother and brother. Nathan liked going to the library. For him, it was a place to release the tensions of home. Before returning the books, Rachael made her son give oral book reports just to make sure he read them. There were few school trips to the library. Twice a year, the classes walked to the library to hear one of the caretakers known as the Story Lady. She told lengthy stories with moral endings like those biblical sonnets at Sunday school. The library was divided into three sections. One posed as a conference room, where large groups could be seated. The main area was subdivided into the children and adult sections. The children's side encompassed a small lounging area that had a record console that seated four where they could listen to recorded stories through headphones.

Summer chores didn't take away the trips to the beach and exploratory walks to Castle Island. The old stone fortress stood on the outer rim of Pleasant Beach, beckoning the curious, only to be stopped by iron rods that blocked every entryway. Pleasant Beach was pristine and blanketed with white sands across its mile-long stretch. It was part of the threshold to the Atlantic Ocean, displaying an array of dead jellyfish lining its shore. There was an occasional shark or two, which was rare. The city eliminated the threat by constructing a rock jetty that enclosed the beach area with a lookout point called the sugar bowl.

It took a couple of years to complete. A person could walk the two-mile hike around the circumference of the beach. The day arrived when the aircraft carrier *USS Enterprise* made a port visit to Boston. It anchored a distance from the Boston Harbor with its presence headlining the radio.

Nathan was interested in seeing the spectacle. He got permission and quickened his pace toward the beach to see the majestic vessel. It was his first experience seeing an aircraft carrier. Nathan raced toward Castle Island just to look at the immensity of the ship. He sat on its banks just staring at the majestic vessel. He sat for what seemed to be hours before making the track back home.

The Fourth of July gave way to wiping foreheads from the steady heat. There were no air conditioners nor fans to provide relief from those hot and humid days. There was the occasional watermelon for quenching the heat. Rachael was creative and sidestepped the cutting the melon up into the usual slices. She took a melon scoop and hollowed the core, making melon balls, and placed them back into the shell. Everyone spooned the melon balls into their bowls, savoring every bite of the mouthwatering treat. The finishing touch was a tuna noodle and pea salad making the afternoon meal bearable.

As the sun sank toward the horizon, the family gathered with the two youngest placed into the carriage. The family followed the crowd over to L Street and onto Columbus Park. It was where the fireworks were being displayed. They passed the bathhouse, giving Nathan a brief tingle down his spine. The carriage ensemble found a place to sit on the top bleacher section, making it easy for everyone to see.

As dusk fell, the fireworks started with a series of ground displays on assorted posts. As darkness ensued, the sky canvased the fire illuminations with the echoes of oohs and aahs with each explosion. It was about a half hour when the sky lit in a series of kabooms, giving the applause of the witnessing public. It took around midnight for the family to arrive home, resting their heads into their feathered pillows.

Time came for Beth and Nathan to pack their clothes for camp. Rachael managed to buy the sleeping bags and toiletries that were on the required lists. Sunday was a travel day with one of the church members arriving at the Andersons' doorstep to help load the older two's luggage into the station wagon. Inside sat a couple of kids from the other side of the city.

It was an odd feeling leaving the confines of Boston and driving out of state. It took a couple of hours driving to Camp Fireside in Barrington, giving plenty of time for the Anderson kids to get acquainted with their fellow journeymen. Nathan couldn't help but notice the road lines went from white to yellow crossing the New Hampshire border. He was intrigued by the very sight of them.

Barrington was a rural town boarding the small city of Rochester. Driving into Camp Fireside made everyone anxious. It was the day when new arrivals registered and got settled. The camp's driveway viewed an extremely wide scenic vista. To its immediate right stood a large gambrel barn that housed the chow hall, and just beyond it stood a souvenir and candy wagon. Across the way lay an open field exposing a half dozen large-sized cabins for the girls. The boys' cabins were farther beyond in a wooded area. Each cabin had a designated name and number. Each section had a building for showering, washing up, and going to the bathroom. They were nothing more than oversized outhouses.

Registration was time consuming as the camp staff took their time verifying the medical sheet that accompanied each camper. Spending money was accredited in the souvenir and candy wagon. The reception committee conducted thorough reviews, looking for any limitations a camper might have for the week's activities. Cabins were assigned, and after giving their sponsors a goodbye, the campers went searching for their bunks.

The camp counselors arrived, welcoming the new members, and went over the list of camp rules and regulations. The counselors were college seniors earning tuition money. Nathan was assigned to cabin 6, which stood on the far edge of a wooded opening. It was surrounded by four other cabins. His counselor was a young middle-set bodybuilder who explained why each cabin's nickname was for a woodland creature. Cabin 6 was nicknamed "Raccoon."

Reveille sounded at six with the blaring horn over the public address system. Nathan awoke, staring at the ceiling rafters of the rustic cabin. He unzipped his sleeping bag, followed by others in the cabin. He grabbed his towel, toothbrush, and toothpaste from his suitcase, making his way to the washhouse. There was already a line where each one took turns washing and using the outhouse. Toilet paper was at a premium, and many brought Kleenex to use instead.

Nathan sauntered back to the cabin, where others were cleaning and straightening their bunks. With everyone returning from their daily hygiene, the counselor divided the campers into groups responsible for certain cleanup duties. It assured everyone in keeping the cabin swept and dusted and the personal gear neatly stowed. They wouldn't have a chance to do it after breakfast.

At reveille, a series of religious songs echoed throughout the campgrounds. They gave inspiration to the campers in their housekeeping duties. The chow hall opened at seven thirty, with cabin 6 walking as a group to the gambrel barn followed by other campers in their wake.

The campers filed into the gambrel structure awaiting their breakfast. Nathan saw the multitude of picnic tables laced with red-and-white checkered tablecloths. Each table was pedestaled with a numbered card surrounded with plates of pancakes, scrambled eggs, bacon, sausage, toasts, and pitchers of milk and orange juice. The card indicated the cabin number, where the campers huddled using their utensils nonstop.

Breakfast was hearty and often required seconds for many tables. The horseshoe area of stoves and ovens corralled the cooks busily making meals for the masses. There was a short rest period before the daily activities went into action.

Activities included softball, archery, arts and craft, and swimming. The activities rotated each day from cabin to cabin, scoring points along the way. The arts and craft shop provided the opportunity to make beaded necklaces, leather pouches, or any other decorative trinkets. Today cabin 6 was in competition with another cabin, shooting archery.

Nathan hadn't held a bow and arrow in his life. The circular straw target was fifty feet away. Nathan stood near the end of the line watching each predecessor take their stance and shoot. Nathan was up. He was guided by a counselor on how to hold, take aim, and shoot. Nathan followed and missed the target on his first try. He realized what he needed to do and adjusted his second shot. He lifted the bow, took aim, and landed the arrow on the outer circle. He was pleased with the shot and himself.

The next competition was softball. The only game Nathan witnessed similar to this was street ball. It was played in the road using car bumpers as bases. A rubber ball cut in half was pitched like a Frisbee to the batter holding a utility stick. It was Nathan's turn up to bat. He took hold of the bat for the first time and, being left-handed, stood on the opposite side of the home plate. He concentrated on each pitch, never once making contact. He wondered if playing softball was new to him or if he just wasn't coordinated enough to hit the ball.

Lunch was served with different platters of sandwich mixtures. Sandwiches were made of cold cuts, peanut butter and jelly, or egg salad, accompanied with french fries and jugs of a bug juice mixture and milk. The noontime meal gave the results of the daily judging of the cabins. The cleanest cabin received a rooster trophy; the dirtiest, a trophy of a pig. The rooster exempted the cabin from the next day's judging.

The first part of the afternoon was personal time. It gave campers time for writing letters or sending a postcard home. It was a necessary item as the outgoing correspondence was needed for getting into the chow hall for supper. Nathan spent the time writing his mother and sending postcards to Flora and his grandparents. Afterward he checked the souvenir and candy wagon on what they had to sell. It also posed as the camp's post office, handling incoming and outgoing mail. Campers were free to roam around experiencing fellowship with other campers. Nathan decided to keep close to his cabin.

For a couple of hours, campers were paraded down the wooded trail to the sparkling lake for a late-afternoon swim. The public address system announced the swim, having the campers change and meet in front of the chow hall. The campers congregated inside their cabins, changing into their swimwear and grabbing a towel for the lake. Nathan changed into his suit along with others in his cabin. He didn't think anything of changing in front of others until later.

After the campers were accounted for, they paraded like ants trailing down to the refreshing waters. Every swimmer needed a buddy, making everyone responsible for each other.

After supper, Bible study was conducted at the camp chapel, lasting an hour. The congregation left the chapel and trailed to the campfire arena for an evening of ghost stories and testimonials by the counselors. As the evening wore on, the campfire dimmed into glowing ambers while the sleepy campers made their way back to their bunks. They were rousted by dawn's reveille blaring throughout the camp accompanied by the religious songs giving inspiration to the day.

Saturday was designated as fun day with an evening that highlighted each cabin performing some comical or entertaining skit. The performance played out on the chapel stage and ended with a religious service before turning in for the last time.

The campers were packed and ready to load into their vehicles for the return home. During the week, Nathan seldom saw Beth, and this was the first time they were able to compare notes. The camping trip was better than what they thought, vowing next year they'd go for two weeks. It was disappointing arriving home, falling back into the daily routines.

In their absence, Rachael and Tracy bought a pair of used bikes. It was Nathan and Beth's new adventure for the remainder of the summer. Beth and Nathan lined the bikes along the curb. Beth pushed herself from the curb, getting her balance. She had to jump down once or twice to prevent herself from falling over. After a couple of tries, she got the knack of peddling while concentrating on her steering.

It was Nathan's turn. He pushed himself out into the road, taking hold of the handlebars. He was unable to rest his foot on the lower pedal, causing him to lose balance and fall onto the asphalt. He was slightly bruised but managed to try again. This time, he couldn't synchronize the balancing and pedaling together. It was after the third try Rachael felt Nathan would be safer learning on the girls' bike with Beth riding the boys'.

It seemed only a week had passed when Rachael arranged a trip to Manomet to celebrate her parents' fiftieth wedding anniversary. They were married on August 10, 1910. The milestone took place at Aunt Ethel's. It would be a crowded affair with all the nieces and nephews, cousins, and a host of family members and friends.

Rachael borrowed a vehicle to drive to the celebration with Beth and Nathan sitting in the back. She had gotten her parents a wall clock with gold metal rods denoting the sun's rays coming from the clock's center. They left before dawn, leaving Tracy to watch the younger ones with Kenneth recuperating from a large gash on his knee. The drive seemed long, taking two hours to reach the Brook Road homestead.

Rachael was the first to arrive. Her parents were already there, having spent the previous night. Sarah wore a lavender dress with a corsage of yellow roses pinned below her left shoulder. Milton sported a yellow rose in the lapel of his gray suit. The whole affair was celebrated by over a hundred people. The weather was clear and warm, highlighting the day's enjoyment. Nathan found himself wanting to be part of the celebration. His mother pulled him aside, requesting he go play with the other kids around back. For some reason, Nathan looked at the younger crowd and realized he didn't fit in. He decided to sit the rest of the afternoon in the back of the car. Beth took a different approach and clung to Aunt Ethel's apron strings.

Ethel displayed a money tree, where donations were pinned to its branches. An elaborate anniversary cake was made by the neighborhood ladies, highlighted with golden wedding bells. The occasion was a hallmarked celebration among the society's social circles. The day was long, and by early evening, Rachael was on the road with her two sleeping in the back heading for home.

TRIALS AND TRIBULATIONS

By fall, Rachael became ill and was confined to her bed. Her skin showed tints of yellow, and her brow was beaded with sweat. Eileen stopped over to help with what she could. She took Rachael's temperature that read 101 degrees. She filled a basin with cold water, soaked a facecloth, and cooled Rachael's forehead. She dipped the facecloth again to wipe down Rachael's arms and hands, trying to cool the woman's body temperature.

Eileen took a break and gathered the younger ones together and tried explaining to them. "Listen, children. Your mother isn't feeling well and probably won't be feeling better any day soon. She needs to stay in bed and rest. What I need all of you to do is to be on your best behavior and keep your voices down while your mother is resting to get better. Do you understand?"

Kenneth and Laura just looked at each other with a hint of mischief in their eyes. Gretchen and Abigail just stood looking up at the woman, not really understanding what she had said. They nodded their heads in agreement as Eileen dismissed them to their new playtime rules.

Tracy called Sarah from work, telling of her daughter's illness. Sarah wasted no time arriving to assess the situation. Rachael had contracted hepatitis. Beth and Nathan shouldered the burden of the household chores. Sarah stayed the week, ensuring the household was being cared for, and the children stayed on their best behavior.

The older two took turns staying home to help clean and do the laundry. The television was wheeled into their mother's room so she could watch her daytime dramas. Other times, Rachael resorted to reading, wearing a pair of flesh-toned glasses. It was the first time the children witnessed their mother wear glasses. She remarked having to wear them only when her eyes got tired. It would take weeks before Rachael felt more like herself.

Food was running low, and Rachael was still weak from her infliction. She wrote an itemized list and sent the older two grocery shopping at the First National supermarket. They rode the transit bus back, carrying the heavy bags. Tracy arrived around suppertime, upholding the household discipline. Nathan made sure Patty went out for her bathroom runs. She had no problem going down the two flights but panted fiercely on the way up.

Tracy stayed around on weekends, giving Rachael a chance to regain her strength. It gave Beth the opportunity of washing her mother's sheets and bedclothes. The first of the month meant the arrival of the support check. Rachael endorsed it, handing it to Nathan to cash at the O and East Fourth Street drugstore. She wrote a note allowing her son to receive the money. The drugstore had cashed checks for Rachael a few times in the past. It would save Nathan the possible loss from walking downtown to the nearest bank. The note gave the manager satisfaction cashing such a large check to a small lad. Nathan looked at the check and noticed it was made out to "Rachael M. Anderson and minor children of Clarence L. Anderson." The amount was for $125. The money was sealed in an envelope and handed back to Nathan. The manager looked straight at the lad, telling him to hide it under his shirt to keep it safe. He did and made it home, handing the bulky envelope to his mother.

Rachael wrote another note, placing it and the cash inside the envelope. She told Nathan to go around the corner on P Street to a building where their landlord lived. She gave him the landlord's name and told him to make sure he didn't give the money to anyone else. He realized the support money paid the rent, leaving Tracy paying the rest. Nathan followed his mother's instructions and came back with a receipt.

Rachael regained her strength, letting Nathan hike to the Boys' Club. He saw a listing for upcoming classes on the bulletin board. He signed up for a woodworking class. The costs covered the wood used for the projects. He wanted to make a three-tier wall shelf for his mother. It would be the first time Nathan worked with wood. The instructor was a hands-on teacher, making sure everyone knew what tools were needed and used. He personally operated the table saw for anything needed sawing. Nathan was left rasping and sanding the rough edges of his handiwork. After a few weeks, he completed the shelf, satisfied on what he accomplished. He decided to make a small two-tier corner display. Both would become Christmas gifts.

Rachael was amazed about Nathan's interest with the Boys' Club. She asked if they had a swimming pool, and the reply was they did.

Then came the infamous question, "Do you have to wear a bathing suit to go swimming?"

What is it with this woman and not wearing bathing suits? thought Nathan.

He pictured the pool entryway and how a few boys got their peeks looking through the door windows at the naked guys walking around inside. Nathan had joined in, looking at what went on the poolside before continuing to the woodshop. He watched as grown guys dove in, then climbed out of the pool naked, displaying their proud chests with water dripping about their pubic hairs above their penises.

There were younger kids that looked like Nathan enjoying the water followed by their older counterparts. It brought flashbacks of Tracy exposing himself.

Snapping back, Nathan answered, "Naw, you don't need a bathing suit."

There was the follow-up with Rachael telling Nathan, "You should go swimming since you're there anyway."

This was getting to him. Nathan decided to put the issue in the back of his mind as part of his sex education. Learning sex was done on the streets through friends and teenage greasers. They often gathered around the street corners listening to their transistor radios while passing their best lines to any beauty queen that passed their way.

Late fall brought the chill of the brisk air weaving through the cracks of the aged buildings. Beth turned eleven and, like girls her age, started the need for a training bra. The cold weather embraced the Anderson children while they were walking the city blocks to attend church service. Beth and Nathan joined other classmates and huddled around the organist as she practiced the hymnals for the service. She encouraged them to sing and noticed the harmonic sounds she had produced. She decided to put together a junior choir. Nathan's voice got the aged organist's attention and enticed him to sing a verse or two by himself. He felt unnerved and somewhat comfortable singing to the small congregation.

The time came to prepare for the grandparents' preholiday arrival. It meant all the bedding needed to be washed, floors scrubbed, bathroom cleaned top to bottom, and everything dusted down. Even the living room carpet got its water sprinkler swept down. The Thanksgiving shopping was complete along with the installation of the plastic window coverings.

Tracy was worried about the holiday expenses. He was behind on the utilities, and the cost of presents would set the family back even more. Even Rachael's part-time job wouldn't be enough to make up for some of the loss. Tracy felt guilty knowing Rachael had figured he was sending money to Gloria. The money was to prevent her from having him arrested for desertion. His drinking after work didn't help matters. He knew Flora lived in Cambridge and had a few dollars to her name. He sat on the bar stool contemplating whether to ask her for help.

Tracy took an afternoon off, riding the city bus to Cambridge. He managed to find Flora's address and knocked on the door. She opened it and recognized the figure standing before her.

"I'm surprised you found the place," responded Flora, letting the man inside. "Was it hard to find?"

"It was a little difficult. You're really out of the way," commented Tracy.

"How's Rachael doing and the children?" inquired Flora.

Tracy gave a solemn look. "That's just it. They're not. You know the family. Truthfully Rachael and I hadn't realized the costs of raising a large family. Even with her support money, we're finding it hard to make ends meet. Rachael's trying to help with the expenses by working at Jordan's during the holidays."

"I know about the hard times. I know what you and Rachael must be going through. She's written me, so what do you want me to do?" asked Flora sternly.

Tracy responded, "Well, the holidays are coming up. I don't know if she told you. We're a few months behind on the utilities, and I don't know how we can even afford to give the children a Christmas this year."

Flora was already three steps ahead of him. "So you want me to help you out. Does Rachael know you're here?"

"No, Flora, she doesn't, and I'm hoping she doesn't find out. All I'm asking is to borrow a few hundred dollars to get gifts for the kids," Tracy pleaded.

Flora asked, "And what about the utilities? How are you planning to get those paid?"

Tracy's only reply was "We'll work on those, paying a little extra each month."

Flora knew that wasn't a reasonable answer. Flora and Rachael knew he was drinking away some of his paycheck along with giving some to Gloria. Flora encountered many hard-luck tales during her lifetime and could read right through them. She understood her niece and had an idea of what hardships she must have been going through with such a large family. Flora knew Tracy and didn't trust him.

The two sat at Flora's table scratching figures on a piece of paper. The dollar amount was underlined. Flora looked straight into Tracy's hollowed brown eyes, still not sure if all this was meaningful.

Flora offered a condition, "I'm going to help you, Tracy, not for you, but for Rachael and the kids, because I don't want to see them go without. The amount I'm giving you should pay for the gifts and unpaid bills. Do you hear me, Tracy? I mean it. You're going to invite me over around Christmas so I can see for myself that my money didn't go to waste. Understood?" She reluctantly gave him a thousand dollars disguised as a bonus from work.

Tracy humbly replied, "Thank you, Flora. Thank you so much. I appreciate what you're doing for the kids. They'll have a great Christmas."

Tracy took the check, leaving her doorway with a slight smirk on his face.

The day arrived when Doris Rines rapped at the door. Sarah and Milton were waiting in the car. The kids again raced down the flights of stairs to help carry the luggage up to the apartment. Doris and Nathan again helped Milton climb the two flights step by step. His arthritis was getting more severe with each passing year. Milton knew he had to keep exercising and develop a routine of walking up and down the hallway.

Rachael was rehired at Jordan Marsh's bargain basement for the Christmas season. She dressed herself conservatively with only a touch of makeup. Working for a well-known clothing store required a certain personal appearance. Occasionally Nathan caught the transit bus and transferred to the subway and stopped at Jordan's to accompany his mother for the ride home. Nathan arrived an hour early, taking another walk through the Enchanted Village. Later the mother and son joined the hordes of holiday shoppers heading for home loaded with shopping bags.

Thanksgiving came and went with all the trimmings, and the Christmas season took its place. Sarah took her usual reprieve back to Plymouth, returning in a week's time to help shop for the Christmas tree. Rachael bought Nathan the small cans of stain, one walnut and one maple for the two sets of shelves. He stained the three-tier walnut that was gifted for his mother and the two-tier maple for his grandparents. Both remained hidden until their debut on Christmas Day.

Flora made a surprise appearance helping with the decorations although her visit was to satisfy her curiosity. Flora remained pleasant and tried being sociable with everyone. She and Nathan sat playing a few card games, chuckling over their outcomes. Their laughter irritated Sarah, who was bothered by her sister's presence. Nonetheless, Flora got to meet the family, who, until now, were just names and pictures. She had only known the top four from their younger days.

Flora shared a cup of cheer before returning to Cambridge, satisfied of her investment.

The Boys' Club sponsored a Christmas dance. Rachael was surprised Nathan had an interest in going. She expressed her curiosity of who he had in mind. Nathan confessed there was a girl in his Sunday school class he wanted to take. Having his mother's approval, Nathan invited Sheila, and she accepted his invitation as the club was only a couple of blocks from her house. This was the first dance he had ever attended. The large game room was transformed into a dance hall paradise. Sheila and Nathan joined in with the large crowd. The local TV cameras were there taking spontaneous film shots of the whole affair. Sheila and Nathan made their way to the camera lenses every time they saw them light up. As the closing hours approached, Sheila and Nathan left. He walked her home, then made his way through the cold of the night.

As New Year's approached, Doris arrived, returning the grandparents back to their own surroundings. Sarah never liked prolonging visits. Her main concern was her own place and belongings. She and Milton spent more time than usual this year, knowing it was for helping their daughter.

A YEAR OF SURPRISES

The new year weathered with more snow and frigid temperatures. The heat from the kitchen stove didn't flow throughout the apartment. Rachael bought a new heating console for the living room. It gave the added warmth to both the living room and the boys' room. It was even more important to catch the weekly oil truck to ensure the five-gallon cans were filled. Otherwise, Beth and Nathan would have to walk the few blocks to the gas station for kerosene.

Winter's melting brought spring cleaning with scrubbing floors and woodwork. The metal folding table that supported the family's meals for the past few years had weakened. The metal legs were losing their stability in holding the weight of food and dishware.

Tracy knew of a wooden table at work that would be a perfect replacement. He persuaded his superiors in taking it off their hands. His plan was to ride the bikes over to his job, then balance the table on them for the trip home. Tracy and Nathan rode across the field, pedaling over to East First Street, and approached the General Electric delivery platform. Nathan suddenly realized that GE was where Tracy worked. At the edge of the platform sat the table.

Tracy worked as a receiving clerk, processing supplies and equipment. Nathan met a few of the coworkers and helped carry the large table off the platform. The plan worked in theory but not into practice. Tracy tried balancing it on both bikes. The plan wasn't thought out for guiding the bikes along its destined path. Both grabbed an end, carried the table, and stopped to rest every twenty or thirty feet. It took a while to get the table home and maneuver it up through the back stairway. The metal table was folded and stored in the back entryway. The new replacement was solid enough to support any dinner arrangement the Andersons could imagine. Rachael sent Beth and Nathan to walk back to the plant to retrieve the bikes.

Spring brought the need to buy new Easter clothes. Beth and Nathan were going through growing spurts. Rachael periodically had them stand back-to-back, seeing who was taller. Beth always stood slightly taller. Laura just turned five and would need a wardrobe to start first grade in the fall.

The beginning of summer brought a period of lice infection throughout the neighborhood. Fine-tooth combs were widely purchased, dissecting the individual strands on adults and children everywhere. A handful of neighborhood children came down with the infectious pests. Some had their heads shaven to reduce and eliminate the infliction. Everyone in the Anderson family except Beth escaped the lice. Not wanting to have her head shaven, Beth resorted to the alternative, which was shampooing her hair with kerosene. It took a few shampoos to free her head of the tiny pests. Rachael supervised the disinfecting of the girls' room. Bedding and clothes were put through the washing machine. The kids scrubbed the wood trim and floor with basins of hot water and Lysol. The bathroom also was given a thorough disinfecting to prevent the further spread.

Summer was in full swing, allowing many folks to become beachgoers. Elementary schools sponsored ice-cream cup giveaways to local kids. Clip-on roller skates became popular with the neighborhood. A metal key adjusted the toe clips, along with widening or lengthening to any shoe size. The key hung as a talisman for those on-the-spot adjustments. Nathan borrowed a pair and enjoyed skating along the neighborhood sidewalks. Summer included the sprouting of Hula-Hoops on neighborhood sidewalks. Kids chalked out various versions of hopscotch on the sidewalks and played game after game. Hide-and-seek was common toward the evening hours, using the utility pole as goals. Beth occupied a lot of her time playing jump rope with the Costello girls while Nathan preferred making the hike to the Boys' Club.

Rachael obtained an old metal bed and placed it on the back porch for Nathan to sleep in the open air. There were days the pantry was too hot and stuffy. The bed was pressed against the wall divider that separated the adjacent apartment. Just lying there gave him a front-row seat hearing a Rolland boy make out with his girlfriend on the opposite side. Nathan could hear their intimate talks that led to the sounds of breasts being fondled and the pulsating sex. Nathan wondered if placing him there was somewhat planned.

It was a short time before Beth and Nathan were packed for their two weeks at Camp Fireside. They remembered the fun and excitement of the previous year. Nathan was surprised being assigned to the same cabin. He toured around the campground familiarizing himself of the whole setup. Things hadn't changed. The routine was very much the same. Reveille at six, followed by washing up, then cleaning the cabins. It continued with going for breakfast, playing an activity, lunch, rest for about an hour, another activity, a swim in the lake, supper, and finally a Bible study at the camp chapel.

Despite the routine, Nathan enjoyed being away from home and doing things with kids that shared the same interests. The campers were from all over New England. The guys that shared the cabin were a self-supporting group. Nathan wondered if any of them came from a troublesome home life. When it came to changing clothes, they had no problem changing in front of each other. Nathan chuckled to himself with thoughts of his mother asking about places where naked guys could be seen.

He realized how little his mother knew the person he was and the person he was becoming. From his innocent exterior, one would think he was just another lost soul needing direction. Nathan never regretted going to Camp Fireside. It exposed him to a different outlook of life and of people. He never realized how shallow minded his home had encased him.

The two weeks went by quickly. It felt strange riding the same station wagon as the previous year back to South Boston. The more Nathan was able to meet new people, the more he felt estranged from his family. The younger ones told of their time at an amusement park.

Laura stood looking at Nathan, swaying with a projecting grin. "We went on rides, and you didn't, so ha ha."

Nathan wasn't amused, showing no interest to what she was saying. His two weeks were far better than anything the neighborhood could offer.

Time harnessed Nathan into the routine of household chores. The day came to pack for Ellis Pond. The trip was different now that Teddy was no longer around. Flora took a breather before getting another tail-wagging companion and walked more adventurous trails both morning and night.

Daybreak broke over the Ellis Pond as Flora woke Nathan for a morning walk on a more difficult and winding trail. She wanted to pick some wild blueberries for making pancakes for breakfast. The hike took them about a mile on a beaten path before coming across the stray blueberry bushes. They picked enough for pancakes and a little extra for muffins. They returned, with Flora whipping up a blueberry pancake batter and suggesting eating out on the picnic table.

Nathan placed the dishes and silverware on the weathered table. Flora stood over the stove busily frying the pancake batter. Nathan finished preparing the toast and coffee. The two sat eating as the sun warmed the morning air.

"How's the new baby?" asked Flora.

"Baby? You mean Rebecca? She's growing. She's starting to crawl," answered Nathan.

"It must be pretty crowded in the apartment," added the grandaunt.

"A little bit, but everyone is doing okay. I like the room Mom made for me," Nathan said, biting into a piece of toast.

"I remember that when I visited last Christmas. I hope your mother isn't planning on any more kids. Where would she put it?" Flora asked with a slight chuckle.

"I don't know."

There was a slight pause.

"Aunt Flora, can I ask you a question? I was thinking everyone seems to be born a year apart. I always wondered about the gap between me and Kenneth. I can't imagine Mom going that long without having a baby. Did something happen?"

Flora remained silent for a brief moment, taking a sip of coffee. "Well, there was the divorce, and that took time." She saw Nathan's attentive look and took another sip of coffee, then continued, "There was another child. Your mother miscarried it right in my house."

Nathan's eyes widened, astonished of what he just heard. "Mom miscarried?"

"Yes, right there in my house. It was just before your mother divorced your father. Keep it to yourself. Not everyone knows about it, okay?" Flora asked with a softness to her tone.

The news was a little hard to understand, but it made sense to Nathan. He tried to recall his memory of the days on South Street. He remembered Tracy being the milkman and some of the augments that went on.

"Did Mom tell you we had the cops come to our door a couple of times talking to Tracy?" asked Nathan.

"No. You had cops come to your door?" asked Flora, surprised at the news.

"They came a couple of times, mostly at night," added Nathan.

Flora sat, looking at her grandnephew for a moment, then ate another forkful of the syrupy pancake. "Gloria must be after him. That seems odd."

"Why's that?" asked Nathan.

"Well, I have a newspaper clipping—I'll show you later—where Gloria is requesting the whereabouts of her husband. She must be applying for state aid or something."

Nathan just nodded, taking the last bite of toast.

"Well, let's get the table cleared, then you can go for a swim. I'll take care of the dishes," ended Flora.

"You want help?" asked Nathan, collecting the plates and silverware.

"No, I've got it. You go for a swim," replied Flora.

The two cleared the table. Flora started washing dishes, sending Nathan out in his bathing suit and a terry towel. Flora thought over what she just learned, figuring she'd talk to a few in her social circle after Nathan left. She was curious as to what Gloria might be up to.

Labor Day was on the horizon. The family cleaned for Karen's upcoming visit. The girls' room was filled, leaving a vacancy in Kenneth's room. Tracy and Rachael made the trip to the airport to meet her. Karen remained pleasant and enjoyed sharing small talk in her soft-spoken voice. The relaxing moments got her up to date on family events, coupled with walks around the neighborhood.

Sunday didn't excuse the kids from Sunday school or church service. Nathan still raked and shoveled the alleyway of all the trash and debris. The spare time let Rachael enjoy her adopted sister. It provided Karen a chance to tell Rachael she was getting engaged and might be relocating somewhere out west. Labor Day passed, sending Karen on the Greyhound to visit her family.

The first day of school added Laura to the waking troop. Beth started breakfast and the school lunches for the four of them. She began feeling overwhelmed with each add-on chore and asked if Kenneth and Laura could help.

Rachael looked at her oldest daughter. "Listen. You're quite capable of making one more lunch. Those two aren't responsible enough to take on chores."

Beth looked at her brother, recalling all the chores they did at their age.

As time went on, Beth streamlined the morning routine. She made Kenneth and Laura responsible for getting themselves ready for school, or they would get left behind. The first couple of days, the three traveled together, giving Laura the feel of walking to school and getting there on time. Beth took the bus for the first couple of days as she was in junior high attending Gavin Middle School. She walked the two-and-a-half-mile track back home with one of her girlfriends.

Mrs. Kendell was still principal and Nathan's sixth-grade teacher. She maintained her stern business attire resembling a cutout of the 1930s. She gave no indication that there was an ounce of compassion within her. She asked for volunteers for safety patrol and school monitor positions. Without taking a second breath, the students flew their hands up throughout the room. All but two safety patrol slots were filled. Another bid for volunteers bolted from Kendell's lips. None responded.

She looked down on her printed diagram of seating arrangements and called out, "Nathan, how about you? Would you like to volunteer?"

The blood rushed to his head and clouded his brain.

Nathan's inner thoughts said, *No, thanks*, but the bold large eyes staring at him somehow forced him to say, "Yes, I don't mind."

No sooner were the words spoken when a rolled-up safety patrol belt was passed his way. Nathan's post would be the O and East Seventh Street corner.

The class became more flexible than all the others with its curriculum of English, math, world history, geography, and more spelling. Thursday mornings still allowed for the class to participate in off-campus catechism, leaving the steadfast trio that included Nathan doing teacher's aide duties. Friday afternoons, the boys spent the last hours in woodworking class located in the basement. The girls attended a homemaker's session, cutting out a pattern and sewing together a full-length apron.

The woodworking project was the same for all the boys. It included the drawing, cutting, sanding, and assembling a small octagon table lamp made out of cedar. Later it was shellacked and assembled with hardware so that it would be a working item.

Late fall, everyone had veered off in their own direction. Beth came home from school with a girlfriend to help with the homework. Nathan was off to the public library or the Boys' Club. Kenneth found a neighborhood friend in Lily Ann. She was a solid, street-smart five-year-old who showed no fear about anything. Her persona was likened to Charlie Brown's Peppermint Patty. The smaller ones had each other. Tracy fished off the Boston pier on Saturdays, catching a flounder or two for Sunday's dinner. During weekday evenings, his time was spent at the East Second Street pub.

Rachael got impatient with him not coming straight home and sent Nathan out to retrieve him. He took the shortcut through the gap in the fence and found Tracy sitting in a booth full of coworkers laughing with their pints of beer. Tracy noticed Nathan at the door and motioned him to come closer to his side. Nathan relayed the message while Tracy bore a smile and patted him on his lower back. He sent Nathan home with the message: he'd be home in a few minutes.

It was a Saturday morning when a rap came to the Anderson's door. It was an unknown gentleman wanting Rachael's attention outside. After a brief conversation, she went down and returned, calling for Beth and Nathan. She pulled them outside the apartment door and told them in a soft tone that their father was downstairs in a car and wanted to see them. She reminded her two how good Tracy had been and his caring for them all these years. Nathan's mind was telling her likewise, reminding himself of all the abuses bestowed upon them. Beth and Nathan raced down the two flights to meet the man called Clarence Anderson.

They approached the car, watching their father slowly climb out of the vehicle with crutches. He was all smiles seeing them for the first time since they were toddlers.

He hugged them, saying, "I can't tell you how long I've waited for this day."

"We've missed you too," answered Beth.

Clarence noticed the two looking at his crutches, telling them, "Don't mind the crutches. I've got a sickness called multiple sclerosis. It's something I'll have the rest of my life. Right now, I can handle it. Tell me, how are the two of you doing? How's school? What grades are you in?"

Beth gave a welcoming smile over her father's explanation of his sickness. She told the man, "We're doing good. I'm in seventh grade, and Nate's in sixth."

Clarence looked over his kids. "Look how tall you both are. Are you being treated okay?"

"We're okay," Beth answered.

Clarence smiled at his children and indicated he wanted to take a picture of them. He was handed a Polaroid camera by his companion.

Clarence got it ready, telling his two, "Go stand over on the sidewalk so I can take a picture to remember you by."

Beth and Nathan stood side by side while Clarence took a couple of shots.

He noticed the figure standing at the third-floor window, knowing his time with his two children was about over. "Come here, you two, so I can give you both a hug. I really miss you two, but I have pictures to remember you both. Maybe someday, when you get older, we'll be able to see each other."

Beth and Nathan replied in unison, "We'd like that. We'd like that a lot."

"So I'll say goodbye and let you go back to your mother. Take care of yourselves, and always know I love you," said Clarence with tears in his eyes.

"We love you too," said Nathan and Beth as they slowly walked away.

Hearing their father's love for them gave a beacon of hope for the future. Rachael questioned the two on what was said, and they only gave their mother generalities.

During Christmas holidays, Nathan's class performed the birth of Jesus as a school play. He played as a shepherd. The players were responsible for their own costumes. Rachael bought a new sewing machine during the year and tried her luck in making clothes for the kids. She took the challenge of making an Arabian robe complete with headdress. Her choice of material was brown corduroy with the conventional white linen headdress. It took her only a couple of days to complete.

The show gave two performances, one during the day for the school classes and another in the evening for the students' families. There were no speaking parts. Everyone performed their roles in concert with the narration being told off to one side. Sacred music was played, giving the dramatic effect to the spectators. The play ended with a loud applause, sending everyone into the winter night for home.

Rachael and Tracy sat in the living room eating supper while watching their favorite television shows. The kids had gone to bed, leaving the couple to themselves. Rachael couldn't help think about Clarence's appearance during the summer. She saw how crowded the apartment was getting and the future cost of transporting her children across the city for school as they got older.

Rachael turned to Tracy. "We need to start thinking about finding a better place for the family. What do you think about moving to the suburbs?"

Tracy turned toward Rachael, looking somewhat curious. "Why would we want to do that? We're great just where we are."

Rachael replied, "The kids are getting older. The expenses alone for school and keeping up with the household finances are going to be more than we can afford. I got a letter from Mom. She says we ought to consider moving back to Plymouth, where the family can help us with the kids."

Tracy thought a moment, trying to understand the bigger picture. He could see Rachael's point. "Let me think about it and ask around for some prospects."

By Christmas, the birthday trio turned another year older. Gretchen turned four, Kenneth turned seven, and Nathan turned eleven. The week flowed with cakes and ice cream and the onslaught of Christmas presents. Another year had come and gone. Surprisingly this was a year Rachael didn't come home with another baby. The music of Guy Lombardo delivered 1962.

THE LAST YEAR

Another season of cold oceanic winds and snow fingered through South Boston's busy streets. Kids were bundled in layers, preventing themselves from freezing on their way to school. Nathan rotated from his safety patrol position to bathroom monitor.

The four Anderson children made the two-mile walk to church in the frigid cold. Their enduring plight was brought to the attention of the church deacon. He and his family lived a couple of streets over from the Andersons and volunteered to pick them up in his already-crowded car. After the service, the Andersons walked the long trek through the snow-beaten paths toward home.

Nathan's appearance was being observed by the Boys' Club officials. It wasn't so much his clothes but the way he walked. Nathan had a terrible instep that made him walk like he had a deformity. He sat in the library when he was approached by a manager. He noticed Nathan's shoes had a prominent inward slant. The manager asked Nathan how long he had them. Nathan shrugged his shoulders, guessing about a year. With a pat on the back, he requested Nathan go with him. They got into the car and drove a couple of blocks to Thom McAn. Nathan's feet felt the comfort of a new pair of sneakers as he thanked his new supporter. The manager and the store clerk wasted no time in tossing the old pair and let Nathan walk home in his new shoes. Nathan didn't realize the awkwardness of his walk but felt the comfort of the new pair. He showed his mother the sneakers and how they came about. Rachael was surprised that someone would go out of their way to buy her son a new set of footwear, leaving her feeling a bit embarrassed.

It was morning when Abigail was changed and placed on the kitchen floor. She crawled around looking for objects that intrigued her. She spotted the can beside the leg of the kitchen stove. She crawled over to satisfy her curiosity and started playing with the small container. It contained the kerosene that dripped from the main distributor. With hand to mouth, she consumed some of its contents. Rachael saw Abigail from the other side of the kitchen and burst into a panic. She ran downstairs pleading with her neighbor to use the phone to call for an ambulance. Abigail was rushed to the hospital and stayed a day or two for observation. Rachael called all the younger ones together, making it perfectly clear certain places were out of bounds.

The summer heat weaved itself over the last of the spring season. Rachael's birthday was Memorial Day. The celebration brought the arrival of a new black kitten sporting white patches on her underside. She was gotten from Paul's corner store on East Fourth Street. Rachael fell in love with it, naming her Penelope Jane—Penny for short. She knew her new addition needed to be neutered before too long.

The last days of school, Nathan's class lined up, making the long walk to the Gavin Middle School. They joined other sixth graders in the Boston area for introduction day. The Gavin auditorium was large and filled to capacity. The principal gave a short lecture of what their upcoming school year would be like and the expectations of each one. They were about to enter another phase of their lives that the elementary school had prepared them. The students were dismissed, making their long walk home saying goodbye to their formative years.

Rachael decided on sending Nathan to Ellis Pond early. She thought the visit would do him good since there would be no attending camp this year.

In the meantime, Rachael asked her son, "Your father is doing a project around Lake Winnipesaukee in New Hampshire. He wants to know if you'd like to go with him for a weekend."

"Is anyone else going?" asked Nathan.

"No. He just thought you might enjoy going with him," Rachael answered.

Nathan knew what Tracy had in mind, remembering all his naked exposures. He knew words like *queer* and *homo* and what they meant. He heard phrases like "Suck my dick" and "Fuck you" many times in the neighborhood and the schoolyard. He knew what Tracy wanted was wrong and thought of telling his mother. Still he decided against it and began thinking she might be in on Tracy's exposures. After all, she was the one encouraging him to swim with naked guys.

Nathan just looked at his mother. "Naw, I think I'll stay here."

Before the July Fourth holiday, Nathan had his suitcase in hand and rode the Greyhound bound for Plymouth. He loved the historic town. It always emitted an aura of calmness and serene atmosphere throughout the neighborhoods. The first stop was checking in with his grandparents while waiting for Flora's arrival. Milton was using two canes to get around. Sarah commented he needed the added support for walking outside on his daily exercise. Flora arrived from having her hair done. This time, they met up with the Duncans for the trip back to Ellis Pond.

The Duncans had a cottage on the next street from Flora. They had known each other for years, often taking the same walks with their dogs. Flora and Nathan still took morning and evening walks around the neighborhood except now it was with a Boston terrier called Buster. He was an anxious and spirited dog. Flora loved the fact that he was small and short haired and more manageable in checking for fleas and ticks.

Flora got Nathan up at dawn for a morning walk before breakfast. Both walked along the dirt road with Buster in tow. They continued for a while when Flora suddenly turned toward her grandnephew.

"What do you think about moving to New Hampshire?"

Nathan paused, with his face turning flushed. The question caught him off guard.

He looked at Flora. "What do you mean moving to New Hampshire?"

Flora smiled in amazement. “Didn’t you know your family is moving to New Hampshire? I thought your mother had told you by now.”

“No, she didn’t,” Nathan replied, being discontented with the news. “Do you know when we’re moving, Aunt Flora?”

“Sometime before school starts. At least that’s what your grandmother told me. I’m surprised your mother hasn’t told you kids. She really didn’t give you a hint?” asked Flora.

“I remember Mom asking me to go on a weekend trip with Tracy to New Hampshire, but I didn’t want to go. She didn’t mention the house or moving. Mom has a habit of not sharing anything unless it involves one of us to help,” replied Nathan.

He thought this might be a good time to share with his grandaunt the reason for not going with Tracy. Still Nathan didn’t trust himself to tell anyone. He kept thinking of all the repercussions that might follow if he did.

The neighborhood friends were getting older and taller. The troop still frolicked off the old diving raft playing water tag and other water sports. Evenings still held the usual card games at the cottage while Flora took a night or two playing penny poker. She’d often played once a week with a group of ladies at one of the beachfront homes. Nathan’s visit was ending, and he would go home acting surprised when told of the family’s impending move.

Nathan was greeted with another addition. The family acquired a small Dutch bunny. His black-and-white coloring was like a tuxedo. It looked very much like a politician with a top hat. Then came the news: the family was moving to New Hampshire. Rachael was excited, knowing everyone would be having their own rooms. The unique feature got everyone enthused about wanting to move sooner.

Beth and Nathan attended Sunday school, delivering the news of their upcoming departure. Nathan’s teacher, Ms. Coleburg, presented him with an illustrated book containing all the Biblical stories as a going-away present. There were a few others saddened by the news and wished the Andersons well. It dawned on Nathan that he wouldn’t have the chance to say goodbye to any of his classmates or his buddies at the Boys’ Club.

It was the later part of August when the moving day arrived. The huge van pulled up, unloading the soon-to-be-assembled boxes used for packing their livelihood. Tracy rented a box truck to carry the sensitive and antique furnishings. The children were sent across the street to be out of the way. The van attracted the neighborhood as they watched the loading from nearby doorsteps. The activity continued throughout the day and into the evening. The last item to leave was the upright piano. A hoist was attached to the roof with the bedroom window removed. The monster was lifted through and lowered to the alleyway before taking its position within the van. By sunset, the van was ready for the journey to the Andersons' new address in New Hampshire.

The family gathered in the apartment that served as their home during the past four years. It was almost cleared except for a couple of boxes and a few household items. They were carefully loaded into the box truck. The Anderson kids loaded themselves—including Patty, Penny, and Michael Jay—in the back on the truck. Rachael, Tracy, Rebecca, and Abigail crowded in the front. In the cloak of darkness, the box truck drove off, leaving the streets of South Boston for the last time.

NEW DURHAM HOMESTEAD

The last few bumps were felt before the box truck came to a halt. The family arrived at their new home in the middle of nowhere. The rear gate opened, letting the kids touch ground from the few hours of steady travel. Before them stood a weathered large barn with a herd of brown-and-white-faced cattle grazing in the pasture. Farther back was an apple orchard where another herd of black-and-white cattle grazed. Nathan was astonished at the sight of them. It was the first time he saw so many cattle, and he asked his mother if the family owned them. They belonged to their neighbor in the house across the street.

Nathan glanced over to the neighboring house and noticed a tall man with silver-and-white hair standing in the doorway. His weathered features pronounced the many years of hard living in running his farm, fuel business, and other small enterprises. He walked across the dirt road, introduced himself as Jake Dawson, and enlightened the Andersons on the history of their place and the lay of the land.

Nathan wasn't impressed with the weathered house and the whole setting. The vast openness of land and breathing fresh country air would have overwhelmed anyone. Somehow he didn't feel it. Nathan joined the entourage into the house and followed the tour throughout the rooms. The back entrance led into the spacious dining room, then turning right, there was the kitchen with the only working toilet.

The two rooms looked like they had been recently painted. Tracy spent weekends with his coworker Cory Nyland painting the kitchen and dining areas. All the other rooms still needed work. The dining room had three other separate doorways leading to various parts of the house. The doorway to the immediate left led to Rachael and Tracy's bedroom. The doorway beside it led into the study. The back wall of the dining room was lined with cabinet space, above and below. The final doorway led into a hallway that hallmarked the front door and the stairway to the second-floor bedrooms.

The main floor of the house was set up with each room interacting with the other. The study had an arched wall that led to the doorway to the front hallway staircase. Continuing into the study, there was a doorway to another bedroom that Gretchen and Rebecca would share. Beside it was a shelved closet ideal for storing books. The next doorway led into the back living room area that featured a doorway leading to a small hallway where there was a stairway to the second floor. The hallway had an exit door leading to the backyard. Another doorway led back into the parents' bedroom, completing the roundabout.

Climbing the back staircase, there stood a bedroom for Nathan with a closet standing across from it. Following the corridor was a corner bedroom for Kenneth with another closet a few steps down the hallway. The front staircase stood a few steps ahead, leading into a large bedroom for Laura and Abigail. To the left of the staircase was a smaller bedroom for Beth that faced the front of the house. To the side of the staircase was a full bath that was in desperate need of repair and had a small hatchway leading to a storage attic over the kitchen.

The immediate focus was to unload the truck of the household necessities. Sensitive items like the marble-top table, sewing machine, boxes of dishes, and antique knickknacks found their destination.

The Mayflower moving van arrived midafternoon with a crew mastering the unloading of each furniture piece and box to their designated rooms. Rachael sent the kids to play in the open field while the van unloaded. They romped and ran through the tall clover-leafed field adjacent to the house. Beth and Nathan were awestruck standing on the gate rails, watching the cattle grazing in the pasture.

By evening, the house was full of disarrayed furnishings and cardboard boxes. Putting the beds together was a priority, complete with the bedding. There would be another day for unpacking and rearranging the furnishings.

Dawn crept over the new landscape. Cold cereal, coffee, and toast made the first breakfast in the Anderson household. The kitchen sink consisted of a long trough. A separate washbasin would be needed to avoid washing dishes in its present state. The unpacking continued with everyone helping to put the clothes and small furnishings in their proper rooms. The few unimportant boxes were stored in the upstairs bathroom. Lunch and supper consisted mainly of sandwiches and milk or Kool-Aid. Each day relieved the house from the organized chaos. The family took a breather exploring the outdoors.

Tracy made a store run, stocking the family with groceries, before driving back to South Boston. He continued working at General Electric, having arranged to live with one of his coworkers. His present income was needed to support the family, and he mailed the remaining paycheck to the farmhouse.

Rachael maintained the household and started assessing the needed repairs. She was infatuated with the barn, wasting no time to explore the inside with Nathan tagging along. The main entrance had an enormous sliding door, exposing a wide walkway that continued to the rear of the building. The hidden interior masked a robust era that had long faded into time. Before them stood a John Deere tractor followed by a four-door pink Ford sedan. A heavy rope hung from the ceiling rafters. Toward the back sat a large hay wagon that only a pair of draft horses could pull. Behind the wagon, in the dark abyss, stood a large covered buggy. The style was symbolic of professionals who traveled during the industrial age.

There was a doorway with a descending stairway that led to the earthen basement. At the bottom lay a couple of dried-out troughs that long awaited some amount of grain to fill its void. Its overhead bay had a few missing floorboards. The overhead bays lining the opposite side of the walkway were full of hay bales destined for the roaming cattle. The baled hay, tractor, and car belonged to Jake Dawson, who used the barn to temporarily store his livelihood.

Walking toward the barn entrance, they found a couple of open stalls, revealing more evidence of penned-in animals like sheep or goats. Few steps onward were a couple of stanchions outfitted for the milking cows.

Next was an open bay where larger animals were housed, coupled with more horse equipment such as reins, neck collars, and other related relics. Rachael returned to the main entrance and noticed three compartment flaps along the left wall. She opened each one and noticed they were hollow, with coats of hay lining the bottom. The compartments gave the appearance of a hideaway for chickens to nest their eggs.

An open doorway exposed a darkened passageway that appeared to have an end wall. Rachael looked at the open bays to the right. One bay displayed a modest number of scattered floorboards with a large packing trunk abutting the enclosed rail. Looking upward gave an open view of the upstairs of the barn's ell addition.

The next bay gave a full view to the earthen ground beneath the main floor. The trunk interested Rachael, and she had Nathan pull it out to reveal its contents. It was full of old clothes and memorabilia from bygone days, none of which Rachael wanted to keep. Instead she removed the relics and put them aside to be trashed. She took one end, with Nathan taking the other, and carried it into the house.

Both continued down a darkened passageway leading into the ell portion of the barn. The back wall gave way to a short sliding door leading to a one-car garage. The garage sliding door opened to the outdoor driveway. Along the garage's back wall were a couple of doorways. One opened to a two-hole privy. Another led to a storage closet with windows, awnings, and a few oblong screens. Between the two doorways stood five five-gallon cans of various paints. The wall laid host to various logging tools and more horse harnesses that had seen better days. A side wall led to an open stable area that occupied more equipment.

The two stepped inside, scoping the room. Along one wall lay more oversized screens that aroused Rachael's curiosity. The opposite wall exposed a staircase leading up to the overhead. The overhead was large and filled with hundreds of baled hay. To the other end was a small mezzanine that followed a stairway heading down to the garage. To one side of the stairway was a workshop that had a work bench occupied by rusty horseshoe nails, old hammers, and other associate paraphernalia. A wall structure containing a multitude of pigeonholes indicated slots where pieces of mail could be inserted. Jake had told them their homestead once served as the area post office during the stagecoach era.

Taking one last glance, Rachael spotted the remains of a couple of bed frames. She examined the condition of each piece before deciding to put them to use. Beds were an issue now that the girls were getting bigger. They proceeded down the stairway and out into the sweeping backyard that surrounded the homestead.

Before tending the family, Rachael and Nathan ventured into the cider shed that stood adjacent to the barn. They slid the door open, and the interior displayed weathered equipment that once worked with precision grinding apples into liquid gold. The equipment was tossed in every direction, giving the appearance that vandals had rummaged through every nook and cranny. A closer look found crumbs of nuts and berries from the last inhabitants. The metal ironworks that once ran with precision were dressed in rust and decay. It was apparent the shed had seen its last days.

Rachael stepped out of the shed, heading for the house, facing the complaints and whining of the smaller ones. The rearranging continued, making up rooms, unpacking clothes boxes, and dusting the furnishings as they found their permanent place.

Beth didn't have a bed and slept in the double bed with Laura. Abigail took the single bed. The room had a walk-in closet that was large enough for both girls while Beth used the closet in her bedroom. The bunk beds in Kenneth's room were assembled and placed against its only straight wall. The bedroom's adjacent wall slanted to the contour of the outer roof. Nathan shared Kenneth's room until his room was put together.

The weekend went fast, with the house resembling a lived-in home. Entertainment was limited. There was no library nearby and no recreational club to join as everyone had to entertain themselves in the greater outdoors. The portable television in the living room was connected to a worn antenna attached to the house's backside. It was the only source of entertainment and news from the outside world. The Andersons were able to pick up Boston's channels 7 and 4 and channel 13 out of Portland, Maine. When on the air, channel 11 transmitted from atop Mount Washington, giving the weather for the New Hampshire region.

Trash became an issue. Rachael noticed the small storage shed attached to the barn outside the garage. She pushed the sliding door open to an empty dirt floor. It was used to store firewood. She decided it would temporarily store the mounting trash with the majority being burned in the furnace. Later Rachael would find a more permanent place to dump the residue.

Labor Day was upon them, and everyone scurried to ensure they had their school clothes ready. Jake told Rachael about the two bus schedules, with one arriving early for high schoolers and a second about an hour later for the elementary grades.

A mail carrier drove the town's back roads providing mail service to every household. The Andersons were new to the area, and the carrier made a deliberate stop, giving them information of how the postal service worked. Bill Blakney introduced himself, having served as the town's mailman for decades. He sold stamps, money orders, stamped envelopes, and any other customer service a post office would provide. He gave Rachael a couple of small brown ordering envelopes for starters. The money orders would come in handy since Rachael never had, nor wanted, a checking account. It was doubtful she even had a savings account since any income received went hand to mouth in support of her seven children.

Beth and Nathan woke to their mother's call. She made sure they got into a routine of meeting the bus in plenty of time. They rushed the first morning, having gotten up around five. The two had a little over an hour to meet the six-forty-five bus. They stepped out of the front door when the bus sped by. Beth and Nathan stood spellbound at the front porch doorway. Jake stood across the way, hollering for them to cross the street and meet it on the return trip. The bus traveled down about a couple of miles to the last family, then turned around for the trip back. Only a couple of minutes passed when the yellow vehicle muscled itself up the small hill, coming to a stop and letting the new students step aboard.

This was Beth and Nathan's second experience riding a school bus. They had no idea where they were going or how long the trip. Both didn't know a soul except watching the occasional stares wondering who and where they originated from. The bus traveled the winding dirt road, stopping at the end of a long drive that could easily be mistaken for a private road. A couple of kids loaded, with the driver saying hello to the oldest lad called Shylock although his real name was Sean Arket. Nathan chuckled after hearing it. Each stop aroused Nathan's curiosity watching each new face climb aboard, filling the myriad of bench seats.

It seemed a half hour passed when the bus drove into a narrow drive that curved around a small white school building. The Anderson children stared out their windows looking at the destination. The opening of the bus door solved their inquisitive minds. It was the collection point where kids from the center of town loaded onboard for the last leg of the journey. It was when the second bus arrived did the journey continue.

The bus drove through the town, stopping at a moccasin-shoe store for more students. It continued crossing the Alton town line, making a few more stops. The bus made a last pickup, stopping where the name on the mailbox read "Ziegler." The irony of the last person boarding would be the last letter of the alphabet. The bus drove through the town of Alton, making a turn at a corner IGA grocery store. It headed down a short distance before stopping in front of a large gray Victorian schoolhouse. Its appearance could have posed as a prop for a haunted thriller. It was attached to a more updated building that provided a systematic educational system.

Once off the bus, Nathan caught up with Beth and got directions to the principal's office. They managed to register themselves, and without wasting a minute, both were escorted to their respective classes. Nathan was motioned into the seventh-grade homeroom headed by a young educator, Mrs. Cummings. He was introduced and made welcomed, taking one of the vacant desks. In the process, Beth vanished to her eighth-grade class.

Nathan was in wonder of the simplicity of the school. The school cafeteria was large enough for eating outside the classroom. A large pasture posed as the school's playground and served as the soccer and football field. It was during the recess Nathan met a few of the guys asking about his background. A few were genuine in offering their friendship while others were testing how tough Nathan was. It would establish his pecking order within the male hierarchy.

The school building was old and rustic. The floorboards gave way to occasional creeks. The main hallway had its majestic staircase to the upper level, denoting the times of the Victorian Era. The day was long, and it was a relief when the last bell rang, releasing the flow of anxious kids yearning to go home. The buses were lined in front of the building, and Nathan made a beeline to the one with the familiar driver. In a matter of minutes, the bus was loaded and heading back on the return route. Nathan wondered what fate had brought him to this.

THE VISITS

The crisp autumn chill flowed throughout the month of October. Rachael received a letter from the Gordons wanting to visit for a weekend. It was a Friday when they arrived in a borrowed car with Tracy. Kyle and Eileen stepped out, followed by their son and the two girls. Eileen took a final drag off her cigarette before rendering it harmless with her foot. Rachael raced out of the house, excited seeing Eileen.

"You're here! You don't know how happy I am to see you. I couldn't wait for you to get here," exclaimed Rachael.

They gave each a hug when Eileen took a quick turn looking at the surrounding countryside. She was in awe, standing in disbelief over what she was seeing. She was amazed over the vast difference from the third-floor apartment where Rachael once lived.

Eileen, still awestruck, turned toward Rachael. "Wow, would you look at this place. Look at those gorgeous fields and those beautiful autumn colors. Is this all yours?"

"Yes, and it's a lot of work," replied Rachael, toning down her excitement. She turned, acknowledging the rest of the family. "Hi, Kyle, Davon, Camila, and you too, Rose. Everyone, follow me into the house for a moment."

Rachael and Tracy led the group into the house. Rachael showed off the rooms while taking Eileen and Kyle to Gretchen and Rebecca's room.

"This is where I'm going to put the both of you. Nathan, take Davon up and show him Kenneth's room. That's where he'll be sleeping. Then take him out and show him the place."

Eileen was still amazed and began feeling a touch of envy of how Rachael was handling everything. "What about the girls?"

"I've got Rose and Camila sharing a bed in the girls' room. Rebecca can share with Beth, and the three girls can share the big double bed in their room," said Rachael.

"That's a bit crowded. I'm so sorry to put you through all this," Eileen replied.

"Don't worry about it. It's only for a couple of nights. The girls won't mind. Now get your things, and afterward I'll take you on a tour of the place," Rachael said with excitement in her voice.

Saturday was spent showing off the farm and the fields while catching up on the local chitchat. Nathan entertained Davon the best he could. His silly disposition reminded Nathan how obnoxious he was. Nathan put on his best face, taking Davon into the barnyard pasture. Jake had loaded his cattle a week prior and driven them to his Farmington barn for the winter. It let the boys roam free from being chased by the curious beasts. They walked among the apple orchard, dodging the cow pies. They climbed a few trees, grabbing an apple or two. They continued the paths throughout the pasture before retracing the crocked path back to the barn.

Rachael took advantage of the Gordons' vehicle and made a grocery trip to Farmington. She made a vat of spaghetti with her homemade meat sauce. Rachael put together cans of tomatoes, tomato paste, ground beef, onions, and garlic in a large skillet, allowing it to simmer until it was ready to serve. It provided enough to serve the large crowd. The adults ate at the kitchen table while the young crowd sat in the dining room. With their bellies filled, the families veered off into smaller segments. The younger crowd amused themselves in the study and living room. The adults remained in the kitchen, indulging in more remembrances, while Beth and Nathan cleaned the aftermath.

Rachael and Eileen recapped their time in South Boston and some of Rachael's earlier years growing up in rural Manomet. She sent Tracy into their closet for some family pictures being kept in the bureau wall. He opened the drawer, retrieving the childhood photos, when he saw a large manila envelope tucked away in the corner. He pulled it out and opened it, noticing all the kids' birth certificates. He smiled at the sight of them until he noticed that their father's name was listed as Clarence Anderson.

Tracy stood feeling slighted. Blood filled his brain with thoughts of revenge. His imagination went further, wondering if it wasn't a spiteful ploy by Rachael for his involvement with Gloria. Tracy calmed himself and began thinking that maybe he should feel lucky, seeing the absence of his name as an act of redemption.

Tracy put the envelope back in the drawer and scooped up a handful of Rachael's formative years. He pretended not having seen the envelope's contents and returned to the sporadic laughter in the kitchen.

Nathan felt grimy, and washing himself in the kitchen was impossible. He got permission to take a basin of warm water up to his room to wash himself. With the entertainment and incoherent voices downstairs, Nathan stripped, washing with the facecloth and soapy water. He continued washing when soft footsteps climbed the back stairs and his bedroom door crept open. Nathan quickly turned and saw Tracy standing there with a sly grin on his face.

He walked over to the naked lad, unzipping his pants. He pulled out his penis and put Nathan's hand around it.

Tracy started feeling Nathan's genitals, asking him, "You like it when I do this?"

Nathan looked at the figure, thinking how sick and demented he was. Nathan remained silent, letting Tracy get his kicks; and after a few moments, Tracy released Nathan's hand and zipped himself up, telling the lad he'd see him later.

Nathan watched as Tracy slowly exited his room, only closing the door partway. Nathan stepped over to the door and heard the footsteps descend the front stairs. It didn't bother Nathan of what just happened; he lived through Tracy's previous advances. He decided to play Tracy's encounters as a tactical game. He dried himself and got dressed, stepped down the stairway, and melted into the crowd.

The final day of the visit went unnoticed. Everyone moped about sluggishly. Nathan filled the wheelbarrow with a few tools and proceeded down to the sawmill. He continued sawing the remaining beams. Rachael wanted the project done before the winter weather set in. Nathan did what he could, stacking the wooden blocks in the shed. As Nathan worked, he thought of those schoolyard talks about chainsaws making the woodcutting go quicker.

Rachael walked down to see how the project was progressing. She was content seeing the many boards stacked by the stone wall. She asked Nathan to walk with her to the far side of the field. Along the tree line was a logging trail that led into the woods. On each side of the path lay the remains of past decades of trash. Rachael told her son that this was where she wanted the trash placed.

Sunday afternoon, the tribe loaded into the vehicle for the drive back to Boston. They returned to South Boston, dropping Tracy off at his East Second Street apartment. The apartment belonged to Al Welton. He preferred to be called Red and worked as the bartender for the East Second Street Bar and Grill. Tracy had a room with the Nylands when the family first moved. The chemistry didn't work between the two. Tracy's drinking was more than they could handle. Before the relationship turned sour, he moved and rented a room from Red. Tracy was a steady customer at the pub and got to know and befriended the barkeep.

Red was middle aged and solid, liken to a football player. His red hair had become sparse over the years from hearing the tales slurred over the beer bottles. Tracy kept to his room having a camper's refrigerator to store his liquor and snacks. He made a call to Gloria, updating her of how he was doing.

"So how's farm life treating you?" asked Gloria.

"There's a lot of acreage and plenty of room for the kids," replied Tracy. "How are the boys doing?"

"They're doing okay. They're into school activities that keep them busy, plus putting a strain on my pocketbook. Right now, they're doing homework," Gloria answered.

"Can I talk to them?" asked Tracy.

Gloria smirked. "I don't think so. They're busy, and besides, I think you need to send more money."

"Why? Isn't what I'm sending you enough? I can't send you any more than what I'm doing," Tracy said, beginning to worry about his wife's next move.

"Well, you better think twice, Tracy. After all, it's your bed, and you chose to lie in it. I bet Rachael is beating her brains out while you're down in Boston. If she only knew what went on behind her back. You're lucky I don't call the police and have you arrested, or should I send Rachael a note?" exclaimed Gloria with a touch of sarcasm.

Tracy cut it short, ending the call before he got himself into a knot. Tracy sent Rachael the remainder of his paycheck. It wasn't enough.

Tracy called his mother-in-law from time to time, letting her know how the family was weathering the farmhouse. He played on her emotions, telling her of the hardships the family was enduring, spending more money than what they had planned. He asked Sarah if she could spare a few dollars helping the family out and not let Rachael know about it. Sarah spared a dollar now and then, knowing what her daughter must have been going through with seven mouths to feed. As the weekend approached, Tracy sat on the edge of his bed preparing himself for the trip to New Hampshire.

The farmhouse celebrated the family's birthdays. It was their main event. Beth's thirtieth birthday enabled her to be a main attraction entering the teenage years. Like all teens, her puberty years continued with skin transformations. She wasn't alone with this change into adulthood; Nathan was right behind her.

Cold weather settled the countryside. The outdoor projects came to a halt, concentrating on cleaning the interior. Beth and Nathan took turns washing floors on their hands and knees. Nathan didn't understand what madness or enjoyment his mother saw in this when a good mop was far better and easier. A large straw-woven basket stood next to the dining room's marble-top table. It was filled with wrinkled clothes that Rachael and Beth needed to iron but often went by the wayside.

The goal was to have everything done by Thanksgiving. It would allow everyone to relax and enjoy the winter's snow. Beth had an idea of having one of her old girlfriends up for a visit. Rachael gave her approval, thinking the girl would decline the invitation since traveling would be difficult. The girl surprised everyone and accepted a weekend trip. Her name was Carol and a former classmate of Beth's while attending Boston Gavin. Beth sent directions to take the Trailways bus to Farmington and to get a cab the rest of the way.

Carol arrived the first weekend of December. Beth was ecstatic, becoming so full of herself. She shared Beth's bedroom and followed her around like a shadow. It was known she had a boyfriend back in Boston but was sending Nathan those occasional looks that would tease any guy. Her visit hadn't exempt Beth from her responsibilities. Carol was more than willing to help and often teased Nathan into the conversations. Beth got around doing some ironing. Nathan wanted to go out to the barn and check the tightly stacked hay.

Jake taught them, if hay was put away with any amount of moisture, the bales sometimes would become hot enough to start combustion. Nathan knew the conditions of the bales when they were stacked. He climbed into the lofts, forcing his arms down between the bales, feeling for any heat source. There were a few bales that were warm enough to separate for cooling and letting in the cold air to circulate.

The trip to the barn enticed Carol to follow. She climbed up into the hayloft, watching Nathan feel down between the bales. They climbed over one bale, then another. In the middle of romping, they coupled together, and Carol planted an affectionate kiss.

Nathan looked at her closely. "What are you doing?"

"Don't you like me?" asked Carol.

"Of course I do. I think you're rather pretty," replied Nathan.

"Well then, don't you want to kiss me back?" whispered Carol.

"Sure I do," Nathan whispered and pulled her close, kissing her deeply.

"I'm fond of you, Nathan," continued Carol.

Nathan looked into Carol's eyes and gave her another deep kiss. The two stood trying to read the other's mind and determining what to do next.

"You're a smart girl," replied Nathan. "But I don't see where this is leading anywhere. Do you?"

Carol just smiled, saying, "You never know. Sometimes things happen unexpectedly."

Nathan just grinned. "Let's finish checking the hay and get back into the house, where it's warm."

The two climbed down from the loft and made their way back into the house.

Rachael came out of the kitchen looking at Carol's smile as she and Nathan entered the door. "How's the hay?"

"There were a few warm bales that had to be separated, but most were okay," responded Nathan.

"And what about you, Carol? Did you help?" asked Rachael.

"It was educational," replied the girl, making her way over toward Beth.

Nathan left the barn episode alone. He knew Carol would fade into the background like all the friends they left behind, and so she did.

The Christmas season was upon the Andersons, with snowstorms blanketing the land throughout the horizons. Holiday shopping needed to be done. Rachael filled a few mail orders from the Sears and Roebuck and Spiegel catalogs, relieving the need to store shop. The time came to put up the tree. Nathan looked forward to the family trudging through the woods for a real Christmas tree. This year broke tradition with the setup of the first artificial tree. Not only did it break the traditional green, but it was bone white. Nathan was a little confused, thinking of the oddity of living in the country, and here he stood before an all-white artificial tree. His mother even had a color scheme of all blue ornaments with the white lights adorning it. It was placed to the right of the living room's entrance.

The living room had a nonfunctional fireplace displaying the mantle where the train station was placed with a sheet of cotton batten. A string of colored lights trimmed the winter scene. The stockings were hung along the mantle awaiting to be filled by the spiritual elf fulfilling every child's pleasant dreams. The Lionel train no longer occupied its traditional place under the spirited tree. Its motor malfunctioned, rendering the iconic rail cars motionless.

Rachael tried bringing out the season's spirit. She sat at the piano playing Christmas carols from the holiday song books as the younger set hovered around singing. Toward the evening, everyone took turns bathing in the portable washtub that sat on the kitchen floor. Afterward they gathered in the living room listening to their mother's rendition of *The Night Before Christmas*.

Christmas week came with the celebrated birthdays of Gretchen turning five, Kenneth turning eight, and Nathan turning twelve. The family's first country Christmas would be missed by the grandparents. Telephone calls substituted their visit, with everyone telling them how they were missed and loved. The enjoyment of presents remained the same, with Santa delivering the much-needed winter clothes.

The winter snowsuits went to immediate use, insulating the girls while they frolicked upon the mounds of snowdrifts. Tracy's morning ritual didn't change. He sat at the kitchen table, swallowing a glass of wine with the raw egg mixture. An ashtray filled with Lucky Strike butts sat an arm's length from him. The holiday breakfast went casual with no formal sitting. It was basically helping oneself to a bowl of cereal, toast, and a glass of milk.

The New Year came with little fanfare for the house that sat in the middle of nowhere. Missing were the muffled sounds of neighboring people shouting from their open windows. For all they knew, it was just another day with the changing of the calendar.

THE ADJUSTMENT DAYS

January crawled with snowstorm after snowstorm. School cancellations accompanied the frigid isolation. The town grader plowed the winding back roads. Its operator, Saul Harper, maneuvered the beast despite having only one hand. School and businesses were closed or delayed due to snow conditions making traveling next to impossible.

Rachael and Nathan bundled up for a walk to the barn. She wanted to explore the upper level now that the truckloads of hay were gone. Rachael noticed an old bench swing, thinking it would look good hanging from the large elm. An old butter churn that once made mass quantities stood nearby, having lost its usefulness long ago. Its four legs and body were solid and in good condition. Rachael visualized it as a possible lawn planter.

They continued down exploring the stalls and the cow stanchions. There was an old milk-and-cream separator along with some large metal pictures depicting various types of cows. It taught Nathan names such as Jersey, Guernsey, Holstein, and Hereford. Discovering these relics told the story of how this barn was a major part in the homestead's operation. As time influenced the New Durham terrain, the once vibrant and historical homestead had lost its soul and deteriorated into weathered decay.

Nathan continued making the trash runs. He burned most of the paper, leaving the bottles, cans, and food stuff. He piled the bags on the sled and trudged through the deep snow to the tree line, where a trash pile stood motionless. Occasionally he'd rake the mounds into leveled blankets.

The coal furnace worked enough to keep the place warm. There were episodes when it backfired, smoking up the house with toxic fumes. The doors flew open, allowing fresh air to circulate. The internal portion of the furnace had to be poked and prodded, making the heating elements functional. The water content was regulated within the scope of the glass tube attached to the furnace's side. The furnace was antiquated and hadn't been used in years. It needed to be looked over before another season took place.

Cabin fever started to settle. Many times, Jake Dawson or Dave Carlson sat at the kitchen table with a warm cup of coffee, engaging Rachael in some neighborhood banter. They didn't stay long. Jake often invited Nathan to help tend his cattle in Farmington. He had no idea why Jake wanted him to tag along, but it was something his mother encouraged. Nathan figured she wanted an adult male in his life.

The sounds of springtime couldn't come fast enough. The coal briskets that were tossed into the driveway were raked evenly. The oversized chunks were added to the compost pile. Spring spawned a visit from the elder matriarch.

Sarah traveled the Greyhound bus to Boston, transferring on Trailways to Farmington and riding the cab the rest of the way. She had read the farm's transformations from Rachael's letters and the phone calls from Tracy. She was curious and wanted to see for herself how the farmhouse was progressing.

The cab arrived, with Rachael and the smaller ones running out, hugging Sarah with shared kisses. Rachael wasted no time taking her mother inside and showing her the house. Sarah was surprised how large and roomy it was. Rachael let her mother rest in the kitchen to catch her breath before taking her on a tour of the farm.

"Well, Rachael, it's a pretty nice place for you and the kids. Are you doing okay?" asked Sarah.

"Somewhat. I can tell you it's not easy. I really didn't realize how much went into keeping a place like this going. The unexpected costs for just the household items are more than what I expected," uttered Rachael, feeling disheartened.

"How are you feeding the kids? How are you keeping everything together?" asked Sarah, looking concerned.

"I have good neighbors," replied Rachael. "I have a neighbor who is a great friend and takes me shopping once a week so I can load up on groceries and get a few household items."

"And how long is that going to last?" asked the elder. "Good will can only last just so long. Have you thought about getting a vehicle?"

"Of course I have. I can only afford one thing at a time," asserted Rachael. "I have Beth and Nathan helping me keep this house going. It isn't easy. Are you ready to see the rest of the farm?"

"I guess so. Let's go out and get some fresh air." Sarah sighed.

The two women stepped onto the backyard with Rachael leading the tour. She took her mother for a walk through the barn and showed her the stanchions, animal pens, and all the antiquities that lie within it. She continued out the back pasture, dodging the old cow pies while pointing out the apple orchard. Rachael mentioned how the kids loved climbing the trees to pick a couple now and then. Sarah was impressed and thought how beneficial it was having an orchard on the property. At least her daughter could make apple sauce, turnovers, and pies to feed her kids.

Rachael returned to the backyard, showing the remains of the cider mill and the fifty-foot well beside it. They continued onto the small field where the sawmill once stood.

"Nathan helped me tear down the lumber mill, and we'll be tearing the cider mill down soon. They're both rotted and only adding to the tax bill. We're using the wood to heat the house and saving somewhat on the coal bill. In another month, I'm going to need a lawn mower, rakes, garden tools, and pruning shears to maintain the outside," added Rachael.

"And how are you going to afford all that?" asked Sarah, expressing her deep concern.

"I'll worry about that when the time comes," replied Rachael.

Sarah just stood, looking at her daughter. "Is Tracy making enough to cover all this? I know your support check must be paying a big chunk, but how much is Tracy helping for all of this?"

Rachael couldn't give her mother a straight answer other than operating a farm was far more than what was expected. Sarah had seen enough for the time being and wanted to go back into the house to understand how things were being handled.

The conversations with her mother churned in Rachael's head. She realized it was more than kindness the Carlsons gave them. They saved their lives, ensuring her family had food on the table and the basic tools to survive. She faced the fact that it would be a matter of time before their favors would see their days waning. Rachael knew a vehicle had to be a priority.

Natalie stopped by to take Rachael shopping and met the elder matriarch. Sarah gave a few dollars to Rachael to get some wallpaper for the girls' room. It was in desperate need for a major uplifting. Rachael left her mother to babysit while accompanying her neighbor on the shopping spree.

Sarah and Rachael set up the foldaway table as a workbench for pasting the new wallpaper. The new print was applied after peeling and tossing the old paper into the furnace. It took two to three days to complete despite a few uneven spots in the tight corners. A week passed when Sarah needed to return home to Milton. She felt satisfied knowing she had a realistic look at the farm conditions.

The Nylands started their weekend trips to their small bungalow at Dexter Corner. They brought Tracy along, saving him the expense of a round-trip ticket. One weekend, they dropped off a dozen chicks along with a twenty-pound bag of grain. They were met by the oohs and aahs from the girls. Each chick was picked up and petted by the small hands that found them soft and cuddly. The chicks rested in a cardboard box on the kitchen table for a day or two before being moved to the entryway. A lamp and a towel lay over the lid, keeping the heat within and Penny's curiosity out.

Jake added more to the Andersons' woes by suggesting they get a cow to compensate for the cost of milk. He tried convincing Rachael that a cow would be cheaper to maintain than buying milk for such a large family. Rachael thought about it and wondered if it was worth doing. She showed an interest if the price was affordable.

Jake assured her he'd keep his eyes and ears open for anything that might turn up.

Jake was well connected, having lived his life in the New Durham–Farmington area. He had dual residencies, living most of the year in his house across from the Andersons. During the winter, Jake lived close to his cattle in Farmington.

The arrival of the warm weather brought Jake's loaded cattle truck. It backed up into his pasture gateway, and he unlatched the backflap and released the herd one by one as they kicked their hindquarters in jubilation.

The season brought the removal of the plastic window coverings and the enticing air circulating throughout the house. The green grass pierced throughout the yard and fields. Tree buds wasted no time sprouting into light pastels before darkening with every exposure to sunlight.

Patty, now thirteen, caught a second wind of life and prided herself in cornering a woodchuck in the adjacent field. Penny was more conservative in her movements and often resorted to resting on the dining room table.

Rachael had Nathan built another rabbit pen that was large enough to allow Michael Jay some breathing space. It was constructed with chicken wire in the same manner as his cage in the back hall. It sat in front of the barn, allowing him to nibble on the vegetation.

A clothesline was strung on pulleys from the back porch to the barn, giving Rachael more line for the bedsheets and blankets. It relieved them from being cramped on the porch or the wooden clothes dryer.

Tracy had a prospect on a used Ford. The price was reasonable but needed a lot of work. It took months to save enough money to purchase it. Tracy wanted someone to make the journey north with him in case the vehicle broke down. Nathan was sent, riding the bus to South Boston, and waited at the Gordons for Tracy's arrival.

Revisiting the old neighborhood gave Nathan an opportunity to see a few former neighbors. Tracy arrived to pick up Nathan, and together they walked the dozen blocks, meeting up with the car's owner. He wrote a bill of sale and handed the keys to Tracy. He motioned to Nathan to hop in and started the drive on the interstate back to New Hampshire. Nathan rode in the front under Tracy's watchful eye. After a while, Tracy asked if Nathan needed to go to the bathroom. He chuckled to himself and looked at Tracy, saying he didn't have to go. Hardly another word was spoken. The journey ended when the four wheels came to a stop on the crusty drive.

Rachael arranged to have the car looked over at Frank's garage. It took a couple of days, and the repairs ended up equaling the cost of the vehicle. It put the family further in financial debt. Rachael dreaded the costs but knew the vehicle would last for the long term.

The chickens were big enough to roam outside. Rachael found more displaced chicken wire and converted the barn's entry storage space into a chicken coop. Rachael and Nathan wired the opening and placed a rail above the floor resting on the wall's support beams. Eventually the chickens would use it for roosting. There were two doorways to the space. One entered the room from the cow stanchions, and another led to the outside. Natalie donated an old chicken feeder and watering pan for the cause.

Rachael wanted a vegetable garden. She used her flirtatious instincts on Dave Carlson's good nature in asking him to plow her an acre. He drove his team of draft horses, dragging a plow behind them. It took all afternoon plowing an acre atop the large pasture. It took another day to repeat the process with a cultivator. It was time to plant. Nathan loaded the wheelbarrow with old manure from beneath the barn and pushed it up the hill, where Rachael waited. She dug a few holes for cucumbers and squashes. The furrowed rows planted a series of carrots, beets, Swiss chard, a variety of beans, and potatoes. It filled the front half of the garden. The back half was sown with hills of corn.

School ended with the bus door opening at the Andersons' front door. Rachael sat on the front porch with scissors and comb lying on the table. Her mission was to give her two boys summer crew cuts. Kenneth normally wore his hair short, but Nathan sported the regular cut, allowing a head of hair to show. Rachael sat them down one after another, clipping away until the scalps came into view. Nathan was bitter staring in the mirror at his crew cut and wishing it was his last.

The following days were geared to demolishing the cider mill. Rachael was able to purchase a sledgehammer, pinch, and crowbars. They started taking the building apart with the same strategy as the lumber mill. The project would take a couple of months. In the interim, Rachael received a letter from Eileen wanting to make another visit. This time, their stay would be longer.

The Gordons arrived mid-July, breaking up the Andersons' normal routine. The group walked around the improvements and demolitions. The cider mill was well on its way being dismantled. Rachael made it clear the area was off-limits to everyone. The summer heat was tolerable, with sweat dripping from any amount of exertion. Everyone was able to drink cold water or iced coffee to quench their thirst. There were packets of Kool-Aid for the younger ones. Eileen made Kyle drive to the supermarket to load up on groceries before returning to Boston. The Gordons were going through marital problems, and Eleanor needed time apart to think.

Kyle returned to the South Boston apartment, sharing it with his oldest son. The place seemed empty with his family up in New Hampshire. He continued to get up and walk to the bus depot, where he worked as a bus driver. Some evenings, Kyle crawled through the fence, taking his place on a stool at the East Second Street pub. The beer made his problems more lucid to anyone who'd listen, including the shadow behind the bar.

Kyle's son was in his late teens sporting a club jacket with his name, Larry, on the back. Larry felt proud wearing his jacket. He earned a few dollars here and there but mostly spent nights behind bars for disturbing the peace or some petty crime.

The girls were cramped sleeping together. Rachael needed to be creative with the sleeping arrangements. She remembered an old iron bed up in the barn's mezzanine. She called Nathan to follow her into the upper level of the ell.

Rachael spoke in an empathetic tone to her son, "Nate, I need you to do me a favor. I need you to sleep up in the loft for a while so I can use your bed for the girls."

"Do you know how hot it is up there?" responded Nathan.

"I know it might be uncomfortable, but it'll be cooler at night. You can sleep in a sleeping bag, and you can use a pillow to make it better," Rachael added.

"Why is it just me?" asked Nathan, being defiant.

"Because I said so," Rachael said sternly.

"What about Davon?"

Rachael was quick to respond. "He can sleep out here too if you make a place for him. That'll help everyone. I'll tell Eileen that you and Davon will be sleeping out here. Now I need you to climb up there and fix the place for the both of you."

Nathan climbed the ladder steps into the mezzanine. There sat the rusted iron bed with an old stained mattress. He retrieved a pillow and a sleeping bag to complete his new sleeping quarters. Davon's bed was nothing more than a fluffed-up bale of hay. He had the other sleeping bag and a pillow to rest his bones. The heat flooded the loft, giving little relief during the dark of night.

Nathan lay there looking at the rafters, wondering where he'd be in the next ten years. The Vietnam War was still going strong. Would it be over by the time he got out of high school? Even if he went to college, would the war still continue? What would the future world be like? America was already heading for the moon. Would the world change that radically in the coming years? Nathan's mind was racing as he realized high school would be over in a few years. Nathan resigned, taking life as it came while his eyes slowly sank into darkness.

Mid-August arrived, and Eileen felt it was time to return home to face her marriage. Rachael thought about sending Nathan to his grandparents for a week. After the Gordons left, she drove him to Farmington and bought a bus ticket at Osgood's Pharmacy.

Sarah took Nathan on a few neighborhood walks upon his arrival. They proceeded on a side street where Clifton Michaels had a small apartment. Esther died, leaving Cliff to sell the home in Manomet. Like the Manters, he wanted to live within walking distance of Plymouth and close to the people that meant the most to him. He still had his car but seldom drove. His eyesight was diminishing, and time had limited Cliff's ability to do things.

The two left Cliff and walked to the top of the street where the Pilgrim forefathers monument stood. It was the first time Nathan had seen such a tall dedication to the Puritan forefathers. After walking around the parkway, they descended back to the apartment. Sarah cooked supper while Milton and Nathan indulged in a game of fifteen-two, fifteen-four.

Flora appeared the next morning, spending most of the day. The first few hours, the three walked downtown shopping for a few odds and ends. Flora was one for stopping in a deli-style restaurant for a quick snack and coffee. She treated these moments as spending quality time with her sister. Once home, Sarah fixed Milton a hearty meal before the three played a game of dominoes. Sarah took time to visit the neighbors while the challengers played. By early evening, Flora left to catch her ride back to the cottage. It would be another year before Nathan visited Ellis Pond.

The news came that the family was getting a cow. Jake had friends who had a pregnant Jersey they were willing to sell. Jake talked the price down by telling them it was for a family with seven kids buying the creature. The sale benefited both families. The Andersons had shelter and the pasture to care for the cow, and the owners could retire from the morning and evening milkings.

Rachael had to shop for a milking pail and all that went with it. Natalie gave her a material list. Besides the pail, Rachael needed bag balm, cheese cloth, liquid Lysol, a couple of pails for watering, milking jars, a large halter, and a couple of bags of grain for starters. Jake offered to sell Rachael a bay full of hay, which she appreciated. With the shopping done, Rachael sat on the back steps wondering what she had gotten herself into. She hadn't realized how much went into owning a cow.

It was a Saturday when the truck arrived, unloading the brown Jersey. Her face was blackened with a white band around the nose. Her red forelocks were cropped with a pair of horns. She fit the ideal description of any Jersey cow. She was placed in the stanchion area, munching on a few layers of hay. There were a few stranded bales of straw that were used as bedding. Natalie stayed a few moments, showing Rachael how to do the milking and what to expect.

Rachael woke Nathan to help her with the milking. The coffee water was heating while Nathan toted buckets of water out to the barn. With every pail, Nathan tried petting the cow between her horns. He stood watching after giving her a scoop of grain in the feed bowl. His initial fear was getting horned in the process. Nathan tried earning the cow's friendship by moving slow and petting her hindquarters, easing his hand toward her head. He stepped back, grabbed the hoe to clean the trough of the manure, and pushed it down the shoot. Nathan just stood studying the Jersey for a few moments before heading in for coffee.

Nathan sat with his mother sipping the hot brew. Something quick and warm added to the comforts of the cool outdoors. Nathan followed his mother into the stall. She grabbed an old stool and positioned herself for her first milking. Nathan sat against the barn wall, watching his mother milk away.

An old radio was placed on the barn shelf giving the news and background music to the cementing silence. Rachael felt the coldness within the stall. She realized the stanchions needed to be enclosed. She and Nathan built a wall next to the cow, reinforcing it with the remaining roll of plastic. They continued insulating the back wall and windows to retain the creature's body heat. The next shopping trip bought a grooming brush and curry comb. Rachael felt an attachment with the cow and wanted to come up with a name. After much brainstorming, the cow became known as Matilda. The name came from her constant moving while being milked as if she was waltzing, becoming waltzing Matilda.

The milk didn't sit well with everyone. It didn't taste the same from the store. During the night, the milk had separated with a layer of heavy cream. Rachael spooned it off, putting it into mason jars.

The garden was ready for harvest. A large amount would be canned and stored away for the winter. Canning was another process needing to be learned. The mason jars, feed for Matilda, school clothes, and car maintenance took its toll on what the family could afford. It came to a point Rachael needed to cut down expenses. The telephone was disconnected, leaving correspondence done by mail. Rachael felt she had no choice but write her mother, explaining her dilemma, asking if she could spare a few dollars.

The last of the haying season came. Jake did Rachael a favor baling what hay was available on the large pasture. It would be the last time the field would be mowed. It needed to be plowed and fertilized before growing another crop. It was something the Andersons couldn't afford. Jake had his large pasture adjacent to his farmhouse. It was thick and rich with tall grass and clover. Rachael felt she had to return Jake's kindness by offering Nathan's help with his haying. The field had been cut, raked, and baled as the hay was ready to be loaded. Nathan followed the wagon, stacking each bale in the crisscross fashion.

Jake turned off the tractor. He motioned to Nathan to follow him up to his house for a water break. Despite Jake's home being built similar to the Andersons, the rooms took on a different dimension. They were more spacious. The kitchen was large and boxlike. The sink hadn't any faucets but a single hand pump that drew the water up from the well. Next was a medium-sized room Jake used as a living room, where he ate his meals while watching his favorite television shows. Nathan noticed the rest of the house was closed off.

It was one of Tracy's letters that told Rachael of Eileen Gordon's passing from lung cancer. It devastated Rachael. The news reflected a time when Rachael lost her cousin to cancer. Eileen was just as close. Rachael took a moment remembering all those morning visits in South Boston. Now another life's chapter was closed.

Cold weather brought on the coal furnace backfiring, sending more toxic fumes throughout the house. Rachael searched around and found a contractor who dealt with their type of furnace. The furnace had outlived its usefulness, but the family couldn't afford replacing it. The internal firing bricks needed to be replaced.

Nathan stayed home from school to meet the repairman. He was elderly and moved at a snail's pace. He followed Nathan into the basement, where the two proceeded in cleaning and tearing out the internal parts of the furnace. It took a few hours replacing the rubber belts and making the furnace work more efficiently. The cost was more than what was anticipated. The aged contractor reminded Rachael it would have been a lot more without her son's help. Rachael bit her lip, holding back her discontent, and, with a polite smile, paid the bill.

Money became tight, and for many days, the family ran the furnace on just wood. The jars of milk were adding up. Disguising it in chocolate was the only way the kids would drink it. Rachael found a gallon-size butter churn at Clark's Grain Store and had Natalie teach them to use the mini machine. It took almost an hour churning the heavy cream before large lumps of butter began to emerge. The butter was scooped and kneaded with a spoonful of salt, then molded into sticks. It passed the children's flavor taste and was used like any store-bought margarine.

The Manters decided they wouldn't be able to visit the farmhouse for the holidays. Sarah discovered she had breast cancer and needed an operation. She planned on being home recuperating before she let the news be known.

Thanksgiving was a few days away. The school lunch period was over, and Nathan's afternoon class was in Ms. Crum's study hall. She was a robust middle-aged woman whose reputation for teaching business made her students focus directly on the lessons. It was a little after one o'clock when word came over the PA system that President Kennedy was shot and died. There was a request for a moment of silence. In an instant, the school became cloaked in utter silence and would remain so until the last bell.

Upon reaching home, Rachael was already glued to the television. The news broadcasted the circumstances leading up and including the assassination. It televised the photo of Vice President Johnson being sworn in as president, with Jacqueline Kennedy standing nearby. It gave the family pause to sit and listen until the moment came to start doing chores.

Thanksgiving became just another Sunday dinner with many more meals to be stretched. The holiday season repeated the previous with the window coverings and the decorated white Christmas tree, along with the other holiday decors.

The snow lay thick and heavy with many more outings with the shovel. Nathan carved out the walkways, spending hours shoveling the lengthy driveway from the road to the barn entrance. Jake suggested clearing the porch roof before it caved. Rachael had Nathan crawl out of the girls' bedroom window, maneuvering the scoop shovel to clear the back-porch roof, then climb over the pitch and begin removing the mounds of snow that blanketed the front.

ANOTHER YEAR, ANOTHER DOLLAR

Another year put the farmhouse in more financial despair. Rachael's survival depended on the car and the mail. Her mother's cancer weighed heavy on her mind. She decided to send Nathan to his grandparents during the February vacation. Rachael needed her son to give her a firsthand report on her mother's health.

Sarah had been home a few weeks recovering from the breast surgery. Nathan served as her extra pair of arms, carrying groceries, taking out trash, and helping with household chores. Up to now, Sarah had nearby relatives and friends stop by making sure she didn't overexert herself.

The morning sun shone through the frosted windows of the Manter apartment. Sarah got up and gingerly walked into the kitchen, starting breakfast.

Nathan watched her from the cot. "You okay, Gram?"

"I'm all right, just going to start breakfast," answered Sarah.

Nathan looked concerned. "Let me help you. I can do the toast and set the table," Nathan said, heading for the kitchen. He glanced over, watching his grandfather sit up on the edge of the bed. "Going to use the bathroom, Gramp?"

"Thought I would while everyone is busy in the kitchen," answered Milton, grabbing his cane and thunder jug.

He made his way toward the bathroom to wash his face and upper body. It took him the same amount of time as it did to cook the Cream of Wheat.

"Is everyone ready?" asked Sarah, dishing the oatmeal into bowls.

"Not quite," replied Milton, returning the jug and putting on his pajama top.

Sarah turned on the television for the morning news. Nathan filled the coffee cups and placed the oatmeal bowls as his grandmother took her place.

They ate while the news announced the headlines around the Boston area. Sarah was more interested in the local weather report. They had taken their last bite when Nathan got up and started clearing the table.

"Gram, why don't you go wash while I do the dishes?"

"Just leave them. I can wash dishes. I'm not that helpless," Sarah stated.

"I know you're not. I just want to help," replied her grandson.

Sarah wasn't used to all the attention but allowed her grandson to help this one time. Milton got his clothes from the bedside chair and started dressing himself.

Sarah brushed her hair the forty strokes before giving herself a facial.

Milton finished buttoning his shirt, calling out, "Hey, Nathan, could you help me with my shoes?"

The grandson peered around the corner, eyeing his grandfather. "Be right there. Let me rinse these dishes first."

Nathan stooped to tie Milton's shoes when Sarah stepped out getting a dress from the closet.

"Nathan, I want to show you something," Sarah said with some solace to her tone.

Nathan turned, looking up at his grandmother. She stood there in her slip, then pulled the top part aside, exposing the massive scar tissue where a breast once stood.

Nathan didn't know what to make of it. "I'm sorry, Gram. I'm sorry you had to go through that."

Sarah let go of her slip and continued putting on her dress. "I just wanted you to see what cancer can do to a person."

"How do you feel?" asked Nathan.

"I feel better, just a little sore," came the reply.

Nathan knew his grandmother wasn't looking for sympathy, just wanted to share the trauma with him. In Nathan's eyes, it only made him realize how strong his grandmother really was.

It was routine for Sarah to visit her neighbors, checking on their health and welfare. These past weeks, they looked at Sarah, ensuring she was able to get about without any discomfort. Nathan accompanied his grandmother downtown, taking casual looks into the store windows. Sarah knew walking was good exercise for her recovery. It was late morning when Flora stepped off the bus to spend the day with her sister. She wanted to check on her sister's health and well-being. It didn't take long before Milton challenged her and Nathan to a game of dominoes. It was Sarah's cue to go visit a neighbor or two.

The threesome played for the remaining hours before Flora had to leave to catch the bus back to Cambridge. Sarah had returned an hour earlier and was puttering with her jigsaw puzzle. She had succeeded in putting a few pieces together. She thanked Flora for stopping by and would call her later in the evening.

The Manters weren't television buffs. They watched the news and had their favorite game shows, then turned it off while doing their hobbies. Sarah loved jigsaw puzzles while Milton either read the newspaper or played variations of solitaire. Nathan enjoyed playing games with his grandfather, spending hours challenging him to cribbage, dominoes, and rummy. By week's end, Sarah was feeling more herself, and Nathan was ready for the long bus ride home.

The bus door opened in Farmington, letting Nathan step onto the sidewalk. He noticed the green Ford parked across the street and climbed into the front seat. Rachael started the car for the drive back to the homestead.

"Good to have you back. How's your grandmother?"

Nathan glanced over at his mother. "She's doing better. She wasn't herself. I'm glad I went to help her. We walked downtown a few times just to window-shop. Saw Aunt Flora while I was there. She's doing okay."

"Oh?" Rachael asked curiously. "What did she have to say?"

"Nothing much. She was just concerned about Gram. She, Gramp, and I played a few games of dominoes. I don't think she likes it when I win," Nathan said with a smile.

Rachael returned the smile and continued driving. The car arrived at the driveway, with Nathan grabbing his suitcase. The kids came out the back door, excited to have Nathan back. The welcoming surprised him.

Rachael looked at her son as she passed the younger set. "They didn't realize how much you did."

Nathan returned doing the chores with the added milking. It would be for a short period as Matilda needed her udder dried up. She was due to calf in the coming weeks. It would be over a week after calving before the cow's milk could be used by the family.

Jake stopped by mentioning there was a Jersey cow destined for the slaughterhouse that Rachael could get cheap. It would help provide more milk for the family. He mentioned the cow had one teat that wasn't working. The Andersons' hardships were general knowledge, and any offering would be accepted. The cow arrived in the predawn days of March and was placed in the stanchion separate from Matilda. She became known as Sandy.

Rachael milked her first to test her temperament. Sandy was more than sound. She was easygoing, and being hornless made her disposition even more welcoming. Her body color was more a light tan, far different from Matilda's. Sandy suffered a condition of mastitis that affected her dysfunctional udder. The area vet arrived providing some meds and a teat dilator, and with tender loving care, Sandy's udder became fully functional.

Michael Jay found his caged surroundings boring. He soon discovered gnawing the wire gave way to his freedom. His explorations went from room to room before being captured and fitted back into his pen. It was Nathan's scent that was most familiar to him. The midnight crusader again chewed through the wire, making his way up the stairs and finding Nathan's bed. He tickled Nathan's nose with his whiskers. It didn't matter how his pen was mended; Michael Jay was determined to get out for his nighttime escapades.

The winter snows melted into pools of water and rushing streams. Matilda was showing signs of getting ready to calve. Her udder became swollen with a little waxing on each teat and dilations under her tail. It was time to place her in the small box stall. The birthing stall was built weeks earlier and big enough for Matilda to move around. Nathan coated the floor with the bale of straw before leading Matilda into the stall. By day's end, the fawnlike calf arrived. Rachael fell in love with the newborn standing on its wobbly legs and covered with a bold-red coat. Rachael adored Matilda's calf, naming her Ivy and deciding to have her dehorned as soon as she was old enough.

For the next few days, Matilda roamed the maternity stall caring for her calf before being confined to her stanchion. Raising a calf was something new to Rachael. Natalie stopped by, lending what little help she could do. She was pregnant herself and due to deliver in a couple of months. She instructed Rachael that the calf would have to be transferred to a nursing pail after the first week. With two milking cows, Rachael went back to milking Matilda, with Nathan milking Sandy. Rachael was overburdened with milk, having to throw most of it away.

The Carlsons suggested raising a couple of pigs. It wouldn't take much to feed them, just a little grain mixed with the excess milk and the food scraps. After a full season, the pigs would be ready for the freezer. It's what Natalie and Dave did for years in cutting down on the food bill. Careful planning was given before the animal population expanded.

The Nylands stopped by, dropping off two Peking ducks. After the ducks came two piglets. They were penned on the ground floor toward the end of the barn. They had the large area to root and dig to their hearts' content. The challenge was stepping down the staircase meeting the two snorting faces who anticipated the bucket of slop. Filling the trough was difficult. The pigs had tipped it over so many times that Nathan's attempt to feed them included a balancing act, holding the bucket at arm's length while trying to upright it.

It was time to open the barn doors and let the fresh air circulate. The rambunctious cows were let out, stretching their legs. Nathan followed his mother along the fence line. They replaced posts made from small poplar trees that were chopped, sawed, and axed. They repaired two large gaps that needed reinforcement.

It was the middle of May when Rachael started thinking about the gardens. The upper garden needed to be plowed. Rachael again asked Dave Carlson to help with the plowing.

Dave asked jokingly, “How much is it worth to you?”

Rachael lightheartedly said, “Why, how much do you want?”

“Something that’ll make it worth my while.” Dave smiled.

“I can give you what you want. All I want to know is, Will you do it?” asked Rachael.

“I’ll lend you the equipment, but you’ll have to do the work,” responded Dave.

Rachael explained to Tracy that the Carlsons were willing to lend the equipment for plowing the gardens but he’d have to do the work. Tracy was reluctant but walked the mile dirt road to the Carlsons. He rode the plow, guiding the team of draft horses back to the garden area. Nathan was called to help guide the draft horses down the rows while Tracy handled the plow. It was a picturesque moment watching Tracy, thin and inexperienced, behind the reins of two majestic draft horses. The two repeated the process cultivating the plowed-up earth the following weekend.

Rachael stood at the head of the plowed-up acre. She thought about where she wanted her crops planted. She knew about rotating and imagined where the vegetables were the previous year. Rachael and Nathan hoed the rows about a foot and a half apart. One area was for vine plants such as cucumbers, summer squash, and zucchini. Nathan pushed wheelbarrows of manure, filling each cavity. It was time consuming and frustrating for Nathan making the many trips back and forth to the manure pile. He stopped a few times to wipe the sweat from his brow. It took over a dozen loads to fertilize the holes for the vine seeds. The remaining rows were planted with potatoes, carrots, Swiss chard, beets, string beans, peas, and lettuce. The hills of corn were seeded on the back end. Rachael and Nathan put the same energy into planting the lower garden with onions, tomatoes, and a variety of squashes.

Beth had developed into the flirtatious teenager like many girls her age. She sparked the attention of boys who were discovering their own hormonal instincts. Beth caught the interest of a local boy. He was Ben Greyson, a rural guy who wasn't afraid of hard work, just hard authoritarians. He had a bay gelding named Bosco. After school, he worked at a horse farm atop the ridge. During his off time, he rode his mount weaving through the wooded trails visiting neighbors. Ben found his way to the Andersons' front yard. A ten-foot hitching log stood alongside the house. It was ideal for tying the gelding while Ben spent a few moments saying hello.

Ben survived his first visit and was invited again. His stopping at the house was on the way to his friend Andy. Andy's father ran a small construction company primarily dealing with heavy equipment. They had a couple of ponies and a Tennessee walker. It wasn't too long before Andy galloped up saying his hellos.

By the end of June, the homestead was looking like a postcard. The lawn was trimmed and extended itself into the small pasture. While mowing the lower field, Nathan discovered stems of black raspberries growing alongside a grapevine. He saw his mother trimming along the backside of the house and called for her to look at the new discovery. Rachael was surprised at what she saw and had Nathan clear the weeded area and construct a wooden trellis for the vines to grow. A charcoal pit was constructed within the stone border. The couple of flower beds were rejuvenated with tulips, daffodils, and irises. The hedges along the stone wall were trimmed, matching the wall's height. The antiquated double-seater made its way hanging from the big elm tree.

The weathered barn and farmhouse were in desperate need of painting. There were a few five-gallon cans of paint in the garage. Using a screwdriver, Rachael opened them up and found three of white and two of cardinal red. The first challenge was repainting the house. Tracy started in the front, painting the high perches. Rachael watched while plucking a weed or two from her flower beds.

Nathan pushed the wheelbarrow with a hoe, rake, and an old sitting cushion up to the garden to weed a few vegetables rows. Beth was busy monitoring the younger ones while doing the wash and ironing.

The pigs were getting bigger, and the ground floor had become a garden of muck. Rachael wanted a pen built with an overhang shelter protecting them in foul weather. She walked the barn pasture following the fence line for possible site. The two cows followed behind with the occasional mounting of each other. Rachael knew this was a sign they were in season and needed to get in touch with the area veterinarian. She glanced at an area just over the stone wall, where the old lumber mill once stood, as a possible location.

The vet arrived, letting Rachael pick the bulls from a pictured pamphlet to service her cows. The vet removed the specimen capsules from his carryall and performed the artificial insemination on both cows.

The construction started on the pig pen next to where the old lumber mill stood. Nathan chopped down a half dozen small poplar trees into fence posts. The mother and son constructed the pen using the boards that were put aside along the stone wall.

The weekend had Nathan leading the pigs with a bucket of slop to their new pen. They snorted through the backyard, scaring the younger kids into the house. Nathan poured the mixture into the trough as the pigs raced to fill their gullet. He returned to the opening and nailed the boards in place. The confining pigs began exploring every corner to escape their new surroundings. Tracy staggered from inside the barn, having visited his hidden liquor bottle. He witnessed the whole proceedings from the doorway. He saw Nathan walking toward the house with the empty bucket.

"You think you're so damn clever!" yelled Tracy. "You think you're smarter than me. Well, you're not and never will be."

Nathan stared at Tracy as he continued walking toward the barn. He realized what Tracy was doing and remained silent.

Tracy continued sparring with Nathan, "You think, just because you're in high school, you know more than me."

Nathan still contained himself, not wanting to get involved with Tracy's intoxicated state.

"Go ahead…big man…Mr. Know-It-All. You'll never amount to much," continued Tracy.

"Well, I don't see your high school diploma," interjected Nathan, having had enough of Tracy's belligerence.

"Who told him? Who told him!" Tracy yelled, turning toward Rachael.

"Don't look at me," answered Rachael. "I didn't tell him anything."

The two continued arguing well into the afternoon.

By the end of July, Sarah wrote asking if they could visit for a few weeks. Rachael wasn't sure the car would make the trip and had Frank give it a once-over. The drive began after Nathan tended the animals, and they arrived in Plymouth late morning. The arduous job was helping Milton to the car. In the meantime, Sarah closed the apartment, giving her goodbyes to a few of the neighbors. She appointed one to collect her mail. By midafternoon, the Ford made the long drive back to New Hampshire.

It was suppertime when they drove into the driveway. Rachael found the only way for her father to get into the house was through Michael Jay's entranceway. It was easier for him to walk into Gretchen and Rebecca's room, where they would be sleeping. The girls doubled up in their sisters' upstairs bedroom. It was the first visit for Milton. He scanned the landscape, reserving his comments while making his way to the doorway.

Milton loved gardening and saw the need of a big garden. Rachael drove him to the upper field, where he sat in the car watching the weeding take place. Milton watched as Rachael and Nathan pulled weeds along the single rows, then hoed the ground between each one. Everything was growing. The mother and son had finished their rows and placed the garden tools in the trunk. Before leaving, they gave the vine plants the once-over for bugs.

The nesting hens cackled, making everyone aware of their peeping hatchlings. The chicks were safe within the secret compartments while the mother hens pecked about the barnyard for food. They flew into the compartments, comforting their small broods.

The mother duck sat on a few eggs, producing one hatchling. The three wobbled out of the barn and around the backyard. They made their way through the pasture and into the flowing stream that fed the apple orchard.

Blueberry season enlisted the help of Beth and Nathan. They got up at dawn, with Beth making the bagged lunches while Nathan did the barn chores. The pickup came by around eight, taking them to Smitty's vegetable stand. A group of kids already gathered awaiting his arrival. Smitty scooped them up and dropped them off at his large blueberry field. The Andersons were given a crash course on how to rake. A large water container stood on the back of his truck for anyone needing to hydrate themselves. The two newbies took advantage of it while most everyone brought cans of soda to wet their whistle.

Lunchtime gathered everyone eating and enjoying a joke or two. By midafternoon, the call came for everyone to climb aboard the truck for the ride to Smitty's farmhouse. The containers were poured through a winnower, separating the berries from the small twigs and leaves. The pickers were paid for what the winnowed pints produced. Beth and Nathan enjoyed raking and the camaraderie that went with it. The experience would last for the next two weeks.

Having the grandparents during blueberry season made life easier on the household. Sarah was able to do most of Beth's chores while Rachael tended to the garden. By August, the vegetables were ready for harvesting. Milton sat on a chair outside shucking peas, snapping beans, and preparing the vegetables for canning. The butternut and blue Hubbard squashes were placed on propped-up boards in the back of the earthen cellar. Beside them stood a wicker basket of potatoes.

The Andersons' food supply was stocked for the winter, but the hay had diminished. Rachael was desperate in need of hay for the three cows. Dave Carlson knew a farmer who sold hay in Pittsfield and could get a truckload. Rachael asked Dave if he'd get a load for her and, in return, would volunteer Nathan's help when Dave was ready to do his haying. Nathan rode the back of Dave's truck all the way to Pittsfield. The two loaded the truck, then off-loaded the bales in the Andersons' overhead bays. Rachael held to her promise in having her son help load the Carlsons' hay bales from the field and stack into their barn, ending the dog days of summer.

Labor Day arrived with Rachael making multiple trips into Rochester. It was school season, and the children needed to be outfitted for school. Rachael could only outfit a couple at a time going up and down the clothing aisles. From the clothing aisles, Rachael wheeled the cart through the school supply rows, filling it with pads of notebook paper, folders, pen, and pencils.

More bread was needed for the additional school lunch sandwiches. Rachael found it cheaper to buy half dozen of day-old bread for a dollar from the thrift store. The final trip was at Clark's Grain Store to load up on grain feed and canning items.

THE KILLING SPREE

The town voted to join a new regional school district with six other towns. It would make riding to school that much longer. The school bus arrived at the Andersons' farmhouse at its usual time, picking up the kids attending the new school in Wolfeboro.

The following weekend, Rachael found time to drive her parents back to Plymouth with a bagful of the year's harvest. Sarah looked forward to using her garden-fresh vegetables and assorted apples. Milton made his way into the provincial building as Sarah unlocked the apartment. She was glad to be home and getting Milton settled. She offered glasses of water to Rachael and Nathan before they journeyed back to New Hampshire.

The early days of October brought an end to the pigs. It was time to have them butchered. The Andersons didn't have a big-enough freezer and sold the hogs to pay some bills. It was a Saturday morning when a truck pulled into the Andersons' driveway. Three farmhands jumped out with rifles and proceeded to the pig pen. Rachael rushed inside, taking the kids with her. Within moments, shots were fired, accompanied with anguishing squeals. Then all was silent. Nathan stood by the backyard apple tree and witnessed the carcasses being dragged into the truck.

Indian summer allowed for more painting on the house. Tracy completed the front and the upper half of the west side. He and Nathan continued painting along the bottom when they heard Kenneth practicing the trumpet. It was his first year playing an instrument. His rustic notes were piercing. One had to close their eyes with persistent concentration to hear the notes of "Mary Had a Little Lamb" to come together as a tune.

"Listen to that," said Tracy. "That kid's got talent. He'll do okay if he keeps it up."

Nathan thought differently and smiled sarcastically back at Tracy.

Tracy noticed Nathan's smirk. "What? You don't think he's got a lot of potential? He's got a lot of talent. You watch."

Nathan shrugged his shoulders and continued stroking the paintbrush.

Kenneth continued to practice, only to make the melody flow intermittently from the trumpet. In the following months, his efforts were unforgiving, and he decided to give up.

Cold weather weaved throughout the countryside. It was time to reinforce the animals' living quarters. Beyond the stanchions was a double pen enclosed with chicken wire. It was ideal for the chickens and ducks. Nathan spread some shavings along the floor before penning them in. He added more plastic insulation around Sandy, enabling her to retain more of her body heat.

The jars of milk started adding up and filling the refrigerator. A small family recently moved into the weathered house down the road. Rachael offered them the excess, retaining the jars of heavy cream.

The house was prepared for the winter's howling winds and snowstorms. There were only enough storm windows for the front and west side of the house. The inside windows were covered with plastic. The family attempted to save coal by burning more wood. There wasn't enough excess wood to last a month, never mind the winter. They burned whatever they could, chopping old weathered boards, tree limbs, barn beams, and anything else they could find. Ben and Andy stopped by with their chainsaws, sawed down a couple of trees, and prepared them for splitable logs.

The holiday season brought Natalie with her newborn for a round of kitty whist. The game put the day's stresses on pause. The spoken lines of wit provided entertainment with each hand dealt. Each partner was confident of winning their bids, only seeing defeat in overestimating the number of tricks. Nathan played as his mother's partner. He had more than a knack in reading her facial expressions. The card game lasted for hours. Nathan stayed on top of the furnace while concentrating on his partner's subsequent moves.

The girls enjoyed being outside. They climbed the slope that led to the upper garden, then hopped on their sleds seeing who could go down the farthest. A pair of old wooden skis were tied together, forming a makeshift sled that added to the fun. Hours fled by before the frigid cold penetrated their bones, forcing the three younger girls inside. Rachael heated some milk for hot chocolate while whipping the heavy cream. The three sat at the kitchen table while their rosy cheeks defrosted. The smiles illuminated the whipped cream with every sip of the hot chocolate.

The holidays came and went. New Year's Eve was celebrated with gingerbread cake topped with spoonfuls of whipped cream. Everyone ate while watching the multitudes blaring their horns in Times Square. The next morning, Rachael took Nathan rummaging through the barn once again. They struggled to determine what other boards could be used to heat the house. Rachael managed to pick out more old beams and a cluster of floorboards for Nathan to chop. With the wood supply exhausted, the Andersons had no choice but bear the expense of a load of coal. Wood wasn't the only thing scarce; hay was dwindling. The amount wouldn't last a month. Rachael asked Natalie what she should do, wondering if she needed to get hay or if she could just feed the cows grain. Natalie suggested getting hay pellets as a substitute. They would provide the animals the same type of nutrients.

The Andersons made it through the frigid winter as it transitioned into warmer days. Before the last hint of snow disappeared, Rachael and Nathan walked the fence line looking for any weaknesses. The stanchion door slid open, releasing Matilda, Sandy, and Ivy. They filed out onto the pasture kicking their hindquarters. Nights were cool enough for the threesome to stay out overnight. Before dawn, Nathan went out searching the pasture of them. He eventually found them under the barn filthier than if they had stayed inside. Nathan had no choice but to get a pan of warm water diluted with a capsule of Lysol and washed both cows' udders before milking them. The milkings wouldn't last long as both Matilda and Sandy needed to have their udders dried up before they calved.

April arrived, and within days of each other, Sandy and Matilda gave births to bull calves. They were sold for veal, and even though the decision was difficult, Sandy was included in the sale.

Time came for getting the ground ready for planting. Tracy couldn't picture himself guiding the Carlsons' draft horses again. Rachael pleaded with Jake to use his tractor to plow and till the gardens. He hesitantly agreed, telling Rachael this was the last favor. The best she could do to show her appreciation was to offer a couple of acres bordering the Cameron Road for raising prime hay and Nathan's help any time he needed. Nathan became Jake's second pair of eyes when plowing not only for the family's garden but with Jake's own hayfield.

The upper and lower gardens were sown in the same manner as previous years. The upper garden was planted with hills of corn in the front half with the vegetables mapped out in the back. Rachael and Nathan hoed out the rows a foot and a half apart. It made pushing the wheelbarrows of manure much harder through the garden ruts. The calloused hands planted the seeds carefully along each furrowed row.

Suddenly a commotion came from the side pasture. Ivy had jumped the fence. Once over, Matilda followed through. Rachael and Nathan stood watching the two cows romp throughout the open vista like newfound criminals. It was senseless trying to corral them toward the barn. The only way to coax them was with a can of grain. Just the sight of the grain can got the cows' attention, and they followed it all the way to their stalls. Nathan needed to chop down a couple of poplar trees to make more posts. They were crowbarred into place as he reinforced the gap with additional strings of barbed wire.

It was nearing the end of the school year when Rachael told Nathan it was time to take Patty to the vets and that she wouldn't be coming back. Numbness fell over him. He couldn't understand why Patty had to go. She seemed content and didn't show any signs of being sick. Nathan hadn't realized how old Patty was in dog years. Still he thought sure Patty would remain on the farm until her final days. Nathan wasn't prepared for this day.

In five minutes, she would be a memory. She had been part of the family since the days of Plymouth. Patty was fifteen, showing signs of difficulty walking, and lay on the dining room floor. Somehow Nathan never noticed her difficulty and knelt before her, giving one last hug. He slowly slipped her collar from around her neck and walked out of the door, staring out into the open field. Tracy and Rachael placed Patty in the back of the Ford and, without wasting a moment, drove down the dusty dirt road.

It was early July when Rachael thought it would be a good time for Nathan to visit Flora. It would sooth the emotional distraught of losing Patty. It was his first visit to Ellis Pond in over two years. Nathan looked forward to visiting his grandaunt and enjoying his distant friends. To welcome his return, Barbara and Alan put on a late-afternoon barbeque. After a short swim, Nathan cleaned up while Flora put together a simple potato salad for the outing. Alan showed Nathan his monstrosity, telling how his hands cemented each stone one after another until it pillared the shoreline.

Alan wasn't an elaborate cook but did his best grilling the traditional burgers and mild sausages. The potato salad and tall glasses of ice tea made the barbeque complete. The conversations were tempered with polite laughter along the backdrop of a brazen sunset overlooking the pond. The moment was warm and comforting. Nathan stood thinking how much he missed the pond. There were times Flora mentioned why he couldn't visit for a couple of weeks. One week was the limit as he was needed back at home.

There were overcast days that brought Flora and Nathan raking leaves. They cleared the excess weeds around the cookout area. Under her cottage was a crawl space that sent Nathan seeing what was hidden. There were a couple of jars of old preservatives that Flora wanted pulled and tossed. They loaded the tub-sized basket with the raked debris and headed toward the front of the cabin.

Along the way, Flora pointed to the back-end corner where the living room wall met her bedroom. "I'm thinking about having a small bedroom built on that corner of the house."

Nathan looked surprised. "A bedroom?"

"Of course, I think a bedroom would look nice. This way, my company would have a place to sleep instead of on the futon," remarked Flora.

"You wouldn't consider building a full bathroom at the same time?" suggested the grandnephew.

"Gosh, no. I don't need a full bath. I'm used to washing without one," answered Flora.

"You sure? A bathroom would be nice," added Nathan.

"I think a bedroom is enough for now. Let's get this basket up by the front fence post."

The two continued the trail to the front, placing the trash basket by the fence post. They day ended as the two went inside to wash.

Nathan returned home just as his mother was in the throes of making the runs to Wolfeboro. She went over the list of chores for Nathan. First was the caring of Matilda and Ivy, tending the chickens, weeding, and hoeing three rows of vegetables, plus hilling the cornstalks. In the afternoon, she wanted the landscape trimmed.

Operation Head Start became a reality in the school district. The project started the first week in July and ended around mid-August. Rachael volunteered to drive the handful of preschoolers for the six-week period. The stipend money helped with the overdue bills.

It had been a couple of weeks since the last rain. Rachael knew the vegetables were in dire need of watering. She wanted Nathan to haul water up for the cucumbers, squashes, and pole beans. It was his fourth trip when his arms began to tire. He continued filling the buckets when Rachael wanted Nathan to do another chore. Nathan felt overwhelmed, feeling the sweat drip from his forehead and his mind snapping under the summer heat.

He continued walking with the heavy pails, yelling back at his mother, "Why can't Kenneth or Laura do it?"

"Because I want you to do it," commanded the response.

Nathan walked toward his mother, placing the two pails on the ground. "I'm doing the chores and the watering. Can't either Kenneth or Laura do it?" asked Nathan.

"No, they can't. I want you to do it," stated Rachael with authority.

"I'm always being told to do everything. Those two aren't doing anything. What makes them so special?" Nathan asked with an anger to his tone.

Rachael stood up, facing her son. "You'll do what I tell you to do. Do you hear me?"

Nathan stood there, feeling the anger penetrate his nerves. He picked up a pail and splashed his mother.

The surprised look on Rachael's face turned into rage over what her son just did as she shouted, "What's wrong with you? What if I were pregnant? Don't you know what could've happened?"

Knowing how desperate their family was, Nathan thought, *She can't be pregnant. She can't be that stupid.*

"Pick up those pails and finish watering the plants. I'm going to have your father take care of you this weekend," yelled Rachael as she went inside to change.

When Tracy arrived, Rachael told what Nathan had done. He yelled for the lad to come down from his bedroom. As Nathan entered the room, Tracy raced toward him with a fist on one arm and a coiled belt in the other.

Nathan was left with a few body welts and a bloodied nose. He returned to his room trying to stop the bleeding from flowing down his chin. Nathan looked out the bedroom window, feeling the anger swell within him. He couldn't wait for the day when he would leave this place for good. He and Beth had these conversations often while doing the dishes. For now, Nathan realized his circumstances mandated him to be obedient.

The trips to Wolfeboro continued with the town's preschoolers and returning them home by midafternoon. Rachael took Kenneth to keep order in the vehicle. Nathan weeded and hoed the vegetable rows along with the hills of corn. He didn't bother hoeing between the corn hills. He continued through the laundry list, mowing the lawns and filling the watering troughs.

Beth had all she could do managing the kids, doing laundry, and tackling the ironing basket. Natalie stopped by checking on things. She knew the family lost Patty and wondered if they would be interested in a puppy. Beth jumped on the idea, convincing everyone she would care for it. Holding to her promise, Beth was allowed the puppy. Nathan accompanied his sister along the dirt road to the Carlsons. The pup was golden with a white strip down its front. Beth fell instantly in love with it. It was a little high strung, but what puppy wasn't? Beth named her new addition Misha.

Beth maintained the household at a snail's pace. She wasn't ambitious and discovered she could get a helping hand with just a pathetic whimper. Beth realized she had the shoulders of two ambitious guys in her life. It gave her a little more confidence while doing her chores. She cooked a little extra, knowing the table scraps would feed her new companion.

Rachael called for Nathan to follow her into the barn. She was curious about the condition of the buggy that sat in the rear. To get a clear view, they pulled the enormous hay wagon outside, followed by the buggy. It was the first time in decades these horse-driven vehicles had seen the light of day. Rachael examined the buggy and noticed the small luggage compartment in the rear. She opened it, exposing a couple of empty liquor bottles. Rachael stood motionless for a moment, letting her mind wonder, then snapped back into the present. She was satisfied of what she discovered and wheeled them back to their former place.

The Andersons realized the number of roosters romping around. It was time to thin the chicken population. There were a half dozen roosters that served no purpose. Nathan hadn't witnessed a creature being killed other than bugs and an occasional snake. To be placed in the middle of a killing spree made Nathan feel jittery even though he knew they were raised for food. These chickens were different. They were barnyard pets having been raised from baby chicks.

Nathan followed Tracy out to the barn. Nathan filled a can of grain, spreading a handful on the barn floor. The roosters came pecking at the floor unknowing the fate that awaited them. As each one was captured, Tracy wrung its neck, then snapped it while the bird flapped its wings in despair.

The birds were strung up by their legs with pieces of baling twine in the stanchion area. Six roosters met their doom all within an hour and were hung in a row waiting to be plucked. Beth was called out to accompany Nathan. They were shown how to pluck the feathers without ripping the skin. Beth started plucking like it was second nature. Nathan felt queasy with every tug.

By the time the feathers were off, the heads had swollen with blood. A couple of hours elapsed before all six were ready to be processed. Plucking was as far as Nathan could handle. The birds were brought inside, where Beth took part in the cutting off the heads and legs, then pulling out the entrails. The heads, legs, and guts were wrapped in newspaper. Nathan wasted no time taking the bundles along with the other trash to the far end of the open field. Nathan hoped it would be the last time he'd take part in these slaughters; it was only the beginning.

The following week began the blueberry season. Nathan was the only one who could pick. Rachael continued driving the preschoolers to Operation Head Start while Beth tended to her younger siblings. The gardens went unattended during the weeks of blueberry season. Nathan did his morning routine feeding the animals and making himself a lunch. The pickup drove in just as he was finishing.

It was Friday evening when a two-toned Chevy convertible drove into the drive. Tracy had invited one of his friends up for a weekend. The guy went by the nickname Red. He was middle aged and physically solid. Red was going through some hard times, and Tracy invited him for a change of scenery. His pleasant personality drew the attention of the family.

Red was given the guided tour of the farm and enjoyed the relaxed atmosphere. He was more enthused about the cows and the chickens roaming around the farmyard. Red gave Tracy an excuse for lighting the stonewall grill. Saturday afternoon gave some enjoyment of cheeseburgers, potato salad, and soda. Rachael had Nathan set up the badminton net for some competitive games. By day's end, Red was given the bed in the parents' downstairs bedroom to sleep. Tracy and Rachael took over Nathan's room, and Nathan was moved in with Kenneth.

The dawning of the next morning rose with the summer heat. Nathan was on his way to the barn and noticed Red sitting in his car. He walked over, watching the guy go through his glove compartment. Nathan looked over the car, then at Red.

"Nice car," commented Nathan. "Did you sleep okay?"

"Slept great," answered Red.

"Like the country?" asked Nathan.

"It's not bad. I'm more adapted to the city life. This is a great place your family has," Red commented.

"Are you from Boston?" inquired Nathan.

"I'm originally from the north end. Lived most of my life in the Boston area." Red smiled.

Nathan looked at the man's thinning red hair, figuring it gave him his nickname. "Can I ask you what's your real name?" asked Nathan with a curious look.

"Al Welton," replied Red.

"Do you work with my stepfather?" continued Nathan.

"You're full of questions. No, I don't work with your father. I'm a barkeep in the south end. That's where I met him. You know, I have a son your age. Here, I'll show you a picture," continued Red.

He took out his wallet and flipped over to a single portrait of a teenage lad. He stood tall with auburn hair. Beside it was Red's driver license verifying the name as Al Welton.

Nathan smiled. "You and your wife must be proud of him."

"I'm divorced," answered Red.

"Guess you know we lived in South Boston a few years. We lived on East Third Street. I sometimes miss the city," reminisced Nathan. His thoughts flashed back for a moment before he commented, "Well, it's nice knowing you, Red. You got a great son. Glad you came up. I got barn chores to get started."

Nathan walked off toward the barn entryway. Red continued shuffling through the papers from his glove compartment, glancing in his rearview mirror, watching Nathan fade into the barn.

The Wolfeboro trips ended along with blueberry season. Nathan felt good having a few dollars for school. Labor Day wasn't far off, and neither was Karen. It was her debut to the farmhouse. Rachael ensured the house was scrubbed and every crevice cleaned. She had Nathan give the lawns a touch-up along with the bushes. Rachael thought of getting the school shopping done before Karen's visit. She took Nathan and Laura, hoping to avoid any last-minute shopping trips.

Karen's flight landed at Boston's Logan International Airport, where Tracy arranged to meet her. They rode the airport limousine to Rochester, where Rachael and Nathan met them for the ride home. The hugs and kisses were numerous, with Rachael and Karen barely having time to catch their second wind between the never-ending sentences. They played catch-up even though the corresponding letters back and forth told the same tale.

Somewhere in the mix, Nathan heard his mother say she was seven months along. It was the first time Nathan understood they were having another baby. The news just floored his insides.

He stared at the back of his mother's head, thinking, *What kind of world are you living in*?

He had heard all the previous arguments of the family not affording much of anything, especially when it came to feeding the animals. Yet she was about to deliver another mouth to feed. Nathan's inner gut told him, when this newborn arrived, things would change for the worse.

Karen's visit brought a little lightheartedness. She became successful at the Caterpillar company, being one of the major supervisors and recently engaged to another manager. Karen couldn't get over Rachael's large family and how she was getting along. Nonetheless, Rachael seemed happy, and that was all Karen wanted to know. She slept upstairs in the parents' room. Saturday morning, Nathan got up caring for Matilda and Ivy and released the chickens out for their backyard scratching. The three ducks came and went although their hideaway was somewhere in the back of the barn.

Karen woke, making her way down for breakfast always consisting of a cup of coffee and toast. She was dressed for the farm in her plaid short-sleeved blouse and dark pair of knickers. The adults sat for a while catching up on old times. Rachael got up, leading the tour through the pasture, showing off the orchards, Matilda, and Ivy. They crossed over the fence line to the upper and lower vegetable gardens. The final stop was on the front porch for another cup of coffee. The three climbed into the car for a drive around the neighborhood and the small hamlet of New Durham.

Sunday was another occasion for lighting the outdoor grill. Tracy performed the chef duties, grilling the burgers and hotdogs, while Rachael put together the potato salad and watermelon. Monday morning rose with Rachael and Tracy driving Karen to Rochester to catch the bus to Boston. Karen was spending the rest of the week visiting her parents at the cape. Tracy stayed behind, taking the remaining week off.

Tracy sat at the kitchen table sipping his morning coffee while smoking a cigarette. He experienced the morning stopovers from Jake Dawson and Dave Carlson. Jake often stopped by for a chat and a cup of coffee. It was his opportunity to ask for Nathan's help, having nicknamed him Speedy. Jake knew all the chores he did and how quick he did them. Today he needed Nathan's help to load hay. He noticed Nathan's worn instep of his shoes. After the last bale was stacked, Jake asked Nathan to climb into his pickup. They drove into New Durham's center, stopping at the moccasin shoe shop. Jake and the salesman deliberated over what shoes to buy for the lad. Nathan walked out with a new pair of sneakers. This was the second time someone outside the family realized Nathan's need for a decent pair of shoes. He thanked Jake, offering his help whenever he needed it.

Dave stopped by on his return from work for a little conversation and morning coffee. It gave him a few moments seeing if Rachael needed any help. Tracy became flustered of these morning Joes and couldn't help letting his imagination get the best of him of who else might be stopping by. The following weeks were compounded with yelling spats over Tracy's aspersions of Rachael's affair with Dave. Rachael sparred back with his associations of his estranged wife.

Rachael's two oldest wanted to take a couple of after-school activities. It took a long debate to convince Rachael, and in the end, she relented in allowing them to participate. Beth became a member of the majorettes, traveling with the band to the many football games. She practiced her twirls and tosses on the side yard wearing her green-and-white majorette uniform, complete with headgear. Nathan joined the cross-country track team and, in the spring, would compete in the tennis matches.

The track team practiced running three miles a day with intervals of competitive track meets. The school provided late buses, which took the students back to their town centers. From there, they found their own way home. Rachael waited for Nathan at the general store, then drove home for the evening chores.

It was the first year the Andersons hadn't any hay, relying mostly on hay pellets. There were plenty of corn stalks the cows could eat while it lasted. Nathan walked around the farm and found a thicket of straw where the old sawmill stood. He scythed them down for bedding. The chicken flock had dwindled to a few hens and two roosters, with the remaining numbers packed in the freezer. Michael Jay found himself back in his indoor pen. He nipped himself to freedom, sensing his way into Nathan's bed and brushing his nose whiskers against Nathan's face.

Rachael, Nathan, and Beth went out raking leaves into piles and wheeling them to the compost heap behind the barn. Beth raked the front lawn with Misha at her side. A car sped by with the dog in chase. In an instant, she got struck, crippling her hind leg. Rachael and Beth whisked Misha into the car for the drive to the vets. The rescue party returned with the injured dog having a crutch attached to her broken leg. It would be about a month before Misha was able to use all fours. Beth needed to give her dog the extra loving attention to ease the burden of the crutch. It was too much for Beth to handle, and she sought a new home for her dog.

A few weeks passed when Rachael decided on another pet for the family. A black puppy appeared that Rachael named Sheri. Sheri was a retriever mix, having a white stripe from her chest to her belly. She was energetic like all puppies and soon found her place in the household.

Penny was always independent, coming and going at will. She always had her resting spot atop the dining room table. She looked at the new addition without concern. She was used to seeing new creatures in her travels. Sheri was just another four-legged roommate.

With the new baby due to arrive, Rachael needed all the help she could muster. The first week of November, Rachael and Nathan drove to Plymouth. Sarah was excited seeing them. She couldn't help brag about her new neighbor Beulah of how they shared the same interest in jigsaw puzzles, and Beulah had many. Milton maintained a look of bewilderment. He couldn't get over the fact his daughter was ready to deliver another child. He checked his pockets, grabbed his walker, and started down the hallway.

Loading took a few moments as they got Milton into the car. With everyone seated, Rachael proceeded north on the interstate. By late afternoon, the Ford arrived onto the beaten driveway, stopping parallel to the farmhouse's back entryway. Milton paced himself using his walker to rest. Michael Jay was the first to welcome him with his striking butler-style markings.

Rachael's timing of her parents' arrival couldn't have been better. In a week, Rachael was rushed to the Frisbie Hospital, where she delivered a son, Thomas Booker. Tracy was elated having a son. Sarah and Milton held their reservations. They only saw another mouth on an already financially strapped family. Milton rubbed his head, still wondering why his daughter wanted another child.

Rachael returned home just before Thanksgiving with the newborn. Sarah dominated the household while Rachael gave her attention to the new arrival. She made the Thanksgiving dinner memorable. The baby's crib was put together, making its home in the parents' downstairs bedroom.

Sarah worked on another braided rug when she found the time. She utilized all kinds of rags, incorporating them into colorful strips. The tedious part was sewing the braids into an oval shape, hiding the stitching with each turn of the braid.

Sarah made her routine trip back to Plymouth during the first week in December, catching up on her mail and bills. She returned a few days with disappointing news that someone had broken into her apartment, stealing her strongbox. The box didn't contain many valuables but had the documentation of Sarah's linkage to the Pilgrims. Nathan recalled his grandmother showing him how the family was linked to one of the original Pilgrims. Milton's sister had heard stories of how she and Milton's lineage connected to other Pilgrim passengers.

Despite the circumstances, the Christmas and the birthday celebrations helped to brighten the spirits. Nathan felt comfortable having his grandparents around for the holidays. Their presence added in calming the family's tempers, plus contributing to a truckload of coal.

The Christmas season was over, and the Manters were driven back to Plymouth. It was a period when winter storms were unpredictable. The Ford made the round trip without any problems although the motor developed a slight rattling noise.

TURNING POINT

The cold winter penetrated the exposed skin of the playful faces weaving amongst the snowdrifts. They trudged through the deep layers, making their way inside with rosy cheeks. Their mother made the usual pan of hot chocolate to warm their souls. The indoor warmth slowly erased the evidence of Jack Frost on the energetic youths.

The barn animals generated their own body heat, keeping the stanchions somewhat warm. It wasn't enough to keep the hands warm during the milking. Rachael brought an electric heater, making the barn chores tolerable. Nathan fed and watered Matilda and Ivy, unplugging the heater as he left. The Andersons needed bedding not only for the cows but for Michael Jay. Rachael scrapped up what money she could for a couple of bales of shavings.

The expenses were mounting. It was time for Tracy to join the family. Rachael figured it would cut down on the money Tracy was spending in South Boston. Tracy knew the day would come when he'd have to leave the city for good. He told Red about Rachael's need for him at the homestead, making sure he was welcome to visit anytime. Tracy called Gloria about his plans.

"What do you mean you've got to move to New Hampshire? Can't Rachael handle the farm?" asked Gloria.

"The kids need help, and we're getting behind on the bills. So I've got to get a job closer to the family," replied Tracy.

"When are you leaving?" Gloria asked, then added, "Can I have your number so we can stay in touch?"

"I don't have a number. I'll call you when I get settled and have a job," responded Tracy.

"No number? What about the money? When am I supposed to get that?" demanded Gloria.

"You're not getting any, at least not now, not until I get a job. You'll just have to wait until I get a chance to call you. It'll be a while. I'm just asking you to be patient," explained Tracy.

Gloria's mind was cascading. She thought Rachael really must have been going through hard times wanting Tracy to be with her. And not having a phone? Gloria couldn't get over that. She decided to leave the ball in Tracy's court, being satisfied the whole bunch of them weren't having an easy life.

Dave Carlson told Rachael about openings at Colby and Sheldon shoe manufacturers along with Clarostat Manufacturing. She had Tracy apply, and he got hired at Clarostat for an assembly line position. His presence at home had the younger ones moving about cautiously.

The new routine didn't continue without spats between Rachael and Tracy. The yelling came and went over the unpaid bills and Tracy's drinking. The arguments carried over, putting pressures on the older two. Beth couldn't stand listening to the constant yelling. It seemed to go on day after day. She realized her only salvation was with Ben and his family. She pulled Nathan aside, telling him she was taking off and wanted him to go with her. Nathan tried convincing her that running wouldn't prove anything but cause more beatings and head games. She decided to go anyway, walking into the cold night and making her way to the Greyson farmhouse. She went unnoticed for the first hour when Rachael called Nathan from his room.

"Nathan!" yelled Rachael. "Have you seen your sister? Do you know where she went?"

Nathan stood, looking down from the stairway at his mother. "She left. She couldn't take the yelling."

Rage filled Rachael's face. "Do you know when and where she went, and why didn't you go with her?"

Nathan stood a bit shaken. "She left about a half hour ago, and don't know where she went off to."

Rachael ordered him back into his room and to stay there. Three hours later, the police chief arrived with Beth and sat down with the two collaborating minds. The talks hadn't changed a thing.

Spring approached with the Anderson household holding their temperaments. Nathan joined the tennis team, still needing a new pair of sneakers and a tennis racket. Beth continued with her majorettes and practiced her twirls and tosses with the baton.

Ben traded his mount for a well-used pickup. He continued his visits, now driving into the driveway. Andy already drove his own muscle car and stopped by saying his hellos. Their occasional visits eased the tensions that were building in the house.

On one visit, Ben asked Nathan if he'd be interested working with him on the horse farm. Nathan had no idea what he meant, nor did Nathan have any interest in horses. Rachael didn't have any objections. She only saw an opportunity for Nathan to earn a few dollars. Saturday morning, Ben drove his pickup into the drive for the day's adventure. Nathan didn't have a lunch prepared, not knowing how long he'd be gone or what was in store. All that didn't matter.

They pulled into the driveway of a huge rustic barn. Nathan followed Ben over to the white estate. A tall able-bodied man on the outer rim of middle age stepped out of the front door and walked over toward them. His white strands of wisdom cropped his roundish head. Ben introduced Nathan to Dr. Roger Goodall. A younger woman displaying a princely ash-blond bob stood at the doorway and was introduced as his wife, Alice. She had recently given birth to a baby daughter. It was the second marriage for both. Doc's previous marriage produced a couple of children, who were now in their late teens. Alice had a couple of preteens of her own. Both met where some would consider comedic: the doctor's office.

The project involved installing fence posts made from cut-to-size telephone poles. The base of each post had to be painted with creosote and piled around back of the farmhouse. Doc marked an outline of a large oval riding ring. He operated the John Deere tractor, drilling three-foot holes every eight to ten feet from each other. Each post was positioned into its upright formation. It took the rest of the morning and afternoon to complete. Alice made cold-cut sandwiches and a handful of chips for the guys' lunch.

It was midafternoon when Nathan followed Ben into the barn. The two cleaned stalls with the scoop shovel and wheelbarrow. The center aisle had two floor hatches where the manured bedding was dropped to the earthen cellar. It took a couple of hours to do the stalls. They finished with the grain feed, watering and haying the long line of horses.

It was evening when Ben pulled into the Andersons' drive. He asked if Nathan could be used the next day in finishing the ring construction. The day was spent nailing the three levels of boards around the track. Most had to be cut to size. When the day ended, Alice wrote a check for the two days' work totaling thirteen dollars.

Summer was on the threshold, and so was the end of another school year. The high school sponsored a summer hiring program for the junior and senior classes. Beth submitted her name hoping to earn a few dollars for her senior year. She recently completed the driver's education course and received her driver's license. She had experience in day care, being the oldest of eight kids. There were a few nanny positions that caught her interests. One opening was out of state for a six-week period. A couple was looking for a caretaker for their two small children in the town on Hamden, Connecticut.

Beth really wanted the job and pleaded with her mother in accepting it. Rachael knew Clarence lived in Hamden and gave Beth's request some serious thought. She decided what harm would come if her daughter met up with her father. She would have to return to finish her senior year. Rachael reluctantly gave her approval, thinking it might broaden Beth's outlook on life. The week after school ended, Beth was on the bus to New Haven meeting her sponsored family.

The homestead was given a new lease on life after receiving its fresh coat of paint. Rachael thought about painting the barn. There were two five-gallon cans of red paint in the garage. Ben stopped by and mentioned his grandfather was a painter and hadn't much to do. He took a moment to drive his grandfather over to scope over what had to be painted. The pitch of the barn's roof was high, and the old man didn't have a problem reaching such heights. All he needed was an extension ladder, and he knew where he could get his hands on one. The buckets of paint managed to cover the front of the barn. The clapboards were so dry they absorbed the paint instantly. The grandfather painted the pitch down to a point where the family could continue.

Letters from Beth arrived, telling of her housekeeping experiences. She was caring for a brother and sister, ages four and six respectively. She was allowed to drive the family vehicle for entertaining the children at the neighborhood pool or to a museum. She mentioned doing some cooking although the mother enjoyed putting the meals together herself.

The lines that got Rachael's attention was reading of her daughter's free time. Beth mentioned having paid a visit to her disabled father, who was being cared for by his mother. Beth had written they lived in an apartment complex a couple of streets over from where she worked. Rachael took it in stride, keeping the information to herself.

It was the end of July when Beth returned to the homestead. She enjoyed her caretaking experience, and the family would have kept her even longer. Returning home wasn't the same. Rachael overheard Beth tell her brother of her travels around the Hamden-New Haven area. She mentioned a few visits with their father and grandmother. Rachael was a little disappointed and hoped her daughter would have kept that part to herself.

It was a humid afternoon. Ben and Andy drove in for a short visit. Andy watched Nathan filling the cows' watering trough with an extended garden hose. He was curious as to why Nathan was filling a trough when there was a stream running through the orchard. He looked up at Andy, explaining the stream often dried up, becoming a line of mud. Besides, his mother wanted the trough filled. Andy looked down where the narrow stream ran. It sparked an idea of creating a small watering hole.

Andy suggested the idea to Rachael, who jumped at it. Andy wasted no time in getting the project started. The next morning, Andy drove in with the dump truck trailing the bulldozer. He bulldozed the stumps and boulders away until a large earthen bowl was forged. A couple of sticks of dynamite were placed and discharged. The underground stream slowly surfaced into a small pond. It took a few days for the water to clear, allowing the cows to drink and the ducks to swim.

The Ford sputtered even louder. It had been overused and outlived its life expectancy. The mechanics were strained with repair estimates more than what the car was worth. The realization came for getting another vehicle. The next vehicle was a used aqua-and-white Chevy Impala. Nathan got a couple of tries driving it in and out of the barn, then a couple of test runs up to and from the garden.

The Greysons were finding it hard to maintain their household. Ben decided to quit school and work full-time to help with the family's expenses. He was hired to drive for R. C. Conrad, hauling wood byproducts, and said his goodbyes to the Goodalls. Ben tried providing a reliable replacement with one of his brothers, but none wanted the job. He asked Nathan if he wanted it, and with Rachael's approval, he accepted.

Nathan walked the miles of dirt road to the top of the ridge, reaching the horse farm. He had little curiosity about what he was about to encounter. Alice explained the job that mirrored what he helped Ben with not long ago. Alice taped a menu on each stall as to the horse's daily feeding. Lastly she wanted the barn floor swept at day's end.

It was the first time Nathan handled horses. He moved them from one stall to another, cleaning each one and spreading a couple of fresh baled shavings. He filled the grain buckets with the prescribed menu, then continued filling the water buckets with the extended hose. A couple of hay slices finished the feeding. It took Nathan a couple of hours doing the barn before finding himself walking the two-mile hike back home.

The Goodalls asked Nathan if he could work mornings. He couldn't, having to accompany his mother on the kindergarten trips to Wolfeboro. During the session, Rachael and Nathan checked out library books to read at the waterfront prier. Afterward Rachael loaded the preschoolers for the drive home. She arrived in time to prepare for her midafternoon soaps, making a deli sandwich and getting herself comfortable on the couch. Nathan gathered a few gardening tools and weeded a few rows before hiking the two-mile stretch.

It took about a week for his legs to get used to the long walk. Hiking up Ridge Road was the hard part before heading toward the rustic barn. Nathan grabbed the wheelbarrow and scoop shovel and started on the first of a dozen stalls. Each stall varied in size, giving any horse enough room to move about. Three vacancies were used for boarding. One was used by a Farmington schoolteacher, Ray Lawson. He owned a Tennessee walker, a tall horse for a guy that was smaller than the average man. The horse appeared intimidating but had a temperament of a gentle giant. The other two were for transient mares, being bred to the farm's headlining stud, Windfield.

Each horse was cross tied on the center floor while the stall was being cleaned. The only exception was Windfield. He had to be placed in an empty stall to keep him from getting excited. He was the stallion whose idyllic looks and bloodline brought breeding fees from all over New England. Alice was the horse enthusiast, and raising horses was her pride and joy. Doc didn't mind his wife having them, provided they paid their way. The spring foals and breeding rights contributed to the upkeep of the farm.

Alice came out, checking how Nathan was adapting. She was interested in having Nathan for the long term and wondered if he would be available weekend mornings, and he replied that he could.

The days were getting shorter as the evening sun faded behind the mountains. Walking home in the night air enabled delusional thoughts while hearing the repetitive sounds of unknown creatures. It allowed one's mind to create hideous creatures ready to pounce at any moment. Once home, Nathan found the family already relaxed in the living room for the evening.

Rachael tried coaxing Kenneth in trying his hand at milking. He didn't feel confident being around cows and couldn't get a hold of the milking technique. He jumped with every movement of the cow's body. Rachael realized she and Beth would have to care for the barn animals.

Blueberry season started with Kenneth being old enough to pick. Nathan remained on the Wolfeboro trips while Beth babysat. This was Kenneth's first job in doing anything. He had linked up with Chuck Paulsen. Chuck had a small place surrounded by large blueberry fields at the end of Ten Rod Road.

At summer's end, the Ford lost its momentum and was finally pushed to the back of the barn. Tracy drove the Impala, which already was a financial hardship. Monthly notices were received for unpaid bills. Rachael accepted the fact she needed to get a job. She asked Tracy to pick up an application at Clarostat. Rachael was interviewed and was hired on the spot. The only problem was finding a babysitter for Tom. Tracy had acquainted himself with the Garfield family, who lived farther down on Ten Rod Road. They hadn't a problem caring for Tom.

All seven kids attended school and ended up policing themselves. The high schoolers and the elementary girls took shifts washing, eating breakfast, making school lunches, and catching their buses. Many of the Andersons didn't like eating oatmeal even though it was what their mother wanted then to eat. They made cups of oatmeal and swished it around the pan and the cereal bowls, giving the impression that they ate. The remainder was fed to Sheri.

Ben stopped by on occasion. Nathan filled him in on the events at the horse farm. Nathan was asked to babysit on a moment's notice while Alice and Doc went out attending horse conferences. It gave Nathan the opportunity of getting acquainted with the kids. The Goodall household was immaculate with everything in its place. Even the kids' rooms showed little disturbance although their persona rapidly changed once their parents left. Nathan was ganged upon and wrestled with. He suspected their energy had been well harnessed during their family time. When bedtime came, the three went willingly, leaving Nathan in the living room watching the color television. Color TV was new to Nathan and the industry; only a few could afford them.

It was close to midnight when the Goodalls arrived. Alice apologized for being so late. Doc appeared to have had a good time, trying to keep his balance from the car to the house. His tie was loosened and the top button undone, allowing his rosy cheeks to resonate from the martinis he had drunk earlier in the evening. Doc tried making small talk as he drove Nathan home. The lad only smiled, wishing Doc a good night, and found his bed for the comforts of a deep sleep.

The garden didn't produce much to make it worthwhile. There really wasn't the time or the effort in caring for it. Nathan earned enough money to pay for his school clothes and provided his mother with a few dollars for gas. Kenneth made a few dollars picking blueberries and was able to buy a few things for himself.

The bus ride started another school year, with everyone showing each other's class schedule and teacher assignments. Beth entered her senior year and Nathan his junior. Kenneth and Laura went to junior high. Gretchen, Abigail, and Rebecca were left to fend for themselves. They made sure Sheri did her bathroom run before locking the doors and catching the bus.

Nathan decided to make use of his time and read while walking the dirt roads to the Goodalls. Most novels were Agatha Christie mysteries with a few Harold Robbins adventures. The walk home was dark, creating more imaginative adventures that coincided with the woodland echoes. Nathan's suspenseful thoughts were transcribed into poetic sonnets and short stories. They became his creative writings for his English course.

The Thanksgiving and Christmas holidays came with a drive to Plymouth bringing the grandparents to the farmhouse. The white artificial tree remained the focal point. Nathan had a few dollars to buy presents and the things he really needed. Somehow the family fared well under the ornamented tree that adorned the living room.

The Goodalls were into the holiday spirit, surprising Nathan with a new winter parka. He was truly thankful since the coat he wore was a Tracy hand-me-down, having no insulation from the winter elements. The family received a portable record player that entertained everyone with a couple of comedic records and a few Western country albums. Rachael entertained the family with her old album collection that had been carefully stored away in the music cabinet.

Another sled was added, giving the girls more enjoyment while trudging through the snow dunes. The days passed, and just like clockwork, the return trip to Plymouth signaled the end of another holiday season. It was New Year, with the Christmas decorations taken down and packed away in the upstairs attic.

ONE STEP FORWARD, TWO STEPS BACK

During the frigid cold of January, Rachael was driven to Frisbie Memorial to undergo a hysterectomy. Tracy wanted to drive into Rochester to check up on Rachael's health and well-being. He planned on leaving once Nathan had returned from work. It was about noon when Nathan arrived from cleaning stalls and weathering the winter winds walking home. Tracy gathered most everyone into the car, placing Nathan and Tom in front while Kenneth, Laura, and Rebecca sat in the back. He drove the route over the ridge, thinking it would be safer than going straight down Ten Rod Road.

The car drove on the downside of the ridge when it swerved and plowed into the banking. The front end landed over a small log, locking the vehicle in place. Nathan stayed with the car while Tracy hiked up the road to get help. He arrived with the Greysons, and with combined force, they released the car from its grips. After a few words of gratitude and thoughts of stupidity, the car continued along its way. The family arrived at their mother's bedside. She looked tired and drained but well enough in coming days to return home.

Nathan managed to keep up with his schoolwork despite working at the horse farm. Rachael never understood why Nathan didn't have the abundance of homework Beth had in prior years. She couldn't piece together Beth's utilization of her free time. Nathan used his study halls for homework while Beth was the social butterfly, engaging herself with the social circles.

Nathan enjoyed working at the horse farm. Apart from cleaning the stalls, he helped Alice prepare the mares for breeding. She wanted the process done soon after his arrival. She'd wash around the mare's tail, wrapping it to prevent any interference. Nathan braced himself against the mare's chest, having a firm grip on her lead chain. Alice handled Windfield, with Nathan exercising the mare afterward, preventing any fluid loss.

A high-strung mare arrived from Massachusetts. She was temperamental, with only a few people capable of handling her. Nathan had difficulty getting her out of the stall. He held the lead chain tight as the horse was cross chained in the center of the barn. He shoveled and deposited the manured shavings down the floor shoot, then gave the stall a couple of fresh bales. Nathan took a firm hold and walked the mare back into the stall, only to have her turn quickly and bite his lower back. It felt like a lightning bolt leaving a mark of a huge beesting. The pain wouldn't let her temperament get the better of him. Nathan's impulse took the back end of the shovel and gave her a healthy whack on her hindquarters. It startled the mare, pressing herself against the wall. In a split second, the mare's disposition changed, so much that everyone was amazed how gentle she had become.

The Goodalls' barn was slowly deteriorating. The outer walls needed to be reshingled. Zachary Newcomb was a man of many talents and agreed to do the job.

Zachary and Katherine Newcomb lived down the road from the Goodalls. They retired from working in the heart of Boston. Zach was an embalmer, and Katherine, an executive secretary. They bought their New Durham farmhouse a few years back. They found new jobs while remodeling their weathered homestead. Katherine found a secretarial position in Rochester while Zach worked at the armory. They eventually retired and were enjoying their golden years. Zach was hired to reshingle a side wall when he noticed a lanky sort of lad with thick brown hair walk from the road and into the barn. He was curious as to who the lad was.

Zach follow inside and introduced himself while catching Nathan's name. Zach was known for telling a good story. He pulled out his pipe and lit the pressed tobacco, taking another ten minutes in sharing his background with the lad. One story led to another, and they learned both of them lived in South Boston at the same time. It amazed Zach of their similarities and invited him to his house to meet his wife.

Doc decided this was the year to grow a vegetable garden on the west side of his estate. He climbed on the John Deere and began plowing the fertile earth while blaring in a song that echoed throughout the estate. It was one of the rare moments Nathan heard Doc being so full of himself. Doc's cavalier moments were few but didn't go unnoticed when they occurred. Nathan noticed they happened mostly when Alice was busy with the horses or at one of her horse shows.

Working at the Goodalls and meeting the Newcombs inspired Nathan in being more self-confident—confidence that gave a slight disconnect from his own home. He did his best to cope with the rigors that clouded his family. Laura was showing signs of entering her teenage years. Tracy noticed her months before, having a few sexual encounters in the barn's hidden alcoves. Nathan often witnessed him from afar, drawing Laura close to his unzippered pants. Nathan always felt empty and shallow whenever Tracy acted out his desires. He wanted so much to expose him but knew telling would destroy the family.

He recalled evenings when taking sponge baths in the kitchen. Tracy would make his way into the room. He'd look for something in the refrigerator or make a bathroom run. Nathan anticipated his appearances and kept his underwear on. As much as he lingered, Nathan pressed against the sink, leaving little room for Tracy to make any advances. It left Tracy frustrated. Nathan took fewer sponge baths, relying mostly on the school gym showers to keep himself clean.

The kitchen baths became a concern to Rachael. The girls were growing and no longer fitting into the large portable tub that hung in the back entryway. Rachael discovered the pipe drain from the upstairs tub didn't leak, but the water pipes leading up to it did. She decided to heat caldrons of water and pour them into the tub, adding the cold to make the bathwater tolerable.

It was prom season for many schools, and Wolfeboro's high school was no different. Beth attended her junior prom and now prepared for the senior prom. Beth couldn't afford buying a full-length gown but had a close friend offering her a three-quarter-length dinner dress for the occasion. Nathan hadn't transportation or an opportunity to socialize with anyone special, giving up the prom and all the other school socials.

The school year was almost over with Beth seeing the last of her high school days. Her graduation allowed for three ticket holders. Sarah wanted to see her first grandchild graduate and wrote asking if she and Milton could make a visit. Rachael made a quick drive to Plymouth, bringing the grandparents up for the ceremony.

It was graduation eve when Nathan returned from work. He walked onto the driveway seeing a vehicle parked with Connecticut plates. With some expectations, he entered the living room and noticed the family gathering. Among the group sat a small plump elderly woman. It was Grandmother Anderson making her appearance.

Rachael sat up. "Ah, Nathan, I want you to meet your grandmother, Hannah Anderson. Hannah, you remember Nathan?"

Hannah smiled. "Of course I do. It was so many years ago. You were such a tiny tyke."

Nathan smiled back. "I remember you too."

Rachael added, "He just got home from working on a horse farm. Nathan, there's some leftovers in the fridge if you're hungry."

Nathan looked around the room, seeing everyone seated in a shape of a horseshoe. He noticed his grandparents sitting together just past the entryway. Sarah looked determined while Milton was expressionless, not really caring. His mother sat on the extended couch with the paternal grandmother, and next to her was Beth. Beth sat tall, being the center of attention. Nathan looked at his sister as if she had somehow turned angelic.

A strange woman sat on the opposite end with Tracy standing behind. She was a full-figured woman, middle aged with her dyed-blond hair well teased and coiffured.

The woman got up and extended her hand toward Nathan. "Hello, I'm Stephanie Cole, a close friend of your grandmother."

Nathan extended his, shaking hands. "Glad to meet you." Then he turned toward Hannah.

Hannah acknowledged Nathan's look. "We drove up for Beth's graduation and to visit you and your sister. Your father sends his love to the both of you." With that, Hannah pulled a small package from her handbag and passed it to Beth. "It's from your father and me."

Beth wasted no time opening it and revealed a gold lady's wristwatch. Everyone was in awe with the gift, except for Rachael and Sarah. They sat giving their polite smiles.

"A watch! Oh, thank you so much," exclaimed Beth as she leaned over to give her paternal grandmother a kiss on the cheek.

Stephanie decided it was time to leave. "Hannah, we ought to be going so we can get plenty of rest for tomorrow."

Rachael was curious, asking, "Where are you staying?"

"We have a room at the Wolfeboro Inn, close to the high school," remarked Stephanie, standing up and grasping her handbag.

Nathan watched as everyone got up to leave the room except for Milton, who continued to sit. Nathan stood motionless as the parade of adults left the room.

Hannah commented to her grandson in passing, "It was good to see you. However, we probably won't be up to attend your graduation."

Nathan could only respond with a respectable smile. He understood how much Beth was the favorite.

He followed behind watching the gathering saying their goodbyes at the back door. The door closed with Rachael looking out the window watching the two disappear around the corner.

"I'm so glad that's over with," commented Sarah. "Did you know they were coming?"

"No, they were a total surprise. Did you know anything, Beth?" asked Rachael.

"Nope, I didn't know anything," replied Beth, remembering the conversation from the previous summer.

Sarah looked at her granddaughter, who was focused on the new watch. "How did they find us?" asked Sarah, turning her attention to Rachael.

"Hannah said they stopped at the general store and asked. So it's not that difficult," Rachael stated with some concern.

"Well, it's over now, so let's just forget the whole thing," ended Sarah, heading back toward the living room.

Nathan walked back in the living room, seeing his grandfather still sitting with his face lowered and rubbing his head with his hand. Nathan helped put the dining room chairs back and continued toward the kitchen to check out the leftovers.

Nathan knew how much his sister looked forward to graduation and couldn't wait to pack and leave. He bought her a five-piece suitcase ensemble for the occasion. On graduation evening, Tracy, Rachael, Sarah, and Beth loaded into the car and drove off into the pomp and circumstances.

The next morning, there was an aura about Beth. She had reached the pinnacle, knowing she could leave at any moment. With diploma in hand, Beth was free to set her own destiny. It was a few weeks before she decided to move. Ben arranged for Beth to live in Farmington with his sister Lydia's family. It was close to home and in finding a job. Living with Lydia was easier on rent and the utility bills.

Beth landed a job waitressing at the Wishnik Restaurant. The job couldn't have come any sooner. The family was served a court summons by Jake Dawson for not paying past invoices on the coal deliveries. Rachael asked Beth if she could help pay the outstanding bill, and she did.

The summer months delivered both calves from Matilda and Ivy. Rachael decided to sell both Matilda and her calf. The family had Matilda for a few years, and she was getting on. Within a week, both had been loaded onto a truck and driven away. Rachael couldn't watch the ordeal since Matilda was her family pet. Ivy would provide whatever milk the family needed. Rachael named Ivy's calf L. C. Ivy.

With Beth gone, Rachael offered Nathan her old room. He thought it over, deciding to keep sharing a room with his brother. Beth's room had no heat and solely relied on the heat flowing in from the hallway. The room faced north and was in direct line of the winter winds striking the window and the inner wall. It did have its own closet, which was an advantage. The downside was anyone sleeping there would be in direct line of Tracy's dead-of-night sexual prowls.

Nathan continued working during the summer. After cleaning the stalls, he'd head down to the Newcombs for a few moments before heading home. He often found Zach doing yardwork, then taking a breather by smoking his wood-grained pipe. Zach enjoyed telling his stories despite Nathan having heard them before. On occasion, Zach took his special friends into the cellar for a glass of what he called the nectar of the gods. It wasn't long before Nathan was escorted into the earthen bowels to meet age-old cider barrels.

It was where Zach brewed his hard cider. One barrel was in use while the other fermented. On a dusty shelf stood three beer glasses which had seen the mouths of many a traveler; Nathan became one of them. Katherine was more on the side of social ethics. She was organized and business minded. She kept the household neat as a pin and the finances in order. She allowed Zachary his weekly allowance and, once spent, wouldn't allow him a penny more until the following week.

It wasn't unusual for Alice to walk out to the barn asking if Nathan could babysit on the spur of the moment. He always was willing, with Alice leaving something simple to cook for the kids. One occasion, Nathan was left to cook a package of spaghetti with a jar of ready-made sauce. It was simple to do. Nathan had made it many times at home. He boiled the water, cooked the spaghetti strands, and heated up the sauce. After draining the spaghetti, Nathan forgot to add butter to moisten the individual strands. He went to the stove for the heated sauce with the spaghetti already placed in each dish. The kids got the enjoyment of tossing the strands onto the celling where they stuck dangling like shoestrings. It took a swipe of the broom to scrap them all down, proving to be memorable moment.

There was a cookie jar that Alice had sitting beside the kitchen sink. She let Nathan know he could help himself to a few should he come down with the munchies. The couple returned from their horse conference, with Alice apologizing for being so late. While Doc drove the workhand home, she emptied the jar, counting just how many were eaten.

Nathan had only the basic courses during his senior year. His English class continued the literary theme with the concentration of poems and poets with the analytical assets of more short stories. Nathan developed an interest in drawing and small watercolor washes. Art class became one of his main interests.

Many in his senior class participated in after-school activities. Nathan's friends encouraged him into doing track. He had participated in the sport in a previous year but refused because of transportation issues. Instead Nathan joined the yearbook club to help put the ageless book together with yearlong memorabilia and wit.

It was the end of September when the car was repossessed, leaving Tracy and Rachael stranded. For weeks, the Andersons remained without a vehicle. Tracy hitchhiked to work while Rachael stayed at home. Without transportation, food and grain supplies ran low with no one really to rely on for help. Saturday morning, Nathan was sent to Farmington on the five-mile hike with a grocery list. His legs were tired, and his leg muscles ached with each step through the grocery aisles. He made it through the checkout counter, then hailed a cab for the ride back. Grain for the barn animals was low, and Nathan kept reminding his mother of their desperate need. It went unanswered, which begun the starvation of the animals. All Nathan could do was keep watering them.

During mid-October, the day of reckoning had come. Rachael walked out to the barn seeing what condition Ivy was along with her calf. It was too late. The cow had died, and the calf was barely breathing. Rachael went into a panic knowing she had to do something. Her impulse was to get to a phone and fast.

The closest was Natalie Carlson. Rachael gathered the kids and made the rush to Dexter Corner. Her pace quickened with every step, telling her brood to keep up. She knew she'd get grief by Natalie, but it was too late for anything. She knocked on the Carlsons' door and explained she needed a phone. Natalie let her in. The two women got into a heated conversation about the animals and how Rachael should have gotten in touch with Natalie if she needed help. Natalie bitterly let Rachael use the phone. Her first calls were to the school and Alice Goodall.

Nathan was called to the principal's office for a phone call. It was his mother instructing him to get off at the Goodalls after school. She told him Ivy had died. In the back of Nathan's mind, he was expecting the news. He saw how weak the cow was early that morning. It wasn't his fault; he told his mother over and over they needed grain. He became nervous throughout the day, not being able to concentrate on anything.

Rachael's following call was to Beth, seeing if she could get Ben to help with the calf and what remaining animals that were around. Beth called around, getting in touch with Ben, telling him about her mother's desperate need of help. Before the day ended, LC was gone. Ben was able to find family friends to take her and the remaining animals.

Rachael paused a moment, looking at her kids standing by her side. She looked over toward Natalie, who sat in her chair still red from the anger boiling within her. Rachael had to make one more call to Tracy. Rachael could hear Tracy's raging fit wanting to kill Nathan for letting the cow die. He took the afternoon off and sped for home.

As the bus approached the top of the ridge, Frank Hudson noticed Alice Goodall waiting at the corner. He stopped, with Alice requesting Nathan to get off the bus. She told Nathan of the situation and allowed him some comfort in dealing with it. After work, Nathan slowly walked the two-mile stretch to face the devastation. By then, the house was engulfed in a cloak of silence. The day's events had to be accepted with the temperaments being restrained. There was nothing more to do but focus on getting another vehicle. Not only did the animal situation become a reality, but the family's very existence was hanging in the balance.

In the days to follow, the mail contained threats from unpaid bills, including the bank foreclosure notice. The family was able to get their hands on a well-used Rambler. Despite needing work, it had four wheels and ran. The car was babied throughout the winter. Rachael was able to return to work, changing the house routine. It went from the days when Beth and Nathan took turns staying home maintaining the house to Kenneth and Nathan sharing the burden.

The holiday season was somber and sobering. There was little enjoyment knowing that Ivy's carcass remained in the barn as a reminder of their desperate times. It became a season the grandparents wouldn't be present. The vehicle wasn't trustworthy, and the wood supply was just about gone.

Beth paid most of the coal bill, putting the Andersons in good standing with Jake delivering more coal. Thanksgiving came, and even though Rachael had gotten the basics for the holiday, the town delivered a Thanksgiving box to their doorstep. The box contained a good-sized turkey, potatoes, and a couple of cans of various vegetables. It was one year the town delivered holiday food boxes to those families in need.

Christmas decorations did their best to add to the festive mood, but the spirit didn't arrive. Nathan's senior pictures were ready as he had picked one pose from the series of proofs. He was prepared to bear the expense toward his graduation. He was thankful for his job. For Christmas, Nathan gave his mother the colored picture of his senior portrait. He forwarded a smaller version to his grandparents. The wallet sizes were traded like baseball cards among fellow classmates. The colorized photo was placed next to the pictures of Beth and Rachael atop the piano.

The Christmas presents provided only the essentials. The stockings were still filled with the traditional fruits and candy. It was a time when Beth, Ben, and Andy arrived for a cup of holiday cheer. During the visit, Tracy stepped outside with Ben and Andy for a few moments. After a while, they reentered in the same joyous spirit.

The new year rang in the usual and never-ending tunes of Guy Lombardo. Nathan began sensing a chill of something unknown was about to happen. By the end of the first week, the bus ride home took its usual course until it stopped at the Greyson farmhouse. Mable stood in the driveway, asking for all the Anderson children except for Nathan. Frank Hudson was aware of what had happened, thanking Mable for taking them. Nathan was confused as to what was going on. At the top of the ridge, Alice waited for the bus and instructed Nathan to get off and go with her. She gently told him that his house was gone and that it was engulfed in a fiery blaze.

Nathan was stunned, realizing the death of Ivy wasn't the worst that had happened but the total loss of the homestead and all its contents gone forever.

GRADUATION

There wasn't much anyone could do to ease the aftermath of the farmhouse. Nathan desperately wanted to see what was left from the residue. He felt his thoughts racing through his head, finally resolving there was nothing he could do and the best thing now was to keep busy. Alice gathered some of Doc's old clothes and a pair of boots for Nathan to wear. Ray arrived for his afternoon ride and walked up to the barn's entrance, seeing how distraught Nathan's face looked.

"I'm so sorry to hear about your house. I heard it on the radio driving up," Ray said condolingly.

"Thanks, Ray."

"Does anyone know how it happened?" inquired the schoolteacher.

"Not yet," replied Nathan.

"Do you know what your family is going to do?" asked Ray, walking Beau out of the stall.

"I don't. I haven't seen them yet. I'm sure something's going to happen," answered Nathan, wondering the same question himself.

He finished the stalls and the feeding, then returned to the back room and changed into the only clothes he possessed.

Alice stepped out. "Nathan, you're going to have supper with us. Your parents are stopping by later. So you can come in and wash up when you're ready."

"Thanks, Alice," replied Nathan, feeling relieved of what was about to happen.

Alice placed the last supper dish into the dishwasher when a knock rapped on the door. Rachael and Tracy were offered chairs at the table. Nathan was sent into the living room pending the outcome. After a lengthy discussion, the consensus was made.

Rachael walked in, taking a seat on the couch next to her son. "The Goodalls are willing to let you stay and finish your last semester. They couldn't see you starting a new school. It's all right with us if you want to stay, if it's okay with you. Do you want to do that?"

Nathan looked at his mother. "It's okay with me. I'd like to finish with my class. They don't mind me staying, do they?"

"No, it's all right with them. What do you think I should do? Do you think we should rebuild the farmhouse?" asked Rachael.

Nathan wasn't expecting the question and thought, *Why would she ask that? Why go back to all the hardships of running the place?*

He wondered what scheme was going through his mother's head.

He looked at his mother. "I think you should sell the place. Rebuilding would only bring back too many memories."

Rachael just nodded, got up, and walked back into the kitchen.

Alice was next, taking her seat next to Nathan. "I want you to know we are more than willing to have you stay with us and finish school. You only have a semester left, and we feel it isn't right for you to start and finish at another school. So if it's all right with you, you can stay and live with us. We're more than willing to have you. We can work out the details later. What do you say?"

Nathan showed an appreciative smile. "Thanks, Alice. I'd like to stay, and I appreciate you and Doc for letting me."

Doc listened to Nathan's decision to stay. Rachael said her goodbyes to her son, promising to check on him later.

Doc waited for the Bookers to leave before turning toward his wife. "We need to get this guy some clothes. He doesn't have anything to wear."

"Not now. Let me ask around and see if I can get a few folks to volunteer something first," suggested Alice.

Nathan remained on the couch thinking over Alice's mentioning of the details. He instinctively knew he would be paying his way without any help from his mother. Alice thought somewhere around 10 percent of Nathan's accumulated monthly wages was fair. Nathan agreed, knowing that any amount would be fair. He wasn't all that disappointed, knowing his family wasn't there to give him some financial support.

Nathan was given the upstairs guest room. Alice found an alarm clock for him to borrow and asked about school lunches and breakfast. Nathan explained how little maintenance he was and would settle for instant oatmeal, toast, and coffee. She provided the breakfast items, letting Nathan put together his own breakfast. The house had a full bath downstairs and a half upstairs. He wanted to use the downstairs bath, but the door was closed. It connected to the master bedroom. Nathan didn't want to disturb the sleeping couple and used the upstairs bathroom to wash his face and brush his teeth. Not having access to the downstairs bathroom made Nathan rely on the gym showers for keeping himself clean.

Going to school the next day was traumatic. Nathan was quiet as a mouse in getting up, washing, and getting ready for school. All he needed was hot water to mix the few packets of oatmeal and a glass of milk. He turned on the water faucet at a low stream, rinsing his bowl, and placed it in the sink. Nathan grabbed his books then tiptoed onto the porch, where he met the Goodalls' golden retriever, Max. It was easier walking to the end of the road meeting the bus than it was getting ready for school.

Nathan contained his composure while the school bus drove past the charred foundation. The next stop was the old white house where the Berch sisters climbed aboard. Nathan noticed a small cage with a rabbit identical to Michael Jay sitting alongside. He was tempted to ask the girls but felt leaving well enough alone. Nathan lived the school day like any other, with the exception of wearing the same clothes.

Alice spent the day grocery shopping and recruiting neighbors in donating clothes for Nathan. She managed to collect a few shirts and dress pants, hoping they would fit. Nathan was thankful for the selection Alice got for him. He still needed to do some shopping on his own.

Evening meals were far different from the standard boiled potatoes and a vegetable. Nathan learned little incidentals like sour cream on baked potatoes, shrimp with brown rice, and venison stew. He tasted dinners that he wasn't accustomed to having. Nathan started to realize how much of life he was missing. The Goodalls had a variety of friends that Nathan met over the coming weeks. They broadened his perspective on life. Alice's persona changed in the company of her fellow horse enthusiasts or when neighbors stopped over. She was more relaxed and personable than the portrayed horsewoman that Nathan got to know.

Nathan's habits suited Alice. She had a live-in farmhand and babysitter. She paid him the agreed amount, which satisfied Nathan knowing he wasn't living off charity. It was a couple of weeks since the fire when Beth called, asking if Nathan wanted to see the family. He thought of the oddity of Beth calling and not his mother. Having Alice's approval, Nathan took Beth's offer. She borrowed Lydia's car, making the long drive.

Nathan had Beth stop at the Globe retail store so he could buy a set of clothes, toiletries, and a few washcloths. Alice wasn't one for minor details unless it involved finances. She was a horsewoman with a business mind who accounted for every dollar. Beth continued the drive into Somersworth.

"Want to thank you for stopping," remarked Nathan. "I really needed these things. The Goodalls are good people, but Alice isn't one for providing incidentals. At least I can wash my face and have a couple of towels for gym class."

"Do you think you made the right choice staying at the Goodalls?" asked Beth.

"Yeah, I wouldn't want to finish a school year in another school. They're good people, and I appreciate them letting me finish my school year."

Beth drove along into Somersworth when she pointed to a motor inn. "That's the inn the family stayed a few nights before getting the rental."

Nathan took a quick glance before looking to where they were headed. Beth drove onto a narrow drive next to a small ranch-style house.

Both entered, with Nathan going through the motions of saying hello to everyone. In the middle of the living room was Sheri. Nathan spotted her right away.

"How did Sheri get here?" asked Nathan.

"Somehow she got out and was rescued," replied his mother. "She's about to have puppies."

Nathan somehow thought that was odd, then remembered seeing the Michael Jay look-alike. He started wondering how the house actually caught fire.

Nathan talked of how well school was going and how generous everyone was treating him at the Goodalls'. His younger siblings had just started school even though it would be for a short time. Rachael commented how the family was surviving and looking for a permanent place to live. Beth wanted to leave, having spent a couple of hours visiting. She had a long drive ahead of her. Nathan couldn't help thinking never once did his mother ask if he needed money for clothes or anything. It didn't surprise him; after all, he was living with a well-to-do family that probably wouldn't mind supporting him. Beth drove into the Goodalls' driveway, letting her brother out.

"Thanks, Beth. I wonder if you could take me shopping again in a couple of weeks when I get paid. I'll be needing more clothes. This is the only time I get to go anywhere."

Life went on at the horse farm. Nathan noticed how at ease everyone was when Alice went on one of her horse excursions. The kids loved it when Nathan babysat. They liked having fun overtaking and wrestling him to the ground. Doc always enjoyed having a martini before supper. Occasionally he'd strike up a conversation just to see what Nathan's points of view were on current events. Nathan's opinions were limited. He had little interactions with evening news, newspapers, or even a radio. What thoughts Nathan projected seemed purely conservative. Doc enjoyed Nathan's other characteristics, especially the fact that he, like Doc, had a German heritage.

Alice realized Nathan had no quality time for himself. She gave him Saturdays off, allowing him time for shopping or visiting family, the Greysons, or the Newcombs. Nathan put Alice on pins and needles when he visited Zachary and Katherine; she was quite aware of his cider barrel. Doc smirked under his breath knowing Nathan was half snookered. Doc was well acquainted with the cider barrels, having visited them on numerous occasions when Alice was away at her horse shows.

Spring came and was marred by the assassination of Martin Luther King. Ray Lawson listened to the news bulletin on his car radio on his way to the Goodalls. He shared the sad news with Nathan, who was already in the middle of cleaning stalls. Ray enjoyed riding Beau. It was the schoolteacher's way of clearing his head before settling down at home doing what all teachers do in the evenings: correcting papers.

Beth spent a few days staying at the Greyson farmhouse. It was a Saturday afternoon. She decided to walk up and visit with her brother. Nathan spotted her walking down the dirt road and walked up to meet her.

"How's it going?" asked the brother.

"Okay," came the response. "I wanted to let you know I'm pregnant."

"You're what?" asked Nathan, surprised at what he just heard.

"I'm pregnant. Ben and I are planning a June wedding. It'll be a small one. We're thinking about having it at the family's new place in Middleton," explained Beth.

"Middleton? When did the family move to Middleton?"

"It was weeks ago. It's a nice place, just a few miles from Diprizzio's Lumber," Beth continued. "I got a letter from Dad with an enclosed check for a little over a thousand dollars."

"A thousand dollars?" gasped Nathan, looking surprised.

"Yeah, its money he saved over the years, and you'll be getting yours in another year."

The news was too much to take. June was also the time for his graduation. He wondered why it took this long to be told where his family was living. The two chatted a while longer before Beth made the track back down the ridge.

For years, Clarence received a small stipend from Social Security in support of "his" four children. He put the money into separate accounts, which, over time, had grown into a tidy sum. Beth, having turned eighteen, received her share of the accumulated amount.

It wasn't long when Rachael decided to visit her son. Nathan was working in the barn when Alice appeared, telling him his mother was at the house. Nathan was surprised seeing his mother.

"How are you doing?" asked Rachael.

"I'm okay," replied Nathan.

"How's school?"

"It's going okay," came the response.

"Have you given any thought to attending school after graduation?" asked Rachael, being curious about her son's future endeavors.

"I was thinking about going to an art school. I've applied to a couple in Boston and have interviews next week," explained Nathan.

"Really. I thought a junior college majoring in something like liberal arts might be better for you. Have you given any thought in attending one of those? You don't have to worry about the tuition. You fall under the War Orphans Act since your father's disability is service connected," reminded Rachael.

"No, I really didn't give any thought to a college. My grades aren't all that hot, and I don't think I'd have a chance getting in," replied Nathan.

"So when are these interviews, and where in Boston?" asked Rachael.

Nathan told his mother of the two around the Boston Common. She mentioned going with him and would call his grandmother to join them at the common. Nathan was a bit surprised and didn't mind having his mother and grandmother tag along. There wasn't anything malicious about the trip. Rachael needed to pay close attention to what her son had in mind for the future, making sure they suited her interests. Nathan watched as his mother drove down the road, then returned to cleaning the stalls.

Rachael continued to convince her son in applying to a junior college. It meant more support money in her pocket. Rachael got in touch with Sarah to meet them at the Boston Common. Sarah stepped off the Greyhound bus and saw her daughter and grandson standing in the terminal. The three proceeded, walking the city blocks to the first interview. After a half hour, the trio walked a series of city blocks, arriving in time for the second.

Nathan did his best convincing the schools of his art interests. Sarah suggested stopping for a late lunch before catching the afternoon bus back to Plymouth. Rachael and her son returned to the parked vehicle for the drive north. She kept repeating to her son the necessity for applying to a junior college. She tried painting a picture of how a liberal arts degree would benefit him in the job market. Nathan just sat storing the information into his brain. Rachael continued to watch her son's movements and ambitions carefully, especially during these final months of school.

Rachael wasn't alone monitoring Nathan's escapades. Clarence called, asking what his plans were after graduation. Nathan told his father he wanted to pursue something in the art field. It wasn't long before Clarence called about an art school in New Haven. He gave Nathan the information on the Paier School of Art. It caught Nathan's attention and would ask for an application. It was one application Nathan would keep to himself, not even telling his sister. Beth was reliable but not one for keeping secrets. Alice supported Nathan's ambition in furthering his education. She wanted him to stay the summer helping with the horses while she exhibited throughout New England.

The Boston schools sent their regrets, thanking Nathan for his application.

He thought, *So this is how it feels to receive college rejections.*

Nathan was relieved getting the letters of regrets; maybe New Haven was his destiny. The family's attention was centered on Beth's upcoming house wedding.

Beth's wedding was planned for the middle of June. The invitations were mailed, and the preparations were simple. The reception would be a small catered affair with tables and a few chairs placed outside. Rachael called a week prior, asking to borrow the Goodalls' lawn mower. Alice was accommodating, but wondered why Nathan's mother hadn't bought one already. Rachael's excuse was that she hadn't gotten around to it.

The exterior of the Middleton house and surrounding lawn were inviting. The rooms were small and the walls needed updating. There wasn't time to make any necessary changes. By early afternoon, Nathan was whisked off along with the lawn mower back to New Durham. Alice was glad having Nathan back as the stalls needed cleaning. The summer heat caused the slime to collect within the water buckets. It was another tedious job for Nathan, scrubbing each one thoroughly before filling them in their respective stalls.

It was Thursday afternoon when Ray drove up for his usual afternoon ride. He heard the news that Robert Kennedy had just been shot at one of his campaign conventions. Ray was the only one Nathan relied on for any updates on current events. The Goodalls didn't have an accessible radio, and supper always took place while the evening news was being televised.

Beth's wedding day arrived. She would be Mrs. Benjamin Greyson by day's end. Rachael arrived at the horse farm, picking up her son. Nathan was dressed in a new black suit and the only one dressed for the ceremony. Sarah and Milton were driven up to witness their granddaughter's wedding. They took their places beside Ben's parents. The justice of the peace arrived, going over the preliminaries. Beth asked her brother at the last moment to stand in as Ben's best man. Andy was to do the honors but couldn't get the time off from his military commitments.

The ceremony took place in the small empty room off the kitchen. The justice was a tall man standing front and center. Ben was dressed in a simple blazer and an open-collared shirt. The Greysons seemed to be dressed for a shopping adventure. The moment arrived. There was no music. Beth walked in wearing the three-quarter dinner dress she had worn at her senior prom. Tracy presented her to Ben.

It was a small affair with just the immediate family. Many family and friends sent their regrets, deciding to meet the newly married couple later. The reception didn't amount to much and could have easily resembled a family supper gathering. The couple left on their honeymoon among the White Mountains. By evening, Rachael drove her son to the ridge, ever glad having the whole affair over. The following weekend was graduation.

Final exams started the last week of school with a few moments staged for rehearsals. The class wanted an outside ceremony with pictures inserted into their yearbook, delaying the memorabilia pages until fall.

Graduation was at four in the afternoon. Alice wondered if Nathan had time to do the stalls. Nathan stood back, thinking this was his day and he wanted it to be carefree and full of celebration, but it wasn't the case. He did the stalls, delaying any ceremonial anticipation. Late morning, Rachael arrived, driving Nathan over to Middleton.

The house was quiet. Nathan was surprised seeing Red and shared a few moments. Red spoke lightheartedly, adding some enthusiasm to the day. Tracy was on his way getting drunk, mumbling obscenities. Rachael just wanted this whole day over with. Nathan's grandparents were back in Plymouth, unable to attend. Nathan's only request was to take a shower so he didn't smell like a horse barn.

It was time to leave for the graduation. It was Rachael, Red, and Nathan that filled the car. Tracy had passed out on the sofa. Nathan sat in the back seat of the vehicle staring out the window while his mother drove the thirteen miles to the high school.

Red turned toward Nathan, asking, "Looking forward to graduating? Did you think you'd ever see this day? How many in your class?"

Nathan glanced up at him, not comprehending what Red just asked. He was deep within his thoughts how this was supposed to be a milestone in his life yet it seemed just like another day.

The weather was full of sunshine, not a cloud in the sky. It gave the class the graduation they dreamed about. The class collected themselves in the school cafeteria, donning their caps and gowns. The class director instructed them on last-minute cues and gave a quick rundown on the ceremonial procedures.

The audience chairs were set up on the side lawn between the school and the parking lot. Within minutes, the class filed out the back door into the parking lot. The school band was already in place beside the stage and podium. The other side of the podium staged the rows of empty chairs for the graduating class. The audience was seated and ready, then the sounds of pomp and circumstances filled the air.

The audience stood as the class of 1968 filed down the walkway, taking their assigned seats. Family members broke ranks, standing in idyllic spots snapping memorable photos of their loved ones. Rachael took her camera and joined other eager photographers taking pictures of the ceremony.

The speeches concluded, signaling the calling of the names one by one in presentation of their diplomas. The ceremony was over, and the members said their final goodbyes while returning their caps and gowns. Nathan didn't have time to say goodbye to any of his close classmates. He headed for the car and took his seat in the back for the return trip to Middleton. Rachael and Red followed behind.

"Well, how does it feel? Glad it's over with?" asked Red with some levity to his voice.

Nathan looked up at Red with a slight smile, then noticed his mother's determined stare in the rearview mirror. Hardly a word was spoken the remainder of the trip. Nathan sat with nothing more than his tassel and diploma in the palm of his hand. It was the only remembrance that highlighted the day. Nothing was arranged for his graduation, not a cake nor a card. Nathan felt disappointed that none of his family felt the need to celebrate this milestone in his life.

He glanced over at Red, thinking, *You're the only one.*

Nathan gave a slight chuckle to himself, wanting to get back to the Goodalls. Rachael prepared a spaghetti supper. It wasn't even Nathan's favorite dish. After the table was cleared, Rachael drove her son back to the ridge.

Sunday mornings, the Goodalls didn't rise until eight. The first thing was caring for the horses. Sitting around the breakfast table made Nathan feel his time at the Goodalls was ending. After all, he finished school, and this was the first day of his new life. Doc started the conversation asking Nathan about his future. Nathan mentioned moving south to live with his father in New Haven. There was an art school he was interested in. The discussion was right on cue when the phone rang.

It was Clarence congratulating his son on graduating. He wondered if Nathan gave any thought to the art school in New Haven. He told his father he wanted to make an appointment for an interview. It put the Goodalls at ease. They enjoyed having Nathan around even for the summer months. However, they wanted some assurance Nathan was well on his way to new horizons.

A letter arrived from Paier giving Nathan a time to meet. It had to be a trip of deep secrecy. Nathan would take the Trailways from Dot's Lunch to Boston and connect onward to New Haven. It would be a day's travel. He planned a three-day trip visiting his father and doing the interview. Hopefully Nathan would pull this off.

He called his father, telling him of his travel plans. It was after supper when he arrived in New Haven. It was a quaint city with over half encompassing Yale University. Nathan stood for a moment absorbing his surroundings. He noticed the ornate buildings and the streets sprinkled with diversified people heading in one direction or another. It was unlike the all-White community he had left hours earlier. He hailed a cab, taking him to his father's apartment in Hamden. The series of brick apartment buildings stood well suited for the middle-class occupants. Nathan stood at his father's door and rang the doorbell. A short-haired elderly woman answered the door. It was Hannah, who welcomed him inside. After a moment of hello, she took Nathan into Clarence's bedroom. He lay in a hospital bed watching his remote-controlled television.

The television went silent, and his smile welcomed Nathan for the first time since that brief meeting in South Boston. Clarence had a spare chair next to his wheelchair. Nathan sat talking with him for a couple of hours while noticing how the multiple sclerosis had crippled his father's legs. Clarence had the air-conditioning running, filling the room with a deep chill. Hannah bedded the couch, telling Nathan lights went out at ten. The appointment with Paier was at nine thirty the next morning. Instead of a cab, Hannah's neighbor Stephanie Cole drove him to the interview.

The building resembled an old English Tudor with a lot of small rooms. The receptionist office was tiny, with Mrs. Paier sitting behind the desk. She and her husband, Edward, founded the school and built it into a successful enterprise. Nathan introduced himself with a warm smile. She had him, along with his portfolio, follow her into one of the small classrooms. He opened the portfolio, where Mrs. Paier went over the sketches. She considered Nathan being on the young side from the usual applicants.

She asked about his background; and he proceeded to tell her of his life in New Hampshire, his interest in art, and his hopes in getting the opportunity of knowing his father. After reviewing the work, they agreed that Nathan really needed more work and experience. Mrs. Paier thought Nathan's direction would be in advertising and that doing a semester at night would adequately prepare him for full-time classes. Nathan agreed to the proposal. After an hour, Mrs. Paier allowed him to leave. He was accepted under these special terms, and said she would follow up with a letter.

Nathan told his father the news. Clarence was thrilled Nathan would be going to Paier. The next step was to set up tuition costs with the VA. Nathan felt relieved knowing the trip was successful and needed to get back to New Hampshire. The next morning, Stephanie drove him down to the center of New Haven. He bought his ticket at the depot for the trip to Boston. Nathan had a layover in Boston for about two hours.

Nathan sat waiting when he heard his name called over the PA system. He walked over to the ticket counter, curious as to who would be calling him. He was handed the phone, surprised to hear it was his mother on the other end. Rachael's voice chastised him for doing what he did. Her angered voice told him she would be picking him up in Farmington. This was the blow Nathan hadn't expected. Nathan stepped off the bus in Farmington, where he was hustled into the back seat of the car. Rachael's voice filled the interior as they drove up to the Goodalls'.

"Who in the hell told you, you could go to Connecticut? What right do you think you have traveling without my permission?" shouted Rachael.

"I want to go to an art school," answered Nathan.

"Well, you can forget that. We're going to the Goodalls', and I want you to pack your things and get back into the car. You're never to make a move without my permission. Is that clear? You're going job hunting until I can figure all this out. Do you hear me?" yelled Rachael.

Nathan sat visibly shaken from looking at his mother's determined eyes in the rearview mirror. The car came to a quick stop in front of the Goodalls' house.

As Rachael kept the engine running, she looked straight at her son. "Go get your things and get back into the vehicle as quickly as you can."

Alice was already in the barn and heard the vehicle come to rest outside her house. She peeked out and saw Rachael's car. She dropped everything and quickened her pace over to meet her.

"Hi, Rachael, what brings you here?" asked Alice, being polite.

"Nathan's leaving. I'm having him pack, and he'll be going with me. I want to thank you for taking care of him," Rachael said with a touch of anger in her tone.

"Let me go and see if he needs any help," replied Alice, feeling the anxiety of the situation.

She went inside and raced up the stairs, catching Nathan placing the last of his clothes in his suitcase.

"Nathan, I'm so sorry for telling your mother where you were. She put me in a bad situation. If you want to leave anything here, you're more than welcome to put it up in the attic. I'll give you a check for what I owe you, and if you want me to save some of it for later, I can do that," Alice said with some helpful assurance.

Nathan paused for a moment, then looked at Alice. "Thanks, Alice. I would like to leave a few things if I could, and if you can save about half my pay for a while, I'd appreciate that. I know my mother will want what I have." Nathan thought for another minute. "Alice, I really appreciate what you're doing to help me. I should have expected this, but I'm glad I did what I did. Maybe something will come out of it in the end."

Alice smiled and went downstairs to write Nathan a check. He placed a few pieces of clothing up in the attic, then descended the stairs with his suitcase.

Alice handed him a check. "Give us a call when you can, telling how you're making out."

Nathan smiled. "I will, and tell everyone I said goodbye and thanks."

Nathan climbed in the back seat of his mother's car with his suitcase. Within seconds, the vehicle drove down the dirt road. The car arrived in Middleton, where Nathan was restricted to the house. The kids were instructed to report on everything Nathan said, did, and went while she and Tracy went to work. Rachael ordered Nathan not to leave the house under any circumstances.

That lasted an hour before Nathan walked about a half mile to the center of Wakefield. He found a pay phone, making a call to Alice, explaining the situation. Nathan's only salvation was Flora. Nathan kept in touch with her off and on while staying at the Goodalls'. He felt good knowing he had written her a few months earlier asking her if he could visit this year.

It didn't take long before word got to her about Nathan's move to Middleton. Flora wrote Rachael, asking when Nathan would be visiting. As the weeks passed, the tension in the household was thick. Rachael gave Nathan the elongated couch to sleep on. It was overly used with lumps that was more torture than comfort. The following weekend, Rachael sent Nathan out with Tracy to job hunt on the Dover route picking up applications. Nathan had no intentions of getting a job. He walked into the various stores, walked around, then returned to the car commenting they weren't hiring.

Finally Rachael caved, letting him visit Flora. Nathan had packed a small suitcase, making the appearance he was just going for a visit. Yet Nathan was packed for the rest of his life. Nathan followed his mother into the car and sat looking at the scenery as she drove to Dover. He bought a ticket to Boston and transferred over to a Greyhound bus for the ride to Plymouth. He checked in with his grandmother while waiting for Flora. Sarah apologized for not being at his graduation, thinking she was becoming ill and wanted to get home. Nathan accepted it even though it meant very little. Flora arrived, saying her hellos. Nathan grabbed his suitcase and followed his grandaunt downtown, meeting up with the Duncans.

Sarah called her daughter, "Hi, Rachael, just calling to let you know Nathan made it down and is on his way to Flora's."

"That's a relief. I didn't think he'd make it. Mom, I don't trust him to come back. What do you think I should do?" asked Rachael.

"Why won't he go home? What's he up to, Rachael?" continued Sarah.

Rachael confessed, "Clarence has gotten to him. He's got Nathan to apply to a school down in Connecticut. I don't want Nathan with him."

Sarah sighed. "I don't know what to say, Rachael. Why wouldn't he go home?"

"Because he wants to go to Connecticut, that's why," answered her daughter.

Sarah thought a moment and offered an idea, "If you want to be sure he makes it home, you can always send one of the girls down. He'll have to make sure she gets home."

The idea sparked with Rachael's approval.

"That'll work. I'll send Laura down to Boston tomorrow if you can meet her there. Then call Flora that she's with you and that Nathan will have to bring her home."

"Okay, Rachael, I'll ride up tomorrow morning and meet Laura at the Trailways station. Tell her to stay there until she sees me," ended Sarah.

Sarah carried out the plan, having Laura spend the remaining week with her, and called Flora.

Upon hearing the news, Nathan told Flora, "I'm going to tell you something I want to be a secret. I'm not going home when I leave here. I'm going to Connecticut to go live with my father. I got accepted to an art school in New Haven. I'm not going back to be my mother's prisoner."

Flora stood surprised. "What do you mean your mother's prisoner?"

"She wants me under her control. She doesn't want me going to art school. When she found out, she had me collect my things at the Goodalls' and took me to Middleton, where she told me to stay in the house. She had the kids rat on me on every little thing I did or said," confessed Nathan.

"No! You're kidding. She really didn't do that?" asked Flora, looking stunned.

"Yes, she really did. My only hope in getting to Connecticut was coming down to see you," Nathan added.

"I can't believe that. Well, good for you. I'm glad you're making the move and getting out from under that household. I'd hate to see your mother's face, never mind your grandmother's, when you don't show up."

"I've got to do it, Aunt Flora, if I'm ever going to make something of myself. I just can't take it anymore," Nathan stated, somewhat nervous.

"You've got to do what you've got to do. I've always liked your father, and so did your grandfather. He's a good man. It's your grandmother that favored Tracy. Just remember, I still have that insurance policy if you ever need it. I promise I won't tell your grandmother. I know she'll call me, telling what kind of a sneak you are. I'll act surprised when she tells me," continued Flora.

Nathan gave a slight smile after hearing Flora's words of support. They boosted his confidence. He felt his inner voice telling him it was time to tell his grandaunt the other reason for going to Connecticut. After all, he wasn't returning to the troubled family he was leaving behind.

"Aunt Flora, there's something else I want you to know. I don't know how much you know about Tracy, but the man is sick and demented."

"What do you mean?" asked Flora, looking concerned.

"I mean he's abusive and has made many advances on us kids. I mean sexual advances," Nathan said nervously.

"What do you mean sexual advances?" Flora asked, looking even more concerned.

"I mean, for years, he's been feeling our crotches and having us touch him. He's been touching me since South Boston, and I know he's been touching a few of the girls," confessed Nathan.

"Does your mother know?" Flora asked, reflecting the anger in her face.

"I don't know if she does or not. Sometimes I think she does and turns the other cheek. I remember a time she always wanted me to be around naked men," continued Nathan.

"You're not serious?" Flora said, looking bewildered.

"I am serious. I've always known why Beth and I did all the chores. Kenneth and the others never had to lift a finger. I always thought Mom made us do everything because we were my father's kids and felt it was one of the reasons Tracy was allowed to abuse us. I learned, long ago, if we didn't give in to his demands, he'd make our life miserable. I never gave in, giving him cause to torment me. I remember the time my father visited us in South Boston. He gave Beth and I hope that we could reach out to him some day. Today is the day. I'm done taking the abuse and being belted. This is my only opportunity to go live with my father," confessed Nathan.

Flora walked over to her chair and sat, giving some thought of what she just heard.

She looked up at Nathan. "And to think I gave him a thousand dollars to help your family one year while you folks were living in South Boston."

Nathan looked dumbfounded upon hearing what his grandaunt had just said. He remembered that year when his mother mentioned how Tracy got a big Christmas bonus and how they should appreciate what he was giving them. Nathan realized the truth behind that bonus.

Flora got up and headed for the kitchen. "I'm not going to tell anyone, Nathan. It would ruin your grandparents and your mother, never mind what would happen to the kids."

Nathan followed behind. "Do you think I'm doing the right thing?"

"Of course you are," Flora reassured her grandnephew. "I know your mother is quite aware of Tracy and what he is. She knew what he was when she first got involved with him. Your mother is just as guilty as Tracy. Now go get changed into your bathing suit and take a swim for yourself. I'm going to get supper started."

Nathan looked at Flora for a brief moment, wanting to hear more, but did what she requested. He changed and sauntered down to the pond. Nathan felt the cool water calming his rattled nerves.

The day of freedom arrived. Alan and Barbara Smyth drove Flora and Nathan downtown, dropping them off at the supermarket.

Flora sent Nathan on his way, not wanting to go any farther. She thought it best not to get into any conversation that might lead into what Nathan was about to do.

Flora watched her grandnephew walk away from her. She thought of everything she just learned about her niece and Tracy. She never trusted him, and she knew how conniving Rachael could be. After all, she had witnessed her behavior over the years. She remembered Rachael's formative years when she was a little mischievous toward her father. It was his fault for spoiling her. It was Sarah who kept her daughter under control. Flora remembered how her niece got the added child support for Kenneth and Laura, realizing that Rachael and Tracy were two of a kind. Suddenly she felt sorry for the younger kids—kids she knew little about.

Nathan made the walk to his grandparents', where Laura was packed and ready to return to New Hampshire. Sarah walked them to the bus stop and watched both board the bus.

It was at Boston Nathan bought Laura's ticket to Farmington and a separate one to New Haven.

It was time for the bus to load for New Hampshire.

Nathan turned, looking at his sister. "I'm not going back with you. You're going back alone. You're to get off in Farmington and go directly to Beth's apartment. Do you understand?"

Laura looked confused. "What about you? Why aren't you going with me?"

Nathan didn't want to tell his sister the plan, just telling her, "I'm going somewhere else. I'm not going home, and that's all I can tell you. So here's your ticket. Now get on the bus before it leaves."

Laura, still not clear of what just happened, climbed onto the bus, taking a final look at her brother. Nathan knew she could handle it as she had been part of the entourage walking those many miles in

South Boston. It would be another hour when Nathan's bus would be leaving southward.

The trip to New Haven took longer. Laura arrived in Farmington, meeting her mother at the corner drugstore. Rachael was livid not seeing Nathan. Nathan sat nervously on the bus, wondering if something would stop him in his tracks. The bus made the trip uninterrupted to New Haven. Nathan stepped off, feeling a sense of relief, and hailed a cab for the final leg to his father's apartment.

It was evening when Nathan rang his father's doorbell. Hannah answered, seeing her grandson standing before her. She invited him in and led the way into his father's room. Clarence smiled with relief that Nathan had pulled it off. Within the hour, the phone rang. It was Rachael calling from the Farmington Police Station. She and an officer were on the other end. The words were loud with accusations spoken among the parties. Finally the officer concluded there wasn't anything the police could do since Nathan wasn't a runaway but was living with his father and basically of legal age.

Rachael wouldn't accept what she was hearing and insisted to talk to her son.

She tried laying a guilt trip by asking Nathan, "What's wrong with you? Don't you love us? Don't you want to be part of this family?"

Nathan paused momentarily, replying, "Of course I do, but I'm not going back. I'm staying here."

Nathan proved to have stepped into another stage of his adulthood. Rachael still saw her son as the child she had full control over. She gave her one last pitch to sway him. The conversation ended, and the umbilical cord cut.

A NEW SUNRISE

Nathan's eyelids slowly opened as the morning daylight crept across the living room. He heard the pedaling of an exercise bike. Hannah was doing her morning ritual as Nathan lay awake on the foldaway bed. He heard the bedroom door open, and his grandmother shuffled into the bathroom to wash her face. It coupled with a few hackings and coughs.

She made her way back to her room, pausing to tell Nathan, "The nurse will be coming around eight, and I want you up and dressed."

Nathan followed suit, making his good mornings to his father and telling him he felt okay from the previous day's aftermath.

The voice from the kitchen gave Nathan a reminder, "Let's get a move on."

Without hesitation, Nathan washed and dressed into what few clothes he had. Hannah was busy making a bowl of cereal, cup of coffee, and toast for Clarence's breakfast tray.

The two sat at the breakfast table eating their last bite when a middle-aged figure appeared at the back door. She wore a nurse's uniform with her eyes hidden behind a pair of oversized sunglasses. She entered the kitchen wearing a generous smile that made up for the mystery she was projecting.

"Nathan, this is Clair Padowski, your father's nurse," said Hannah.

"So you're Nathan. Finally glad to meet you. Your father has talked a lot about you," replied Clair.

The young man smiled. "Yup, I'm Nathan. Glad to meet you too."

"Your father said you're going to attend Paier. Will you be looking for a job?" asked the nurse.

"Well, I'd like to get a job, but I don't know the area, and I haven't got a driver's license," admitted Nathan.

"That shouldn't be a problem. There's a supermarket down the hill in the plaza that is always hiring students. You might check with them since most of the kids will be going back to school," suggested Clair.

Nathan raised his eyebrows, not knowing what surrounded the apartment complex. He was anxious to get out and explore the neighborhood. Nathan took the last sip of his coffee and followed Clair into his father's room.

"Morning, Clarence. Just met your son."

Clarence was glad seeing the two meet.

She continued, having removed the breakfast tray, "I told him about the plaza and Pegnataro's in case he's looking for a job."

Clarence nodded, looking at his son. "That's right. They're down the road and always hiring. You might check them out." He then added, "Clair lives in West Haven with her husband, Ned, and has a teenage son. She's quite a person. I hope you two will get along."

"I think we will." Clair smiled. "Did you know your son doesn't have a license?"

"Yeah, he told me. That's something I'll have to set up," replied Clarence.

They continued to tell Nathan about Hamden, the plaza, and the different ways to get about. Clair explained the bus routes on Whitney and Dixwell Avenues. Nathan was taking in all this information. It sounded too good to be true. He became anxious about going out and explore. Clair saw the excitement in Nathan's face and excused him while she started working on the disabled man.

Pegnataro's was privately owned, having three stores in the Hamden-New Haven area. Nathan saw the supermarket sign as he descended the apartment complex hill. He walked straight into the store and approached the receptionist's counter. The timing was perfect in asking for an application as the high school and college kids were returning to school. Nathan was offered a job in the produce department even before completing the application.

Nathan was shown the departments and led through the underground, where the packaging, grocery stowage, break room, and employee restrooms were located. They asked how soon he could start. The earliest was the following Monday. Nathan was seventeen and needed working papers. The receptionist gave him directions to Hamden's town hall.

Nathan left the store and stood momentarily in total amazement. He hadn't been in Hamden twenty-four hours and was now living with his father and had a job supporting himself. Nathan wasted no time following the map to the town hall. It took about thirty minutes to obtain his working papers. Nathan's excitement followed him all the way back to the apartment.

Hannah sat at the kitchen table enjoying her cup of tea. Nathan entered the back door, excited he'd got a job. Hannah smiled. She saw her grandson as a threat and wouldn't mind having him occupied both day and night. His announcement was heard in the living room, where his father and Clair were sitting. They were astonished how quick Nathan had gotten a job. Nathan sat, retracing his steps of his morning adventures with them. Hannah remained in the kitchen cooking dinner, showing no interest in her grandson's revelations.

Clair left for the day, feeling good about meeting Nathan. He sat at the kitchen table sensing something amiss about his grandmother. He tried engaging her in a conversation while she sat across from him sipping her afternoon tea. She admitted she wasn't used to having young adults around. She wasn't there watching him and Beth grow up like their cousins in Illinois.

Hannah had a few allergies, having a handkerchief hooked around her watchband for those occasional sniffles. She had her share of daily meds, like most people of her generation. Hannah wasn't a TV watcher, turning it on for the evening news. Most of her time was spent climbing the stairs to the second-floor apartment, visiting Stephanie Cole. Nathan noticed his grandmother's antics weren't that far off from what he was familiar.

Nathan took a few moments sitting with his father, hearing him reminisce of bygone years. He heard the tales of how Clarence left Plymouth and made his way to the New Haven area. He kept doing law enforcement as he moved from one town to another. Clarence kept the television on while they talked. As each adventure was told, Nathan noticed his father's attention span on a television show was short lived. After five or ten minutes, he'd click the channels from one station to another. There were about five channels to choose from. Nathan would get interested in a show when it was clicked to another. It flustered Nathan, but he realized the television was there for his father.

At quarter to eight, Nathan stood at Pegnataro's front door. The store receptionist opened the door and led Nathan to the produce manager, Lucian D'Marro. He showed Nathan the produce line and how to work the phone hanging on the side counter. It was used to order more produce crates from the preparation room below. He followed Lucian through the swinging back doors adjacent to the meat department. It led to a descending stairway.

Before stepping down, Lucian showed Nathan the back door. It was where the vendors made deliveries. Along the back wall was a descending conveyor sending the delivered crates down to the processing area. The goods were stored into a room-sized cooler. Nathan was introduced to the processing crew—Willie, Val, Maria, and Tony. He felt as if he stepped into little Italy as everyone was of Italian descent. A knee-length red coat was given to Nathan, identifying him as a clerk. He put it on and followed his supervisor up the stairs and back to the produce section. His job was to keep the displays replenished by placing the old on top and the new underneath.

By midafternoon, two high schoolers punched in, handling the evening shift. Just prior to closing, all the unwrapped produce was sent down and placed in the cooler. Come morning, the day shift reversed the process for the early shoppers. It took a couple of weeks for Nathan's first paycheck. It was enough to buy some new clothes and put a few dollars away for school.

Nathan made the two-and-a-half-mile walk to the art school's main building. He noticed the houses, the apartment buildings, and the large variety of stores along Dixwell Avenue. His journey stopped when he stood before the huge cement block exposing a few colorful doors. The building had no windows. Nathan went inside, feeling the cool air circulating about him. He heard voices echoing throughout the building as if he had stepped inside a seashell. Nathan approached the receptionist, introduced himself, and asked about his class schedule. The receptionist had a basket ready with organized files on the oncoming freshmen. She pawed through the layers and found Nathan Anderson. She handed him his evening schedule and took him on a quick tour of the school. The basement had a few open-bay classrooms plus a school store, where students could purchase art supplies. Nathan took advantage of the store, getting the basics he needed for that first night.

Nathan walked the plaza, shopping for a toolbox to carry the art supplies. Anything else could wait until his Monday, Wednesday, and Friday evening classes. Clarence called a few driving schools and set up training classes for his son on Tuesday and Thursday evenings. The course would last six weeks, and upon completion, Nathan would be driven to the police station for the tests.

Nathan studied the booklet that outlined the driving rules and regulations. By mid-October, Nathan took the tests, passing both with flying colors. It was another milestone he was proud to complete, and he was thankful to his father.

Attending Paier led Nathan in meeting many interesting people, some novice and some professionals. The night semester trained students on painting still-life objects monotone in color. The shadow boxes contained items from all black to all white with a few shades of color. The lighting affixed to the shadow boxes allowed the students' eyes to see other hues reflecting from the solid objects. Still-life drawing gave them the training to draw objects and buildings from one- or two-point perspective. The instructors were hands-on, going around and giving each setup their individual attention. The classes prepared the artists for the upcoming months.

Letters from Plymouth started arriving from Sarah and Flora. Flora heard Nathan made the move, keeping his secret and acting stunned when told of his great escape to Connecticut. She hoped he was doing well and felt sorry for all he went through. She wanted to hear about his new life living with his father. The letter from Sarah was forgiving, hoping Nathan would keep in touch.

He started writing to them both, telling them about his job and school. Flora decided to install a phone in case Nathan wanted to call. Her goal was getting the cottage functioning to where she could live there year-round. Until then, she continued closing the place in early fall and making the trip back to Cambridge.

November brought the election of Richard Nixon as president, followed by Beth giving birth to her daughter, Angela. Clarence felt proud hearing the news of becoming a grandfather. He enjoyed the ribbings from both his mother and Stephanie Cole.

Christmas was in full mode. Nathan followed Hannah to where the Christmas decorations were stored in the basement. Each apartment was assigned a six-by-eight-foot area for storage surrounded by chicken wire. He carried the boxes up and placed each artificial tree limb together. Nathan used his artistic eye for decorating. Hannah didn't like getting involved. She was content with the few decorative knickknacks strategically placed throughout the apartment. Nathan carried the decorating into his father's room, extending the Christmas spirit.

Clair liked the decor. Clarence's collection of Christmas albums played on the turntable. Clarence loved music and possessed an eight-track player on his nightstand. The stand spotted trays of various tapes he would listen to anytime. His selections were mostly made up of Ray Conniff and his orchestra. During the night, Clarence wore his headset, falling asleep to the never-ending tunes.

Christmas dawned with Hannah being her usual self. Nathan got up, placing the foldaway bed back in his father's room while wishing him a merry Christmas.

Clarence chuckled. "Thanks. I wish I could have some real Christmas cheer."

Nathan smiled, leaving the room to get washed and dressed. Hannah was preparing a ham and had invited Stephanie down for dinner. Nathan turned on the television for the Christmas parade.

He sat thinking of his father in one room and his grandmother in the other.

He went into the kitchen. "Gram, do you think Dad would want to get up for Christmas?"

Hannah looked up from her puzzle. "It's not a bad idea. Let's ask him."

Nathan followed his grandmother toward Clarence's room.

She peeked in, asking her son, "Nathan wants to know if you'd like to get up for Christmas. He'll help with the lift, getting you into the wheelchair."

Clarence was surprised by the suggestion. "Sure, I'd like to get up if it's all right with everyone."

Hannah turned toward her grandson. "Let me clean him up, and I'll let you know when he's ready."

Nathan nodded and returned to watching the television. Hannah got a washcloth and washed her son's face and arms. Nathan operated the lift, raising his father out of bed, and placed him gently into the wheelchair. Clarence already felt better being up and joining his son in the living room.

There wasn't too much to do for excitement. Nathan learned neither his grandmother nor his father played card games. Clarence's hands lacked control, often losing their ability to grip. Hannah just wasn't a game player. By early afternoon, Stephanie arrived, being somewhat surprised at seeing Clarence up and rolling around. Hannah called everyone to the dinner table, where she had placed the prepared plates. Stephanie livened the room with her enthusiastic conversations. After the meal, she helped Hannah with the dishes while the father and son returned to watching television.

It was time for Stephanie to leave and check on her mother before the night air settled. Clarence began feeling tired from sitting most the day and asked Nathan to wheel him back to bed.

Hannah suggested making calls to distant family members and wishing them merry Christmas. Clarence dialed, making one call after another from his bedside phone. Nathan shared in the conversations on the kitchen extension. The day ended as it always did around 10:00 p.m., with everyone drifting off into a deep sleep.

The next morning celebrated Nathan's eighteenth birthday. He was able to enjoy the vacation time from school. The important part of the day was driving to the Selective Service office to register for the draft. Attending Paier gave Nathan a deferment. In another week, Nathan rescheduled his working hours to fit his daytime semester.

Lucian wasn't pleased about Nathan's change of hours, having no choice but to go along with it. The new shift was noticeable in Nathan's paycheck. It gave him little to spend, but some money was better than none. The new year came with little fanfare with Nathan focused on school.

The first days at Paier indoctrinated the expectations and supplies that were needed. The classes alternated from the main contemporary building to the old English Tudor on the other side of Hamden. Homework had them creating various designs with incorporated lettering, watercolors, acrylic paintings, and still-life drawings. Most assignments were started in class and finished up at home.

Nathan ended his school day and drove straight to work, teaming up with one of the high schoolers. Most of the management had left for the day, leaving only a couple of supervisors for the evening shift. Nathan didn't realize how relaxed the evening shift was and the foolery that went behind the department walls.

He worked with Jeff during the five-hour shift with a fifteen-minute break. He led Nathan into the basement, where he hid a package of hotdogs. Jeff cooked them on the hot plate and had a couple of soda cans to wash them down. Nathan witnessed the ingenious way Jeff had prepared the hotdogs. They consumed the package, hiding the evidence within the depths of the garbage boxes. Jeff assured Nathan not to worry as other employees did things just as radical.

The meat department entertained themselves with a six-pack they hid in the meat cooler. They succeeded with the drink fest by displaying the illusion of keeping busy. The evidence was placed outside the back door and disappeared when the crew left for home.

Arriving at the apartment, Nathan found his grandmother sitting at the kitchen table. He made a quick hello to his father and reminisced about his day. It was just about time for lights out when

Nathan broke out the art supplies to do his homework. It put Hannah on edge, expecting everyone in bed by ten. Nathan continued doing his homework, staying up for as long as it took.

Hannah put up with it for a couple of evenings before complaining about the paint, glue, and any other nonpaper item that triggered her allergies. Hannah was adamant in making her point. She'd wait for Nathan to start his projects, then come out of her room deciding on a cup of tea. It prolonged Nathan's ability to do his homework. After a week of trying to accommodate his grandmother, Nathan went to his father for some sort of resolution. Clarence saw what his mother was doing and tried reasoning with her. He tried making her aware of the bigger picture of having Nathan around. She reminded her son he could always get someone else to care for him.

Nathan had an idea of transforming the basement storage into a work area. It would be ideal, having plenty of heat and convenience. Nathan only had to trust his grandmother not locking him out once she went to bed. Nathan shared the drama with Clair. She thought Hannah was being unreasonable and that he wasn't alone in his grandmother's head games. Clair shared her encounters of the tit for tat she had with Hannah. It wasn't long before Nathan's secret nickname for his grandmother was Super Bitch.

In subsequent moments while having tea with Hannah, Nathan learned she had no use for men. They had only one purpose, and that was to procreate. Other than that, women were just as capable as men in getting things done. Nathan was taken aback after hearing this.

Winter was more than half over when Beth wanted to visit. The only glitch was she needed a ride down and back since Ben was working. Clarence got an idea of having his son drive up on a weekend to bring Beth and Angela down for the visit. Nathan had no problem driving to get his sister and niece. He saw the excitement in his father's face, knowing it would be the first time seeing his granddaughter. Nathan looked at the visit differently, knowing Beth was on a mission.

The trip gave Nathan a chance to visit with a few folks. As he drove over the New Hampshire border, the snow began piling up and drifted for miles. It displayed a landscape of glistening white while Connecticut had little in comparison. The snowbelt lay along the Massachusetts Turnpike. Nathan arrived at the Greyson farmhouse for the evening. He got up just before dawn and drove to Farmington to pick Beth up bag and baggage. During the ride, she told her brother of Ben's parents giving them some land to build a house. It would be a long process in getting the land cleared with the installation of a well and septic system. Beth had just confirmed the reason for the visit.

They arrived at the Mix Avenue complex, meeting Hannah at the back door. She was introduced to her great-granddaughter and was led into Clarence's room. He had longed for this moment for quite a while and became teary-eyed holding his granddaughter for the first time. Beth and Nathan unloaded the car bringing in the suitcases. Hannah placed a small blanket on her bed for Angela. She had no objections of having both girls sleeping in her room. Angela slept in the carryall while Beth bunked with Hannah. Clarence couldn't wait to call family members and friends about having Beth and his granddaughter down for a visit. Hannah made a beeline up to Stephanie's and invited her down to meet them.

The excitement lasted well into the evening before the lights dimmed for another restful night. Monday arrived with Nathan attending his classes and going to work. He made his usual appearances for lunch. Clair found time to chat with Beth about things women normally found interesting. Nathan took Beth down into the basement and showed her his setup, explaining the difficulties their grandmother had put him through. He popped in the apartment before ten, getting his bed in position as not to disturb anyone.

The week passed, and they made the return trip back to New Hampshire. Beth hinted that their mother wanted to see him. Nathan refused. He asked what the family was up to. Beth's description was more disturbing with every sentence. She told Nathan about Tracy and Rachael buying the Richard's Block and selling the Middleton home. She described the sexual abuses Tracy was doing on the girls. It made Nathan numb hearing it.

Nathan spent the night at the farmhouse. He played a couple of games of cribbage, tuning his strategic abilities on the Greyson boys. The gang went outside, engaging in a few snowball fights before the sky turned dark. By Sunday evening, Nathan was back in Connecticut, where peace and quiet resumed.

The young Greyson couple managed to afford their Farmington apartment. Ben traveled into Massachusetts making deliveries for a warehouse company while Beth still waited on tables. The expenses were mounting with utility bills and babysitting costs. Both realized they needed to move to the farmhouse if they wanted to save money in preparing the lot.

The news traveled about the Goodalls losing their barn to an electrical fire that consumed most of their livestock. The shortage sparked the fire into the haylofts. The Goodalls tried saving a few of the horses, but the extreme heat relaxed the barn door springs to the point it made it difficult to hold up the barn door. The door was an oversized garage door. Doc held the door up as much as he could while Alice tried rescuing those closest to entrance, including Windfield.

It was weeks before the news trickled down to Nathan. A couple of days passed before his father allowed his son to call Alice. She had sold a couple of the young yearlings a few months earlier, only to buy them back from generous owners. As the conversation ended, the Goodalls made Nathan promise to stop by and visit the next time he was up.

Nathan made a couple of trips up to the North Country, stopping at the Goodalls'. Doc and Alice were glad seeing him and invited Nathan to work for them during the summer if he had no other plans. They were in the process of completing the new barn designed with posts and beams. The outer doors would operate on rollers, sliding back and forth, preventing any difficulty in the future. Alice converted the car garage into more stalls for breeding.

Nathan felt it was time to visit his grandparents. He drove to Plymouth for the first time since his escape and pulled in the provincial building's driveway. Sarah rushed out, greeting her grandson with overwhelming hugs and kisses. He walked into the studio apartment seeing his grandfather sitting in his chair with the walker placed in front. Nathan gave his grandfather a heartfelt hug.

"Tell me, how have you been?" asked the anxious grandmother.

"I'm doing good," replied the grandson.

"How do you like your school?" asked Sarah.

"I like it. I'm learning a lot about advertising."

"Is that what you're majoring?" continued Sarah.

"Yeah, I'm doing lettering, design, watercolors, perspective drawing, and a couple of other classes," replied Nathan.

Milton sat listening, expressing an interest in his grandson.

Sarah continued, wanting to know more about her grandson's new life, "How's your job at the supermarket?"

"I like it. I'm still doing produce. The money helps getting some clothes and the supplies I need for school," answered Nathan.

"How's your grandmother and father?" Sarah asked with curiosity.

"They're doing good. I'm glad to get to know my father."

Sarah came to the point where she had to ask the question that bothered her the most, "What happened between you and your mother?"

Nathan paused and wrestled on what to say. "Gram, I had a chance to go to art school. Mom wanted me to stay with her and hopefully go to a community college. All the time we lived in New Durham, she wouldn't let me have friends, meet people, or anything. She didn't even want me having a driver's license. Even when I was living at the Goodalls', she didn't even bother to see if I had clothes to wear. When my father called asking what I wanted to do after high school, he helped me get into a school and even made sure I got my license."

Nathan paused, noticing his grandmother's face go pale, then continued, "When Mom took me to Middleton, she didn't have room for me. She had the kids spy on my every move and report to her what I did and said. It was either be her prisoner or go to Connecticut. I couldn't take it anymore. I had to leave."

"I can't believe she'd do all that. Was there anything else?" asked the grandmother in disbelief.

"No, there's more. I couldn't stand Tracy's sexual abuses," commented Nathan.

"What do you mean?" Sarah said, looking stunned over what she just heard.

"I mean Tracy made advances on me and a few of the girls, especially Laura. That's what I mean. Gram, I'm talking times when we lived in South Boston. I remember all the beatings with the belt and having to deal with Tracy touching me and making me touch him. I wasn't the only one. He was touching Beth. When we lived in New Durham, he made passes at me several times, and he was having Laura touch him. Mom wouldn't let me have friends or do much of anything even though Beth was allowed her friends. Cripes, Mom was okay with Beth getting pregnant before getting married. Beth was allowed to do more than I ever could. I just couldn't take it anymore. I had to leave," explained the grandson.

Sarah remained stunned, and Milton just sat rubbing his head. It would take more than a few moments to digest what they had just been told. Sarah put the explanation aside and would relive it another day. For now, she realized the young boy she once knew had grown.

Nathan notified Pegnataro's of his plans of working in New Hampshire for the summer. The management wished him luck and reassured Nathan there'd be a job in the fall should he decide to stop by. Clarence and Clair felt disappointed in Nathan's leaving. Nathan knew it was for the best. He needed a change of scenery and couldn't see spending the summer putting up with Hannah's constant criticisms.

He rode the bus to New Hampshire, turning into Dot's parking lot. Nathan saw Doc playing ball with two of the kids on the open field. Everyone was all smiles when Nathan stepped off the bus. One of the first concessions Doc and Alice gave Nathan was letting him have Saturday afternoons for himself.

The new barn was built with a few stalls filled with the lost bloodline. Windfield's stall was still at the front of the barn's entrance. His stall had a back door leading into an enclosed fenced area where he could exercise during the day. Alice had plenty of stalls available for breeding mares. Ray Lawson bought a new gelding to ride. This one was smaller and more in proportion to Ray's body.

Nathan fell into the routine of cleaning the stalls and doing landscaping and any other job Alice had in mind. In the evenings, he teamed up with Doc, doing more fencing. He taught Nathan how to use the posthole attachment. Nathan thought they'd be an eventual end to the construction, but somehow it seemed like an endless job. In the meantime, the farmhand continued creosoting the series of fencing posts.

Doc offered his car if Nathan wanted to visit his sister in Farmington. Doc was a stick-shift man, and Nathan had very little experience using it. He only knew shifting gears from operating the John Deere. Doc took him out for a crash course up and down the road. He didn't see Nathan having any real problems, provided he stayed on the main roads.

Saturday Nathan hiked down to the farmhouse, having the need to interact with guys his own age. Other times, he didn't mind hearing the stories from Zachary and Katherine Newcomb. Both spent their free time sitting outside sipping on a cocktail. Katherine was the expert on managing money. She'd tell the various ways of investing money for the future. Nathan listened intently on how to invest in certificate of deposits and mutual funds and how his money would earn compounded interests. Nathan took Katherine's advice to heart, knowing he was starting out in life and needed every dollar that came along. Zach's stories were lengthy, often ending with a glass of the magic potion from the fermented barrel. Doc always chuckled of Nathan's deliverance from the Newcombs. His glassy eyes always gave him away.

With the end of summer, the bus ride returned Nathan to Connecticut. Clarence was glad having his son back; even more so was Clair. Clair said it was like working in a morgue. Hannah remained being self-centered, spearheading any gayety that surfaced. Clair and Nathan joked at Hannah's expense, even with thoughts of putting a vibrator in her bed just to see if it might brighten her mood.

Clarence traded his Mercury for a sportier Oldsmobile Toronado. It was tan with camel-colored interior and roof, with features of powered windows, seats, and headlights. It was the ideal chick mobile. Fall classes were a continuation of the previous semester. Pegnataro's rehired Nathan for evening shift but could only use him as a bagger. Sometimes he was sent to other departments to help. It really didn't matter what job it was; he was earning a few dollars. As a bagger, Nathan got acquainted with a few other students, making the working hours fly by.

Clarence allowed his son a couple of weekends to New Hampshire visiting Beth and the neighboring folks. She and Ben had moved into the farmhouse. Their lot was located on one of the town's side roads. The road was seldom used and marked as officially closed. Years of adverse weather had eroded the dirt road with a myriad of ruts that ran erratically along their traveled paths. The dirt road was garnished with potholes the size of manhole covers that challenged any vehicle driving on it. Ben and his brothers slowly steered their pickups along the furrowed veins, arriving at the assigned lot. It took weeks to clear the lot of any standing wood. Ben networked with folks in construction to help rid the lot of the many stumps and boulders. The team got it accomplished, with Ben and Beth envisioning themselves living on the property before the winter's snow.

The weeks allowed Ben to have a well drilled and a septic system installed. He had prospects on a house trailer that would be temporary until he could afford a place of his own. Ben hated trailers, but for the next couple of years, it was all he could afford. The only glitch was getting a loan. Ben had overextended his credit through the many vehicles he had driven over the years. He treated vehicles rough, often disabling them sooner than expected. Beth wasn't working, and financing a house trailer was next to impossible.

Ben's parents talked over a financial solution with their son and Beth. They would apply for an equity loan to buy the house trailer. The younger Greysons would have to make the monthly payments without putting the farmhouse into jeopardy. The bank approved the loan, allowing the house trailer to be moved on the freshly prepared lot.

Beth felt uncomfortable about the equity loan, knowing Ben wasn't reliable in making enough money at any one time. She had to come up with another way to obtain the loan without putting herself, Ben, and the Greyson farmhouse in turmoil. Beth's only resort was asking her father for a loan.

Thanksgiving was over the horizon, and Clarence was interested having Ben and Beth visit. They were strapped but needed someone to watch the place while they were gone. The underbelly of the trailer wasn't completely insulated, and both were afraid of the pipes freezing. Beth told her father they wouldn't be able to find anyone to watch the place on short notice. She asked if Nathan could drive up and watch the place. Nathan found it hard to believe, figuring Beth had something in mind she didn't want him to know about. Nathan agreed to do it for his father's sake.

Nathan drove up Thanksgiving eve, having the four-day weekend. It allowed Ben and Beth to do the swap. Beth left her brother the eight-pound turkey to cook if he wanted. Nathan thought preparing it wasn't that much of a challenge, having watched his family cook turkeys over the years.

Ben, Beth, and Angela arrived at the Mix Avenue apartment. Hannah was excited meeting them at the door. Their presence couldn't have brightened Clarence and Hannah's holiday any better. Clarence held his granddaughter every chance he could, making Angela the center of attention.

Hannah enjoyed having her granddaughter to talk to. She invited Stephanie down from her apartment to join in on the girls' chitchat. Ben felt out of his element being cooped up in the small apartment. He found comfort talking to Clarence about his new place and all the plans that went with it. Beth could hear the conversations between the two men as it laid the groundwork for what she was about to ask her father.

Clair stopped by performing her nursing duties. She had met Beth before and was introduced to Ben. Ben was surprised and a little envious at seeing Clair. Even as a middle-aged woman, she had kept her figure and her platinum-blond hair neatly styled. Ben thought Clarence was lucky in finding her.

Beth peeked her head into her father's bedroom. "Hi, Dad, thought I'd sit and talk with you for a while."

"Come in. Have a seat. Angela is quite a handful," Clarence stated with a smile.

"That she is. She's at the stage of noticing everything around her. Listen, Dad. I wanted to talk to you about something, just between you and me," Beth said, downplaying her tone.

"Sounds serous. What is it?" asked Clarence.

"Well, it's about the house trailer. Ben and I weren't able to get a loan because we weren't making enough money. We've spent all we could just getting the land cleared and prepping for the well and septic. His parents took an equity loan on their farmhouse to help us out buying the house trailer. Dad, they've gone out of their way giving us the land as a wedding gift, and they already have a houseful to feed, never mind the bills that come with it. I don't feel right taking their equity loan knowing what they've done so far."

Clarence concentrated on what his daughter was about to ask him.

She continued, "I was wondering if you could help and lend us the money for the house trailer. With Ben's work schedule, I know we can eventually pay you back."

Clarence looked at Beth, wondering how serious she really was or if she was using him. "How much was the house trailer?"

"Its three thousand dollars," replied Beth, looking a little dismayed.

"Three thousand dollars! That's a lot of money," Clarence said, sounding doubtful.

The room went silence for a moment. Beth stared at her father, wondering if he would give her the money. Clarence thought just how much he needed to contribute to his daughter's happiness. He thought over how much the Greyson family had helped Ben and Beth. First was with the land, the clearing, and the installation of the well and septic system. And now they had to support Angela and any other children that would soon come along.

Clarence reluctantly came to a decision. "Beth, I'm not sure what to say, but I'll lend you and Ben the money. Just make sure you reimburse me when you can afford it, okay?"

Beth began to smile. "Thanks, Dad. You don't know how much this will help. You won't regret it."

"I'll tell your grandmother to make out a check before you leave. Now let's see what's on the TV," said Clarence, trying to change the subject.

Beth spent a few more minutes sitting in the room, watching the drama unfold on the television, before getting up to tend to her daughter.

Nathan was enjoying his stay at the trailer. He washed the turkey, placing pads of butter under the skin. He capped the bird with a sheet of aluminum foil before placing it into the oven. Nathan took care basting the browning bird during the couple of hours of baking. He boiled a couple potatoes, making mashed potatoes. He looked at the bird, deciding it was well cooked, and watched it collapse once out of the pan. Nathan chuckled over the spineless bird, blaming it on over basting. Not letting the juices go to waste, he made a mixture of flour and milk, then spooned it into the turkey broth, making enough gravy for a couple of meals.

A few neighbors stopped by saying hello, having nothing to do over the holiday. Nathan smiled and welcomed them in sharing a holiday brew. He realized any one of them could have watched the place. Early Saturday afternoon, the young Greyson family returned home from their Thanksgiving holiday. Nathan gave Beth the itinerary of what he did while they were gone. He packed his things and made the drive back to Connecticut.

Nathan continued writing his grandparents and Flora. They sent letters of support, hoping he wouldn't forget them. A letter from Sarah left Nathan wondering about her health. She wrote about spending a few days in the hospital with a follow-up in a nursing home. He was hoping the cancer hadn't reoccurred. Nathan planned a trip to visit them, but school and work were a priority.

Nathan struggled doing the homework in the basement. It was getting stressful on Hannah as she had to walk down and get him whenever he had a telephone call. Clarence reminded her it wouldn't be such a struggle if she only let Nathan do his schoolwork in the kitchen.

RICHARD'S BLOCK

The Middleton house ran like any other suburban home. Rachael and Tracy continued their predawn drive to Clarostat, passing Tom off to one babysitter or another. The kids were on their own eating breakfast, getting dressed, and catching the Farmington school bus. Red had given up his hold on South Boston and decided to move to New Hampshire. Rachael allowed him to stay at the house until he got settled. Red did what he could to help the family and noticed Tracy's drinking was taking its toll. It formulated his imagination to control his cognizant thinking.

Red heard and looked forward to seeing Nathan with his upcoming graduation. It seemed he became part of the family one day and gone the next.

Red drove about Rochester, answering want ads. Nothing stood out, and he made his way back to Middleton. He'd pass Farmington's favored pub a few times and decided to stop for a quick beer. Red began talking with the barkeep and discovered the building rented rooms that suited his wallet. He rented a room and was hired as a second-shift barkeep. It amazed him that, in a matter of moments, his life changed to living and working under the same roof. Patrons looked forward to having a brew and sharing their stories with the new barkeep. Red humored the beer drinkers by reciprocating with tales of his worldly adventures.

The Richard's Block was the center of Farmington and had a beehive of boarding rooms. Red enjoyed the down-to-earth folks that occupied the barstools. They weren't that much different from South Boston's blue-collar workers residing around East Second Street.

Only a few barstool stories became dramatic with every sip. And with every sip, the drama became more intense. Red was used to these intensities and used his pleasant persona in putting a damper on the heated debates.

Rachael and Tracy picked up Tom from the babysitters and often stopped at the Richard's Block. They checked on Red, seeing how he was progressing. His reviews entertained them, spawning an idea in Tracy's head about getting involved with the bar. Tracy thought it might be worthwhile investigating instead of traveling to Dover every day. Rachael had her doubts but would give the idea some serious thought. She was mainly concerned about Tracy's thirst for alcohol.

The couple arrived home. Kenneth and Laura had everyone fed and the aftermath cleaned. They did the routine the older two had done many years before. Kenneth used his talents in keeping the landscape around the house trimmed and mowed. He found others in the neighborhood wanting their lawns mowed and their bushes trimmed. There were offers Kenneth couldn't resist, and solicited himself trying to make some extra money.

The sun slowly faded behind the trees when Kenneth wheeled the lawn mower into the garage. Tracy stood in the corner, having a few sips from his hidden whiskey bottle. He approached Kenneth, pinning him against the wall. Tracy looked eye to eye into the young lad, placing his hand into Kenneth's crotch, and started rubbing his genitals.

"You like this? You like it when I do this to you? You want it, don't you?"

Kenneth had all he could do, smelling Tracy's toxic breath. He pushed Tracy back, making a straight line into the house. Tracy just smirked and staggered behind.

Laura cooked, did dishes, and tended to the younger ones. For the most part, they were content watching television. Laura had blossomed into a flirtatious teenager. Her blond hair had exceeded her shoulders. Her fair skin and shapely figure caught the eyes of many of her contemporaries. She was still the object of Tracy's dark room advances.

The babysitters changed from week to week, which varied their route going to and from work. Rachael and Tracy's frequent stops at the Richard's Block laid the foundation for subsequent sips from the hidden liquor bottle. It took a couple of beers or slugs of whiskey to trigger Tracy's lustful mind.

Tracy's alcoholism usually kicked in right after supper. He noticed the girls were growing and could have his pick of any of them. Laura had been an object of his lust over the past years. Gretchen was developing into a fine young girl and knew of her sister's escapades with Tracy. Gretchen ignored Tracy's advances and found refuge among her siblings. Next in line was Abigail, who was more receptive like her older sister Laura.

The evening at the Middleton house was quiet. Rachael lay on the couch, having Kenneth rub her feet and ankles from the poor circulation. The group sat around watching television in the cloak of darkness. Kenneth slipped out and went to bed while his mother dozed off. He was followed by the younger ones crawling into their beds. Tracy had consumed a couple of beers, spawning a moment. His eyes looked upon Laura, and he motioned for her into an empty room. The thrusting sounds woke Rachael and caught them in the act.

Rachael went into a rage, kicking Tracy in the groin over and over. His wailings woke the rest of the household. She'd have him arrested if it wasn't that she'd be implicated. Rachael forced him into getting psychiatric treatment for his sexual disorder.

Rachael thought long and hard about the Richard's Block. She wondered if it might work in her favor. She thought of the benefits of being in the vicinity of her home and children. There would be Red to help manage the place and keep watch over Tracy. Saturday morning, Rachael stopped at the Farmington bar while on her way grocery shopping. Red was surprised seeing her walk through the door.

"Hi, Rachael, what's up?"

"Thought, if you had a minute, I'd like to talk to you about the bar," replied Rachael.

"What do you want to know that you didn't know already?" asked Red.

Racheal continued, "Remember when we talked about getting involved with the bar a few weeks ago?"

"Yes. What about it? You serious?" inquired Red.

"I might. How difficult is it? I mean, what would I have to do to operate it? What if you stayed to help me keep it going?" asked Rachael, sounding a bit curious.

"Well, it's what you make of it. It can be as difficult or as easy as you want. Are you interested in selling just drinks and chips, or are you including a kitchen menu? I can help you run the bar if you want to do the kitchen. Mark handles the books and arranges the deliveries. You already know he does an open kitchen early in the evenings for burgers and fries. So if you want to continue that, it's your option," explained Red.

"I need to think about Tracy. I don't want him behind the bar. I need to think about what to do about him," remarked Rachael.

"You can use him in the kitchen and busing tables. I can watch him out in the bar area and keep him away from the drinks," replied Red.

"Where's Mark? I want to talk to him about the books and a few other things," inquired Rachael.

"He's in the kitchen. Go ahead. He'll be glad to see you. Catch you later. Good luck." Red smiled.

Red turned to a waiting customer while Rachael went through the swinging doors to the kitchen. She talked to the aged man sitting at the kitchen counter. Mark was the owner and felt it was time to retire and enjoy life. Hearing Rachael's interest brought a smile to his face. She sat down and got a snapshot of the operating procedures. Rachael decided it wasn't anything she couldn't handle. She gave it a day or two before making her final decision. The deal was made, and the family's life changed once again.

Red agreed to manage the operations. He was already accustomed to those notables that frequented the place. He knew the credible ones who paid their tab from those looking for a free beer. Rachael took advantage of exploring the boarding rooms and the rest of the building. Tracy tried keeping his sober streak and his doctor's appointments. He helped with busing the tables, often taking a seat and being the socialite. When Rachael wasn't looking, Tracy sneaked in the back room grabbing a few beers for his friends while enjoying the laughter with their empty pockets.

At the bar sat a regular who was curious about Tracy. His name was Toby Sullivan. He was a husky man whose determined eyes and stubbed beard intimidated anyone in close proximity. He arrived daily taking his usual barstool that conformed to his weight. He had come to know the barkeep and was carefully observing the new owner. Toby knew how to handle himself and to manipulate others. He watched Tracy and saw how vulnerable he was. Toby encountered him with softened eyebrows and a welcoming smile.

Tom needed babysitting while his parents operated the bar. The babysitter lived close by should an emergency arise. It was late when Rachael and Tracy arrived home. Everyone was in bed and asleep. Rachael let the dog out for a bathroom run before turning the lights off for the night.

It had been a while since Rachael saw Karen Adams, and it would be a while longer before they would meet again. Rachael kept up the correspondence between them. In one letter, Rachael learned Karen had married the man of her dreams and would be moving to New Mexico. Rachael was elated yet disappointed of the distance that was occurring between them. Rachael needed help with the household while she got a foothold on the block. She called her mother, and Sarah was on her way.

Sarah arrived, taking control of the house. She decided to spend a week relieving the babysitter from watching Tom. Sarah noticed how much was needed to be done around the house. She helped with the usual laundry, mended clothes, and tackled the ironing. Kenneth and Laura could only do so much with their daily routines. Rachael realized maintaining the bar and the household was wearing her down. She saw an opportunity to buy the block despite its deteriorating condition.

Rachael already visualized sectioning off a portion of the building for her family's living quarters. There'd still be enough available rooms left for renting. It seemed to make sense to run a business and live under the same roof. Rachael's presence in the bar allowed her to network with a lot of the townspeople. They came from all walks of life, and Rachael took advantage of their backgrounds. The sale was approved, with the Bookers taking ownership of Richard's Block.

The family spent their last holiday season in the Middleton home and made the transition into the family living quarters. It was the early months of 1969 when they officially moved, putting the Middleton home up for sale.

It seemed Rachael had made the idyllic decision. She underestimated Tracy's erratic behavior. Tracy drank more, making insinuations toward Red over his managing the bar. Tracy's insults were spun by Toby during his friendly interventions. He knew Tracy's weaknesses and stroked his brain with accusations, knowing Tracy would take them seriously.

Red was popular, and people enjoyed sharing stories with him. Tracy's jealousy caused him to verbally abuse Red with accusations of scalping the profits from the business. Rachael managed the finances and couldn't see what Tracy was arguing over. The more Rachael tried to quiet Tracy, the more belligerent he became.

The bar conflicts left the kids fending for themselves. They no longer had a spacious backyard to play. The Farmington streets became their playground. Kenneth realized he had to step up and become the caretaker for his siblings. Laura found being outside sparked the interests of many of the guys in the area that enraged Rachael. She noticed Laura was gaining weight and losing her waistline.

Rachael made a doctor's appointment to have her daughter examined. She conned Laura into the car for a shopping trip. The car stopped at the medical office parking lot. Laura got out, knowing her mother had suspected her secret. Rachael was overbearing throughout the examination. The doctor confirmed Laura's pregnancy, probably three months along. It put Rachael into a self-contained rage. She knew Laura couldn't bring it to term, especially at her young age and it being Tracy's. Before leaving, Rachael wanted an abortion set up for her daughter. The doctor would get in touch with Rachael in another week for the procedure.

The drive back to the block left little words. Laura continued her outside love interests. It put Rachael on edge, realizing she couldn't get through to her daughter. The two became outspoken with daily confrontations. Rachael's internal rage took over, deciding to curtail those love interests by lopping off Laura's golden locks.

Kenneth was upset over the verbal abuses his mother was getting from Tracy. He stepped in and confronted Tracy, hoping to protect his mother from the attacks. Having made his stance, Kenneth returned to the living quarters, making sure the kids were fed and settled for the evening. Rachael decided she couldn't tolerate Tracy's attitude much longer. Alcoholism had taken over, with the therapy sessions ending long ago.

Rachael looked long and hard into the mirror. She saw a woman aging before her time. The strains of gray started to highlight her thick brown head of hair. Her face sported a few wrinkles but not enough to bother. Rachael developed a few female allies in Farmington. One of them would gladly give Rachael a perm with a blond tint to cover the gray. Others came to her aid, involving themselves with her kids.

Kenneth helped in the kitchen when time allowed. He often peered into the bar looking at the congestion of drinking mugs and smoke-filled laughter. He watched Tracy and a few of his so-called buddies, especially Toby Sullivan. He saw how protective he was of Tracy. All Toby had to do was give Tracy a few laughs and a friendly arm about his shoulders, and Tracy felt secure. It wasn't long before Toby made his way to other assets of the bar.

Rachael sent Kenneth to the cellar to get a case of beer for Red. Upon reaching the bottom step, Kenneth encountered Toby putting a case outside the back door with a beer in his hand. Kenneth called him out. Toby turned, closing the door after completing his mission. He rushed up to Kenneth, knocking him against the wall.

"You mention one word of this, and it will be your last. You hear me, boy?" Toby whispered sternly, holding Kenneth by the neck.

Kenneth became numb, his nerves shaken. All he could hear was his heart pounding in his throat. The smell of Toby's breath was a reminder of a previous time of being pinned.

Kenneth managed to squeak out, "I hear you."

Toby raised his fist, making Kenneth squirm into a fetal position. Toby relaxed his fisted arm and gave Kenneth another fierce warning. Kenneth stood watching the massive hulk go out the back door along with the lifted case.

Kenneth was stressed by the confrontations with Tracy and his barroom associates. Rachael decided to send him to visit his grandparents for a couple of weeks. She was determined not to see her investment or her family fall to ruins. Tracy's tantrums became less violent as time went. He accepted Rachael putting him off as she sported a new look. She became more personable and involved herself with her patrons.

One patron caught Rachael's eyes. His name was Ron Fillbright. He was an entrepreneur who lived in Rochester and had friends in Farmington. Before heading home, he stopped in the town's watering hole for a beer. Rachael and Ron became friendly, sharing ideas and past experiences. Ron had similar interests of operating a hotel with a lobby bar. The more visits Ron made, the more familiar he became with Rachael.

She looked at Tracy and saw his burdensome relationship with the glasses of whiskey and bottles of beer. He indulged in them more than his family. Rachael's inner thoughts dictated she didn't have to stay with Tracy; after all, she wasn't married to him. The only link they had were the kids. She could release him and let him go back to Gloria. Rachael gave a hard look at Tracy and the same to Ron. Rachael had reached rock bottom and decided Ron might be the answer to her salvation. She encouraged Ron's involvement in her life. Tracy became bitter, deciding to resurrect telephone calls to his estranged wife.

Fall was on the horizon, and so was Red. He had taken enough of Tracy's accusations and gave his notice on moving. Red met a guy who ran a bar in Rochester. He sought the opportunity to resettle, alleviating himself from all the toxic drama.

Bartending suited Red for a while. He wanted more out of life yet knew the ultimate family life he dreamed about was beyond reach. He had lost contact with his son and former wife. Through meeting new professionals, Red moved to Dover, operating a sanitation route. He inspired his subordinates with pride and professionalism by doing the best job possible. Red's enthusiasm was only a facade for the deep emptiness he felt inside. He felt isolated, falling into periods of deep depression with each passing week. One evening, he stared out the window watching the mild traffic drive by accompanied with a few people strolling up and down the sidewalks. Red wondered how many thought their lives were mundane and systematic and felt the way he did. He stared out the window for a while longer. Before going to bed, he went into the bathroom. Red looked long and hard into the medicine cabinet mirror, then slipped under the bedcovers, never to wake up.

Tracy remained belligerent, becoming drunk before evening. He needed attention and flaunted his money to any of his fly-by-night friends. The bar was flooded with beer mugs tapping to the beat of the overwhelming jukebox. Tracy used the opportunity to stagger up the stairs with a lustful grin for one of the girls.

It was a long day for Kenneth. He was tired and climbed the stairs heading for his room. He passed his parents' room and heard a commotion going on. He carefully cracked the door open and saw Abigail sprawled out on the bed sparsely dressed. He caught Tracy grabbing his pants and running into the closet. Kenneth raced in grabbing his sister and her clothes, placing Abigail in another room for her safety. The family that once lived by founded ethics had decayed into an aura of intoxication and deceit.

A NEW DECADE

Three-dimensional designs became more intricate in the creation of liquor boxes, snack packages, vacation pamphlets, raised billboards, and magazine ads, along with fifteen-second television ads. Watercolor classes turned into oil paintings. Still life graduated from a few objects to drawing human models. Basic lettering and design became creative photography as one would learn color separations in producing billboards. Nathan sat looking at his sketches for a design project. He reflected how far he had come from those earlier years of shadow boxes.

The previous decade brought the era of the Beatles, long hair, tie dyes, bell-bottoms, platform shoes, and music far from the normal rock and roll. By the end of the 1960s, the conservative look was no longer the norm. Protesting became fashionable, including the war in Vietnam. The mottos were "Give peace a chance" and "Flower power."

Nathan's mind was being filled with ultimatums and possibilities. A classmate, Phyllis Brown, got into a conversation of disabled veterans and how they could make differences in their lives. Nathan entered the conversation about his father's situation and how he just accepted life. It was common knowledge Nathan went home for lunch. Phyllis suggested inviting her to lunch so she would have an opportunity to express her views to his father.

Clair liked the idea of having Nathan's friend over for lunch. Phyllis was a love child, and her clothes and demeanor reflected that. Her appearance was a little shocking to the lunch crew. Still they were interested in what Phyllis had to say. She was polite and cordial and promoted her ideology of how people could improve their lives no matter what their situation. She presented her point without being harsh and was taken with a grain of salt. Nathan couldn't get over what he just witnessed and appreciated Phyllis saying what she did.

Spring came when Clarence wanted to visit the VA hospital. It was a breakthrough for him, and Nathan couldn't help wonder if the words from Phyllis impacted his father. It surprised Nathan and Clair, who decided in making a trip on a Saturday morning. A special ramp was constructed for wheeling Clarence down the front steps and onto the walkway. Nathan operated the car lift, transferring his father onto the front seat. It was the first time in years Clarence had ridden in a vehicle. It took a little over a half hour driving to the East Haven VA hospital. Nathan wheeled his father into the elevator, stopping at the sixth floor where the disabled inhabitants lived.

It took a while for Clarence to catch his bearings. He wheeled around trying to recognize anyone from those bygone years. There were too many new faces. One veteran lay strapped on a wooden slab, disabled from the neck down. He was in the middle of doing a painting while holding a brush between his teeth. The painting showed unique creativity. To his side was an attached tray with an extended buzzer for getting the attention of any nurse. Clair and Nathan were awestruck and amazed of the courage and determination of these veterans. Nathan was overwhelmed seeing the many extreme disabilities. He couldn't get over how they tried for a better quality of life.

Clair looked at Clarence's face, then at Nathan. She felt gratified knowing the visit was worth the effort. There were only a few faces Clarence recognized and could reacquaint himself with. The visit lasted a few hours when Nathan drove his father home and put him to bed. Hannah was glad to see her son get out for a change. It was a long but worthwhile day. Nathan drove Clair home, reflecting on those extraordinary veterans.

Nathan planned on working for the Goodalls during the summer months. Clair tried talking him out of it as she considered Nathan the only ray of sunshine in the place. Beth called with the news of their mother's cancer and that she was undergoing treatment.

The news didn't bother Nathan but gave him more incentive to head north. School ended, and within a week, Nathan was riding the bus to New Hampshire. Doc stood waiting for him at Dot's Lunch.

He brought his portfolio with some of his artwork. The Goodalls gave him his own room instead of doubling up with their son. The routine of the barn chores and landscaping rebounded without missing a beat. The new barn was well used with every stall filled. It hadn't a foundation, so cleaning stalls involved the use of the John Deere and the spreader. It was a change from the usual wheelbarrow. Nathan drove the tractor, spreading the manure onto the neighboring fields. Alice knew of Rachael's condition and gave Nathan extra time for himself. She continued the training for the upcoming competitions throughout New England.

For one show, Alice decided taking her kids. Doc had a few pregnancies that were about to be delivered, leaving him and Nathan watching the farm. The first night, the phone rang, and Nathan answered. Tracy was on the line wanting an update on his wife's status. He didn't recognize Nathan's voice. Doc gave the man the prognosis. After the call, Doc sat Nathan down, telling him that his mother was dying of cervical cancer. Nathan put Doc's mind to rest, saying Beth had told him weeks earlier.

The second night, the two walked down to see Zachary. He was surprised and enthused seeing Doc and Nathan standing at his door. Zach didn't waste a moment inviting them in while Katherine sat comfortably watching her favorite television show. Zach knew not to disturb his wife and led the visitors down into the dark abyss. Zach turned on each light fixture along the earthen cellar, where shared stories could be told and the cider barrel listened.

The glasses were filled from the wooden spigot while the former embalmer started telling tales of past days in preparing the departed. His voice accentuated everything, from washing the body, draining the blood, and injecting the embalming fluid to the cosmetic secrets on making the corpse look presentable. Doc interjected how his surgical blade repaired the wounded bodies during the war in the South Pacific. The tales were mouthed from one to another although the cider had taken control, overlapping their spoken lines. Nathan took sip after sip, listening and watching these two veterans enjoy their never-ending life adventures. A few hours had passed when the cider glasses clashed when placed back onto the shelf. Doc and Nathan felt no pain as they stumbled the better part of the evening back to the estate now silhouetted by the nighttime sky.

June was ending when Beth called asking if Nathan wanted to visit their mother at the Frisbee Hospital. Nathan decided it was time, knowing she no longer posed a threat. Alice had no objections, telling him not to rush. Beth picked Nathan up along with the portfolio. It was the initial greeting that would be the hardest even though that wasn't difficult.

The sister and brother walked into the hospital room where their mother sat in her bed. The room was a double occupancy with the curtain divider. Rachael had deteriorated, appearing thin and frail. She welcomed her son with a hug, letting him know there were no hard feelings. She asked about school and how he was getting along. Nathan responded to the frail figure that he enjoyed school and a little of his social life.

His gut wanted to belittle her on being a self-centered and abusive bitch. He desperately wanted her to know how she robbed him of his childhood—not allowing friends, denying him of his high school memories, and forcing all those household responsibilities. But her cancerous state wouldn't let him. Instead Nathan spoke of how much he appreciated her raising him. In a way, those years of abuse molded Nathan into being a stronger and outgoing person. It was a far cry from those formative years of being shy and reserved. Nathan had developed the fortitude to meet and handle any adversities life passed his way.

He knew she wanted to know more about his present life but decided to break into the portfolio. Nathan showed his mother the many pieces of acrylic and watercolor paintings, giving the inspiration on each one. Even a nurse popped in and fell in love with one of the acrylics and bought it on the spot. She didn't have any money on her. Nathan asked if she knew Dr. Goodall. She nodded and was told to give the money to him. Beth and Nathan spent an hour before leaving. One last request Rachael made of Nathan was to get in touch with Aunt Ethel. Beth was amazed how her brother handled the visit. She realized it took a lot of guts to do what he just did. In a few days, they made another visit. This time, it was in Manchester.

Rachael's cancer had gotten worse with her days numbered. Beth and Nathan entered her room, finding Tracy standing on the opposite side of the bed. They gave their mother a kiss on the cheek, and Nathan took a seat beside the bed. Rachael slowly reached for her son's hand and held it for the duration. She wasn't vocal and was more in an unconscious state with the oxygen tubes connected to her nose. Tracy looked at the two, whom he was well familiar, saying his hellos. Neither of them gave him the time of day.

When Rachael regained some resemblance of consciousness, Nathan talked about his job at the supermarket and how he was looking forward to starting school. Beth couldn't take looking at her mother or staying another moment with Tracy in the room. She wanted to leave, not knowing when they'd make the next visit. Beth thought about one in another week—a visit fate wouldn't deliver.

It was an early July morning. Alice and Doc were already up. Nathan had just finished washing in the upstairs bath. He was making his way down the stairs when a knock came at the door. Nathan's descend came to a halt. Alice answered with Mable Greyson at the door. She brought the news that Rachael had passed, offering any help. Alice accepted her willingness to help and would get with her later in the morning. First Alice wanted to break the news to Nathan.

Nathan continued descending when Alice came around the corner telling of his mother's passing. He kept in control, hearing the news for a second time. She told him to take whatever time he wanted to help his family. Nathan decided on keeping his mind occupied and headed for the barn.

The wheels were already in motion between Alice and Mable. Tracy was in no condition, nor was he concerned about, getting the kids prepared for the funeral. Beth knew all the girls needed clothes for the funeral.

Sarah had placed herself and Milton in a nursing home, feeling her health was on a downturn. The home got the news, notifying a local minister to tell the aged couple of their loss. Alice walked to the barn telling Nathan his grandparents were on their way and would be staying with them. After supper, the knock on the door met with Doris Rines. She had driven up with Milton and Sarah. Alice welcomed and allowed them to get settled. She let the grandparents have her bedroom downstairs as it was accessible to the adjoining bathroom. Doc and Alice took their old bedroom upstairs.

Doris stayed at the Greyson farmhouse since they had a spare bed. The morning light, Alice grabbed Nathan and drove to the farmhouse where she, Mable, and Beth discussed the children's needs firsthand. Mable and Beth would shop, getting the girls new dresses with Alice contributing the funds for their purchases. It was apparent neither of the two women had any money.

The funeral took place after a two-day wake at Peaslee's. Alice kept the grandparents company while Nathan did the barn. By evening, Alice let him use her vehicle to drive his grandmother to the funeral home to view her only child. Sarah asked Nathan if he had a camera and to bring it. They drove down, finding they were the only ones there. Peaslee led them into the parlor and allowed their private moment with their loved one. Sarah bent over and kissed her daughter.

Sarah stood staring at her beloved Rachael. "Did you know she was dying?"

"Not until recently. Beth was the one who told me," responded Nathan.

"I wished somebody told me. I wished I could have spent time with her before she died," whimpered the aged woman. "Did you bring your camera?"

"Yes, Gram, I have it here," Nathan replied, showing it to his grandmother.

"I want you to take a picture of her for me," requested his teary-eyed grandmother.

Nathan stood at the foot of the coffin and took a couple of shots of his deceased mother.

They stood together side by side, looking over the open casket. Rachael looked at rest, laid out with her dyed hair neatly coiffured. The makeup slightly contoured her face as she wore her gold-and-white printed dress. She wore a gold cornucopia watch around her neck that accented the outfit.

Sarah looked at her daughter's folded hands, noticing the wedding ring. "You know, that ring was your grandfather's."

Nathan looked at the ring as if to notice it for the first time, then turned toward his grandmother. "It's Gramp's ring?"

"I told her, if she was going to live as a married couple, she should give the appearance as a married woman. Your mother didn't want to wear the band your father gave her, so your grandfather insisted she wear his."

Nathan was overwhelmed of what he just heard. He was going to ask if she wanted it back but thought otherwise. He knew his grandfather would've wanted a piece of him buried with his one and only daughter. Fifteen minutes passed before the vehicle made its way back to the ridge.

The funeral day arrived with Doris driving the grandparents. Nathan traveled with Alice, ensuring everyone had coordinated their rides. The parlor was filled with the Greyson family, Tracy, and the girls, along with a few family friends. Among the group was Tracy's estranged wife, Gloria, and her two sons. They surprised everyone with their presence. A few minds drew wild conclusions as to why they were there. Tracy called Gloria about Rachael's death. She didn't have any remorse for Rachael and wanted to drive up and witness the service firsthand. She wanted to see the woman who had taken her husband all these years. Gloria got her two sons together, making the trip to New Hampshire. Tracy met them and arranged for their stay at the block.

The service was short. The caravan of people filed out, lining their vehicles. Milton made no bones that he wanted to kiss his one and only daughter goodbye. As the funeral room emptied, there was a realization there wasn't any pallbearers. The Greyson boys volunteered, carrying the gray-drabbed coffin into the hearse. The long convoy of lighted vehicles slowly made their way to the Pine Grove gravesite. Nathan walked over, meeting the pastor and Mr. Peaslee. He introduced himself as Nathan Anderson, Rachael's oldest son.

It caught them by surprise. They naturally thought that every child Tracy listed was a Booker.

Nathan's grandparents were still in a state of shock. Sarah tried hard to control her emotions. Milton wept over the stark realization his daughter was dead. The following morning, Doris arrived, collecting the elderly couple for the long trip back to Plymouth. Sarah expressed her eternal thanks to both Doc and Alice for their hospitality, noting how rare it was for anyone to open their home to total strangers. Nathan was proud of the moment and could only echo his grandmother's words.

It was time to get back to some resemblance of normalcy. Doc was impressed with Nathan's grandparents, especially the stories Milton told about his early farming days. One involved a group of farmers taking their horse and wagons to the seashore collecting seaweed to use as fertilizer on the gardens. Most didn't have or couldn't get the needed cow or horse manure.

Nathan reflected on how relieved he felt having the funeral over with. The whole orchestration, procedure, and aftermath had come and gone. He didn't regret his mother dying. The years growing up, Nathan only knew her as Mom who dominated as a strict disciplinarian. There were only a few blips he could remember her with any affection. Many of the memories were of the abuse.

It dawned on him how she never shared how or where she grew up, where she went to school, how she met his father, when they got married, and what led to their divorce. Most of which, Nathan learned through stories from either his grandmother or Flora. Over time, Ethel added a few more tidbits. After some afterthought, he realized how little he knew of the buried woman called Mom.

Nathan was fortunate having to know his father. He was a quadriplegic and couldn't perform like other fathers. Yet he was alive and didn't get overwrought with emotion. Having multiple sclerosis not only made Clarence physically disabled but sometimes clouded his thinking.

Nathan sat reevaluating himself. His paternal ancestry was of German heritage, contributing for his hardworking and determined demeanor. His maternal grandparents were Anglo-Saxon, teaching him to be humble and proud and to treat people fairly. Flora taught him to plan and be financially secure with a retirement plan, words Nathan would remember.

He reminisced about Karen Adams and why she wasn't at the funeral. He talked to Beth about it. She made him aware Karen was married and living in New Mexico. It had been years since he last remembered her. Nathan wanted to write, telling her about his mother's death. Beth gave her brother the address. He wrote and received no response. Nathan saw less of Beth in the following weeks. She was involved in getting guardianship over the younger siblings. They had to be taken from Tracy before school started. All Beth could think about was the abuse Tracy might be inflicting on them.

Alice came and went to the horse shows. A few of the neighbors stopped by for a cocktail or two. Nathan entertained the kids in the backyard pool, followed with some roadside walks. Doc busily worked in his vegetable garden. It was his second year trying to grow one. It was his pride and joy having Nathan help with the weeding. The summer routine went on, including visits to the cider barrel that accompanied Zach's repetitive stories of his growing-up years.

August started with little dilemma. The first week ended with Mable and Nelson Greyson knocking at the Goodalls' door. They were experiencing more financial hardships. Over the years, they had taken out second and third refinancing loans to make ends meet. The Greysons needed money to pay some of their immense bank debt. They offered their upper field to Alice and Doc. It was prime pastureland ideal for haying. The Greysons felt selling the land to the Goodalls would allow the land to remain in its present state. It wasn't the first time the Greysons sold property to keep their household together. Nathan felt pity on seeing large farmlands reduced to small parcels to financially secure the raising of large families.

The time came to return to Connecticut and focus on getting back to school. Alice settled with Nathan, but he insisted she keep his earnings from July. He wanted to reimburse her for the money spent on the clothes for his younger sisters. Without them, they wouldn't have anything presentable for their mother's funeral. She appreciated the gesture and assured Nathan their door was always open and to stop by when he could.

Nathan rode the long bus ride back, reflecting on what he was going to do with his life. He was halfway through school, and the Vietnam War was still in full force. President Nixon wasn't making any progress in ending it. Somehow Nathan felt alienated from all fronts. He didn't belong in New Durham, nor could he see himself hanging around New Haven. For now, Nathan concentrated on school.

Beth petitioned the court and became her siblings' legal guardian. They were divided into various foster homes. Beth took Rebecca and Gretchen. Mable took Laura and Tom, and the Tibbitts family took Abigail. Kenneth stayed with close friends in Farmington.

Ben and Beth's house trailer became overcrowded. Adding two teenage girls brought more confrontations. The dramas between Beth and the girls headlined the daily routines. Gretchen and Rebecca looked at their older sister as being ruthless and controlling. Ben saw the drama destroying his household and realized the conflict of interest. He knew to get back any order of stability was to send the two sisters living elsewhere. Gretchen was sent to live with another Greyson brother who had a small family of his own. Rebecca was accepted by the Olson family atop the ridge.

The summer events presented nothing more than chaos. The death of Rachael Anderson and the guardianship of her children sidetracked everyone from enjoying the summer. The saddest event was the celebration of Milton and Sarah's sixtieth wedding anniversary. It was their daughter who kept track of everyone's celebrations. With Rachael gone, the grandparents' milestone went unnoticed by her grandchildren. It was Sarah's church that put together a small celebratory party for them. During the event, Sarah and Milton wept, unable to share this momentous occasion with their beloved Rachael. Nonetheless, nearby relatives and friends made the celebration, giving support and comfort to the enduring couple who withstood so much over their sixty years of marriage.

Nathan found he no longer could have his workshop in the basement. Hannah maintained her stand that his art supplies caused her allergies to erupt. Nathan found himself in a position he needed help. He called around finding some classmates willing to let him do his projects. Nathan knew, if he was to succeed, he had to move from his father's place.

Students were always looking for new roommates. The combination of graduating, changing schools, or just moving out of the area led to a few vacancies. Nathan was introduced to three advertising majors looking for a fourth roommate. The apartment was in West Haven. It had three bedrooms with a possibility of a fourth. It provided a large living room, dining room, kitchen, and a full bath. Behind the living room was an enclosed porch that could easily be transformed into a bedroom. The space was offered to Nathan. The room was ideal except for the wall-to-wall high windows and no door. Each window had its own shade, which helped, and adding a curtain door would complete the space.

Clarence was between a rock and a hard place. To ease the tension, he allowed his son to move. With Clair's help, Nathan got a monthly allowance from his father. In return, Nathan would have lunch at his father's. It assured Nathan having one good meal and giving Clair and Clarence an update on how he was doing. Clarence allowed his son to use the foldaway bed, which saved a lot of worrying. If Nathan needed any other furnishings, there was always the Salvation Army's secondhand store.

Nathan sat in the first-floor apartment on Central Avenue wondering how he was going to cope through all this. Paier was a twenty-minute drive. He bought an old 1963 Dodge vehicle that needed its leaf springs replaced. It was time to get in touch with Flora about the college fund she had set aside. It was an insurance policy that wouldn't fully mature until Nathan was twenty-one. He scratched his head, thinking that collage usually starts right after high school. The insurance fund amounted to eight hundred dollars, giving Nathan a cushion for emergencies.

It wasn't long before meeting the girls living on the second floor. There were four rooming together with three attending Southern Connecticut. They were friendly and outgoing. Pam and Jane were studying to be social workers, and Susan was studying to be a teacher.

The fourth just needed a place to stay while she worked for a living. Pam, Jane, and Susan were always involved with intense homework consisting of simulated modules of family issues. They kept to themselves and, on occasion, stopped by on weekends for a beer or two.

Nathan became comfortable with his new surroundings. He felt at ease with the freedom of doing what he wanted. He could make calls to his grandparents and Flora. His grandfather's birthday was mid-October, and Nathan decided making a trip to celebrate. It was the year that Flora attempted to live at the cottage year-round. Before making the trip, the muffler blew a hole, announcing Nathan's presence on every road. He had no choice but bear the expense of replacing both the exhaust and the leaf springs.

He called Sarah and Flora of his impending trip out to see them. The drive wasn't as long as Nathan expected. He drove the interstate coastline to Route 44 and into Flora's backyard. He picked her up and continued the drive to his grandparents. Nathan made a pit stop as Flora wanted to get a cake to make the visit more enjoyable.

Sarah looked tired, having gone through a series of emotional stresses. She showed her grandson the newspaper article of their sixtieth wedding anniversary. Nathan stared at the article and felt the despair in the corresponding picture. It showed the distraught faces of his grandparents standing behind the celebratory cake. He handed the article back to his grandmother, who, in turn, placed it back into her album. Nathan felt even more gratified about the visit, having spent a good part of the afternoon with his grandparents. It was time to leave, with Nathan kissing both grandparents on their cheeks and wishing them well. He drove Flora home, stopping at a local supermarket, allowing his grandaunt to load up on groceries. By nightfall, Nathan was back at Central Avenue.

Being around his newfound peers made Nathan enjoy and experience life. They possessed different political and social views, changing Nathan's outlook on life. They lifted each other's spirits with weekend beer parties and sometimes a few during the week.

Halloween arrived. It was the first time in years Nathan saw trick-or-treaters come to the door. It brought back memories of bygone years. Some students celebrated by painting Halloween decorations on their faces and wearing them to class.

Nathan made the effort to stay in Connecticut during the Thanksgiving and Christmas season. He made it over to decorate his father's Christmas tree, allowing the spirit to flow throughout his place. There were enough weekends for heading north. Nathan decided his father needed someone to celebrate the holidays. New Year's was a time Nathan wanted to celebrate with his friends on Central Avenue. The celebrated glasses were shared in every hand. Nathan's glass was filled with never-ending boilermakers, making the Times Square ball fall into a haze.

CLOSING THE DOOR

There was a calmness to the winter months on Central Avenue. The avenue's aura welcomed sidewalk strollers captivated by the snowy landscape. Around the corner was the large park lined with nineteenth-century lighting along its walkways. A rippling stream flowed alongside its beaten path, making the picturesque garden resemble paintings that hung on many hallway walls. A stone arch bridge adorned with cascading ivy stood over the flowing waters while philosophical poets mumbled their never-ending sonnets. The park attracted many, who sauntered the winding trails with their creative minds. Nathan walked the stately landscape, having an appreciation of its natural wonder. It was his last year, and he was pondering about his future. He thought of where he might be after school ended. It was something Nathan contemplated repeatedly in his mind.

The classes became more intense; the projects, more defined. It was exhausting to design and put the tedious projects together before collapsing into bed. The occasional nighttime raps at Nathan's window continued from the girls upstairs. They always managed to convince him in going to Dunkin' Donuts for coffee and a roll. Nathan knew that using the front door would alert his roommates. Instead he climbed out his window and joined the mad hatters. Their performance was a comedic skit, as the four crammed into Pam's Volkswagen Beetle with everyone in their PJs. Nathan wore his shorts and a T-shirt. It showed guts walking into a Dunkin' Donuts during the midnight hour. It was a college city, and most vendors were used to the unusual attire entering their doors.

By spring, Nathan made another trip visiting his grandparents. He took his portfolio with a small collection of acrylic paintings and advertising projects. Sarah appeared tired and worn, still able to function about the apartment. The three were having dinner when Sarah suddenly put down her fork and looked straight at her grandson.

"Nathan, there's something that has been gnawing at me. If you don't mind, I want to ask about the abuses Tracy did to you and the girls."

The topic caught the grandson off guard, but he understood why his grandmother wanted to know.

"Gram, Tracy's abuses on us were sexual. He'd drop his pants and have us touch him. He did it to me, Beth, and I know he had Laura do it many times. I got the belt so many times I was afraid to say anything. I don't know if Mom knew or not. I can remember, when we lived in South Boston, she was always trying to get me to be around naked men. When we lived in New Durham, there was a couple of times Tracy put his hands on my crotch and felt me. I tried to avoid him as much as possible. I don't know what he did to the others. I have to tell you I hated those years."

There was a slight pause.

Then Nathan continued, "Looking back, I think it made me stronger. I think it got me where I am today."

Nathan could see his grandmother's face turning pale. She remained silent, carefully taking another forkful of her meal. Nathan could see she was trying to fully understand what she just heard. Milton had the same unresponsive expression, looking somewhat distraught at his wife.

"Well, thank you for telling me. I needed to know." Sarah looked over to her husband and, in a soft tone, said, "Milton, there's nothing we can do now, so just accept it and let it go."

After spending a few moments coming to terms with their disparities, the grandparents turned their interests to Nathan's artistic endeavors. He opened his portfolio, going over each painting and his thoughts behind them. It was early evening when Sarah turned on the television for the news while preparing supper.

The first week in May, Ethel wrote Nathan about his grandmother. Sarah's health had taken a turn for the worse. She was losing her balance and collapsing on the floor. Ethel needed someone to intervene before things got terribly worse. She was elderly herself and in no condition to look after the two of them. If worse came to worst, Ethel could look after her brother for a short while. There wasn't any family member in the area that could or would spare the time to help.

Nathan called Beth, only to satisfy his own instincts about his sister intervening. Her response was just as he suspected. She couldn't help, having issues of her own.

He convinced himself that Ethel had to give some serious thought of who to contact. Nathan knew he had to be the one to handle the situation. He accepted the fact he'd be spending most of the summer in Plymouth and responded to Ethel, saying he'd be there just as soon as school was done for the semester.

The news didn't sit well with Nathan's father or Clair. Clarence was especially fond of Milton and was glad his son was going to help. Clair supported Nathan even though she wanted him around for those daily luncheons. Hannah just wished him well and didn't comment either way. Before leaving, Clarence asked his son if he needed any money. Nathan had enough for the time being and appreciated knowing he could count on his father's support.

He drove back to Central Avenue, notifying the guys he'd be gone for a while, leaving them the following month's rent and a few extra for utilities. The girls upstairs were sorry to hear about Nathan's grandparents. Pam wanted the phone number, thinking she and one of the girls might take a trip out to Plymouth just to say hi. He appreciated the thought and gave her the number.

The drive to Plymouth was met with dire situations. Sarah had entered the hospital, leaving Ethel to stay with her brother. Nathan's arrival was a relief as Ethel was getting flustered, not knowing what to do next. He drove his distraught grandaunt back to Manomet. She told how Sarah's health began failing and how grave the whole situation was. The bottom line meant Milton would have to be placed into a nursing home. The sooner, the better, if Nathan was to take care of his grandmother's affairs. Ethel would be around for the summer to give Nathan any help. She already had plans to move to Arizona in the fall to live with her two sons. Nathan was tired from the long day's drive but managed to cook supper for himself and his grandfather.

He tried getting his grandfather to talk about how Sarah fared these past weeks. Milton's stories left Nathan to wonder how serious his grandmother's situation was. The two men turned in for the evening, leaving Milton the bed while Nathan took the cot.

The morning was sunny, and the warmth projected some feeling of promise. Milton got up following his usual routine while his grandson fixed breakfast. Nathan's goal was to visit his grandmother and talk to the doctors. He turned on the television, giving Milton some sort of company. Nathan drove to Plymouth Memorial to see his grandmother's condition firsthand.

He found his grandmother in bed appearing somewhat rested from her ordeal. He took a seat beside her and let her know Gramp was okay and being cared for. Nathan listened to his grandmother. She could only say a few words, but they were enough that Nathan felt comfort in them. It was time to return to the apartment, knowing Sarah had some assurances that her husband and the apartment were being looked after.

Nathan walked to the nurses' station trying to find anyone who could tell him what the real story was on his grandmother's health. He learned the cancer was terminal and was spreading throughout her body. Within days, she was transferred to the Brockton Hospital for the duration.

Brockton had facilities to care for the terminally ill. It was a crushing blow to Nathan. He knew his next step was to break the news to his grandfather and make him realize he had to go into a nursing home. It was the hardest thing Nathan had to do. The thought of going into a nursing home hit Milton like a brick wall. He wanted his grandson to call Beth and see if she would take him. Nathan knew his sister had no place or condition to care for the old man. Nathan sat at the dining table staring at the place mat, thinking how their family had experienced so much over the past years. They had lost their home, mother, and now their grandmother.

He called various nursing homes, looking for vacancies. The Plymouth Nursing Home had a vacancy that would be available the following week. Milton's situation was no stranger from other patients under their care. Nathan's grandfather was losing his self-esteem. The thought of it made him weep, and he wondered why he couldn't live with Beth. There was no choice in the matter. Nathan had to be strong for the both of them. Milton despairingly told his grandson where the landlord lived. It was a few doors up from the main building.

The next morning, Nathan knocked on the door with a gray-headed man answering. Nathan let the gentleman know he was closing the Manter apartment. The landlord indicated the rent was paid until the end of July, so there wasn't any rush. He gave a list of furnishings belonging to the apartment. Nathan left with the instructions to drop off the keys when it was time.

The drive to Brockton was time consuming. The hospital was situated in a wooded section of town. The outside decor presented the illusion of a large millionaire's estate. Nathan followed a nurse to an open ward. Sarah sat in a wheelchair among other elderly women. Her hands held a photograph of the deceased daughter lying in the casket. The picture was the last of what his grandmother remembered of her beloved Rachael.

Sarah looked worn and seemed to fade in and out of reality. She recognized her grandson, giving him a warm smile. Her face no longer presented her well-kept hair or the touch of makeup that made her presentable. Her hair showed flyaway strands reaching out into every direction. Nathan carefully got up and gently combed his hand over her head, making the strays conform to the shape of her head. He noticed a large open sore in the back. It was the cancer that was rapidly devouring her.

Nathan decided to make daily trips to see his grandmother. Ethel called for an update on Sarah. He told her how his grandmother was deteriorating and about the opening at the Plymouth Nursing Home. Ethel was relieved hearing about the opening and could be at peace knowing Milton was going to be cared for. Nathan delayed any housecleaning until his grandfather was safely placed in the home. He would spare Milton the pain of seeing his wife's belongings moved to points unknown. Nathan called his sister to plan a trip to pick up what furnishings were left. Beth was reluctant, but the mere mention of their grandmother's cedar chest and small winged dinner table and chairs quickly changed her mind.

The day came to move Milton to the nursing home. Nathan would make this day a memorable one. He packed a couple of paper bags with his grandfather's shirts, pants, socks, shoes, slippers, and personal gear—all with his name attached as required by the home. Nathan ensured Milton had a few sweaters and his gray suit when packing his grandfather's clothes into the car. Milton resigned to the fact this was the end and would go reluctantly.

He slowly made his way down the walkway and into the front seat of Nathan's Dodge. Nathan gave him a few moments to look over the building that had been his home for over ten years. He slowly drove to the top of the hill so his grandfather could view the grand forefathers monument. From there, they drove to the shore, where Nathan parked in front of the open bay. The view encompassed all the fishing vessels and motorboats that were moored.

Milton appreciated his grandson stopping. He told Nathan stories of how he and Cliff Michaels would drive down to see the boats sail in and out of the harbor. Milton remembered trying to get Sarah to find a place on the waterfront, but she couldn't or wouldn't and called her a "fucking bitch." It was the first time Nathan heard his grandfather refer to his loving wife as anything foul.

A half hour passed. It was time to get Milton settled into the home. The place sat majestically on a hill located on the south end of town. There was an ample amount of paperwork to be filled out before carefully unloading his belongings into a shared room. Milton would have his own bureau but shared a closet with two other gentlemen. The room had a large window overlooking Plymouth Bay. The Atlantic Ocean was right within his sight. Nathan felt comfortable about leaving his grandfather and told him he'd stop by to say hello in the coming days.

Nathan drove back to the apartment and started the major cleanup. He went through the drawers and cabinets, unloading their contents into disposable bags. He unhung the many dresses in the closet, going through the pockets of each one. Nathan found money his grandmother hid. He boxed the wardrobe for Beth, thinking some of the dresses might fit her neighbors. Nathan put aside a plain but eloquent aqua dress. His grandmother loved it, telling him once it was her favorite and she would love to be buried in it. On the closet floor sat the bag of blocks along with a croquet set that brought back childhood memories. Nathan debated on keeping them but decided they should remain memories and tossed them into the trash.

Emptying the bureaus led Nathan to find hidden envelopes taped to the back end of the drawers with twenty-dollar bills. Nathan never realized how cautious his grandmother was. The collection totaled about three hundred dollars. It was money that Nathan could use paying for gas and surviving while staying in Plymouth. All the underclothes and miscellaneous items went to the trash. By day's end, he filled the trash cans that stood outside the building.

By morning, the cans had been picked over. The buzzards had been watching as Nathan buried the garment bags under the metal lids. Late morning, he got a call from Beth telling him she'd be down that weekend to pick everything up. Nathan made sure she drove down with a big-enough truck to take everything. Nathan set aside a carload of belongings for himself, including heirlooms of photo albums, a couple of antiquated dolls, wall pictures, his grandfather's three canes, and even the corner shelf Nathan had made back in South Boston. There were pieces of dishware, along with a few books, and his grandmother's Bible.

Pam called asking how Nathan was making out. She and a friend wanted to make a visit. He felt good getting the call, giving Pam a weekday to visit. Nathan made another drive to Brockton. He noticed all the patients were in wheelchairs. His grandmother was slightly bent to one side, enduring a catnap. He tapped on her shoulder, making her aware of his presence. Sarah smiled, slurring her words of hello. She had deteriorated to the point her false teeth no longer fitted her mouth.

Nathan held her hand, noticing her sense of reality faded from the present into the past. He could only stay so long before getting emotional about her condition. The attending nurse gave him a brown envelope containing her rings, watch, and the photo of his coffined mother. She explained that his grandmother's time was ending. Nathan sat momentarily in the car. He became teary eyed, trying to get a hold on what he needed to accept.

Nathan drove to Ethel's, giving her the update on her brother and of Sarah's failing health. Ethel tried giving some words of comfort and insisted Nathan stay for supper. She offered the guest room if he decided to stay. Molly Baker and Katie Freeland stopped by for a quick hello. Nathan recognized Molly from his youth and was surprised of her presence. They lived on Brook Road all their lives and more than likely would end their days there. Nathan took Ethel's offer and spent the night, only returning to Plymouth the next morning. Nathan was proud of how much he had accomplished in such a short time. The complex had a laundry in the basement, and he managed to do a couple of loads of wash.

A rap on the door the following morning announced the appearance of Pam and a fellow girlfriend. Nathan opened the door, seeing the two girls standing before him. He gave Pam a hug and welcomed both inside. Pam looked around, noticing how efficient and homey the place was.

"This is your grandparents' place?" asked Pam.

"What's left of it. I've been clearing out a lot of the belongings and getting it ready for my sister's trip down this weekend. She's coming for most of the furnishings, clothes, and most everything else," replied Nathan.

"It's cute. How's your grandmother doing?" asked Pam, adding some comfort in her tone.

"Not so good. She hasn't much time left. That's why I've been trying to clear this place. I had to put my grandfather into a nursing home. It was tough doing that, especially since it broke his heart to go there," continued Nathan.

"I'm so sorry to hear that. What can we do to make your day better?" asked Pam, turning to her companion. "Nathan, I forgot to introduce you to Donna. Donna, this is Nathan. Donna is a friend from school."

Donna smiled, nodding her head, recognizing the introduction.

"First we can all get into my car, and I'll show you all around Plymouth," Nathan stated with some enlightenment.

Pam's visit relieved Nathan from most of the stresses that overwhelmed him. For the next couple of hours, the weight of responsibility was lifted from his shoulders. He posed as a tour guide, showing the two visitors all that Plymouth had to offer. Nathan took them to the various historical monuments, the bay, the *Mayflower II*, and the rock. They toured the popular wax museum that featured multitudes of Pilgrim historic scenes of their arrival into the New World. They ended the day stopping at a side restaurant for a small lunch. Nathan sighed with a smile, thanking Pam for the visit and giving him a chance to catch his breath. He ended the visit giving her an approximate date he planned on returning to New Haven.

Saturday came, and it was around noon when Beth and Ben arrived with the truck. They looked over the apartment noticing how everything was packed and ready to load. Ben and Nathan started loading the cedar chest, leaf table, and the three wicker-seated chairs. Beth helped with the boxes of clothes and dishes. She was amazed how much Nathan had accomplished.

The apartment was almost bare except for the few essentials, which included the bed, desk and chair, and a nightstand. Beth noticed a few more boxes and a suitcase in the closet and wondered about them. Nathan told his sister they were put aside for himself. He asked Beth if she wanted to see their grandfather since she was in Plymouth. Beth hadn't time to make visits to either of the grandparents and wanted to get started on the road. Within minutes, they were gone.

The place looked bare. It no longer looked or felt like the loving studio apartment where Sarah and Milton enjoyed their many years together. The remainder of the day, Nathan walked around the waterfront, breathing the salt air of the Atlantic Ocean.

Sunday morning, Nathan drove to Ethel's and picked her up to see both his grandparents. The nursing home was right on the route into Plymouth. Milton was happy seeing his sister and was getting adjusted to the place. He pulled his sister close, asking if he could live with her. Ethel gently explained to her brother that his wife was failing and this place would give him the care he needed. They spent about an hour visiting Milton before leaving him in tears.

While driving onto Brockton, Ethel told Nathan about going to the town hall and notifying them of his grandparents' situation regarding their Social Security checks. Brockton bore no promising news. Sarah was laying in her bed exhausted. Her hair was matted, and her lips slightly drooped to the side of her mouth. She was a little coherent, taking every effort on her part to make conversation. It was only a half hour before Ethel and Nathan wanted to leave, knowing that Sarah's end was just a matter of time.

Nathan completed packing the apartment the best he could and needed a change of pace. He called Flora, giving her an update on his grandmother. She invited him over, which Nathan accepted for a night. The cottage relaxed Nathan. He stared at the white tiled ceiling while listening to his grandaunt's words of comfort. The constant traveling back and forth was beginning to weigh on his soul. The morning sunrise over Ellis Pond was refreshing, uplifting Nathan's spirits. He drove Flora to Brockton to see her sister one last time. The visit was brief as Flora couldn't bear to see how much her sister had deteriorated. She didn't want any more visits. Flora just wanted to remember Sarah in better days. Nathan stayed with Flora until evening before returning to the apartment.

Nathan packed his car with the remaining remnants of his grandparents. Before making the trip to New Haven, he wanted to experience Plymouth's July Fourth one last time. He made the slow walk to Cole's Hill, taking a seat on the grass with hundreds of others. Darkness shrouded the bay. Within moments, the heavens lit up with sparkling kabooms. It was followed by the oohs and aahs echoing from the crowd. Then, in one final blast, daylight sparked the night with the orchestra of rapid firings of crackling kabooms. Darkness fell, and all was silent for a moment. There was the rustling of cheering crowds funneling their way back to their cars and the side roads for their way home. Nathan followed the shoreline back to the provincial building.

The sky was full of sunshine the next morning. Nathan made calls to Ethel, Flora, and his father, informing them of his plans. Walking out of the building, Nathan informed a few of the neighbors he'd be gone for a few days and would be back. He stopped at the post office, giving them his grandparents' forwarding address to his Central Avenue apartment. Within the hour, the Dodge drove west on Route 44.

Nathan arrived at Central Avenue tired and worn. He lay on his bed and napped for a few hours. He awoke, still feeling he could use a few more hours of sleep. He managed to call his father of his return to the neighborhood and would stop by the next day. He asked if he could store his grandparents' belongings in the storage space. Clarence had no objections and looked forward in seeing his son.

The rest of the evening, Nathan lay back catching up on the news around the apartment. He paid his portion of the rent and bills before heading out on more errands. Clair was overwhelmed seeing Nathan back even though it was only temporary. He still had to return to Plymouth to settle things. Clair let him in on all the adventures she encountered with Super Bitch. At this point, Nathan didn't care what his grandmother's head games were. He was emotionally drained, not allowing anything else to affect him. The following days, Nathan felt better emotionally and more at ease with himself, then the call came from Ethel.

PASSING OF THE MATRIARCH

It was the crack of dawn when Nathan woke and sat on the edge of his bed. He tried getting his head together for the trip back to Plymouth. He packed a few things along with his grandmother's favorite dress. He phoned his father and sister, notifying them of Sarah's passing, and went back to arrange for her funeral. Nathan's first stop was Beaman's Funeral Home. The home had serviced the Manter family for decades. There was no extravagance; the funeral would be small and simple. Next was the drive to the nursing home and breaking the news to Milton. Nathan asked the home to have his grandfather ready in a couple of days for his wife's funeral. He checked the closet, making sure Milton's gray suit was still there.

Nathan returned to the apartment, focusing on what he was about to face. He called Flora, who was already aware of her sister's passing but wasn't sure whether she'd make it. His next call was to Beth.

"Hi, Beth, just letting you know Gram's funeral will be Wednesday at eleven. I need you to drive down with a couple of the kids. Is that okay?"

Beth's response was disheartening. "I can't, Nate. We've got too much going on, and I just can't break away."

"What do you mean you got a lot going on? This is our grandmother for Christ's sakes. What do you think it'll look like with none of the family attending? Listen, I've traveled to New Haven and back, cleaned out the apartment, put our grandfather into a nursing home, and now arranging for our grandmother's funeral. Most of all, it's not going to cost you a dime. I'm the one buying the flowers and the extra funeral expenses. How about it? The least you can do is bring some of the family down," raged Nathan, keeping his anger tempered.

Beth could feel her brother's rage as his anxiety filled her brain. She took a few shallow breaths, trying to calm herself enough to let the blood flow back into her extremities. She knew her brother would have blared out how insensitive she was if she didn't make the journey.

"Okay, Nate, I'll see who I can get to go. I can't make any promises. I don't think the younger ones should go, do you?"

"No, they didn't know Gram or Gramp, so you can leave them behind. Get the older ones, okay? It's important the family be there." Nathan paused only to calm his anger. "Thanks. I'll meet all of you Wednesday morning at Beaman's Funeral."

Beth didn't like long, distant trips. She called around seeing if Kenneth, Laura, and Gretchen wanted to attend the funeral. At least she'd have Ben do the driving.

Nathan stopped by the florists, ordering the family flowers. He arrived at the funeral home, spending a few moments with Reverend Anthony, who pastored at Plymouth's Congregational church. Nathan sat telling him the highlights of his grandmother's life story, then sat with the funeral director, settling the costs, relying mostly on funds from the town. One relief was the Manters had their own cemetery plots. The responsibility for the pastor, funeral hall, and casket lay with Nathan. As evening fell, Nathan drove to Manomet, spending the night at Ethel's.

The morning sun rose with Nathan lying in bed, praying for this day to be over. He knew it would be long and tiresome. Ethel and Nathan pawed over a small breakfast before starting on the long day ahead. They gauged themselves being at the nursing home early, hoping Milton would be ready. Milton was just about dressed when the two arrived. The head nurse offered Nathan a wheelchair to help the old man move about. Nathan appreciated the gesture knowing it was a time saver.

They drove into the funeral parking lot. Nathan wheeled his grandfather inside for a few private moments with his wife and for him to give her a final kiss goodbye. Ben and Beth arrived with Kenneth, Laura, and Gretchen. Other close friends and relatives began entering the parlor. Marie and Flora arrived with their nephew Lance Nickerson and his wife. The funeral went as scheduled with Reverend Anthony recapping the life of the woman that lay before them.

As the funeral proceeded, Nathan was deep within his memories. He reminisced about his grandmother and all that she meant. He recalled all those baking escapades when he was little living in the Harold estate, those times when Sarah let him put the dry ingredients into the mixing bowl and lick the spoons and mixing utensils. Nathan recalled the walks downtown, sometimes just to window-shop. Sarah was a great influence in his life. She instilled family values and personal ethics although he learned there were exceptions. She taught him to play and treat people fairly. Sarah taught Nathan to be strong willed and to believe in himself even though peer influences would dominate his shortcomings.

Nathan remembered his grandmother being such a proud woman who was generous in helping others. Like his grandfather, she possessed an eighth-grade education. In her day, an eighth-grade education was equivalent to modern-day high school diplomas. Sarah knew hard work and hard times, always dignifying herself in her mannerisms and her dress. She believed in God although she wasn't an overly religious person. She attended church when time allowed and participated in the church's auxiliary club, sewing and knitting items for the church bazaars.

Sarah loved people, especially her daughter, Rachael, and her grandchildren. She made trips throughout the year, especially during the holidays when she and Milton would spend Thanksgiving and Christmas with their grandchildren. Little did Nathan realize those memories would become such precious moments. One of Sarah's proud findings was her ancestral link to the *Mayflower* Pilgrims. Sarah Manter was a remarkable woman and, like all grandmothers, would forever be engraved in people's hearts and minds.

Reverend Anthony ended his remarks. Nathan looked around the room, seeing old familiar faces like Molly Baker, Katie Freeman, Lisa Duncan, and a few others.

He looked at his grandfather, thinking, *Gramp, what's to become of you now that Gram has passed? How are you ever going to manage without the woman you spent sixty years with?*

Nathan sighed, realizing the funeral was over and it was time to move on. The procession led to the gravesite. Nathan followed the hearse, allowing his grandfather to stay inside the car yet close enough to witness the graveside proceedings. The reverend ended the benediction, with Ben and Beth, along with their siblings, saying their goodbyes. Their car left the graveyard for the interstate back to New Hampshire. Nathan watched as their vehicle disappeared down the road. He felt contented having the family show up and would follow them to the North Country another day after closing the apartment.

Nathan arrived at Beth's early in the afternoon for a couple of days before heading back to New Haven. He was tired of driving and needed a break from all the responsibilities. The summer heat invited many to swim at Merrymeeting Lake. Nathan needed to feel the cool waters to sooth his frayed nerves. He joined a few others diving off the dam and swam about the water's surface. Suddenly he forced himself underwater, feeling isolated while the cool water cleansed the stresses of the past weeks. Nathan surfaced, feeling renewed while changing his clothes. He returned to the center of town, stopping at Dot's Lunch for a bite to eat. He needed the restaurant's atmosphere to enjoy a meal without the company of any family member. He paid his bill, taking one last look toward the horizon, before climbing into his car and heading south.

School began, bringing the fold back to their residences and classrooms. It felt good getting back into the routine. The summer was exhausting and now part of the past. Nathan had one more semester before moving on to who knows where. Most everyone would be staying the full year, and Nathan had the same option. He was reminded of the war and losing his deferment. His bank account told of a different story. Nathan had enough to carry him the rest of the year and knew his time in New Haven was ending.

The advertising classes brought on even more challenging projects. Clarence insisted his son take his credit card for school supplies. It helped putting together the detailed projects that were sometimes costly. The girls upstairs continued kidnaping Nathan for the midnight Dunkin' Donut runs. The midnight get-togethers caught everyone up on all the dramas headlining their building. Nathan's apartment wasn't any different from other places. Their differences were small as they found their talks benefited everyone's outlook.

During the fall, Nathan made the effort to check on his grandfather, letting him know he wasn't forgotten. Milton still begged to live with Beth. Ethel had moved to Arizona, living in a loft apartment over her son's garage. Flora returned to Cambridge, not chancing another winter at Ellis Pond. There was no one left in Plymouth to give Milton any moral support.

The holidays were on the horizon, and Nathan decided to spend them in Connecticut. He felt it might be the last chance spending them with his father. Winter snows came early, giving some credence to the community decorations. City lights reflected from the overcast clouds, and the sounds of crushing snow by anxious footsteps added to the holiday spirit.

The winter semester ended for Christmas vacation. The whole experience was over. Nathan was a different person from the country bumpkin who arrived three years earlier. His outlook on life was an open door filled with new approaches and attitudes. He decided to return where simple minds ruled the neighborhood. Nathan outgrew the family and friends that resided in New Durham. His return to them would be for a short time. He just needed to relax his head from the past year's events. He needed to surround himself of simpler times.

Nathan bunked at the Greyson farmhouse for a few weeks. He went around visiting his siblings and how they were surviving. Gretchen was content living with one of the Greyson families. Rebecca was happy, enjoying her own bedroom with the Olsons atop the ridge. Tom and Laura were making do at the farmhouse while

Kenneth kept to himself living with friends in Farmington. It was a drive to see Abigail at the Tibbitts. It seemed she was doing all right. She wasn't too talkative nor revealing of what was going on with her life.

Nathan started mailing job applications to every major company. He started getting nervous about the draft. One evening, having a few beers, Nathan decided to enlist in the navy. Sooner or later, he knew he'd have to serve. Unbeknown to anyone, he drove to the Rochester recruiting station.

The Portland AAFES station called, telling him to bring nothing except a few toiletries. Whatever belongings he had, Nathan placed them in the trunk of his car and left it to rest at his sister's doorstep. Nathan rode with others, making the trip to Portland, Maine. They took the oath of service, then loaded into the navy vans for the trip to the Portland airport. The recruits boarded a plane for the first time, having their flight sail into the endless sky.

EPILOGUE

The recruits landed in Chicago and bused to the navy recruit training center at Great Lakes. It taught them to live and grow inside a unit of mixed backgrounds, cultures, and ethnicities. Nathan's first assignment in July 1972 was Fleet Composite Squadron 10 at Guantanamo Bay, Cuba. He found his exposure to navy life far different from the outside world. Like his recruit training, Nathan worked among a camaraderie of diversified members from all over the country. He listened to and learned different traditions that were unknown to him.

The squadron performed its mission as a well-oiled machine in monitoring the open seas around Cuba.

They worked hard and played hard, often indulging in the various recreations that the base provided. Many participated in deep-sea fishing, swimming, volleyball, outdoor movie theaters, and a host of other activities. It provided Nathan everything he wanted to enjoy during his formative years.

Nathan's siblings experienced the births of their own children, along with the deaths of elderly family members. Beth built her home while giving birth to more children. Ben found it profitable working for himself, buying his own equipment. He drove the daylong roads hauling deliveries to nearby states. Beth continued getting her father's support when meeting the household bills.

Kenneth remained on a personal crusade getting his life together. He had networked himself throughout the town of Farmington. He made a point to go through the Richard's Block, scavenging family belongings before they were lost to Tracy's social friends. He didn't receive the financial support entitled to him, which he needed to support himself. Kenneth eventually dropped out of school, getting hired at the local shoe company. He spent the next few years making the best of his life. Occasionally he was seen weaving in and out of the town's social endeavors and family events.

Laura remained high spirited and couldn't take sitting all day at school. She had an itch to do something more with her life. Like some of her contemporaries, she dropped out of school, having the urge to move on with her life. She was well familiar with the social life on the streets of Farmington. She dated a few locals, settling down with a guy who had ambitious dreams in faraway places.

Gretchen graduated, finding a local job waitressing. She was self-supporting and ended up marrying the first guy that came along that made her smile. She had no career ambitions and stayed in a town she was familiar with and raised a family of her own.

Abigail was traded off to one foster home after another. Her teenage years lead to a few upheavals and confrontations. She became pregnant and married the father of her child. Her situation caused her to drop out of school in supporting herself and her newborn. She sought an opportunity to move out of the area for a better life. After a chain of marriages and divorces, she returned full circle blending in with the local community and her family roots.

Rebecca entered the workforce after graduating, trying to discover her individuality. She was a strong character and knew what she wanted in life. Rebecca eventually married a local boy, producing her own family. She involved herself in the town and contributed to the school's extracurricular activities.

Tom grew being the brunt of multiple teasings from his foster family. Their intentions were good, making him feel as one of their own. His sensitivity put him on the defense and, in the end, made him a stronger person. He graduated high school finding the girl of his dreams. They moved to new horizons to raise a family, parting themselves from the scars of a troublesome past.

The family lost Flora in May of 1973. She believed in eating healthy and kept fit with her daily walks. It was a heart attack that took her from this world. Her sister Marie finalized her estate and, once settled, informed other family members of her passing. Milton continued his long life until his ninety-seventh year. He had the strength to live to a hundred. A deep depression took his will to live.

Rachael kept the Richard's Block operating while she lived. Upon her death, Tracy maintained the bar with little success. His friends swooped in to help maintain the building's operations. Many filled their pockets, knowing Tracy's real love was a whiskey bottle and a six-pack. In the months to follow, Tracy found he was unable to pay the bills. He called Gloria from time to time seeking forgiveness—forgiveness that never came.

Tracy realized there was no reason to remain in New Hampshire once Beth became legal guardian over her younger siblings. Despite Beth's efforts, Tracy drove around the town trying to recoup a few of the girls, all fleeing his advances. Tracy sank to a point where he packed what was left of his belongings and returned to his childhood neighborhood of Lynn, Massachusetts. The Richard's Block defaulted and was taken over by financial institutions.

Word reached the Farmington stronghold that Tracy died penniless in Lynn during December of 1973. In the course of two years, he had squandered every dollar acquired while owning the town's favorite water hole and was buried in a pauper's grave. The news allowed everyone to live their lives with a sigh of relief, no longer having to keep their peripheral vision on alert.

Nathan moved from one duty station to another. He continued to grow and experience life, no longer the family's caretaker. Nathan loved living in different parts of the country, exchanging cultural experiences. Deployments enabled him to visit history and historic places such as Naples, Rome, Venice, Athens, and the Italian Alps. He wrapped himself in the biblical history of Jerusalem, Bethlehem, and Haifa and the Egyptian pyramids.

As Nathan's journey continued, he remembered those words from his grandparents, Flora Atwood, and Katherine Newcomb. They instilled in him to live for today and prepare for tomorrow. In retrospect, Nathan enjoyed traveling and being adventurous like his Pilgrim forefathers. In time, he'd anchor down in a country setting but not until he satisfied his thirst for knowledge and the world.

Throughout the decades, the Andersons endured a myriad of trials and tribulations that many families experience in one way or another. For the Andersons, it started with an only child of middle-aged parents—parents with little possessions making a living helping others, coupled with a loving community that enabled their abilities. Rachael grew having ambitions of a large family and the ideal home to raise them. She led a nomadic life while producing a family along the way, eventually settling on a spacious farm in a small country town that contributed toward making those dreams a reality.

Her ambitions were overwhelming and contributed to the crumbling of her idyllic life. Rachael's reality became severely handicapped from the lack of finances and a lover who was ridden with abuses. In time, the pressures of her desires gave way in losing the farm, the surfacing of Tracy's inner demons, and eventually losing her life.

Rachael's children were consumed by their mother's excessive ambitions, with her two oldest taking hold of responsibilities larger than themselves. They witnessed the loss of their home, mother, grandmother, and friends and eventually separated from the alcoholic and sexual abuses of Tracy Booker.

Time doesn't heal wounds but gives pause, allowing for closure. It gave the Anderson children time to examine their own lives. Growing up in the Anderson household expressed all the human emotions, including the seven deadly sins. Some experienced the love of family, matched with the financial and social struggles of raising one. There were rewards, disciplines, and abuses that weaved into the family fabric of those struggles. Over time, each confronted the challenges of growing up, coming out either stronger or failing to face their own demons. Their experiences were no different from families living similar harrowing aspirations. The Anderson children became survivors with most staying in town, marrying and raising a family. Others were content with traveling a more adventurous future.

ABOUT THE AUTHOR

Wayne E. Held was born in Plymouth, Massachusetts, in 1950, living his formative years in South Boston. His family moved to New Hampshire in 1962, where he graduated from Kingswood Regional High School, Wolfeboro, New Hampshire, in 1968. He always had an avid interest in literature and cultural arts. He attended and graduated from Paier School of Art, Hamden, Connecticut, in 1972.

With the Vietnam War still in progress, Wayne enlisted in the US Navy, specializing in administration. Upon retiring in 1994, Wayne continued his education, receiving an associate degree in business administration from the Hudson Valley Community College, Troy, New York, in 1995. He returned to New Hampshire, settling in the Emerald Lake Village District (ELVD) within the township of Hillsborough. He worked for many years with the McLane Northeast Concord Food Distribution in Contoocook, New Hampshire, until permanently retiring in the summer of 2013.

Wayne has been an active participant in the political affairs within his community. He enjoys the comforts of his ELVD home, having morning coffee on his deck. His hobbies include reading, painting, landscaping, fishing, and hiking.

CPSIA information can be obtained
at www.ICGtesting.com
Printed in the USA
JSHW012243301122
34152JS00001B/47

9 781684 987436